정재현 新토익 실전 1000제 RC 문제집

영단기

정재현 新토익 실전 1000제 RC 문제집

저자	정재현
연구원	송다영(수석) 최민정 김은영 임정길 함윤희 유정수 우중민 송인지 박승원
	Kirsten Avila Jooch Nam Michael Putlack Peter Morton
기획 총괄	김효신
기획 · 편집	정유상 한미선 김혜민
디자인 총괄	김지원
표지 디자인	김유선
내지 디자인	닷츠
펴낸날	초판 1쇄 2017년 3월 15일
	7쇄 2024년 8월 3일
펴낸이	김정택
펴낸곳	(주)에스티유니타스
등록번호	제25100-2022-000072호
홈페이지	eng.conects.com
고객센터	카카오톡 플러스 친구 [영단기] / 영단기 1:1 게시판
주소	서울시 구로구 경인로 662 타워동 30층/31층
ISBN	979-1-161310-13-8

머리말

여러분, 안녕하세요.
여러분의 토익 선생님 정재현입니다.

2016년 5월 이후 토익에 기존에 없던 새로운 문제 유형이 추가되면서
토익의 전반적인 체감 난이도는 상승하였고 따라서 이를 제대로 대비할
좋은 토익 실전 문제에 대한 필요가 더욱더 커지게 되었습니다.

그렇다면 제대로 된, 좋은 토익 실전 문제는 무엇일까요?
어떤 문제를 풀고 공부해야, 단기간에 최고의 토익 점수를 얻을 수 있을까요?

좋은 토익 실전 문제는,
실제 토익 문제와 같거나 조금 더 높은 난이도의 문제가 되어야 합니다.
그런 문제로 연습해야 단기간에 가장 많은 점수를 올릴 수 있습니다.
좋은 토익 실전 문제는,
가장 많이 출제되는 유형을 빠짐없이 담고 있어야 합니다.
또한, 신유형의 출제 패턴을 정확히 분석해 반영하는 것은 기본이고,
문제를 구성하는 문장과 어휘까지도 반드시 토익에 출제되는 것이어야 합니다.
그렇게 되면, 한 문제를 공부하면서도 5점이 아니라, 10점, 15점의 점수 상승을
기대할 수 있습니다.

이를 위해, 정재현어학연구소에 토익 분석만을 담당하는 숙련된 토익 전문가들과 토익 문제
출제에 경험이 많은 원어민을 초빙했습니다. 탄탄한 기존 연구진과 새롭게 구성된 연구진의
피나는 노력으로 문제에 숨어 있는 출제자의 의도와 유형의 변화 패턴을 파악하였습니다.
그리고 문제에 쓰인 문장과 지문의 길이, 어휘, 난이도를 실제 토익 시험 대비에 최적화된
상태로 모두 조절하였습니다.

이러한 정재현어학연구소의 노력의 결과는 신토익이 시행되면서 더욱 높아진 적중률이 말해
주고 있습니다. 그리고 그 결과의 진수를 바로 이 책 〈정재현 新토익 실전 1000제 RC〉에
모두 담았습니다.

적중,
단기간의 점수 상승,
이것이 〈정재현 新토익 실전 1000제 RC〉가 관심을 두는 모든 것입니다.

이 책이 여러분의 토익 졸업을 분명히 앞당겨 줄 것이라 확신합니다.

정재현 드림

정재현의 新토익 RC
끝내기 비법 FAQ

Q1 신토익으로 바뀌면서 ETS에서 바뀐 토익 규정이 있나요?

A 네, 있습니다. 기존에는 토익 응시자들이 고사장 변경을 원하는 경우, 정기/특별 추가 접수 기간에 동일 지역에 한해서만 고사장 변경이 가능했습니다. 하지만 신토익으로 바뀌면서 인터넷 접수 기간 이내라면 얼마든지 응시 지역과 관계없이 고사장 변경이 가능하게 되었답니다. 이 부분과 관련해서는 ETS 토익 관련 규정에서 확인하실 수 있어요.

Q2 신토익으로 바뀌면서 Part별로 어떻게 바뀌고 난이도는 얼마나 달라졌나요?

A Part 5는 40문제에서 30문제로 줄어든 대신 Part 6는 4지문에 총 16문제로 4문제가 늘어났어요. 무엇보다 Part 6에는 '문맥상 적절한 문장을 선택'하는 신유형이 추가되었습니다. Part 7 역시 문제 수가 6문제 늘었는데, 여기에도 몇 가지 신유형이 추가되었어요. 특히 세 지문을 읽고 문제를 풀어야 하는 트리플 지문이 15문제를 차지하게 되어서 독해에 자신이 없는 학생들에게는 체감 난이도가 높아졌다고 할 수 있습니다. 한정된 시간 안에 다량의 문제를 풀어야 해서 이전보다 긴 지문을 빠르고 정확하게 읽는 독해력이 요구됩니다.

Q3 신토익의 경우 Part별로 어떻게 시간을 배분해야 할까요?

A 상대적으로 Part 6, 7에 시간이 더 소요되기 때문에 최대한 Part 5에서 시간을 줄여야 해요. 따라서 Part 5를 '10분' 정도로 속도감 있게 푸시고 Part 6는 '8분' 안에 풉니다. 그리고 Part 7을 '54분' 안에 푸시고 나머지 '3분' 정도는 마킹하는 데 배분하시면 되겠습니다.

Q4 RC를 시간 내 모두 풀기가 힘들어요. 시간을 좀 더 효율적으로 관리할 수 있는 방법이 있을까요?

A 파본 검사 시간이나 LC 디렉션 시간을 잘 활용해야 합니다. 이 시간에 RC의 Part 5를 대략 5문제 정도 푸실 수 있습니다. 또한, Part 7의 경우 기사 지문이나 진위 확인 유형과 같이 단서가 지문 전체에 걸쳐 있어서 시간이 많이 소요되는 유형은 가장 마지막에 푸시는 것이 좋아요. 무엇보다 평소에 실제 시험처럼 시간을 재고 실전 문제를 푸는 연습을 꾸준히 하셔야 합니다.

Q5 OMR 카드에 답안을 마킹할 때 시간 내 실수 없이 답안지를 옮기는 방법을 알려 주세요.

A 시험 막판에 모든 Part의 답을 옮기려고 하면 자칫 실수할 수가 있어요. 따라서 Part별로 답안을 마킹하시는 것을 추천합니다. Part 5, 6를 풀고 나서 한꺼번에 OMR 카드에 마킹하세요. Part 7은 한 지문씩 문제를 풀고 답을 옮기는 것이 좋습니다. 예를 들어, 편지 지문에서 두 문제를 푸셨다면 바로 답안지에 옮기고 다음 지문으로 넘어가서 푸시면 됩니다.

Q6 목표 점수가 900점 이상인데 몇 달째 800점 후반에서 오르지 않고 있어요. 특히 Part 7에서 많이 틀리고 시간도 부족합니다. 독해를 잘할 수 있는 방법에 대해 조언해 주세요.

A 독해의 경우 가장 중요한 건 어휘력입니다. 따라서 평소에 토익에 자주 출제되는 단어와 숙어 표현을 공부해 두셔야 합니다. 기출 어휘집이 있으시면 시험 직전까지 반복해서 암기해 주세요.
다음으로 직독 직해를 빠르게 하시려면 정독과 다독을 통해 독해의 기본기를 쌓으시는 것이 필요합니다. 토익 지문은 물론 평소에 실용문(영어로 된 편지, 광고, 공지문, 기사 등)을 접하시면서 다양한 영어 지문을 통해 독해 연습을 하시는 것도 영어 지문을 빠르고 정확히 읽는 데 많은 도움이 됩니다. 토익 문제집에 나온 지문은 반드시 끊어 읽기를 하면서 해석하시는 연습과 함께 틀린 문제는 지문의 단서가 어디였고, 어떤 부분을 놓치셨는지 오답을 정리하는 것도 필요합니다.

정재현의 新토익 RC
끝내기 라인업

新토익 끝내기 5단계 라인업

초보/입문	기초/중급	실전 대비	최종 점검	시험 당일
영단기 新토익 스타트 RC	영단기 新토익 RC	적중특강	정재현 新토익 실전 1000제 RC	정재현의 적중노트

토익 단기 고득점을 위해서는 분명한 공부 전략과 시험에 반드시 나오는 유형만을 짚어 주는 1등 강사에게 배워야 합니다.

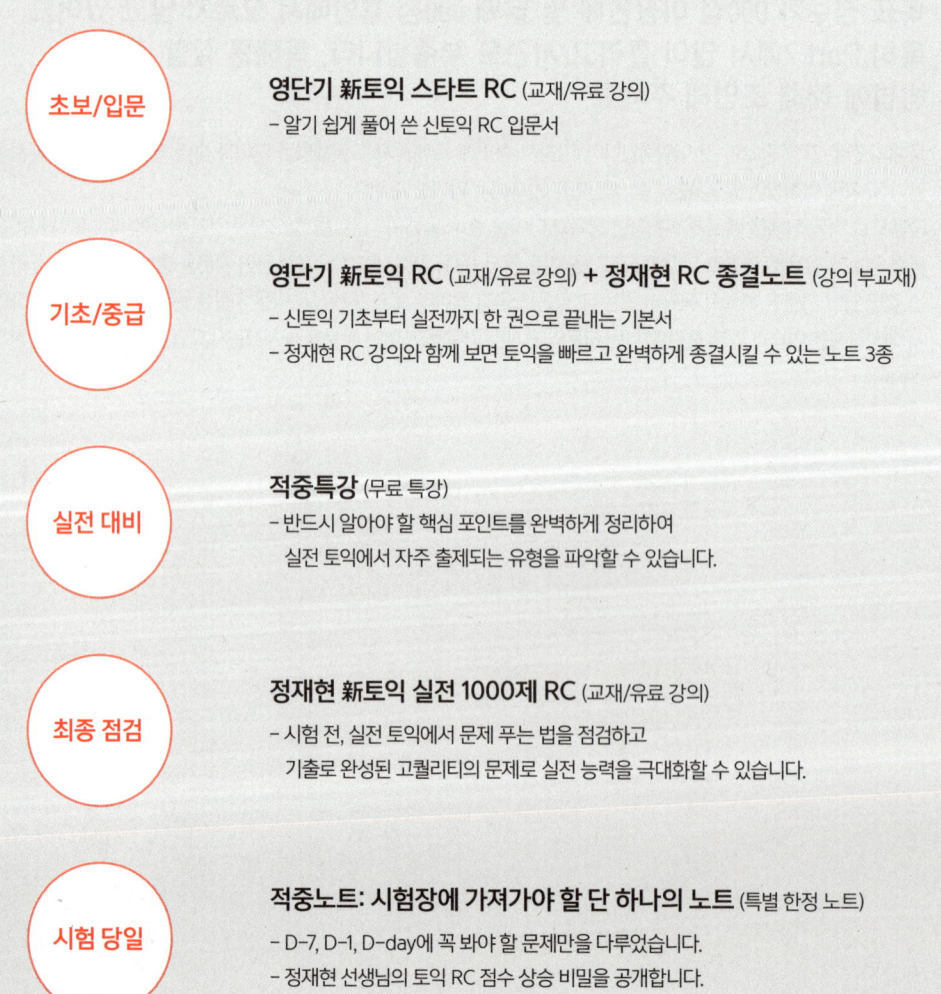

초보/입문

영단기 新토익 스타트 RC (교재/유료 강의)
– 알기 쉽게 풀어 쓴 신토익 RC 입문서

기초/중급

영단기 新토익 RC (교재/유료 강의) **+ 정재현 RC 종결노트** (강의 부교재)
– 신토익 기초부터 실전까지 한 권으로 끝내는 기본서
– 정재현 RC 강의와 함께 보면 토익을 빠르고 완벽하게 종결시킬 수 있는 노트 3종

실전 대비

적중특강 (무료 특강)
– 반드시 알아야 할 핵심 포인트를 완벽하게 정리하여
  실전 토익에서 자주 출제되는 유형을 파악할 수 있습니다.

최종 점검

정재현 新토익 실전 1000제 RC (교재/유료 강의)
– 시험 전, 실전 토익에서 문제 푸는 법을 점검하고
  기출로 완성된 고퀄리티의 문제로 실전 능력을 극대화할 수 있습니다.

시험 당일

적중노트: 시험장에 가져가야 할 단 하나의 노트 (특별 한정 노트)
– D-7, D-1, D-day에 꼭 봐야 할 문제만을 다루었습니다.
– 정재현 선생님의 토익 RC 점수 상승 비밀을 공개합니다.

정재현의 新토익 RC
적중 사례

단순한 예측이 아닌, 진짜 적중된 문제를 경험해 보세요!

정확한 예측과 적중은 강의를 몇 년 한다고 아무나 할 수 있는 것이 아닙니다.

10년 이상의 치밀한 분석과 연구로 완성된 <정재현 新토익 실전 1000제 RC>로 남들보다 더 빠르게 토익을 끝낼 수 있습니다.

2016년 12월 적중특강 문제	2017년 1월 토익 시험
------- Mr. Carpenter hired a new company to make the firm's advertisements, sales began to rise at a rapid pace. (A) Along **(B) Once** (C) So (D) Finally	------- you have submitted all the necessary documents for your great proposal, the evaluation process will begin. (A) Then (B) Next **(C) Once**　　정답 적중! (D) Always
2016년 11월 적중특강 문제	**2017년 1월 토익 시험**
The opening of the newly designed downtown civic center was postponed ------- construction delays. (A) without (B) as if **(C) due to** (D) instead of	The Violet Café is closed today ------- problems with its heating system. (A) while (B) whereas (C) as for **(D) due to**　　정답 적중!
2016년 11월 적중특강 문제	**2017년 1월 토익 시험**
The Human Resources Department recently altered the company Web site ------- potential applicants could submit all relevant documents electronically. **(A) so that** (B) if (C) why (D) because of	Please fill out the feedback forms ------- conference organizers can improve future workshops. **(A) so that**　　정답 적중! (B) in order to (C) because of (D) as well as
2016년 9월 적중특강 문제	**2017년 1월 토익 시험**
It is ------- that all hospital personnel immediately report incidents affecting employee or patient safety. (A) critic (B) critics **(C) critical** (D) critically	It is ------- that clients be made aware of inventory shortages as soon as they occur. (A) sudden **(B) critical**　　정답 적중! (C) eventful (D) actual
2016년 9월 적중특강 문제	**2017년 1월 토익 시험**
On account of the low number of passengers, Destiny Air's weekly flights to Samoa have been cancelled until **further** notice.	Rinax employees will continue to receive a discount on in-store purchases until **further notice** 　　유형 적중!

新토익 시험 정보의 모든 것

新토익 소개

TOEIC 시험이란?

TEST OF ENGLISH FOR INTERNATIONAL COMMUNICATION의 약자로, 모국어가 영어가 아닌 사람이 일상적인 생활 또는 업무에서 의사소통이 가능한지를 평가하는 시험입니다.

시험 구성

듣기(LC) 4개 파트 100문제와 읽기(RC) 3개 파트 100문제로 총 7개 파트에 걸쳐 200문제가 출제됩니다. 200문제 모두 선택지 중에서 정답을 찾는 객관식 문제로 출제됩니다.

구성	PART 구성	출제 내용	문항수	시간	점수
LC (Listening Comprehension)	PART 1	사진 묘사 (사진 보고 문제 풀기)	6	45분 내외	495점
	PART 2	질문-대답 (질문 듣고 답변 고르기)	25		
	PART 3	짧은 대화 (두 명이나 세 명의 대화를 듣고 질문에 답하기) 신유형	39		
	PART 4	설명문 (전화 메시지, 연설문, 안내방송, 일기예보 등을 듣고 질문에 답하기) 신유형	30		
RC (Reading Comprehension)	PART 5	문장 빈칸 채우기 (하나의 문장 안에 있는 빈칸에 알맞은 말(문법&어휘) 고르기)	30	75분	495점
	PART 6	지문 빈칸 채우기 (짧은 지문 안에 있는 빈칸에 알맞은 말(문법&어휘&문장) 고르기) 신유형	16		
	PART 7	싱글 지문 (1개의 지문을 읽고 질문에 답하기) 신유형	29		
		더블 지문 (2개의 지문을 읽고 질문에 답하기)	10		
		트리플 지문 (3개의 지문을 읽고 질문에 답하기) 신유형	15		
총계			200	약 120분	990점

출제 범위 및 주제

일상생활 및 업무에 대한 영어 의사소통 능력을 평가하기 때문에 특정 분야의 전문 지식 또는 이와 관련된 어휘는 출제하지 않습니다. 국제 업무 환경에 맞게 다양한 국가의 지명과 성명이 등장하며, 듣기 평가에서는 미국, 영국, 호주 발음이 고르게 섞여 출제됩니다. 다음 주제를 참고해 봅시다.

기업 일반	이사회, 편지, 공지, 전화, 팩스, 이메일, 사무실 장비 및 가구, 사무실 규정, 계약, 협상, 합병 및 인수, 판매, 보증, 사업계획, 회의, 노사관계
공식 연회	식사 및 연회, 장소 예약
엔터테인먼트	영화, 공연, 전시
재무	은행업무, 투자, 세금, 회계, 청구
의료	건강보험, 병원 방문 및 예약
부동산	건설 및 보수 내역, 부동산 구매 및 임대, 기타 설비
제조	제품 조립, 공장 경영, 품질 관리
채용	모집, 고용, 퇴임, 승진, 급여, 일자리 지원서, 구인광고, 연금, 시상
구매	쇼핑, 주문, 배송, 송장
기술	전자장비, 기술지원, 컴퓨터, 연구실과 관련 장비
여행	교통 관련 일정, 교통 관련 각종 공지, 렌터카, 호텔 예약, 연착 및 취소

006 정재현 新토익 실전 1000제 RC 문제집

1. 토익 접수 방법

- 토익 시험의 인터넷 접수 기간을 한국 TOEIC 위원회 사이트(www.toeic.co.kr)에서 확인합니다.
- 사이트에서 인터넷 접수를 선택하고 시험일, 고사장, 수험정보 등의 정보를 입력합니다.
- 시험 접수 시 최근 6개월 이내 사진(JPG 형식)이 필요하니 미리 준비합니다.

TIP 시험 D-30부터는 특별추가접수에 해당하여 약 5천원 정도의 추가 비용이 발생합니다. 미리 시험을 접수하는 것이 좋습니다.

2. 시험 당일 꼭! 챙겨야 할 준비물

- **규정 신분증**
  성인의 경우, 주민등록증, 운전면허증, 기간 만료 전 여권, 공무원증 등이 인정됩니다. 중고등학생에 한하여 학생증(국내 학생증만 허용)도 신분증으로 인정됩니다.
- **연필 (볼펜, 사인펜은 No!)**
  연필 끝을 뭉뚝하게 만들어 준비하면 답안 마킹을 더 쉽게 할 수 있습니다.
- **지우개**
- **아날로그 손목시계 (전자식 시계는 No!)**

> **토익 고수의 Tip!**
> 뭉뚝한 연필 준비!
> 마킹이 쉽고 빨라져요.

3. 입실 전 유의사항

- 시험 시간이 오전일 경우, 오전 9:20까지, 시험 시간이 오후일 경우 오후 2:20까지 입실합니다.

TIP 오전 시험은 오전 9:50 이후, 오후 시험은 오후 2:50 이후로는 절대 입실할 수 없으니 꼭 시간을 지켜 미리 입실합니다.
시험 시간 직전에는 독해 문제를 풀기보다는 듣기 연습을 충분히 하여 귀를 훈련시키는 게 더 효과적입니다.

4. 시험 진행 안내

오전 시험	오후 시험	시험 진행
9:30~9:45 (15분)	2:30~2:45 (15분)	답안지 작성 오리엔테이션
9:45~9:50 (5분)	2:45~2:50 (5분)	쉬는 시간
9:50~10:05 (15분)	2:50~3:05 (15분)	신분증 확인
10:05~10:10 (5분)	3:05~3:10 (5분)	문제지 배부, 파본 확인
10:10~10:55 (45분)	3:10~3:55 (45분)	듣기 평가 (LC)
10:55~12:10 (75분)	3:55~5:10 (75분)	독해 평가 (RC)

5. 성적 확인 및 성적표 발급 방법 알아보기

- 시험일로부터 19일 후 오후 3시에 한국 TOEIC 위원회 사이트(www.toeic.co.kr) 혹은 ARS 060-800-0515로 성적 확인이 가능합니다. (단, ARS 성적 확인에 '동의'한 수험자에 한하여 ARS 성적 확인이 가능함)
- 성적 수령은 온라인 출력이나 우편 수령을 택할 수 있습니다.
- 온라인 출력 시, 성적 유효기간 내 홈페이지를 통해 출력 가능합니다.
- 우편 수령 시, 성적발표 후 접수 시 기입한 주소로 성적표가 우편 발송됩니다. (약 7~10일 소요)
- 온라인 출력과 우편 수령은 1회 발급만 무료이며, 이후에는 유료로 발급됩니다.

新토익 RC 출제 경향

2016년 5월~12월 新토익 시험 분석

PART 5 Trends 분석

1 어휘 문제보다 문법 문제의 출제 비중 편차가 크다.

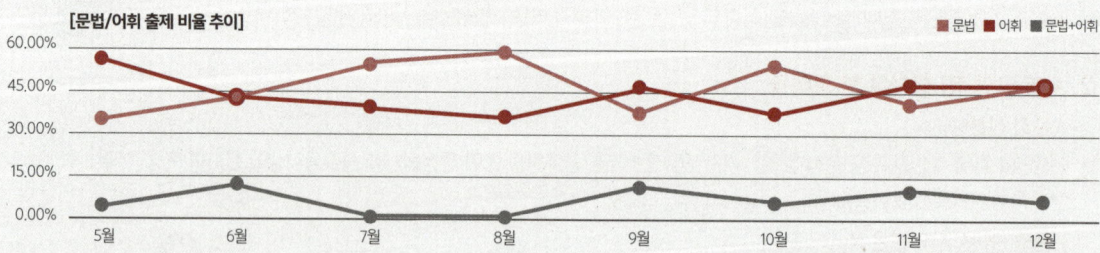

위의 그래프는 신토익 이후 출제된 토익 시험의 '문법/어휘/문법+어휘' 문제 유형의 출제 비중 변화를 추적한 것이다. 위의 그래프를 보면 문법 문제의 출제 비중 변화 폭이 크며 상대적으로 어휘 문제의 출제 비중 변화 폭은 작다. 이는 '문법+어휘' 유형의 출제 비중 폭을 나타내는 그래프의 모양이 어휘 문제와 거의 같은 것에서 그 이유를 찾을 수 있다. 위의 그래프에서 또 하나 발견할 수 있는 것은 2~3개월 주기로 출제 비중의 역전 현상이 일어나고 있으며 그 폭은 점차 감소하고 짧아지고 있다는 점이다. 5월 첫 시험 이후 문법 문제가 8월까지 3개월간 상승하고 9월부터 12월까지는 매월 등락을 거듭하고 있으나 11월과 12월에 시험에서는 어휘와 문법의 출제 비중이 거의 동일하다.

2 품사별 출제 비중은 구토익과 거의 동일하다.

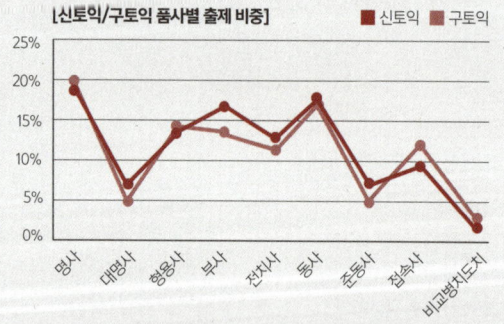

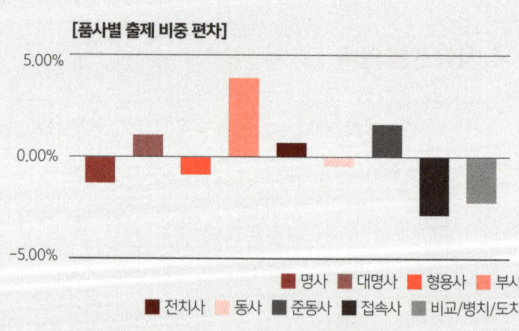

ETS는 신토익으로 변경하면서 기존 시험과 난이도와 출제 경향은 거의 비슷할 것이라고 발표하였는데, 정말 그렇게 구현될 것인지에 대해서는 회의적이었다. 위의 그래프를 분석해 보면, 왼쪽 그래프에서 신토익과 구토익의 그래프 모양이 거의 유사한 형태를 가지고 있다는 것은 실제로 두 시험 간의 품사별 출제 비중은 큰 차이가 없음을 알 수 있다. 오른쪽 그래프는 품사별 실제 출제 비중의 편차를 보여 주는 것이다. 40문항에서 30문항으로 줄어든 것을 고려하면, 부사와 준동사는 구토익보다 1문항 더 출제되며, 접속사는 1문항 덜 출제된다.

3 동사 관련 문법 문제는 복합유형이 늘었다.

구토익에 비해 10문항이 줄어들었기 때문에 기존에 자주 출제되던 문법 항목의 출제 비중은 줄어든 대신 다양성은 늘었다. 예를 들어, 동사 관련 문제는 동사의 형태, 수일치, 시제, 능수동태로 네 가지로 나눌 수 있다. 기존 시험에서 시제와 능수동태 문제가 동시에 출제되는 경우가 많았으나 신토익 이후에는 단독으로 묻는 대신 '시제+수일치', '시제+능수동태', '수일치+능수동태'와 같이 복합유형을 묻는 문제의 비중이 늘었다. 비교구문을 예로 들면, 출제 빈도가 가장 높던 비교급 문제의 비중이 줄어들고 원급과 최상급 문제의 비중이 늘어난 것이다. 기존의 기본 문법 지식을 확인하는 문제보다 난이도가 중/상에 해당하는 문제의 출제 비중이 늘었다고 결론을 내릴 수 있다.

월	핵심 문법	핵심 어휘
5월	대명사 someone	notwithstanding, concentrated
6월	가정법과거완료	부사 since
7월	현재분사구문	equivalent, selective
8월	수량표현+of+관계대명사	a wealth of
9월	명사절 접속사 whichever	traditionally, likewise
10월	등위접속사 yet	marginally
11월	be set to V	marked
12월	기수+최상급	seldom

1년 총 20회의 시험 중에서 1회 정도 출제되거나 한 번도 출제되지 않을 만한 유형들이 매월 출제되었다. 그중에서 6월에 출제된 가정법 과거완료의 경우 능수동태와 함께 출제되어 난이도를 높였고, 8월에는 관계대명사 문제 중에서 선행사의 종류와 동사의 수(數)까지 고려해야 하는 '수량표현+of+관계대명사' 유형이 출제되었고, 9월에는 명사절 접속사 중 복합관계형용사 'whichever'가 출제되어 난이도를 높였다. 처음 출제되는 유형은 아니지만, 문장 전체를 수식하는 현재분사구문을 묻는 문제의 출제 비중이 높다. 어휘 문제 중에서는 5월에는 'notwithstanding(~에도 불구하고)', 분사형용사 'concentrated(집중된)', 7월에는 'selective(선택적인)', 8월에는 '많은, 풍부한'이라는 의미를 가진 숙어 'a wealth of'에서 명사 'wealth', 9월에는 부사 'traditionally(전통적으로)'가 처음으로 토익 시험에 등장하였다. 이외에 6월 시험에서 전치사와 접속사로 출제 빈도가 높은 'since'가 부사로 출제되었고 출제 비중이 아주 낮았던 유형이었다. 그리고 12월 시험에서는 부정을 나타내는 빈도 부사 'seldom'이 전치사구와 출제되어 어휘 문제의 난이도를 높였다.

PART 6 Trends 분석

1   어휘 문제의 출제 비중이 높다.

구토익과 신토익의 문법/어휘 문제의 출제 비중을 분석해 보면 12문항으로 구성되어 있던 구토익과 신토익 모두 출제 비중이 거의 유사하다. 신유형을 제외하면, 대략 6:4로 어휘 문제의 비중이 높다. 2016년 1월부터 4월까지 실시된 구토익 시험을 분석해 보면 대부분 어휘 7문항, 문법 5문항으로 어휘 문제의 비중이 높았으며, 이는 신토익에서 16문항 중 신유형인 문맥상 알맞은 문장 넣기 4문제를 제외한 12문항의 출제 비중과 거의 동일하다.

[문제 유형 출제 비중]

- 32.81% 문법
- 40.63% 어휘
- 1.56% 문법+어휘
- 25.00% 신유형

2   부사와 준동사의 출제 비중이 상승하였다.

신토익에서 Part 6는 12문항에서 16문항으로 늘어났으나 늘어난 4문제는 모두 신유형인 문맥상 알맞은 문장 넣기로 구성되기 때문에 기존 유형의 품사별 출제 비중을 살펴보는 것은 의미가 있다. 뒤의 그래프를 살펴보면 신토익에서는 명사, 형용사, 전치사, 동사의 출제 비중이 감소하였고 부사와 준동사의 비중은 상승하였다. 대명사와 접속사의 출제 비중은 거의 이전과 동일하다. 부사의 경우 앞뒤 문장의 내용으로 정답을 찾는 접속부사의 비중이 상승하였고, 준동사의 경우 주로 Part 5와 동일하게 to부정사와 분사 문제로 구성되었으며, 동명사의 출제 비중은 높지 않았다. 동사의 경우 어휘 문제와 시제 복합 문제의 출제 비중이 높다.

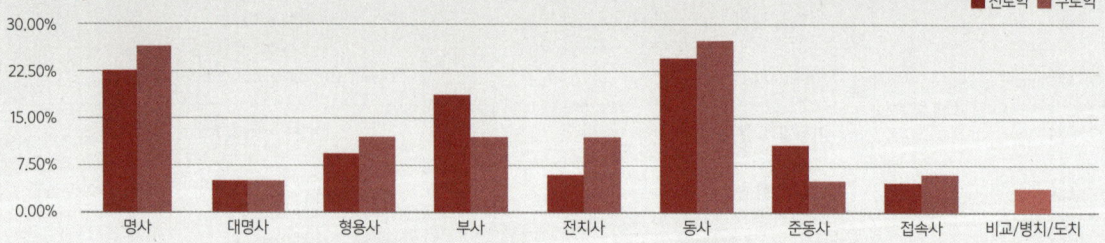

3 신유형은 두 번째와 세 번째 문제의 출제 비중이 높다.

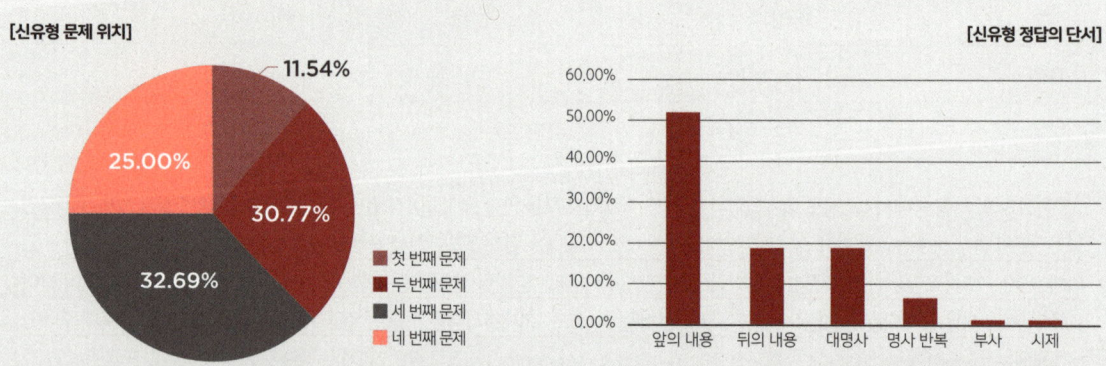

신유형인 문맥상 알맞은 문장 넣기의 경우 신유형 문항이 출제되는 위치와 정답의 단서가 어디에 위치해 있는지에 따라 난이도가 결정된다. 문제의 위치의 경우 앞쪽에 위치할수록 난이도는 상승할 수밖에 없다. 그 이유는 빈칸 이후의 내용을 근거로 정답을 찾아야 하기 때문이나. 빈칸 뒤의 내용을 기반으로 역추론하는 것이 앞의 내용을 근거로 순서대로 추론하기보다 더 어렵기 때문이다. 신유형의 문제 위치를 살펴보면 세 번째 문항>두 번째 문항>네 번째 문항>첫 번째 문항 순이다.

정답의 단서를 살펴보면 빈칸 앞의 내용이 단서인 경우가 50%가 넘는다. 지시형용사/지시대명사/의미가 같은 명사 사용/순서를 나타내는 형용사 또는 부사와 같이 정답 보기 문장 안에 단서가 있는 경우가 대략 30%를 차지하고 있다. 따라서 Part 6의 신유형 문제를 해결하기 위해서는 빈칸 앞의 내용과 보기 내의 단서를 찾는 것이 가장 빠르고 정확한 방법이다.

PART 7 Trends 분석

1 세부사항과 추론 유형의 출제 비중이 가장 높다.

신토익 이후 Part 7의 난이도는 거의 중상 이상으로 고정되어 있다. 문항 수는 48문제에서 54문제로 6문제가 늘어났을 뿐이지만 트리플 지문으로 인해 읽어야 할 지문의 수 또한 총 15지문에서 21지문으로 문항 수와 똑같이 6지문이 증가하여 가장 난이도 상승이 높은 Part이다. 문항 수가 2문제로 정해져 있는 주어진 문장이 들어갈 알맞은 위치를 찾는 유형과 의도를 묻는 유형을 제외하면 세부사항이 가장 많이 출제되며 그 뒤를 추론, 진위, 주제/목적 순으로 비중을 차지하고 있다. 특히 기존 구토익에 비해 진위(NOT/TRUE) 유형보다 추론 유형의 출제 비중이 높은 것이 가장 큰 특징이다. 동의어 문제는 신토익 실시 이후 최대 6문제까지 출제되었으나 점차 감소하여 12월 시험에서는 3문항으로 구토익 출제 비중까지 떨어졌다.

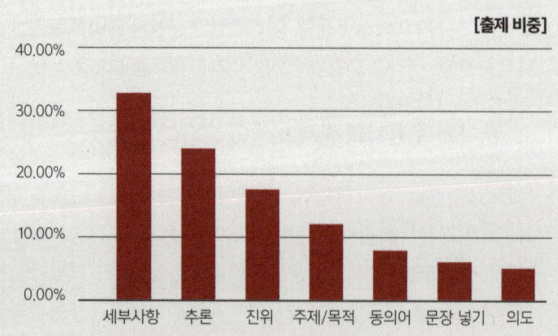

[출제 비중]

2 싱글 지문과 더블 지문에서 이메일과 편지의 출제 비중이 가장 높다.

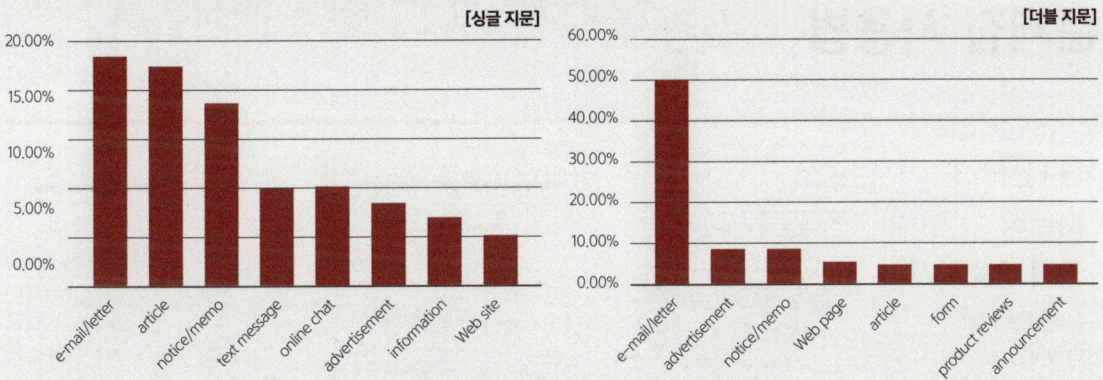

기존 유형인 싱글 지문과 더블 지문의 지문 종류별 출제 비중을 살펴보면 전혀 다른 양상을 보이고 있다. 싱글 지문과 더블 지문에서 가장 출제 비중이 높은 종류는 이메일과 편지이다. 하지만 싱글 지문에서는 20% 미만이나 더블 지문에서는 거의 50%에 육박하는 비중으로 출제되고 있다. 싱글 지문에서는 이외에도 기사 지문과 공지 지문이 비슷한 비중으로 출제되나 더블 지문에서는 기타 다른 지문의 경우 그 출제 비중의 차이가 너무 크다. 이는 더블 지문의 경우 두 지문 중 한 지문은 거의 이메일 또는 편지일 확률이 높다는 것을 의미한다.

3 트리플 지문에서 Web page와 기사 지문의 출제 비중이 가장 높다.

트리플 지문의 경우 더블 지문과 거의 유사한 출제 비중을 보이고 있으나 하나의 세트에서 3개의 지문이 출제되기 때문에 더블 지문에 비해 기타 다른 지문 유형이 출제될 확률이 높다. 오른쪽 그래프에서 알 수 있듯이 Web page와 기사 지문의 출제 비중이 상대적으로 높다. 특히 최근 들어 Web page 관련 지문이 다양한 내용으로 출제되고 있는 것에 주의한다. 2개 이상의 지문에서 정답의 단서를 찾아야 하는 연계 문제의 경우 세트당 1~2문항이 출제되고 있다. 정답의 단서 또한 1-2지문, 2-3지문, 1-3지문에 걸쳐 다양하다.

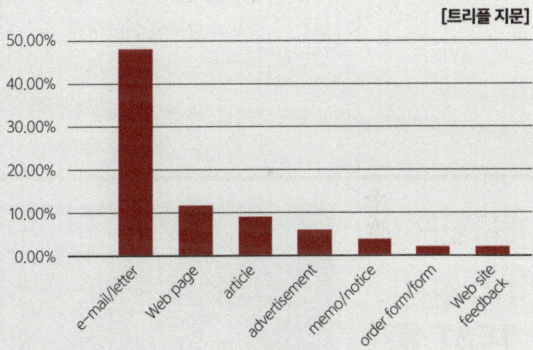

4 주어진 문장이 들어갈 알맞은 위치를 찾는 신유형은 이메일/편지, 기사 지문에서 출제 빈도가 높다.

신유형인 의도를 묻는 문제 유형은 LC와 달리 모든 문제가 의미하는 바 또는 암시하는 바를 묻는 문제로 구성되어 있으며, 시험마다 2문제가 출제되며, text message chain과 online chat discussion에서 각각 1문제씩 출제된다. 이와는 달리 문장이 들어갈 알맞은 위치를 찾는 유형의 경우 다양한 지문 종류에서 출제되고 있다. 이메일/편지, 기사에서 거의 85%가량 등장하며, 이외에는 안내, 보고서, 메모에도 출제되었다. 정답의 위치로는 3번과 4번에 위치할 확률이 높으며, 정답의 단서로는 '순서를 나타내는 형용사 및 부사', '앞의 문장을 요약하는 지시대명사', '접속부사', '앞의 지문 내용에 대한 부연설명', '예제 문장' 등이 제공된다.

정재현 新토익 실전 1000제 RC
문제집 사용법

STEP 1

신토익
준비 운동하기

신토익 경향을
파악하고
전략을 세우자!

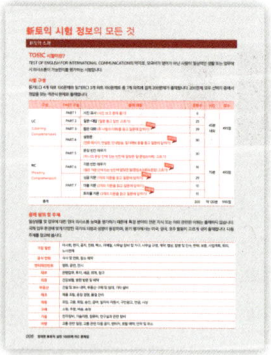

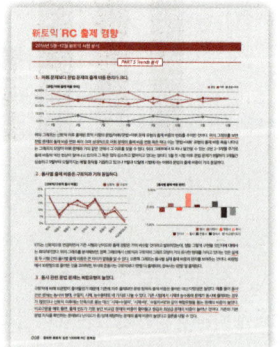

**정재현의 新토익 RC
끝내기 비법 FAQ**

신토익을 준비하는 수험생들이 자
주 하는 질문을 모아 정재현 선생
님만의 핵심 노하우로 상세하게
답변하였습니다.

**세상에서 가장 친절한
新토익 시험 가이드**

토익 접수 방법부터 시험 당일
팁까지 유용한 정보를 수록
하였습니다.

新토익 RC 출제 경향

신토익 시행 이후 출제 경향을
Part별로 철저히 분석하여
신토익에 효과적으로 대비할
수 있도록 하였습니다.

STEP 2

RC 실전
TEST 풀기

신토익 출제 경향을
철저히 반영한
새로운 문제!

잠깐! TEST를 시작하기 전에 ❶

시작 시각과 종료 시각을 적으세요.
시계까지 옆에 챙겨 두었다면
당신은 완벽한 토익커입니다.

잠깐! TEST를 시작하기 전에 ❷

문제집 맨 뒤에 수록되어 있는
ANSWER SHEET 중 한 장을
잘라냅니다. 이제 마킹이 잘 되
는 뭉뚝한 연필을 들고 시험을
시작해볼까요?

신토익 RC 실전 TEST 10회분

〈정재현 新토익 실전 1000제 RC 문제집〉은 신토익 시행 이후의
최신 출제 경향을 완벽 분석하여 제대로 정밀하게 반영하였습니
다. 정기 토익 시험에 응시하기 전 실전 TEST 10회분을 모두 풀
고 꼼꼼히 복습하여 진정한 토익 고수가 되어 보세요.

STEP 3

채점 및
복습하기

자신의 실력을
확인하고 점검하자!

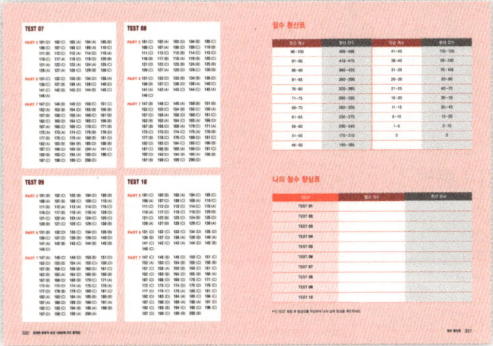

정답표/점수 환산표/점수 향상표

각 TEST를 마친 후 교재 뒤에 수록된 정답표를 통해 채점을 한 뒤, 점수 환산표에서 자신의 점수를 확인하세요. 각 TEST가 끝날 때마다 점수 향상표에 점수를 기록함으로써 자신의 실력을 파악하고 학습 계획을 세울 수 있습니다.

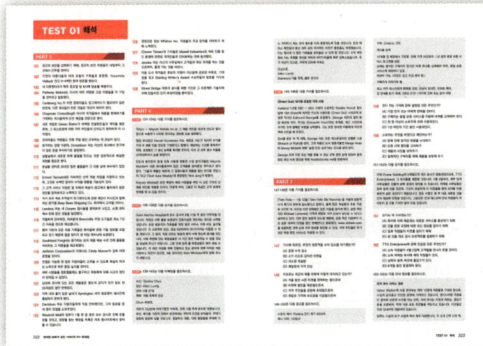

해석 전문 수록

교재에 수록된 모든 문제와 지문 해석을 수록하였습니다. 이해가 잘 되지 않았던 문제와 지문은 반드시 해석을 확인하여 이해한 뒤 학습을 이어가세요.

STEP 4

부가자료
활용하기

신토익
고득점으로 가는
가장 빠른 지름길!

정재현 RC 종결노트(유료)

eng.conects.com

정재현 RC 강의를 들으며 종결노트 3종을 활용하면 토익을 빠르고 완벽하게 종결시킬 수 있습니다. 강의만으로 부족할 때, 좀 더 확실한 학습을 원할 때 종결노트 3종으로 더욱 완벽하게 공부할 수 있습니다.

단기 고득점 달성을 도와주는 적중특강(무료)

eng.conects.com

정재현 선생님의 적중특강으로 시험 전 실전 문제에 익숙해지고 꼼꼼히 대비할 수 있습니다. 토익 시험 전에 적중특강을 학습하고 목표 점수를 달성해 보세요.

목차 및 학습 플래너

페이지	TEST	공부한 날	풀이 소요 시간	점수	해석 페이지	복습 여부
016	**TEST 01**	☐ 월 ☐ 일	_____ 분 75분 내에 완료했나요? ○ｌ✕	맞은 개수 _____ 환산 점수 _____	322	○ｌ✕
046	**TEST 02**	☐ 월 ☐ 일	_____ 분 75분 내에 완료했나요? ○ｌ✕	맞은 개수 _____ 환산 점수 _____	330	○ｌ✕
076	**TEST 03**	☐ 월 ☐ 일	_____ 분 75분 내에 완료했나요? ○ｌ✕	맞은 개수 _____ 환산 점수 _____	339	○ｌ✕
106	**TEST 04**	☐ 월 ☐ 일	_____ 분 75분 내에 완료했나요? ○ｌ✕	맞은 개수 _____ 환산 점수 _____	348	○ｌ✕
136	**TEST 05**	☐ 월 ☐ 일	_____ 분 75분 내에 완료했나요? ○ｌ✕	맞은 개수 _____ 환산 점수 _____	358	○ｌ✕

페이지	TEST	공부한 날	풀이 소요 시간	점수	해석 페이지	복습 여부
166	**TEST 06**	☐ 월 ☐ 일	_____ 분 75분 내에 완료했나요? ○ ㅣ ✕	맞은 개수 _____ 환산 점수 _____	367	○ ㅣ ✕
196	**TEST 07**	☐ 월 ☐ 일	_____ 분 75분 내에 완료했나요? ○ ㅣ ✕	맞은 개수 _____ 환산 점수 _____	376	○ ㅣ ✕
226	**TEST 08**	☐ 월 ☐ 일	_____ 분 75분 내에 완료했나요? ○ ㅣ ✕	맞은 개수 _____ 환산 점수 _____	384	○ ㅣ ✕
256	**TEST 09**	☐ 월 ☐ 일	_____ 분 75분 내에 완료했나요? ○ ㅣ ✕	맞은 개수 _____ 환산 점수 _____	393	○ ㅣ ✕
286	**TEST 10**	☐ 월 ☐ 일	_____ 분 75분 내에 완료했나요? ○ ㅣ ✕	맞은 개수 _____ 환산 점수 _____	403	○ ㅣ ✕

*환산 점수는 p. 321의 '점수 환산표'를 참고하세요.

TEST 01

PART 5
PART 6
PART 7

토익 Reading Comprehension은 75분 동안 진행됩니다.
현재 시각과 지금부터 75분 후인 테스트 종료 시각을 기록해 두고,
반드시 종료 시각 전에 문제 풀이와 답안지 마킹을 완료하세요.

  현재 시각  시 분
테스트 종료 시각  시 분

READING TEST

In the Reading test, you will read a variety of texts and answer several different types of reading comprehension questions. The entire Reading test will last 75 minutes. There are three parts, and directions are given for each part. You are encouraged to answer as many questions as possible within the time allowed.

You must mark your answers on the separate answer sheet. Do not write your answers in your test book.

PART 5

Directions: A word or phrase is missing in each of the sentences below. Four answer choices are given below each sentence. Select the best answer to complete the sentence. Then mark the letter (A), (B), (C), or (D) on your answer sheet.

101. ------- security at the warehouse, full-time guards will be on duty there starting tomorrow.

(A) Enhanced
(B) To enhance
(C) Enhancement
(D) Enhance

102. ------- for natural beauty and opportunities for outdoor adventure, Yosemite Valley is visited by 3 to 4 million people yearly.

(A) Eligible
(B) Important
(C) Renowned
(D) Prepared

103. The new documentary is ------- to air every Saturday night at eight o'clock.

(A) committed
(B) scheduled
(C) proved
(D) considered

104. Parkway Motors announced that it will purchase more luxury vehicles for its ------- fleets.

(A) rent
(B) rental
(C) to rent
(D) rents

105. While ------- of the Carlsberg, Inc. computers is in need of an upgrade, the ones made by other companies need to be improved.

(A) nothing
(B) no one
(C) not
(D) none

106. Chapman Consulting ------- in the provision of advice for companies looking to sell their products in Asian countries.

(A) considers
(B) differs
(C) specializes
(D) senses

107. After the newly opened Green Bistro contracted marketing consultants, the local residents' awareness of the restaurant became ------- better.

(A) chiefly
(B) markedly
(C) affordably
(D) tightly

108. Neither the managers ------- the employees are interested in working during the holiday weekend.

(A) and
(B) nor
(C) but
(D) yet

109. ------- increasing competition, Mr. Donaldson has decided to invest more money into research at his company.

(A) To
(B) Amid
(C) During
(D) Within

110. Making new chemicals in the laboratory typically requires a ------- process.

(A) complicate
(B) complicated
(C) complicates
(D) complicating

111. Many of the items that had been turned in to the lost and found center were not ------- the next day.

(A) retrieves
(B) retrieval
(C) retrieving
(D) retrieved

112. Ernest Tannehill supports continuing work on the new medicine, ------- has the potential to generate millions of dollars in revenue.

(A) that
(B) who
(C) which
(D) whatever

113. The customer service representative is trying to ------- the cause of several shipments never being sent from the warehouse.

(A) instruct
(B) determine
(C) develop
(D) afford

114. A ------- to upgrade the fleet of delivery trucks will be considered at the quarterly Busy Bees Shipping Co. meeting with board members.

(A) conclusion
(B) proposal
(C) shift
(D) degree

115. Ms. Landers went out looking for the new Coryne dishes and found ------- for sale at the shopping center.

(A) they
(B) their
(C) them
(D) themselves

116. ------- proper care, your Bronoville kitchen gadgets are expected to last at least seven years.

(A) For
(B) To
(C) About
(D) With

117. All paper-based medical records are stored in a locked file cabinet because they contain ------- information about patients.

(A) confidential
(B) confided
(C) confiding
(D) confidentiality

118. Southfield Freight has retrained its employees in handling items because of an increasing number of glassware -------.

(A) shipped
(B) shipments
(C) ship
(D) shipment

119. The Jackson Corporation's subsidiary will ------- under the direction of Cindy Mercer.

(A) conduct
(B) evolve
(C) operate
(D) direct

120. Interviews will be conducted ------- day in an effort to ensure that as many candidates as possible may be considered.

(A) only
(B) full
(C) all
(D) some

GO ON TO THE NEXT PAGE

121. The cause of the accident could not be determined by the committee despite their having reviewed -------.

(A) specifics
(B) specify
(C) specific
(D) specifically

122. All items that are in the menswear department are on sale for 25% off ------- otherwise noted.

(A) despite
(B) afterward
(C) neither
(D) unless

123. The poor weather in the local area prevented Mr. Symington's flight ------- departing on time.

(A) with
(B) from
(C) in
(D) onto

124. Mr. Davidson contacted the applicants -------, but three of his coworkers helped with the interviews.

(A) herself
(B) myself
(C) yourself
(D) himself

125. If you wish to accept the position with our company, be sure to sign the attached document and return it by e-mail or fax ------- three business days.

(A) by
(B) within
(C) about
(D) over

126. Management always ------- to recognize the major achievements of the employees at Whitner, Inc.

(A) creates
(B) assumes
(C) strives
(D) conforms

127. Reporters at the *Devon Times* ------- to interview individuals who are involved in the ongoing dispute with Maxell Industries.

(A) agreeing
(B) were agreed
(C) agreement
(D) have agreed

128. Ms. Jacobs avoids going on business trips, ------- to conduct video conferences with clients from her office.

(A) prefers
(B) preferring
(C) preferred
(D) preference

129. Children's book authors have awaited the announcement of the Starling Writer's Award winners with anticipation since ------- were made public last month.

(A) subscriptions
(B) nominations
(C) creations
(D) venues

130. The timeframe for finishing the Street Bridge was ------- an estimate made by an engineer on the project.

(A) shortly
(B) merely
(C) strongly
(D) slightly

PART 6

Directions: Read the texts that follow. A word, phrase, or sentence is missing in parts of each text. Four answer choices for each question are given below the text. Select the best answer to complete the text. Then mark the letter (A), (B), (C), or (D) on your answer sheet.

Questions 131-134 refer to the following article.

Tokyo—Mayoto Mobile Inc. released information today that ------- would begin exporting its line of
131.
products to India and the Philippines next year.

The vice president of sales, Mr. Haruki Kurosawa, said he expects the new endeavor to nearly

double revenue for the company. To meet the anticipated demand, factories will expand their

production capabilities. -------.
132.

Market analysts familiar with cell phone use in India and the Philippines believe Mayoto Mobile will

attract many customers from other companies. "Their sales will quickly excel well ------- of those of
133.
their competitors," said Yani Jung, editor for *Tech Asia Weekly*.

Mayoto Mobile will also be developing a new line of lower-priced devices specifically for the foreign

markets. -------, they will be able to sell to a wider demographic of consumers.
134.

131. (A) it
(B) he
(C) anyone
(D) someone

132. (A) The relocation will help to make
operations more centralized.
(B) All five are set to increase manufacturing
rates by forty percent.
(C) However, local regulations significantly
held back profits.
(D) The device features video and camera
capabilities.

133. (A) above
(B) before
(C) ahead
(D) aware

134. (A) Likewise
(B) In this way
(C) In particular
(D) Alternatively

GO ON TO THE NEXT PAGE

Questions 135-138 refer to the following notice.

The renovation at Saint Martha Hospital will take place during the week of June 11. Work will commence with the west supply room being converted into a nurse's station. -------. During this
135.
project, patient rooms 9208 through 9215 will not be accessible. -------, staffing will be reduced to
136.
match the number of patients on the unit. Please note that the restrooms on the west side will be unavailable during this time. The east hall restrooms may therefore experience ------- use. If you
137.
have any questions or comments on preparations ------- for this improvement process, please talk
138.
to the ninth floor director, Matt Whitaker.

135. (A) The building will soon be leased to Saint Martha Hospital.
(B) A visitor and family self-serve coffee bar will also be installed.
(C) Supplies will be sold at the gift shop during this time.
(D) It ensures that all nurses are rewarded for working overtime.

136. (A) In other words
(B) Nevertheless
(C) As a result
(D) On the other hand

137. (A) long-term
(B) heavy
(C) correct
(D) available

138. (A) being made
(B) making
(C) will be made
(D) have made

Questions 139-142 refer to the following e-mail.

To: Tabitha Chun
From: Allen Lundy
Date: September 27
Subject: Autumn Festival Success

Dear Ms. Chun,

I have been busy since we last spoke, preparing for the annual Autumn Festival. First, I ------- your
                                                                                        139.
advice to change the layout from the previous one, so that the stage would be in the center of the

park. As you said, having other activities ------- close to the stage should make the event more
                                            140.
united. I have also arranged for additional children's activities like face painting and balloon art.

-------. The planning committee and I are really pleased ------- your ideas to improve the festival. If
141.   **142.**
you have any further input, please call me.

Sincerely,

Allen Lundy
Starwood Autumn Festival, Logistics Director

---

139. (A) will take
(B) took
(C) having taken
(D) would take

140. (A) also
(B) just
(C) rather
(D) soon

141. (A) The April Festival was also held in the same place.
(B) This will allow us to attract more families to the occasion.
(C) A large crowd is expected to attend the competition.
(D) The stage was previously located further from the center.

142. (A) to
(B) after
(C) with
(D) over

GO ON TO THE NEXT PAGE

Questions 143-146 refer to the following article.

Local Bookstore Hosts *Dried Out* Author

Aukland (December 3)—The Attic bookstore owner, Natalie Yoon, ------- Edmond George,
                                                          143.
celebrated author of the book series *Dried Out*, to the 12th Street location of her store Sunday.

Following a question and answer session with Mr. George, the author read an excerpt from the

latest addition to the series, subtitled *Eleventh Hour*. -------.
                                                          144.

In addition to this acclaimed book, Mr. George also wrote the stand-alone novel *Breach of Risk*, a

best seller. His ------- has been praised as a "remarkable achievement" by book reviewers Marge
         145.
Hass and Benny White.

For ------- about where to find Mr. George's most recent book, and for a recording of the question
   146.
and answer session, visit theatticbooks.net.

---

143. (A) recommended
    (B) invited
    (C) notified
    (D) interviewed

144. (A) He also signed copies of his books for those in attendance.
    (B) Ms. Yoon occasionally invites authors to her bookstore.
    (C) Moreover, the author spent his childhood years in Spain.
    (D) After that, the author went on to write a subsequent novel to the series.

145. (A) work
    (B) contract
    (C) service
    (D) deal

146. (A) detail
    (B) details
    (C) detailed
    (D) detailing

PART 7

Directions: In this part you will read a selection of texts, such as magazine and newspaper articles, e-mails, and instant messages. Each text or set of texts is followed by several questions. Select the best answer for each question and mark the letter (A), (B), (C), or (D) on your answer sheet.

Questions 147-148 refer to the following article.

(Twin Falls—January 12) Twin Falls Ski Resort has reported an unexpected decrease in the number of visitors this winter. Given this year's large amount of snowfall and cold temperatures, the lower number of ticket sales has surprised many. Park director Michael Lemme believes the area's increase in gasoline prices may be the cause. In response to the decline in numbers, the park has announced a sale on tickets from now until the end of the season. Visit www.skitwin.com for information on pricing details. Additional special offers are also available for local residents.

147. According to the article, what caused the decrease in the number of visitors?

(A) A decline in the number of parks
(B) The costly tickets for the ski resort
(C) An excessive amount of snowfall
(D) An increase in the price of gasoline

148. How is the resort dealing with the recent change in sales?

(A) By selling season tickets during the winter
(B) By providing a discount on tickets
(C) By inviting local residents to the park
(D) By subsidizing gasoline prices

GO ON TO THE NEXT PAGE

Questions 149-150 refer to the following advertisement.

Posted by owner: Perkins Lawn Mower 4200X
Asking price: $110
Location: Ontario, OR

Posting Description

Bought at a store 10 months ago. Original price $450. Mower has two months remaining on a 1-year factory warranty.
Mower in great condition but has one broken wheel to be replaced by buyer, not covered by warranty.
Cash only. (Pictures not available, see in person.)

Buyer must pick up.

Will be sold to highest bidder; if interested, call to reserve.
For directions, call or text (562) 272-1747.

149. What has been described about the lawn mower?
(A) It will be sold to the one who comes first.
(B) The buyer should use the warranty to replace a wheel.
(C) It has been used by more than one owner.
(D) It has been in use for less than a year.

150. What does the owner offer to do?
(A) Repair the broken part before selling
(B) Consider a discount upon request
(C) Show photographs of the item
(D) Hold the item for a prospective buyer

Questions 151-152 refer to the following notice.

Now that the six-month renovation of the Evans Building has been completed, TTG Enterprises will reorganize its departments. Starting from April 2, the finance team's offices can be found in the south wing of the building. The marketing offices will be in the east wing, as it is the only space large enough to keep these employees together. The change will be reflected in the new building directory within a few weeks. The receptionists at the front desk are happy to show you where to go in the meantime.

151. Why was the notice written?

(A) To promote a new service offered by the company

(B) To report updates to a building regulation

(C) To announce the relocation of some employees

(D) To explain an upcoming renovation project

152. What is mentioned about TTG Enterprises?

(A) Its employees will not see clients on April 2.

(B) Its marketing department has the most employees.

(C) It has entrances on the south and east side.

(D) It has been in operation for six months.

GO ON TO THE NEXT PAGE

Maintenance Services Information

The maintenance department at Upton Station, with its team of approximately fifteen people, contributes to the smooth and safe operation of the facility. While the engineering staff makes repairs to the trains and tracks, our department is responsible for all other aspects of the station, including lighting, restrooms, entrances, and more. These are outlined in the staff handbook.

Duties vary widely depending on the needs of the facility. At the beginning of each shift, we perform all urgent tasks first followed by routine maintenance and repairs. We maintain an equipment log to show what has been checked in or out. This is hanging on the door of the storage room.

All entry points are examined daily upon the opening and closing of the station. For after-hours access to the facility, call 555-7878.

153. Who is the intended audience of this information?

(A) Passengers at a bus terminal
(B) Professional travel agents
(C) Employees at a train station
(D) Current engineering students

154. According to the information, how can readers get more information about borrowing equipment?

(A) By calling a helpline
(B) By reading a posted document
(C) By speaking to a supervisor
(D) By checking a Web page

155. How often are the entrances checked?

(A) Once a day
(B) Twice a day
(C) Once a week
(D) Twice a week

Questions 156-158 refer to the following memo.

Kathryn Morrison Marathon after-race Banquet

The Kathryn Morrison Marathon after-race spaghetti feed will continue as originally scheduled on September 20 at 5 PM, the evening after the race. Due to double booking, however, the event will be held at the Gold Gate Festivities Hall on Cole Road rather than at the Alphonsus Center.

Directions to the Gold Gate Festivities Hall from Leif Stadium (Race starting line)

Begin west on Vermont Road, following it through two stop lights until it becomes Granite Street. Continue on Granite for one mile. Then turn right onto Phillmore. Take an immediate left on Gold Street and the parking lot of Gold Gate Hall will be on your right. The staff at the welcome desk will direct you to the correct room.

Please note that onsite parking is abundant. You will be issued a parking ticket upon pulling into the parking lot at the Festivities Hall. Simply have the ticket validated before leaving the dinner and no payment will be necessary.

156. Where was the event originally planned to take place?

(A) At the Gold Gate Festivities Hall
(B) At the Alphonsus Center
(C) On Cole Road
(D) At the gate of the race

157. Where will the race start?

(A) Granite Street
(B) Phillmore Road
(C) Gold Street
(D) Vermont Road

158. According to the memo, how can the parking fee be waived?

(A) By finding a valid parking place
(B) By leaving before the dinner ends
(C) By attending the marathon race
(D) By having an eligible ticket

GO ON TO THE NEXT PAGE

Questions 159-160 refer to the following text message chain.

Alita LaGrande   10:14 A.M.

I thought my meeting would last until 11 A.M., but it's finished. So I'm headed to Birmingham now.

Walter Lind   10:17 A.M.

You didn't have any trouble changing your train ticket, did you? I booked you a flexible fare so you could take any train on that route.

Alita LaGrande   10:18 A.M.

It was fine. But I want to make sure I can check in at the Ewell Hotel as soon as I arrive. I told them I would check in at 2, but I'll be there about an hour early. Could you call them for me and make sure that's okay?

Walter Lind   10:20 A.M.

Of course. I'll text you after I'm done with that.

Alita LaGrande   10:21 A.M.

Thank you!

---

159. When does Ms. LaGrande want to check in at a hotel?

(A) At 11 A.M.
(B) At 1 P.M.
(C) At 2 P.M.
(D) At 5 P.M.

160. At 10:20 A.M., what does Mr. Lind most likely mean when he writes, "Of course"?

(A) He will pick Ms. LaGrande up.
(B) He will book a train ticket.
(C) He will contact a hotel.
(D) He will call the train station.

Questions 161-164 refer to the following letter.

Joyce Wallace
629 Park Boulevard
Roxbury, MA 02119

January 8

Sergio Bianchi
881 Valley Street
Collingswood, NJ 08108

Dear Mr. Bianchi,

My name is Joyce Wallace, and I am the head of the research department of Vernon Pharmaceuticals. I am aware that you have a job opening for a senior lab technician, and I believe that James McCarty would be an excellent candidate for this role.

Mr. McCarty joined our company six years ago as a volunteer trainee and was hired permanently after the three-month program ended. After just six months of working as a lab technician, he assumed the role of project manager, which is usually given to much more senior staff members. I have been his immediate supervisor since that time. While working with Mr. McCarty, I was impressed with how he was able to come up with solutions to the project delays and unexpected challenges. He always completed tasks with energy and enthusiasm, and he was happy to put in the necessary effort to increase his knowledge about his field.

I'm confident that should you bring Mr. McCarty on board, you will benefit greatly from his work ethic and experience. I'm happy to answer any questions you may have, and I may be reached at (617) 555-7041.

Sincerely,

Joyce Wallace

161. What is the purpose of Ms. Wallace's letter?

(A) To submit an application for a job opening
(B) To offer Mr. Bianchi a lab technician job
(C) To recommend an employee for a position
(D) To explain job duties to a new employee

162. What is suggested about Mr. McCarty?

(A) He worked with Ms. Wallace for six months.
(B) He has never had a management role.
(C) He was Ms. Wallace's immediate supervisor.
(D) He has not always been a paid employee.

163. The word "assumed" in paragraph 2, line 3, is closest in meaning to

(A) assigned
(B) supposed
(C) accepted
(D) created

164. What is NOT indicated as one of Mr. McCarty's qualities?

(A) Time-management skills
(B) An energetic attitude
(C) Problem-solving skills
(D) A willingness to learn

GO ON TO THE NEXT PAGE

Restaurant License Updates

Numerous restaurants in the Greater Detroit area will be affected by the upcoming changes to the restaurant license legislation currently under review by state officials. — [1] —. Proponents of the bill point to increased government revenues as an important consideration.

Industry observers predict that, following an above-inflation raise last year of 6%, restaurant license costs will probably jump by approximately 8% if the regulations pass a vote and are implemented in early January. — [2] —. They expect to see a negative effect on service industry job growth, which has enjoyed 10% and 11% increases in the last two years, respectively.

"This change could have harmful consequences for the food and beverage industry as a whole," said Restaurant Association Chairman Sol Adams. "— [3] —. Further administrative costs could prove too much for some." Legislators must decide whether the benefits outweigh the risks to the business community. — [4] —.

---

165. According to the article, how much are license fees likely to rise next year?

(A) 6%
(B) 8%
(C) 10%
(D) 11%

166. What do experts believe is a possible consequence of the legislation?

(A) Fewer jobs will become available.
(B) Inflation will continue to rise.
(C) Administration fees will be simplified.
(D) Business closures may decline.

167. In which of the positions marked [1], [2], [3], and [4] does the following sentence best belong?

"With increases in the costs of ingredients, many restaurants are already strained."

(A) [1]
(B) [2]
(C) [3]
(D) [4]

Questions 168-171 refer to the following online chat discussion.

Huan Wu 5:24 P.M.
Since we didn't have time to meet today, I wanted to see how everything is coming along for the Classic Movies Celebration.

Dale Gracey 5:26 P.M.
We've just begun advertising for the festival.

Ravi Gupta 5:27 P.M.
I've dropped our posters at all the restaurants and shops around town, and they'll be posted in prominent areas.

Huan Wu 5:29 P.M.
That's wonderful. I know a lot of business owners had promised that, but I thought they might not follow through.

Dale Gracey 5:30 P.M.
You don't have to worry.

Ravi Gupta 5:31 P.M.
I'm expecting high attendance, but that creates another problem. Neither the lot behind the theater nor the one across the street can hold many vehicles.

Amber Vanuolo 5:32 P.M.
That's why I'm working on getting permission to use the Tresson Mall lot and have a shuttle bus running between the two sites.

Huan Wu 5:33 P.M.
That'll work perfectly. Thanks! Amber, do we know which special guests will be there?

Amber Vanuolo 5:34 P.M.
Some of the directors, but I don't have a final list yet. Also, Carlton Fletcher is planning to be there. He said his article about the event will most likely be on the front page of *the Peoria Daily Times*.

---

168. What is the online chat mainly about?

(A) An awards show
(B) A community parade
(C) An anniversary celebration
(D) A film festival

169. At 5:29 P.M., what does Ms. Wu most likely mean when she writes, "but I thought they might not follow through"?

(A) She is surprised that the event attendance will be high.
(B) She thought a project might not be completed on time.
(C) She was worried they could not put up some advertisements.
(D) She believed some business owners would not make donations.

170. What does Mr. Gupta think will happen?

(A) A mall will close early.
(B) Some parking areas will fill up.
(C) A shuttle bus will not run on time.
(D) Some tickets will sell out quickly.

171. Who most likely is Mr. Fletcher?

(A) A director
(B) A building owner
(C) An entertainer
(D) A journalist

GO ON TO THE NEXT PAGE

To:	Katherine Jarvis <katherine.jarvis@phc.net>
From:	Geraldine Grayson <g.grayson@reachcomp.com>
Date:	January 17
Re:	PHC Proposal

Dear Ms. Jarvis,

Many thanks for your informative presentation last week. You did an excellent job outlining PHC's market saturation and reader engagement. — [1] —. Unfortunately, we have determined that PHC is not a good fit for us, so we are going to pass this time.

We have seen diminishing returns across the board from print media advertising. — [2] —. We believe this is due to the impact Web-based channels have had over the past five years, which we have found work well for us. We have also committed to other projects that have a strong track record, such as mailing flyers to consumers directly and sponsoring sporting events. — [3] —.

In addition, we do see some success with monthly and quarterly magazines, and these still form a core part of our strategy. However, daily papers fare worse and sometimes do not provide a return on investment, as we have found with yours in the past. — [4] —.

Thank you for your understanding, and I wish you all the best.

Sincerely,

Geraldine Grayson
Marketing Communications Director, Reach Computers

172. Why did Ms. Grayson write the e-mail?

(A) To propose a business arrangement
(B) To pass on a computer order
(C) To make suggestions to a business
(D) To decline an advertising opportunity

173. What is NOT mentioned as an effective marketing technique for Reach Computers?

(A) Exhibition attendance
(B) Corporate sponsorship
(C) Online channels
(D) Direct mail

174. What kind of business most likely is PHC?

(A) A monthly magazine
(B) A news Web site
(C) A mobile app
(D) A daily newspaper

175. In which of the positions marked [1], [2], [3] and [4] does the following sentence best belong?

"Our board members reviewed your materials during their meeting and discussed these points at length."

(A) [1]
(B) [2]
(C) [3]
(D) [4]

GO ON TO THE NEXT PAGE

Kovar Aquarium and Marine Preservation (KAMP)
Quarterly Summary Review: Curtis Rafferty

Tasks/Accomplishments:

Organized press event for the groundbreaking of the new wing of the Marine Preservation Center, which will house the penguin habitat exhibition next year. Representatives from 16 media outlets were in attendance. [April]
Planned and operated a booth at the Avery Career Fair in Dallas for the third year in a row, assisted by Jamie Halstead. Interest in our booth was much higher than last year. [May]
Accompanied Director Lionella Monaldo as she presented her research at the Progressive Environmental Conference in Vancouver, Canada. Met with researchers to discuss KAMP projects. [May]
Conducted training sessions for employees to inform them of new government regulations regarding animal welfare. Brought all KAMP sectors into compliance with these regulations. [June]

Aquarium Under New Leadership
By Dorothy Langston, *Kovar Herald Community News* Journalist

SEPTEMBER 14—Kovar Aquarium and Marine Preservation (KAMP) has announced the hiring of Ruben Caro as its new director. Caro will take over for Lionella Monaldo, who served as the aquarium's director for fifteen years. She is leaving her position to go into retirement. Although Caro has worked as a researcher at KAMP for five years, his appointment has been surprising to some, as all previous directors had come from a management background rather than an academic one. However, Caro's passion for the facility, along with his strong background in the field and innovative ideas for generating interest in the site, will certainly have a positive effect on KAMP. Caro is scheduled to give a talk on rescued marine mammals at the upcoming Progressive Environmental Conference, held next year in Sydney, Australia. There he will work to not only educate his colleagues but also draw attention to the invaluable work that KAMP does for the ocean environment.

176. What happened at KAMP in April?

(A) Funds for protecting the habitat of penguins were raised.

(B) Visitors were welcomed to a newly opened exhibit.

(C) Some groundbreaking research was announced.

(D) Construction was begun on a new building section.

177. What most likely was the purpose of Mr. Rafferty's visit to Dallas?

(A) To network with potential donors

(B) To learn about new regulations

(C) To promote KAMP's job openings

(D) To advertise a new service

178. What is suggested about Ms. Langston?

(A) She recently visited the aquarium.

(B) She used to work for KAMP.

(C) She plans to leave her position soon.

(D) She is employed by a local newspaper.

179. What is indicated about the KAMP director position?

(A) It requires five years of experience.

(B) It is usually not held by a researcher.

(C) It had to be filled unexpectedly.

(D) It is appointed by board members.

180. What is implied about the Progressive Environmental Conference?

(A) Its host country changes.

(B) Its popularity is growing.

(C) It is held every other year.

(D) It is intended for scientists only.

GO ON TO THE NEXT PAGE

Questions 181-185 refer to the following flyer and e-mail.

Be Changed by The Power of Art!

Is your business located in the downtown commercial district? Would you like to bring attention to your business while helping our community at the same time? Then you should consider enrolling in The Power of Art (TPOA) program. TPOA is commissioning the painting of colorful murals in the city center to help bring more visitors to Norfolk City. The city council has determined that the number of tourists has been declining steadily over the past few years. This has prompted the city council's decision to take measures to prevent a further drop in visitors.

By enrolling in TPOA, you are giving permission for a mural to be painted on the exterior of your building. You can select an image created by one of our professional artists or design one yourself. Should you choose to make your own design, it must follow the theme of "Historical Norfolk City." The design cannot contain any business name or logo.

Inquiries and registration requests should be sent to Hubert Fletcher at h.fletcher@norfolkcity.gov. Registration is free, and submissions will be accepted until April 15. Owners of the selected sites will be notified no later than April 25. Painting of small-scale murals (50–250 square feet) will begin on May 10, while painting of large-scale murals (251+ square feet) will begin on June 1.

If you are interested in donating paint, paintbrushes, buckets, ladders, etc., please visit www.norfolkcity.gov/tpoa. This will help us to maximize our budget and produce as many murals as possible.

To: Marilyn Raya <rayam@sunnydayflorist.com>
From: Hubert Fletcher <h.fletcher@norfolkcity.gov>
Date: April 20
Subject: The Power of Art (TPOA)

Dear Ms. Raya,

Congratulations! Your site (154 Ames Street) has been selected for the TPOA program. You submitted your own image, with the following description:

8′x15′ mural (120 sq. ft. total) depicting Main Street as it appeared 100 years ago. Mural includes several buildings and people, along with the Sunny Day Florist logo in the bottom left-hand corner and the artists' signature in the bottom right-hand corner.

We made some alterations to your submission, as it did not fit our criteria in its original state. Please see the attached altered version. You do not need to make any special preparations for the painters other than removing items from the area. The team will take care of the rest.

Thanks!

Hubert Fletcher
Director, The Power of Art (TPOA)

181. What is the purpose of TPOA?

(A) To clean up the downtown area
(B) To start more local businesses
(C) To provide training for artists
(D) To attract more people to the city

182. In the flyer, the word "prompted" in paragraph 1, line 6, is closest in meaning to

(A) initiated
(B) acted quickly
(C) allowed
(D) provided assistance

183. According to the flyer, what can be done on the Web site?

(A) Submitting project ideas
(B) Viewing past entries
(C) Making supply donations
(D) Reviewing program rules

184. What most likely is the problem with Ms. Raya's submission?

(A) It failed to follow the requested theme.
(B) It contained a reference to a specific business.
(C) Its site does not fall within the city center area.
(D) It was not designed by a professional artist.

185. When will a team most likely start working at Ms. Raya's business?

(A) April 25
(B) May 10
(C) May 25
(D) June 1

GO ON TO THE NEXT PAGE

Questions 186-190 refer to the following notice, review, and article.

NOTICE TO COOL BEANS COFFEE PATRONS

Cool Beans Coffee will be relocating to 176 Irving Street on October 1. Driving directions to the new site are available on our Web site at www.coolbeansc.com. We hope you will visit us there and continue to support locally owned businesses such as ours. We are committed to bringing you the finest coffee drinks in town. Please note that our last day of business at the Wentzville Mall will be September 20.

We will be holding a special event during our first week in business to celebrate the move. There will be specialty drinks crafted by our creative baristas, discounts on hot beverages, and live folk music. Check us out from October 1–7 to make sure you don't miss out on the fun. We look forward to serving you for many years to come!

Cassandra Marquez
Owner, Cool Beans Coffee

---

www.wentzvillenow.com/chamber-of-commerce/reviews

Business: Aloha Coffee   Date Posted: October 28

I recently tried Aloha Coffee for the first time because it took over the rental space that was previously used by Cool Beans Coffee. The coffee itself was satisfactory, and the coffee shop offers all of the standard drinks that you would expect. However, big chains like this just can't provide the level of personal and friendly service that locally owned businesses do. In this community, Cool Beans Coffee has set the standard for excellence in customer service, and I'm afraid Aloha Coffee falls short.

Shopping Center Remains at the Center of Business

With over two hundred retail shops, the Wentzville Mall has always been a major attraction for both local shoppers and tourists. Under new ownership, it has received some upgrades to the parking lot and security system, and plans to renovate the food court and restrooms are underway. However, the changes taking place behind the scenes will significantly shape the site in the long run.

One of the first changes was an increase in the rental fees for shops in the mall, going into effect as each individual lease expires. This has forced several businesses off site, including locally owned businesses such as Evelyn's Boutique and Cool Beans Coffee. These types of businesses are being replaced by major chains that can benefit from name recognition and national advertising campaigns.

While small business owners are concerned about the trend, it doesn't seem to be negatively affecting the mall's image. "I love shopping at the Wentzville Mall," said one shopper, Alice Russell. "It has everything I need under one roof."

186. Why most likely did Ms. Marquez relocate her business?

(A) She thought the new location was more convenient.

(B) She needed more seating for customers.

(C) She could no longer afford the rent.

(D) She wanted to be in a newer facility.

187. What is suggested about Aloha Coffee?

(A) It has a partnership with Cool Beans Coffee.

(B) It occasionally features live music.

(C) It is located in the Wentzville Mall.

(D) It has many regular customers.

188. In the review, the word "set" in paragraph 1, line 5, is closest in meaning to

(A) established

(B) rested

(C) calculated

(D) placed

189. What is mentioned about the Wentzville Mall?

(A) It has recently been sold.

(B) It is currently recruiting staff.

(C) It will expand its building.

(D) It advertises nationally.

190. What does Ms. Russell like about the Wentzville Mall?

(A) Its modern appearance

(B) Its wide variety

(C) Its low prices

(D) Its friendly staff

GO ON TO THE NEXT PAGE

	E-mail
To:	Saiki Kojima <kojimas@hoshinotech.com>
From:	Namiyo Fujimoto <fujimoton@hoshinotech.com>
Date:	January 9
Subject:	Business trip details

Dear Mr. Kojima,

I am writing in response to your inquiry about your business trip to Singapore in March. The regulations for expenses are the same as those for domestic trips, as listed below.
- The company will pay for your hotel and flight directly.
- You should use the corporate credit card for all other expenses. It is not necessary to keep receipts for small purchases up to $100 such as food, transportation, and client entertainment, as these can be reviewed on the credit card statement.
- For any expense that exceeds that amount, you must turn in the receipt to me upon your return.

Please observe the following notes regarding transportation.
- Free shuttle bus services will be available when traveling to and from the airport, Novena Convention Center, and Aspella Hall.
- We will arrange a hired car for your visit to Sunrise Restaurant.

I am happy to answer any further questions you may have.

Sincerely,

Namiyo Fujimoto
Human Resources Officer, Hoshino Tech

Saiki Kojima
Hoshino Tech
33-4 Sakanoshita, Kamakura
Kanagawa Prefecture 248-0021, Japan

Dear Mr. Kojima,

Thank for your registering for the International Tech Design Conference (ITDC). We have received your booking and $300 registration fee. Enclosed you will find the receipt for this charge. This year's conference will feature notable leaders in the field, including Keith Noster of OBC. We are still working out some scheduling details, but as soon as the speaker schedule is settled, we will post them on the Web site.

I recommend that you do not delay in booking your hotel room, as hotels in the neighborhood are expected to fill up quickly. Please note that, in addition to the scheduled conference sessions, there will be a welcome breakfast on the first day of the conference for members of the Global Technology Alliance. There will also be a closing banquet for all conference presenters on March 24.

Enjoy your time at the ITDC!

Felicia Lim
Event Coordinator, International Tech Design Conference

Weekly Calendar of Events / Saiki Kojima

Mach 21	March 22	March 23	March 24	March 25
2:10 P.M. Flight DS384 departs from Narita International Airport	8 A.M. Welcome breakfast at Novena Convention Center	10 A.M.–6 P.M. Conference sessions at Novena Convention Center	10 A.M.–2 P.M. Conference sessions at Novena Convention Center	8 A.M. Meeting with Zi Mai at Jave Hotel
8:55 P.M. Arrival at Changi Airport Check in at Jave Hotel	10 A.M.–6 P.M. Conference sessions	7:30 P.M. Dinner with Norman Kelly at Sunrise Restaurant	3:00 P.M. Tour of Aspella Hall	11:50 A.M. Flight DS1609 departs from Changi Airport
				8:11 P.M. Arrival at Narita International Airport

191. According to Ms. Fujimoto, what should Mr. Kojima do for purchases over $100?

(A) Use a different credit card
(B) Get approval in advance
(C) Submit proof of purchase
(D) Make a bank transfer

192. In the letter, the word "settled" in paragraph 1, line 5, is closest in meaning to

(A) finalized
(B) paid
(C) ended
(D) relieved

193. What does Ms. Lim suggest doing?

(A) Reviewing a schedule of events
(B) Arranging accommodation right away
(C) Downloading conference materials
(D) Making dinner reservations in advance

194. What is indicated about Mr. Kojima?

(A) He will give a presentation at the conference.
(B) He used to be an employee of the ITDC.
(C) He will attend a meeting with Ms. Lim.
(D) He is a member of the Global Technology Alliance.

195. When will Mr. Kojima use a private car?

(A) On March 22
(B) On March 23
(C) On March 24
(D) On March 25

GO ON TO THE NEXT PAGE

Product Testers Wanted

RP Investigators is currently seeking members for a consumer panel that will taste test a variety of drinks and snacks from major food producers. You must be at least 18 years old to participate. The panel members will evaluate the products on several factors and share their opinions both in written form and through small group discussions. The session will last from 1 P.M. to 4 P.M., and you must be able to attend the entire session without interruption. For more information, visit www.rpinvestigators.com.

● ● ●	e-mail

To: Lila Valente
From: Darshan Bassi
Date: August 14
Subject: Consumer Panel Update

Dear Ms. Valente,

Regarding the August 28 consumer panel, I've moved the session to 6–9 P.M. because many people in our target demographic (18- to 30-year-olds) work during the day. We had 45 applicants, and 40 of them were accepted. The others were rejected because they were allergic to wheat or nuts, which are ingredients in some of the products to be tested.

I've decided to use two conference rooms. Participants will start in Conference Room A. We have space for individual tables there, so participants won't chat and influence each other's opinions. They will try each product on their own and write a full description of their experience. I'll then have everyone move to Conference Room B, where the room will be set up for small group discussions.

We will test products from the following companies:
    Lee's Beverages: three soda flavors
    Duncan Farms: one fruit juice flavor
    Neosho: four cracker flavors
    Jarmill Co.: two potato chip flavors

I will contact the clients with a full report after the session is completed.

Sincerely,

Darshan

To: Anthony Fowler
From: Darshan Bassi
Date: August 30
Subject: Consumer Panel Results

Dear Mr. Fowler,

RP Investigators has completed the consumer testing of your products. Attached you will find the complete report of the participants' comments as well as recommendations from our staff. In brief, customers liked your products' flavors, rating both of them higher than 90%. If you would like to have further testing performed, or explore other factors such as packaging, please do not hesitate to contact me.

Warmest regards,

Darshan Bassi
Lead Researcher, RP Investigators

196. What is NOT indicated about the members of the consumer panel?

(A) They must be available for three hours.
(B) They cannot have certain food allergies.
(C) They must meet a minimum age requirement.
(D) They should be frequent shoppers.

197. According to Mr. Bassi, why was a session's time changed?

(A) To avoid double-booking some meeting rooms
(B) To accommodate a certain age group
(C) To comply with a government regulation
(D) To ensure enough employees can attend

198. In the first e-mail, the word "full" in paragraph 2, line 3, is closest in meaning to

(A) detailed
(B) occupied
(C) satisfied
(D) crowded

199. Why does Mr. Bassi want to use two rooms?

(A) To host two groups simultaneously
(B) To avoid mixing the various products
(C) To have access to different equipment
(D) To get independent opinions

200. Where does Mr. Fowler most likely work?

(A) At Lee's Beverages
(B) At Duncan Farms
(C) At Neosho
(D) At Jarmill Co.

This is the end of the test. You may review PART 5, 6, and 7 if you finish the test early.

정답 p. 318 / 점수 환산표 p. 321 / 해석 p. 322

TEST

02

PART 5
PART 6
PART 7

토익 Reading Comprehension은 75분 동안 진행됩니다.
현재 시각과 지금부터 75분 후인 테스트 종료 시각을 기록해 두고,
반드시 종료 시각 전에 문제 풀이와 답안지 마킹을 완료하세요.

 현재 시각   시   분

테스트 종료 시각   시   분

READING TEST

In the Reading test, you will read a variety of texts and answer several different types of reading comprehension questions. The entire Reading test will last 75 minutes. There are three parts, and directions are given for each part. You are encouraged to answer as many questions as possible within the time allowed.

You must mark your answers on the separate answer sheet. Do not write your answers in your test book.

PART 5

Directions: A word or phrase is missing in each of the sentences below. Four answer choices are given below each sentence. Select the best answer to complete the sentence. Then mark the letter (A), (B), (C), or (D) on your answer sheet.

101. All employees are requested to use the back ------- to the building while the lobby is being renovated.

(A) entrant
(B) entered
(C) enters
(D) entrance

102. Marqui Flowers provides its ------- customers with a complimentary bouquet of flowers every year on their birthdays.

(A) reserved
(B) established
(C) approximate
(D) solitary

103. Employees who are planning on taking this Friday off should ------- their hours worked to their supervisors no later than this Thursday.

(A) involve
(B) submit
(C) resolve
(D) propose

104. Two Oaks sells ------- priced good-quality furniture for both residences and office environments.

(A) reason
(B) reasons
(C) reasonable
(D) reasonably

105. Parabolic Ventures intends to release several revolutionary devices ------- the next few years.

(A) past
(B) over
(C) among
(D) since

106. ------- at Vecker Laboratories revealed that it would be possible to cure heart disease within the next few years.

(A) Research
(B) Researcher
(C) Researched
(D) Researches

107. The county fair was a big success, ------- the relative lack of advertising that was done for it.

(A) because
(B) whereas
(C) notwithstanding
(D) however

108. The home listed for sale at 2472 E. Grapewood Drive boasts ------- space for a large garden and an already installed watering system.

(A) sufficient
(B) a lot
(C) considerate
(D) mandatory

109. The vice president ------- everyone in the R&D Department that the budget would not be reduced in the coming year.

(A) observed
(B) assured
(C) pleased
(D) inspired

110. The coordinator of the company retreat told everyone that ------- would complete the arrangements by the end of the day.

(A) his
(B) he
(C) him
(D) himself

111. Pollard Clothes outlines its exchange policy both on its Web site and ------- a sign at the cash register.

(A) to
(B) until
(C) on
(D) under

112. ------- Ms. Langford completed the assignment for Mr. Nugent, she was sent to the vice president's office to brief him on her progress.

(A) Except
(B) As soon as
(C) So that
(D) Also

113. After many studies showing the importance of recycling, a ------- of 135 municipalities now have some form of mandatory recycling program.

(A) goal
(B) total
(C) search
(D) result

114. Given the popularity of tennis, it is no surprise to see ------- numbers of young children starting to play it these days.

(A) many
(B) large
(C) broad
(D) sudden

115. When listing ------- during an interview, only focus on those that are relevant to the job you're applying for.

(A) accomplishing
(B) accomplished
(C) accomplishments
(D) accomplishes

116. Throughout its 30 years in business selling kitchen appliances, Dean & Gold Co.'s sales have increased ------- almost every year.

(A) arguably
(B) currently
(C) productively
(D) incrementally

117. Lessons in Russian and German ------- to both students who wish to study by themselves and those who want to learn with others.

(A) have offered
(B) to be offered
(C) are offered
(D) offering

118. Staff members who transfer to branches abroad ------- rely upon someone in HR to find accommodations for them and their families.

(A) norm
(B) normed
(C) normal
(D) normally

119. The Pollard Award recognizes ------- in engineering and is given to a deserving individual each year.

(A) to innovate
(B) innovator
(C) innovating
(D) innovation

120. Please be advised that no one ------- hotel patrons and guests has access to the Winchester Hotel pool facilities.

(A) out of
(B) for
(C) except
(D) among

GO ON TO THE NEXT PAGE

121. ------- speaking to large audiences, it is important to avoid looking at one's notes for the majority of the talk.

(A) For
(B) As
(C) In order to
(D) When

122. Ms. Johnson is ------- to provide assistance to the clients from Berlin since it will give her the chance to speak German.

(A) delighting
(B) delighted
(C) delightful
(D) delights

123. Please note that bloggers do not necessarily reflect the ------- of *Greenwich News and Report* or its contributors.

(A) differences
(B) effects
(C) views
(D) exchanges

124. According to Mr. Marshall, information ------- to employees should be restricted only to those working on the Bentley project.

(A) distributes
(B) distribute
(C) distributed
(D) distributing

125. The decision to reduce the number of workers on the team was opposed by virtually ------- in the office.

(A) everyone
(B) anything
(C) whatever
(D) one another

126. There are more than ten ethnic restaurants ------- walking distance of the Mandarin Hotel.

(A) by
(B) usually
(C) within
(D) until

127. Meredith Wesley, the CFO, ------- the bonuses recently given to some employees at tomorrow's shareholders' meeting.

(A) had addressed
(B) is addressing
(C) will be addressed
(D) can be addressed

128. Hartford Manufacturing attributes its success to the quality of its products ------- the marketing campaign conducted by Jefferson Media.

(A) as for
(B) except
(C) rather than
(D) after all

129. While market experts had long predicted a drop in sales this holiday season, consumers ------- continued to surprise analysts by turning out in record numbers.

(A) furthermore
(B) despite
(C) nevertheless
(D) neither

130. Portions of Westmill Mall will be closed ------- renovations during the month of January, and a list of affected stores can be found on our Web site.

(A) in
(B) to
(C) for
(D) of

PART 6

Directions: Read the texts that follow. A word, phrase, or sentence is missing in parts of each text. Four answer choices for each question are given below the text. Select the best answer to complete the text. Then mark the letter (A), (B), (C), or (D) on your answer sheet.

Questions 131-134 refer to the following notice.

New recreation facilities ------- to the community of Hernsdale. Yesterday, *The Hernsdale Press* ran
          131.

a story announcing that a 3 million dollar sports complex was approved by the city council parks

committee. -------.
    132.

Construction begins on November 10 at the site of the field located next to Willis Park. The Blue

Ridge Sports Complex, as it will be known, will open on June 22. The facilities may be reserved for

local sports teams ------- of the time, but will normally be available to anyone ------- regular hours.
      133.   **134.**

131. (A) has come
    (B) will have come
    (C) are coming
    (D) came

132. (A) The vote was held on Tuesday, September 2.
    (B) Thousands of fans enjoyed watching sports there.
    (C) Members agreed that funds should be spent elsewhere.
    (D) Even so, supporters will appeal to the council.

133. (A) some
    (B) many
    (C) little
    (D) all

134. (A) for
    (B) to
    (C) during
    (D) with

GO ON TO THE NEXT PAGE

Questions 135-138 refer to the following article.

Irving (9 July)—Jonathan Melle has been promoted to director of the Irving School District. He was

------- chosen at the board meeting on Monday night. -------. In his new role, he will be responsible
135.   **136.**

for overseeing the budget, staff and facilities of all the schools in the district. -------, he will chair
                                                              137.

the school board starting at the next meeting on August 11. Ms. Adel Keene is the outgoing director

------- the board during her last five years.
138.

135. (A) numerously
(B) unanimously
(C) singly
(D) greatly

136. (A) The positions have been vacant
throughout the whole month.
(B) Several schools have been newly added
to the school district.
(C) During the meeting, Mr. Melle talked
about the upcoming merger.
(D) Mr. Melle has been the principal at JPC
High School for six years.

137. (A) In addition
(B) Nevertheless
(C) As a result
(D) Instead

138. (A) that chairs
(B) who has chaired
(C) whose chairs
(D) chairing that

Questions 139-142 refer to the following letter.

Karlee Wood
Hiring Manager of Habitat Advertising
342 Marsh Lane
Sun Valley, ID 83353

Dear Ms. Wood,

We've had the pleasure of having Mr. Andrew Nelson work with us here at Yountville Marketing

Agency for more than three years. ------- the very beginning of his employment with our company,
139.

he has proven to be a reliable and dedicated asset. -------. As a result, we have witnessed an
140.

increase in the overall productivity of our staff.

Of course, I truly ------- seeing Andrew leave Yountville Marketing, yet I give nothing short of my
141.

highest recommendation for him to your company. Undoubtedly, he ------- a remarkable asset to
142.

Habitat Advertising just as he has been to us.

Sincerely,

Joshua Shroud
Yountville Marketing Agency, Director

---

139. (A) Along
(B) Given
(C) From
(D) Without

140. (A) Over the past 10 months, he has been
in charge of training new hires.
(B) This is why Mr. Nelson is eligible for a
promotion.
(C) I have interviewed many candidates for
the position.
(D) Our intellectual property is handled with
much care.

141. (A) regret
(B) excuse
(C) apologize
(D) disapprove

142. (A) has been
(B) will be
(C) would have been
(D) is being

GO ON TO THE NEXT PAGE

Questions 143-146 refer to the following e-mail.

To: Kyra Thompson <k.thompson@mail.org>
From: Trista Whitaker <trista@harvestgrain.com>
Date: April 4
Subject: your application

Dear Kyra,

I received your application for pastry chef posted at our Capitol Street bakery. The ------- has not yet
                                                                                                    143.
been filled. -------. I ------- that you have some work experience baking bread and cakes in another
              144.   **145.**
bakery. Therefore you probably understand some of the duties this job entails. My co-owner and I

are quite impressed that your credentials are so strong. I have an opening for an interview on April

9 at 3 P.M.

If you are interested, call me to ------- the appointment. Thank you for your interest.
                                 146.

Sincerely,

Trista Whitaker
Harvest Grain Bakery, Co-owner

---

143. (A) document
(B) position
(C) bakery
(D) form

144. (A) In addition, is it possible for you to work on weekends?
(B) In other words, can you send us two references?
(C) All bread products at our bakery is dairy-free.
(D) If you are still interested, the next step is to schedule an interview.

145. (A) see
(B) will see
(C) was seen
(D) would see

146. (A) confirm
(B) finish
(C) authorize
(D) ask

PART 7

Directions: In this part you will read a selection of texts, such as magazine and newspaper articles, e-mails, and instant messages. Each text or set of texts is followed by several questions. Select the best answer for each question and mark the letter (A), (B), (C), or (D) on your answer sheet.

Questions 147-148 refer to the following e-mail.

---

e-mail

To: gamer1985@mail.com
From: taladipro@shop.taladi.com
Subject: New Taladi Active Pro
Date: August 31

As a gaming enthusiast, you may have already heard that the Taladi Active Pro Gaming Console will be released soon.

As a previous customer of Taladi Inc., you are receiving a special invitation to preorder the Taladi Active Pro, scheduled to be on the market November 1. Supplies are limited and expected to be sold out well into the holiday season. Orders can be made by visiting www.taladi.com/activepro and entering your special invitation code W23YU1.

Happy Gaming
Taladi Gaming Consoles Promotions

---

147. What is the purpose of the e-mail?

(A) To announce a new game company opening
(B) To notify its customer of a seasonal sale
(C) To introduce an upcoming product
(D) To extend an invitation to an event

148. What is suggested about Taladi Active Pro?

(A) It is exclusively for new customers.
(B) It is popular among young professionals.
(C) It requires a six-digit code in order to play.
(D) It is not yet available.

GO ON TO THE NEXT PAGE

Questions 149-150 refer to the following invoice.

Inside Out Pest Control
3510 Market Street
Milton, Nebraska 68858

Date: May 9   Bill to:
Account Number: X32433MV   Marito Resort and Spa
                                               PO Box 695
                                               Milton, Nebraska 68858

Invoice for April 23 comprehensive seasonal pest control treatment

Materials used: $96.50
Labor: $135.20
Subtotal: $231.70
Tax: $13.90
Total: $245.60

Next treatment date: May 23
Thank you for your business.

*Please send the requested amount prior to the next monthly treatment date. If payments are not received on time, the next scheduled appointment may be delayed or canceled. Late fees of 10 percent of the outstanding amount will also be added to the bill. Our records show that your facility is scheduled through August only, so to arrange for fall services, please call our office at 585-711-3620 no later than August 10.

---

149. What is Marito Resort and Spa asked to do?

(A) Reply in writing to Inside Out Pest Control
(B) Make a payment within two weeks
(C) Choose the date of the next treatment
(D) Confirm the amount of total payment

150. When was the work performed?

(A) March 9
(B) April 23
(C) May 23
(D) August 10

Questions 151-152 refer to the following notice.

Attention English-speaking professionals living in Manila. The International Association of Business and Marketing (IABM) is opening its first chapter in Manila. The first meeting will be held June 3 from 6-9 P.M. in unit 3C located at 2342 Rizal Avenue.

Due to the size of the facilities rented, attendance is limited to 150. No membership fee is required to attend the first session. However, those interested should call 5442-5467 to reserve a seat.

Vice president Samyra Duete of IABM will be the featured speaker. She will outline the many functions of IABM and the contributions its members have made in business and marketing around the globe. Those who attend can learn about the many opportunities for professional development that IABM offers.

We are excited to expand IABM into the Philippines. Membership details and our chapter's scheduled speakers and events can be found at www.iabm.org/manila.

---

151. Where would the notice be found?

(A) At a broadcasting facility
(B) In a book about business and marketing
(C) In an international newspaper
(D) In a community newsletter

152. What is indicated about IABM?

(A) It has been gathering its members internationally.
(B) Manila is the first location where it started its business.
(C) No membership fee is required for its new employees.
(D) Requests to open a chapter can be made online.

GO ON TO THE NEXT PAGE

Rosanna Cosmetics

Highly esteemed by his colleagues for his expertise and business sense, William Terry is the replacement for Judith Perkins, who recently stepped down from her CEO position. Mr. Terry has already outlined a five-step strategy to take Rosanna Cosmetics to the next level and launch our award-winning brand in Europe.

Mr. Terry founded a small cosmetics distribution company fifteen years ago and ran it successfully for five years before he joined the Rosanna Cosmetics team and worked his way up to the chief marketing officer position. His brand management has helped the company to make gains each quarter. During his six years as chief marketing officer, Mr. Terry used his networking skills to connect to an impressive number of colleagues across the country and beyond. Prior to his time at his own business and Rosanna Cosmetics, he was a veterinarian at a small practice in his hometown.

153. Why was the information posted?

(A) To promote a product launch
(B) To profile a new executive
(C) To announce an award winner
(D) To outline a business procedure

154. What is NOT mentioned about Mr. Terry?

(A) He is respected by others.
(B) He helped to improve profits.
(C) He is originally from Europe.
(D) He has extensive business contacts.

155. What is indicated about Mr. Terry?

(A) He worked at Rosanna Cosmetics for fifteen years.
(B) He decided to change his career path.
(C) He does not have experience in public speaking.
(D) He sold his company to Rosanna Cosmetics.

Questions 156-157 refer to the following text message chain.

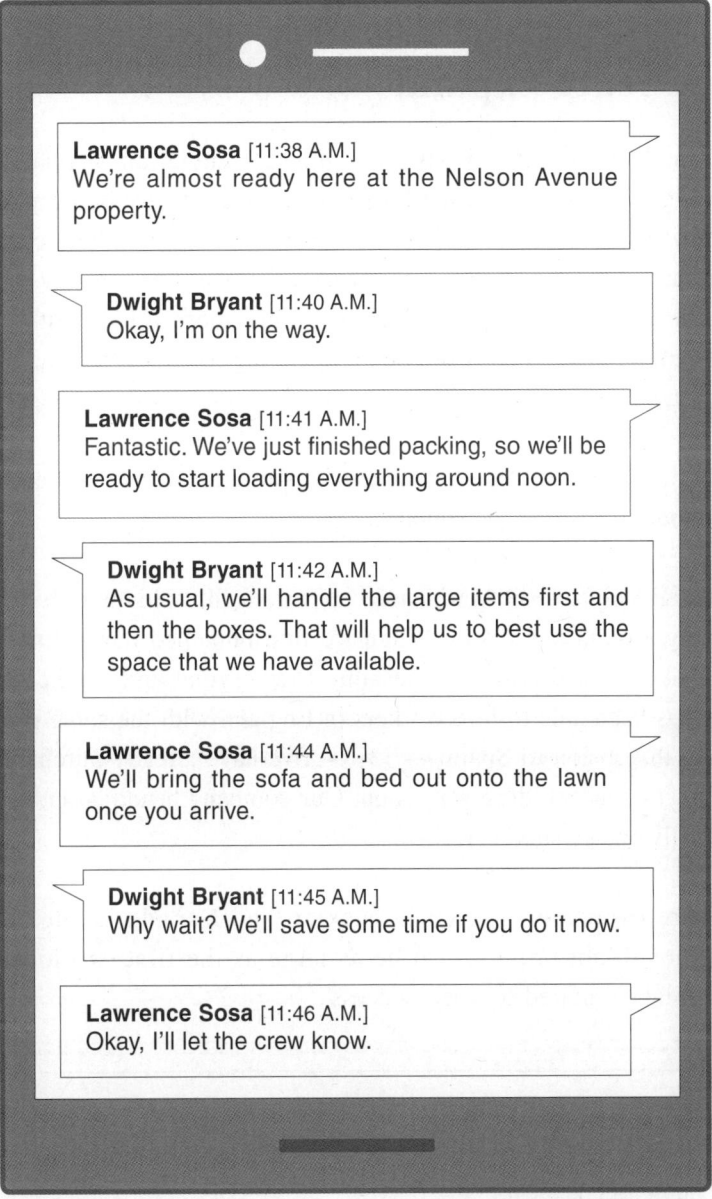

Lawrence Sosa [11:38 A.M.]
We're almost ready here at the Nelson Avenue property.

Dwight Bryant [11:40 A.M.]
Okay, I'm on the way.

Lawrence Sosa [11:41 A.M.]
Fantastic. We've just finished packing, so we'll be ready to start loading everything around noon.

Dwight Bryant [11:42 A.M.]
As usual, we'll handle the large items first and then the boxes. That will help us to best use the space that we have available.

Lawrence Sosa [11:44 A.M.]
We'll bring the sofa and bed out onto the lawn once you arrive.

Dwight Bryant [11:45 A.M.]
Why wait? We'll save some time if you do it now.

Lawrence Sosa [11:46 A.M.]
Okay, I'll let the crew know.

156. Who most likely is Mr. Sosa?

(A) A truck mechanic
(B) A professional mover
(C) A construction worker
(D) A property manager

157. At 11:45 A.M., what does Mr. Bryant most likely mean when he writes, "Why wait"?

(A) He suggests letting the crew take a break now.
(B) He is confused about missing a deadline.
(C) He thinks some furniture can be sold immediately.
(D) He wants the team to start a task right away.

GO ON TO THE NEXT PAGE

Bookstore Set to Expand

February 9—Intelecto Mundial Books announced completion of plans to expand its business starting this summer. Three bookstores are currently being planned to open in the next few years, each in a different country. — [1] —. The company, which specializes in the sale of rare books from around the world, is a major source for hard-to-find books of varying languages and origins. While most of its profits currently come from its online store, the company did begin operating its first brick and mortar store in England two years ago. — [2] —.

The new bookstore has been hugely successful attracting locals and even becoming a major draw to tourists visiting the country.

Intelecto Mundial Books CEO Mariana de la Torre said, "This is only the first step in reviving reading around our world. When we first launched our online Web site, our goal was to make great literature accessible to everyone and to encourage reading. Our company has been able to hire workers in England with the same goal as ours. We will soon bring this vision to Spain. — [3] —. We have already purchased property in Barcelona and will start building very soon. Our company headquarters is in Madrid so it's good to finally open a shop here."

More stores are expected to open in Mexico and Canada in the coming years. — [4] —. Although not projected to be as large as the first two locations, careful planning will still be required for their success.

158. What is mentioned about Intelecto Mundial Books?
(A) Most profit currently comes from the London branch.
(B) Its headquarters is planned to be built in Spain.
(C) New stores will be greater in size than its first branch.
(D) It offers people opportunities to read more literature.

159. Where is the next store expected to open?
(A) In England
(B) In Spain
(C) In Mexico
(D) In Canada

160. In which of the positions marked [1], [2], [3], and [4] does the following sentence best belong?

"With the huge interest in global literature in Europe, the London branch is on track to eventually outsell even the international sales from the Web site."

(A) [1]
(B) [2]
(C) [3]
(D) [4]

```
•  •  •                              E-mail
```

To:	Pandara Nishad <p_nishad@bellhurst.net>
From:	Ross Dillard <r_dillard@bellhurst.net>
Date:	April 18
Subject:	Assignment

Dear Ms. Nishad,

I've completed the task you've assigned me regarding the possibility of starting an employee investment program. After looking into the options for our company, I have determined that implementing such a program would be feasible within the timeframe you suggested. I've attached a summary with the details.

While there are many factors to consider, I believe that Abner Investments would suit our needs best. The company has experience working with firms whose employees are mainly very far from retirement age, providing extensive resources to help people make informed decisions about investments, so I think it would be perfect for Bellhurst. We can start a contract as soon as we make the final decision.

I know you'll be out of the office later today. I'll be out of town next week, so I'd like to get together before that. Please let me know your availability.

Thanks!

Ross Dillard

161. What is the purpose of the e-mail?

(A) To submit some research
(B) To reject a suggestion
(C) To give approval
(D) To assign a task

162. What is implied about Bellhurst?

(A) It specializes in financial products.
(B) It has young staff members.
(C) Its workforce is growing quickly.
(D) It has not been operating long.

163. When would Mr. Dillard most likely want to have a meeting?

(A) Later today
(B) Later this week
(C) Next week
(D) In two weeks

GO ON TO THE NEXT PAGE

http://www.oakridgecleaning.com/company_information

| HOME | **COMPANY INFORMATION** | PRODUCT LIST | ORDER PAGE | CONTACT US |

Our Products

Oakridge Cleaning is Oakridge's largest supplier of cleaning products used commercially and in residential settings. We work with top manufacturers to ensure our selection is of the best quality. Each product is non-toxic and specifically designed to clean a specific area. Our staff members are fully trained to recommend products for difficult tasks and stain removal.

Our Story

Oakridge Cleaning was founded twenty-five years ago by Joseph Jordan, who got the idea for the business when he was frustrated with the lack of options for the cleaning products to be used at the hotel he managed. Jordan wanted to make it easy for people to get what they needed right here in Oakridge so that they could support the local economy. The business was kept in the family upon Jordan's retirement, when he handed over the business to his daughter.

Our Expansion

Thanks to loyal customer support, Oakridge Cleaning is ready to expand operations to Evansville. Our shop there will allow for faster delivery to that area and—just like at our initial branch—will be open daily for in-store purchases. It will also be the exclusive site of weekly product demonstrations aimed at teaching customers the best ways to clean surfaces and fabrics of all kinds.

To keep up-to-date about everything going on at Oakridge Cleaning, e-mail us at info@oakridgecleaning.com and we will add you to our newsletter mailing list. We look forward to serving you at Oakridge Cleaning!

Paula Kirchner, Owner
Craig Ramos, Store Manager (Oakridge Location)

164. What is indicated about Oakridge Cleaning?

(A) It advertises its products in commercials.
(B) It is the largest business of its kind in the country.
(C) Its products do not contain harmful chemicals.
(D) It is a manufacturer of cleaning products.

165. What is suggested about Ms. Kirchner?

(A) She plans to move to Evansville.
(B) Her father used to manage a hotel.
(C) She has twenty-five years of experience.
(D) She will pass the business on to Mr. Ramos.

166. How will the Evansville site differ from the Oakridge site?

(A) It will be open every day of the week.
(B) It will offer a wider selection of goods.
(C) It will provide cleaning demonstrations.
(D) It will have a delivery option.

167. Why should customers e-mail the address provided on the Web page?

(A) To request some complimentary samples
(B) To sign up for a rewards program
(C) To share feedback about the products
(D) To stay informed about company news

Adam Sanderson
428 Ridgewood Drive
Aberdeen, SD 57401

Dear Mr. Sanderson,

Under your extended warranty for your Dargo 4-door sedan, serial number 683495-97, you are eligible for a complimentary inspection every six months. — [1] —. Tyson Garage offers this inspection, called the Basic Preventative Maintenance Package (BPMP), to all owners of Dargo brand vehicles. The package includes testing the on-board electric circuits, making sure the air conditioner is in good operation, monitoring brake function, and more. — [2] —. We also vacuum and polish the inner surfaces of your car for your comfort. The BPMP is a way to make sure that all of your vehicle components are running smoothly, and it gives us a chance to look for possible repairs that may be needed. — [3] —.

You may claim your package between June 8 and 20. These sessions are by appointment only. Please contact us at 555-5950 to set one up. — [4] —. If you are unable to bring in your vehicle within the timeframe mentioned, we may be able to issue you a voucher for a later date, but this is at the discretion of the manager.

Sincerely,

The Tyson Garage Team

168. What is the purpose of the letter?

(A) To provide an urgent safety warning
(B) To introduce a customer loyalty program
(C) To notify a customer of a free service
(D) To update some warranty information

169. What is NOT mentioned as part of the BPMP?

(A) Cleaning a vehicle's interior
(B) Checking electronic components
(C) Replacing worn brakes
(D) Testing a cooling system

170. What is Mr. Sanderson asked to do?

(A) Upgrade to a newer package
(B) Make an appointment by phone
(C) Check a voucher's expiration date
(D) Confirm a serial number

171. In which of the positions marked [1], [2], [3], and [4] does the following sentence best belong?

"If any are identified, we will inform you before moving forward."

(A) [1]
(B) [2]
(C) [3]
(D) [4]

GO ON TO THE NEXT PAGE

Questions 172-175 refer to the following online chat discussion.

Madison Lynch [1:11 P.M.]		Hey, Evan. Sorry to bother you. Would you help me with a technical question about the database?
Evan Norris [1:13 P.M.]		If I can. I don't think I know any more about it than you do, though.
Madison Lynch [1:14 P.M.]		I just tried to log on, and I got an error message. I'm trying to access some information for Kent Feldman of HF Enterprises. I need to prepare a marketing strategy for their new soda line, and I wanted to review some government regulations.
Evan Norris [1:16 P.M.]		Didn't you hear? The system has been upgraded. You need to use the new password you were assigned at yesterday's staff meeting.
Madison Lynch [1:17 P.M.]		I wasn't there.
Evan Norris [1:18 P.M.]		Talk to Ben in the IT department. He can assign you a password. I had the same problem this morning.
Madison Lynch [1:19 P.M.]		I'll do that. Thanks!

SEND

172. At 1:13 P.M., what does Mr. Norris most likely mean when he writes, "If I can"?

(A) He hopes to meet Ms. Lynch later.
(B) He is unsure about his schedule.
(C) He will try to give assistance.
(D) He will report a technical problem.

173. Where does Mr. Feldman most likely work?

(A) At a beverage manufacturer
(B) At a research institute
(C) At a marketing firm
(D) At a government office

174. What is indicated about Ms. Lynch?

(A) She is a new employee.
(B) She was absent from a meeting.
(C) She added files to a database.
(D) She upgraded her computer.

175. What did Mr. Norris do in the morning?

(A) Contacted a client
(B) Assigned Ms. Lynch a password
(C) Spoke to an IT worker
(D) Got his computer repaired

GO ON TO THE NEXT PAGE

Ride the Rails Drawing Contest: Your Ticket to Adventure

For a one-of-a-kind experience, see the beautiful scenery of the Pacific Northwest from the window of a train! The Northwest Folk Festival is partnering with Seattle Train Tours to offer you a chance to win a free train ride for you and two guests.

Buy anything at the Northwest Folk Festival, taking place throughout the month of August, and you will be issued a six-digit code for the prize drawing. Input the code on our Web site, www. northwestff.org/contest, to enter. You must be at least 18 years old to participate. One entry per person. The drawing will be held the morning after the submission period ends, and the winner will be contacted that same day. Check out the fabulous prizes below!

Prize	Submission Date
Mount Rainier Railroad Tour	August 1–7
Cascade Railroad Tour	August 8–14
Coastal Railroad Tour	August 15–21
Heritage Park Railroad Tour	August 22–28

Whether you're a visitor or a resident of the Seattle area, we hope you'll make the most of your summer by visiting the Northwest Folk Festival and participating in this contest. Good luck!

To: Lillian Brewer <brewer.l@star-inbox.net>
From: Curtis Flynn <curtis@northwestff.org>
Date: August 15
Subject: You're a Ride the Rails Winner!

Dear Ms. Brewer,

Congratulations! I'm pleased to inform you that you are this week's winner in the Ride the Rails drawing contest. Attached you will find a schedule of the upcoming tours that are offered. Please e-mail me back with your first and second choices for the days you would like to take the tour, and I will do my best to accommodate you. I recommend doing this as soon as possible, as the tours are popular and they tend to sell out in a short time. Your tickets will arrive by mail on approximately August 27 at the address provided on your entry form. Tours vary slightly in time, lasting up to six hours. The company also regularly conducts surveys to find out how it can further improve its services, so you may be asked to complete a form at the end of your trip. If you have any questions, please let me know.

Sincerely,

Curtis Flynn

176. What is NOT mentioned about the Ride the Rails drawing contest?

(A) A purchase is required to enter.
(B) Each prize is valid for three people.
(C) Participants may only enter one time.
(D) It is held in the area every year.

177. Which prize did Ms. Brewer most likely win?

(A) The Mount Rainier Railroad Tour
(B) The Cascade Railroad Tour
(C) The Coastal Railroad Tour
(D) The Heritage Park Railroad Tour

178. What is suggested about Ms. Brewer?

(A) She attended the Northwest Folk Festival.
(B) She had trouble downloading a schedule.
(C) She wants to change the tour time.
(D) She requested her tickets by e-mail.

179. What is Ms. Brewer asked to provide?

(A) Her mailing address
(B) Proof of her identity
(C) Her date preferences
(D) A valid receipt

180. In the e-mail, the word "conducts" in paragraph 1, line 7, is closest in meaning to

(A) accomplishes
(B) administers
(C) guides
(D) behaves

GO ON TO THE NEXT PAGE

To: Albert Chapman <alchapman@grantviewmail.com>
From: BB-Card <info@bb-card.com>
Date: May 23
Subject: A Message from BB-Card

Dear Mr. Chapman,

On behalf of BB-Card, I would like to thank you for using our services. Our records indicate that you recently redeemed your rewards points for the first time. In order to help us monitor customer experience, we ask that you fill out the attached form. It is a questionnaire on which you can share your feedback freely. The form can be returned via e-mail to this address.

To show our appreciation for your time, you will receive a free BB-Card leather-bound day planner if the form is completed and returned on or before June 15. Customers who submit forms after that date will receive a BB-Card pen set. We hope you enjoy the free gift.

Sincerely,

Kevin Salas
Head of Customer Services, BB-Card

Thank you for completing this survey from BB-Card!

Name: Albert Chapman   Survey completion date: June 29

1. Why did you sign up for the BB-Card? It was recommended to me by a friend.
2. How often do you usually use your BB-Card, and where do you use it? I use it almost daily, mainly for regular purchases such as at gas stations and supermarkets.
3. How would you rate your experience of redeeming your rewards points?
[✔] Excellent   [   ] Good   [   ] Okay   [   ] Poor
Comments: I liked that there was a wide variety of items available for me to purchase with my BB-Card points. At first, I had trouble figuring out how to access my account to check my point balance, but once I read the online user guide everything became clear. After placing the order, I was surprised that I received my goods within just a few days. I will keep shopping with this card so I can earn more points.

181. What is the purpose of the e-mail?

(A) To thank a customer for upgrading a service

(B) To gather opinions from a customer

(C) To remind a customer to make a payment

(D) To request information for an order form

182. What is true about BB-Card?

(A) It offers a rewards program.

(B) It has a low interest rate.

(C) It can be used internationally.

(D) It gives a gift to first-time customers.

183. In the e-mail, the word "monitor" in paragraph 1, line 2, is closest in meaning to

(A) supervise

(B) retain

(C) detect

(D) observe

184. What will probably be sent to Mr. Chapman from BB-Card?

(A) A voucher for gas

(B) A set of writing utensils

(C) A supermarket sample

(D) A leather day planner

185. What does Mr. Chapman indicate about BB-Card?

(A) Its online user guide was confusing.

(B) Its items were dispatched quickly.

(C) Its policy changes are fair.

(D) Its Web site access was temporarily unavailable.

GO ON TO THE NEXT PAGE

Questions 186-190 refer to the following advertisement, form, and e-mail.

Glitz Cleaning
Leave your cleaning to us!

At Glitz Cleaning, we understand that cleaning chores are difficult to fit into your busy lifestyle. That's why we offer one-time and weekly cleaning services. We are committed to creating a fresh and welcoming environment in your home, and our team of professionals can handle jobs of any size.

We send a team of three cleaners, and our rates are calculated in blocks as follows: $80/1 hour, $150/2 hours, $215/3 hours, $280/4 hours. Work exceeding 4 hours should be negotiated ahead of time.

Our staff will bring all of the cleaning supplies and appliances with them, so you don't need to prepare anything. If you have tasks that require special attention, please let us know at the time of booking an appointment. Contact us today at www.glitzcl.com.

---

http://www.glitzcl.com/booking
Glitz Cleaning / Work Request

Date of Request: October 14   Request #: 9820
Customer: Vivian Pharr   Address: 592 Brook Road, Fredericksburg, VA 22401
Contact: [   ] Phone _____ / [✔] E-mail vpharr@espinozainc.com
Have you used Glitz Cleaning before? [   ] Yes [✔] No
Size of the property to be cleaned: Five-bedroom house, all rooms

Preferred Date of Service: October 20   Preferred Time of Day: Morning
Type of Service: [✔] One-time   [   ] Weekly   Number of hours: 2

Customer Notes: The cleaners will need a tall ladder to dust the light fixtures attached to the ceiling. This will have to be provided, as I don't have one.

Special Instructions: In the living room, I have an old armchair that I would like taken away, so I'm wondering if you can handle that. Please let me know.

```
● ● ●                          E-mail
```

To: Vivian Pharr <vpharr@espinozainc.com>
From: Glitz Cleaning <appointments@glitzcl.com>
Date: October 14
Subject: Cleaning Request

Dear Ms. Pharr,

I would like to confirm your cleaning appointment for October 20 at 10 A.M. Due to the size of your property, we've booked you for one hour more than you requested. It seems this will be necessary due to the size of the property, especially since it's our first visit. Three employees will be sent to your home, and they can be identified by their green Glitz Cleaning name tags. Please remember that our employees cannot accept cash payments from customers. Therefore, you should arrange payment by bank transfer at least twenty-four hours before the appointment. I have attached the invoice and the instructions for making the transfer. You will be issued a receipt by e-mail. You may keep this for your records, but it is not necessary to present it to the employees.

Regarding the request you made in the Special Instructions section of our request form, I'm happy to say that we can accommodate you. And because you are a new customer, we will perform this service free of charge.

If you have any questions, please do not hesitate to contact me at this e-mail address or by phone at 555-2907.

Sincerely,

Alan Jordan
Glitz Cleaning Customer Service Representative

---

186. In the advertisement, the word "committed" in paragraph 1, line 2, is closest in meaning to

(A) limited
(B) contributed
(C) accustomed
(D) dedicated

187. What does Ms. Pharr indicate about her home?

(A) It has some broken lights.
(B) It is more than one story tall.
(C) It has high ceilings.
(D) It was renovated recently.

188. How much will Ms. Pharr's bill most likely be?

(A) $80
(B) $150
(C) $215
(D) $280

189. What does Mr. Jordan remind Ms. Pharr to do?

(A) Move items out of the way
(B) Make a payment in advance
(C) Confirm an address
(D) Check an account number

190. What is suggested about Glitz Cleaning?

(A) It plans to expand its workforce.
(B) It offers furniture removal services.
(C) It advertises its business locally.
(D) It performs outdoor maintenance.

GO ON TO THE NEXT PAGE

NOTICE

The management team is pleased to announce that our hotel will be featured in *Urban Outdoors Magazine*. There will be an article about our private gardens. Photographs of the gardens, along with a group picture of the relevant staff members who help to maintain them, will accompany the article. A photographer will visit our hotel on Tuesday, May 20, for a photo shoot at 2 P.M. If you will be part of the group photo, please wear a professional-style button-up shirt and trousers (no jeans, please) for the picture. You should bring along something to change into after that so you can continue your work. If you have any questions, please talk to Antonia Suhr.

E-mail	
To:	Antonia Suhr <antoniasuhr@merrillhotel.net>
From:	Jessie Weiss<jessie@urbanoutdoorsmag.com>
Date:	May 16
Subject:	Upcoming photo shoot

Hello Ms. Suhr,

The weather is supposed to be warm and sunny on next week's photo shoot day, so I think the pictures will turn out great. I'll take the group picture first so people can get back to work. That won't take more than ten minutes, and I think the best place would be near the fountain, so please have people meet me there. I'll then go on to photographing the rest of the gardens, and I plan to have everything wrapped up by 4 P.M. I look forward to meeting you in person on Tuesday!

Sincerely,

Jessie Weiss

Merrill Hotel: A Nature Break in the City

by Ralph Cross

For those staying in Hammond City, the Merrill Hotel—with its four acres of gardens surrounding the building—offers a welcome break from the hustle and bustle of the city. At the main entrance on the north side of the hotel, guests are greeted by beautiful rose gardens featuring twelve different varieties of roses. At the rear of the building, to the south side, there is a functioning marble fountain designed by artist Fausta Udinesi. To the west, guests can enjoy an outdoor patio area that is attached to the hotel's on-site restaurant. And to the east, there are six elaborate hedge sculptures.

Every year, when Merrill Hotel opens in the spring for the tourist season, visitors and locals flock to the hotel to enjoy the beauty of the site. "When the gardens are in full bloom, it is a feast for the eyes," says regular hotel guest Andrew Deleon. "I love the calming environment in these gardens. It always helps me relax."

The Merrill Hotel accepts bookings on its Web site, www.merrillhotel.net.

191. Who most likely will Mr. Weiss take a photo of?

(A) Housekeepers
(B) Receptionists
(C) Groundskeepers
(D) Hotel guests

192. What are some staff members asked to do on May 20?

(A) Stay out of the garden area
(B) Bring extra clothing to work
(C) Come early for a shift
(D) Wear an employee ID badge

193. Where will a group photo be taken?

(A) North of the hotel
(B) East of the hotel
(C) South of the hotel
(D) West of the hotel

194. What is suggested about the Merrill Hotel?

(A) It is not open year round.
(B) It has more than one branch.
(C) It is the largest hotel in the city.
(D) It hosts an annual flower festival.

195. What does Mr. Deleon like about the hotel's gardens?

(A) The natural wildlife
(B) The variety of plants
(C) The comfortable seats
(D) The peaceful surroundings

GO ON TO THE NEXT PAGE

Autumn Lecture Series at Laurel Community Center

Thursday, September 15 / "Improving Decision-Making" / Granite Room / 7:30 P.M.–9:30 P.M.
Professor JieKuo, who teaches psychology at Bergan University, will explain the principles behind how people make decisions and teach you how to avoid the most common mistakes. There will be a collection for the Laurel Homeless Shelter after the talk. Everyone is encouraged to give generously.

Thursday, September 29 / "The Science of Health" / Slate Room / 7:30 P.M.–9:00 P.M.
Dr. Arthur Cardoso of Russell University will discuss the latest research in the field of health and well-being, including topics such as vaccinations, work-related stress, and the effects of too much screen time. Dr. Cardoso will be collecting donations on behalf of the 8th Avenue Clinic.

Thursday, October 13 / "International Politics" / Granite Room / 7:00 P.M.–9:00 P.M.
A great way to stay informed! Cynthia Ebert will cover the hottest political issues of our time, with insights you won't hear anywhere else. Participants will have the opportunity to make a financial contribution to the Worldwide Relief Fund.

Thursday, October 27 / "Exploring Classic Literature" / Granite Room / 7:00 P.M.–9:30 P.M.
Professor Isabella Folliero of Charlotte College will examine some of the best-known novels in history, highlighting the aspects that set them apart as masterpieces. Participants may donate to the Laurel Library at the event.

E-mail Britney Maxwell, b.maxwell@laurelccenter.org, for tickets ($6.50 each). Please note that seating in the front row is reserved exclusively for employees of the municipal government.

To: Britney Maxwell <b.maxwell@laurelccenter.org>
From: Hayden Lester <lesterhayden@epic-mail.com>
Date: September 10
Subject: Autumn Lecture Series

Dear Ms. Maxwell,

I'm interested in reserving a ticket for your Autumn Lecture Series. I have already ordered—and received—my ticket for the "Improving Decision-Making" lecture. I'm so pleased that I'll be able to sit in the first row. The ticket I would like to add is "International Politics." Please send me one adult ticket and charge the credit card I provided for my original purchase (Invoice #7592). Thank you!

Hayden Lester

To: Hayden Lester <lesterhayden@epic-mail.com>
From: Britney Maxwell <b.maxwell@laurelccenter.org>
Date: September 11
Subject: RE: Autumn Lecture Series

Dear Mr. Lester,

I'm sorry to inform you that we cannot fulfill the request you made yesterday. Unfortunately, that lecture has been canceled and replaced with a talk by Glenda Fesno called "The Social Media Age." Unfortunately, a ticket for the canceled lecture has already been sent to you and your credit card was charged. If you would like to attend the new lecture, we will just exchange your old ticket for a new one. We would hold the ticket for you at the information desk, and you could pick it up on the day of the event. Please e-mail me back to let me know whether you would like to attend the new lecture or receive a refund.

Sincerely,

Britney Maxwell
Ticketing Agent, Laurel Community Center

196. What is the same about all of the lectures?

(A) They are all in the same room.
(B) They are all the same duration.
(C) They are all taking donations.
(D) They are all given by professors.

197. What is suggested about Mr. Lester?

(A) He thinks his first ticket was lost.
(B) He attended last year's event.
(C) He is a community center member.
(D) He works for the government.

198. When will the lecture entitled "The Social Media Age" take place?

(A) On September 15
(B) On September 29
(C) On October 13
(D) On October 27

199. In the second e-mail, the word "hold" in paragraph 1, line 5, is closest in meaning to

(A) host
(B) carry
(C) grasp
(D) keep

200. What is Mr. Lester asked to do?

(A) Provide a mailing address
(B) Express a preference
(C) Show proof of payment
(D) Select a seat

This is the end of the test. You may review PART 5, 6, and 7 if you finish the test early.
정답 p. 318 / 점수 환산표 p. 321 / 해석 p. 330

TEST

PART 5
PART 6
PART 7

토익 Reading Comprehension은 75분 동안 진행됩니다.
현재 시각과 지금부터 75분 후인 테스트 종료 시각을 기록해 두고,
반드시 종료 시각 전에 문제 풀이와 답안지 마킹을 완료하세요.

 현재 시각 시분

테스트 종료 시각 시 분

READING TEST

In the Reading test, you will read a variety of texts and answer several different types of reading comprehension questions. The entire Reading test will last 75 minutes. There are three parts, and directions are given for each part. You are encouraged to answer as many questions as possible within the time allowed.

You must mark your answers on the separate answer sheet. Do not write your answers in your test book.

PART 5

Directions: A word or phrase is missing in each of the sentences below. Four answer choices are given below each sentence. Select the best answer to complete the sentence. Then mark the letter (A), (B), (C), or (D) on your answer sheet.

101. The manager of Lexon Construction has proposed changes to make operations less ------- by recycling the building materials.

(A) wasting
(B) wastefully
(C) wastes
(D) wasteful

102. The company restricts ------- to the main laboratory to senior technicians because the research conducted there is highly sensitive.

(A) accessible
(B) access
(C) accessed
(D) accesses

103. The wheat harvest is ------- to be excellent on account of the pleasant weather this summer.

(A) completed
(B) maximized
(C) seemed
(D) expected

104. The Mahawai Resort Hotel has a reputation for being ------- to the requests of its guests, no matter how large or small the matter.

(A) attentive
(B) comprehensive
(C) noteworthy
(D) partial

105. Parking is not allowed on either side of Waterstone Road because it is the narrowest ------- in the entire town of Clarksville.

(A) any
(B) one
(C) each
(D) which

106. Thanks to the state-of-the-art technology it uses, the Brotan-630 printer is able to ------- plenty of professionally printed materials.

(A) duplicates
(B) duplicated
(C) duplicate
(D) duplicating

107. According to a recent survey, many customers at Harding's are ------- of the existence of its exclusive shoppers club.

(A) willing
(B) entitled
(C) unaware
(D) undecided

108. The national marketing campaign for Camping Express generated a great deal of interest in its ------- line of tents.

(A) updated
(B) updates
(C) update
(D) updating

109. Officials reported that the population of the southern suburbs of the city is growing at a ------- fast pace.

(A) surprising
(B) surprises
(C) surprised
(D) surprisingly

110. Your selected shipping method can be upgraded to one-day air for an additional ------- of just $7.99.

(A) pay
(B) charge
(C) revenue
(D) money

111. At Gold's Gym, it was announced that the costs of attending group classes will differ ------- in January.

(A) started
(B) starts
(C) to start
(D) starting

112. The president met with several ------- economists to discuss ways to prevent a downturn in the export market.

(A) notably
(B) notable
(C) noting
(D) note

113. A survey is going to be conducted over the next two weeks to ------- customer satisfaction at the Moreland Department Store.

(A) gauge
(B) administer
(C) invent
(D) please

114. More in-depth details ------- the annual journalism conference can be found at www. hughesjournalism.org/conference.

(A) pertaining to
(B) despite
(C) along
(D) through

115. Participation in the Sustainability for Life event gives entrepreneurs wide ------- to investors who may financially support their projects.

(A) exposed
(B) exposure
(C) exposing
(D) expose

116. The funds raised at the annual banquet will be distributed to ------- charity is in the greatest need.

(A) whichever
(B) every
(C) several
(D) any

117. Companies will not ------- approve requests to transfer departments until an employee has worked a minimum of six months in the same position.

(A) generally
(B) exactly
(C) currently
(D) largely

118. The Carthage project, ------- the direction of Ms. Luther, is expected to be completed two weeks from tomorrow.

(A) before
(B) under
(C) beside
(D) regarding

119. The Municipal Transit Department is developing a card that ------- passengers to travel by bus, subway, and taxi with one payment.

(A) allow
(B) was allowed
(C) has allowed
(D) will allow

120. Critics who attended the concert of pianist Melissa Keen were impressed by her uniquely ------- playing.

(A) precisely
(B) preciseness
(C) precise
(D) precision

GO ON TO THE NEXT PAGE

121. The research of Marie Hollister, professor of Political Science at Wrenton University, is published ------- in the *Journal of Current Events*.
(A) shortly
(B) thoroughly
(C) finely
(D) regularly

122. Due to its ------- to public schools, parks and shopping centers, the Meadow Lake Village is very popular among people.
(A) area
(B) proximity
(C) resource
(D) direction

123. ------- the airline found Ms. Camacho's missing luggage, she had already taken her return flight.
(A) Whenever
(B) By the time
(C) Thanks to
(D) Unless

124. ------- being one of the most popular vacation spots in Central America, Belize is known among nature lovers for its remarkable wildlife.
(A) In search of
(B) Regardless
(C) Aside from
(D) Seeing that

125. The VIP lounge on the top floor of the building is to be ------- solely by executives and their guests.
(A) use
(B) usage
(C) using
(D) used

126. To improve safety in the parking lot, the maintenance team will replace the dim lights with ------- ones.
(A) brightest
(B) brighter
(C) brightly
(D) brightness

127. On March 9, sales ------- from top selling brands across the country convened for the Conference on Brand Marketing.
(A) associates
(B) revenue
(C) products
(D) priority

128. The organizers of the international conference have hired over thirty interpreters, ------- are native speakers of the target language.
(A) most of whom
(B) insofar as
(C) many of them
(D) because of them

129. Every fax machine ------- a one-year agreement to provide service or repairs free of charge.
(A) includes
(B) fixes
(C) locates
(D) accommodates

130. Zaga Inc. manufacturing plants use the most time-efficient machinery available, ------- increasing production capabilities.
(A) nevertheless
(B) in spite of
(C) likewise
(D) therefore

PART 6

Directions: Read the texts that follow. A word, phrase, or sentence is missing in parts of each text. Four answer choices for each question are given below the text. Select the best answer to complete the text. Then mark the letter (A), (B), (C), or (D) on your answer sheet.

Questions 131-134 refer to the following advertisement.

Natural hot springs, delicious food and a peaceful river nestled in beautiful wooded mountains

------- you at Sawtooth Spa. -------. With nearby accommodations abundantly available in any style
131.   **132.**
and price range, visiting Sawtooth is ------- anyone's budget.
                                      133.

For more details or to purchase a pass, simply visit sawtoothspa.com. Inquiries can be made under

the tab 'Contact Us'. All questions and requested materials will be responded to -------, because we
                                                                              134.
believe planning a vacation should never be stressful!

131. (A) await
(B) awaited
(C) was awaiting
(D) had been awaiting

132. (A) We hope you enjoyed having time to relax
at our site and that you'll come again.
(B) Thank you for inquiring about our
massage services and beauty treatments.
(C) Located only 15 minutes off Exit 21B of
Interstate 84, getting there is easy.
(D) Sawtooth Spa will go through renovations
starting January 12.

133. (A) to
(B) among
(C) within
(D) by

134. (A) nearly
(B) promptly
(C) suddenly
(D) again

GO ON TO THE NEXT PAGE

Questions 135-138 refer to the following information.

Thank you for your ------- of the Belmore Evening Gown size 4 in blue. We value your business and
        135.

wish you the highest satisfaction with our product. If you are not satisfied, you may request a refund

of any unused item within 60 days of purchase. To return an eligible item, submit a request through

your online account and we will send you a shipping label. Your item ------- with the original price
        136.

tags. ------- Return shipping and handling costs may be deducted from the total. We appreciate your
    137.

business and we hope you will ------- with us again.
        138.

135. (A) purchasing
(B) purchased
(C) purchase
(D) purchases

136. (A) will send
(B) is sending
(C) must be sent
(D) has been sent

137. (A) We can offer you the same item in two different shades.
(B) Please bring the receipt in person when returning your gown.
(C) We make sure our customers receive high-quality service.
(D) Allow 30 days for your request to be processed.

138. (A) meet
(B) shop
(C) tour
(D) work

Questions 139-142 refer to the following letter.

Manning's Groceries
945 East Front Street
Placerville, CA 95667
May 19

Jon Mauk or Current Resident
2700 Foothills Dr.
Placerville, CA 95667

Dear Valued Customer,

Manning's Groceries' participation in the state-wide effort to reduce plastic use will commence on

June 1. We would like to inform you of the effects this ------- will have on our grocery store. We will
                                                      139.
begin by eliminating plastic bags at our check-out lines, and replacing them with either purchased

reusable bags or boxes left over from our merchandise shipments. To ------- either option, simply
                                                                   140.
speak to your cashier at the register.

As a result of this project, we actually expect to lower sales costs, ------- our customers about $10
                                                                    141.
per year.

Thank you for partnering with us to protect the planet. For more information you can visit

manningsfood.com or ask a store manager. -------.
                                        142.

Sincerely,

Silvia Bundy, Store Manager
Manning's Groceries

---

139. (A) initiative
(B) research
(C) negotiation
(D) environment

140. (A) inquire
(B) agree
(C) explain
(D) request

141. (A) will save
(B) being saved
(C) saving
(D) savings

142. (A) The state has emphasized the importance of the project.
(B) Thus, the effort should benefit the customers as well as nature.
(C) We hope that you will take pride in the participation of this project.
(D) We will be giving out 200 free reusable bags on June 1.

GO ON TO THE NEXT PAGE

Dear Mr. Hanson,

We have received and processed your ------- for a loan which you submitted through our Web site
143.
on January 6. It is our desire to not only provide our customers with the funds they need, but also to

ensure the contracts are viable. Your file has been carefully reviewed and the status of your request

is -------. Please, contact ------- loan officer, Ms. Sienna Toledo at 253-5545, who will provide you
144.   **145.**
with further information. -------.
                          146.

Zenque Credit Union looks forward to finalizing this contract and partnering with you to strengthen

your financial future.

Cordially,

Gwen Hughes
Chief Loan Officer
Zenque Credit Union

---

143. (A) invitation
(B) notation
(C) application
(D) suggestion

144. (A) approved
(B) postponed
(C) rejected
(D) addressed

145. (A) their
(B) his
(C) our
(D) your

146. (A) She will be available to answer your questions.
(B) We also provide cash insurance and retirement plans.
(C) This information includes your address and phone number.
(D) We appreciate your interest in a career with us.

PART 7

Directions: In this part you will read a selection of texts, such as magazine and newspaper articles, e-mails, and instant messages. Each text or set of texts is followed by several questions. Select the best answer for each question and mark the letter (A), (B), (C), or (D) on your answer sheet.

Questions 147-148 refer to the following e-mail.

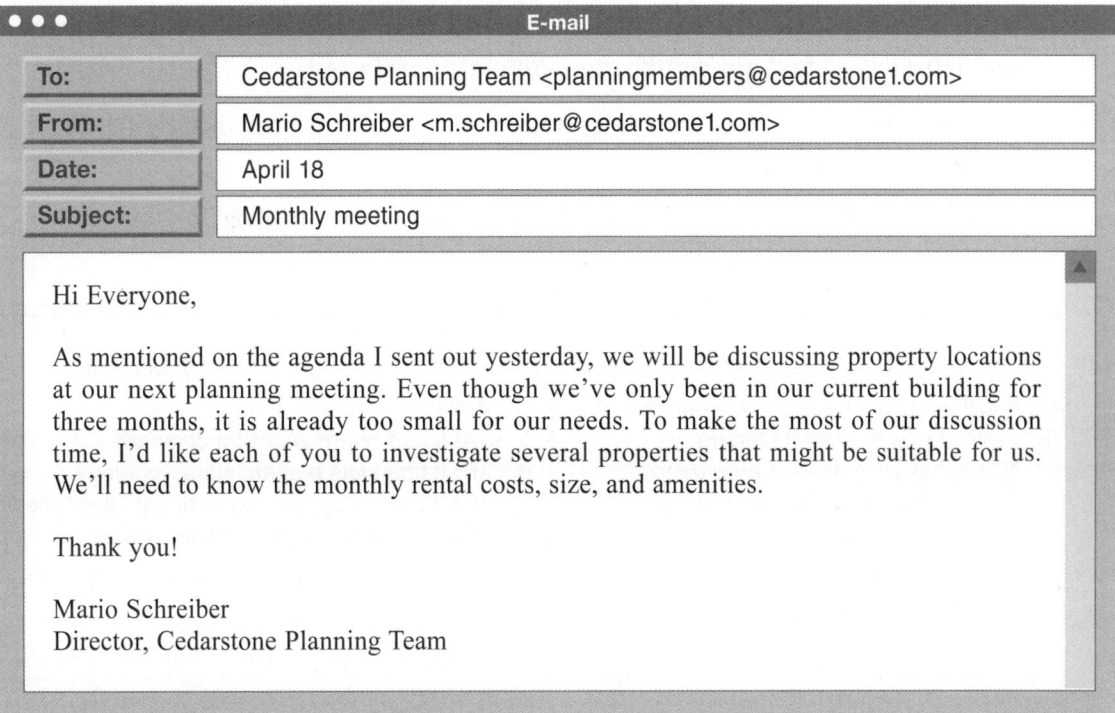

To:	Cedarstone Planning Team <planningmembers@cedarstone1.com>
From:	Mario Schreiber <m.schreiber@cedarstone1.com>
Date:	April 18
Subject:	Monthly meeting

Hi Everyone,

As mentioned on the agenda I sent out yesterday, we will be discussing property locations at our next planning meeting. Even though we've only been in our current building for three months, it is already too small for our needs. To make the most of our discussion time, I'd like each of you to investigate several properties that might be suitable for us. We'll need to know the monthly rental costs, size, and amenities.

Thank you!

Mario Schreiber
Director, Cedarstone Planning Team

147. What does Mr. Schreiber suggest about Cedarstone?

(A) It has more than one branch.
(B) It is recruiting employees now.
(C) It has grown quickly.
(D) Its planning meeting has changed.

148. What are the e-mail recipients asked to do?

(A) Perform some research
(B) Divide into discussion groups
(C) Take photos of properties
(D) E-mail a location preference

GO ON TO THE NEXT PAGE

Questions 149-150 refer to the following advertisement.

The Wildview Youth Ranch has an opening for three student interns to assist the research team with several projects related to the human psychological benefits of working with farm animals.

- Successful applicants will have completed at least one year of postgraduate training in the areas of psychology or counseling by June 10.

- A basic working knowledge of animal training is essential to the job function, as is a desire to work with children.

- Candidates with a first aid certification are highly preferred.

Those interested should submit a portfolio detailing any previous fieldwork, written reports or statistical analysis.

Apply online by visiting wvyouthranch.org/summerinternship prior to November 10.

149. What is NOT a qualification for the interns?

(A) Knowledge in the area of animal habitat
(B) Familiarity with animal training
(C) Medical skills in case of emergency
(D) Postgraduate education in counseling

150. What is stated about The Wildview Youth Ranch?

(A) It is a pharmaceutical company.
(B) It conducts research in psychology.
(C) It has an opening for a project supervisor.
(D) It manages several small farms.

Questions 151-152 refer to the following information.

Providence Electronics

At Providence Electronics, we understand that our customers appreciate and depend on our commitment to quality and reliability. We guarantee you the best products, and your welfare is important to us. That's why we have decided to voluntarily recall our Spirit-22 rechargeable battery packs. We have received reports that these devices can overheat, causing a risk of fire.

Customers who have purchased this product are eligible to receive a refund. Please note that we will not attempt to fix these devices at the workshops in our retail locations. We will simply collect them and issue a refund. For further information, call our helpline at 1-800-555-7676 daily from 7 A.M. to 9 P.M. Eastern Standard Time, or visit www.providenceelectronics.com. Thank you for your business.

151. Why was the information written?

(A) To request opinions from regular customers
(B) To introduce a new method of ordering goods
(C) To inform customers about a safety issue
(D) To show appreciation for customer loyalty

152. What is true about Providence Electronics?

(A) Its devices come with a lifetime warranty.
(B) Its helpline is available twenty-four hours a day.
(C) It can only refund items if a receipt is presented.
(D) It offers a repair service at its retail stores.

GO ON TO THE NEXT PAGE

Questions 153-154 refer to the following text message chain.

Natasha Mann [3:02 P.M.]
George, could I check something about the TV news clip you wanted me to shorten?

George Atkins [3:04 P.M.]
Of course.

Natasha Mann [3:05 P.M.]
I noticed that there weren't any captions at all. Do I need to add them, or will someone else do it?

George Atkins [3:07 P.M.]
That will be done at a later time. We're still waiting on some information.

Natasha Mann [3:08 P.M.]
All right. I'll send it over to the news team then.

George Atkins [3:09 P.M.]
I wouldn't do that yet.

Natasha Mann [3:10 P.M.]
Oh, really?

George Atkins [3:10 P.M.]
You'd better have Marty look it over first to give his approval. Otherwise, you might have to make changes later.

Natasha Mann [3:11 P.M.]
That's true.

George Atkins [3:12 P.M.]
I just don't want it to be sent back to you.

---

153. Who most likely is Ms. Mann?

(A) A TV repair person
(B) An advertising executive
(C) A newspaper reporter
(D) A video editor

154. At 3:11 P.M., what does Ms. Mann most likely mean when she writes, "That's true"?

(A) She should talk to the team in person to avoid confusion.
(B) She thinks that Marty will be the best caption writer.
(C) She agrees that she should have a task reviewed.
(D) She will have more time to make changes later.

To the editor of the *Easton Times*,

When the major storm moved through Easton last week, I was concerned about how the city would handle it. A natural disaster is always difficult for a community to deal with.

In the city center, trees that had fallen down were lying across Roosevelt Street, so cars couldn't get through. There was also a power outage that affected buildings in some neighborhoods. In addition, the Tyce River overflowed its banks, leaving parts of Jackson Park underwater.

I have to say that I was impressed with how quickly these issues were addressed, and I commend all of the municipal workers. I found the city's social media page, run by Daniel Roberts, to be particularly helpful. It allowed everyone in town to check the latest news easily. Thank you to everyone involved for a job well done.

Amelia Cho

155. Why did Ms. Cho send the letter?

(A) To provide a storm warning
(B) To recommend a municipal policy
(C) To explain a maintenance procedure
(D) To praise an emergency response system

156. What is NOT indicated as a problem in Easton?

(A) There was a loss of electricity.
(B) A roadway was obstructed.
(C) A river was polluted.
(D) A park was flooded.

157. What is suggested about Mr. Roberts?

(A) He predicted a natural disaster.
(B) He kept residents up to date.
(C) He managed some city workers.
(D) He made repairs to a facility.

Ian Danley Branching Into New Genres

By Shelly Haagenson

Los Angeles (9 December)—Ian Danley is known for producing numerous musical hits of all genres, often used in advertisements and movies. You may recognize his work from the popular jingle on the ads for *Zippy Cakes* desserts. Some of his pieces, such as *Twilight Breeze* and *Mint Leaves*, have made him famous across the United States and into parts of Europe. Now, in collaboration with composer Kate Evans who has worked with him on other occasions, Danley is creating the score for a production set to hit the big screen next summer. The two have been contracted to write for the animated full-length film, *Zoo Run*, produced by Michael Straight. Mr. Straight has won a Trendy Award for his work on *Mully's Day Out*.

While this is the first time Danley has written for an animation, he is optimistic about the effort. "I really enjoy how different and fun animation is. It's much more light-hearted than some of the other movies I have worked on. In a lot of ways it's the same—making the score fit the scene— but I get to experiment a bit more."

The film is ready to screen in Los Angeles on June 1 and hit theaters across the country on June 22. It will play in London and Sydney on June 24 and likely other parts of the world soon after.

As for Mr. Straight, he expects the film to be popular. In an interview last week he said, "I can't see why *Zoo Run* won't be number one at the box office, especially with such talented writers like Kate and Ian. The story line is also fascinating and will be enjoyed by all ages."

158. Who is Mr. Danley?

(A) An advertisement producer
(B) An animation movie director
(C) A screen writer
(D) A music composer

159. What is suggested about Mr. Straight?

(A) He will be writing the score for the new film.
(B) He has worked in collaboration with Kate Evans before.
(C) He spoke to Ms. Haagenson recently.
(D) He interviewed Kate and Ian last week.

160. What is mentioned about the film *Zoo Run*?

(A) It is the first animation film Mr. Straight has written.
(B) It has become popular among all age groups.
(C) The film consists of animated scenes only.
(D) Its producer has worked on more light-hearted films.

| Home | **About** | Products | Customer Service | Careers |

Flintglass Eyewear is an online retailer of prescription and non-prescription corrective eyewear and sunglasses for all ages. Being in business since 1928, we specialize in meeting the vision and fashion needs of our clients. — [1] —.

With more than three thousand different styles, we offer the largest assortment of specialized eyewear available anywhere. And each style can be custom engraved and altered to meet the sizing needs of the customer. — [2] —.

The ordering process cannot be more straightforward. — [3] —. Simply make an account and upload a photo of yourself looking directly at the camera. Follow a few simple steps and then our software will allow you to preview how you look in different frames. — [4] —. Then enter the specifics of your lenses and click the order button. Our products usually ship in 2-3 business days and can be sent anywhere in the world.

For any questions or concerns, our customer service specialists are able to help you by phone or online chat around the clock. See our customer service page for a list of phone numbers specific to your country.

161. What is NOT true about Flintglass Eyewear?

(A) It offers custom-made eyewear to meet the needs of the customers.
(B) It takes less than a week on average until shipment.
(C) Customers can inquire about their concerns at any time.
(D) Customers can try on various styles of eyewear at its retail shop.

162. According to the Web page, what is a part of the ordering process?

(A) Designing a frame for your selected photo
(B) Using the software Flintglass Eyewear provided for a preview
(C) Directly uploading your photo for recommendations on frames
(D) Sending a photo of yourself to customer service through e-mail

163. In which of the positions marked [1], [2], [3], and [4] does the following sentence belong?

"All you have to do is choose the frames you want!"

(A) [1]
(B) [2]
(C) [3]
(D) [4]

GO ON TO THE NEXT PAGE

Questions 164-167 refer to the following text message chain.

Mina Yoon [9:07 A.M.]	I hope you all had a nice weekend. Sorry we had to cut the July 5th HR planning meeting short last week. We didn't have a chance to brainstorm what to do about the poor survey results, so I'd like to get your thoughts.
Stan Berry [9:08 A.M.]	We were all surprised by the responses from last month's survey. I'm not sure what we should do.
Andrew Geneva [9:10 A.M.]	Yeah, normally when we give questionnaires to employees, they report being satisfied overall with the working environment. So, we need to find a way to get them motivated again.
Stan Berry [9:11 A.M.]	That's right. How about having a special banquet to recognize employees' achievements?
Megan Dawson [9:12 A.M.]	Why not? That would be a fun way to show our appreciation. It's the busy season for most conference centers these days, though. How about I call today to book a venue? We don't want to miss out.
Mina Yoon [9:14 A.M.]	You'd better get approval from the finance director first. We have to make sure there's room in the budget.
Megan Dawson [9:15 A.M.]	Good point. I'll do that now and let you know later what happened.

SEND

164. Why did Ms. Yoon start the text message chain?

(A) To report some results
(B) To request some solutions
(C) To announce a project
(D) To postpone a meeting

165. When was a survey conducted?

(A) In May
(B) In June
(C) In July
(D) In August

166. At 9:12 A.M., what does Ms. Dawson most likely mean when she writes, "Why not"?

(A) She doubts there will be a scheduling conflict.
(B) She thinks a banquet is a good idea.
(C) She is confused about a policy.
(D) She believes Mr. Berry deserves an award.

167. What will Ms. Dawson most likely do next?

(A) Speak to a department head
(B) Approve a budget proposal
(C) Contact a conference venue
(D) Send information to employees

To: Carla Earhart <earhartc@falcoind.com>

From: Benjamin Reeves <ben.reeves@ddcsecurity.com>

Date: July 19

Subject: Please read

Dear Ms. Earhart,

Thank you once again for making time for a visit from one of our technicians on July 3. I sent you a list of our recommended security upgrades following the visit but have not yet heard whether you'd like to go forward with these. — [1] —. We have devised an initial plan to cater to your exact specifications. — [2] —. We have recently opened in the area and already have many satisfied customers. — [3] —. These range from shopping centers and art galleries to construction firms, so we are confident that we can provide a high level of service for Falco Industries, one that meets or exceeds that of your current provider. So that you don't have to go back through your previous e-mails to find the original, I've attached the document for your accounting company to this e-mail again for your convenience. — [4] —.

I hope to hear from you soon,

Benjamin Reeves

168. What is the purpose of the e-mail?

(A) To submit an updated price estimate
(B) To resend some recommendations
(C) To schedule a visit to a site
(D) To point out an error in a proposal

169. What is suggested by Mr. Reeves?

(A) DDC Security has hired some new technicians.
(B) Mr. Reeves and Ms. Earhart have met in person.
(C) Ms. Earhart is using DDC Security's competitor now.
(D) Falco Industries has recently opened in the area.

170. What kind of business most likely is Falco Industries?

(A) An accounting firm
(B) A shopping center
(C) A construction company
(D) An art gallery

171. In which of the positions marked [1], [2], [3], and [4] does the following sentence best belong?

"Additionally, we can adjust our services as your needs change over time."

(A) [1]
(B) [2]
(C) [3]
(D) [4]

GO ON TO THE NEXT PAGE

Labor Market Looking Bright in Stansbury

STANSBURY—Stansbury is showing strong job prospects with the announcement that Ziemer Software will open a branch in Stansbury, making it one of a growing number of tech companies centered in Stansbury. Although Belding City is still the area's largest provider of jobs in the field of technology, thanks in part to its generous tax breaks to attract companies to the city, Stansbury is starting to make a name for itself in its own right. With top-class programs at Vanderhoof University's branch in Stansbury, there is a wealth of recent graduates who are locally based and highly qualified.

Robotics engineering company Emeral Inc. has been a major employer in the area for years, and it recently reconfirmed its plans to keep its operations in Stansbury. A spokesperson for Emeral Inc. said that the company has been pleased with the workforce pool in Stansbury. "In some of our offices, like St. Petersburg, Russia, and Madrid, Spain, it takes a long time to recruit the right candidate because we only accept the top talent. In Stansbury, we always find recruitment easier because there are so many great candidates to choose from. We are fortunate to have had so much success. Financial support from investors and first-rate goods are only part of the equation. You need creative employees to drive the process."

Private businesses are not the only sector boosting employment opportunities in Stansbury. Business Connect is a government-run program that helps job seekers to find work locally. The program began two years ago in an effort to draw more people and businesses to Stansbury. What began as a part-time operation with just two employees has grown to a staff of six full-time workers. Marjorie Barnes, the director of Business Connect, said that the program is dedicated to providing support to local businesses. "When our local businesses succeed, our community is enriched," Barnes said. "We're here to make that happen."

172. According to the article, why do businesses find Stansbury attractive?

    (A) It has a large transportation network.
    (B) It is growing in population quickly.
    (C) It is easy to find skilled workers there.
    (D) It provides tax services to businesses.

173. What is true about Emeral Inc.?

    (A) It tries to attract foreign investors.
    (B) It moved its headquarters to Stansbury.
    (C) It has overseas branches.
    (D) It outsourced its recruitment efforts.

174. What is NOT indicated as a factor in Emeral Inc.'s success?

    (A) High-quality products
    (B) Innovative staff members
    (C) Investment funds
    (D) An efficient review process

175. What is implied about Ms. Barnes?

    (A) She is a former employee of Emeral Inc.
    (B) She started her own business in Stansbury.
    (C) She has a degree in a technical field.
    (D) She is employed by the government.

GO ON TO THE NEXT PAGE

● ● ●

To: Gateway Accounting Staff <allstaff@gatewayaccounting.com>
From: Robert Garza <r.garza@gatewayaccounting.com>
Date: March 7
Subject: MTC Incorporated

Hello Everyone,

As we announced at yesterday's meeting, the negotiations for our merger with MTC Incorporated have been completed, and the agreement is finalized. I know that many of you were concerned about how this merger would affect the company and your role in it. I want to reassure you that there are many clear advantages to this decision. The newly formed company (MTC Gateway) will have approximately 35% of the market share, giving us a competitive edge. Like Gateway Accounting, MTC Incorporated has a reputation for working on complicated tax filings. In addition, MTC Incorporated has a department that provides legal advice, which will allow us to bring a new dimension to our business.

To help make the transition smoother, departmental meetings will be held next week with one meeting leader from each company. The Gateway Accounting representative will evaluate everyone's job responsibilities to see how to best combine the two workforces. The MTC Incorporated representative will give a talk on the policies going forward under MTC Gateway.

Sincerely,

Robert Garza
Office Manager, Gateway Accounting

Departmental Meetings: Gateway Accounting Headquarters
Thursday, March 16, 1 P.M.–4 P.M.

Department	Room	Meeting Leaders
Sales	Conference Room A	Semhar Tewelde [Gateway Accounting] Carol Nicols [MTC Incorporated]
Marketing	Room 304	Rohini Sharaf [Gateway Accounting] Mitsuo Daijou [MTC Incorporated]
Human Resources	Conference Room B	Terry Woodard [Gateway Accounting] Joseph Decker [MTC Incorporated]
Finance	Employee Lounge	Gabriel Cardoso [Gateway Accounting] Yan Siu [MTC Incorporated]

The current CEOs of both firms will visit all departments except Human Resources, whose staff has already had a private meeting with them.

176. What is one reason that Mr. Garza sent the e-mail?

(A) To emphasize the benefits of a change
(B) To thank employees for their hard work
(C) To announce a corporate merger
(D) To describe a negotiation process

177. What is indicated about MTC Incorporated?

(A) It held 35% of the market share.
(B) It is known for handling difficult tax cases.
(C) It caters to individuals and businesses.
(D) It has some offices overseas.

178. In the e-mail, the word "dimension" in paragraph 1, line 8, is closest in meaning to

(A) obstruction
(B) characteristic
(C) commitment
(D) proportion

179. What is most likely true about Mr. Cardoso?

(A) He will assess some staff duties.
(B) He will meet with the office manager.
(C) He will take over for Ms. Siu.
(D) He will discuss new policies.

180. What is suggested about the March 16 meetings?

(A) The leaders were selected by the staff.
(B) The Human Resources meeting will be cut short.
(C) The departments will meet before lunch.
(D) The CEOs will not visit Conference Room B.

GO ON TO THE NEXT PAGE

Questions 181-185 refer to the following flyer and e-mail.

Get a Free Rain Barrel for Your Home or Business!

In an effort to reduce pressure on the Burwell City Water System, which often lacks sufficient water to meet the city's needs, rain barrels will be distributed to Burwell residents on May 3 at Valencia Park. Residents are eligible to receive one free rain barrel (per address), and business owners may buy one for just $40, which is far below the retail price. This event is sponsored by the city of Burwell and the Association for Environmental Responsibility. The barrels must be picked up in person, and they are only suitable for homes or commercial buildings with slanted roofs and a gutter system. Please note that a pickup truck may be required to transport the barrel, depending on the barrel size.

The water collected in these barrels can be used for gardening, washing vehicles, and more. The city is continuing to seeking creative solutions like these, which can dramatically reduce the impact we have on nature. For more information, visit www.cityofburwell.gov/water.

---

e-mail

To: Tammy Damian <damiant@telebiz.com>
From: Hinako Okamura <h_okamura@cityofburwell.gov>
Date: May 18
Subject: Rain Barrel Program

Dear Ms. Damian,
I am writing to you regarding the rain barrel that you bought at the May 3 event at Valencia Park. After getting some complaints from users, we realized that the spout at the bottom of the barrel was the wrong size. Therefore, even when assembled correctly, the barrel will leak. Please complete the attached form so that we can send you a new spout. It is not necessary to return the original one. In fact, we will be using that size on our rain barrels next year, so you might want to hang onto it if you plan to participate in the program again. The form can be sent by mail or e-mail.

Thank you for your participation,

Hinako Okamura
Program Coordinator

181. What kind of information is NOT provided in the flyer?

(A) The building requirements
(B) The available barrel sizes
(C) The event's supporters
(D) The reason for an event

182. What is stated about Burwell?

(A) It suffers from low water supplies.
(B) Its rainiest month is in May.
(C) It has opened a new park.
(D) Its population is growing rapidly.

183. In the flyer, the word "dramatically" in paragraph 2, line 3, is closest in meaning to

(A) strictly
(B) artistically
(C) substantially
(D) environmentally

184. What is suggested about Ms. Damian?

(A) She is using a barrel at her business.
(B) She volunteered to distribute goods.
(C) She is not a resident of Burwell.
(D) She made a complaint to Mr. Okamura.

185. What does Mr. Okamura suggest doing?

(A) Reviewing some assembly instructions
(B) Signing up for next year's event
(C) Checking some equipment for problems
(D) Keeping a component for future use

GO ON TO THE NEXT PAGE

Questions 186-190 refer to the following e-mails and meeting minutes.

To: EP Committee <ep@marietta-co.com>
From: Melissa Trevino <m_trevino@marietta-co.com>
Date: October 10
Subject: Mr. Kovar's retirement

Hello Everyone,

As you all know, Jack Kovar will be retiring next month after nearly thirty years of service to Marietta Co. The event planning committee is in charge of organizing a retirement banquet for him to celebrate his time at the company and to send him off in style. I'd like to set up a meeting for sometime this week. Please let me know the best day and time for you, and I'll try to accommodate everyone's schedules.

I have already booked the venue—the ballroom of the Laredo Center—for November 21. However, the rest of the planning still needs to be done. Because our time is somewhat limited, I've asked Chelsea Ebert to do some preliminary research to find a caterer. She will assess a few places, including Fairfield Catering, which we have used in the past but is now under new ownership.

Please think about this party and bring your best ideas to the meeting. Mr. Kovar has performed his duties with the utmost integrity and determination. Therefore, it is important that he be honored properly.

Sincerely,

Melissa Trevino

To: EP Committee <ep@marietta-co.com>
From: Chelsea Ebert <c_ebert@marietta-co.com>
Date: October 11
Subject: Catering Options

Hi All,

Ms. Trevino asked me to look into the catering companies that might be available for Mr. Kovar's retirement dinner. I have it narrowed down to Bryant Creations and Fairfield Catering, either of which would be suitable for the event. I'll provide more details at the meeting, but a quick comparison is provided below.

Menu Options: Bryant Creations focuses on high-end food for those with sophisticated tastes. The high standard of food would reflect positively on the event as a whole. On the other hand, Fairfield Catering has a much larger menu, and it can accommodate vegetarians, vegans, gluten-free diners, and more.

Price: Bryant Creations is about 50% more expensive than Fairfield Catering. However, if we have some flexibility in the budgets for other categories, we could still afford it.

Availability: Both companies are available on the event day, but we should decide soon to secure the services. Additionally, both companies recommended hiring one server for every ten guests, since we want a sit-down meal rather than a buffet.

Meeting: Event Planning Committee
Date and Time: Thursday, October 13, 10 A.M.–11 A.M.
Location: Conference Room 2
Chairperson: Melissa Trevino
Present: William O'Connor, Deborah Hughes, Chelsea Ebert
Absent: Lewis Eastman

Meeting Notes:

1. Ms. Ebert presented a detailed comparison between Fairfield Catering and Bryant Creations. The committee selected Fairfield Catering by a unanimous vote. Ms. Ebert will contact Fairfield Catering to pay the deposit and will also inform Bryant Creations that we will not be using their services. The estimated guest count is 150 people, and Fairfield Catering can provide the necessary number of servers.

2. Budgets for each of the event categories were set, and a committee member was assigned to each one to help with the research, though the committee will still make major decisions as a group. The categories are Venue (Melissa), Food/Beverages (Chelsea), Entertainment (William), and Decorations (Deborah). Lewis will be asked to assist where needed.

3. The next meeting will be held on Friday, October 21 at 1 P.M. We will select colors and a theme so we know how to decorate the venue.

186. What is the purpose of Ms. Trevino's e-mail?

(A) To report a change in a meeting time
(B) To recruit volunteers for a committee
(C) To determine a meeting time for a retirement party
(D) To announce the retirement of a coworker

187. In the first e-mail, the word "performed" in paragraph 3, line 2, is closest in meaning to

(A) presented
(B) entertained
(C) achieved
(D) carried out

188. What is NOT indicated about Fairfield Catering?

(A) It has a wider selection of food than Bryant Creations.
(B) It specializes in providing buffet dinners for events.
(C) It has provided food for Marietta Co. events in the past.
(D) It is a cheaper option compared to Bryant Creations.

189. How many servers will the company most likely hire?

(A) 10
(B) 15
(C) 20
(D) 25

190. What is scheduled to happen at the next meeting?

(A) Sampling food items
(B) Preparing invitations
(C) Choosing a guest speaker
(D) Discussing decorations

GO ON TO THE NEXT PAGE

● ● ●

To: All Members <memberslist@sunnydalecommunity.org>
From: Sally Fordwich <s.fordwich@sunnydalecommunity.org>
Date: September 23
Subject: Update

Dear Members,

To begin, I'd like to thank you all for your hard work during last week's fundraising event. We exceeded our target by 12%! Our finances are now looking very strong for the next year, and we'll be announcing several exciting projects soon.

Also, as some of you may know, Bob Harknett will not be able to attend the upcoming city council meeting due to a medical appointment. Karl Rogers has agreed to cover the presentation in his place. He will bring up the following three issues on our behalf:
– Using public funds to allow entry fees for older residents to be reduced
– Adding speed bumps outside the community center's main gates to improve safety
– Hiring two more security guards to allow for full-time coverage overnight

Yours sincerely,

Sally Fordwich
General Secretary, Sunnydale Community Center

Sunnydale City Council Meeting Proposed Agenda
September 28, 3:00 P.M. [Last updated September 18]

3:00 P.M.	Call to Order and Roll Call, Reading and approval of previous meeting's minutes
3:15 P.M.	Guest Speaker: Daniel Fashanu, State Deputy Governor
	Speech: "Building Community Connections"
3:45 P.M	Education Report: Elise LeBlanc, Sunnydale High School Principal
4:00 P.M.	Resident Presentation: Alice Rickards
4:15 P.M.	Resident Presentation: Bob Harknett
4:30 P.M.	Resident Presentation: Shannon Jackson
4:45 P.M.	Debate among council members on presented topics
5:15 P.M.	Selection of a city council member to replace Millie Lentz as head of the Workforce Development Committee (Council members who expect to be absent may cast their ballots in advance.)
5:30 P.M.	End of proceedings

Changes Ahead for Sunnydale Community Center

October 25—After many struggles with the city council, the Sunnydale Community Center (SCC) was able to celebrate a number of successes following last month's meeting. Speaking outside the gates of the center, where new speed bumps have been installed, Sally Fordwich, General Secretary for the SCC, said that the traffic-slowing measures had already had positive results in the form of fewer "near-miss" accidents reported. In addition, she was pleased that the council agreed to subsidize community center fees for the elderly. While Ms. Fordwich praised the city council members for their actions, she also mentioned that she already has plans to request further financial support next month.

191. Why does Ms. Fordwich thank the group members?

(A) They participated in a building renovation.
(B) They made useful project suggestions.
(C) They attended a city council meeting.
(D) They assisted in a successful donation drive.

192. What time did Mr. Rogers most likely address the city council members?

(A) At 3:45 P.M.
(B) At 4:00 P.M.
(C) At 4:15 P.M.
(D) At 4:30 P.M.

193. What is true about the September 28 meeting?

(A) Its main speech took place at the end of the meeting.
(B) It featured a debate between council members and residents.
(C) It included a vote to elect an official.
(D) It was not open to members of the press.

194. What change requested by Mr. Rogers was NOT made by the city council?

(A) Putting in speed bumps outside the center
(B) Decreasing entry fees for senior citizens
(C) Increasing the number of security personnel
(D) Making improvements in disabled access

195. What will Ms. Fordwich most likely do in November?

(A) Run for a city council position
(B) Ask for more funding
(C) Start some new projects
(D) Request a building expansion

GO ON TO THE NEXT PAGE →

To: Finn Holmberg
From: Graycliff Outfitters
Date: April 8
Subject: RE: Inquiry

Dear Mr. Holmberg,

Thank you for your interest in purchasing 20 backpacks for your new nature guide business. You mentioned that you are looking for a model that is lightweight, as you cater solely to beginner hikers who may not be used to vigorous physical activity. In addition, because the hikes will take place regardless of the weather, you need the backpacks to be made of waterproof or water-resistant materials. We have a wide range of backpacks in our inventory, so I'm sure you can find something that suits you. I have attached some product information about the items that are within your specified price range. Please let me know if you have any questions.

Sincerely,

Trina Sherman
Customer Service Agent, Graycliff Outfitters

Graycliff Outfitters

Backpacks: $150.00-$199.99
All backpacks come with a free 3-year warranty, except Trailz, whose warranty must be purchased separately.

Trailz-$154.99
Wide shoulder straps to distribute weight evenly. Twelve compartments of various sizes. Made with waterproof fabric.
Colors: Blue, Red, Gray.
Capacity: 36 liters.

Camplife-$169.99
Padded waistband for all-day comfort. Water-resistant canvas keeps interior dry in light rain. Six outside pockets and three inside pockets for easy organization. One of the lightest frames on the market.
Color: Black.
Capacity: 34 liters.

Sierra-$174.99
Lightweight design with five interior sections and four outer pockets. Sierra outsells its competitors by nearly two to one. Retractable chain for keys.
Colors: Black, Dark Green.
Capacity: 60 liters.

Cougarex—$189.99

Two interior sections and five exterior pockets, including one mesh pocket for drying damp items. Made from heat-and water-resistant fabric. Mid-weight frame.
Colors: Black, Blue, Red.
Capacity: 80 liters.

Businesses Respond to Tourism Shift
By Rebecca Keiser

June 20—Summer is always a busy time for hotels, airlines, and other tourism-related businesses. However, this season has also seen a significant rise in visits to natural areas such as wildlife sanctuaries and national parks. On account of the growing need for experienced guides for hiking and camping excursions, businesses have sprung up to fill the gap. While visitors are allowed to tour the parks on their own, many of the sites include hazardous sections of the trails. People are willing to pay extra to have professional assistance, as safety counts. Two businesses that have been leading tours for years are Forrista, operating advanced and intermediate tours in the Hickman Mountains, and Ace Tours, operating beginning-level tours in Evergreen Park. Two newcomers to watch are DC Excursions, providing hikes exclusively to beginners in Mesa Park, and Sunshine Tours, providing hikes of all levels in the Marshall Nature Reserve.

196. What is suggested about Sierra?

(A) It is the largest backpack.
(B) It is the most popular item.
(C) It has a padded belt.
(D) It is recommended by professionals.

197. Which feature is common to all four brands?

(A) They all come in more than one color.
(B) They are all designed to dry quickly.
(C) They all have numerous compartments.
(D) They are all covered by a free warranty.

198. Which backpack would be most suitable for Mr. Holmberg's company?

(A) Trailz
(B) Camplife
(C) Sierra
(D) Cougarex

199. In the article, the word "counts" in paragraph 1, line 7, is closest in meaning to

(A) considers
(B) includes
(C) calculates
(D) matters

200. Where most likely does Mr. Holmberg's company operate?

(A) Hickman Mountain
(B) Evergreen Park
(C) Mesa Park
(D) Marshall Nature Reserve

This is the end of the test. You may review PART 5, 6, and 7 if you finish the test early.
정답 p. 319 / 점수 환산표 p. 321 / 해석 p. 339

TEST

04

PART 5
PART 6
PART 7

토익 Reading Comprehension은 75분 동안 진행됩니다.
현재 시각과 지금부터 75분 후인 테스트 종료 시각을 기록해 두고,
반드시 종료 시각 전에 문제 풀이와 답안지 마킹을 완료하세요.

 현재 시각 시 분

테스트 종료 시각 ⬜ 시 ⬜ 분

READING TEST

In the Reading test, you will read a variety of texts and answer several different types of reading comprehension questions. The entire Reading test will last 75 minutes. There are three parts, and directions are given for each part. You are encouraged to answer as many questions as possible within the time allowed.

You must mark your answers on the separate answer sheet. Do not write your answers in your test book.

PART 5

Directions: A word or phrase is missing in each of the sentences below. Four answer choices are given below each sentence. Select the best answer to complete the sentence. Then mark the letter (A), (B), (C), or (D) on your answer sheet.

101. The display tables for the farmers market used to require partial setup by vendors every Saturday, but now they remain ------- assembled.
    (A) fuller
    (B) full
    (C) fullest
    (D) fully

102. Mr. Lambert's secretary called to ------- for Mr. Stewart to meet him on the fifth of June.
    (A) specify
    (B) connect
    (C) arrange
    (D) conduct

103. Due to the unfortunate lack of funds, the first ever National Reader's Education Conference will be rescheduled ------- next year.
    (A) in
    (B) by
    (C) at
    (D) for

104. ------- the guests report any issues with their hotel rooms, please make an effort to resolve them as quickly as possible.
    (A) If
    (B) Whether
    (C) Though
    (D) So that

105. The hourly wages offered in rural areas are ------- lower than those paid by companies in urban centers.
    (A) significance
    (B) most significant
    (C) significantly
    (D) more significant

106. Since Mr. Taylor believed he had been contacted in -------, he did not make a return phone call.
    (A) demand
    (B) error
    (C) problem
    (D) mistake

107. Those who need some refreshments will ------- the employee lounge on the first floor of the building across from the elevators.
    (A) find
    (B) sit
    (C) relax
    (D) stay

108. New employees are encouraged to direct any complaints to the manager rather than try to handle them -------.
    (A) theirs
    (B) their own
    (C) they
    (D) themselves

109. The publishing company is requesting the edited ------- in its entirety no later than October 1.

(A) appliance
(B) property
(C) volume
(D) result

110. When you attend Friday's staff meeting, you should be ready to report your ------- of the proposed business model.

(A) to analyze
(B) analysis
(C) analyzes
(D) analyzed

111. The amount of the loan that can be granted is ------- on the business' annual revenue as well as its credit history.

(A) dependable
(B) depends
(C) dependent
(D) depend

112. Yoon Financial Consultants work ------- with clients to establish plans that fit their personal goals and earning capabilities.

(A) nearly
(B) closely
(C) lately
(D) newly

113. Because of the ------- nature of their work, medical professionals abide by a strict code of confidentiality in all matters related to their patients.

(A) appropriate
(B) effective
(C) careful
(D) sensitive

114. While the roof of the Harrisville branch is being repaired, the staff must move ------- of the site's inventory to an off-site warehouse.

(A) everything
(B) each
(C) all
(D) such

115. The library's board members decided to release funding for a new computer lab after much -------.

(A) deliberated
(B) deliberate
(C) deliberation
(D) deliberates

116. Johno's Wool sells the finest wool products to individuals and businesses located all ------- Australia.

(A) across
(B) along
(C) wide
(D) from

117. At Roof Videos, all rentals should be returned within 7 days, and late rentals are ------- to additional charges.

(A) subject
(B) entitled
(C) accountable
(D) compared

118. The committee in charge of the art contest will review the entries ------- all of the paintings have been collected and displayed.

(A) whether
(B) now that
(C) by
(D) how

119. According to the *Journal of Rock and Soil*, researchers estimate the ------- for minerals used in cosmetics will peak in the next 20 years.

(A) population
(B) appearance
(C) correlation
(D) demand

120. A recent report ------- a need to lower prices in order to prevent more customers from purchasing goods elsewhere.

(A) commented
(B) indicated
(C) allowed
(D) collected

GO ON TO THE NEXT PAGE

121. Ms. Maguire was asked to provide a list of ------- venues for the upcoming product launch of the company's new athletic shoes.

(A) prefers
(B) preferring
(C) preferred
(D) preference

122. ------- the paperwork for Mr. Herbert's home mortgage was incomplete, the bank was unable to process his request.

(A) Unless
(B) Until
(C) Because
(D) Given

123. Because Dr. Carter has a ------- of expertise, he is frequently contacted by local hospitals when they have patients with unknown illnesses.

(A) wealth
(B) height
(C) number
(D) fame

124. The person who delivers the take-out food has a device to collect ------- by credit card if the customer prefers that to cash.

(A) payment
(B) pay
(C) payer
(D) paying

125. Be sure to save and back up all documents in ------- for the installation scheduled between 2 A.M. and 4 A.M. tomorrow.

(A) calculation
(B) operation
(C) preparation
(D) exception

126. No one is supposed to leave the building ------- scanning his or her ID card at the security counter.

(A) without
(B) unless
(C) merely
(D) though

127. Due to the high rate of failure in the industry, investors are ------- cautious about backing restaurants.

(A) financed
(B) financial
(C) financially
(D) finance

128. Due to urgent and unexpected repairs at the Ragland Theater, the community play will hold its first showing on June 5 -------.

(A) alike
(B) instead
(C) already
(D) too

129. If Ms. Symington had accepted the transfer to Beijing, she ------- a large pay raise from her firm.

(A) would have received
(B) has received
(C) is being received
(D) would have been received

130. Using company computers for non-work related activities is not considered ------- for employees except during designated break times.

(A) useful
(B) tentative
(C) significant
(D) appropriate

PART 6

Directions: Read the texts that follow. A word, phrase, or sentence is missing in parts of each text. Four answer choices for each question are given below the text. Select the best answer to complete the text. Then mark the letter (A), (B), (C), or (D) on your answer sheet.

Questions 131-134 refer to the following article.

After opening its first bakery three years ago, Hogan's Donuts has ------- grown throughout the
131.
northern United States and now seeks to expand abroad. -------. In a recent interview with *Timely*
132.
Business, its CEO Kirk Mason said that two other locations are expected to open within a year in

the same country. -------, the company has yet to secure franchise owners able to open shops in
133.
the country itself. Prospective ------- should visit hogansdonuts.com for a list of requirements and
134.
steps. The company is prepared to assist franchisees with difficulties associated with international

business laws.

131. (A) quick
     (B) quicken
     (C) quickly
     (D) quickness

132. (A) Then the store will be able to
         accommodate up to 150 people.
     (B) He will be visiting several countries in
         Asia this month.
     (C) Hogan's Donuts will be selling beverages
         along with donuts.
     (D) The chain already runs two stores located
         in Canada.

133. (A) Therefore
     (B) However
     (C) Even so
     (D) In particular

134. (A) chefs
     (B) candidates
     (C) clients
     (D) technicians

GO ON TO THE NEXT PAGE

Questions 135-138 refer to the following article.

Emmet (May 28)—Lewiston Auto Dealer, the city's most popular seller of used and new vehicles, will change its notification system. The dealership ------- routine auto service to hundreds of its
135.
customers every month. Starting soon, the company will primarily use mobile ------- to send service
136.
date reminders. The current system is time-consuming, relying on letters to be printed and sent through the mail.

"We expect the change to be much more -------," said Tanya Kay, the site manager. -------. However,
137.   **138.**
anyone can reply STOP to opt out of the new system and continue to receive physical notifications.

135. (A) provided
(B) provides
(C) had provided
(D) will be providing

136. (A) alerted
(B) alerting
(C) alerts
(D) to alert

137. (A) fair
(B) efficient
(C) profitable
(D) important

138. (A) The text notification service will begin on July 1.
(B) A message will be sent to the managers first as a trial.
(C) Customers may receive an e-mail notification as well as a letter.
(D) Inevitably, the cost of the new system is expected to rise.

According to CEO Gretchen Hun of Billington Air Group, the Westmore Airport runway ------- to allow
139.
for additional incoming and outgoing flights. ------- the steady growth in the city's population over
140.
the last five years, the airport has experienced increasing air traffic. Ms. Hun stated that engineers

now expect the venture to take about six months. -------. Ms. Hun noted that airfield security must
141.
remain a top priority. Additionally, "travelers should expect a reduction in flight availabilities, which is

likely to result in a higher ticket price. -------, this is the only viable choice," said CEO Hun.
142.

139. (A) was expanded
(B) will be expanded
(C) is expanding
(D) to expand

140. (A) In case of
(B) Along
(C) Even if
(D) Owing to

141. (A) The original estimate of four months was
revised to allow for daily security checks.
(B) The Westmore Airport runway is renowned
for its security system.
(C) The air traffic has inevitably caused
delays for the flights.
(D) The airport has contacted experts in the
field.

142. (A) Regrettably
(B) Surprisingly
(C) Accordingly
(D) For example

GO ON TO THE NEXT PAGE

Questions 143-146 refer to the following memo.

From: Alyssa Brundige
To: All Staff
Date: January 2
Subject: Director of Development Position Filled

I am excited to share that Alex Yoon ------- as the new Development Director of Alumbaugh
                                       143.
University.

Mr. Yoon has 10 years in fundraising and promotion, and has raised more than five million dollars

for institutions of higher education. Such ------- has well equipped him to contribute to our university,
                                            144.
but it is not the only reason.

In addition to being an alumni of Alumbaugh University, he is a charismatic individual with many

unique ideas which he will employ to make this institution ------- as our student population grows.
                                                            145.
-------.
146.

You can look forward to meeting Alex on January 7 at our first staff meeting of the year.

Sincerely,

Alyssa Brundige

143. (A) will be appointing
(B) appointed
(C) has been appointed
(D) being appointed

144. (A) experience
(B) analysis
(C) charity
(D) efficiency

145. (A) remodeled
(B) successful
(C) decisive
(D) specialist

146. (A) Mr. Yoon has organized numerous
fundraising events for charity.
(B) The final interview will take place in this
facility.
(C) The population in Alumbaugh has recently
increased to 3 million.
(D) I am confident he will be an invaluable
addition to the Alumbaugh family.

PART 7

Directions: In this part you will read a selection of texts, such as magazine and newspaper articles, e-mails, and instant messages. Each text or set of texts is followed by several questions. Select the best answer for each question and mark the letter (A), (B), (C), or (D) on your answer sheet.

Questions 147-148 refer to the following letter.

Skylark Air Rewards
2310 Kings Avenue
Auckland, NZ
0800-313-555

Jenny Smith
1600 First Street
Apt. 12B
Auckland, NZ

March 15

Dear Ms. Smith,

Welcome to Skylark Air Rewards program! Our members benefit from the ability to view and use rewards points from any computer or mobile device. The application is free and you don't have to be tech savvy to navigate it. For more information or to sign up for free, visit skylarkair.com/rewards today.

On the back of this page is an easy one-point guide to take you through the process.

Happy flying,

Isaac Yoon
Skylark Air Rewards
Director

147. What is the purpose of the letter?
(A) To encourage a previous customer to return to a program
(B) To promote a service of the Skylark Air Rewards Program
(C) To guide Ms. Smith about how to use an application
(D) To promote a new version of computer software

148. What is included with the letter?
(A) An advertising flyer
(B) Instructions
(C) Ms. Smith's points status
(D) A sign-up form for the program

GO ON TO THE NEXT PAGE

Questions 149-150 refer to the following Web site.

Home >> Services >> E-Account >> fujisawa_yuiri

Welcome, Ms. Fujisawa! We have updated our Web site to make it easier for you to perform functions associated with your electricity account. Using the new site, you can do the following:
- Settle your electricity bill by online money transfer
- Set up text alerts regarding power outages and safety warnings
- Contact our customer service team with any issues with your power line
- Read tips on how to conserve energy at your home or office

Click here to read our Terms and Conditions.

149. Who most likely is Ms. Fujisawa?

(A) A customer service representative
(B) An online banking user
(C) A customer of a utility company
(D) A job applicant

150. What is NOT indicated as an activity done on the Web site?

(A) Making a payment on an account
(B) Reporting problems with a service
(C) Requesting to receive informational messages
(D) Scheduling a safety consultation

Questions 151-152 refer to the following text message chain.

Marilyn Cooper [1:15 P.M.]
I'm at the bakery picking up the cake for tonight's banquet. I won't have time to stop back at the office. Can you help me? I can't get a hold of Eric in the maintenance department.

Ettore Arcuri [1:18 P.M.]
What do you need?

Marilyn Cooper [1:19 P.M.]
There are three boxes of decorations in my office. Could you please bring them to the conference center?

Ettore Arcuri [1:20 P.M.]
For sure. What time do you need them?

Marilyn Cooper [1:22 P.M.]
Around 2:30 would be good. My office is locked, though, so you'll have to get Eric to help you.

Ettore Arcuri [1:23 P.M.]
Okay. He's probably back from his lunch break by now. I'll go check.

Marilyn Cooper [1:24 P.M.]
Thanks! See you in about an hour.

151. At 1:20 P.M., what does Mr. Arcuri most likely mean when he writes, "For sure"?

(A) He plans to attend a company banquet.
(B) He agrees to transport some containers.
(C) He is certain that some information is correct.
(D) He knows where to buy some decorations.

152. Where will Mr. Arcuri probably go next?

(A) To the maintenance office
(B) To the convention center
(C) To Ms. Cooper's office
(D) To a bakery

GO ON TO THE NEXT PAGE

Hannigan's   May 1

200 Bannock St.
Eagle, Montana
(435) 555 – 9293

Receipt of Purchase #2742953

#1040	Allen wrench(1/4 Inch)	$7.99
#2311	2 gallon custom mixed interior paint (1 at $21.25)	$42.50
#0232	Fiberglass claw hammer	$8.35
#5499	Mini power tool combo set	$127.00

Invoice Total	$185.84
Tax(7%)	$13.00
Total	$198.84
Payment method:	
Gift card 013945	$100 (Balance $0)
Cash	$98.84
You just earned 68 Rewards Points!	
Total rewards points: 325	

This period of Rewards Points accumulation is from April 1 through May 31.

Present this receipt on your next visit by the end of this month to use
your rewards points for a reduced price.

We have a no-questions-asked return and exchange policy on items
purchased within 60 days.

If you do not have this receipt at time of return, you will be issued a store credit.

Thank you for shopping at Hannigan's!

153. What should be done in order to receive a discount?

(A) Visit the store within 60 days starting from May 1
(B) Bring the receipt to the store before June begins
(C) Purchase items using a gift card within a month
(D) Earn more rewards points by buying more items

154. What is NOT stated on the receipt?

(A) The refund policy of Hannigan's
(B) The delivery date for the purchased items
(C) The date when rewards points stop accumulating
(D) The price of custom mixed interior paint per gallon

155. What kind of business most likely issued this receipt?

(A) An art store
(B) A hardware store
(C) A gift shop
(D) An auto repair shop

March 17—City officials have announced the approval of the construction of a large-scale sports stadium in the neighborhood of Tyler Valley. In addition to the usual concession facilities, the building will also feature several restaurants, including a fine-dining establishment. The stadium will incorporate a portion of the former VF Plastics plant, which was the driving force in the area for decades before closing down four years ago. The new facility will make use of sustainable technology such as solar panels and a system that reuses water for irrigating the field. It will also have a roof that can be taken off on sunny days. Boosters will be installed throughout the stadium to ensure fans have Wi-Fi access at all times, and planners hope this will enable promotion on social media as fans share their experiences live. The on-site lot will hold 25,000 parking spots, a portion of which will be under a protective canopy. The stadium is expected to bring in tourists from the region and will be the perfect complement to the massive Alexia Convention Center, just ten miles away in the Evergreen neighborhood.

TEST 04

156. What is suggested about the Tyler Valley neighborhood?

(A) Its main business is a convention center.
(B) It is the site of several restaurants.
(C) It used to be the home of a manufacturing business.
(D) Its sports stadium will be expanded.

157. What is NOT mentioned as a feature of the stadium?

(A) An underground parking area
(B) A water-recycling system
(C) A removable roof
(D) A reliable Internet connection

GO ON TO THE NEXT PAGE

November 8

Dr. Lanae Harding
5498 Newport Beach Road
Newport Beach, OR 97352
United States

Dear Dr. Harding,

Thank you for choosing to attend the first ever Conference on Neuro Genetics at the Evergreen Convention Center. — [1] —. The remaining $100 is due to be paid in full by November 30. Included with your attendance to the conference are breakfast and lunch on Friday, Saturday, and Sunday as well as all necessary session materials. There are multiple restaurants open in the evening within walking distance of the convention center. A complete list along with reviews is available on the conference Web site. — [2] —.

There are several options for lodging near the convention center, but please be aware that accommodations are not included in your registration payment. — [3] —.

Enclosed in this packet are the convention program along with a detailed list of hotel amenities and their prices. It is our recommendation that you review the program in advance to choose from the many seminars and workshops that will be taking place. — [4] —.

Once again, thank you for registering for the Conference on Neuro Genetics.

Best regards,

Jon Simmons
Jon Simmons

Chairperson of the Association for Neuro Genetics

158. Why did Mr. Simmons write the letter?

(A) To announce an annual conference in November
(B) To ask about the coverage of the payment
(C) To provide information on the exact location
(D) To confirm the completion of the registration

159. What information is Dr. Harding invited to check ahead of time?

(A) Which sessions are planned to take place
(B) The facilities and services available at each hotel
(C) Materials included in the registration fee
(D) The locations of the restaurants for dinner

160. In which of the positions marked [1], [2], [3], and [4] does the following sentence best belong?

"Your payment of $100 has been processed and a place has been reserved for you."

(A) [1]
(B) [2]
(C) [3]
(D) [4]

To:	Neil Bergeron <neilb@thismail.com>
From:	Caroline Wells <cwells@mercuryfinancial.com>
Date:	April 3
Subject:	Mercury Financial

Dear Mr. Bergeron,

After careful consideration, I have found that you are the most qualified of all the applicants for the position of senior financial analyst at Mercury Financial, so I would like to offer you the position. As a senior financial analyst, you will be expected to personally handle the accounts of some of our top clients. You will also oversee some of our junior analysts, provide advice to them and mentor them. Finally, we require all of our senior financial analysts to produce weekly reports on different sectors of the economy. Yours would be on the foreign and domestic automobile industry.

You will be paid a salary of $120,000 each year and also receive a quarterly performance bonus as well as company stock. You should start your employment with us no later than May 1, so you have to find a place to stay in Dallas before that date while you are getting ready to move from St. Louis. The company will pay for your moving expenses and will also cover your housing costs until you can find a permanent residence.

If you accept this offer, then you will be contacted by Melissa Patterson, who works in the HR Department. She will send you a number of employment forms, including your contract, which you need to fill out in full, sign, and return to her no later than April 20.

I am looking forward to working with you in the near future.

Sincerely,

Caroline Wells

TEST 04

161. What is the purpose of the e-mail?

(A) To propose working on a joint project
(B) To extend an invitation to a seminar
(C) To request advice on an employment matter
(D) To discuss a hiring decision

162. What is NOT listed as one of the responsibilities of a senior financial analyst?

(A) Providing assistance to other employees
(B) Writing reports on a weekly basis
(C) Leading meetings with other analysts
(D) Working closely with certain clients

163. What is mentioned about Mr. Bergeron?

(A) He has never met Ms. Wells in person.
(B) He has a decade of experience in the field.
(C) He lives in St. Louis at the moment.
(D) He reports directly to the HR Director.

164. What does Ms. Wells ask Mr. Bergeron to do?

(A) Complete some paperwork
(B) Make a payment for his order
(C) Visit the St. Louis office
(D) Contact Ms. Patterson

GO ON TO THE NEXT PAGE

Questions 165-168 refer to the following online chat discussion.

Brian Roebuck [5:31 P.M.]
Hello, everyone. I've just had a request from Danielle Roy. She wants our team to complete the interior design work for her business one month early. I'm wondering if that's possible.

Rick Lloyd [5:32 P.M.]
I think we have enough time. The locker rooms and workout rooms are planned, but the lobby area needs to make a good impression on gym members.

Chang Tung [5:34 P.M.]
I've finished the preliminary drawings for the lobby, but I can't present anything until the budget estimates for materials are done. Where are you on that, Amanda?

Amanda Vicini [5:35 P.M.]
I hadn't started that yet because I thought I had more time.

Brian Roebuck [5:37 P.M.]
How soon could you get it done? I don't want to book the work crew until we know exactly when to start.

Amanda Vicini [5:39 P.M.]
I don't mind putting in some extra hours. I'll have it on your desk first thing tomorrow morning.

Brian Roebuck [5:40 P.M.]
Great! Thank you! Then I think we can meet her new deadline of March 15th.

Chang Tung [5:43 P.M.]
Does Ms. Roy know that we recently raised our fees?

Rick Lloyd [5:44 P.M.]
Yes. I gave her a brochure with the updated figures when we arranged the contract.

SEND

---

165. At 5:31 P.M., what does Mr. Roebuck most likely mean when he writes, "I'm wondering if that's possible"?

(A) He is making sure a budget is sufficient.
(B) He is unfamiliar with a policy.
(C) He wants to alter a schedule.
(D) He doubts that a service is offered.

166. What type of business is Ms. Roy opening?

(A) A fitness facility
(B) A hotel
(C) An apartment complex
(D) An institute

167. Who most likely will work late today?

(A) Mr. Roebuck
(B) Mr. Lloyd
(C) Ms. Tung
(D) Ms. Vicini

168. What is indicated about Ms. Roy?

(A) She has recommended a business.
(B) She needs service at multiple locations.
(C) She wants to negotiate the contract.
(D) She is informed about the new rates.

```
● ● ●                           E-mail
```

To: All Staff
From: Oliver Sondreal
Date: October 23
Subject: For your immediate attention

Dear Staff,

Due to time constraints, we weren't able to discuss everything on the agenda at this morning's staff meeting. Therefore, I'd like to take a moment to tell you about the upcoming Toronto Design Contest (TDC). — [1] —. This competition is held annually and is open to all companies within Canada that have been in operation for less than twelve months. The management team of Media Max would like you all to make TDC a top priority. — [2] —.

This competition is an excellent opportunity because it will introduce our talents to the wider market. Last year's winner received a great deal of attention because of the contest, and this fueled growth that would otherwise be very difficult to accomplish without heavy investment in advertising. — [3] —.

Please see Marcus Ness in the administrative office if you are willing and able to put together an entry with others. — [4] —. Updates about the guidelines will follow next week, but we would like a general idea of who is interested by Friday, if possible. We hope you will all consider it.

Sincerely,

Oliver Sondreal

169. Why did Mr. Sondreal write the e-mail?

(A) To explain the guidelines of a contest
(B) To remind recipients about a staff meeting
(C) To encourage participation in an event
(D) To request opinions from employees

170. What is stated about Media Max?

(A) It was founded by Mr. Sondreal.
(B) It is less than a year old.
(C) It is based in Toronto.
(D) It won a competition last year.

171. What benefit of TDC does Mr. Sondreal mention?

(A) Networking with colleagues in the industry
(B) Applying for funding from the government
(C) Introducing a new product to the market
(D) Receiving an increase in publicity

172. In which of the positions marked [1], [2], [3], and [4] does the following sentence best belong?

"This will assist us in assembling the best possible team."

(A) [1]
(B) [2]
(C) [3]
(D) [4]

GO ON TO THE NEXT PAGE

Chicago (17 May)—In a move that has many speculators surprised, long-standing president and founder of Tilliman Beverages, Norman Chapin announced he will step down from his leadership role. Mr. Chapin is renowned for successfully aiding the company in the transition from marketing its beverage line to commercial distributors, such as restaurants, to selling its products directly to consumers. By changing its focus from corporate to individual clients, the company widened its base of customers and became one of the most popular beverage makers.

Due to the company's success, Milton Snacks made a bid to the owners of Tilliman Beverages last November in hopes of acquiring the market leader. After several months of negotiations and meetings, a deal was reached to merge the two industry giants. The merger is scheduled to occur next month.

CEO Heather Moore of Milton Snacks said in a press conference yesterday afternoon that the two companies will continue to retain the same great flavors that made them popular, but will also join forces to research the creation of new products. Although no details were given, Ms. Moore did say that Mr. Chapin would play an important role in this process.

173. What is the purpose of the article?

(A) To propose a merger between two snack industries

(B) To announce the resignation of the founder of Milton Snacks

(C) To notify customers about the changes in a product line

(D) To announce some changes at Tilliman Beverages

174. In what way did Tilliman Beverages change in recent years?

(A) They created new lines of beverages.

(B) They began selling their beverage line to restaurants.

(C) They expanded the range of customers.

(D) They intended to acquire another corporate giant.

175. What is NOT true about the merger?

(A) It will eventually alter the type of beverages of Tilliman Beverages.

(B) It has been discussed for several months.

(C) It is between two of the most prosperous companies.

(D) It will take place in June.

GO ON TO THE NEXT PAGE

Arya Sehgal, Head of Human Resources
NWT Sports Corporate Office
4355 Drummond Street
Dallas, TX 75207

April 10

Dear Ms. Sehgal,

I am currently working as the store manager at the NWT Sports store in Austin. I heard that the store manager at the Laredo branch, Patrick Soto, will retire soon, and I would like to be considered for the store manager position there. I have had a great deal of success at the Austin store. When I turned up on my first day, the store was a mess. Employees were unmotivated and undertrained and sales were the lowest in the region. Also, customer satisfaction ratings were terrible. Within just a few months, I was able to correct these issues and make Austin the second-most-profitable store in the region. I am looking for a new challenge, and I believe that Laredo is the best place to implement my skills.

I would be more than happy to set up an interview—by phone or in person—to discuss this matter further. Please contact me at your earliest convenience.

Sincerely,

Susan Quinn
Austin Branch Manager, NWT Sports

To: All Laredo Branch Employees
From: Susan Quinn
Date: January 8
Subject: To all employees

Hello Everyone,

I've reviewed the figures for the quarter that just finished, and I'm pleased to let you know that we reached our sales goal. Great job, everyone! The goal was ambitious, even for the holiday season, but you all worked together to accomplish what we set out to do. By keeping the store well organized and providing excellent customer service, we were able to significantly improve sales compared to last year.

I was also impressed with the teamwork you showed. As you know, the demand for our products has grown, so we hired about twenty additional people. The way you all assisted these newcomers in getting adjusted to our work environment was amazing. This kind of behavior helps to make NWT Sports a pleasant working environment. It is a pleasure to be managing this store, and I look forward to the upcoming year. Keep up the fantastic work!

Susan

176. Why did Ms. Quinn write the letter?

(A) To provide requested job figures
(B) To inquire about a company's mission
(C) To recommend a colleague for a position
(D) To show interest in a job opening

177. In the letter, the phrase "turned up" in paragraph 1, line 4, is closest in meaning to

(A) moved
(B) discovered
(C) arrived
(D) increased

178. What is one purpose of the e-mail?

(A) To explain the reason for a change
(B) To congratulate the staff on an achievement
(C) To thank the staff for their suggestions
(D) To outline the next year's goals

179. What is indicated about the Laredo branch?

(A) It is the most popular branch.
(B) It holds training sessions regularly.
(C) Its staff has grown in size.
(D) It had to undergo an inspection.

180. What is probably true about Ms. Quinn?

(A) Her request for a transfer was approved.
(B) She was eligible to receive a bonus.
(C) Her suggestion for a holiday sale was followed.
(D) She used to work in Ms. Sehgal's office.

GO ON TO THE NEXT PAGE

Questions 181-185 refer to the following flyer and Web page.

Towry Center

Goldcliff Building, 1488 34th Street, Indianapolis, IN 46203

The Towry Center is a privately funded organization dedicated to the community. We provide free classes and online resources to help individuals and families take control of their debt and spending through learning the best ways to manage their finances. Group classes are taught every month by Reynalda Palermo. There is no enrollment fee for classes. We also offer one-on-one counseling, provided by Scott Brenner, for a nominal fee.

In addition to getting helpful articles, those who subscribe to the monthly newsletter will receive a free e-book on budgeting by Jeremy Caruso. This step-by-step guide has helped thousands of people.

For more information, visit our Web site at www.towrycenter.org or stop in during our business hours, which are Monday through Friday from 10 A.M. to 5 P.M.

---

www.towrycenter.org/upcomingevents

| HOME | UPCOMING EVENTS | CONTACT US | FAQs |

Tuesday, August 3
Monthly Group Class (Free Admission)
This month's topic: Planning for Taxes
7:30 P.M. – 9:00 P.M., Logan Hotel (Conference Room 106)

Saturday, August 28
Visit our booth at the Annual Indianapolis Fair, at the Hickory Convention Center, for a free 10-minute consultation to assess your finances. You can also talk to our staff to learn more about the programs we offer.

Wednesday, September 1
The Affordable Housing Commission (AHC) has announced that it will offer grants for first-time home buyers starting from September 1. There are only twenty-five grants to be issued in our region, and they are given on a first-come, first-served basis. Applications are accepted from September 1 and the grants are expected to run out within the first few days. Visit the AHC office in person in the Rex Building (475 Searcy Street) or call Margaret Garza at 555-4856 for more information.

181. What is the purpose of the Towry Center?

(A) To give support to small businesses
(B) To advise people on handling money
(C) To provide private loans to people
(D) To raise money for community projects

182. According to the flyer, how can people get a complimentary book?

(A) By joining a mailing list
(B) By making a purchase
(C) By sharing their feedback
(D) By attending a class

183. Who will most likely lead the event in the first week of August?

(A) Scott Brenner
(B) Jeremy Caruso
(C) Margaret Garza
(D) Reynalda Palermo

184. Where will the Towry Center representatives be giving free consultations?

(A) At the Goldcliff Building
(B) At the Hickory Convention Center
(C) At the Logan Hotel
(D) At the Rex Building

185. What is implied about the AHC?

(A) It plans to provide a tour of homes.
(B) It will relocate in September.
(C) It holds events at the Towry Center.
(D) Its offer is in high demand.

GO ON TO THE NEXT PAGE

3rd Annual Woodridge Environmental Festival
Saturday, October 15, 9 A.M.–8 P.M. at Fleming Park

Eco-Warriors, Meet at the outdoor stage, 9 A.M.–noon
Turn your attention to the environment by volunteering for this cleanup project. We will collect trash from the shores of the James River and leave the area in pristine condition. Please bring your own gloves.

Trash to Treasure, Hosted by the Loredo Gallery, 1 P.M.–3 P.M.
Show your creativity by making unique crafts from recyclable products. Contest entries will be judged by festival visitors throughout the day, and the winner will be announced at the closing ceremony. One entry per person.

Zany Zoo, Hosted by the Woodridge Health Association, 4 P.M.
Dress up as your favorite animal for a fun and memorable 5K run. Prizes will be awarded for both the fastest runners and the best costumes!

Super Stalls, Hosted by the Environmental Alliance, All Day
The area's largest outdoor market, with a wide variety of stalls selling health foods, natural beauty products, upcycled clothing, and more. Support the sale of sustainable goods in our region.

Closing ceremony at 7:30 P.M. at the outdoor stage

To: Addison Evans <addisonevans@communityconnex.org>
From: Jackson Lewis <j.lewis@woodbridgecity.gov>
Date: October 12
Subject: Woodridge Environmental Festival

Dear Ms. Evans,

I've checked the weather forecast for this weekend, and it looks like it's going to be quite cold on the morning of the festival. I'm worried that the cold temperatures will discourage participants from coming to the river cleanup event. I know that Community Connex has already committed to bringing twenty people to the activity, but I'm wondering if you could find five to ten additional helpers. Sorry for the short notice, and please rest assured that the emcee will recognize your group's hard work in his comments at the closing ceremony.

Thank you!

Jackson Lewis

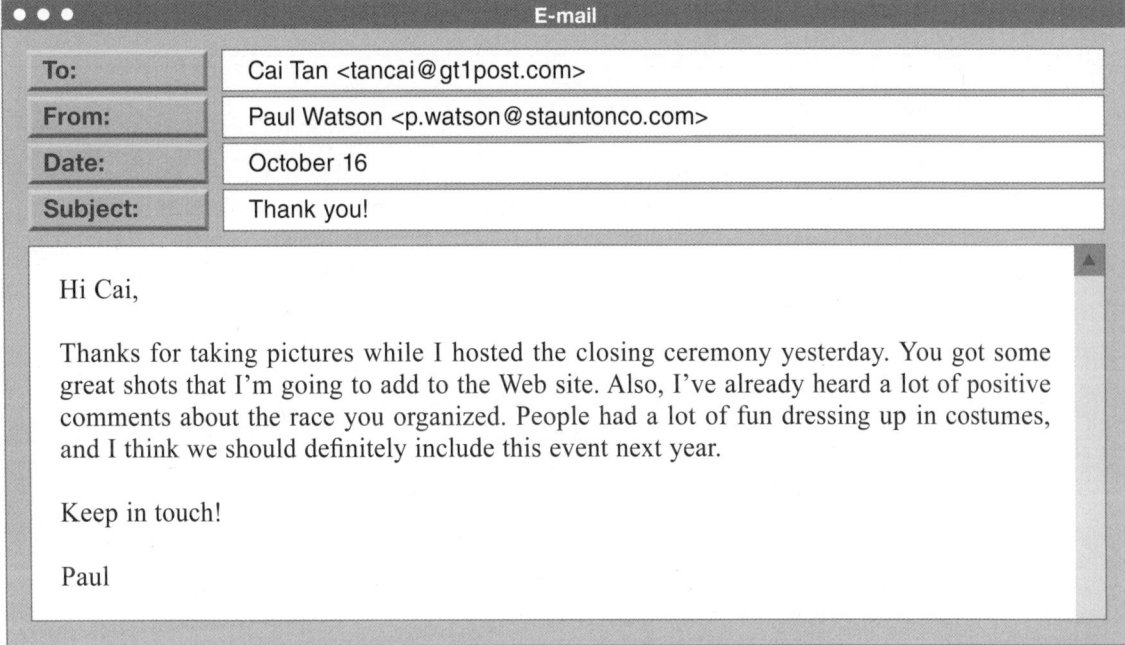

186. In the schedule, the word "Turn" in paragraph 1, line 1, is closest in meaning to

(A) Direct
(B) Adapt
(C) Convert
(D) Spin

187. What is indicated about the craft competition?

(A) Its winner will be announced at 3 P.M.
(B) Its competitors cannot be professional artists.
(C) It will be judged by a gallery owner.
(D) It limits a person's number of entries.

188. Why did Mr. Lewis send the first e-mail?

(A) To announce a location change
(B) To recruit more volunteers
(C) To adjust a schedule
(D) To check a weather forecast

189. What is implied about Mr. Watson?

(A) He wants to get together with Mr. Tan in person.
(B) He is a member of the Woodridge Health Association.
(C) He attended last year's Woodridge Environmental Festival.
(D) He mentioned Community Connex at an event.

190. Which event did Mr. Tan lead?

(A) Eco-Warriors
(B) Trash to Treasure
(C) Zany Zoo
(D) Super Stalls

GO ON TO THE NEXT PAGE

Questions 191-195 refer to the following letter, e-mail, and advertisement.

To Whom It May Concern:

The Sapphire Theater Association is holding a talent show to raise funds for a restoration project at Sapphire Theater. Budget shortfalls resulted in numerous delays in essential repairs and restoration work, but we simply cannot stand this any longer. Now is the time to act, and you can help.

Become a sponsor and support this worthwhile project while also gaining publicity for your company.

Donation Tier	Donation Amount	Complimentary Advertising Placement	Other Benefits
Bronze Level	$250	Theater Web site	–
Silver Level	$500	Theater Web site & printed program	–
Gold Level	$1,000	Printed program & stage banner	VIP seating in the center section (6 people)
Platinum Level	$2,500	Stage banner & newspaper advertisement	VIP seating in a private box (8 people)

Gold- and Platinum-level donors should select a representative to pose for a picture at the talent show with Mayor Ryan Campbell and the theater's general manager, Nino Shaw; this will appear in the Sunday edition of *the Stone Valley Times*.

We hope you will join us in preserving this beautiful historic building and prominent downtown landmark.

Sincerely,

Elise Hart
President, Sapphire Theater Association

To: Elise Hart <e.hart@sapphiretheater.com>
From: Neerav Chambal <chambaln@bramptonltd.com>
Date: May 14
Subject: RE: Sapphire Theater Fundraiser

Dear Ms. Hart,

I'm pleased that you received Brampton Ltd.'s check for one thousand dollars. We are happy to make a financial contribution to this important cause. The person we have chosen to represent our company is Ms. Shannon Gardner. She will report to the stage at 6:45 P.M. on the event day as you requested. We wish your organization all the best in its fundraising efforts, and we hope that you meet or even exceed your goals.

Warmest regards,

Neerav Chambal

Sapphire Theater Talent Show
Brought to you by the Sapphire Theater Association
Saturday, June 2, 7:30 P.M.

We're looking for singers, comedians, magicians, and more for the first-ever Sapphire Theater Talent Show. Share your talents with the community and help raise money for renovation projects at Sapphire Theater. No auditions needed! Prizes will be awarded by the theater's general manager at the end of the show.

Not a performer? You can still support the event by being a part of the audience. Tickets are only $15 per person and include a free soft drink at intermission.

191. To whom most likely was the letter sent?

(A) Theater critics
(B) Professional musicians
(C) Club members
(D) Local businesses

192. In the letter, the word "stand" in paragraph 1, line 3, is closest in meaning to

(A) locate
(B) rise
(C) tolerate
(D) remain

193. Where will Brampton Ltd. receive free advertising?

(A) On a Web site only
(B) On a Web site and in a program
(C) In a program and on a banner
(D) On a banner and in a newspaper

194. What is indicated about Ms. Gardner?

(A) Her photo will appear in a newspaper.
(B) She is the owner of Brampton Ltd.
(C) Her seat will be in a private box.
(D) She plans to sing in a talent show.

195. What is true about the June 2 event?

(A) Mr. Campbell will give a speech.
(B) Performers should arrive one hour in advance.
(C) Prizes will be distributed by Mr. Shaw.
(D) Tickets include a prize drawing entry.

GO ON TO THE NEXT PAGE

Questions 196-200 refer to the following Web page, schedule, and e-mail.

● ● ● www.musicshop99.com

| HOME | **GENRES** | TODAY'S DEALS | CONTACT |

Search: Janice Brown

4 Results Found:

On the Edge
This upbeat album showcases Brown's lyrical talent as she and hip-hop star Ferrari G join forces for a unique blend of music styles focusing on inner-city life. The single "Wouldn't You" spent 18 weeks at the top of the charts.

For Always
Brown teamed up with a number of legends in the music world for this fast-paced rock album. All proceeds from the album go toward the Hurricane Relief Fund, which serves communities that have suffered from natural disasters around the world.

Simple Things
A departure from Brown's usual fast beats and electric sound, *Simple Things* features slow love ballads. Each song is a duet with another artist with only acoustic guitars serving as accompaniment.

Footsteps
A live recording from a tour performance in Dallas, Texas. Brown performed with her tour band and with singer Rhonda Cook to a crowd of thousands of enthusiastic fans. The album includes Brown's hits as well as new material.

103.5 FM Radio Afternoon Schedule: Monday, June 4

1:00 P.M. Politics and Promises / Episode 2 of this 6-part series that explores corruption at the state and national level. Narrated by Joe Rayburn.

2:00 P.M. Jazz Hour / Hosted by Tara Watkins, this program features a variety of jazz hits for your enjoyment. Call the station at 205-555-2940 to make a request.

3:00 P.M. On the Pulse / A look into the entertainment industry, with the latest news on musicians, actors, directors, and more. This week, host Gregory King interviews singer Janice Brown about her fundraising album to help hurricane victims.

4:00 P.M. News Corner / A collection of stories from around the world to keep you informed on current events and the up-to-the-minute news on issues you care about most.

Weather and traffic reports at the top of each hour.

To: <feedback@103-5radio.com>
From: Ashley Lemon <lemona@scopemail.net>
Date: June 6
Subject: Program comment

To Whom It May Concern:

I wanted to express my appreciation for your fine afternoon programming, particularly On the Pulse. I got hooked on this show several years ago when Lee Parker was the host, as I'm a huge fan of pop culture. I think that Gregory King is doing an excellent job, and he seems very natural on air even after only a few weeks on the show. It's easy to see that he has a great deal of talent for communicating with others and bringing out the most fascinating aspects of their lives. I also enjoy the selection of guests, and I was delighted to hear the interview with Janice Brown. I attended the show where she made her live recording, and I was thoroughly impressed. It was interesting hearing about her creative process and the inspiration behind the music. I will continue to be a loyal listener of this show. Keep up the good work!

Sincerely,

Ashley Lemon

196. What do all of Janice Brown's albums have in common?

(A) They involve collaboration with other musicians.
(B) They are accompanied only by acoustic guitars.
(C) They have love as their main theme.
(D) They contain songs with a fast rhythm.

197. Which album was the focus of Mr. King's show?

(A) *On the Edge*
(B) *For Always*
(C) *Simple Things*
(D) *Footsteps*

198. What is suggested about Mr. King?

(A) He used to be a professional singer.
(B) He changed his show's time slot.
(C) He is new to his position.
(D) He is a well-known radio host.

199. In the e-mail, the word "see" in paragraph 1, line 4, is closest in meaning to

(A) recognize
(B) ensure
(C) consult
(D) predict

200. What is implied about Ms. Lemon?

(A) She called the station to request a song.
(B) She went to a concert in Dallas.
(C) She owns all of Janice Brown's albums.
(D) She listens to 103.5 FM every afternoon.

This is the end of the test. You may review PART 5, 6, and 7 if you finish the test early.
정답 p. 319 / 점수 환산표 p. 321 / 해석 p. 348

TEST

PART 5
PART 6
PART 7

토익 Reading Comprehension은 75분 동안 진행됩니다.
현재 시각과 지금부터 75분 후인 테스트 종료 시각을 기록해 두고,
반드시 종료 시각 전에 문제 풀이와 답안지 마킹을 완료하세요.

현재 시각  시  분

테스트 종료 시각 ☐ 시 ☐ 분

READING TEST

In the Reading test, you will read a variety of texts and answer several different types of reading comprehension questions. The entire Reading test will last 75 minutes. There are three parts, and directions are given for each part. You are encouraged to answer as many questions as possible within the time allowed.

You must mark your answers on the separate answer sheet. Do not write your answers in your test book.

PART 5

Directions: A word or phrase is missing in each of the sentences below. Four answer choices are given below each sentence. Select the best answer to complete the sentence. Then mark the letter (A), (B), (C), or (D) on your answer sheet.

101. The responsibilities of the floor manager include ------- the performances of employees.

(A) advertising
(B) purchasing
(C) establishing
(D) reviewing

102. The staff cafeteria on the ground floor of the building is required to comply with all --- health guidelines.

(A) localize
(B) local
(C) locals
(D) localizing

103. ------- needs to report that there is extensive water damage in the lab due to last night's storm.

(A) Someone
(B) Them
(C) We
(D) Any

104. According to the film festival's Web site, the entrance fee ------- admittance to all screenings and workshops.

(A) is included
(B) have included
(C) includes
(D) including

105. The rental prices of apartments differ ------- by neighborhood, with high-end properties nearly triple those at the low end.

(A) substantiality
(B) substantially
(C) most substantial
(D) substantial

106. In order to be reimbursed for travel expenses, all receipts for business trips must be turned in ------- the end of the year.

(A) within
(B) until
(C) for
(D) by

107. Haritas Express plans to ------- for qualified applicants for its open positions by advertising extensively.

(A) apply
(B) complete
(C) search
(D) send

108. Changes cannot be made to buildings in the historical district until the ------- permit applications are submitted and approved.

(A) relevancies
(B) relevant
(C) relevance
(D) relevantly

109. ------- an increase in concern over ingesting harmful chemicals, the demand for organically grown produce has risen sharply.

(A) In addition to
(B) Rather than
(C) Because of
(D) Instead of

110. At your -------, we have canceled your recent purchase of 24-pack Vanilla Scented Soy Candles.

(A) idea
(B) request
(C) position
(D) claim

111. Because Ms. Lee will arrive ------- to the weekly budget meeting starting 9 A.M., the meeting cannot start as scheduled.

(A) late
(B) soon
(C) nearly
(D) once

112. As their schedules for the upcoming week are various, the delegates from Collins Inc. will go to the conference ------- by car.

(A) separated
(B) separations
(C) separately
(D) separate

113. The Graphics Center at CDV Apparel allows customers to ------- the design that appears on the front of their T-shirts.

(A) customizing
(B) customize
(C) customized
(D) customizes

114. System updates from last month ------- need to be completed on one quarter of the computers used by employees.

(A) recently
(B) precisely
(C) ever
(D) still

115. The director of the Indianapolis Homeless Shelter is ------- the budget needs of the site for the upcoming year.

(A) consider
(B) considerable
(C) considered
(D) considering

116. Mr. Thompson became incredibly wealthy by ------- advice on how to enter foreign markets to large corporations.

(A) provide
(B) provided
(C) provides
(D) providing

117. The stories that are contained in the collection are ------- on folk tales that are told by people in the countryside.

(A) depended
(B) based
(C) heard
(D) read

118. Complimentary lunch will be provided for all the conference participants, ------- donations are welcome.

(A) but
(B) if
(C) as long as
(D) rather than

119. The chief computer programmer, ------- extensive expertise enabled the team to finish the software, will give a talk at the upcoming convention.

(A) that
(B) who
(C) which
(D) whose

120. Mayor Stephenson will attend a ceremony to ------- those who contributed financially to the city stadium's renovation fund.

(A) acknowledge
(B) accomplish
(C) indicate
(D) extend

GO ON TO THE NEXT PAGE

121. Organizational practices are ------- revisited to ensure that they reflect the company vision in a reasonable and meaningful way.

(A) formerly
(B) periodically
(C) extremely
(D) mutually

122. ------- of interest in the topic resulted in the academy canceling its plans to offer classes in biology.

(A) Lack
(B) To lack
(C) Lacking
(D) Having lacked

123. A group of government lawyers is determining ------- any laws were violated during the merger between the two firms.

(A) rather
(B) given
(C) since
(D) whether

124. Mr. Oh will send the agenda ------- Wednesday's monthly business meeting no later than 5 P.M. on Friday.

(A) by
(B) to
(C) near
(D) for

125. ------- are doctors at Grand View Hospital permitted to spend more than four days in a row away from the office.

(A) Even
(B) Yet
(C) None
(D) Seldom

126. While Mr. Morrow has never studied marketing, he is the most ------- employee at the company when it comes to nanotechnology.

(A) authorized
(B) knowledgeable
(C) comprehensive
(D) confirmed

127. After receiving favorable reviews, Karen Smith has agreed to write another ------- for the opinion column of *the Shaw Mountain Daily Newspaper*.

(A) sense
(B) article
(C) news
(D) print

128. By subscribing to a year-long membership with *Warren Global News Magazine*, you will receive a ------- issue of *Modern Travel Weekly*.

(A) complimentary
(B) variable
(C) presumable
(D) subsequent

129. The relocation of Genome Software Inc. to London is expected to generate a(n) ------- demand for computer engineers in the city.

(A) accomplished
(B) plenty
(C) sizable
(D) careful

130. For the past ten years, Ms. Rosewood has ------- a number of art books from her own personal collection to the university's library.

(A) written
(B) published
(C) drawn
(D) donated

PART 6

Directions: Read the texts that follow. A word, phrase, or sentence is missing in parts of each text. Four answer choices for each question are given below the text. Select the best answer to complete the text. Then mark the letter (A), (B), (C), or (D) on your answer sheet.

Questions 131-134 refer to the following article.

Annual Sentinel Springs Marathon

Early bird registration has opened for the 23rd annual Sentinel Springs Marathon. -------. This year
131.
the race will fall on April 30 and will start at 7 A.M. ------- in Hide Park, the 26.2 mile course follows
132.
the scenic Coastal Boulevard with participants ending in Meyer Stadium.

Based on the turnout from last year, the number of ------- is expected to exceed 10,000. All runners
133.
must complete registration no later than April 15.

------- fee before February 1 is $70. Those registering after the early bird deadline will need to pay
134.
$90.

---

131. (A) The long-distance footrace will take place as usual on the last Sunday of April.
(B) The weather was the perfect combination for runners, dry and cool.
(C) City officials are pleased to offer this activity to the community for the first time.
(D) You can find the directions to the event place on the Web site.

132. (A) Leading
(B) Walking
(C) Training
(D) Beginning

133. (A) trainers
(B) spectators
(C) participants
(D) visitors

134. (A) Entered
(B) Entrance
(C) Entrant
(D) Entering

GO ON TO THE NEXT PAGE

Questions 135-138 refer to the following notice.

Hanauma Children's Community Center is sponsoring a concert to be held on November 3 at 4 P.M. at Diamond Head Park Amphitheater. The center announced that the ------- of the gathering is to

135.

generate funding for the creation of an interactive natural science children's museum.

Oahu Youth Jazz Ensemble will perform, along with Kailua Children's Choir. Soloist Ailani Kane

------- as a vocalist. The event will be family friendly and free to all children under the age of 12. Seats

136.

can be reserved on hanaumaccc.org and grass space will be available on the day of the ------- on a

137.

first come, first served basis. Ticket prices will vary based on location and availability. -------.

138.

135. (A) action
(B) goal
(C) mark
(D) view

136. (A) featuring
(B) will be featured
(C) has been featured
(D) used to feature

137. (A) contract
(B) preservation
(C) contest
(D) performance

138. (A) These include educational programs for local children.
(B) We appreciate your volunteering for the coming concert.
(C) All proceeds will benefit the local children's museum project.
(D) As a result, the ticket prices are the same for all age groups.

From: m.hassel@d&bequipment.com
To: D&B Equipment employees
Subject: Discounted Ski Park Passes
Date: October 31

As many of you know, Hatons Resorts, the company which operates the Millet Basin Ski Park, is one of our most long-standing -------. We have supplied and installed ski lift equipment for them at
139.
nearly all of their 17 locations across the country. -------. These will be available to any employee for
140.
only 20 percent of the regular price. ------- you plan to take advantage of this unique offer, write me
141.
back to confirm. The regular season pass price is $300, so each employee would only pay $60. We expect there will be a lot of ------- in these passes.
142.

Thanks for your hard work.

Marge Hassel
D&B Equipment, Director

139. (A) performances
(B) guests
(C) clients
(D) patterns

140. (A) They are looking to open more ski parks in Switzerland.
(B) In appreciation, they are offering us low-cost season passes.
(C) Moreover, Hatons Resorts is famous for its exquisite activities.
(D) We have organized a trip to one of the ski parks as an incentive.

141. (A) If
(B) Whether
(C) Unless
(D) Whereas

142. (A) interest
(B) interested
(C) interesting
(D) interests

GO ON TO THE NEXT PAGE

Questions 143-146 refer to the following memo.

From: olivestone@advantagedental.org
To: All Staff
Subject: Dental Excellence Award
Date: April 7
Attachment: Meal options

Dear Advantage Dental Professionals,

I am so proud of our dental professionals who ------- significantly to the oral health and wellbeing
                                                                      143.
of this community. Our patients have been giving our services the highest ratings. -------, we
                                                                                              144.
have been presented for the third consecutive year with the Dental Excellence Award. -------. The
                                                                                                    145.
Advantage Dental administrators are therefore pleased to host a congratulatory catered dinner on

April 23 at the Running Y Resort. Please view the ------- list for your meal selection.
                                                          146.

With greatest appreciation,

Olive Stone
Advantage Dental Director

143. (A) contributing
(B) contribute
(C) were contributing
(D) are contributed

144. (A) On the contrary
(B) By comparison
(C) In fact
(D) However

145. (A) This award is offered to the dentists who
excelled in their research.
(B) Also, Advantage Dental is equipped with
professional appliances.
(C) We are honored to receive such a
prestigious award for the first time.
(D) This is one of the reasons our patient
numbers continue to grow.

146. (A) attach
(B) attaching
(C) attaches
(D) attached

Directions: In this part you will read a selection of texts, such as magazine and newspaper articles, e-mails, and instant messages. Each text or set of texts is followed by several questions. Select the best answer for each question and mark the letter (A), (B), (C), or (D) on your answer sheet.

Questions 147-148 refer to the following form.

Angwin Gardens Vineyard: Wedding Facilities

Congratulations and welcome to the Angwin Gardens Family! We are excited that you have chosen Angwin Gardens Vineyard to celebrate this important moment in your life. Please take a moment to tell us more about your plans for this special day.

One of our event organizers will contact you with plan and pricing details needed to meet the needs of your wedding.

– Name of principal parties: _____ and _____ .

– E-mail: _____ Contact number: _____ Date: _____

– Site Selection: St. Helena: { } 1200 Blue Vintage
Calistoga: { } 9530 Hot Springs Dr.
Angiwn: { } 913 Clark Road { } 25 Angwin Way

– Facilities needed: { } Chapel { } Dressing rooms { } Reception hall { } Other: _____

– Estimated number of guests: { } 15-29 { } 30-69 { } 70-99 { } 100-149 { } 150+

– Equipment needed: { } Tables { } Chairs { } Sound system

147. What is an event organizer likely to do next?
(A) Prepare the facilities and equipment for the special day
(B) Post a notice online for the wedding participants
(C) Provide information on hotel accommodation costs
(D) Give an estimate based on the details provided on this form

148. What is suggested about Angwin Gardens Vineyard?
(A) It offers meals for guests when requested.
(B) It has four different locations to choose from.
(C) It is equipped with various utensils.
(D) It has guest rooms available for use.

GO ON TO THE NEXT PAGE

NOTICE TO 8TH STREET HARDWARE CUSTOMERS

The management team of 8th Street Hardware would like to inform you of an important change. After thirteen years being operated by the Jackson family, the business has been sold to a local entrepreneur, Carl Lugo. We wish him the best of luck in his endeavors, and we are confident that he will maintain the high-quality customer service that you have come to expect from 8th Street Hardware. For the first three months under the new management, there will be no changes to the exchange policy. The prices on goods will also stay at their current level. We hope you will continue to make 8th Street Hardware your first stop for all of your building and home repair needs.

149. Why was the notice written?

(A) To introduce the winner of an award
(B) To announce a change in ownership
(C) To promote an anniversary event
(D) To explain an exchange policy

150. What is mentioned about the store's merchandise?

(A) It is considered to be of high quality.
(B) Its repairs will be done for free.
(C) It can be returned within three months.
(D) Its prices will remain the same.

Smithson Educational Conference

December 4
Andrew McCoy
726 McKinley Street
Westborough, MA 17344

Dear Mr. McCoy,

This letter is to confirm your attendance at the Smithson Educational Conference from December 20 to December 22 in Princeton, New Jersey. Your presentation will be delivered on December 22.

On the last day of the conference, there will be a dinner for all the participants of the seminar. It will take place at the Triple Crown Hotel, just downstairs of where the seminar will be conducted. It will start at 9 p.m. You are welcome to join the dinner if possible.

My assistant, Jordan Genovia, has arranged a reservation for your stay at the Grand Tree Hotel. The hotel is conveniently located in the downtown area of the city, and the conference is only a five minute walking distance away from the hotel. For any question about your stay, please contact my assistant at jgenovia@smithsonec.com.

I would like to remind you that you need to send in the copies of your presentation and the materials related to it in order for us to examine its quality and appropriateness before you give your speech. We ask you to do this as soon as possible.

We heard great things about your career at the Johnson Education Center from your colleagues. We are more than delighted to hear your speech at the seminar.

Sincerely,

Grace Page
Event Operator, Smithson Educational Conference

151. Why was the letter sent?

(A) To recruit a seminar leader
(B) To give details about the conference
(C) To advertise an educational event
(D) To inquire about a room reservation

152. Where will Mr. McCoy be giving a presentation?

(A) At Grand Tree Hotel
(B) At a dinner reception
(C) At Johnson Education Center
(D) At Triple Crown Hotel

GO ON TO THE NEXT PAGE

Questions 153-155 refer to the following advertisement.

Join an interactive Italian art history tour!

Do you love art, history and culture? Combine all three next summer and take a two-week tour through Italy, led by an art history expert.
Included on the itinerary:
• Visits to Italy's most famous museums
• Walkthrough lectures on the Renaissance
• Hands-on classes on the techniques of sketching, painting and sculpting
• Delicious meals at authentic Italian restaurants

Guests will stay at luxury hotels in cities such as Florence, Venice and Rome. All museum entry passes, meals and accommodations will be included. However, participants should be capable of several hours of light to moderate walking each day. Tours will begin in Rome and each guest should secure his or her own plane ticket.

Three tours are currently still available. These begin May 30, June 18 and July 5. Register before January 1 to save up to 15 percent.

For pricing specifics and detailed itineraries, please visit www.italianarthistoryculture.org.

153. What is being advertised?

(A) A vacation package
(B) Tickets to art museums
(C) A special event held in Italy
(D) Three lectures in art and history

154. What are guests asked to do?

(A) Write an online review
(B) Sign up for an art history class
(C) Check the vacancy of rooms at hotels
(D) Book a flight to Rome

155. According to the advertisement, what is available on the Web site?

(A) Directions to local attractions
(B) The schedule of activities
(C) A list of luxurious hotels
(D) The cost of entry to museums

MARY SCHMIDT 12:40 P.M.
I sent you a text message this morning about the Comic Book Expo to be held on Friday. Did you receive it?

MARSHALL GRIMES 12:55 P.M.
I just checked my messages a moment ago. It said that there aren't many tickets remaining, right? I hope we can still get in. I really want to have my *Cloaked Rider* series signed by their author.

MARY SCHMIDT 1:00 P.M.
You mean you didn't buy the tickets yet?

MARSHALL GRIMES 1:03 P.M.
No, but it shouldn't be too big of a problem. The box office is on my way home. I'll go buy two of them right now.

MARY SCHMIDT 1:04 P.M.
It's too late. They sold out an hour ago.

MARSHALL GRIMES 1:07 P.M.
It will work out. We'll just have to buy them from someone else online. They'll be twice as expensive, though.

MARY SCHMIDT 1:13 P.M.
Not necessarily. A friend of mine works at the event, and he might be able to get me tickets.

MARSHALL GRIMES 1:15 P.M.
Okay. I'll keep my hopes up.

156. What type of event do the writers plan to attend?

(A) A sports competition
(B) A book convention
(C) A street parade
(D) A fashion show

157. At 1:07 P.M., what does Mr. Grimes mean when he writes, "It will work out"?

(A) He is confident that plans will not change.
(B) He does not believe what Ms. Schmidt told him.
(C) He is happy that many people will be at the event.
(D) He is not willing to change his schedule.

GO ON TO THE NEXT PAGE

Regional News
By Andrea Vaughn

August 19—Local businesses are winding down from their busy season as summer visitors head back to their homes, reports Chad Nelson, CEO of Stats Watch, a company that monitors consumer behavior. — [1] —. While most hotels and airlines serving the region experienced similar figures to last year, there has been a rise in revenues for businesses offering nature-related adventures. Companies such as Cliff Inc. and Campex guide visitors through national parks on overnight excursions that are bringing in top dollar. — [2] —. Campex opened with just five guides, but has plans to hire two more next month to keep up with demand, which is expected to hold steady until the late fall, when the weather starts to get colder. — [3] —.

"The draw of these types of businesses is that they promise a unique experience for participants. — [4] —. It's no wonder people are lining up to take in the area's nature at its best," said Nelson.

Area officials suspect the trend will continue next year and beyond. Matters of increased regulation to ensure visitor safety will be discussed over the coming months.

158. Why was the article written?

(A) To announce plans for a business merger
(B) To give an update on the tourism sector
(C) To introduce a new corporate CEO
(D) To explain a proposal to support businesses

159. What will Campex do in September?

(A) Expand its workforce
(B) Form a partnership with Cliff Inc.
(C) Donate to a national park
(D) Begin offering indoor services

160. In which of the positions marked [1], [2], [3], and [4] does the following sentence best belong?

"A walk to beautiful Winona Falls is just one example of the trips being offered."

(A) [1]
(B) [2]
(C) [3]
(D) [4]

Sunshine Home and Garden Customer
1149 Lindale Avenue
Berkeley, CA 94707
May 15

Dear Customer,

At Sunshine Home and Garden, we've been working hard to implement changes to improve our store and shopping options. We hope you will come check out the improvements next month. — [1] —.

If you've visited Sunshine Home and Garden recently, you've probably noticed construction on the north end of the building. — [2] —. From June 1, our gardening tools section will be double the size of the original. The added space also makes it possible for us to add outdoor chairs and tables to our inventory for the first time ever.

We plan to celebrate these exciting improvements on Sunday, June 7. — [3] —. Throughout the day, we will be offering free gardening demonstrations as well as complimentary refreshments. Also, our store will stay open until 9 P.M. every day instead of 8 P.M. — [4] —. To show our appreciation for your loyalty, please find enclosed several store coupons, which are valid until June 30. You will also find a sample pack of Venetar brand flower seeds.

Warmest regards,

Jessica Cerrone
Store Manager, Sunshine Home and Garden

161. What is the purpose of the letter?

(A) To invite the reader to a store relocation party
(B) To promote a brand of power tools
(C) To announce the expansion of a store
(D) To clarify the terms of a seasonal sale

162. When will a special event be held at Sunshine Home and Garden?

(A) May 15
(B) June 1
(C) June 7
(D) June 30

163. What is NOT indicated in the letter?

(A) The store's business hours will be extended.
(B) The gardening tools area will be larger.
(C) A customer loyalty card will be introduced.
(D) Outdoor furniture will be for sale.

164. In which of the positions marked [1], [2], [3], and [4] does the following sentence best belong?

"This was part of a project to increase the store's display area by 7,500 square feet."

(A) [1]
(B) [2]
(C) [3]
(D) [4]

GO ON TO THE NEXT PAGE

Questions 165-167 refer to the following Web site.

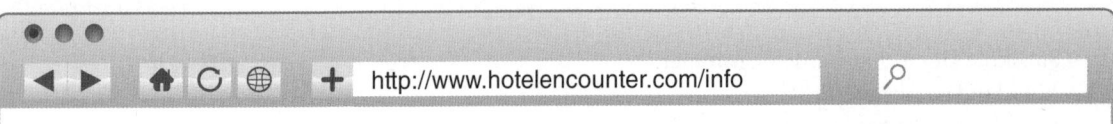

Get the best deals on hotels with the Hotel Encounter smartphone app!

Hotel Encounter helps you to find the best prices on hotels at the touch of a button. Whether you're making a last-minute booking or planning ahead, you're sure to find a hotel that suits your needs. You can search by location, price, or rating. Premium members can also get special offers on airport transportation, fine dining, travel insurance, and more.

Once you've made your selection, you will be taken to the hotel's Web site to finalize the booking. We can provide information about the hotel, but please note that refunds and cancellations must be processed through the hotel itself. However, if you discover that our listed prices do not match those of the hotel, you may call us at 1-800-555-6879 to tell us about the problem. We will correct the error online and ensure that you get the advertised price.

165. What is suggested about Hotel Encounter?

(A) Its customers can rate their hotel experiences.
(B) It matches the prices of its competitors.
(C) Its results can be based on different criteria.
(D) Its last-minute bookings are the cheapest.

166. What will be provided to premium members?

(A) Discounts on related services
(B) Free travel insurance
(C) Advance notice of sales
(D) Express airport check-in

167. According to the Web site, why should customers contact Hotel Encounter?

(A) To make a complaint about a hotel
(B) To request a refund for a cancellation
(C) To provide payment details
(D) To report price inconsistencies

Questions 168-171 refer to the following online chat discussion.

Fang Qin [4:20 P.M.]	Thanks for attending today's meeting, everyone. I know we have a lot of work ahead of us trying to make up for the loss of Sharber Enterprises.
Raktim Maraj [4:21 P.M.]	It was such a disappointment that they decided to move to our competitor.
Ashley Cohen [4:22 P.M.]	Yeah, it's going to take a handful of new companies just to compensate for the loss.
Fang Qin [4:24 P.M.]	That's why I've made a plan to restructure the sales territory so our team is more efficient. I'm sorry the handout with the map wasn't ready at the time of the meeting. There was a problem with the printer.
Victor Rocha [4:25 P.M.]	Can you send it by e-mail?
Fang Qin [4:29 P.M.]	I just did. Take a look to see how I have things divided.
Ashley Cohen [4:32 P.M.]	It looks like senior and junior salespeople have their own areas rather than working together. But pitching an idea to a new client is difficult without a lot of practice first.
Victor Rocha [4:33 P.M.]	Right. Ms. Waleck started here in March.
Fang Qin [4:34 P.M.]	I want to stick with the original plan, but maybe a workshop with some role-playing activities would be useful for the newer employees. Does anyone have time to be in charge of that?
Raktim Maraj [4:35 P.M.]	I could put something together.

168. What is implied about Sharber Enterprises?

(A) Its representatives recently met with Ms. Qin.
(B) It plans to move its business overseas.
(C) It was a major client of the writers' company.
(D) Its contract was lost during a relocation.

169. Why does Ms. Qin apologize?

(A) She made a client upset.
(B) She forgot to order a new printer.
(C) She used an incorrect e-mail address.
(D) She did not have a document prepared.

170. At 4:33 P.M., what does Mr. Rocha mean when he writes, "Ms. Waleck started here in March"?

(A) He thinks a coworker cannot handle a task.
(B) He has identified the reason for a change.
(C) He wants to clarify a colleague's error.
(D) He requests some help from a team member.

171. What does Mr. Maraj volunteer to do?

(A) Lead a training session
(B) Recruit new staff members
(C) Assemble some furniture
(D) Proofread some reports

GO ON TO THE NEXT PAGE

Peter Tulip Appointed Nutriglow Director

Finance Monthly

Los Angeles (July 6)—Nutritional supplement manufacturer Nutriglow announced this week that it will bolster its roster of industry experts in its boardroom with the addition of Peter Tulip. Mr. Tulip is widely regarded within his field as being one of the leading authorities on marketing, overseeing the successful development of rival company WellEat, Inc. Nutriglow hopes that his presence in the boardroom will see a similar increase in profits. The company has been struggling since January of this year, with reduced income thought to be related to a change in pricing strategy made at that time.

The choice to hire Mr. Tulip was made following a conference in May, in which senior directors expressed their concern over the direction in which the company was heading. According to chairman Sean Masters, Mr. Tulip was one of the few people qualified for the role. "We are under no illusions over the size of the job at hand to turn Nutriglow around", Mr. Masters told a press conference. "We're confident that Mr. Tulip will bring a fresh perspective that we've been sorely lacking in recent months." Mr. Tulip, also present at the press conference, added that he was delighted with his new role. "There's no doubting the potential of Nutriglow", he told gathered reporters. "It's my job to make sure I nurture the potential of everybody here."

Peter Tulip went on to tell journalists covering the story that his first move will be to relaunch the popular supplement Strawberry Supreme, the price of which is presently undetermined. This was a popular flavor amongst young customers, but was previously discontinued to allow for the development of new flavors.

To close the press conference, Tulip also took the time to thank his old employers, and expressed his satisfaction of the job achieved under his stewardship. "During my time, I saw WellEat, Inc. develop from a small, family business into the number one nutrition company in the country," he said. "I leave with nothing but fond memories."

172. What is the article about?

    (A) The merging of two companies
    (B) The recruiting of a specialist
    (C) The opening of a new factory
    (D) The closing of a business

173. According to the article, what took place in May?

    (A) An executive meeting was held.
    (B) A new manager was hired.
    (C) A change in pricing strategy was made.
    (D) A promotional offer began.

174. What is still to be determined regarding the relaunched supplement?

    (A) The packaging color
    (B) The list of ingredients
    (C) How much it will cost
    (D) Where it will be sold

175. What is mentioned about WellEat, Inc.?

    (A) Its products are available for purchase by mail order.
    (B) It offers over one hundred products.
    (C) It was founded in Los Angeles.
    (D) It is a market leader.

GO ON TO THE NEXT PAGE

Questions 176-180 refer to the following notice and calendar.

Bloomfield Community Center Notice

Thanks to a generous donation from one of our community members, the Bloomfield Community Center is able to expand its programs. The first activity that will be added to our schedule is Tai Chi. The class will be taught by martial arts expert Sheng Hou two mornings a week. It is recommended that participants wear loose-fitting clothing and sturdy athletic shoes. The first class will begin as soon as fifteen people have signed up. However, after the class starts running regularly, signing up in advance will not be necessary. If you would like to suggest new activities for the Bloomfield Community Center, please fill out a comment card at the Information Desk. The aim of our facility is to provide a wide variety of healthful activities for the community, so your opinions matter to us.

Bloomfield Community Center Activities Schedule: February
Main Court Activities

Sundays
   12:30 P.M. Family Aerobics, Heart-healthy exercises for all ages
   3:00 P.M. Ballet for Beginners (1st and 2nd week only), Shoes available for rent

Mondays (Closed)

Tuesdays
   11:00 A.M. Indoor Tennis, Singles or Doubles
   2:00 P.M. Tai Chi, All levels welcome

Wednesdays
   10:00 A.M. Beginner Yoga (1st, 2nd, and 4th week)
   3:00 P.M. Indoor Tennis, Singles or Doubles

Thursdays
   10:00 A.M. Indoor Tennis, Singles or Doubles
   5:00 P.M. Young Adult Basketball

Fridays
   2:00 P.M. Tai Chi, All levels welcome
   6:00 P.M. Kickboxing, Pre-registration requires

Saturdays
   1:00 P.M. Young Adult Basketball (canceled last Saturday of the month so the court can be used for the regional tournament)

A printed schedule of activities is available from the front desk, or you may download it from www.bloomfieldcc.org.

176. Why was the notice written?

(A) To request donations for a community center
(B) To introduce a fitness instructor
(C) To recruit members for the park staff
(D) To invite participants to a new activity

177. In the notice, the word "aim" in paragraph 1, line 8, is closest in meaning to

(A) direction
(B) intention
(C) perception
(D) indication

178. What is most likely true about the Tai Chi class?

(A) It requires a special uniform.
(B) It is one of the most popular activities.
(C) It meets at a later time than originally planned.
(D) Its instructor was changed for February.

179. Which activity is scheduled to happen exactly three times in February?

(A) Family Aerobics
(B) Indoor Tennis
(C) Young Adult Basketball
(D) Beginner Yoga

180. What is suggested about the Bloomfield Community Center?

(A) It will host a competition in February.
(B) Its tournament schedule is subject to change.
(C) It was founded by Sheng Hou.
(D) It has more than one basketball court.

GO ON TO THE NEXT PAGE

E-mail

To:	Elaine Andell <andell.e@ibsconsulting.net>
From:	Chen Li <li.chen@ibsconsulting.net>
Date:	March 28
Subject:	Inquiry

Dear Ms. Andell,

I'm wondering if you are able to help me with something. The company sent me abroad, along with a few of my team members, to the International Leadership Conference in Taipei last month. We learned a great deal of information there, and I was particularly impressed with a talk by Dr. Arnav Gera of Chennai University, who led a session on group dynamics. I wanted to read the research paper that he wrote on this topic so that I could use that data in my upcoming talk at the orientation session.

Unfortunately, when I searched our electronic reference library, I discovered that we do not have a subscription to the journal in which the paper appeared, *The Journal of Strategic Management*. I was wondering if it would be possible for IBS Consulting to purchase a subscription to this journal. If we go with this option, we'll have access to not only Dr. Gera's work but also other articles that I think would be valuable resources for our company.

Please let me know whether or not you'll be able to get this subscription before April 8, as that is the orientation day.

Thank you,

Chen Li

To: Chen Li <li.chen@ibsconsulting.net>
From: Elaine Andell <andell.e@ibsconsulting.net>
Date: March 29
Subject: RE: Inquiry

Dear Mr. Li,

I'm sorry to inform you that the company's budget for this year has already been set, and items cannot be added to it. Therefore, I won't be able to purchase the subscription you requested at this time. However, there might be another way. I browsed Chennai University's Web site to try to get the e-mail address of Dr. Gera. He was not listed, as it appears he recently left the university, but there were details for Professor Leya Sahota, who was Dr. Gera's co-author. I've attached a copy of the directory so that you may reach out to her directly. She may be able to supply you with what you need. Please feel free to e-mail me inquiries or talk to me at the weekly staff meeting tomorrow.

Sincerely,

Elaine Andell

181. What did Mr. Li have trouble doing?

(A) Logging into a reference library
(B) Scheduling an orientation session
(C) Finding information about a study
(D) Hiring speakers for a conference

182. In the first e-mail, the phrase "go with" in paragraph 2, line 4, is closest in meaning to

(A) select
(B) discuss
(C) accompany
(D) count

183. What did Ms. Andell do to provide assistance?

(A) Sent some contact information
(B) Recommended a different speaker
(C) Checked a report for errors
(D) Changed the date of an event

184. What is suggested about Ms. Sahota?

(A) She plans to get in touch with Mr. Li directly.
(B) She recently left Chennai University.
(C) She had her work printed in a journal.
(D) She has agreed to participate in Mr. Li's event.

185. What is NOT indicated about IBS Consulting?

(A) It does not permit budget changes.
(B) It sends employees to events overseas.
(C) It is seeking a partnership with a university.
(D) It holds a staff meeting once a week.

GO ON TO THE NEXT PAGE

Questions 186-190 refer to the following Web pages.

---

http://roxburyinstitute.com/classes

| HOME | **CLASSES** | REGISTER | REVIEWS | CONTACT US |

Art Classes at the Roxbury Institute: June

The Roxbury Institute is the new addition to Maryville's art community and has already gained popularity in just a few weeks. Our instructors teach just one class per week. We offer different classes every month so participants can learn a variety of skills.

Watercolor Landscapes: Mondays 7:00–9:00 P.M. / Instructor: Donald Bernier
Students will recreate landscape scenes using photographs as a guide. Donald Bernier will walk you through practical techniques that can be applied no matter what your level is.

Oil Portraits: Tuesdays 6:30–8:30 P.M. / Instructor: Geneva Winters
Capturing an individual's personality in a portrait is a fun challenge, and Geneva Winters will use her expertise to help you get there. Please note that you must have taken Oil Basics or an equivalent class in order to enroll.

Shading and Color Mixing: Wednesdays 6:30–8:30 P.M. / Instructor: Chantel Hernandez
This class is especially helpful for beginners, but artists of all levels can improve their results by practicing these essential techniques.

Nature Painting: Thursdays 7:00–9:00 P.M. / Instructor: James Roble
From animals and flowers to mountains and streams, nature has endless possibilities to inspire participants. Final projects will be included in a community exhibition at the Hadley Gallery.

Members of the National Arts Association will receive a 25% discount.

Click here to enroll!

---

http://roxburyinstitute.com/register

| HOME | CLASSES | **REGISTER** | REVIEWS | CONTACT US |

Enrollment Date: May 19
Student: Cynthia Morton
Are you a National Arts Association Member? No

Session: June
E-mail: c.morton@crmpost.net

Class Description	Class Dates	Enrollment Fee
Watercolor Landscapes	June 5, 12, 19, 26	$89
Nature Painting	June 8, 15, 22, 29	$112

Upon receipt of payment, you will be e-mailed a confirmation code. Please present this code to the instructor on the first day of class.

| HOME | CLASSES | REGISTER | **REVIEWS** | CONTACT US |

Review by Cynthia Morton / Posted, July 5

I was extremely satisfied with the painting classes I received from Roxbury Institute. I am somewhat new to this hobby, and I found both of my instructors to be knowledgeable and patient. Donald Bernier was especially enthusiastic about the class. He clearly has a deep love of art, as well as a talent for sharing it with others.

When I found out that there would be around fifty people in Mr. Roble's class, I thought that I wouldn't get much individual attention. However, to me, the balance between working independently and getting feedback from the instructor was perfect. Next month, I plan to sign up for another class and even try to recruit my friends to come along.

186. What is NOT indicated about the Roxbury Institute?

(A) It changes classes monthly.
(B) It has opened recently.
(C) It offers bulk discounts.
(D) Its instructors work part-time.

187. Which class requires previous experience?

(A) Watercolor Landscapes
(B) Oil Portraits
(C) Shading and Color Mixing
(D) Nature Painting

188. What is probably true about Ms. Morton?

(A) She is interested in learning more about portraits.
(B) She had an opportunity to display her work publicly.
(C) She was eligible for a twenty-five percent discount.
(D) She signed up for a class taught by Ms. Hernandez.

189. What did Ms. Morton suggest in her review?

(A) Watercolor Landscapes was too crowded.
(B) Nature Painting was more difficult than expected.
(C) Watercolor Landscapes had a passionate instructor.
(D) Nature Painting was taught by an expert.

190. What does Ms. Morton say she will do in August?

(A) Work with the same instructors again
(B) Encourage friends to take a class
(C) Sign up for two painting classes
(D) Post another review about the institute

GO ON TO THE NEXT PAGE

Questions 191-195 refer to the following e-mails and attachment.

To: Jia Bansal, Timothy Reeves, Genji Taihei

From: Lara Strehlow

Date: November 4

Subject: Banquet

Attachment: venue_details.dox

Hello Everyone,

It was great to make progress on the anniversary party plans for our company during our meeting at the Spirit Café on November 2. I'm looking forward to the event because we'll be able to meet some of the authors whose novels our company has launched. I'm glad we decided not to use a party planning service, since we can make the arrangements ourselves at a fraction of the cost. As promised, I have spoken to several venue owners throughout the city and have summarized the top options in the attached document. Please look it over so we can decide which one would be best for our purposes. Since all of us are busy these days, we won't meet in person again until November 19. However, in the meantime, we can share our ideas by e-mail.

Cheers,

Lara Strehlow, Doyle Incorporated

Hatton Hall / A modern building near the airport, Hatton Hall has plenty of free underground parking for guests. The main hall has recently been equipped with a state-of-the-art sound system, and it has received top ratings for its service. Main hall rental fee: $1,950

The Lexington / The Lexington has fantastic views of the city center from its rooftop terrace, which is available for rent. It is a very short drive from the airport. Portable heaters can be set up outside if the weather is cold. Rooftop terrace rental fee: $1,600

Morgan Plaza / Morgan Plaza has spacious rooms for overnight guests and is just a few minutes away from the airport. The Grand Hall features beautiful woodwork as well as a large stage, which can be decorated for free by the venue. Grant Hall rental fee: $1,800

Wakefield Center / Located downtown, Wakefield Center offers a complimentary shuttle service to and from the Riley Street Mall. It has rooms for overnight guests upstairs and offers discounted rates for guests attending on-site events. Main ballroom rental fee: $1,750

To: Jia Bansal, Timothy Reeves, Lara Strehlow
From: Genji Taihei
Date: November 5
Subject: RE: Banquet

Dear fellow committee members,

Sorry I couldn't be at the recent Spirit Café meeting. I planned to be there, but I was in San Francisco discussing contracts with a very promising client, and my flight home was delayed by a few hours. Thanks, Lara, for putting together this helpful list. I've finally had some time to review it. I'm not sure what the rest of you are thinking regarding the venue, but to me, I think we'd better choose a place near the airport. A lot of our attendees will be flying in from out of town, and they won't want to travel far after they arrive. In addition, the majority of them will need to stay overnight, so it would be best to have a venue that also offers guest accommodations. I'd love to hear your thoughts.

Thank you all for sending me the pricing estimates for your various categories (venue, food, and decorations). Also, Timothy, I still need the phone number of the graphic designer you recommended to do the invitations. I'd like to have a sample done by the November 19 meeting.

Thanks!

Genji

191. Where does Ms. Strehlow most likely work?

(A) At a financial institution
(B) At a publishing company
(C) At a coffee shop
(D) At a party planning service

192. What is mentioned as an amenity offered by one of the venues?

(A) A built-in seating area
(B) An on-site dining facility
(C) A modern security system
(D) A free transportation service

193. What did Mr. Taihei do on November 2?

(A) Appointed a committee
(B) Returned from a trip
(C) Toured a venue
(D) Misplaced some contracts

194. Which site would Mr. Taihei most likely select?

(A) Hatton Hall
(B) The Lexington
(C) Morgan Plaza
(D) Wakefield Center

195. What is suggested about Mr. Reeves?

(A) He will be absent from the next meeting.
(B) He sent Mr. Taihei some figures.
(C) He works as a graphic designer.
(D) He visited some venues with Ms. Strehlow.

GO ON TO THE NEXT PAGE

Cerda National Park: Cross-Country Skiing Trails

Arrowhead Trail / Difficulty: Beginner / Length: 9.3 miles
A flat terrain makes this trail excellent for beginners. The trail takes you through beautiful forest scenery as well as past Fort Robinson, a former military outpost.

Prairie Trail / Difficulty: Intermediate / Length: 18.1 miles
This trail includes some steep inclines, but the view of White Lake from the trail is well worth the effort.

Bell Valley Trail / Difficulty: Intermediate / Length: 15.8 miles
Thanks to its proximity to active wildlife areas, this has become our most popular trail. A picnic shelter is located on the east side of the trail, and visitors are reminded to take all trash with them.

Harmony Trail / Difficulty: Advanced / Length: 19.4 miles
This trail requires advanced pole use and turning skill, so it is only recommended for experienced skiers. If trouble arises, a ranger station is located along the trail at Mile 7.

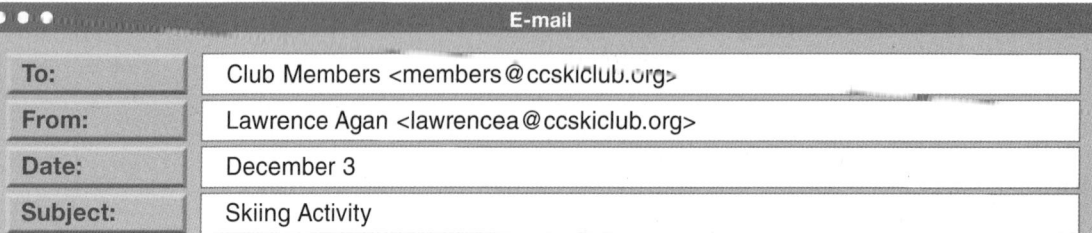

E-mail	
To:	Club Members <members@ccskiclub.org>
From:	Lawrence Agan <lawrencea@ccskiclub.org>
Date:	December 3
Subject:	Skiing Activity

Dear Cross-Country Ski Club Members,

We have selected Cerda National Park as the site for our next skiing activity, which will take place on Saturday, December 8. Many of you commented that last month's trail was too easy, so this time, we will take an intermediate level trail. There are two available at Cerda National Park, and we can decide on the activity day which one is better for us. We will meet at 9 A.M. at the Visitor Center. Be sure to bring your own packed lunch and snacks, as we expect to stay at the park until about 3 or 4 P.M.

I'm looking forward to seeing you all!

Lawrence

NOTICE

Due to safety hazards caused by falling rocks, Prairie Trail is closed for the remainder of the winter season. It will reopen again in the spring after the rocks have been cleared and the area is considered safe, after which time it is expected to remain open for the rest of the year. A red sign marks the head of the trail. No access is allowed beyond that point. For more information, stop by the Visitor Center, located near the western entrance of the park.

Effective from December 6

196. What can skiers visit along the longest trail?

(A) A ranger station
(B) A lake
(C) A picnic shelter
(D) A military site

197. Which trail will the group most likely take?

(A) Arrowhead Trail
(B) Prairie Trail
(C) Bell Valley Trail
(D) Harmony Trail

198. What is suggested about Cerda National Park?

(A) It is open year-round.
(B) It will construct a new trail.
(C) It provides skiing lessons.
(D) It charges an entrance fee.

199. In the notice, the word "point" in paragraph 1, line 5, is closest in meaning to

(A) feature
(B) purpose
(C) location
(D) idea

200. Where will the group meet on December 8?

(A) Near the trail head
(B) At the main gate
(C) Near the western entrance
(D) In a parking lot

This is the end of the test. You may review PART 5, 6, and 7 if you finish the test early.

정답 p. 319 / 점수 환산표 p. 321 / 해석 p. 358

TEST

PART 5
PART 6
PART 7

토익 Reading Comprehension은 75분 동안 진행됩니다.
현재 시각과 지금부터 75분 후인 테스트 종료 시각을 기록해 두고,
반드시 종료 시각 전에 문제 풀이와 답안지 마킹을 완료하세요.

 현재 시각 시분
테스트 종료 시각 　시　분

READING TEST

In the Reading test, you will read a variety of texts and answer several different types of reading comprehension questions. The entire Reading test will last 75 minutes. There are three parts, and directions are given for each part. You are encouraged to answer as many questions as possible within the time allowed.

You must mark your answers on the separate answer sheet. Do not write your answers in your test book.

PART 5

Directions: A word or phrase is missing in each of the sentences below. Four answer choices are given below each sentence. Select the best answer to complete the sentence. Then mark the letter (A), (B), (C), or (D) on your answer sheet.

101. Mr. Yang developed a Web site to rate local business establishments since consumers like ------- were being treated unfairly at some places.

(A) himself
(B) someone
(C) they
(D) any

102. Professional basketball player Bryan Jones recently signed a contract agreeing to ------- Bevelia Athletic Shoes for five years.

(A) dispose
(B) endorse
(C) relate
(D) inquire

103. Due to careful planning, Hiltz-Steen Inc.'s finances surprisingly remained ------- throughout the significant economic downturn.

(A) authorized
(B) resigned
(C) mutual
(D) stable

104. Bain Capital has earned a good reputation by ------- addressing its customers' complaints.

(A) prompt
(B) prompts
(C) promptly
(D) prompting

105. The customer service desk ------- the front entrance handles all returns and exchanges.

(A) near
(B) between
(C) from
(D) next

106. ------- three months, Ralph Electronics Corporation requires each supervisor to conduct an employee performance evaluation and submit a report.

(A) During
(B) About
(C) All
(D) Every

107. Most consumers were surprised to hear that the prices for HG Electronics' new flat screen TVs are ------- low.

(A) gradually
(B) rapidly
(C) mainly
(D) relatively

108. As soon as the new proposal for the online marketing initiative receives -------, the supervisor will hire an outside design agency.

(A) approval
(B) approved
(C) approvingly
(D) approves

109. The decline in the number of staff members at HT Corporation was ------- the result of its failure to provide better benefits.

(A) large
(B) largely
(C) largest
(D) largeness

110. Merchandise with any minor product ------- should be offered at a reduced price and placed in the clearance section.

(A) defects
(B) launches
(C) quotas
(D) rebates

111. Once a store establishes a ------- inventory of items, it will be fairly easy to update it on a regular basis.

(A) completes
(B) completion
(C) complete
(D) completely

112. The team of consultants ultimately found the mistake after the ------- review of corporation accounting records.

(A) depleted
(B) exhaustive
(C) numerous
(D) reluctant

113. The owner of the recently opened Italian restaurant La Ciccia said that the second location will ------- be in operation in the Durham area, on the opposite side of the state.

(A) yet
(B) soon
(C) ever
(D) previously

114. The checklist that the team leader has sent can help the final ------- make sure all the details are included in the document.

(A) reviews
(B) reviewed
(C) reviewer
(D) to review

115. ------- located in the neighborhood of Sunset Beach, Heaven Resort is widely known as one of the best tour destinations.

(A) Convenient
(B) Convenience
(C) Conveniently
(D) Conveniences

116. Filomena Books is offering a 50% discount off prices listed ------- the pamphlet while items are in stock.

(A) over
(B) about
(C) in
(D) among

117. The marketing team attending the technology conference will prepare a(n) ------- presentation to promote the newest line of computer security software.

(A) industrious
(B) comprehensive
(C) conclusive
(D) presumable

118. After months of construction, the remodeling project is in the final ------- and set to be completed next week.

(A) degree
(B) basis
(C) phase
(D) impact

119. Payments submitted after 10 P.M. may not appear on billing statements ------- we open for business the following day.

(A) while
(B) on
(C) whether
(D) until

120. Last month, the local company Birdwell Inc. ------- for its exceptional contributions to the advancement of communication technology.

(A) was honored
(B) honors
(C) honored
(D) is honoring

GO ON TO THE NEXT PAGE

121. J&T Enterprises' goal for its yearly sales figures has ------- been exceeded due to its employees' commitment to service quality.

(A) early
(B) already
(C) soon
(D) yet

122. The employees from ACN Co. have found most of the activities and programs led by industry experts each day very -------.

(A) attractive
(B) attraction
(C) attracted
(D) attracts

123. For ------- reasons, Human Resources will not release any individual's personal information to a third party without a signed release form from the individual.

(A) secure
(B) secured
(C) security
(D) securely

124. Regular exercise is highly recommended, ------- for office workers who spend most of their time working at their desks.

(A) particular
(B) particulars
(C) particularity
(D) particularly

125. Franz Daily Deli will hire three additional waiters in order to ------- increased demand during the summer tourist season.

(A) accommodate
(B) succeed
(C) propose
(D) remain

126. ------- the Keller Institute received a large grant from the Jackson Foundation, it intends to hire more researchers within the next couple of months.

(A) Unless
(B) Since
(C) Even
(D) Therefore

127. Several attempts were made to convince local residents to agree to a tax increase, ------- of which met with any success.

(A) neither
(B) nothing
(C) none
(D) no

128. Froth Beverages Inc. is currently working with international market specialists to expand its ------- into parts of Asia and Europe.

(A) presence
(B) vicinity
(C) incentive
(D) estimate

129. Please inform Ms. Kennedy of any intentions to take time off this summer ------- work schedules can be amended accordingly.

(A) in spite of
(B) due to
(C) so that
(D) while

130. A series of new online games developed by Newmont Tech are ------- to a variety of age groups.

(A) market
(B) marketing
(C) being marketed
(D) to market

PART 6

Directions: Read the texts that follow. A word, phrase, or sentence is missing in parts of each text. Four answer choices for each question are given below the text. Select the best answer to complete the text. Then mark the letter (A), (B), (C), or (D) on your answer sheet.

Questions 131-134 refer to the following brochure.

Galington-Ling Partners is a world renowned name in the luxury housing market. Our professional

------- are experts at combining size and style into a single blueprint.
 131.

------- your needs are large or small, elaborate or simple, our specialists can ensure your
 132.
satisfaction. -------. A consultant ------- you with all of the necessary information and estimates and
          133.   **134.**
guide you through every step of the process.

131. (A) architects
  (B) constructors
  (C) decorators
  (D) realtors

132. (A) Either
  (B) Despite
  (C) As it were
  (D) Whether

133. (A) There are many reasons for changing the style of your home.
  (B) Garlington-Ling Partners is involved in a consulting business.
  (C) Schedule an appointment with us by calling 919-736-4291.
  (D) Please send us any feedback that you might have by e-mail.

134. (A) to provide
  (B) provided
  (C) will provide
  (D) would have provided

GO ON TO THE NEXT PAGE

Questions 135-138 refer to the following e-mail.

To: Cody Black, Plant Supervisor
From: Darrel Reagan, Safety and Repairs Department
Date: March 12
Subject: Re: Equipment inspection

Mr. Black,

Thank you for contacting the safety and repairs department with your concerns regarding the -------
                                                                                              135.
gauge in warehouse C2. -------.
                         136.

The gauge was registering notably warmer than the settings necessary for proper storage of fresh

produce. However, although there appeared to be a problem, the gauge proved to be -------. It is
                                                                                    137.
correctly detecting what may be a problem with the refrigeration system.

Despite this, our technicians are testing the cooling system to find out why it is not cooling properly.

In the meantime, please ------- all perishable items out of warehouse C2.
                         138.

Thank you for your cooperation.

Sincerely,
Darrel Reagan

---

135. (A) distance
(B) temperature
(C) sound
(D) pressure

136. (A) We will soon begin searching for the exact cause.
(B) Your feedback about our service is always appreciated.
(C) Our department is situated close to the warehouse.
(D) My team has been looking into the matter.

137. (A) dangerous
(B) concerning
(C) functional
(D) adaptable

138. (A) are transferring
(B) transfer
(C) to transfer
(D) transferred

June 3

Dear Mr. Peralta,

Thank you for your purchase on May 28. Steel and Stone Hardware values all of your questions

------- criticisms specific to your business with us.
139.

We always hold the client's perspective in the highest regard.

For this reason, we request that you complete a brief survey to express your opinion regarding our

products, services, pricing and various other ------- related to the quality of your experience with us.
140.

The survey has been designed to help us improve our strengths and discover our weaknesses.

Most importantly, your reply to the questionnaire ------- our customers to receive the quality they
141.

desire. -------.
142.

Sincerely,
Steel and Stone Hardware

139. (A) except for
(B) as well as
(C) far from
(D) despite the fact

140. (A) elements
(B) departments
(C) payments
(D) installments

141. (A) could have enabled
(B) will enable
(C) has been enabling
(D) is enabled

142. (A) We thank you in advance for your input.
(B) We are looking forward to being fully operational soon.
(C) Customers are welcome to organize a survey on their own.
(D) Please visit my office to receive our high-quality product samples.

Questions 143-146 refer to the following letter.

Internal Applicants

One benefit of working for a large company like St. Luke's National Real Estate is that after one

year, employees are ------- to request international transfers or company-wide promotions. -------.
                143.   **144.**
Internal applicants may not necessarily be chosen over external applicants. -------, if qualified for
                                                     145.

the position, internal applicants will always be given -------.
                                           146.

---

143. (A) exclusive
     (B) prompt
     (C) selective
     (D) eligible

144. (A) Those interested can find openings on the company's intranet site.
     (B) Employees are still required to report their duties to their managers.
     (C) For example, financial incentives will be given to all employees.
     (D) This change indicates the transfer of the business ownership.

145. (A) In addition
     (B) However
     (C) Consequently
     (D) Then

146. (A) prefer
     (B) preferred
     (C) preference
     (D) preferential

PART 7

Directions: In this part you will read a selection of texts, such as magazine and newspaper articles, e-mails, and instant messages. Each text or set of texts is followed by several questions. Select the best answer for each question and mark the letter (A), (B), (C), or (D) on your answer sheet.

Questions 147-148 refer to the following certificate.

This certificate confirms that Rachel Torsten was present at a series of workshops at the Stansfield Professional Institute entitled "Ethics in the Financial Sector: The Principles of Fair Practice in Trading" on April 26. She scored 86 points on the post-session exam, earning the classification of 'extremely competent' in accordance with the Institute's ranking system.

Daniel Payet

Daniel Payet, Workshop Leader
Stansfield Professional Institute

147. What did Ms. Torsten do on April 26?

(A) She conducted workshops.
(B) She attended some sessions.
(C) She applied for a teaching position.
(D) She checked out of a hotel.

148. Who most likely is Ms. Torsten?

(A) An athlete
(B) A computer professor
(C) A stockbroker
(D) A property developer

GO ON TO THE NEXT PAGE

Questions 149-150 refer to the following notice.

Once a month, *The Bartlett Journal* features the submissions of vintage photographs for its three-page "Bartlett Looks Back" column. This monthly feature celebrates moments in the city's history as documented by members of our community.

Photographs taken more than forty years ago of notable places and events in the city's history are of particular interest.

Photos can be submitted to Jennifer Cook via e-mail at jencook@bartlettjournal.com. Provide as much information about the photo as possible, including names of people, the location, and the approximate date. Submissions must be received no later than the second Friday of the month of publication. Note that all photos in our paper edition will be printed in black and white.

149. For whom is the notice intended?

(A) Magazine editors
(B) Historical writers
(C) Local celebrities
(D) Residents of Bartlett

150. When would *The Bartlett Journal* most likely refuse a submission?

(A) When the sender submits a color photograph
(B) When the submission is less than three pages
(C) When the submission deadline has passed
(D) When the sender shares private information

Tariq Jha   2:07 P.M.
Have you arrived at the airport yet? I know you left the office later than expected and had to take a cab.

Valarie Cortez   2:09 P.M.
I'd say I'm about ten minutes away, so I should easily catch my flight.

Tariq Jha   2:10 P.M.
I'm glad to hear that.

Valarie Cortez   2:11 P.M.
Has the courier delivered the contract from Parsons Co. yet?

Tariq Jha   2:13 P.M.
Yes, it just came in. I'm not sure what to do with it, though.

Valarie Cortez   2:15 P.M.
Please give it to Cynthia. She was handling it.

151. Where most likely is Ms. Cortez now?

(A) At the office
(B) In a taxi
(C) At the airport
(D) On a bus

152. At 2:15 P.M., what does Ms. Cortez most likely mean when she writes, "She was handling it"?

(A) Cynthia made the travel plans for Ms. Cortez.
(B) Cynthia might have made an error with the paperwork.
(C) Cynthia is familiar with the Parsons Co. arrangements.
(D) Cynthia will follow up with paying for a delivery.

GO ON TO THE NEXT PAGE

Questions 153-154 refer to the following e-mail.

To: b.cooper@bcauto.net

From: terrypritchard@quickmail.com

Date: October 2

Subject: Repair work

Dear Bradley,

We brought back one of our company cars from you last week and it has been working fine since then. However, when I tried to drive it to a workshop this afternoon, it wouldn't turn on and some error lights flashed on the dashboard. According to the manual, these indicate that the oil needs changing and that part of the engine requires replacement. I really need these issues resolved as quickly as possible, as we would incur substantial financial losses if one of our vehicles was off the road for a long time. Would you be able to carry out the repair work today? I would be willing to pay extra if you can guarantee a prompt service.

Sincerely,
Terry Pritchard

153. What is the purpose of the e-mail?

(A) To negotiate a car price
(B) To request a service
(C) To order a manual
(D) To schedule a workshop

154. What is suggested about Mr. Cooper?

(A) He was late for work.
(B) He supplies light fittings.
(C) He made a mistake on the last invoice.
(D) He is a mechanic.

Questions 155-157 refer to the following notice.

Attention Passengers

Thank you for purchasing a ticket with Atlantic Airlines. Before you check in, please take note of the following points.

- Passengers are permitted to check in one bag that weighs no more than 20 kilograms. Those checking in any extra bags or exceeding the weight allowance will be subject to a fee that will be determined at the time of check-in. — [1] —.

- Passengers may take one carry-on bag onto the flight. — [2] —. No flammable items or weapons are allowed in any carry-on bags. — [3] —. Carry-on bags will be checked by an Atlantic Airlines employee prior to boarding, and illegal or unpermitted items will be confiscated. — [4] —.

If you have any questions, please feel free to call 1-888-555-4094 to use our new automated system. Simply press 5 at the beep, and you will be connected.

Thank you for flying with Atlantic Airlines.

155. What is the purpose of the notice?

(A) To explain how to cancel a reservation
(B) To publicize some new weight restrictions
(C) To outline a company's policy
(D) To promote the airline's newest routes

156. Why might passengers have to pay more money?

(A) Because they failed to check in two hours before boarding
(B) Because they are carrying illegal items in their carry-ons
(C) Because they are checking in two items of luggage
(D) Because they have exceeded the weight limit for carry-ons

157. In which of the positions marked [1], [2], [3], and [4] does the following sentence best belong?

"This includes laptop bags and backpacks, but each passenger may also carry a purse or handbag."

(A) [1]
(B) [2]
(C) [3]
(D) [4]

Questions 158-161 refer to the following online chat discussion.

Renee Alocer 2:24 P.M.	Do any of you want coffee? Café Reno has two-for-one lattes. I'm going to place an order.
Fiona Brown 2:25 P.M.	Yes, please!
Kenneth Graham 2:26 P.M.	I'll take one.
Oliver Whitworth 2:26 P.M.	None for me, thanks.
Fiona Brown 2:28 P.M.	Kenneth, it's not a problem to bring drinks into the afternoon meeting, is it?
Kenneth Graham 2:31 P.M.	You'd better finish them beforehand. I'll be demonstrating the new security equipment, and we can't afford to have it spilled on.
Fiona Brown 2:32 P.M.	Okay. You'll all be there, right?
Renee Alocer 2:33 P.M.	Of course. We don't have a choice.
Oliver Whitworth 2:35 P.M.	Kenneth, you're presenting? I thought Larry was doing it.
Kenneth Graham 2:37 P.M.	I was asked to cover for him at the last minute since he can't make it.
Fiona Brown 2:38 P.M.	Oh, right. I heard he went home early yesterday because he was sick. Do you need help with anything?
Kenneth Graham 2:39 P.M.	Larry had already prepared a slideshow presentation. But I need to borrow someone's ID card to demonstrate the system because I can't use mine. It behaves differently since I'm on the security team.
Renee Alocer 2:41 P.M.	I don't mind if you use mine. Do you need it in advance?
Kenneth Graham 2:42 P.M.	No, just bring it to the meeting. Thanks!

158. At 2:25 P.M., what does Ms. Brown most likely mean when she writes, "Yes, please"?

(A) She will use a coupon.
(B) She would like a beverage.
(C) She will go with Ms. Alocer.
(D) She needs some office supplies.

159. What is implied about the afternoon meeting?

(A) It will introduce a new employee.
(B) It was scheduled at the last minute.
(C) It is mandatory for staff members.
(D) It will be led by Mr. Whitworth.

160. What is indicated about Larry?

(A) He is absent today.
(B) He is setting up a system.
(C) He arrived at the office early.
(D) He lost a presentation file.

161. Whose ID card will be used in the presentation?

(A) Ms. Alocer's
(B) Ms. Brown's
(C) Mr. Graham's
(D) Mr. Whitworth's

Connect Media: Your link to the world

Are you searching for experienced professionals to deliver a professional Web site for your business? Then why not hire the services of Connect Media, a design company that specializes in making quality Web sites for the food industry, including information such as your menus, ingredients, opening times and reservation details.

We at Connect Media have produced high-end interfaces for over 40 businesses in the local area, and have received many positive testimonials from our previous customers. Those who enlist our services before the end of the month or use our services for more than a year will receive a 20% discount.

Visit www.connectmedia.net to get started. Here, you can choose your color scheme, read the customer reviews, and pay your subscription costs.

Please note: You will need to provide us with the written content for the site. If you feel unwilling to produce this yourself, you can enlist the help of our in-house writer, contactable at 555-3920-4225, who charges a rate of $30 per hour.

162. Who is the advertisement most likely intended for?

(A) Professional writers
(B) Internet bloggers
(C) Financial advisors
(D) Restaurant managers

163. What is indicated about Connect Media?

(A) It is a renowned culinary school.
(B) It requires a 1-year commitment.
(C) It is running a promotion.
(D) It employs 40 staff members.

164. What is NOT mentioned as an action that may be performed on the Connect Media Web site?

(A) Making a reservation
(B) Reading customer testimonials
(C) Paying a fee
(D) Selecting preferred colors

GO ON TO THE NEXT PAGE

The management team request your presence at an event toasting

Mr. Dean Lewis

As we celebrate his record-breaking sales figures
As Director at Capital Automotive

Friday, 19 September
Pinetree Hotel Ballroom
Pine Valley
Massachusetts 84932

7 P.M. Banquet
8 P.M. Speeches and toasts
8:30 P.M. Disco by DJ Turquoise

Instead of gifts, Mr. Lewis has stated that contributions to the Bexley fund for deprived children would be well-received.

Please R.S.V.P as soon as possible to sales assistant Yvonne Setts at 555-3455- 2214 or ysetts@capital.com.

165. What is the purpose of the event?

(A) To discipline some staff members
(B) To celebrate the opening of a hotel
(C) To recognize an employee's achievement
(D) To toast a job promotion

166. What are guests being advised to do?

(A) Bring a present
(B) Donate to a charity
(C) Dress in smart clothing
(D) Pay a deposit

167. What is suggested about Ms. Setts?

(A) She is employed by Capital Automotive.
(B) She is a part-time DJ.
(C) She is Mr. Lewis' assistant.
(D) She has a new e-mail address.

Questions 168-171 refer to the following e-mail.

E-mail

To: John Heyward
From: Wilma Caraway
Re: Your Order
Date: March 27

Dear Mr. Heyward,

Thank you for the e-mail that you just sent us. We at Simpson's Sporting Goods are always pleased to hear from our customers and do our best to assist them in every way possible. — [1] —.

According to your e-mail, there was a problem with your most recent order. You wrote that you ordered item 495-RRE3 (right-handed baseball glove) and item 302-WAW2 (32-ounce baseball bat). However, instead of receiving a 32-ounce baseball bat, you received one that weighs 30 ounces. — [2] —. Unfortunately, while you were charged for both of the items ordered, you were additionally billed for a bat that you did not desire.

We sent you the bat you ordered early this morning by using a special courier service, so you will receive the item sometime this evening. — [3] —. You can return it to us at no cost to yourself, or you can purchase it at a discount of fifty percent. Please tell us which of these two options you like better. If you indicate your intention to return the bat, we will send you a postage-paid box in which you can mail it to us. — [4] —. If you prefer to keep the bat, we will make the necessary adjustments to your account.

We are terribly sorry about the inconvenience and hope that this unfortunate event does not discourage you from continuing to shop with Simpson's Sporting Goods.

Sincerely,

Wilma Caraway
Customer Service Representative

168. What is the purpose of the e-mail?

(A) To thank a customer for returning a product
(B) To explain why an item is no longer available
(C) To address a problem reported by Mr. Heyward
(D) To describe a special deal available to Mr. Heyward

169. What will Mr. Heyward receive upon request?

(A) A shipping box
(B) A baseball glove
(C) A company catalogue
(D) A new invoice

170. What is mentioned about item 302-WAW2?

(A) It will arrive on March 27.
(B) It is being offered at half the regular price.
(C) It was sent to Mr. Heyward together with item 495-RRE3.
(D) It is no longer sold by Simpson's Sporting Goods.

171. In which of the positions marked [1], [2], [3], and [4] does the following sentence best belong?

"Regarding the bat which you received, you have two choices."

(A) [1]
(B) [2]
(C) [3]
(D) [4]

GO ON TO THE NEXT PAGE

Come to Eccleston Theme Park

Eccleston, CA (June 9)—Are you searching for a fun day out for all your family during the summer holidays? Then why not visit Eccleston Theme Park? Although the park is open to visit all year round, next month is the best time to experience the live dolphin show, as the animals are generally happier in the warmer waters of summer. In addition to this, the brand new water ride 'The Drencher' will be unveiled soon.

As Eccleston is an eco-friendly park, it is only accessible by shuttle bus from the city center, with customers unable to arrive via private transportation. This is to minimize the effects of traffic and pollution on the local community. Spaces on a bus can be reserved in advance on the bus company's Web site. Discounted family rates are available for those travelling with children younger than 12.

Tickets to visit the park can be purchased either directly from the park itself, or from one of many independent retailers in the local area. It is advised that customers use only approved venders, as there have been reports of counterfeit tickets being sold by dishonest businessmen, which will not gain you access to the park. Tickets are currently being sold at a discounted rate by Adventurex, with customers qualifying for this promotion when purchasing any of its computers or TVs.

For more information on ticket prices, opening times and show scheduled, please visit www.ecclestonpark.net.

172. According to the article, which month is recommended for visiting Eccleston Theme Park?

(A) April
(B) May
(C) June
(D) July

173. What is implied about Eccleston Theme Park?

(A) It is closed in the wintertime.
(B) It was featured on a TV documentary.
(C) It has no car parking spaces.
(D) It is hiring new staff members.

174. What are visitors encouraged to do?

(A) Sign up to receive the company's newsletter
(B) Purchase tickets from verified businesses
(C) Wear special clothing when using water rides
(D) Reserve seats to view animal performances

175. What type of business most likely is Adventurex?

(A) A childcare facility
(B) An advertising agency
(C) An electronics retailer
(D) A regulatory body

GO ON TO THE NEXT PAGE

Latest Seminar Schedule
Provided by Pumisville College

We at Pumisville College have finalized our latest sequence of seminars for lawyers and associated professionals. The seminars will take place at the college's Darkford Road campus, and will be led by respected figures from the sector who are eager to pass on the knowledge gained through their years of experience. Each seminar costs $20 to attend. Participants are required to arrive ten minutes before scheduled start times.

Monday, 24 March, 8 P.M., Lecture Theater B
Speaker: Robin Terrance, Thompson Solicitors
Document preparation: Learn how to prepare your files in accordance with industry standards.

Wednesday, 26 March, 6 P.M., Lecture Theater A
Speaker: Brian Pinkman, retired judge
Courtroom delivery: Find out the most persuasive language to best represent your client.

Friday, 28 March, 4 P.M., Room 72
Speaker: Sue Perm, Acorn Advertising
Promoting your business: Learn techniques to attract new customers to your firm.

Sunday, 30 March, 12 P.M., Room 8c
Speaker: Freddie Campbell, partner at Campbell & Frazer Ltd
Climbing the ladder: Discover how to impress your boss and quickly rise through the ranks of your company to a more senior position.

All enquiries should be directed to Lucy Wilcox at l.wilcox@pumisville.net or 555-2929-5036.

To: Lucy Wilcox <l.wilcox@pumisville.net>
From: Joseph Whitel <josephwhitel@hmail.com>
Subject: Seminar Series
Date: 29 March

Dear Ms. Wilcox,

I attended the latest seminar series. I was quite excited to attend the session conducted by a retired judge, as I felt I could learn a lot from his experience. However, when I went to the room, I found that he was replaced at short notice by a different speaker. As such, I was no longer interested in attending and left immediately. I would be grateful if you would return the seminar fee that I paid in advance.

Sincerely,
Joseph Whitel

176. In the brochure, the word "figures" in paragraph 1, line 3, is closest in meaning to

(A) statistics
(B) diagrams
(C) textbooks
(D) people

177. What is mentioned about the seminars?

(A) They are free to attend.
(B) They may run ten minutes behind schedule.
(C) They are designed for workers in the legal sector.
(D) They all take place in the same room.

178. What is the main topic of the seminar on March 28?

(A) How to be persuasive in a courtroom setting
(B) How to attract prospective clients
(C) How to prepare documentation
(D) How to earn a job promotion

179. Whose seminar was Mr. Whitel interested in attending?

(A) Mr. Terrance's
(B) Mr. Pinkman's
(C) Ms. Perm's
(D) Mr. Campbell's

180. Why did Mr. Whitel write the e-mail?

(A) To apply for a teaching position
(B) To obtain a brochure
(C) To ask for directions
(D) To request a refund

GO ON TO THE NEXT PAGE

Questions 181-185 refer to following notice and form.

PACKAGE CHANGES

Dear customers,

As part of our effort to provide the best possible service for our customers, we at Teleview Cable have been renegotiating the terms of our partnership with Viewpoint Media, and are delighted to announce that all premium customers will receive access to 3 new movie channels from next month. To celebrate this deal, existing base-rate customers are now able to save $5 off their monthly bill when they upgrade to our premium service. Furthermore, customers will not be penalized with the $50 charge normally incurred for altering an existing contract with us. Customers must upgrade before the end of the month for these terms to apply.

Customers desiring to upgrade to the premium service should call our hotline on 555-923-5894. Customers are also able to do so online by visiting www.teleview.net/upgrade. In order to complete the upgrade procedure, you will need to give your account number and password. In addition, please ensure that you quote promotional code SWITCHME in order to receive the benefits mentioned above. Customers must be over 18 and be resident in the United States for this offer.

Teleview Cable Feedback Sheet

Customer Details
Name: Helen Webbings
Account Number: 939238
Date: August 18
E-mail address: hwebbings@quickmail.net
Details of Complaint: My subscription

I upgraded my cable package last week and the changes came into effect yesterday. I have been delighted with most of the service so far, and I was particularly excited about watching the three movie channels provided by Viewpoint Media. However, I tried to access these channels last night and was greeted with the error message 'Channels Unavailable'. I have read over your terms and conditions carefully, and it is clear that there has been a mistake, as these channels are a feature of the package that I have subscribed to. I would be grateful if this could be amended as soon as possible. This is not the standard of service that I expect from a well-known company such as yours.

181. What is the main purpose of the notice?

(A) To announce discontinued partnership with Viewpoint Media

(B) To alert customers that an upgrade is mandatory

(C) To inform customers of a change of company ownership

(D) To advertise the addition of some cable channels

182. What is indicated about the $50 charge?

(A) It will gather interest if not paid immediately.

(B) It will not be applied when existing customers upgrade.

(C) It is not applied to new customers.

(D) It will be donated to local charities.

183. What is NOT required to take advantage of the special offer?

(A) A password

(B) A discount code

(C) An Internet connection

(D) An account number

184. What is most likely true about Ms. Webbings?

(A) She has signed up for the premium package.

(B) She has applied for a job at Viewpoint Media.

(C) She needs to pay $5 for the new service.

(D) She requested more than 3 channels.

185. What does Ms. Webbings expect Teleview Cable to do?

(A) Remove her from a mailing list

(B) Send her a remote control

(C) Issue her a new password

(D) Correct a service error

GO ON TO THE NEXT PAGE

Community Beat
Vol. 438, April 28

The 5th Annual Summer Music Festival is scheduled to be held once again at Redding Park from July 6 to 8. The festival features a wide variety of musicians over the three-day span, and this year the program will include Annie Jarvis, the Gray Foxes, and the Dallas Quartet. In addition to the musical performances, local businesses can rent outdoor booths to sell their goods. The booths do not have to be music-related. Figures from past events suggest that food, clothing, and craft booths had the most success.

Registration has already begun for the booth rental, and slots are starting to fill up, especially those near the main stage and the baseball fields. Interested businesses are encouraged to secure a booth as soon as possible so as to avoid disappointment. To do so, visit www.mysummerfest.com and follow the instructions on the Retail page. All booths are the same size and are offered for a fee of $350 for all three days. Please note that business owners who participated in last year's event will be given 15% off the fee if they sign up again this year.

More information about the musical acts for the festival will be uploaded as they are confirmed. Questions can be directed to the event coordinator, Melody Adkinson, at m.adkinson@mysummerfest.com.

● ● ●

To: Melody Adkinson <m.adkinson@mysummerfest.com>
From: Raymond Colby <raymondcolby@colbyprints.com>
Date: June 2
Subject: Summer Music Festival

Dear Ms. Adkinson,

I am interested in renting a booth at the 5th Annual Summer Music Festival at Redding Park. One of my friends, Sabrina Ta, said she had great success with her booth there last year. She is renting one again this year, and she highly recommended that I do the same. I tried signing up on the Web site, but the system wouldn't process my request for some reason. Therefore, I hope I can reserve a booth by e-mail instead.

I looked at the map of available booths on the Web site. I'd like to be located in the west section of the park. I prefer to be as close to the main entrance as possible, but most importantly, please assign me a booth that is not right next to one selling clothing, since I run a T-shirt business. Please e-mail me back at your earliest convenience.

Thank you,

Raymond Colby
Owner, Colby Prints

| Parking Lot | Main Entrance | (Available) W1 | Jill's Dresses W2 | Games Plus W3 | Wonder Crafts W4 | (Available) W5 |
| | | (Available) W6 | Ace Florists W7 | Candy Creations W8 | Scoops Ice Cream W9 | (Available) W10 |

186. Why was the article written?

(A) To assess a community organization
(B) To recruit musicians to perform
(C) To attract businesses to a festival
(D) To announce a park renovation project

187. What is indicated about Redding Park?

(A) It is near a body of water.
(B) It has on-site sports facilities.
(C) It has more than one parking lot.
(D) It is located in the city center.

188. In the article, the word "follow" in paragraph 2, line 4, is closest in meaning to

(A) pursue
(B) monitor
(C) grasp
(D) obey

189. What is suggested about Ms. Ta?

(A) Her goods are similar to Mr. Colby's.
(B) She is eligible for a discount.
(C) She will have a booth in the west section.
(D) She will rent two booths this year.

190. Which space would be most suitable for Mr. Colby?

(A) W1
(B) W5
(C) W6
(D) W10

GO ON TO THE NEXT PAGE

Questions 191-195 refer to the following notice and e-mails.

Upcoming Exhibit at the Seattle Science Museum:
Robot Revolution: July 10 – August 1

"Robot Revolution" is a hands-on exhibit that highlights the latest in the field of artificial intelligence. Created by Todd Vega, the exhibit features one-of-a-kind robots that respond to human commands and actions. From using verbal skills to performing physical tasks, the robots "learn" by interacting with humans. Because the robots will show more and more skills as the exhibition progresses, we strongly recommend visiting the exhibit at least twice.

In addition to working with the interactive robots, visitors can read about the history of robotics and discover the future possibilities of this field. With the perfect combination of facts and fun, "Robot Revolution" will delight children and adults alike.

To learn more about this field, don't miss the academic lectures presented by Todd Vega at Hillside Hall (July 12) and Bartlett Hotel (July 20). You can also read more about his work in *Robo-World*, which was co-written by Jacqueline Stanfill.

Tickets for the exhibit are $18 each and can be purchased on site. The Seattle Science Museum is open Tuesday through Sunday from 9 A.M. to 8 P.M.

To: Todd Vega <t.vega@lexingtonmail.com>
From: Georgina Mizrahi <mizrahi_g@techtracking.com>
Date: July 21
Subject: Interview Proposal

Dear Mr. Vega,

After seeing your amazing exhibit at the Seattle Science Museum, I signed up for one of your lectures. I attended the one held yesterday, and I was intrigued by your ideas. I run a technology blog called Tech Tracking, and I think my readers would enjoy reading about your knowledge of robots and artificial intelligence. This would also be excellent exposure for your research, as the blog gets over 200,000 unique visitors per month, and it has received a Web Excellence Award from the Doyle Center.

I am currently living in Seattle. We could conduct the interview by phone, or I would be happy to visit your office in Los Angeles anytime between August 1 and 4, as I'll be there for the Hendrix Innovation Expo. Thank you for your consideration. I look forward to hearing from you.

Sincerely,
Georgina Mizrahi
www.techtracking.com

To:	Georgina Mizrahi <mizrahi_g@techtracking.com>
From:	Todd Vega <t.vega@lexingtonmail.com>
Date:	July 22
Subject:	RE: Interview Proposal

Dear Ms. Mizrahi,

Thank you for the interview invitation. I think it would be best to meet in person at my office. That way, you could take some photos of some of our models and prototypes. Please call my assistant, Jamie Lucas, at 555-5934 to set up a time that doesn't interfere with your expo activities. I'll also have my writing partner join us as well, as I'm sure she'll have some unique insights to share.

Warmest regards,

Todd Vega

191. Why are people encouraged to visit the museum more than once?

(A) Visitors can get a discount on tickets.
(B) Different experts will give lectures.
(C) The exhibit will change over time.
(D) It will be the museum's last exhibit.

192. What is stated about the exhibit?

(A) It will run for one month.
(B) It admits children at no cost.
(C) It is closed all weekend.
(D) It is aimed at visitors of all ages.

193. Where did Ms. Mizrahi attend a lecture?

(A) Hillside Hall
(B) Bartlett Hotel
(C) Seattle Science Museum
(D) Doyle Center

194. What is most likely true about Mr. Vega?

(A) He wants to meet in Los Angeles.
(B) He will add more lectures to his tour.
(C) He has been nominated for an award.
(D) He will send a prototype to Ms. Mizrahi.

195. What does Mr. Vega say he will do?

(A) Invite Ms. Stanfill to a meeting
(B) Have his assistant print some forms
(C) Give a lecture at the Hendrix Innovation Expo
(D) Promote the interview on his Web site

GO ON TO THE NEXT PAGE

Questions 196-200 refer to the following e-mail, Web page, and text message.

To: Steve Irving <steve.i@hmtllc.com>
From: Colin Mountebank <colin.m@hmtllc.com>
Date: February 2
Subject: Contracts – Urgent!

Hi Steve,

In addition to the other tasks I assigned you today, could you please call TransState Couriers to arrange a collection? I'm not going to be back in the office today (my meeting is running a lot longer than originally expected) and the contracts I've prepared for Adam Harrison and his partner need to go out this afternoon. We don't need any special services, but I'd like the documents to arrive by tomorrow. They are in the two envelopes in the top left drawer of my desk. You should use our account number, #563886A, at their online booking screen so that the charges will be billed directly to our company's account.

Thanks!

Colin Mountebank
Senior Partner, Hope, Mountebank & Tweed

◀ ▶   🏠 C 🌐   +   http://www.transstatecouriers.com/services   🔍

TransState Couriers

| Home | About | Services | Package Tracking | Contact |

Services >> Under 0.7 kg >> Documents

At TransState Couriers, we understand the importance of getting your documents sent on time. With our competitive rates and reputation for reliability, you can get the peace of mind you need at a price you can afford.

	Basic Account	Corporate Account
Standard (delivered within 3 business days)	$16.95	$12.95
Express (delivered by 5 P.M. the next day)	$23.95	$19.95

Click here for rates on additional services such as contents insurance, proof of delivery (by signature), and refrigerated transport.

We will make two delivery attempts. In the event that we are unable to deliver the package, it will be returned to the nearest warehouse (click here for addresses and maps), where it can be collected in person up until 11:00 P.M. A text message will inform the recipient.

To: (312) 555-8922
From: (312) 555-1001

To recipient Adam Harrison: TransState Couriers tried to deliver a package (Ref# 822744532) but you were out. The package has been taken to our warehouse at 283 Doyle Lane and can be picked up anytime before 11 P.M. Alternatively, you may visit our Web site to reschedule the delivery.

196. Who most likely is Mr. Mountebank?

(A) Mr. Irving's supervisor
(B) Mr. Irving's assistant
(C) Mr. Harrison's manager
(D) Mr. Harrison's partner

197. In the e-mail, the word "originally" in paragraph 1, line 3, is closest in meaning to

(A) initially
(B) formally
(C) creatively
(D) generally

198. What is NOT mentioned as a service offered by TransState Couriers?

(A) Insuring what is inside the package
(B) Providing evidence that the package was delivered
(C) Using temperature-controlled transportation
(D) Transporting hazardous materials

199. How much did Mr. Irving most likely spend on the delivery?

(A) $12.95
(B) $16.95
(C) $19.95
(D) $23.95

200. What is suggested about Mr. Harrison's package?

(A) The delivery address was incorrect.
(B) The courier tried delivering it twice.
(C) It will be returned to the sender.
(D) It was damaged while in transit.

This is the end of the test. You may review PART 5, 6, and 7 if you finish the test early.
정답 p. 319 / 점수 환산표 p. 321 / 해석 p. 367

TEST 07

PART 5
PART 6
PART 7

토익 Reading Comprehension은 75분 동안 진행됩니다.
현재 시각과 지금부터 75분 후인 테스트 종료 시각을 기록해 두고,
반드시 종료 시각 전에 문제 풀이와 답안지 마킹을 완료하세요.

 현재 시각 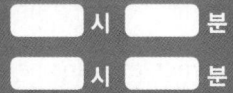시　　분

테스트 종료 시각 　　시　　분

READING TEST

In the Reading test, you will read a variety of texts and answer several different types of reading comprehension questions. The entire Reading test will last 75 minutes. There are three parts, and directions are given for each part. You are encouraged to answer as many questions as possible within the time allowed.

You must mark your answers on the separate answer sheet. Do not write your answers in your test book.

PART 5

Directions: A word or phrase is missing in each of the sentences below. Four answer choices are given below each sentence. Select the best answer to complete the sentence. Then mark the letter (A), (B), (C), or (D) on your answer sheet.

101. Ms. Dickinson's ------- for boosting employee morale has had a significant impact on both the productivity and sales increase.

(A) enthuse
(B) enthusiast
(C) enthusiastically
(D) enthusiasm

102. Quarterly sales reports are published for investors in the company journal, but monthly reports are ------- only to employees.

(A) necessary
(B) active
(C) accessible
(D) impossible

103. In the morning, Patricia Cooper let everyone know that the documents that would be faxed soon were -------.

(A) hers
(B) her
(C) she
(D) herself

104. During a press conference last night, GLM Biomedical CEO Godfrey Miranda made known his ------- not to retire despite reports stating otherwise.

(A) decision
(B) recognition
(C) progress
(D) result

105. Cranton-Taft Mechanics will open a new manufacturing plant and hire 150 technicians specifically to ------- the brand's extensive line of bicycles.

(A) cooperate
(B) assemble
(C) proceed
(D) specialize

106. Happy Beauty plastic surgery center offers a zero interest payment plan if paid ------- 30 days.

(A) on
(B) off
(C) within
(D) until

107. A good team leader should know how to define each team member's task so that they can work -------.

(A) productive
(B) productivity
(C) productively
(D) productiveness

108. Many experts noted that the engineering industry is now growing much ------- than any other part of the country's economy.

(A) fastest
(B) more faster
(C) fastness
(D) faster

109. Mr. Jansen, the chief executive officer of First Tech, called an emergency meeting, but the meeting itself did not ------- of the company's financial problems immediately.

(A) dispose
(B) disposal
(C) disposes
(D) disposing

110. ------- age, anyone who has a valid ticket will be granted admission to the museum's newest exhibit.

(A) In so far as
(B) Nevertheless
(C) Regardless of
(D) Namely

111. The training workshop scheduled to be held throughout next week ------- to increase office efficiency.

(A) has expected
(B) is expected
(C) will be expecting
(D) expected

112. One of the best Greek restaurants is located across from the historic museum in the city, and a famous bronze statue of spiders is ------- as well.

(A) nearly
(B) nearness
(C) nearby
(D) nears

113. Morning Star Clothing emphasized that it uses the best fabrics for its items, but the survey findings suggest -------.

(A) otherwise
(B) in contrast
(C) on the way
(D) instead

114. Ms. Brown volunteered to write a ------- explanation of the new electronic database to include in the employee manual.

(A) spacious
(B) projected
(C) skilled
(D) detailed

115. AME Industries has launched a ------- redesigned Web site featuring user-friendly functions and a new layout.

(A) completely
(B) completion
(C) competing
(D) completed

116. Customers returned ------- of the merchandise that they deemed unsatisfactory and received rebates from the store.

(A) this
(B) anything
(C) all
(D) everything

117. During summer months, Little Critters Apparel will expand its hours and offer weekly promotions in an effort to ------- additional customers.

(A) attract
(B) reimburse
(C) subscribe
(D) contribute

118. Mr. Thomson, one of the most ------- negotiators in the industry, was instrumental in helping our company obtain an affordable contract for the renovations of the Falaman Hotel.

(A) skill
(B) skills
(C) skilling
(D) skilled

119. With his broad experience in sales, Mr. Poe is a welcome ------- to our department.

(A) treatment
(B) outcome
(C) response
(D) addition

120. The report that was sent to the board of directors yesterday ------- Quantum Enterprises' new business strategies regarding reorganization guidelines.

(A) to highlight
(B) highlights
(C) have highlighted
(D) highlighting

GO ON TO THE NEXT PAGE

121. Among the ------- accomplishments listed in Ms. Hill's résumé is her award-winning career as a journalist.

(A) many
(B) little
(C) most
(D) more

122. Rewster Pharma's education officers select articles ------- academic sources for the monthly *Pharmacist's Reading List*.

(A) instead of
(B) besides
(C) from
(D) past

123. Thanks to Terragin Beverage Company's innovative marketing team, their revenues continue to surpass the ------- year's profits.

(A) previous
(B) forward
(C) ahead
(D) immediate

124. According to the practices of the university, any unattended items that are not ------- by the end of each semester will be sent to local charities.

(A) claimed
(B) claim
(C) claims
(D) claiming

125. Mr. Henderson had to conduct an ------- four-month study to come up with an idea for the design of the new office building.

(A) extensively
(B) extension
(C) extensive
(D) extend

126. Should online sales continue to outpace competitors', the plan to open a retail store in New York will be -------.

(A) accelerated
(B) overtaken
(C) conformed
(D) extended

127. There will be a series of meetings with project team members to decide ------- marketing strategies to implement.

(A) which
(B) who
(C) how
(D) why

128. Our data shows that the clients who have used our Internet services for three years or more are less ------- to switch providers than newer customers.

(A) probable
(B) usual
(C) likely
(D) frequent

129. Inspectors are scheduled to arrive at the Merriweather factory ------- confirm that all of the equipment complies with safety standards.

(A) in addition to
(B) in order to
(C) leading to
(D) owing to

130. Mr. Peterson failed to pay attention to ------- and clarity in his analysis report on the findings about the market trends.

(A) organize
(B) organizer
(C) organized
(D) organization

PART 6

Directions: Read the texts that follow. A word, phrase, or sentence is missing in parts of each text. Four answer choices for each question are given below the text. Select the best answer to complete the text. Then mark the letter (A), (B), (C), or (D) on your answer sheet.

Questions 131-134 refer to the following notice.

Thank you for choosing Pocatello Medical Equipment. We always work to ship orders within 24 hours of payment confirmation. If at any time you have questions about the whereabouts of your order, please ------- these important details. -------. The length of time for delivery to occur ranges
           131.   **132.**
from 2 to 15 days, depending on the mode of transport. While it is our goal to always deliver on time, some delays are not avoidable. This can result in items taking ------- to arrive. If you have
                                       133.
questions or concerns, call 800-245-1000 to inquire further about your ------- status.
                                                      134.

131. (A) refer
(B) indicate
(C) note
(D) prepare

132. (A) However, the items you purchased are not eligible for refund.
(B) We are highly recognized for the quality customer service.
(C) All customers are required to select a shipping method at checkout.
(D) A new set of products are updated on our website on a weekly basis.

133. (A) length
(B) longer
(C) longest
(D) lengthy

134. (A) employment
(B) subscription
(C) learning
(D) shipment

GO ON TO THE NEXT PAGE

To: Melissa Ryan <mryan@mail.com>
From: Benjamin Raja <braja@ejconsultants.org>
Subject: Final step
Date: February 29

Dear Ms. Ryan,

Congratulations! -------. Your experience and certifications appear more than ------- for this position.
135. **136.**

Please send me a list of three ------- as per required for applicants in the final stage of review. It is
137.
highly preferable that these include one previous work supervisor, one coworker and one professor

or instructor.

Be sure to e-mail me the requested information as soon as possible. Assuming all goes smoothly,

the selected applicant ------- promptly on May 10. Until you receive our reply, please continue to
138.
closely monitor this e-mail account.

Best regards,

Benjamin Raja
Director of Human Resources
EJ Consulting Firm

135. (A) You have reached the final step for the job
you applied for.
(B) Sufficient amount of educational
background is necessary.
(C) We are receiving résumés for the opening
of consultant.
(D) Your proposal for the project has been
thoroughly reviewed.

136. (A) abrupt
(B) accessible
(C) adequate
(D) acquainted

137. (A) identifications
(B) references
(C) records
(D) choices

138. (A) could commence
(B) would have commenced
(C) are commencing
(D) commenced

Mr. Kenneth Grey
5100 Front Street
Cincinnati, OH 45205
April 15

Dear Mr. Grey,

We appreciate the time you took to apply for the graphic design internship at Reba Sheer Clothing

Co. However, after careful consideration, we are sorry to notify you that you were not chosen to

------- this year's internship program.
139.

-------. However, due to recent budget cuts, our department is restricted to contracting only two full-
140.
time design interns this year.

Despite not being chosen, the advertisements in your portfolio, like ------- for Tippy Electronics and
141.
Young's Jewelry, are promising.

Your talents would be ------- valued at our company. Upon your graduation, please consider
142.
applying for our new graduates training internship.

Best regards,

Naomi Lang
Manager, Graphic Design and Marketing
Reba Sheer Clothing Co.

139. (A) substitute for
(B) commit to
(C) participate in
(D) advertise about

140. (A) Last year, the number of key contracts
with textile companies rose.
(B) A free lunch buffet will be provided on the
first day of the program.
(C) No other candidate was able to exceed
my expectations.
(D) We were previously able to select five
individuals as interns.

141. (A) this
(B) you
(C) those
(D) every

142. (A) high
(B) highly
(C) higher
(D) highest

GO ON TO THE NEXT PAGE

Questions 143-146 refer to the following notice.

Attention Employees,

Our office has recently received several reports of computer viruses gaining access to company computers. Unfortunately, we have not yet determined the source of the problem. ------- you
                                                                                        143.
discover your work computer to be infected with a software virus, immediately turn it off and contact an IT specialist.

-------. Moreover, if you receive any unwanted e-mails, especially from unknown addresses, try not
144.
to open them.

If you do open a ------- message by mistake, be sure to take precautions such as not clicking on any
                  145.
links or replying to the sender. If ------- are followed, you will greatly reduce your risk of contracting
                                   146.
a computer virus.

IT Services
ext. 3203

143. (A) Pending
(B) Even if
(C) Consequently
(D) In the event that

144. (A) We will be focusing on clarifying
maintenance procedures.
(B) Please take precautions when
downloading programs from the Internet.
(C) All employees are reminded to check their
e-mail accounts regularly.
(D) Our anti-virus software is sold at a
reasonable price.

145. (A) defective
(B) lengthy
(C) suspicious
(D) double

146. (A) these
(B) few
(C) either
(D) many

PART 7

Directions: In this part you will read a selection of texts, such as magazine and newspaper articles, e-mails, and instant messages. Each text or set of texts is followed by several questions. Select the best answer for each question and mark the letter (A), (B), (C), or (D) on your answer sheet.

Questions 147-148 refer to the following online chat discussion.

Veronica Stroud	[3:22 P.M.]
Hi, Gustavo. You set up the coffee machine in the break room, right?	
Gustavo Baretto	[3:24 P.M.]
Yes, this morning. Why? Did we run out of coffee already?	
Veronica Stroud	[3:24 P.M.]
No, but it's flashing an "Error" message.	
Gustavo Baretto	[3:25 P.M.]
Did you check that the lid is closed tightly?	
Veronica Stroud	[3:26 P.M.]
Yes. And it is fully stocked with fresh grounds.	
Gustavo Baretto	[3:27 P.M.]
It probably has to be reset.	
Veronica Stroud	[3:27 P.M.]
I've never done that before. Do I need to get out the manual?	
Gustavo Baretto	[3:28 P.M.]
No. Just hold down the button on the right-hand side for five seconds.	
Veronica Stroud	[3:29 P.M.]
Is that it? If I had known that, I wouldn't have bothered you. Thanks!	

147. What is Ms. Stroud's problem?

(A) She missed an important message.
(B) A break schedule had an error.
(C) Some supplies have run out.
(D) A device is not working properly.

148. At 3:29 P.M., what does Ms. Stroud most likely mean when she writes, "Is that it"?

(A) She does not think Mr. Baretto can arrive very quickly.
(B) Some directions are easier than she expected.
(C) She is surprised that the office only has one manual.
(D) A button can be reattached without difficulty.

GO ON TO THE NEXT PAGE

Premier Getaways

Nobody can beat our prices to the best places in Europe.

Rome $349
London $265
Paris $299
Barcelona $388
Athens $321

Visit our Web site at www.premiergetaways.com in order to book your dream trip. Don't forget to stay on our Web site to check out some of the tours and special hotel deals that we offer as well.

Terms & Conditions:
Prices are for individual round-trip tickets on flights departing from Boston.
Those making reservations on our Web site will receive complimentary shuttle bus service from the airport to their hotel.

Individuals using us to reserve a hotel will receive a daily voucher for a free buffet dinner.

149. What most likely is Premier Getaways?

(A) A public transit office
(B) A car dealer shop
(C) A vacation resort
(D) A travel agency

150. What will people who purchase plane tickets receive?

(A) Special discounts on hotels
(B) Complimentary dinner
(C) A ride on a shuttle bus
(D) A guided tour of the city

SPACE FOR SALE

Restaurant facility in the food court on the second floor of the Cloverdale Shopping Mall. It is perfect for a fast-food establishment. There are a kitchen, counter space, and a shared eating area, and it is available for a below-market rate as the owner wants to sell quickly. The refrigerator and cash registers are yours for the taking at no additional charge. Call 1-800-409-4334 for more information or to set up an appointment to see the facility.

151. What is indicated about the facility?

(A) It is located on the ground floor of the shopping center.
(B) The owner is willing to lease it.
(C) It costs less to buy than the other restaurants beside it.
(D) It comes with a private seating area.

152. What is included in the price of the sale?

(A) Some equipment
(B) A storage area
(C) Electricity and gas payments
(D) Parking spaces

GO ON TO THE NEXT PAGE

The City Arts Committee is hosting an exhibition.

On Display: Paintings and Sculptures by the Winners of
Mountainville's Student Art Contest

Tuesday, June 23 from 6:00 p.m. to 9:00 p.m.
Ed Klein Community Center
94 Southeast Front Street
Mountainville, TX 77028

Admission is $5 per person and includes a selection of drinks and light snacks.
Tickets can be purchased at the Mountainville Municipal Center during
regular office hours.

---

153. What type of event is being held?

(A) A play
(B) An art show
(C) A concert
(D) A contest

154. What is indicated about the event?

(A) It is free for students.
(B) It will be hosted by Ed Klein.
(C) It is a weekend event.
(D) It will feature local artists.

Wimberley, Inc.

Wimberley, Inc. is a small-sized medicine manufacturer that has its headquarters in Panama City, Panama. The company produces medicines that are derived from natural products found in the country's rainforests. Most of the company's products are sold in Panama and adjacent Central American countries, but it has begun exporting small amounts of the products to both Europe and the United States. The company has seen its rise in sales by more than 35% in the past two years, and its profits have risen by nearly the same amount. As a result, it has hired more than 65 new employees this year and will spend several million dollars on research and development soon. The company has two manufacturing facilities, both of which are located in Panama. Vice president Ernesto Carrera joined the company last December, and he is expected to expand the company's research to develop products that are more likely to appeal to environmentally conscious individuals.

Wimberley, Inc. has a promising future ahead of it, and it should become one of the leading companies in Panama within the next decade.

155. Who will most likely purchase the products of Wimberley, Inc.?

(A) A mechanic
(B) A patient
(C) An event organizer
(D) A caterer

156. What did Wimberley, Inc. do last year?

(A) It opened several new locations.
(B) It employed a new executive.
(C) It advertised its products worldwide.
(D) It trained its employees on a regular basis.

157. What is suggested about Wimberley, Inc.?

(A) It is one of the largest companies in Panama.
(B) It will enhance its research capability.
(C) The value of its stock has risen for the past two years.
(D) It increased its profits by 35% in the past quarter.

GO ON TO THE NEXT PAGE

Micon Event

Micon has announced that it is hosting a recruitment drive to cover shortfalls in its workforce for an upcoming building project to convert the former Wexley Fabrics factory into apartments. Electricians, plumbers, and construction workers are needed urgently. The conversion of the Wexley Fabrics building is a reaction to the recently enacted policy targeted at increasing the number of homes in the city for low-income families. The event is scheduled for February 17 at the Fairway Center from 8 A.M. to 3 P.M.

Interviews will be conducted on the day of the event, so applicants are asked to bring a completed application form with them. The form can be downloaded at www.micon-inc.net/forms. There you can also sign up for the event. Those who do so before February 17 will be sent an application packet with a company brochure containing details about Micon's mission, working conditions, and hiring process.

158. Why most likely would people want to attend the event?

(A) To tour an apartment complex
(B) To apply for financial assistance
(C) To seek a job opportunity
(D) To join a community club

159. What is the purpose of the policy mentioned in the article?

(A) To provide housing for some citizens
(B) To attract tourists to the city
(C) To reduce urban pollution
(D) To protect historic buildings

160. What will happen to people with advance registration?

(A) They will be allowed into a facility early.
(B) They will be given premium tickets.
(C) They will receive company information.
(D) They will have a fee reduced.

Prabha Shah [2:33 P.M.]
I'm setting up the buffet at the Nero Hotel. It looks like we'll need one more warming tray, though.

Funato Ozaki [2:37 P.M.]
I'm wrapping up the luncheon at Olivia Gardens, but I can bring one when I'm done.

Prabha Shah [2:38 P.M.]
That'll be perfect.

Funato Ozaki [2:39 P.M.]
We're one server short for tonight's event because Carly's sick. Can we get by with just 8?

Prabha Shah [2:40 P.M.]
I don't think so. We cater for Bridge Enterprises regularly, and I don't want the service to be slow.

Funato Ozaki [2:40 P.M.]
Let me add Jason to this conversation.

Prabha Shah [2:41 P.M.]
Jason, we need someone to cover Carly's 6–10 shift. Are you free?

Jason Irving [2:45 P.M.]
Sign me up.

Prabha Shah [2:46 P.M.]
Thanks! I'll text you the details. Please come dressed in the same uniform you wore to the Glendale Hall event.

Jason Irving [2:47 P.M.]
Okay. Fortunately, I've just had it cleaned.

Funato Ozaki [2:48 P.M.]
See you soon, Prabha. And thanks, Jason.

161. What type of business does Ms. Shah most likely work for?

(A) A restaurant supplier
(B) A catering company
(C) A transportation service
(D) A hotel chain

162. At 2:45 P.M., what does Mr. Irving most likely mean when he writes, "Sign me up"?

(A) He can give a talk to the Bridge Enterprises staff.
(B) He wants to register for a training event.
(C) He is able to fill in for a coworker.
(D) He thinks a business arrangement is a good idea.

163. What is Mr. Irving asked to do?

(A) Perform a cleaning task
(B) Get some instructions from Carly
(C) Bring some equipment to Ms. Shah
(D) Wear certain clothing items

164. Where does Mr. Ozaki plan to go next?

(A) Bridge Enterprises' Office
(B) Glendale Hall
(C) Nero Hotel
(D) Olivia Gardens

GO ON TO THE NEXT PAGE

Questions 165-167 refer to the following announcement.

Silvertown Transportation Department
Service Advisory

There is going to be road maintenance between Liberty Stadium and Broadwell Boulevard this weekend from 6:00 A.M. on Saturday until 10:00 P.M. on Sunday. — [1] —. The bus is going to run in two sections. It will run from Liberty Stadium up to Madison Street, and from Riverside Park to Broadwell Boulevard. Apple Avenue will not be accessible for road repairs. — [2] —. For those individuals wishing to go from the Madison Street stop to the Broadwell Boulevard stop, there will be shuttle buses connecting the two streets. — [3] —. The shuttle buses will run every 20 minutes and will be available at no cost for bus passengers. The shuttle buses will cease running as soon as the road work is complete. — [4] —. No other buses are going to be affected by the construction.

We apologize for any inconvenience that this may cause passengers.

165. Where is work scheduled to happen?

(A) At Liberty Stadium
(B) At Riverside Park
(C) On Apple Avenue
(D) On Broadwell Boulevard

166. According to the announcement, what are the shuttle buses for?

(A) To move passengers affected by repairs to a subway station
(B) To connect two bus stops
(C) To take people to Liberty Stadium
(D) To make up for overcrowding on a bus

167. In which of the positions marked [1], [2], [3], and [4] does the following sentence best belong?

"During that time, there will be some changes in the bus 10 service."

(A) [1]
(B) [2]
(C) [3]
(D) [4]

From: Ted Sanders, CEO

To: All Staff

Date: September 10

Subject: Greg Henderson Named Regional Manager

Ever since Ernest Mathieu announced his intentions to retire at the end of September, we at JPR Corporation have been searching to find his replacement. I would like to let you all know that Greg Henderson, who currently works at our headquarters in Chicago, is going to take over as the regional manager for South America at the beginning of October. Mr. Henderson is going to oversee all of our operations in South America, in which we have seen extensive growth in the past several months.

Many of you know Mr. Henderson well since he has been an employee at JPR for the past seven years. Prior to working here, he was employed at Krieg International and worked at that firm's Brazilian offices in both Rio de Janeiro and Brasilia for five years. Mr. Henderson is familiar with the working environment in South America, and he has a number of valuable contacts at companies there that will surely be helpful in his new position. He is going to be based in Buenos Aires, Argentina, but we expect him to visit our facilities throughout South America at various times of the year.

To honor Mr. Mathieu, who has served JPR for more than thirty-two years, we are going to have a farewell event for him on Friday, September 29. It will be held at Marino's, an Italian restaurant located near company headquarters, from 6:00 P.M. until 9:00 P.M. To learn more about the event, please get in touch with my secretary, Corrine Wise, at extension 5830. If you have any questions about the staffing changes, please speak with Stephanie Bush, the director of Human Resources, at extension 9043.

168. From what position will Mr. Mathieu retire?

(A) Chief executive officer
(B) Director of Human Resources
(C) South American regional manager
(D) Secretary

169. What is mentioned about Mr. Henderson?

(A) He is a native of South America.
(B) He worked at Krieg International last year.
(C) He knows many people in the industry.
(D) He is going to be based at JPR's headquarters.

170. Why will the event be held on September 29?

(A) To celebrate the promotion of Mr. Henderson
(B) To announce the retirement of Mr. Sanders
(C) To acknowledge the accomplishments of Mr. Mathieu
(D) To discuss JPR's plans for the South American market

171. Where will the event take place?

(A) In Buenos Aires
(B) In Chicago
(C) In Rio de Janeiro
(D) In Brasilia

TEST 07

From: Julie Hamilton <jhamilton@skydreamsairlines.com>
To: undisclosed recipients
Subject: Annual meeting
Date: November 5

This is a reminder that Sky Dreams Airlines' annual meeting is going to be held on Friday, November 6. — [1] —. Please be aware that more people than expected have indicated their desire to attend the meeting. On account of that, we have changed the location of the meeting. — [2] —. Instead, it has been moved to the East Rutherford Convention Center. The rest of the event including the schedule remains the same as indicated in my e-mail dated October 25.

All Sky Dreams Airlines employees are welcome to attend the event. Our CEO, the board of directors, and most members of upper management are going to be present. In addition, all of our major shareholders and some potential investors will be in attendance. — [3] —. There will be a question and answer session at the meeting, and everyone, no matter what your position, is welcome to contribute during that time. Following the meeting, CEO Travis Carter is going to host a reception at which refreshments will be served. — [4] —. Employees must register in order to attend, so your name will be checked before you are permitted to enter the meeting. Feel free to contact me if you have any questions.

172. Why was the memo written?

(A) To publicize a new venue for a meeting

(B) To mention that Mr. Carter will resign as CEO

(C) To state that some new investors have been found

(D) To encourage employees to register for an event

173. What is mentioned about Ms. Hamilton?

(A) She sent an e-mail about the event last month.

(B) She works in the office of the CEO.

(C) She is going to attend the meeting tomorrow.

(D) She reserved the convention center for the meeting.

174. What does Ms. Hamilton ask the attendees to do?

(A) Make reservations for the reception

(B) Have their questions prepared in advance

(C) Sign up to attend the meeting

(D) Contact Ms. Hamilton to receive instructions

175. In which of the positions marked [1], [2], [3], and [4] does the following sentence best belong?

"It is no longer going to be held in the auditorium at Sky Dreams Airlines headquarters."

(A) [1]

(B) [2]

(C) [3]

(D) [4]

GO ON TO THE NEXT PAGE

Historical Preservation Society (HPS)

The HPS invites you to participate in our upcoming Internet seminar entitled "How to Preserve Historical Documents". The seminar is going to focus on the best methods to ensure that aging documents of a historical nature can be preserved and not be allowed to suffer any kind of damage.

The event will be led by Steven Rohm, who has a PhD in history and currently works as a professor at Parker University. The seminar is set to take place on July 30 from 1:00 P.M. to 4:00 P.M. Those who wish to attend it must register no later than July 1. Information about the cost of the seminar and other details may be obtained by visiting www.hps.org/seminar.

When you register, you will be given the chance to submit a question for Mr. Rohm. He will do his best to respond to as many of them as possible during the seminar. Those questions which he cannot answer live will receive written responses to be posted on our Web site no later than August 10.

● ● ●   e-mail

From: srohm@inthistfound.org
To: sarahhallstead@hps.org
Cc: guybouchrad@parker.edu
Subject: Regrets
Date: June 12

Dear Ms. Hallstead,

I regret to inform you that I cannot fulfill my role at the upcoming seminar being sponsored by your organization. On the day of the seminar, I have to fly to Paris to participate in the restoration of a manuscript from the fourteenth century. I spoke with one of my former classmates, current Parker University professor of history Guy Bouchard, to take over my role at the seminar, and he agreed. He will be contacting you to make the necessary arrangements soon.

Mr. Bouchard has specialized in the restoration and preservation of historical documents for more than fifteen years. He works with both the American Smithsonian Institute and the Vatican, so he is extremely competent. I hope you find him a suitable replacement for me.

Again, I sincerely apologize for my inability to be present on the day of the seminar.

Best,
Steven Rohm

176. What is suggested about the event?

- (A) It is intended for professors at universities.
- (B) It is going to take place over the course of two days.
- (C) It will be held at the headquarters of the HPS.
- (D) It will provide information on how to take care of documents.

177. What is mentioned about people who want to participate in the event?

- (A) They can ask Ms. Hallstead questions.
- (B) They have to sign up for it in advance.
- (C) They are all students at universities.
- (D) They should have a membership in the HPS.

178. When will Mr. Rohm fly to Paris?

- (A) On June 12
- (B) On July 1
- (C) On July 30
- (D) On August 10

179. What does Mr. Rohm indicate that he has done?

- (A) Asked a colleague to fill in for him at the event
- (B) Done some restoration work for the Vatican
- (C) Acquired a fifteenth-century document for the seminar
- (D) Recorded the seminar to show to those who cannot attend it

180. What is suggested about Mr. Bouchard?

- (A) He was recently appointed to his current position.
- (B) He has extensive experience in his field.
- (C) He hopes to work full time at the Smithsonian Institute.
- (D) He spends most of his time working in Europe.

GO ON TO THE NEXT PAGE

For Sale: Ninkovich NK100 Industrial Stapler

Two weeks ago, I purchased the NK100 in order to staple some of the large reports that are produced by my company. However, I was unaware that the NK100 is only capable of stapling a small number of pages together. (I intend to purchase a machine capable of stapling 130 pages.)

The NK100 is ideal for those who wish to staple reports of 50 pages or fewer. The stapler which I purchased has never been used and is still in its packaging. According to its Web site, Ninkovich Inc. will service the stapler anytime that it fails to work properly. It will also provide spare parts should any part of it need to be replaced even though this particular machine is no longer being made by Ninkovich as of this Monday. On account of this announcement, which I just read, I am only requesting $15 instead of $25 for it.

Please contact me at the number listed below if you would like to purchase this item. I can send you some pictures of it to your cell phone if you would like to see what it looks like.

Jeremy Summers (617) 905-1743

Model #	Maximum Number of Pages Stapled	Price
NK50	50	$25
NK100	100	$35
NK150	120	$45
NK200	150	$60

Ninkovich Inc.

Ninkovich Inc. provides industrial staplers that can meet the demands of every office. They will put staples through the thickest reports and will not suffer problems such as becoming loose. The staples used in all Ninkovich Inc. industrial staplers are the same size, so the staples you purchase from us are interchangeable. The above chart should give you an idea of which industrial stapler is right for your office. For a demonstration, call (405) 444-3854 to set up a personal appointment.

181. Why is Mr. Summers offering to sell his machine?

(A) He does not need a stapler anymore.
(B) He has a similar model.
(C) It breaks down on occasion.
(D) It cannot handle large reports.

182. According to the flyer, why is the machine being sold at a low price?

(A) It is no longer being manufactured.
(B) It has been used for a longtime.
(C) It is not in new condition.
(D) It requires spare parts.

183. How can those interested in Mr. Summers' machine see it?

(A) By visiting his homepage
(B) By requesting he send them pictures
(C) By going to his office
(D) By going to a local store

184. According to the Web site, what is a common feature of all Ninkovich Inc. industrial staplers?

(A) They staple the same number of pages.
(B) They accommodate identical staples.
(C) They come in the same colors.
(D) They do not weigh too much.

185. Which model will Mr. Summers most likely purchase to replace the one he previously bought?

(A) NK50
(B) NK100
(C) NK150
(D) NK200

GO ON TO THE NEXT PAGE

Internship Recruitment Drive at Delarosa Co.
Spend your summer at the headquarters of one of the top retailers in the country!

Delarosa Co. is looking for summer interns in New York City. By working as an intern, you'll gain valuable experience, learn about how your department operates, and build useful industry contacts. We're holding a one-time recruitment event on April 28 at our headquarters in the Mendoza Building (348 127th Street). All applicants will attend a group interview, and the strongest candidates will be passed on to individual interviews. Applicants will also complete a test to assess their writing skills. Applicants should apply to only one department, and they may do so by sending a résumé and cover letter to Glenn Powell at powellg@delarosaco.com. Please note that while refreshments will be served, interviewees should make their own lunch plans.

Department	Group Interviews	Individual Interviews	Location
Accounting	8:00 A.M.–10:00 A.M.	10:00 A.M.–Noon	Conference Room A
Finance	8:00 A.M.–10:00 A.M.	10:00 A.M.–Noon	Conference Room B
Public Relations	1:00 P.M.–3:00 P.M.	3:00 P.M.–5:00 P.M.	Room 205
Marketing	1:00 P.M.–3:00 P.M.	3:00 P.M.–5:00 P.M.	Room 206

Hiring Committee Summary Report
Written by Glenn Powell, Submitted April 30

Following the April 28 recruitment event, the Delarosa Co. Hiring Committee met to discuss job candidates. A number of factors were considered, including experience, education, exam scores, and personality. The committee makes the following recommendations for internship positions:
    Accounting: Colleen Mack
    Finance: Kyle Atherton
    Public Relations: Patricia Silas
    Marketing: Benjamin Avila

If the top-selected candidates are not available, we recommend as backups Harvey Elliot (Accounting), William Duffy (Finance), Joelle Hudson (Public Relations), and Yolanda Greer (Marketing).

From: Glenn Powell
Received: May 4, 2:48 P.M.
To: Samuel Walburn

Hi, Sam. Kyle Atherton, the first-choice candidate for your department, has declined the internship position. Unfortunately, he has decided to take a job at Benson, Inc., instead. I'll contact the backup candidate and let you know if we need to search any further. If that's the case, I'll send you some résumés to look over. In the meantime, I've e-mailed you the form you need to request supplies for training. Those will be ordered next Wednesday.

186. What is NOT true about the April 28 event?

(A) It was held at the company's head office.
(B) Its attendees were served a meal.
(C) It included a written exam.
(D) Its applicants could attend more than one interview.

187. Where most likely did Ms. Silas have an interview?

(A) In Conference Room A
(B) In Conference Room B
(C) In Room 205
(D) In Room 206

188. What problem does Mr. Powell mention?

(A) He is having difficulty choosing among candidates.
(B) An applicant didn't have the right qualifications.
(C) Some interviews lasted longer than expected.
(D) A candidate accepted a job somewhere else.

189. Who does Mr. Powell plan to contact?

(A) Harvey Elliot
(B) William Duffy
(C) Joelle Hudson
(D) Yolanda Greer

190. What has been sent to Mr. Walburn?

(A) An order form
(B) A training schedule
(C) Interview questions
(D) Some résumés

GO ON TO THE NEXT PAGE

Questions 191-195 refer to the following information, e-mail, and online review.

Product Information/Curtains

Brand: Orem

Orem curtains are made from 100% polyester and have a thick lining to block sunlight. They are sold in sets of two panels, and they have a concealed tab top.

Panel width(inches): 54
Panel length(inches): 63, 84, 95, 108, and 120
Fabric options: Gray-Black Diamonds, Solid Forest Green, Black-White Stripes, Navy Floral, and Solid Navy
Price: $25-$50 per set, dependent on length

For all Orem curtains, customers can receive a free pair of rope tie backs when purchasing two or more sets.

E-mail	
To:	Sales Associates
From:	Jessie Austin
Date:	August 29
Subject:	Orem Curtains

Dear Sales Associates,

I have been informed by our supplier, Rick Brody, that the information sheet for Orem brand curtains prepared by Sophia Mills is out of date. One of the patterns—Navy Floral—is no longer available for this line. In addition, the 120 inch length has been discontinued. New information sheets will be available in the break room sometime next week. In the meantime, please tear out the other one from the product information manual and discard it. This will prevent confusion when the new sheet is added.

I will be away on vacation from September 1 to 9, but you may address any urgent questions to the assistant manager, Michelle Rowe. Otherwise, you can bring them up with me when I return.

Sincerely,

Jessie Austin
Store Manager, Perrine Home Supplies

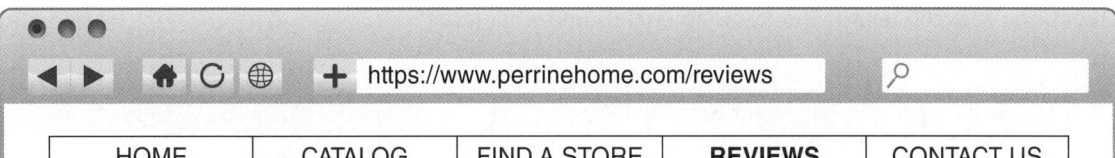

 https://www.perrinehome.com/reviews

| HOME | CATALOG | FIND A STORE | **REVIEWS** | CONTACT US |

Product Category: Home Furnishings, Curtains   Brand: Orem
Reviewer: Walter Kuhl   Posted: September 8

On my most recent visit to Perrine Home Supplies, I purchased some curtains for my master bedroom and my guest room. Although the selection for the blackout curtains was somewhat limited, I found two styles that matched my current decorations. I was confused by the dimensions offered, only knowing that I wanted to make sure that the curtains would reach the floor. The salesperson who helped me was new and didn't have much experience. However, I did get some excellent advice from the assistant manager. Overall, I'm very pleased with my purchase. I sleep a lot better now that the light from the street is completely blocked out. I would definitely buy this brand again.

191. How many fabric patterns can customers choose from?

(A) Two
(B) Three
(C) Four
(D) Five

192. What are the e-mail recipients asked to do?

(A) Check a storage area for supplies
(B) Remove a page from a handbook
(C) Inform customers about a change
(D) E-mail their sales figures

193. What is suggested about Mr. Kuhl?

(A) He shops at Perrine Home Supplies regularly.
(B) He special-ordered a certain pattern.
(C) He was eligible for a free gift.
(D) He purchased his curtains at a discount.

194. In the review, the word "reach" in paragraph 1, line 4, is closest in meaning to

(A) touch
(B) attain
(C) cover
(D) develop

195. Who did Mr. Kuhl talk to during his visit?

(A) Jessie Austin
(B) Rick Brody
(C) Sophia Mills
(D) Michelle Rowe

GO ON TO THE NEXT PAGE

To: Alliance Property Management <info@alliancepm.net>
From: Dawn Koffler <d_koffler@citytimemail.com>
Date: January 14
Subject: Please respond

To Whom It May Concern:

I live on the 4th floor of Raymond Tower, and I asked for a repair for the air conditioner in my living room three days ago (Request #4950). I haven't heard anything back yet, and I'm wondering how soon you can schedule a maintenance visit. Whenever I run the air conditioner, it starts dripping water from the right-hand side. I think there's a problem with the drainage pan, so it might be a good idea to bring a spare one along when checking the appliance. I will leave the key with my next door neighbor, Charles Wade in 405, so you can let yourself in. Mr. Wade will be in the building all day while working from home. Thank you for your prompt attention to this matter.

Sincerely,

Dawn Koffler

Alliance Property Management

Maintenance Report, January 15 / Technician: Edward Hinton

Property	Unit	Working Time	Status
Jewel Apartments	406	9:00–9:25 A.M.	Need to order parts
Jewel Apartments	315	9:30–11:45 A.M.	Completed
Raymond Tower	404	1:30–1:50 P.M.	Completed
Raymond Tower	218	1:55–2:35 P.M.	Need to order parts

To: Dawn Koffler <d_koffler@citytimemail.com>
From: Jonah Rodriguez <rodriguezj@alliancepm.net>
Date: January 15
Subject: RE: Please respond

Dear Ms. Koffler,

We are sorry you had to wait a few days for your repair request to be completed. Two of our technicians have recently left our team, so we are having trouble keeping up with requests. This issue will be resolved soon. Anyway, Edward Hinton completed the work at your home today. He brought a drainage pan with him, so he was able to make the repair without delay. For the next few days, please take note of whether or not there is any water dripping from the air conditioner when you run it. If so, please notify us immediately.

Sincerely,

Jonah Rodriguez
Maintenance Supervisor, Alliance Property Management

196. What is the purpose of the first e-mail?

(A) To inquire about a policy
(B) To reschedule a repair
(C) To follow up on a request
(D) To report water damage

197. What is implied about Ms. Koffler?

(A) Her apartment key is not working.
(B) She normally works from home.
(C) Her recommendation saved some time.
(D) She is a new tenant in the apartment building.

198. When was Ms. Koffler's apartment most likely visited?

(A) At 9:00 A.M.
(B) At 9:30 A.M.
(C) At 1:30 P.M.
(D) At 1:55 P.M.

199. What does Mr. Rodriguez say about Alliance Property Management?

(A) It charges a fee for on-site repairs.
(B) It lost some of the work orders.
(C) Its maintenance team is short staffed.
(D) Its technician will visit Ms. Koffler again.

200. In the second e-mail, the word "run" in paragraph 1, line 6, is closest in meaning to

(A) show
(B) manage
(C) flow
(D) operate

This is the end of the test. You may review PART 5, 6, and 7 if you finish the test early.

TEST

PART 5
PART 6
PART 7

토익 Reading Comprehension은 75분 동안 진행됩니다.
현재 시각과 지금부터 75분 후인 테스트 종료 시각을 기록해 두고,
반드시 종료 시각 전에 문제 풀이와 답안지 마킹을 완료하세요.

 현재 시각 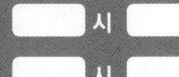 시 분

테스트 종료 시각 시 분

READING TEST

In the Reading test, you will read a variety of texts and answer several different types of reading comprehension questions. The entire Reading test will last 75 minutes. There are three parts, and directions are given for each part. You are encouraged to answer as many questions as possible within the time allowed.

You must mark your answers on the separate answer sheet. Do not write your answers in your test book.

PART 5

Directions: A word or phrase is missing in each of the sentences below. Four answer choices are given below each sentence. Select the best answer to complete the sentence. Then mark the letter (A), (B), (C), or (D) on your answer sheet.

101. Ledge Sporting Goods Store ------- numerous outdoor activities as part of its summer recreation program for children.

(A) inquires
(B) focuses
(C) offers
(D) remains

102. According to reports in the press, ------- by local entrepreneurs to charities in the area have exceeded three million dollars this year alone.

(A) contributions
(B) contributed
(C) contribution
(D) to contribute

103. The company party tentatively scheduled for December 19 can't proceed ------- management's consent.

(A) regarding
(B) under
(C) along
(D) without

104. It doesn't seem that H&J Corporation can achieve the ------- 5% increase in its yearly profits because the firm has failed to create an attractive advertisement.

(A) desire
(B) desired
(C) desiring
(D) desires

105. All participants in the annual job fair should report to the reception booth ------- upon arrival at the venue.

(A) closely
(B) timely
(C) immediately
(D) nearly

106. ABX International has confirmed that it will cut down on recruitment after ------- debate.

(A) lengthily
(B) lengthen
(C) lengthy
(D) length

107. During its 30 years in business, Aerocom Inc. has established a ------- for designing high quality interiors for luxury aircraft.

(A) reputation
(B) caption
(C) confirmation
(D) recognition

108. Mr. Mason intends to remain as the vice president of marketing ------- his replacement has been hired.

(A) over
(B) as for
(C) except
(D) until

109. Due to ------- manufacturing problems, all orders placed during the first week of the month are likely to be delayed 7-10 days.

(A) whole
(B) late
(C) recent
(D) last

110. By adopting a few simple steps into the daily work process, Devon Energy ------- reduced the production defects.

(A) considerable
(B) considerably
(C) considerate
(D) consideration

111. CRP Bank and North Broad Bank have announced they will merge in an effort to expand the ------- of their services in the Piedment area.

(A) available
(B) avails
(C) availability
(D) availably

112. The second edition of *Financial Strategems* ------- Herman Olerud will be released online next summer.

(A) towards
(B) on
(C) by
(D) alongside

113. In order to provide better customer service, Eureka Family Insurance's homepage has ------- been upgraded to include new features such as real-time consulting.

(A) usually
(B) recently
(C) commonly
(D) fairly

114. Salamanca Cuisine has become one of the most visited restaurants in the city since it ------- Best Restaurant of the Year.

(A) named
(B) will be naming
(C) was named
(D) is named

115. All travel expense ------- requests must be submitted no later than five business days after returning to the office.

(A) reimburse
(B) reimbursed
(C) reimbursing
(D) reimbursement

116. Outback Trails is ------- the highest rated adventure tour companies in all of Australia.

(A) until
(B) among
(C) throughout
(D) around

117. To best prevent work-related accidents, ------- safety inspections are carried out on a weekly basis.

(A) confident
(B) routine
(C) aware
(D) durable

118. ------- who would prefer to have a vegetarian meal at the end of the year party should contact Teresa Masters at extension 504.

(A) Those
(B) Others
(C) Whoever
(D) Whichever

119. ------- Ducky's restaurant, all the restaurants located in the Springfield area reported increased profits during the third quarter of the year.

(A) Considering
(B) Except for
(C) Rather than
(D) Whereas

120. In ------- to overwhelming demand from consumers, Cooper's Sporting Goods has decided to develop more options for children's sportswear.

(A) responds
(B) responded
(C) response
(D) respondent

GO ON TO THE NEXT PAGE

121. In order to switch to the computerized medical record system, Dr. Kolpacoff's office staff first ------- all patient records.

(A) contributed
(B) proceeded
(C) inclined
(D) compiled

122. Tammy Butler of Aqua, Inc. has expressed interest in ------- the manufacturing division of her firm's primary rival.

(A) acquire
(B) acquired
(C) acquiring
(D) to acquire

123. Aropagus Water Purification Center offers a tour ------- the award-winning facility to anyone interested.

(A) after
(B) of
(C) so
(D) next

124. You are strongly advised to take an intensive class led by a personal trainer in order to make your workout more -------.

(A) effect
(B) effective
(C) effects
(D) effectively

125. It is recommended to review each page of the information booklet ------- before filling out the registration form.

(A) relatively
(B) thoroughly
(C) seldom
(D) incidentally

126. The health professional ------- wins the International Healthcare Awards will be scheduled to lead a series of educational classes next month.

(A) what
(B) each
(C) who
(D) which

127. It is ------- that starting next year TR Motors will expand its product line and begin opening assembly plants in Asia.

(A) probable
(B) constant
(C) careful
(D) strong

128. Mr. Jackson retired from the company a few months ago, but the ------- has yet to be filled.

(A) open
(B) openness
(C) opens
(D) opening

129. If ------- requires an extension on the deadline, please inform Ms. Hampton at once.

(A) other
(B) every
(C) anyone
(D) each other

130. ------- her experience working with the Cartwright Group, Mary Landers was the ideal choice for the new project based in San Antonio.

(A) To give
(B) Given
(C) Giving
(D) Gives

PART 6

Directions: Read the texts that follow. A word, phrase, or sentence is missing in parts of each text. Four answer choices for each question are given below the text. Select the best answer to complete the text. Then mark the letter (A), (B), (C), or (D) on your answer sheet.

Questions 131-134 refer to the following announcement.

Starbuilt Construction Co. is dedicated to the promotion of an occupational hazard-free work zone.

-------.
131.

In order to continue our record of maintaining worker safety in construction areas, a company -------
132.

has been prepared.

All regular and contracted workers are required ------- an eight-hour construction zone traffic safety
133.

instructional session on May 17. -------, all employees will be provided with an updated manual
134.

highlighting the newest recommendations for work zone safety which will be explained during the

class.

131. (A) Our records show that we are in need of more equipment.
(B) Starbuilt Construction boasts its cutting-edge manufacturing technology.
(C) In fact, we have kept a safe environment for the last three years.
(D) Moreover, the safety process will protect you from potential hazards.

132. (A) site
(B) location
(C) procedure
(D) seminar

133. (A) attendance
(B) to attend
(C) attending
(D) to be attended

134. (A) However
(B) In addition
(C) Actually
(D) For example

GO ON TO THE NEXT PAGE

Questions 135-138 refer to the following letter.

June 13

Dear Ms. Pacheco,

The broadcasting space that you purchased for Greenwall Bakery was scheduled to begin running

on June 12. -------. This problem interfered with the ------- of your commercial.
        135.   **136.**

Our technicians are looking into the problem to ensure it does not reoccur. It seems that it may

------- to the extreme weather conditions.
137.

To apologize for the inconvenience, we will extend your advertisement time by three days.

If ------- additional problem arises, we will contact you immediately. Feel free to call me at 332-878-
  138.
5645 if you have questions. Thank you for your patience.

Sincerely,

Jason Fromme
KGRM Station Manager

---

135. (A) Thank you again for signing a contract
      with KGRM Station.
    (B) We would like to offer our best wishes to
      Greenwall Bakery.
    (C) Customer perception changes due to their
      exposure to TV commercials.
    (D) Unfortunately, our broadcasting system
      went off the air for a while.

136. (A) approval
    (B) transmission
    (C) designation
    (D) retrieval

137. (A) be relating
    (B) to be related
    (C) have been related
    (D) relates

138. (A) your
    (B) most
    (C) other
    (D) any

Attention all Sureway Grocery Store Shoppers:

You may expect to see some changes in the Sureway checkout process throughout the next month.

The Fremont store will be the testing site of a new computerized cashier machine.

-------, the checkout process is conducted manually.
 139.

Beginning on May 10, it will be computerized by the use of automated cash registers. ------- will
                                                                                          140.

scan items for purchase, bag merchandise, and process payments.

We expect this new technology to facilitate customer checkout, possibly resulting in shorter wait

times. While some worry that the machines will prove inefficient, we think there will be an overall

increase in -------.
          141.

-------.
 142.

Sincerely,

Flora Alvarez
General Manager, Sureway Grocery Store

---

139. (A) At present
(B) For example
(C) Even so
(D) Lastly

140. (A) It
(B) That
(C) They
(D) When

141. (A) productivity
(B) cost
(C) personnel
(D) error

142. (A) Please stop by next month and give the
new process a try.
(B) Sureway Grocery Store is gaining
popularity among young shoppers.
(C) Four computerized cash registers have
been successfully installed.
(D) We believe that manual process is safer
than the new technology.

GO ON TO THE NEXT PAGE

Questions 143-146 refer to the following e-mail.

To: Arianne Fredericks <afredericks@MaritonHerald.com>
From: Susan Lee <slee@MaritonPostOffice.gov>
Date: December 18
Subject: Relocation Announcement
Attachment: Photos

Dear Ms. Fredericks,

Mariton City post office will be moving to 4010 Twelfth Avenue, and resuming normal business hours

on January 30. -------, we would like to make an advertisement in the *Mariton Herald* newspaper.
       143.

Please create a simple advertisement that includes the date and address of the new location, as

well as a small map to help residents ------- our new address with ease.
          144.

-------. Incorporate these images at will, and do whatever you judge to be most effective in most
145.
clearly communicating our relocation.

I will be ------- information regarding the cost of the ad space.
    146.

Susan Lee, Director
Mariton Post Service

---

143. (A) Moreover
(B) Furthermore
(C) Accordingly
(D) Nonetheless

144. (A) locations
(B) located
(C) locate
(D) locating

145. (A) I have attached photos of the new building to include in it.
(B) The residents will be delighted to meet the editor in person.
(C) We are open to any further inquiries about the newspaper article.
(D) Call us at 219-136-100 today and learn more about the renewal.

146. (A) conducting
(B) inquiring
(C) awaiting
(D) releasing

PART 7

Directions: In this part you will read a selection of texts, such as magazine and newspaper articles, e-mails, and instant messages. Each text or set of texts is followed by several questions. Select the best answer for each question and mark the letter (A), (B), (C), or (D) on your answer sheet.

Questions 147-148 refer to the following postcard.

Show this postcard to any one of our managers when visiting a branch of Archie's Restaurants for a meal. You'll receive a 30% discount on any bill over $50!

One offer per customer only. This offer may not be used in conjunction with our summer time special or winter spectacular discounts. This offer is not valid for use in any of our airport branches. For full terms and conditions, please visit our Web site.

Note: You have received this special offer as you spent over $100 on your last visit to Archie's. To learn more about branches close to your local area, just text "Show Me" to 99542.

Archie's Restaurants Ltd.
PO Box 93250
Seattle, Washington 93027

Thomas King
57b King James Street
Lexington, WV 20042

---

147. What does the postcard suggest about Mr. King?

(A) He is the manager of Archie's Restaurant.
(B) He has visited the restaurant before.
(C) He is applying for a managerial role.
(D) He is a Web site designer.

148. Why might the recipient send a text?

(A) To activate a new phone contract
(B) To confirm that the details of an order are correct
(C) To receive information about restaurant locations
(D) To view some terms and conditions

GO ON TO THE NEXT PAGE

Questions 149-150 refer to the following text message.

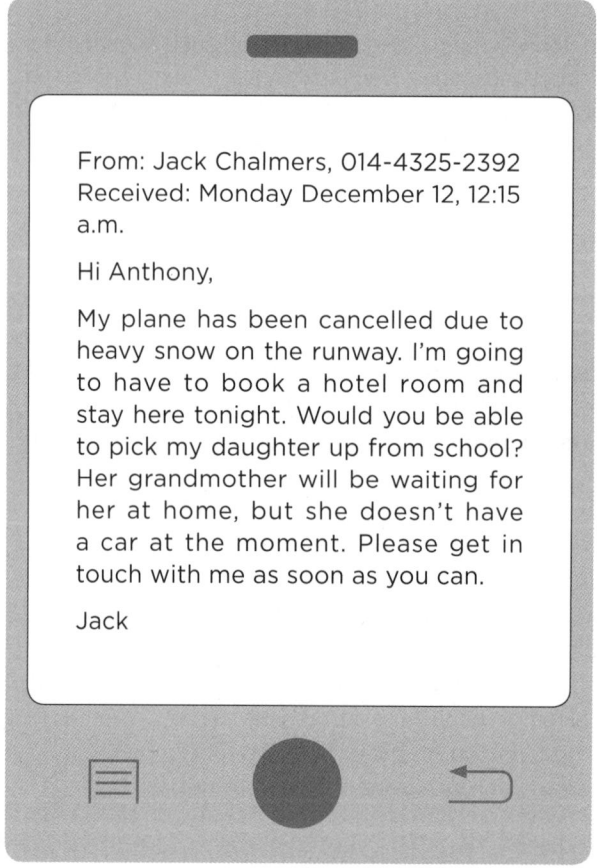

From: Jack Chalmers, 014-4325-2392
Received: Monday December 12, 12:15 a.m.

Hi Anthony,

My plane has been cancelled due to heavy snow on the runway. I'm going to have to book a hotel room and stay here tonight. Would you be able to pick my daughter up from school? Her grandmother will be waiting for her at home, but she doesn't have a car at the moment. Please get in touch with me as soon as you can.

Jack

149. Why did Jack send the message?

(A) To arrange the pick-up of his daughter
(B) To ask about a weather forecast
(C) To organize a car rental
(D) To enquire about the price of a hotel room

150. What is Anthony asked to do quickly?

(A) Arrange transportation
(B) Make contact
(C) Visit his grandmother
(D) Confirm a reservation

Kavariso Sandwich Shop
2320 East Fulton St
Jefferson, WY 82310
(307) 555-1212
www.kavarisosandwich.com

Do you ever wish you could share the great taste of Kavariso's sandwiches with your friends, family, and coworkers without having to visit one of our stores? We're happy to say that now you can! Starting August 1, Kavariso will serve its delicious sandwiches at group events.

We offer three sandwich sets ranging from basic to broad:
Monster Sandwich (Feeds 10-15) A two-meter sandwich that can be served pre-cut or whole and bottled soft drinks. $64
Monster Sandwich Meal (Feeds 15-20) A Monster Sandwich, a fresh vegetable platter, and bottled soft drinks. $88
Monster Sandwich Full Meal (Feeds 20-30) A Monster Sandwich, a fresh vegetable platter, bottled soft drinks, assorted potato chips in single-serving bags, and dessert (brownies and cookies). $116

Orders of three or more sets will receive a 20 percent discount. Orders must be placed at least four hours in advance by phone or through our Web site.

151. What is the purpose of the advertisement?

(A) To promote the opening of a store
(B) To announce a new catering service
(C) To describe recent menu changes
(D) To compare sandwich serving sizes

152. How can customers receive a discount from Kavariso's?

(A) By ordering through the Web site
(B) By ordering the meal in advance
(C) By ordering at least three sets
(D) By ordering from a group event

TEST 08

GO ON TO THE NEXT PAGE

Lucy Crouse   8:38 A.M.

I have some bad news. My car wouldn't start this morning, so I have to take the bus into the city. It looks like I'll be about twenty minutes late.

Jane Levy   8:40 A.M.

Oh, no! So, you won't get here in time to set up the projector for my 9 A.M. presentation.

Lucy Crouse   8:41 A.M.

Could you move to another room with a built-in projector? Or start at 9:30 instead?

Jane Levy   8:42 A.M.

Unfortunately, I can't change the presentation time, and all the rooms are booked. But I'll find someone else to do it for me. Who would have the expertise to handle it? Jim Burke from the IT department?

Lucy Crouse   8:44 A.M.

He's the one. Sorry again and tell him thanks for me.

---

153. What does Ms. Levy plan to do?

(A) Move to another room
(B) Set up some equipment
(C) Ask a colleague for help
(D) Take public transportation

154. At 8:44 A.M., what does Ms. Crouse most likely mean when she writes, "He's the one"?

(A) She reported the problem to Mr. Burke.
(B) She is confident in Mr. Burke's abilities.
(C) She left some equipment with Mr. Burke.
(D) She thinks Mr. Burke has reserved a room.

```
┌──────────────────────────────────────────────────────────────────────┐
│                              e-mail                        ▣ ▦ ☒       │
├──────────────────────────────────────────────────────────────────────┤
│                                                                     ▲  │
│  To: Committee members                                                 │
│  From: Susan Coyle                                                     │
│  Re: Funding                                                          │
│  Date: 27 January                                                     │
├──────────────────────────────────────────────────────────────────────┤
```

I would like to thank you all again for helping to bring the modern art exhibit to the Cubix gallery. We really couldn't have done it without your hard work.

I am always on the lookout for exciting new artwork to display in the gallery; this is to ensure that the people of our city get the chance to experience modern culture first-hand. At the moment, I am currently negotiating with the artist Patrick Cabaye. We are hopeful of exhibiting his work in the summer.

As you know, we rely on the funding of our members in order to cover operating costs. In order to help finance the Cabaye exhibit, please visit www.cubix.com/members and give as much as you can. We at the gallery really do appreciate your continued support.

I hope you can support the gallery in this latest endeavor. The Cubix gallery frequently attracts visitors to the city of Redbridge, which is beneficial to all local businesses. On behalf of everyone here, I would like to once again thank you for your continued support.

Faithfully,

Susan Coyle
Chief Curator, Modern Art Exhibits

155. What is the purpose of the e-mail?

(A) To thank staff for attending a meeting
(B) To provide a biographical profile of an artist
(C) To invite donations from members
(D) To provide directions to a local business

156. What is stated about Ms. Coyle?

(A) She manages the content of displays at Cubix.
(B) She has recently moved to Redbridge.
(C) She will submit artwork this summer.
(D) She is an exciting and upcoming artist.

157. What is mentioned about Cubix?

(A) It sells tickets online.
(B) It has been open for over a decade.
(C) It is being closed for maintenance work.
(D) It has become a tourist attraction.

GO ON TO THE NEXT PAGE

TEST 08

Questions 158-160 refer to the following information.

Choose Geronimo Inc. For Your Business Needs

Do your staff often fail to secure the deal through their sales pitches? Do they lack confidence when presenting to managers of other businesses? Then Geronimo Inc. might just solve all your problems!

Our unique training DVDs will empower your employees through teaching them a range of presentation skills, making them more likely to land those important deals. The material is delivered by Hollywood actor Ryan Minute, making them engaging and enjoyable. On average, businesses report a sales increase of 12% after using our product.

To place an order, please visit www.geronimo.org. If spending over $200, please e-mail our operations leader Dan (dan@geronimo.inc) to receive 15% off the purchase. Our delivery drivers will be standing by to get your order to you as soon as possible.

Geronimo Inc.

158. What is the purpose of the information?

(A) To promote some instructional DVDs
(B) To inform of delivery rates
(C) To announce a sales meeting
(D) To advertise a forthcoming movie

159. Who would most directly benefit from using Geronimo Inc. products?

(A) Business managers
(B) Seminar leaders
(C) Computer dealers
(D) Sales staff

160. What is mentioned about Geronimo Inc.?

(A) It is seeking to hire a new operations leader.
(B) It has reported its increased sales figures.
(C) It offers discounts to qualifying customers.
(D) It has a telephone ordering system.

Nicole Gannon [10:23 A.M.]
Thank you both for responding to my e-mail so quickly. You seemed to have some concerns, so I thought I'd address them here.

Denise Shulte [10:24 A.M.]
I was confused when you said you will be reassigning some of our team's work for creating logos.

Youngsik Park [10:26 A.M.]
Right. Will our current projects be interrupted?

Nicole Gannon [10:27 A.M.]
That depends on the project.

Denise Shulte [10:28 A.M.]
I'm currently working on some images for Bond Tech. Because of previous projects, I know their tastes, so I'd rather not give up this project.

Nicole Gannon [10:31 A.M.]
I understand that. But I've decided to assign high-profile accounts to the most experienced designers. That's why Youngsik will cover Bond Tech.

Youngsik Park [10:33 A.M.]
I may have more experience, but let's look at the bigger picture.

Nicole Gannon [10:34 A.M.]
What do you mean?

Youngsik Park [10:35 A.M.]
The representatives at Bond Tech would probably prefer to work with someone they're familiar with.

Nicole Gannon [10:36 A.M.]
You have a point.

Denise Shulte [10:38 A.M.]
In this case, how about I continue with the work and have Youngsik review it?

Nicole Gannon [10:41 A.M.]
I'm okay with that. I'll make some adjustments to the assignment list and send you a new one shortly.

161. Which department is Ms. Gannon most likely in charge of?

(A) Sales
(B) IT
(C) Graphic design
(D) Accounting

162. What is implied about Ms. Shulte?

(A) She has more experience than Mr. Park.
(B) She has worked with Bond Tech before.
(C) She did not respond to Ms. Gannon's e-mail.
(D) She cannot meet the deadline of a project.

163. At 10:33 A.M., what does Mr. Park mean when he writes, "let's look at the bigger picture"?

(A) He disagrees with a strategy.
(B) He requested working with a client.
(C) He thinks a company will grow.
(D) He wants to hold a meeting.

164. What will Ms. Gannon probably do next?

(A) Send a new contract
(B) Contact a Bond Tech representative
(C) Change some employee assignments
(D) Review Ms. Shulte's work

GO ON TO THE NEXT PAGE

Attack of the Drones to visit Spartsville

2 Dec.— — [1] —. New movie *Attack of the Drones* will be visiting Spartsville Movie Theater in order to provide fans with an opportunity to attend an advanced screening on the weekend of 19-20 December. This has been arranged by city mayor Russell Padrino as part of the city's bid to raise its artistic profile. The film will be released for general viewing the following week.

— [2] —. Each guest shall also be provided with a hot drink at no charge. All attendants shall receive a courtesy magazine, featuring images from the movie.

The film is scheduled to begin at 4 p.m. on Saturday, and 5 p.m. on Sunday. — [3] —. Furthermore, on Sunday, director Dan Scremington will be on hand to take questions from the audience about his film. This additional event will take place after the showing in Room E of the theater. — [4] —. To view the full timetable, and to enter the competition, please visit www. attackofthedrones.net.

165. What is the purpose of the article?

(A) To advertise a film screening
(B) To offer a magazine subscription
(C) To inform of a mayoral election
(D) To announce the opening of a convention center

166. What is indicated about Mr. Scremington?

(A) He is a billionaire.
(B) He is a competition winner.
(C) He visits Spartsville at least once a year.
(D) He will answer questions on December 20.

167. In which of the positions marked [1], [2], [3], and [4] does the following sentence best belong?

"The movie screening is free to all, and ticketing will be allocated on a first-come first-served basis."

(A) [1]
(B) [2]
(C) [3]
(D) [4]

Announcement: Trade Fair in Stockholm

Posted: February 22

Our senior management team is delighted to announce that staff at Readyflex Electronics will once again be travelling to Sweden for the Quantum Future trade fair next month. All managers are expected to organize and pay for their own room at The Chilview Hotel, which will be reimbursed by our company on the last day of the trade fair. We also require 6 members of our sales team to attend the event. Those wishing to volunteer for this opportunity must contact Mark Kennedy by February 26.

The trade fair itself is located in The Alexander White Building, and will be open 9 a.m.–5 p.m. every day between 20-24 March.

Our products will be on display as follows:
> Readyflex T500d model: Tuesday and Thursday, Quantum Main Hall; Stand B
> Advanced battery and memory card packs: Wednesday, Quantum Main Hall; Stand B
> Readyflex Bluejaw model: Friday, External Area C
> Innovations in Auto Body Repair: Thursday, Quantum Main Hall; Stand B

All of our prices for the trade fair have been reduced by 20% in order to attract first-time customers. Please make sure items are clearly marked with the offer price.

As per the terms of your contract, staff are not required to attend this event. However, those that do volunteer will be eligible for a $500 bonus to be added to their regular salary next month. Once again, please contact Mr. Kennedy if you wish to participate.

Leonard Schulz, Director
Readyflex Electronics Personnel Office

168. What is the purpose of the notice?
(A) To promote a particular chain of luxurious hotels
(B) To give details of the launch of a new product
(C) To advertise a managerial vacancy
(D) To provide information on a business trip abroad

169. What is NOT suggested about Readyflex Electronics?
(A) Its products will be displayed on every weekday.
(B) It has attended the Quantum Future trade fair before.
(C) Its items will be available for a discount.
(D) Its products will be displayed in more than one location.

170. When will accommodation reimbursement be issued?
(A) On February 22
(B) Before March 20
(C) On March 24
(D) Before February 26

171. According to the notice, why might staff be interested in attending the event?
(A) They will receive a financial reward.
(B) They will be eligible to receive a promotion.
(C) They will be tested on new procedures.
(D) They need to describe new products to customers.

GO ON TO THE NEXT PAGE

Antonio's Stationery

Claire Darras
Supervisor, Shawcross Services 193 Bridge Street
Chicago, IL

Nov 4

Dear Mrs. Darras,

I am writing to inform you that we at Antonio's are planning to make changes to the way we operate. — [1] —. As such, we now need to carry out much-needed expansion work on our storage warehouse. Once complete, we will be able to provide stationery services to a greater numbers of clients than we do presently. We assume that we will reopen on December 10.

— [2] —. Our business will be closed between November 14 and December 9, meaning your usual service will be temporarily cut off. On the reopening day, we will invite customers to visit our premises, where we will hold a celebratory barbecue. All clients attending will receive a coupon entitling them to 15% off their next purchase. We hope that as many people attend as possible.

— [3] —. We hope that you will be patient while we carry out these much-needed changes to our business. We truly appreciate the business of companies such as yours, which have standing orders to purchase goods each week. Furthermore, we pledge to offer you free delivery next year as our way of apologizing for the inconvenience. — [4] —.

If you have any queries with regard to the above information, please don't hesitate to get in touch. We are reachable by telephone at 555-3954-322. We look forward to resuming normal service and being able to serve your stationery needs.

Sincerely,

Antonio Cinelli

CEO, Antonio's Stationery

172. What is suggested about Antonio's Stationery?

(A) It will upgrade its delivery services.
(B) It will move to another place in March.
(C) It will soon serve more customers.
(D) It has a Web site.

173. The phrase "cut off" in paragraph 2, line 2, is closest in meaning to

(A) improved
(B) divided
(C) reduced
(D) discontinued

174. What is NOT indicated about Shawcross Services?

(A) It is located in Chicago.
(B) It regularly receives goods from Antonio's Stationery.
(C) It is an accountancy firm.
(D) It will be exempt from shipping costs next year.

175. In which of the positions marked [1], [2], [3], and [4] does the following sentence best belong?

"Since we opened in March this year, we have seen a steady increase in regular buyers."

(A) [1]
(B) [2]
(C) [3]
(D) [4]

GO ON TO THE NEXT PAGE

Questions 176-180 refer to the following e-mails.

```
●  ●  ●                          E-mail

From:        Tony Burrows <tburrows@supersaver.com>

To:          Lucy Vixen <lucyvixen3@guardian.net>

Date:        Monday, March 7 11:40 A.M.

Subject:     Business Partnership
```

Dear Ms. Vixen,

My co-workers and I enjoyed meeting you last Thursday (March 3). After further discussion among ourselves, we would like to inform you that we are excited by the prospect of stocking Guardian Inc. products in our megastore outlets. We would like to invite you back to our offices to arrange the terms of the contract. As I mentioned at the time, this meeting will be conducted by managing director Robert Ruins. He was also personally impressed by your range of make-up products, and feels they perfectly represent the spirit of stocking environmentally-friendly goods that we hold here at SuperSaver.

Are you available to come by our offices this Thursday (March 10)? If this does not work for you, Mr. Ruins has a gap in his schedule on Friday afternoon that it would be possible to hold discussions in. As you may imagine, his schedule becomes filled up extremely rapidly as the week progresses, so please let me know your preference as soon as possible. Alternatively, you may contact his personal assistant Tina Coggins directly at 555-292-5200 to arrange this. We look forward to further discussions.

Sincerely,
Tony Burrows
Product Decision Manager

From: Lucy Vixen <lucyvixen3@guardian.net>
To: Tony Burrows <tburrows@supersaver.com>
Date: Monday, March 7 4:00 P.M.
Re: Business partnership

Dear Mr. Burrows,

I was thrilled to read your e-mail expressing your willingness to stock our products in your stores. As you may imagine, this is a huge success for a small manufacturer such as ourselves. Regrettably, I have checked my diary and I have a business trip scheduled for the Thursday that you suggest. However, I would be able to meet with you on Friday and I am available any time after midday.

Furthermore, I spoke to my colleague Phil Satters about the prospect of producing some promotional materials as we discussed last week. He agreed that this would be extremely beneficial in promoting our goods to your customers.

I look forward to Friday.

Sincerely,
Lucy Vixen

176. What is the purpose of the first e-mail?

(A) To schedule a delivery
(B) To arrange a meeting
(C) To place an order
(D) To provide some directions

177. What type of products does Guardian Inc. most likely manufacture?

(A) Electronics
(B) Cosmetics
(C) Kitchenware
(D) Office supplies

178. According to the first e-mail, why does Mr. Burrows want to arrange a meeting with Ms. Vixen?

(A) To discuss product details
(B) To make a complaint
(C) To negotiate a contract
(D) To produce an advertising campaign

179. When is Ms. Vixen expecting to be on a business trip?

(A) On March 3
(B) On March 7
(C) On March 10
(D) On March 11

180. Who is NOT an employee of SuperSaver Inc.?

(A) Mr. Ruins
(B) Mr. Burrows
(C) Ms. Coggins
(D) Mr. Satters

GO ON TO THE NEXT PAGE

Kingsville Business Weekly

On June 14, two-weeks before the week-long closure of the city's airport for planned expansion work, the Kingsville Association of Businesses (KAB) published a brochure entitled *Keep Your Business Flying*. This brochure was produced to provide local firms with strategies for mitigating the impact to normal business operations during the scheduled closure. The brochure was delivered to all KAB-registered businesses directly, and the demand from other businesses was so great that extra copies needed to be printed.

The KAB is currently modifying its initial publication to produce a new version. This is in light of the city council's recent announcement affecting further work to the area's infrastructure, with a month-long closure of High Road planned for essential maintenance work.

The new version, which the association hopes to release at the start of September, will feature a foreword penned by a business owner who was forced to take steps to deal with the airport closure. In order to cut back on expensive printing costs, an online-only version of this brochure will be released.

KAB is currently soliciting opinions from other companies which were impacted by the previous disruptions. Store owners prepared to give an interview are asked to get in touch with Marcus Holmes. He can be contacted by telephone at 555-3934-3178, or by email at marcusholmes@kab.gov.com.

Keep Your Business Flying (Second Edition)
Foreword

Due to the large number of orders taken through our Web site, we at Ryan Clothing rely on long-distance transportation for shipping a lot of our products around the country, with 60% of our business passing through Kingsville Airport. As such, we assumed that we would incur a huge loss of income when it was announced that the airport was closed for a whole week. That was until the brochure from KAB landed on my doorstep. It contained a lot of useful, practical tips, such as how to make use of the country's extensive rail network during this time. While the airport ended up being closed for three weeks, we only saw a 20% downturn in sales, compared to the 60% that our accountants had forecasted. KAB deserves a lot of credit for this, as their tips allowed us to minimize the disruption to our business.

As well as similar tips in minimizing disruption to your business, this new brochure features accounts from CEOs detailing how they coped with the airport work taking more time than anticipated. I urge you to reap the benefit of their experience to help you through this disruptive period.

Ryan Waynefield

181. What is mentioned about KAB's publication in the article?

(A) It was designed two weeks ago.
(B) It was distributed at a charge.
(C) It was extremely popular.
(D) It was written by only one author.

182. Why would a company's representative probably get in touch with a KAB official?

(A) To protest the airport closure
(B) To apply for a job
(C) To purchase a copy of a book
(D) To offer their views

183. In the foreword, the word "credit" in paragraph 1, line 8, is closest in meaning to

(A) donations
(B) interviews
(C) power
(D) recognition

184. What is NOT indicated about Ryan Clothing?

(A) It experienced some reduced profits.
(B) It is owned by Waynefield.
(C) It excluded trains when delivering goods.
(D) It receives online orders.

185. What is suggested about the airport closure?

(A) It was beneficial to Ryan Clothing.
(B) It caused many businesses to go bankrupt.
(C) It was closed for longer than planned.
(D) It was harmful to the city's tourism industry.

GO ON TO THE NEXT PAGE

Berkshire Film Festival
Timeless Films for All Ages

The Berkshire Artists Association is sponsoring the area's first ever film festival at the Cessna Theater from Tuesday, May 12, to Friday, May 15. Each evening during the festival, audience members will be able to enjoy a different classic film. All films begin at 7 P.M., and tickets can be purchased from the Cessna Theater box office and various venues around town. Buy five or more tickets for any given film, and you will get 10% off.

Schedule of Showings:
    May 12: *The Journey to New Orleans*
    May 13: *Mystery of Silver Cave*
    May 14: *Susanne's Dream*
    May 15: *Train in the Night*

To: Conrad Varga <c.varga@npinbox.com>
From: William Riggs <riggsw@trujilloinc.com>
CC: Annie Lockwood <lockwooda@trujilloinc.com>
Date: May 2
Subject: Upcoming Visit

Dear Mr. Varga,

I'm pleased that you will be able to come to the Trujillo Inc. branch in Berkshire. The members of the hiring committee were impressed with your responses to the phone-based questions, and we look forward to interviewing you in person. We have divided our prospective employees into Group A and Group B, and those groups will have visits to the branch on May 13 and 14, respectively. You have been assigned to Group A. After the day's activities, the group members will attend the local film festival. It's our way of showing our appreciation. Please let me know if you have any questions.

Warmest regards,

William Riggs

To: Annie Lockwood 397-555-1695
From: William Riggs 397-555-7940

Due to a train scheduling error, Conrad Varga has to move to Group B. We don't have to change anything with the tickets because Amelia Raff is moving to Group A. So, I can still get the bulk discount for both groups' tickets. Please be sure to have all of the visitor passes ready for everyone when they come. I've e-mailed you a photo of each visitor to include on the pass. Thanks!

186. What is mentioned about the Berkshire Film Festival?

(A) It has been sponsored by the city.
(B) It is being held for the first time.
(C) It is intended for adults only.
(D) It will have two showings per day.

187. What is the purpose of Mr. Varga's visit to Trujillo Inc.?

(A) To perform an inspection
(B) To conduct a training session
(C) To attend an interview
(D) To negotiate a sale

188. Which film was Mr. Varga originally supposed to see?

(A) *The Journey to New Orleans*
(B) *Mystery of Silver Cave*
(C) *Susanne's Dream*
(D) *Train in the Night*

189. What does Mr. Riggs ask Ms. Lockwood to do?

(A) Prepare ID badges
(B) Buy another festival ticket
(C) Make a meal reservation
(D) Confirm a guest list

190. What is suggested about Mr. Riggs?

(A) He will meet some visitors at a train station.
(B) He is a member of the Berkshire Artists Association.
(C) He has met Ms. Raff in person before.
(D) He will purchase at least ten tickets.

GO ON TO THE NEXT PAGE

Questions 191-195 refer to the following Web page and e-mails.

---

www.weddingbliss.net

Wedding Bliss
We provide big help for your big day!

HOME	SERVICES	PHOTO GALLERY	TESTIMONIALS	CONTACT

Planning a wedding is a time of excitement and joy, but it can also be stressful. Hire Wedding Bliss and enjoy any or all of the services below:

– Elegant flowers and decorations to complement your selected colors
– Pianist or organist to provide music throughout the ceremony
– DJ for dinner and reception
– Valet parking for guests
– Professional photographer to capture your memories
– A wide selection of catering options

We have sites in the Columbia Building (288 Chapman Lane) and in the Ritter Complex (1434 Jefferson Street), and we also assist with off-site weddings. We work with you every step of the way to make sure everything is just the way you want it. Click here to contact one of our experienced event planning professionals today.

---

e-mail

To: Alysa Frederick <fredericka@whitleyinc.com>
From: Jennifer Morton <j_morton@garlandsales.com>
Date: September 14
Subject: Wedding Bliss

Dear Ms. Frederick,

I am currently in the process of planning my wedding, and I'm considering hiring Wedding Bliss. The company provided some references, but I wanted to check with someone independently. I work at the Jackson Center, and an accountant at my office, Daniel Crawford, gave your contact information to me. He said you used Wedding Bliss's services in April. I'm wondering if you could tell me about your experience, and whether you used a Wedding Bliss venue or another site. Were there enough choices provided by the caterer? Also, how was the pianist who performed during the ceremony? Any information you could give me would be greatly appreciated.

Thank you!

Jennifer

To: Jennifer Morton <j_morton@garlandsales.com>

From: Alysa Frederick <fredericka@whitleyinc.com>

Date: September 14

Subject: RE: Wedding Bliss

Dear Ms. Morton,

I'm glad you got in touch with me. I know how overwhelming wedding planning can be, so it's my pleasure to help. Overall, I was very pleased with Wedding Bliss' services. Originally, we wanted to use the services off site, at Villa Hall, but it was booked for the day we wanted. We decided to use Wedding Bliss' facility on Jefferson Street, as the one on Chapman Lane wasn't open yet at that time. We had about 300 guests and many of them were vegetarians. The dishes offered by the caterer were diverse enough to accommodate all of our guests' tastes. I also loved the decorations prepared by the Wedding Bliss staff. They were festive yet elegant, and they captured my style perfectly.

Because an event like this is so personal, I suggest making an appointment with one of their consultants. You can do this for free, and it will help you to see exactly what they have to offer.

Best of luck!

Alysa

191. What is stated about Wedding Bliss?

(A) Its decorations are set up the day before the event.

(B) It provides a piano player for the dinner.

(C) It offers a photo-taking service.

(D) Its services must all be used together.

192. Where did Ms. Morton get Ms. Frederick's e-mail address?

(A) From the Wedding Bliss Web site

(B) From a relative

(C) From a Wedding Bliss representative

(D) From her coworker

193. What did Ms. Morton ask about that was NOT addressed by Ms. Frederick?

(A) Decorations

(B) Pricing

(C) Menu options

(D) A musician

194. What advice does Ms. Frederick give?

(A) Negotiating an offer

(B) Setting up a consultation

(C) Requesting a free catalog

(D) Using an off-site facility

195. Where is Wedding Bliss' newest facility?

(A) Columbia Building

(B) Jackson Center

(C) Ritter Complex

(D) Villa Hall

GO ON TO THE NEXT PAGE

Questions 196-200 refer to the following information, online forum, and message.

Standing Desks and Accessories by Lloyd Designs

Research shows that sitting for long periods of time can be harmful to the body. A standing desk by Lloyd Designs is the perfect solution. Desks can be adjusted to suit most people, and we have the accessories you need to create the perfect workspace.

– Standing Desk   32"x52" work surface with a height range of 24"–50". Available in black, white, and gray. Price: $499 / Model: G284

– Adjustable Stool   Cushioned stool covered in black leather with a height range of 22"–36". Price: $149 / Model: T175

– Monitor Arm   The easiest way to position your screen perfectly. Holds up to 20 pounds. Gray design with black trim. Price: $99 / Model: W422

– Standing Mat   Soft surface to help prevent fatigue while standing. Features a non-slip textured surface. Available in black. Price: $29 / Model: K398

Order online at lloyddesigns.com.

---

http://www.realfeedbackforum.com

Company: Lloyd Designs   Thread opened: January 8

Fabian Roscoe   Posted 51 minutes ago

I purchased the Lloyd Designs standing desk for my home office, and overall I am pleased with the results. Adding this desk to my workspace has significantly reduced the back pain I suffer from. I like the ability to sit and stand throughout the day and work in several positions. Standing has also helped me to strengthen my leg muscles and improve my balance.

While I highly recommend the desk, I can't say the same for the accessories. I do have some concerns about model T175. It is a compact size, but it doesn't seem strong enough to hold an adult. I also purchased model K398, but it left black marks on the floor.

---

http://www.realfeedbackforum.com

Private Message   To: Fabian Roscoe   From: Lloyd Designs

Dear Mr. Roscoe,

I am a customer service representative of Lloyd Designs. We are glad that you are pleased with our standing desk, and we appreciate your kind comments. Regarding our accessory leaving marks, you are not the only customer to have this problem. We have recalled that item for the very reason you described. We are now using a new material, and I would be happy to ship a free replacement to you. Please send me back a private message with your e-mail address, and I will e-mail you the necessary form to get a free replacement. As for your concerns about model T175, I want to assure you that it has been thoroughly tested in our laboratory and can withstand more than 350 pounds of weight.

Sincerely,

Kevin Siegel, Lloyd Designs

196. What does Mr. Roscoe mention about his desk?

(A) It has a sophisticated design.
(B) Using it has resulted in pain relief.
(C) It comes in a compact size.
(D) Assembling it was easy to do.

197. In the online forum, the word "balance" in paragraph 1, line 5, is closest in meaning to

(A) remainder
(B) steadiness
(C) productivity
(D) harmony

198. What does Mr. Siegel offer to send to Mr. Roscoe?

(A) A discount voucher
(B) A monitor arm
(C) A standing mat
(D) A product catalog

199. What is Mr. Roscoe asked to do?

(A) Return an item by mail
(B) E-mail a picture of some damage
(C) Respond to the private message
(D) Provide a phone number

200. What is probably true about the Lloyd Designs stool?

(A) Its material has been changed.
(B) It has been recalled.
(C) It comes in different colors.
(D) It is very durable.

This is the end of the test. You may review PART 5, 6, and 7 if you finish the test early.

정답 p. 320 / 점수 환산표 p. 321 / 해석 p. 384

TEST

PART 5
PART 6
PART 7

토익 Reading Comprehension은 75분 동안 진행됩니다.
현재 시각과 지금부터 75분 후인 테스트 종료 시각을 기록해 두고,
반드시 종료 시각 전에 문제 풀이와 답안지 마킹을 완료하세요.

현재 시각 시 　 분

테스트 종료 시각  시 　 분

In the Reading test, you will read a variety of texts and answer several different types of reading comprehension questions. The entire Reading test will last 75 minutes. There are three parts, and directions are given for each part. You are encouraged to answer as many questions as possible within the time allowed.

You must mark your answers on the separate answer sheet. Do not write your answers in your test book.

PART 5

Directions: A word or phrase is missing in each of the sentences below. Four answer choices are given below each sentence. Select the best answer to complete the sentence. Then mark the letter (A), (B), (C), or (D) on your answer sheet.

101. New ------- should fax a copy of their bankbooks so that the finance department can set up the monthly salary payment.

(A) employed
(B) employees
(C) employer
(D) employment

102. ------- a certified valuation of the property when applying for a home mortgage with our financial institution.

(A) Included
(B) Including
(C) Include
(D) Includes

103. The registration documents for the trade expo have been filed ------- in a secure location in Ms. Grayson's office.

(A) numeral
(B) numerically
(C) numerals
(D) numerical

104. The mail room staff members at the Helena Building usually deliver packages and letters about thirty minutes after receiving -------.

(A) this
(B) it
(C) him
(D) them

105. The countertop and appliances in the kitchen need to be replaced, but the light ------- is still in fine condition.

(A) mark
(B) fixture
(C) design
(D) barrier

106. By negotiating with co-founder Samuel Lars upon his retirement, Gail Hendricks was able to gain a(n) ------- share of the company.

(A) significant
(B) extended
(C) virtual
(D) cooperative

107. ------- efforts to fulfill the terms of the agreement on time, not enough products were shipped from the facility by the end of February.

(A) Neither
(B) Despite
(C) Unless
(D) Though

108. Customer service employees are always working hard to ------- that each Mariana Resort guest experiences the highest level of comfort and convenience.

(A) notice
(B) consent
(C) ensure
(D) inform

109. Though ------- believed the museum was being too ambitious, it managed to acquire a world-class collection of art in just five years.

(A) any
(B) herself
(C) many
(D) both

110. Company CEO Hu Chang implemented a plan that requires extensive collaborations ------- the various departments.

(A) among
(B) besides
(C) pertaining to
(D) before

111. Every passenger using Seaside Express must purchase a ticket with a valid credit card and ------- the receipt in case a refund or exchange is requested.

(A) retained
(B) retain
(C) retaining
(D) to retain

112. The flexibility to work weekends, nights and some overtime is a ------- for the secretarial position at Fremont City Hospital.

(A) requirement
(B) reservation
(C) registration
(D) replacement

113. Jules Electronics Inc. is ------- that its new tablet prototype will be refined and on the market before the holiday season.

(A) hopeful
(B) probable
(C) powerful
(D) cautious

114. The engineer team was having difficulty solving the weight problem regarding the bridge ------- Hamilcar Moreno came up with a useful solution.

(A) unless
(B) as though
(C) because
(D) until

115. Award-winning writer Jeremy Keith has published 12 novels, several of ------- were best-sellers for many years.

(A) whose
(B) this
(C) which
(D) other

116. The cost of Ralling Internet and phone services has increased ------- $10 a month.

(A) between
(B) at
(C) onto
(D) by

117. Beginning next year, residents in the Chula Vista area ------- their utility bills electronically rather than by mail.

(A) has received
(B) will receive
(C) receiving
(D) will be received

118. The solar power system has been designed ------- to meet the demand of local hotels.

(A) specifically
(B) specific
(C) specifies
(D) specify

119. Although the hours of operation change based on the season, the state's parks and recreation centers are open ------- the year.

(A) throughout
(B) since
(C) on
(D) under

120. After researching alternatives, it has been determined that installing new air conditioning units is the ------- of all solutions available in the foreseeable future.

(A) cheaply
(B) cheapness
(C) cheapen
(D) cheapest

GO ON TO THE NEXT PAGE

121. After a long delay, the budget proposal for the new building construction project was ------- approved by the board of directors.

(A) exactly
(B) totally
(C) finally
(D) currently

122. The marketing department is scheduled ------- its strategic plan to increase the company's name recognition in the coming months.

(A) to outline
(B) outlining
(C) to outlining
(D) has outlined

123. Samples of our delicious ice cream flavors are available ------- request to any of our store visitors.

(A) upon
(B) about
(C) for
(D) behind

124. Due to the efforts of dedicated employees, the deadline for submitting the financial aid requests has been -------.

(A) meet
(B) meets
(C) met
(D) meeting

125. ------- Total Catering Services expands its family restaurant business into South America depends on the company's ability to utilize money and workforce.

(A) Whatever
(B) Despite
(C) Whether
(D) Nearby

126. All meals served in public school cafeterias must ------- with government nutritional requirements.

(A) observe
(B) comply
(C) adhere
(D) conform

127. Newcomers are permitted to take part in the annual seminar ------- they pay the registration fee in advance.

(A) whether
(B) so that
(C) as long as
(D) due to

128. The real estate prices in the Henderson area ------- in the quarterly report have been compiled from information gathered by local agents.

(A) will quote
(B) are quoted
(C) quoted
(D) quoting

129. A company vice president will ------- the appointment of Mark Poe as the new chairperson of Kit Foods.

(A) inform
(B) earn
(C) announce
(D) interfere

130. Hullet Laboratory is well known for winning many ------- research awards for its work in developing low-cost pharmaceutical products.

(A) successful
(B) prestigious
(C) alternative
(D) reluctant

PART 6

Directions: Read the texts that follow. A word, phrase, or sentence is missing in parts of each text. Four answer choices for each question are given below the text. Select the best answer to complete the text. Then mark the letter (A), (B), (C), or (D) on your answer sheet.

Questions 131-134 refer to the following notice.

Welcome to Dilantin Windows and Doors! Since we were ------- 35 years ago, our engineers have
                                                          131.

been designing the best-made windows and doors in the industry. Our highest objective is to make

certain that each product ------- our logo functions in accordance with brand standards.
                           132.

-------. Our employees consider every customer suggestion as though it were from one of our very
133.

own product inspectors.

We hope to provide our customers with the quality products and services. -------, we invite you to
                                                                          134.

participate in a real-time chat session with one of our representatives. He or she will be happy to

answer any questions you may have regarding our products.

131. (A) related
     (B) founded
     (C) conducted
     (D) indicated

132. (A) carries
     (B) carried
     (C) has carried
     (D) carrying

133. (A) We are listed among the top 10 popular
         companies.
     (B) Our products are inspected every three
         months.
     (C) We are willing to hear from our customers.
     (D) However, employee satisfaction is very
         important.

134. (A) For instance
     (B) Interestingly
     (C) Afterward
     (D) To that end

GO ON TO THE NEXT PAGE

Questions 135-138 refer to the following notice.

Dear Santorini Bank Employees,

-------. The specialists in the department will ensure each system ------- as it is intended.
135.   **136.**

Specifically, if any issue does come to your attention, a report can be completed at santorinibank.

itservices.com. Be sure to specify your contact information, which computer you were using, and a

description of the -------.
137.

Also, it is advised to provide all possible details in order to facilitate the repair process.

Kindly note that IT Services may at times require more than 24 hours to completely analyze

problems and react -------.
138.

Thank you for your cooperation and patience.

---

135. (A) A banking conference for all departments
will be held in October.
(B) In case of any problems, please contact
IT Services.
(C) Please turn off computers and monitors
when leaving the office.
(D) We have recently launched a new system
for our valued customers like yourself.

136. (A) workable
(B) to work
(C) is working
(D) worked

137. (A) arrangement
(B) publication
(C) account
(D) problem

138. (A) frequently
(B) accordingly
(C) collectively
(D) regularly

From: jhill@westernwaterplant.gov
To: heather.kim@uod.edu
Date: 22 April
Subject: Re: Soil usage

Dear Ms. Kim,

Thank you for the e-mail in which you suggested we make use of the soil ------- when purifying the
139.
city's water supply by marketing it as fertilizer for local farms and gardens.

After careful consideration, our management team believes this is a very ------- alternative to our
140.
previous methods of waste disposal. A committee has already been formed to establish the most

cost-effective marketing and distribution methods.

------- matter is very important to us and we appreciate your taking the time to write us.
141.

We wish you the best in your studies at the University of Dranton. -------. Your initiative and
142.
innovation would be highly valued at Western Water.

Sincerely,

Joe Hill
Western Water Plant
Director

139. (A) are removed
(B) to remove
(C) removing
(D) removed

140. (A) visible
(B) abbreviated
(C) able
(D) practical

141. (A) This
(B) Their
(C) Our
(D) Her

142. (A) I am certain that you will succeed in your
new position as a manager.
(B) Consider applying for our student
internship during the summer.
(C) In addition, we would like to inform you of
our new fertilizing system.
(D) The university is located in the East
Waterloo district.

Questions 143-146 refer to the following notice.

Attention All Passengers:

During the month of March, the subway system will be undergoing a variety of changes, necessitating a modified train schedule. Such changes will include the modernization of passenger cars and train depot renovation.

We plan to have this ------- completed before March 25.
                           143.

The temporary timetable, which will be ------- beginning March 2, will be available through the public
                                              144.
transit smartphone application. -------.
                              145.

All updates regarding this project ------- on the Public Transit Authority Web site(PTA.gov/
                                   146.
CloverCity). Questions can be directed to subway@ccpta.gov. Type "March renovations" in the subject line.

Best regards,

Samuel Lee
Clover City Public Transit Authority

---

143. (A) event
(B) simulation
(C) process
(D) analysis

144. (A) out of date
(B) in effect
(C) on the contrary
(D) in particular

145. (A) The renovation project has been approved by the city council.
(B) The alternative schedule is meant to reduce inconveniences.
(C) Free subway passes will be provided to passengers for a limited time.
(D) Passengers are advised to avoid using the subway if possible.

146. (A) to post
(B) had posted
(C) were being posted
(D) will be posted

Directions: In this part you will read a selection of texts, such as magazine and newspaper articles, e-mails, and instant messages. Each text or set of texts is followed by several questions. Select the best answer for each question and mark the letter (A), (B), (C), or (D) on your answer sheet.

Questions 147-148 refer to the following notice.

For Your Convenience

We have a few heated blankets that our guests may borrow. You may request to have one placed in your room when you make your reservation. You may also speak with the person working at the front desk to borrow appliances such as coffee makers and blenders, which are available on a first-come, first-served basis.

Those individuals bringing electric razors or other small appliances from foreign countries should be sure to request a voltage converter as their item will almost surely require one. Simply call the front desk, and it will be brought to your room immediately.

147. Where would this notice most likely be found?

(A) In a hotel
(B) At a hair salon
(C) At a supermarket
(D) In an electronics store

148. What items can readers NOT request?

(A) Coffee makers
(B) Blenders
(C) Electric razors
(D) Voltage converters

Questions 149-150 refer to the following text message chain.

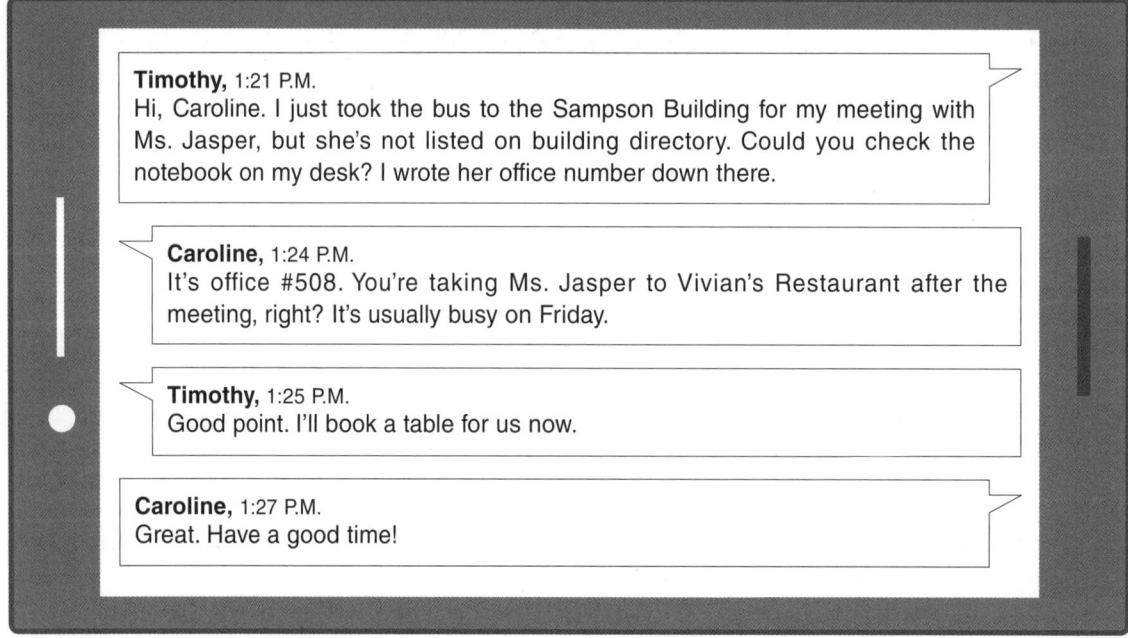

Timothy, 1:21 P.M.
Hi, Caroline. I just took the bus to the Sampson Building for my meeting with Ms. Jasper, but she's not listed on building directory. Could you check the notebook on my desk? I wrote her office number down there.

Caroline, 1:24 P.M.
It's office #508. You're taking Ms. Jasper to Vivian's Restaurant after the meeting, right? It's usually busy on Friday.

Timothy, 1:25 P.M.
Good point. I'll book a table for us now.

Caroline, 1:27 P.M.
Great. Have a good time!

149. Where is Caroline when she writes to Timothy?

(A) At a restaurant
(B) On the bus
(C) At the Sampson Building
(D) At his office

150. At 1:24 P.M., what does Caroline most likely mean when she writes, "It's usually busy on Friday"?

(A) Ms. Jasper will probably be late.
(B) A dinner reservation should be made.
(C) Timothy might get stuck in traffic.
(D) She was not able to make an appointment.

Guest Statement

Guest Name: Jacob Irwin
Company: T.Y. Saks
Address: 45 Robinson Road, Des Moines, IA

Reservation Code: 459-549MV
Reservation Date: April 11

Arrival Date: April 20
Departure Date: April 22

Number of Guests: 1 Adult
Room Type: Deluxe

Date	Description	Amount	Notes
April 20	Deluxe Room	$150.00	
April 20	Room Service (Dinner)	$42.99	
April 21	Deluxe Room	$150.00	
April 21	Room Service (Lunch)	$18.00	
April 21	International Telephone Call	$12.75	10-minute call
April 22	Room Service (Breakfast)	$22.00	

Sub-Total $395.74
Tax $27.29
Total $423.03
Amount Paid $423.03
Amount Owed $0.00

Rudolph Hotel
45 Baker Street, Seattle, Washington

Payer: T.Y. Saks
Credit Card Number: ****9804

Thank you for staying at the Rudolph Hotel. We hope you come again.

151. When did Mr. Irwin check out the Rudolph Hotel?

(A) On April 11
(B) On April 20
(C) On April 21
(D) On April 22

152. What is indicated on the receipt?

(A) Mr. Irwin ordered dinner in his room everyday.
(B) The entire hotel bill was not paid.
(C) The hotel Mr. Irwin stayed at is located in Des Moines.
(D) Mr. Irwin's employer paid for his stay.

TEST 09

GO ON TO THE NEXT PAGE

Cousteau Pro Pool Care

Crestville's most trusted pool care provider for over 30 years!

The weather is getting warmer and now is the time to get your pool ready for summer! For the month of May only, Cousteau Pro Pool Care is offering a special price on our "Season Starter" equipment inspection and pool opening package. Whether you schedule the "Season Starter" online or by phone, simply provide the discount code MAY16 to receive $50 off the regular price. Our technicians are professionally trained, and we guarantee that they will have your pool clean and ready for use within two days.

After your pool is open, keep it sparkling clean all summer long with one of our weekly maintenance packages. We also offer certified safety inspections and affordably priced repairs for both private and commercial swimming pools. Call Cousteau Pro Pool Care at (314) 555-1212 or visit our Web site at cousteauppc. com.

153. What is indicated about the company?

(A) It offers training for new employees.
(B) It is an established business.
(C) It is a service for public pools.
(D) It is having a sale for its anniversary.

154. What does the company promise with its "Season Starter" package?

(A) Fast results
(B) Free repairs
(C) Safety classes
(D) Swimming lessons

Great Harvest Bank
2300 Windsor Street
Atlanta, Georgia

October 5

Peter Oh
2511 Amberidge Trail
Unit 3
Sandy Springs, GA 30319

We at Great Harvest Bank are honored that you have chosen us to safeguard your financial future. Your membership in our bank is highly valued and the security of your personal information is one of our highest priorities. Effective November 1, our online services will be requiring a code to verify your identity at each login.

To establish this code, you will receive an automated telephone call to the phone number on our file, xxx-xxx-0693. The system will prompt you to enter a six-digit number which you will use when logging into your account. If you have questions or prefer to establish the code with a live person, call 800-232-5242 to speak with a Great Harvest Bank representative.

Best regards,

Jenny Kim
Great Harvest Bank

155. What is the reason for this letter?

(A) Mr. Oh has established membership at Great Harvest Bank.
(B) A security breach has recently occurred.
(C) A change in the current login system has been made.
(D) A new online account is ready to function.

156. What is mentioned about establishing the code?

(A) It is replacing an existing code.
(B) All members need to log into their accounts to do it.
(C) Mr. Oh can choose whether to use a code or not.
(D) It can be done by talking to bank personnel.

157. The word "prompt" in paragraph 2, line 2, is closest in meaning to

(A) persuade
(B) lead
(C) halt
(D) activate

GO ON TO THE NEXT PAGE

Questions 158-160 refer to the following letter.

Trenton Courier
67 Fairmont Drive
Vancouver, Canada

Bill Hamilton
Hamilton Consulting 309 W. Pacific Avenue
Vancouver, Canada

Dear Mr. Hamilton,

We at Trenton Courier appreciate the fact that we have been business partners for more than five years. — [1] —. We take great pleasure in providing you and your company with speedy overnight service everywhere in Canada and the United States. — [2] —. Trenton Courier has a spotless record when it comes to transporting important packages quickly and at the lowest rates. — [3] —. We would like you to know that we have expanded the services that our company provides. — [4] —.

* We now provide next-day airmail service to every country in Europe.
* We now provide three-day airmail service to every country in Asia and South America.
* We now provide custom shipping of large objects (up to 2 tons), such as pianos, to anywhere in Canada and the United States.

To find out more about these new services and to learn about our pricing schemes, call us anytime.

Sincerely,

Russell Peterson
Owner, Trenton Courier

158. Why was the letter written?

(A) To offer a discount to a business partner
(B) To mention where new offices will be opened
(C) To provide information about new services
(D) To advertise positions available in other countries

159. What is indicated about Trenton Courier?

(A) It has reduced its rates to selected customers.
(B) It offers transport of oversized packages.
(C) It is moving its headquarters to the United States.
(D) It has employees that can speak various Asian languages.

160. In which of the positions marked [1], [2], [3], and [4] does the following sentence best belong?

"Here is what we have done:"

(A) [1]
(B) [2]
(C) [3]
(D) [4]

Questions 161-163 refer to the following advertisement.

All of the residents of Springwater are invited to attend a unique event this Saturday. The Springwater Community Center is finally ready to open. After more than two years of construction, the community center is now complete. It has several outdoor facilities, including tennis courts, a jogging track, a park, and a swimming pool. Also, there are many indoor facilities, such as a basketball court and an aerobics area, and several rooms for language and arts classes.

Visitors to the community center will be given a tour of the entire area, which covers more than twenty acres. They will learn about the benefits of becoming a member of the center. And they will learn about all of the classes and the sporting events that will be provided exclusively for members. Staff members of the center will be on hand to answer any questions.

This center is located at 90 Valley Road in the Golden Fields neighborhood of Springwater. Visitors are welcome to come anytime on Saturday between the hours of 9 A.M. and 6 P.M. Anyone who cannot attend the opening event can feel free to check out the Web site at www.springwatercommunitycenter.org. Information regarding the fees for the membership can be found online or can be discussed with a staff member at the center itself.

161. What event is being held at 90 Valley Road?

(A) A seminar on the classes being offered to residents
(B) A meeting regarding the building of a new facility
(C) An introduction to new public amenities
(D) A presentation about getting involved in the local community

162. What is indicated about the Springwater Community Center?

(A) It exceeded its budget during the construction process.
(B) People can take part in various activities there.
(C) Only members may use the center's outdoor facilities.
(D) It is offering a special discount on membership this weekend.

163. What is provided on the Website?

(A) Information on paying for a service
(B) Pictures of the community center
(C) A list of the names of the staff members
(D) All of the classes being offered next month

Chapman Manufacturing to Upgrade Facilities

AUGUSTA (June 12)—Chapman Manufacturing, one of the largest manufacturers of electronic appliances in the United States, announced that it is going to upgrade the facilities at its factory in Augusta. "We just signed a couple of new deals with corporations in Spain and Japan. — [1] —." said company president Gerald Powell. "We need to increase the production while simultaneously keeping our labor force the same size."

Mr. Powell said that the assembly lines in the company's factory will be improved by adding state-of-the-art machinery to them. — [2] —. As a result, the efficiency of the workers is expected to improve by up to 40%. The machines that will be installed are manufactured by Deco, Inc.

Mr. Powell mentioned that Chapman Manufacturing has no intentions of reducing the company's workforce. — [3] —. "We are anticipating getting several more contracts this year," he stated at a press conference. "And we have no intentions of letting any of our workers go as it would be foolish for us to let any of our competitors get their hands on such highly trained individuals."

He added that most of the employees will have to be trained to use the new machinery. Chapman Manufacturing is going to have seminars and training sessions on the machinery led by engineers from Deco. Mr. Mastroeni is one of the workers who anticipates getting trained. — [4] —. "I'm looking forward to learning how to do my job better and faster," he said. "And it will be great to acquire new skills as well."

164. What is NOT mentioned as a reason that Chapman Manufacturing is going to upgrade its machinery?

(A) Chapman Manufacturing does not want to hire more workers.
(B) Chapman Manufacturing has gotten more business overseas.
(C) The machinery will let the employees do their jobs better.
(D) The competitors of Chapman Manufacturing are purchasing new machinery.

165. According to Mr. Powell, what will some of the workforce at Chapman Manufacturing do?

(A) Transfer to facilities in other countries
(B) Receive guidance on improving their skills
(C) Look for a new job in the same field
(D) Get promoted and receive pay raises

166. What type of work does Mr. Mastroeni currently do?

(A) He creates new designs for better machinery.
(B) He operates machinery on the assembly line.
(C) He manages the employees of the factory.
(D) He receives training for the new machinery.

167. In which of the positions marked [1], [2], [3], and [4] does the following sentence best belong?

"That will enable the workers to accomplish their duties much more quickly and more accurately than before."

(A) [1]
(B) [2]
(C) [3]
(D) [4]

Acrex Customer Service Online Help Desk

Representative James Turner 9:42 A.M.
Good morning. I'm James from the Acrex Customer Service team. How can I help you today?

Charlotte Farrell 9:43 A.M.
I purchased your Book Tracker 230 software program and downloaded it from your Web site. However, I'm not able to sign in.

Representative James Turner 9:44 A.M.
I can help you with that. First, go to the sign-in page. Your username should appear automatically according to the name you used for the purchase.

Charlotte Farrell 9:46 A.M.
I'm looking at the sign-in page now. It has the username cfarrell.

Representative James Turner 9:47 A.M.
All right. Now, type in the password you selected when you set up the software.

Charlotte Farrell 9:48 A.M.
It's my first time using it.

Representative James Turner 9:50 A.M.
I see. Then, instead of using your own password, you need to use the initial password that was generated by our company. It's a twelve-character string of letters and numbers.

Charlotte Farrell 9:51 A.M.
Where would I find that?

Representative James Turner 9:52 A.M.
You should have been sent an e-mail with your purchase receipt, and then another one—the welcome e-mail—with that twelve-character string.

Charlotte Farrell 9:53 A.M.
I only received the receipt. Let me check my Spam folder.

Charlotte Farrell 9:56 A.M.
It's not there.

Representative James Turner 9:57 A.M.
That's no problem. I can issue you a new one by e-mail. It'll take a few minutes.

Charlotte Farrell 9:59 A.M.
Thank you.

Representative James Turner 10:00 A.M.
Please stay in the chat to let me know that you got it.

Charlotte Farrell 10:01 A.M.
Okay, I will.

168. Why does Ms. Farrell need assistance?

(A) She was not sent the software she purchased.
(B) She downloaded the wrong program.
(C) She deleted some necessary data.
(D) She cannot access a software program.

169. At 9:48 A.M., what does Ms. Farrell most likely mean when she writes, "It's my first time using it"?

(A) She needs to restart her computer.
(B) She didn't create a password.
(C) She doesn't know her username.
(D) She cannot find a sign-in page.

170. What does Mr. Turner suggest about the welcome e-mail?

(A) It has instructions for changing the username.
(B) It will take a few days to arrive.
(C) It was sent separately from the receipt.
(D) It confirms the purchase price.

171. Why is Ms. Farrell asked to stay in the chat?

(A) To confirm receipt of an e-mail
(B) To receive some warranty information
(C) To download another product
(D) To get a more detailed explanation

GO ON TO THE NEXT PAGE

Standish Metals, Inc.
2020 Watson Road
Dublin

October 17

Daniel Hampton
Manager, Hampton's Place
209 Burlington Avenue
Dublin

Dear Mr. Hampton,

I am writing this letter to thank you for hosting the award banquet for one of my colleagues on Friday, October 12. While I had never had the pleasure of frequenting your establishment, it is one of the favorite spots of Mr. Roy Capers, who was being honored that night. I really enjoyed the food there so much that I intend to visit your business sometime soon in the presence of my wife and some of our friends.

Of particular note was the degree of professionalism displayed by everyone on your staff. The servers were pleasant, and the chef was even kind enough to speak with us for a few moments.

Again, thank you very much for what turned out to be an extremely pleasant evening. I anticipate contacting you again soon as we are trying to find a place to hold our year-end party this December.

Sincerely,

Ed Standish
CEO, Standish Metals, Inc.

172. What is Hampton's Place?

(A) A mining company
(B) A restaurant
(C) A caterer
(D) A cooking academy

173. What is indicated about Mr. Capers?

(A) He has been promoted recently.
(B) He was celebrating his fifth year of employment.
(C) He secured a new contract for Standish Metals, Inc.
(D) He was recognized by Standish Metals, Inc.

174. The word "degree" in paragraph 2, line 1, is closest in meaning to

(A) level
(B) type
(C) appearance
(D) expectation

175. What does Mr. Standish imply in his letter?

(A) He thought the prices at Hampton's Place were a bit too expensive.
(B) He learned about Hampton's Place from one of his friends.
(C) He expects to do business with Hampton's Place in the future.
(D) He hopes that Mr. Hampton will respond quickly to his letter.

GO ON TO THE NEXT PAGE

Questions 176-180 refer to following schedules and Web page.

The Ninth Annual Marketing Conference
The Rocky Point Hotel
Presentation Schedule

10:00 A.M. How Can I Use Social Media to Market My Product?
Persephone Jones of Tillis Media will speak about the best ways to make use of social media to spread the word about products to customers as well as potential advertisers. She will analyze several recent attempts to use social media that were successful.

11:30 A.M. Getting the Most out of Your Advertising Budget
Shamus O'Conner, a manager at Watson Advertising, will discuss ways that marketing managers with limited funds can make the most of them. He will present two case studies of instances in which advertising budgets were well spent.

1:30 P.M. Surveys: Are They Useful?
This panel discussion, which will feature Jessica Wilder of Kilburn Advertising, Mark Lemay of Sanderson, Inc., and Mary Harper of Green Media, will provide insights on surveys and how they can best be used.

4:00 P.M. Marketing through Print Media
Karl Jesse, a marketing professor at Central University, will speak about the advantages and disadvantages of marketing goods and services through print media. Professor Jesse is a proponent of using the print media so he will present several ideas as to why print media shouldn't be avoided solely to focus on the Internet.

● ● ●

**The Ninth Annual Marketing Conference
Attendee Feedback**

I work for a small company that doesn't really think that much about marketing. In fact, we have a limited amount of funds that I can spend, so I need to work hard and stay occupied to make the money go as far as possible. In the session that I attended, I learned some great ways to make every dollar count, and I'll be sure to use them in the future.
Tammy Howell, posted July 19, 9:14 A.M.

Even though I made sure to be on time for all the sessions I attended, I couldn't always find a seat. That was especially true for the panel discussion. More than half of the people in attendance were standing against the walls or in the aisles. The Rocky Point Hotel needed to put these events into larger rooms. Or the organizers need to move to a different venue next year.
Joe Buckley, posted July 20, 4:55 P.M.

Sadly, I only made it to the last session of the day since my schedule was full of meetings with clients for most of the day. I loved the ideas that Professor Jesse proposed. They made me think about print media, which I have mostly ignored during the past few years.
Naomi Watkins, posted July 20, 6:33 P.M.

Your comments are welcome. Please submit one.
Name:
Comment:

176. What was the topic of Mr. O'Conner's presentation?

(A) The efficient use of money
(B) The advantages of social media
(C) How to raise funds for advertisements
(D) The best ways to utilize surveys

177. What is mentioned about Professor Jesse?

(A) He used to work as a newspaper reporter.
(B) He is unfamiliar with how to market products on the Internet.
(C) He gives a presentation at the conference every year.
(D) He supports marketing efforts in newspapers and magazines.

178. At what time did Ms. Howell participate in a presentation?

(A) At 10:00 A.M.
(B) At 11:30 A.M.
(C) At 1:30 P.M.
(D) At 4:00 P.M.

179. What presentation most likely attracted the most individuals?

(A) How Can I Use Social Media to Market My Product?
(B) Getting the Most out of Your Advertising Budget
(C) Surveys: Are They Useful?
(D) Marketing through Print Media

180. How are Ms. Howell and Ms. Watkins alike?

(A) They work at advertising firms.
(B) They live and work in the same city.
(C) They are both busy at work.
(D) Their companies are small firms.

GO ON TO THE NEXT PAGE ▶

Questions 181-185 refer to the following article and letter.

The Saratoga Daily
August 30
Place to Eat: Jimmy's Lakehouse
Reviewed by Daniel Simon

Jimmy's Lakehouse has been the talk of the town since it opened this month. The restaurant is located at 65 Patterson Lane and overlooks Lake Hamilton. Despite its closeness to the water, the restaurant is very close to both the tourist and business district, so it is in a prime location. Diners particularly approve of the spacious parking lot, which means they don't have to waste any time looking for parking spots in the area.

After being seated, my party and I enjoyed looking through the menu. It was unusually extensive for a medium-sized restaurant so we decided to settle on the buffet in order to sample a bit of everything. Unsurprisingly, the fish, especially the salmon, was cooked to perfection. The fried chicken and beef tenderloin were delicious. The numerous vegetable dishes were filled with fresh, colorful foods. Despite the relatively low price, the food was of high quality, which was a pleasant surprise. The wine list was also nice and featured plenty of outstanding wines at affordable prices.

The only drawback was the wait time. We failed to make reservations, so we had to wait more than one hour to get seated. We simply had to wait in the lobby at the front until our table was ready, which was something a couple of members of my party complained about. The owner of the restaurant, however, indicated to me that this wouldn't be a problem much longer.

Jimmy's Lakehouse is open every day of the week from 5:00 P.M. to 11:00 P.M. It is definitely a restaurant you should visit. Just be sure to make a reservation by calling 904-2900 before you go.

The Saratoga Daily
Letter to the Editor
September 3

To the Editor,

We at Jimmy's Lakehouse were pleased to read your August 30 review of our restaurant. We are proud of the food we serve to our customers as well as the fact that we do not charge prices too high.

However, I would like to point out one thing. The article mentioned that the reviewer had to wait a long time to be seated. I would like to let you know that we are in the process of expanding our restaurant so that it will have 30% more seats than it does now. So as of September 20, we anticipate that our guests will have much shorter waiting times once they arrive even if they don't have a reservation.

Sincerely,

Tim Morrow
Owner, Jimmy's Lakehouse

181. What is mentioned about Jimmy's Lakehouse?

(A) It is not particularly new.
(B) It has lots of expensive menus.
(C) It is located near commercial buildings.
(D) It takes a long time to prepare food.

182. In the article, the word "prime" in paragraph 1, line 3, is closest in meaning to

(A) ideal
(B) acceptable
(C) relevant
(D) nearby

183. What aspect of the restaurant does the reviewer find uncommon?

(A) The amount of food
(B) The size of the place
(C) The choices of dishes
(D) The number of customers

184. Why was the letter sent?

(A) To provide some updates
(B) To correct an error
(C) To apologize for a mistake
(D) To mention a new menu item

185. When did Mr. Morrow talk to Mr. Simon?

(A) In July
(B) In August
(C) In September
(D) In October

GO ON TO THE NEXT PAGE

Pyramid Security Systems

You've worked hard to build a business, and at Pyramid Security Systems, we work hard to protect that business. Whatever your business' needs, we can find a solution that works for you. We offer a complimentary 30-day trial so you can make sure our services are a good fit. In addition, our equipment doesn't leave holes in the walls, like many other systems do. This is perfect for those renting their business space. Call us today at 1-800-555-9778 to speak with one of our agents, who can suggest the best way to move forward. Or complete the Contact Us form at www.pyramidsecsys. com. Check out our standard packages below.

Package Type	Number of Cameras	Motion Sensor Lights	Digital Recording	Emergency Response
Starter	2	2		
Pyramid-Pro	3-5	4	✔	
Pyramid-Premium	6-9	6	✔	✔
All-Inclusive	10+	8	✔	✔

Pyramid Security Systems: Contact Us

Name: Sharon Wenzel   Date: July 24

Summary of your inquiry: I heard about you through Carl O'Connor, a friend of mine who uses your services for his bakery in Bonner City. I understand that your headquarters is in Stevensville. I'm also operating there, so I think it would be convenient to set up an initial meeting. I'm interested in security services for my eye clinic. My problem is that while I'm giving examinations, my receptionist is sometimes in the back room repairing glasses, or in our display area helping customers select frames. When both of us are busy, it means that some areas of the property are left unattended. I'd like to find out more about what you offer. Thanks.

https://www.pyramidsecsys.com/testimonials

I had Pyramid Security Systems install cameras at my business about two months ago. I originally had one camera each in my waiting room, main hallway, display area, and reception desk. After a few weeks, I decided to add a camera outside and in my personal office. I am pleased with the high level of customer service, and I like the digital recording feature, which allows me to back up the footage on my computer easily and store it for later. In addition, I received a 10% discount for being a locally owned business. I would highly recommend Pyramid Security Systems to any small business owner.

–Sharon Wenzel

186. What is NOT indicated about Pyramid Security Systems?

(A) Its products do not cause damage to walls.

(B) Its prices are lower than those of its competitors.

(C) Its services can be used free for a limited time.

(D) Its agents can make recommendations to clients.

187. What is implied about Mr. O'Connor?

(A) He is not eligible for a discount.

(B) He supplies eyeglasses to Ms. Wenzel.

(C) He used to work for Pyramid Security Systems.

(D) He will move his business to Stevensville.

188. What does Ms. Wenzel suggest about her business?

(A) It needs a new receptionist.

(B) It provides free eye exams.

(C) It recently had a security issue.

(D) It has a very small staff.

189. In the form, the word "unattended" in paragraph 1, line 7, is closest in meaning to

(A) lonely

(B) avoided

(C) unfurnished

(D) empty

190. Which security package is Ms. Wenzel currently using?

(A) Starter

(B) Pyramid-Pro

(C) Pyramid-Premium

(D) All-Inclusive

GO ON TO THE NEXT PAGE

www.cleanwatersymposium.co.uk/about

| HOME | **ABOUT** | SPEAKERS | BOOTHS | REGISTER |

The Clear Water Symposium is an annual event held in the UK to discuss water issues facing our growing world population. Due to the symposium's popularity, this year's event will be held at the Valle Complex, which can accommodate a much larger crowd than last year's venue.

Below you can find just a few of the activities that will be available. Visit the Speakers and Booths pages for a complete list.
– Keynote speech by Dr. Sheng Kang, founder of the Water United Foundation
– Question-and-answer session with Member of Parliament Kieran Harper
– Craft activity directed by Professor Lauren Wilkinson of Stokes University: building your own water filter
– Field trip led by Jodie Mellor, President of the National Environmental Association: guided tour of St. Ives Bay

---

e-mail

To: Elizabeth Palmer <e.palmer@eil1.co.uk>
From: Curtis Volk <c.volk@eil1.co.uk>
Date: March 18
Subject: Clear Water Symposium

Dear Ms. Palmer,

My time at the Clear Water Symposium has been well spent, and I think it was a great idea sending me here. I'm learning a lot of valuable information that I believe will be of interest to our subscribers. I had the opportunity to meet Kieran Harper after his appearance. In addition, I got some excellent photos during the bay tour. The most enjoyable activity by far, which was educational as well, was creating a water filter out of items normally found in nature. This is something that people could also try at home, so I might include step-by-step instructions in my article.

Tomorrow I will watch a demonstration of a solar-powered water pump, and I've already arranged an interview with the inventor. I'll spend the rest of my time talking to representatives at the various booths.

Talk to you soon,

Curtis

To: Amil Kota <kotaamil@atwmail.com>
From: Curtis Volk <c.volk@eil1.co.uk>
Date: March 20
Subject: Thank you!

Dear Mr. Kota,

I just wanted to thank you once again for taking the time to meet with me after your demonstration yesterday. It was fascinating to hear your insights into solutions for the world's water crisis. If you provide me with your mailing address, I can send you a copy of the edition in which you will appear.

Warmest regards,

Curtis Volk

191. According to the Web page, what is true about this year's Clear Water Symposium?

(A) It will be held in a different location.
(B) Some of its speakers will give multiple talks.
(C) Its admission fee has been increased.
(D) It will last for three days in total.

192. Who most likely is Mr. Volk?

(A) A magazine publisher
(B) A photographer
(C) A journalist
(D) A business owner

193. Whose activity does Mr. Volk say he liked most?

(A) Dr. Kang's
(B) Mr. Harper's
(C) Ms. Wilkinson's
(D) Ms. Mellor's

194. In the first e-mail, the word "rest" in paragraph 2, line 2, is closest in meaning to

(A) support
(B) remainder
(C) break
(D) assignment

195. What is suggested about Mr. Kota?

(A) He invented a device.
(B) He has recently moved.
(C) He left the symposium early.
(D) He is Mr. Volk's coworker.

GO ON TO THE NEXT PAGE

Workplace Injury Report

As requested by Everest Manufacturing, Ashford Automotive Consulting (AAC) carried out a review of the company's workplace safety record. Because many minor injuries are not formally reported, AAC developed a questionnaire to gather precise details about what is happening at the plant. These were distributed to shift managers, who are believed to be the best source of information on these matters.

The survey was conducted from August 15 to 28 at the Elmhurst, St. Charles, and Pine Valley branches of Everest Manufacturing. Based on the initial findings, three main areas of improvement were identified. These were injuries caused by the misuse of production equipment or failure to wear the required safety gear, injuries caused by either malfunctioning machinery that had worn or incorrectly installed components, and injuries caused by falling on slippery surfaces or off ladders and other high places. AAC will submit recommendations for resolving these issues.

To: Jin Ni <jin.ni@everestmfg.com>

From: Alex Vinson <alex.vinson@everestmfg.com>

Date: September 20

Subject: AAC Report

Dear Ms. Ni,

I am in complete agreement with AAC's advice to change our equipment training from annually to every six months. To carry out this task without having production delays, employees will have to be paid overtime so that they can attend sessions outside their normal work schedules. It will be no problem to secure the funding for this, as it is essential not only to the safety of our employees but also to the company's ability to pass governmental inspections. The next inspection is scheduled for October 27, so I hope we can take action before that time.

Thanks,

Alex Vinson

Everest Manufacturing Newsletter
Pine Valley Branch, Vol. 127

Mandatory Workshop for All Staff

Workers at Everest Manufacturing will undergo safety training this month following recommendations by Ashford Automotive Consulting (AAC). In addition to AAC's original surveys in August, two more Everest Manufacturing sites—Beachville and Wright City—were reviewed by the consultancy firm. It was found that further safety training was needed. The first workshop to address this issue will be held on October 20 and will be conducted by Alex Vinson. Those who are unable to attend the workshop should speak to their immediate supervisor for further instructions.

196. Why was a survey given to shift managers?

(A) To request feedback about a new process
(B) To get accurate information about incidents
(C) To identify employees who should be promoted
(D) To look for ways to reduce operating costs

197. How many sites were reviewed by AAC in total?

(A) Two
(B) Three
(C) Four
(D) Five

198. What recommendation did AAC make to Everest Manufacturing?

(A) Installing more modern equipment
(B) Distributing employee safety manuals
(C) Increasing the frequency of training sessions
(D) Purchasing protective gear for workers

199. In the e-mail, the word "secure" in paragraph 1, line 4, is closest in meaning to

(A) obtain
(B) confirm
(C) fasten
(D) protect

200. What is suggested about Mr. Vinson?

(A) He will lead a workshop one week before an inspection.
(B) He wants to schedule a meeting with Ms. Ni.
(C) He disagrees with some of AAC's recommendations.
(D) He has recently transferred to the Pine Valley branch.

This is the end of the test. You may review PART 5, 6, and 7 if you finish the test early.

정답 p. 320 / 점수 환산표 p. 321 / 해석 p. 393

10

PART 5
PART 6
PART 7

토익 Reading Comprehension은 75분 동안 진행됩니다.
현재 시각과 지금부터 75분 후인 테스트 종료 시각을 기록해 두고,
반드시 종료 시각 전에 문제 풀이와 답안지 마킹을 완료하세요.

 현재 시각 시분

테스트 종료 시각 ☐시☐분

READING TEST

In the Reading test, you will read a variety of texts and answer several different types of reading comprehension questions. The entire Reading test will last 75 minutes. There are three parts, and directions are given for each part. You are encouraged to answer as many questions as possible within the time allowed.

You must mark your answers on the separate answer sheet. Do not write your answers in your test book.

PART 5

Directions: A word or phrase is missing in each of the sentences below. Four answer choices are given below each sentence. Select the best answer to complete the sentence. Then mark the letter (A), (B), (C), or (D) on your answer sheet.

101. Industry experts predict that Karl Amundson will be named the Author of the Year for ------- creative writing in the *Westward Adventures* series.

(A) him
(B) himself
(C) his
(D) ho

102. During the meeting with potential investors, Mr. Demitri suggested a ------- marketing strategy for the company's new wireless headphones.

(A) numerous
(B) bold
(C) variable
(D) grateful

103. For insurance purposes, all workers on the production floor are required to complete an extremely ------- safety course every year.

(A) demanding
(B) demanded
(C) demand
(D) demands

104. The works of ------- architect Jackson Black of Australia have been on display in the famed Drake Center convention building.

(A) solitary
(B) founded
(C) renowned
(D) clear

105. NewPage Hotel Group ------- its hotel chain as soon as agreements with various competitor companies are signed.

(A) will be expanded
(B) is being expanded
(C) will expand
(D) has expanded

106. Interpublic Incorporated, a widely recognized global -------, is now planning to launch a variety of new software programs.

(A) supplier
(B) supplying
(C) supplement
(D) supplies

107. MGU Holdings Corp. is one of the companies that ------- invest in small and medium-sized local businesses.

(A) highly
(B) shortly
(C) accordingly
(D) rarely

108. On behalf of the organizing committee of the concert, the event coordinator Mr. Wilson will apologize for ------- inconvenience caused by the delay of the performance.

(A) many
(B) those
(C) any
(D) both

109. All individuals in the facility will be asked to show their identification badges to security personnel ------- they are seen on the premises after 6:00 P.M.

(A) when
(B) rather than
(C) thus
(D) meanwhile

110. The Ghepo Tech marketing department is distributing complimentary passes ------- admittance to its annual tech show.

(A) near
(B) between
(C) for
(D) among

111. Due to the ongoing drought, many ------- farmers are forced to increase the price of their crops.

(A) close
(B) entire
(C) local
(D) near

112. Our customer service representatives are standing by twenty-four hours a day every day of the year to solve your problems ------- you give them a call.

(A) so that
(B) although
(C) as far as
(D) whenever

113. Business conference presenter Jillian Hull's core area of ------- is international marketing laws and strategy.

(A) treatment
(B) estimate
(C) expertise
(D) possibility

114. Carlos Falconi will lead a seminar on the new software to ------- the accountants in the department with its use.

(A) familiarity
(B) familiar
(C) familiarize
(D) familiarizing

115. Any employee who desires a parking ------- must pay a $15 monthly fee.

(A) permit
(B) permitting
(C) permitted
(D) permits

116. Customers are encouraged to contact a company representative for details ------- the Web site's contents.

(A) about
(B) into
(C) like
(D) except

117. According to a company spokesperson, ------- of the renovation work on the factory will take place over the course of two months.

(A) every
(B) several
(C) both
(D) most

118. Employees should have all changes to the work schedule ------- by the manager in charge of staffing.

(A) reported
(B) transferred
(C) approved
(D) refrained

119. Bissell Business Magazine ------- publishes articles outlining survey findings to show recent changes in consumer trends.

(A) greatly
(B) moderately
(C) almost
(D) frequently

120. Newly employed interns have been ------- since they participated in a workshop held in March.

(A) producing
(B) productive
(C) production
(D) productively

GO ON TO THE NEXT PAGE

121. The new line of items manufactured by Space Technology can interest consumers ------- tastes in electronics and home appliances are luxurious.

(A) who
(B) which
(C) whose
(D) that

122. Mr. Nixon is expected to receive a(n) ------- promotion if the retail branch that he manages continues to outperform its competitors.

(A) frequent
(B) significant
(C) tentative
(D) observant

123. ABT Industries should come up with practical measures to ensure its long-term ------- plan for the newly introduced production systems.

(A) stable
(B) stabilize
(C) stability
(D) stabilizer

124. Paper Planes International ventured into the field of video gaming ------- the acquisition of Hero Graphics, Ltd.

(A) between
(B) with
(C) across
(D) in

125. Peterman International provides consulting services in Europe, ------- it has not yet entered the Asian market.

(A) thus
(B) and
(C) after
(D) but

126. Lere Kitchen Appliances is engaged in an ongoing ------- to improve the quality and functionality of our products.

(A) effort
(B) growth
(C) strength
(D) rise

127. Mr. Kim has hired an advisor to help his employees ------- their ideas to potential investors.

(A) create
(B) promote
(C) interfere
(D) respond

128. After ------- review of the portfolio submitted by Jason Cochran, the human resources director has decided to have an interview with him.

(A) cares
(B) cared
(C) careful
(D) carefully

129. Every participant should thoroughly read the instructions posted at the entrance ------- loading their display items for the exhibition.

(A) as for
(B) along
(C) before
(D) behind

130. The address can be changed ------- the receiver can get in contact with the courier one hour before the package is scheduled to be delivered.

(A) provided that
(B) rather than
(C) in addition
(D) as though

PART 6

Directions: Read the texts that follow. A word, phrase, or sentence is missing in parts of each text. Four answer choices for each question are given below the text. Select the best answer to complete the text. Then mark the letter (A), (B), (C), or (D) on your answer sheet.

Questions 131-134 refer to the following letter.

March 24
Mr. Stephen Garland
162 Strathtay Road
Dundee, Scotland, UK

Dear Mr. Garland,

I am writing to confirm that we have ------- your order for *The British Journal of Electrical*
          131.
Engineering and *Contemporary Econ Journal*. -------. It should arrive within one week.
             132.

-------, the shipment will not include *The British Journal of Electrical Engineering* due to printing
133.
issues, and you will not be able to view a couple of our online features until April 15th due to the

current maintenance of our Web site. Our journal archive will not be ------- to view until late April.
                  134.

Once our Web site and journal archive become fully functional, we will send a notification message

to the e-mail address you provided.

Best regards,

Mary Chilton
Subscription Services Manager

131. (A) suspended
(B) delivered
(C) rejected
(D) processed

132. (A) Information on the subscription procedure is found on our Web site.
(B) We have launched a new scholarly journal which you may be interested in.
(C) *Contemporary Econ Journal* was shipped out yesterday.
(D) Members will no longer receive printed copies of our journals.

133. (A) Moreover
(B) Whereas
(C) Unfortunately
(D) For example

134. (A) access
(B) accessibly
(C) accessibility
(D) accessible

GO ON TO THE NEXT PAGE

Questions 135-138 refer to the following e-mail.

To: Winny Lancet
From: Edwind Real Estate Online
Date: February 15
Subject: Membership Issues

Ms. Lancet,

We recently attempted to automatically renew your yearly account with Edwind Real Estate Online.

-------. Please log into your online account and check that your name and address match those on
135.
the credit card we have on file. If ------- has changed, please update the information within 10 days,
136.
or your account may be deleted.

Additionally, be sure to submit proof of ownership for any property you have for sale or rent on your

account, unless this has ------- been done.
137.

New company policies which were not in place at the time of your original ------- now require that
138.
each property being advertised on Edwind Real Estate Online be under the account of the current

owner only.

Sincerely,

Edwind Real Estate Online

---

135. (A) Subscriptions can be renewed online or
       by telephone.
   (B) You have been approved as a member of
       Edwind Real Estate Online.
   (C) The recent software update has enhanced
       efficiency in transactions.
   (D) However, an error occurred regarding
       your payment information.

136. (A) every
   (B) either
   (C) another
   (D) little

137. (A) hardly
   (B) primarily
   (C) instantly
   (D) already

138. (A) listing
   (B) tour
   (C) statement
   (D) receipt

Questions 139-142 refer to the following article.

Hudson Lanny Gallery will feature Tara Hidalgo's images of ------- living all throughout the month of
139.
August. -------. Contributions will go to the Hidalgo Children's Art Education Fund.
140.

Known internationally for her unique work focused on poverty in small farming towns, few artists

have such a rich connection with their work as does Ms. Hidalgo. Her ------- are said to reflect much
141.
of her own childhood.

------- by her experience of living in various country settings across the American Midwest,
142.
Ms. Hidalgo continues to give the roots to her work not just artistically but as a philanthropist as well.

139. (A) city
    (B) rural
    (C) artistic
    (D) corporate

140. (A) Entrance to the gallery will be by donation
       only.
    (B) In the meantime, Ms. Hidalgo is publishing
       a book on farming.
    (C) Several galleries started bidding on the
       project.
    (D) Many artists have been requested to
       contribute their artwork.

141. (A) songs
    (B) buildings
    (C) photographs
    (D) performances

142. (A) Inspiring
    (B) Inspire
    (C) Inspired
    (D) Inspires

Questions 143-146 refer to the following e-mail.

To: Danielle Lim
From: Huckle Books Customer Service
Re: Textbook Order
Date: November 3

Ms. Lim,

We have processed your order ------- October 30 for the following titles:
                                       143.
Epidemiology: *A Microscopic World* 8th edition by Jennifer Schwarzen $67.85
Hospital Administration 4th edition by Adrian Flemming $84.00
Nursing Research: *A Look into Change* 5th edition by Michelle Stevenson $45.50

-------. However, after searching our database, we discovered that the third book you ordered is
144.
not currently in stock. We have asked for a copy and will expedite it to you free of charge once it is

-------.
145.

We apologize for the ------- and hope that it has not caused you any inconvenience. Please accept
                                    146.
the attached 10 percent off coupon for your next purchase.

Sincerely,

Dana Henry
Huckle Books Customer Service

---

143. (A) dated
    (B) was dated
    (C) to date
    (D) is dating

144. (A) You can place an order for these books
        online at any time.
    (B) Unfortunately, we no longer provide
        shipping service.
    (C) In addition, we have posted a listing of
        new titles on our Web site.
    (D) *Epidemiology and Nursing Research*
        were both shipped today.

145. (A) repaired
    (B) available
    (C) ordered
    (D) expected

146. (A) defect
    (B) accident
    (C) delay
    (D) malfunction

Directions: In this part you will read a selection of texts, such as magazine and newspaper articles, e-mails, and instant messages. Each text or set of texts is followed by several questions. Select the best answer for each question and mark the letter (A), (B), (C), or (D) on your answer sheet.

Questions 147-148 refer to the following information.

Zenith Supplies
Order Details

Item Description / Quantity	Price
16″ round fiberglass serving tray / x 12 at $18.99 each	$227.88
20″x20″ cloth napkins (pack of 12) / x 10 at $23.99 each	$239.90
8-quart stainless steel warming dish / x 3 at $169.99 each	$509.97
13″ stainless steel serving spoon / x 6 at $3.99 each	$23.94
Subtotal	$1,001.69
Delivery and taxes	$134.95
Total	$1,136.64
Payment type: Credit card ending in 8946 / Charge of $1,136.64 applied on February 3	

Date of order: February 3   Estimated delivery: February 9
Customer name: Anuj Misra   Business reference number: F53R98

Special instructions: Napkins will be printed with the Misra Co. logo.

147. What type of business does Mr. Misra most likely operate?

(A) A clothing shop
(B) A hardware store
(C) A catering company
(D) A laundry service

148. What is stated about the order?

(A) It will be delivered to Mr. Misra's home.
(B) Its payment was made in full.
(C) It included clearance sale items.
(D) Its delivery fee was waived.

Questions 149-150 refer to the following Web page.

http://www.lunjaninc.com

Lunjan, Inc.

Now offering moving vans along with our regular fleet of cars and trucks!

In addition to the daily usage charge, you can add a number of features to suit your needs such as:

– GPS Navigation Device
– Heavy-duty Folding Cart
– Bicycle Rack
– Ski Rack

Fees are dependent upon the package selected, and a deposit is required. Click here for more information. Please note that all payments must be made by credit card or bank transfer only, as we do not keep cash on the premises.

149. What type of business most likely is Lunjan, Inc.?

(A) A sporting goods store
(B) A real estate agency
(C) A moving company
(D) A vehicle rental agency

150. What is suggested about the deposit?

(A) It can be paid in installments.
(B) It is reduced for regular customers.
(C) It is not accepted in cash.
(D) It can be returned quickly.

Questions 151-152 refer to the following online chat discussion.

👤	**Ken Johnson** [10:43 A.M.]	Hey, Blake. Have you selected a hotel for Nicky Sutton's crew yet?
👤	**Blake Hurst** [10:45 A.M.]	I just did it this morning. They'll be staying at the Columbus Inn. It's within walking distance, so it will be easy for them to come over here and set up our stage.
👤	**Ken Johnson** [10:46 A.M.]	Great. Please forward the booking information to Ms. Sutton's agent.
👤	**Blake Hurst** [10:47 A.M.]	I will. And Ms. Sutton is arriving on a Buena Airlines flight at 2:05 P.M. on June 1. Do you think we should send a limo to pick her up?
👤	**Ken Johnson** [10:49 A.M.]	Certainly. She's a big celebrity.
👤	**Blake Hurst** [10:51 A.M.]	Then I'll make the necessary arrangements to greet her in style.

SEND

151. Where do the people most likely work?

(A) At a travel agency
(B) At a hotel
(C) At a theater
(D) At an airport

152. At 10:49 A.M., what does Mr. Johnson most likely mean when he writes, "Certainly"?

(A) He thinks the suggested transportation is a good idea.
(B) He agrees that using Buena Airlines is the best option.
(C) He plans to pick Ms. Sutton up from the airport himself.
(D) He has stayed at the Columbus Inn in the past.

GO ON TO THE NEXT PAGE

Harrison Towers
at 372 Stratford Drive
Opening Event on Saturday, August 28

On behalf of Woodland, Inc. you are cordially
invited to view the luxury properties Harrison
Towers has to offer.

Rental options available in various sizes!

Drop in from 1 P.M. to 7 P.M. to tour the site at your leisure.

Call Erin Varner at (212) 555-2054 for
unit layouts and sample lease
agreements.

153. What is the purpose of the event?

(A) To publicize a construction plan
(B) To recruit more staff members
(C) To promote a new housing complex
(D) To introduce a change in leadership

154. Who most likely is Erin Varner?

(A) A museum tour guide
(B) A real estate agent
(C) A construction crew manager
(D) A financial expert

Questions 155-158 refer to the following text message chain.

8:11 A.M.
PAUL: I'm heading to the business center on the 3rd floor. I'm going to make extra copies of the event schedule and bring down another chair.

8:12 A.M.
VANESSA: I'm at our booth. I thought the banner we brought would be too small, but it's the perfect size because we're only using half of the booth. And, we got lucky with Ralston Co.'s color scheme.

8:13 A.M.
WILLIAM: I'm not following you.

8:15 A.M.
VANESSA: I mean that their decorations are really different from ours, so it's clear that we're two different companies.

8:17 A.M.
PAUL: That's great. Visitors will start arriving in an hour. Let's take turns watching the booth so we can go around and see the rest of the expo.

8:18 A.M.
WILLIAM: Good idea. I'd love to see the demonstration by Jarvis Enterprises on the main stage this afternoon.

8:19 A.M.
VANESSA: Me too. The Nixon-44 is one of the most highly anticipated smartphones of the year.

8:21 A.M.
PAUL: Yeah, it'll be great. By the way, there are some gift bags for exhibitors up here too, but I can't carry everything down in one trip.

8:22 A.M.
WILLIAM: I'll come to the business center to help you.

---

155. What is suggested about the group's booth?

(A) It is getting a lot of visitors.
(B) It comes with a free banner.
(C) It is shared with another group.
(D) It is near the business center.

156. At 8:13 A.M., what does Mr. William most likely mean when he writes, "I'm not following you"?

(A) He thinks some decorations should be changed.
(B) He doesn't understand what was said.
(C) He wants to use his own ideas.
(D) He doesn't have time to go with Vanessa.

157. What is implied about the Nixon-44?

(A) Its demonstration will begin in an hour.
(B) It is a best-seller at the writers' company.
(C) It is manufactured by Jarvis Enterprises.
(D) It will be given away to exhibitors.

158. What will William probably do next?

(A) Go to the third floor
(B) Find a place to park
(C) Make copies of a schedule
(D) Meet Paul at the main stage

GO ON TO THE NEXT PAGE

Sardis
Job Openings

Massage therapists: Part-time massage therapist positions (3 total). Candidates must be licensed by the state and have at least two years' related experience. — [1] —. We are open every day from 7 A.M. to 10 P.M., so candidates must be available days, evenings, and weekends. You will be scheduled to work five days a week. — [2] —.

Receptionist: Full-time receptionist (1 total). The receptionist is responsible for taking incoming calls, arranging appointments for massages and other beauty treatments, and handling incoming and outgoing bills. — [3] —. Working hours are Sunday to Thursday, 7 A.M. to 4 P.M. Applicants with experience are preferred, but we are willing to train the right person.

Please fill out an online application at www.sardis.net/careers on or before June 14. — [4] —.

159. What type of business most likely is Sardis?

(A) A training institute
(B) A spa facility
(C) A mental health clinic
(D) An insurance company

160. According to the advertisement, what is required of workers in both positions?

(A) Having prior experience
(B) Being available until 10 P.M.
(C) Working five days a week
(D) Holding a valid state certification

161. In which of the positions marked [1], [2], [3], and [4] does the following sentence best belong?

"You may also be asked to make updates on our social media page."

(A) [1]
(B) [2]
(C) [3]
(D) [4]

Maritime Event Supply
1024 Maritime Street
Miami, Fl 33114

Lease Agreement

Today's date: June 10   Reservation date: August 1
Lessee: Marshal Wendt
Contact preference: ___ e-mail   ___ home phone   X mobile phone: 305-208-6666
Lease Length:
___ Morning (6 A.M. to 1 P.M.)
___ Full day (6 A.M. to 8 P.M.)
 X Overnight (6 A.M. to 10 A.M. next day)

Item	Quantity	Price
Chairs (natural wood; folding)	100	$300.00
Tables (round 6′)	12	$168.00
Table clothes (peach; round)	12	$60.00
Tables (long 8′)	6	$90.00

	Total	$618.00
	Amount paid	$309.00
	Refundable security deposit paid	$100.00
	Remainder due by July 25	$309.00

NOTE: You will be requested to provide photo identification and sign upon pick-up. Be sure to pay remaining rental fee on time, or the reservation may be lost. A full deposit can be expected pending the condition of the items and timelines of return. For items returned after the designated time, a 10 percent hourly late fee may apply. Cost for damages outside of normal use will also be deducted from the security deposit. While fees for basic cleaning are included in rental costs, we do request that tables and chairs be free of food and generally well maintained. Please be advised that additional charges will apply if items are stained or require specialized cleaning. Such charges will be deducted from the security deposit, unless they exceed the $100 amount, in which case you may receive an additional bill.

162. What is indicated about Maritime Event Supply?

(A) It requires information on the customer's credit card.
(B) It rents items which are used in a kitchen.
(C) It returns the deposit once items are back.
(D) It allows rental of items for a maximum of ten hours.

163. When are the rented items due to be returned?

(A) By 6:00 A.M.
(B) By 10:00 A.M.
(C) By 1:00 P.M.
(D) By 8:00 P.M.

164. What expenses are NOT deducted from the deposit?

(A) Cleaning fee
(B) Hourly late fee
(C) Cost for damages
(D) Remaining rental fee

GO ON TO THE NEXT PAGE

Questions 165-167 refer to the following e-mail.

To: Diane Hines <d.hines@ingrammail.com>
From: Roy Monroe <monroeroy@stepbystepgoods.com>
Date: April 20
Subject: Product R-490 (Gigi Cube)

Dear Ms. Hines,

Thank you for your participation in testing the Gigi Cube, which is the safe play structure for toddlers that we are currently developing to accompany our line of toys and supplies. You will receive the item by courier sometime next week at the address you provided us. Feel free to track the delivery of the package on our Web site using the following code: TWLHO90.

We request that you incorporate the Gigi Cube into your everyday lifestyle, using it in your home and also taking it with you when visiting friends, family, and public spaces. You are required to file weekly comments about the product on our Web site at stepbystepgoods.com/testing using the login details previously provided. Please be as detailed as possible about the convenience, appearance, and quality of the item as well as anything else you think may be helpful for us to know. Because we use real customers instead of professionals at this stage in the development process, we can figure out what people really want and need.

At the end of the six-week testing period, the Gigi Cube is yours to keep. It's our way of saying thank you for participating in this process.

Warmest regards,

Roy Monroe
R&D Director, Step by Step

165. What is the purpose of the e-mail?

(A) To explain why a shipment was delayed
(B) To give instructions regarding a task
(C) To thank a customer for making a purchase
(D) To introduce a new line of children's clothing

166. What is mentioned about Step by Step?

(A) It involves ordinary consumers when developing its goods.
(B) Its R&D department is short-staffed at the moment.
(C) It will make extensive changes to its Web site.
(D) It supplies volunteers with discount shopping codes.

167. What can be suggested about the Gigi Cube?

(A) It is made from recyclable materials.
(B) It can be washed in the washing machine.
(C) It comes in several kinds of fabric.
(D) It is intended to be portable.

Diego Milanesi
4368 Oliverio Drive
Satanta, KS 67870

Dear Mr. Milanesi,

I am writing regarding your submission to the Globe Photography Contest. Your landscape photo entitled *Walk in the Woods* impressed our judging panel due to its unique use of light. Therefore, I am delighted to let you know that your photo has made it to the final round of the competition. Congratulations! — [1] —. Just for making it this far, you will receive a $50 gift card from Russell Printing, where you can get photos printed in all sizes.

Your photo will be enlarged and put on display, along with those of other semi-finalists, at the Middleton Gallery on 18th Street. — [2] —. Photos will be available for public viewing from Tuesday, September 6 through Saturday, September 10. On Saturday, the winners will be presented plaques and prizes at a wine and cheese reception at 7 P.M. The first-place winner will be getting the photo printed in *Nature Monthly* magazine. — [3] —. And we're confident that the public exposure would be highly beneficial for the first-place contestant.

In order to help us prepare the right amount of refreshments, please mail back the enclosed form to let us know if you plan to participate in the reception. — [4] —. We ask that you do so by August 23 at the latest. If you have any questions, feel free to call me at 555-4950, extension 45.

Joyce Parker

168. Why did Ms. Parker send the letter to Mr. Milanesi?

(A) To confirm that an entry is original work
(B) To ask him to vote for his favorite photo
(C) To request that he join a judging panel
(D) To inform him of his status in a contest

169. When will finalists most likely attend an event?

(A) On August 23
(B) On September 1
(C) On September 6
(D) On September 10

170. What information is Mr. Milanesi asked to provide?

(A) Additional examples of his work
(B) Where he would like materials sent
(C) Whether or not he will join an event
(D) His preference for photo sizes

171. In which of the positions marked [1], [2], [3], and [4] does the following sentence best belong?

"This is the most exciting prize we have ever offered."

(A) [1]
(B) [2]
(C) [3]
(D) [4]

Meadowbrook (October 15)—The baseball stadium near Reynolds Street subway station is now formally renamed Hennepin Stadium in recognition of the local employer Hennepin Manufacturing, which provides jobs to thousands of people in the area.

"The decision to rename the stadium to honor Hennepin Manufacturing was based not only on the company's good standing in the community, but also its generous investment last year of $3 million toward a plan for site improvements at the stadium," commented John Ross, the chairman of the city council, at a press conference yesterday.

"We were delighted with the news that the baseball stadium would bear the Hennepin name, since it is such a key facility of the community," said Hennepin Manufacturing's public relations director, Kelly Woodruff.

"It's also an exciting event to coincide with our 20-year anniversary in business. We know our employees are proud to support the improvements at the stadium and we hope that Meadowbrook residents will enjoy the facility for years to come."

The building improvement project was approved after a survey of visitors revealed that the most common complaint was difficulty in getting to and from the stadium. In response, the stadium's multi-story parking structure was expanded to accommodate more vehicles. Additionally, two bus stops were added to the city bus line—one at the east end and one at the west end.

Planners used the remaining funds to install solar panels on a portion of the stadium's roof. This will allow the complex to operate with less electricity from the city's grid.

172. According to the article, what has been recently announced?

(A) The winning of a baseball competition
(B) The opening of a production facility
(C) The renaming of a sports complex
(D) The resignation of a city council member

173. What did Hennepin Manufacturing do last year?

(A) Examined feedback from visitors
(B) Moved its headquarters to Meadowbrook
(C) Donated money to a project
(D) Encouraged employees to do volunteer work

174. The word "bear" in paragraph 3, line 2, is closest in meaning to

(A) recall
(B) uncover
(C) try
(D) carry

175. What is NOT mentioned as a benefit of the improvements?

(A) The reduction of energy usage
(B) The expansion of a public transportation route
(C) The addition of more parking spaces
(D) The creation of construction jobs

GO ON TO THE NEXT PAGE

Questions 176-180 refer to the following advertisement and letter.

Simpson Industries is seeking a hard-working and team-oriented factory supervisor for its branch in Detroit. Simpson Industries is one of the leading producers of automotive components in the nation and has been for the past three decades. These components have a reputation for their high quality and are used throughout the world.

The factory supervisor will oversee all activities on the production floor. The duties of this position include ensuring safe working conditions in compliance with state and federal regulations, organizing the maintenance and purchase of equipment, and communicating company policies to workers. At least three years of management experience is required.

Our facility is open 363 days a year, including most national holidays, and applicants availability must be able to accommodate this schedule. Managing staffing levels and adapting to changing manpower needs is essential for staying within our labor budget. We use COBRA scheduling software on-site, so applicants must be proficient in using it.

Those interested in joining our team should download an application at www. simpsonind.com/careers. This should be completed in full and mailed with two letters of recommendation to Attn: Manuel Watts, Simpson Industries, 405 Woodbridge Street, Detroit, MI 48205.

October 16

Attn: Manuel Watts
Simpson Industries
405 Woodbridge Street
Detroit, MI 48205

Dear Mr. Watts,

I am writing on behalf of Mr. Pai, who has applied for the factory supervisor position at Simpson Industries. For the past six of Mr. Pai's eight years with us, I have been his direct supervisor and have worked closely with him on a daily basis. While working for Newton Co. as a production floor manager, Mr. Pai excelled in promoting cooperation among team members, resulting in a low turnover rate compared to industry averages. I have also been pleased with his contributions to weekly management meetings. He has shared numerous helpful ideas, many of which have been implemented at our company.

I have reviewed the job requirements in your advertisement and can confirm that Mr. Pai meets all of them. Furthermore, surveys from employees, as well as our internal investigations, have indicated that Mr. Pai is fully dedicated to preventing injuries and creating excellent working conditions. We have even sent him to other facilities to advise the managers at those sites.

If you choose to hire Mr. Pai, I am certain that you will be more than satisfied with his talents and attitude. I would be happy to discuss his employment at our company in further detail should you find it necessary. You may contact me at my office at 555-8923, extension 24.

Sincerely,

Jessie Hoyle
Facilities Director, Newton Co.

176. What is indicated about Simpson Industries?

(A) It has job openings in several departments.
(B) It plans to expand its business to Detroit.
(C) It specializes in manufacturing parts for vehicles.
(D) It has been in operation for three years.

177. According to the advertisement, what may be required of the factory supervisor?

(A) Moving heavy items
(B) Passing a health exam
(C) Taking business trips
(D) Working on holidays

178. What is the purpose of the letter?

(A) To make a job offer to an applicant
(B) To find out more about an open position
(C) To give a favorable assessment of an employee
(D) To describe a hiring process

179. What is suggested about Mr. Pai?

(A) He knows how to use COBRA scheduling software.
(B) He uploaded his résumé to a Web site.
(C) He has taken team-building courses.
(D) He has experience developing policies.

180. For how long was Mr. Pai employed at Newton Co.?

(A) Three years
(B) Six years
(C) Eight years
(D) Ten years

Questions 181-185 refer to the following schedule and e-mail.

Gazelle Wine Merchant Delivery Schedule

	Tuesday	Wednesday	Thursday	Friday
Morning	Lynwood	Seattle (North)	SeaTac	Renton
Afternoon	Edmonds	Seattle (South)	Tukwila	Bellevue (North)
Evening	Shoreline	Burien	Kent	Bellevue (South)

Deliveries for shops in the greater Seattle area are as above, excluding holidays.

No regular deliveries are scheduled for Mondays, as those are reserved for picking up goods from area wineries. Should you be unable to accept delivery at your regularly scheduled time, please contact Shipping Manager Sabine Korovina at s.korovina@ gazellewinemerchant.com.

---

e-mail

To: George Hoffman <george@regalgoods.net>
From: Sabine Korovina <s.korovina@gazellewinemerchant.com>
Date: October 28
Subject: RE: Delivery request

Dear Mr. Hoffman,

I hope I can clear up some of the confusion you expressed in your e-mail yesterday. Firstly, it's correct that the regular delivery schedule will be amended for the week beginning November 7 due to the national holiday on Friday, November 11. We plan to move all deliveries up by one day for that week only. That means delivery personnel will visit your store on Wednesday, November 9, rather than Thursday, November 10. You will receive the goods at the usual delivery time, so right after lunch in your case. Our team will be making delivery rounds on Monday, November 7, so I'm afraid we cannot accommodate your request for help in setting up a merchandising display.

The normal delivery schedule will resume from November 14, and I will send one of our merchandising specialists to your shop on that day at 10 A.M. to assist you in preparing the holiday display for Cordova Wines. Don't forget to remove shelving, standing signs, and other items from the place where you want the display to be erected. This will expedite the process. If you have any further questions, please feel free to e-mail me anytime.

Sincerely,

Sabine Korovina

181. What happens on Mondays?

(A) Deliveries have an extra charge.
(B) The warehouse is closed.
(C) New stock is gathered.
(D) Delivery vehicles are inspected.

182. Why did Ms. Korovina write the e-mail?

(A) To introduce a new product
(B) To thank Mr. Hoffman for his purchase
(C) To apologize for an out-of-stock item
(D) To explain changes to a schedule

183. Where most likely is Mr. Hoffman's shop?

(A) Bellevue
(B) Burien
(C) Seattle
(D) Tukwila

184. For when did Mr. Hoffman most likely request merchandising assistance?

(A) November 7
(B) November 9
(C) November 10
(D) November 11

185. What does Ms. Korovina remind Mr. Hoffman to do?

(A) Order materials for a display
(B) Submit a formal request by e-mail
(C) Clear an area for a display
(D) Confirm his employees' availability

GO ON TO THE NEXT PAGE

E-mail

To:	Newscast Radio <feedback@newscastradio.net>
From:	Wesley Vincent <w.vincent@wv-enterprises.com>
Date:	April 21
Subject:	Listener Opinion

To Whom It May Concern:

I have been a big fan of Newscast Radio for many years, particularly the international business broadcasts, as I am the owner of a small steel manufacturing business. I was considering purchasing a Newscast Radio membership, but it seems the membership resources are not very different from what is offered for free to the public. However, if you added transcripts of your radio shows to the membership section, I would definitely sign up. I think a lot of people would like to have access to show transcripts because their schedules may prevent them from listening to your radio channel reliably. Thank you for considering my opinion.

Sincerely,

Wesley Vincent

To: Newscast Radio Reporters
From: Kong Wei
Date: May 3
Subject: Weekly Meeting

For those of you who weren't at this morning's meeting, I wanted to provide a brief overview of what we covered.

Construction is well underway on Florence Tower, which will be our new headquarters building. We are scheduled to move in sometime in September, when the work is completed. Details about preparing for the relocation will be provided as the moving date nears.

In addition to the daily news, we have identified several topics for in-depth analysis, each forming a four-part series to be broadcast next month. The selected topics are the increase in the popularity of digital currencies, the prime minister race in Canada, and the bankruptcy proceedings for Reyna Enterprises. These will be researched by Sara, Yuiko, and Manjit, respectively.

Patrick, from the IT department, was supposed to give us a demonstration of the new video conferencing equipment, but this was postponed, as he is still awaiting the shipment. Most likely, this will be done next week.

https://www.newscastradio.net/updates

Changes at Newscast Radio

Posted November 4

Newscast Radio is delighted to announce an upgrade to its membership services. Transcripts of all broadcasts will now be available to download from the membership section of our Web site. Click here to enroll in our membership program for just $3.95 per month.

We will be moving into our new headquarters building this month. In addition to offering more space for our staff, it will have a visitor area on the first floor where members of the public can learn about our business, listen to live broadcasts, and enjoy a drink from the on-site café.

We're also thrilled to welcome back to our team Mr. Reynaldo Carter. Many of you may remember him from his "Fact Focus" interviews.

186. What is suggested about Mr. Vincent?

(A) He travels internationally for his business.
(B) He is a new Newscast Radio listener.
(C) He will most likely sign up for a membership.
(D) He thinks the Newscast Radio signal is unreliable.

187. Who will research a national election?

(A) Kong
(B) Sara
(C) Yuiko
(D) Manjit

188. What is mentioned about the video conferencing equipment?

(A) It is easy for users to operate.
(B) It can be checked out from Patrick.
(C) It was funded with a budget surplus.
(D) It was not delivered by May 3.

189. What is implied about Florence Tower?

(A) Its construction was delayed.
(B) It is near public transportation.
(C) It has a high level of security.
(D) It will be featured in a news story.

190. What is indicated about Mr. Carter?

(A) He worked for Newscast Radio in the past.
(B) He is in charge of the membership program.
(C) He will interview a local celebrity.
(D) He provides tours of Florence Tower.

To: Derek Mohr <d.mohr@jarvissolutions.com>

From: Clara Campbell <c.campbell@jarvissolutions.com>

Date: March 14

Subject: ERS United

Dear Mr. Mohr,

I am waiting at the airport for my return flight to Seattle. I gave the sales presentation to representatives from ERS United. Because the prototype for our water filtration system was too large to take on the plane, I shipped it directly to the ERS United offices using Dobbs Couriers. However, due to a problem with the shipment, I had to skip the thirty-minute demonstration that I had planned for the last part of the talk. Fortunately, some of my slides included video clips of the device in use, but I don't think it was enough. I'll have to arrange another trip here to give a full demonstration.

I contacted Dobbs Couriers earlier today and made a formal complaint about the matter. I'll give you more details about ERS United tomorrow at the office.

Sincerely,

Clara Campbell
Sales Representative, Jarvis Solutions

Dobbs Couriers Weekly Incident Report: March 10-16

Submitted by Jacqueline Roberts

The number of incidents with customer deliveries was higher than last week but was still within the accepted range. The summary is included below.

Incident Reported	Transaction ID	Description of Incident	Insurance Purchased	Status
March 11	48502	Lost package	$100	Trace placed on package
March 12	59641	Incorrect address	None	Package rerouted
March 14	29482	Damaged contents	$500	Pending
March 16	37709	Late delivery	$200	Pending

To: Clara Campbell <c.campbell@jarvissolutions.com>
From: Dobbs Couriers <cservice@dobbscouriers.com>
Date: March 16
Subject: Your Delivery
Attached: voucher_#01125

Dear Ms. Campbell,

On behalf of Dobbs Couriers, I would like to sincerely apologize for the disappointing experience you had with your recent delivery (transaction #29482). We understand that this was a great inconvenience for you. You had requested a reimbursement of $1,200 for travel expenses related to this matter. Unfortunately, we cannot reimburse you for any losses other than those directly related to the package. As you insured the contents, you will receive the full amount of your insurance coverage, and this will be sent to your company's bank account directly. Also, I have attached a voucher for $50 off your next shipment with us by way of apology.

Thank you for your understanding,

Jacqueline Roberts
Customer Service Agent, Dobbs Couriers

191. What is indicated about Ms. Campbell's presentation?

(A) It was supposed to be given by Mr. Mohr.
(B) It resulted in a new client contract.
(C) It included a question-and-answer session.
(D) It was shorter than originally planned.

192. What is suggested about ERS United?

(A) It plans to form a partnership.
(B) It is located in Seattle.
(C) It needs to be visited again.
(D) Its meeting was canceled.

193. In the report, the word "range" in paragraph 1, line 2, is closest in meaning to

(A) variety
(B) limit
(C) distance
(D) ability

194. What problem did Ms. Campbell have with her delivery?

(A) It could not be found by Dobbs Couriers.
(B) It was sent to the wrong address.
(C) It arrived at the site in damaged condition.
(D) It was delivered later than scheduled.

195. How much will be sent to Jarvis Solutions' bank account?

(A) $100
(B) $200
(C) $500
(D) $1,200

GO ON TO THE NEXT PAGE

Instructions for Song Submissions

Congratulations on having your song selected to be featured in an upcoming film by Coburn Studios. Please follow the instructions below to expedite the approval process.

- Review the terms and conditions of the licensing agreement carefully before signing it.
- Because some of the words may be difficult to understand, please supply us with the lyrics to the song that will be used.
- If other musicians are in your recording (for example, background singers, drummers, guitarist, etc.), you must get their consent for the song to be used. This must be done even if you are the song's writer. Consent forms for this purpose are available at www.coburn-studios.com/consent. The signed forms can be submitted by mail or scanned and sent by e-mail.
- Please note that the song may be used only partially or in its entirety, at the discretion of the director.

Coburn Studios
469 Athens Avenue
New York, NY 10021
www.coburn-studios.com

September 27

Daphne Gallagher

3198 Ferguson Street

Westborough, MA 01581

Dear Mr. Gallagher,

I have received all the necessary consent forms, so I can confirm that your song *Daylight Dreams* will be used in our upcoming documentary, *Beyond Politics*. I'm also pleased to hear that you will be able to attend the debut screening onsite at our studio on December 10. I have enclosed four tickets for you and any guests you may want to bring along. Someone from my team will pick you and your party up at your hotel to transport you to the studio.

We're glad you can be a part of this event, and we thank you once again for your contribution. Feel free to call me at (212) 555-9785 if you have any questions, but please note that I only take calls on this number during business hours.

All the best,

Jerald Hornsby
Junior Producer, Coburn Studios

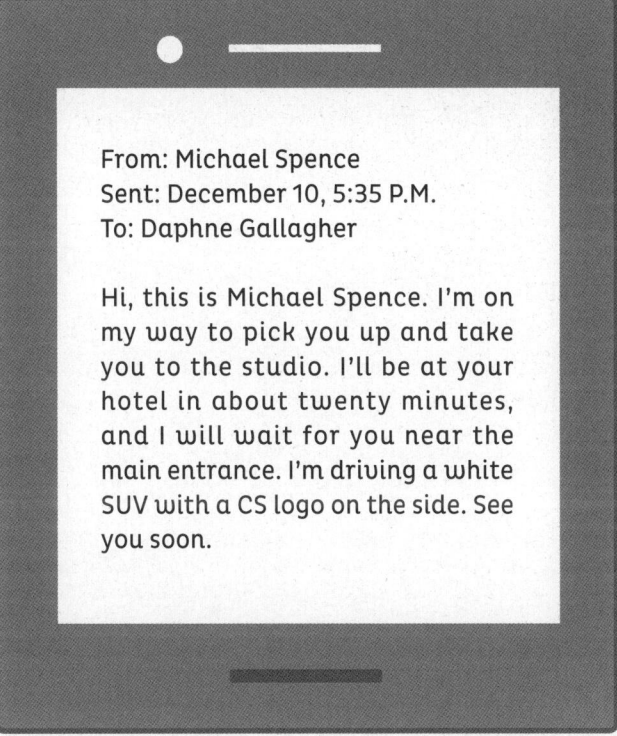

From: Michael Spence
Sent: December 10, 5:35 P.M.
To: Daphne Gallagher

Hi, this is Michael Spence. I'm on my way to pick you up and take you to the studio. I'll be at your hotel in about twenty minutes, and I will wait for you near the main entrance. I'm driving a white SUV with a CS logo on the side. See you soon.

196. What do the instructions tell musicians to do?

(A) Shorten the length of the song
(B) Offer different versions of the song
(C) Provide words to the song
(D) E-mail a copy of the song

197. What is suggested about *Daylight Dreams*?

(A) Its duration is much longer than average.
(B) It has appeared in several documentary films.
(C) It was originally written by Mr. Hornsby.
(D) It includes performances by multiple musicians.

198. According to Mr. Hornsby, what will Coburn Studio do in December?

(A) Send a payment to a film's contributor
(B) Start an ad campaign for *Beyond Politics*
(C) Show a movie for the first time
(D) Enter a documentary contest

199. In the letter, the word "take" in paragraph 2, line 3, is closest in meaning to

(A) choose
(B) accept
(C) carry
(D) remove

200. Who most likely is Mr. Spence?

(A) The director of *Beyond Politics*
(B) Mr. Hornsby's coworker
(C) A hotel employee
(D) Ms. Gallagher's manager

This is the end of the test. You may review PART 5, 6, and 7 if you finish the test early.

정답 p. 320 / 점수 환산표 p. 321 / 해석 p. 403

정답&해석

정답
점수 환산표
해석
ANSWER SHEETS

ANSWER KEYS 정답

TEST 01

PART 5	101 (B)	102 (C)	103 (B)	104 (B)	105 (D)
	106 (C)	107 (B)	108 (B)	109 (B)	110 (B)
	111 (D)	112 (C)	113 (B)	114 (B)	115 (C)
	116 (D)	117 (A)	118 (B)	119 (C)	120 (C)
	121 (A)	122 (D)	123 (B)	124 (D)	125 (B)
	126 (C)	127 (D)	128 (B)	129 (B)	130 (B)

PART 6	131 (A)	132 (B)	133 (C)	134 (B)	135 (B)
	136 (C)	137 (B)	138 (A)	139 (B)	140 (C)
	141 (B)	142 (C)	143 (B)	144 (A)	145 (A)
	146 (B)				

PART 7	147 (D)	148 (B)	149 (D)	150 (D)	151 (C)
	152 (B)	153 (C)	154 (B)	155 (B)	156 (B)
	157 (D)	158 (D)	159 (B)	160 (C)	161 (C)
	162 (D)	163 (C)	164 (A)	165 (B)	166 (A)
	167 (C)	168 (D)	169 (C)	170 (B)	171 (D)
	172 (D)	173 (A)	174 (D)	175 (A)	176 (D)
	177 (C)	178 (D)	179 (B)	180 (A)	181 (D)
	182 (A)	183 (C)	184 (B)	185 (B)	186 (C)
	187 (C)	188 (A)	189 (A)	190 (B)	191 (C)
	192 (A)	193 (B)	194 (D)	195 (B)	196 (D)
	197 (B)	198 (A)	199 (D)	200 (D)	

TEST 02

PART 5	101 (D)	102 (B)	103 (B)	104 (D)	105 (B)
	106 (A)	107 (C)	108 (A)	109 (B)	110 (B)
	111 (C)	112 (B)	113 (B)	114 (B)	115 (C)
	116 (D)	117 (C)	118 (D)	119 (D)	120 (C)
	121 (D)	122 (B)	123 (C)	124 (C)	125 (A)
	126 (C)	127 (B)	128 (C)	129 (C)	130 (C)

PART 6	131 (C)	132 (A)	133 (A)	134 (C)	135 (B)
	136 (D)	137 (B)	138 (B)	139 (C)	140 (A)
	141 (A)	142 (B)	143 (B)	144 (D)	145 (A)
	146 (A)				

PART 7	147 (C)	148 (D)	149 (B)	150 (B)	151 (D)
	152 (A)	153 (B)	154 (C)	155 (B)	156 (B)
	157 (D)	158 (D)	159 (B)	160 (B)	161 (A)
	162 (B)	163 (B)	164 (C)	165 (B)	166 (C)
	167 (D)	168 (C)	169 (C)	170 (B)	171 (C)
	172 (C)	173 (A)	174 (B)	175 (C)	176 (D)
	177 (B)	178 (A)	179 (C)	180 (C)	181 (B)
	182 (A)	183 (D)	184 (C)	185 (C)	186 (D)
	187 (C)	188 (C)	189 (B)	190 (B)	191 (C)
	192 (B)	193 (C)	194 (A)	195 (D)	196 (C)
	197 (D)	198 (C)	199 (D)	200 (B)	

TEST 03

PART 5 101 (D) 102 (B) 103 (D) 104 (A) 105 (B)
106 (C) 107 (C) 108 (A) 109 (D) 110 (B)
111 (D) 112 (B) 113 (A) 114 (A) 115 (B)
116 (A) 117 (A) 118 (B) 119 (D) 120 (C)
121 (D) 122 (B) 123 (B) 124 (C) 125 (D)
126 (B) 127 (A) 128 (A) 129 (A) 130 (D)

PART 6 131 (A) 132 (C) 133 (C) 134 (B) 135 (C)
136 (C) 137 (D) 138 (B) 139 (A) 140 (D)
141 (C) 142 (C) 143 (C) 144 (A) 145 (C)
146 (A)

PART 7 147 (C) 148 (A) 149 (A) 150 (B) 151 (C)
152 (D) 153 (D) 154 (C) 155 (D) 156 (C)
157 (B) 158 (D) 159 (C) 160 (C) 161 (D)
162 (B) 163 (D) 164 (B) 165 (B) 166 (B)
167 (A) 168 (B) 169 (C) 170 (A) 171 (B)
172 (C) 173 (C) 174 (D) 175 (D) 176 (A)
177 (B) 178 (B) 179 (A) 180 (D) 181 (B)
182 (A) 183 (C) 184 (A) 185 (D) 186 (C)
187 (D) 188 (B) 189 (B) 190 (D) 191 (D)
192 (C) 193 (C) 194 (C) 195 (B) 196 (B)
197 (C) 198 (B) 199 (D) 200 (C)

TEST 04

PART 5 101 (D) 102 (C) 103 (D) 104 (A) 105 (C)
106 (B) 107 (A) 108 (D) 109 (C) 110 (B)
111 (C) 112 (D) 113 (D) 114 (C) 115 (C)
116 (A) 117 (A) 118 (B) 119 (D) 120 (B)
121 (C) 122 (C) 123 (A) 124 (A) 125 (C)
126 (A) 127 (C) 128 (B) 129 (A) 130 (D)

PART 6 131 (C) 132 (C) 133 (C) 134 (B) 135 (B)
136 (C) 137 (B) 138 (A) 139 (D) 140 (D)
141 (A) 142 (A) 143 (C) 144 (A) 145 (B)
146 (D)

PART 7 147 (B) 148 (B) 149 (C) 150 (D) 151 (B)
152 (A) 153 (B) 154 (B) 155 (B) 156 (C)
157 (A) 158 (D) 159 (A) 160 (A) 161 (D)
162 (C) 163 (C) 164 (A) 165 (C) 166 (A)
167 (D) 168 (B) 169 (C) 170 (B) 171 (D)
172 (D) 173 (D) 174 (C) 175 (C) 176 (D)
177 (C) 178 (B) 179 (C) 180 (A) 181 (B)
182 (A) 183 (B) 184 (B) 185 (D) 186 (A)
187 (D) 188 (B) 189 (D) 190 (C) 191 (D)
192 (C) 193 (C) 194 (A) 195 (C) 196 (A)
197 (B) 198 (C) 199 (A) 200 (B)

TEST 05

PART 5 101 (D) 102 (B) 103 (A) 104 (C) 105 (B)
106 (D) 107 (C) 108 (B) 109 (C) 110 (B)
111 (A) 112 (C) 113 (B) 114 (D) 115 (D)
116 (D) 117 (B) 118 (A) 119 (D) 120 (A)
121 (B) 122 (A) 123 (D) 124 (D) 125 (D)
126 (B) 127 (B) 128 (A) 129 (C) 130 (D)

PART 6 131 (A) 132 (D) 133 (C) 134 (B) 135 (B)
136 (B) 137 (D) 138 (C) 139 (C) 140 (B)
141 (A) 142 (A) 143 (B) 144 (C) 145 (D)
146 (D)

PART 7 147 (D) 148 (B) 149 (B) 150 (D) 151 (B)
152 (D) 153 (A) 154 (D) 155 (B) 156 (B)
157 (A) 158 (B) 159 (A) 160 (D) 161 (C)
162 (C) 163 (C) 164 (B) 165 (C) 166 (A)
167 (D) 168 (C) 169 (D) 170 (A) 171 (A)
172 (B) 173 (A) 174 (C) 175 (D) 176 (D)
177 (B) 178 (C) 179 (D) 180 (A) 181 (C)
182 (A) 183 (A) 184 (C) 185 (C) 186 (C)
187 (B) 188 (B) 189 (C) 190 (B) 191 (B)
192 (D) 193 (B) 194 (C) 195 (B) 196 (A)
197 (C) 198 (A) 199 (C) 200 (C)

TEST 06

PART 5 101 (A) 102 (B) 103 (D) 104 (C) 105 (A)
106 (D) 107 (D) 108 (A) 109 (B) 110 (A)
111 (C) 112 (B) 113 (B) 114 (C) 115 (C)
116 (C) 117 (B) 118 (C) 119 (D) 120 (A)
121 (B) 122 (A) 123 (C) 124 (D) 125 (A)
126 (B) 127 (C) 128 (A) 129 (C) 130 (C)

PART 6 131 (A) 132 (D) 133 (C) 134 (C) 135 (B)
136 (D) 137 (C) 138 (B) 139 (B) 140 (A)
141 (B) 142 (A) 143 (D) 144 (A) 145 (B)
146 (C)

PART 7 147 (B) 148 (C) 149 (C) 150 (C) 151 (B)
152 (C) 153 (B) 154 (D) 155 (C) 156 (C)
157 (B) 158 (B) 159 (C) 160 (A) 161 (A)
162 (C) 163 (C) 164 (A) 165 (C) 166 (B)
167 (A) 168 (C) 169 (A) 170 (A) 171 (C)
172 (D) 173 (C) 174 (B) 175 (C) 176 (D)
177 (C) 178 (B) 179 (C) 180 (D) 181 (D)
182 (B) 183 (C) 184 (C) 185 (B) 186 (C)
187 (B) 188 (D) 189 (C) 190 (C) 191 (C)
192 (D) 193 (B) 194 (A) 195 (A) 196 (A)
197 (A) 198 (D) 199 (C) 200 (B)

TEST 07

PART 5 101 (D) 102 (C) 103 (A) 104 (A) 105 (B)
106 (C) 107 (C) 108 (D) 109 (A) 110 (C)
111 (B) 112 (C) 113 (A) 114 (D) 115 (A)
116 (C) 117 (A) 118 (D) 119 (D) 120 (B)
121 (A) 122 (C) 123 (A) 124 (A) 125 (C)
126 (A) 127 (A) 128 (C) 129 (B) 130 (D)

PART 6 131 (C) 132 (C) 133 (B) 134 (D) 135 (A)
136 (C) 137 (B) 138 (A) 139 (C) 140 (D)
141 (C) 142 (B) 143 (D) 144 (B) 145 (C)
146 (A)

PART 7 147 (D) 148 (B) 149 (D) 150 (C) 151 (C)
152 (A) 153 (B) 154 (D) 155 (B) 156 (B)
157 (B) 158 (C) 159 (A) 160 (C) 161 (B)
162 (C) 163 (D) 164 (C) 165 (C) 166 (B)
167 (A) 168 (C) 169 (C) 170 (C) 171 (B)
172 (A) 173 (A) 174 (C) 175 (B) 176 (D)
177 (D) 178 (B) 179 (A) 180 (B) 181 (D)
182 (A) 183 (B) 184 (B) 185 (D) 186 (B)
187 (C) 188 (D) 189 (B) 190 (A) 191 (C)
192 (B) 193 (C) 194 (A) 195 (D) 196 (C)
197 (C) 198 (C) 199 (C) 200 (D)

TEST 08

PART 5 101 (C) 102 (A) 103 (D) 104 (B) 105 (C)
106 (C) 107 (A) 108 (D) 109 (C) 110 (B)
111 (C) 112 (C) 113 (B) 114 (C) 115 (D)
116 (B) 117 (B) 118 (A) 119 (B) 120 (C)
121 (D) 122 (C) 123 (B) 124 (B) 125 (B)
126 (C) 127 (A) 128 (D) 129 (C) 130 (B)

PART 6 131 (C) 132 (C) 133 (B) 134 (B) 135 (D)
136 (B) 137 (C) 138 (D) 139 (A) 140 (C)
141 (A) 142 (A) 143 (C) 144 (C) 145 (A)
146 (C)

PART 7 147 (B) 148 (C) 149 (A) 150 (B) 151 (B)
152 (C) 153 (C) 154 (B) 155 (C) 156 (A)
157 (D) 158 (A) 159 (D) 160 (C) 161 (C)
162 (B) 163 (A) 164 (C) 165 (A) 166 (D)
167 (B) 168 (B) 169 (A) 170 (C) 171 (A)
172 (C) 173 (D) 174 (C) 175 (A) 176 (B)
177 (B) 178 (C) 179 (B) 180 (D) 181 (C)
182 (D) 183 (B) 184 (C) 185 (C) 186 (B)
187 (C) 188 (B) 189 (A) 190 (D) 191 (C)
192 (D) 193 (C) 194 (B) 195 (A) 196 (B)
197 (B) 198 (C) 199 (C) 200 (D)

TEST 09

PART 5 101 (B) 102 (C) 103 (B) 104 (D) 105 (B)
106 (A) 107 (B) 108 (C) 109 (C) 110 (A)
111 (B) 112 (A) 113 (A) 114 (D) 115 (C)
116 (D) 117 (A) 118 (A) 119 (A) 120 (D)
121 (C) 122 (A) 123 (A) 124 (C) 125 (C)
126 (B) 127 (C) 128 (C) 129 (C) 130 (B)

PART 6 131 (B) 132 (D) 133 (C) 134 (D) 135 (B)
136 (C) 137 (D) 138 (B) 139 (D) 140 (D)
141 (A) 142 (B) 143 (C) 144 (B) 145 (B)
146 (D)

PART 7 147 (A) 148 (C) 149 (D) 150 (B) 151 (D)
152 (D) 153 (B) 154 (A) 155 (C) 156 (D)
157 (B) 158 (C) 159 (B) 160 (D) 161 (C)
162 (B) 163 (A) 164 (D) 165 (B) 166 (B)
167 (B) 168 (D) 169 (B) 170 (C) 171 (A)
172 (B) 173 (D) 174 (A) 175 (C) 176 (A)
177 (D) 178 (B) 179 (C) 180 (C) 181 (C)
182 (A) 183 (B) 184 (B) 185 (B) 186 (B)
187 (A) 188 (D) 189 (D) 190 (C) 191 (A)
192 (C) 193 (C) 194 (B) 195 (A) 196 (B)
197 (D) 198 (C) 199 (A) 200 (A)

TEST 10

PART 5 101 (C) 102 (B) 103 (A) 104 (C) 105 (C)
106 (A) 107 (D) 108 (C) 109 (A) 110 (C)
111 (C) 112 (D) 113 (C) 114 (C) 115 (A)
116 (A) 117 (D) 118 (C) 119 (D) 120 (B)
121 (C) 122 (B) 123 (C) 124 (B) 125 (D)
126 (A) 127 (B) 128 (C) 129 (C) 130 (A)

PART 6 131 (D) 132 (C) 133 (C) 134 (D) 135 (D)
136 (B) 137 (D) 138 (A) 139 (B) 140 (A)
141 (C) 142 (C) 143 (A) 144 (D) 145 (B)
146 (C)

PART 7 147 (C) 148 (B) 149 (D) 150 (C) 151 (C)
152 (A) 153 (C) 154 (B) 155 (C) 156 (B)
157 (C) 158 (A) 159 (B) 160 (C) 161 (C)
162 (C) 163 (B) 164 (D) 165 (B) 166 (A)
167 (D) 168 (D) 169 (D) 170 (C) 171 (C)
172 (C) 173 (C) 174 (D) 175 (D) 176 (C)
177 (D) 178 (C) 179 (A) 180 (C) 181 (C)
182 (D) 183 (D) 184 (A) 185 (C) 186 (C)
187 (C) 188 (D) 189 (A) 190 (A) 191 (D)
192 (C) 193 (B) 194 (C) 195 (C) 196 (C)
197 (D) 198 (C) 199 (B) 200 (B)

점수 환산표

맞은 개수	환산 점수	맞은 개수	환산 점수
96-100	465-495	41-45	115-155
91-95	415-470	36-40	95-130
86-90	380-425	31-35	70-105
81-85	350-390	26-30	55-90
76-80	320-365	21-25	40-70
71-75	290-335	16-20	30-55
66-70	260-305	11-15	20-45
61-65	230-275	6-10	15-30
56-60	200-245	1-5	5-15
51-55	170-215	0	5
46-50	145-185		

나의 점수 향상표

TEST	맞은 개수	환산 점수
TEST 01		
TEST 02		
TEST 03		
TEST 04		
TEST 05		
TEST 06		
TEST 07		
TEST 08		
TEST 09		
TEST 10		

▶각 TEST 채점 후 향상표를 작성하여 나의 실력 향상을 확인하세요.

PART 5

101 창고의 보안을 강화하기 위해, 정규직 보안 직원들이 내일부터 그곳에서 근무할 것이다.

102 자연의 아름다움과 야외 모험의 기회들로 유명한, Yosemite Valley는 매년 3~4백만 명이 방문한다.

103 새 다큐멘터리가 매주 토요일 밤 8시에 방송될 예정이다.

104 Parkway Motors는 자사의 대여 차량용 고급 차량들을 더 구입할 것이라고 발표했다.

105 Carlsberg Inc.의 어떤 컴퓨터들도 업그레이드가 필요하지 않은 반면에, 다른 회사들이 만든 것들은 개선이 되어야 한다.

106 Chapman Consulting은 아시아 국가들에서 제품을 판매하기를 기대하는 회사들에게 조언을 제공하는 것을 전문으로 한다.

107 새로 개업한 Green Bistro가 마케팅 컨설턴트들과 계약을 맺은 후에, 그 레스토랑에 대한 지역 주민들의 인지도가 현저하게 더 나아졌다.

108 관리자들도 직원들도 연휴 주말 동안 근무하는 데 관심이 없다.

109 증가하는 경쟁 가운데, Donaldson 씨는 자신의 회사에서 연구에 더 많은 돈을 투자하기로 결정했다.

110 실험실에서 새로운 화학 물질을 만드는 것은 일반적으로 복잡한 과정을 필요로 한다.

111 분실물 센터로 보내진 많은 물품들이 그 다음 날에 회수되지 않았다.

112 Ernest Tannehill은 지속적인 신약 개발 작업을 지원하고 있는데, 그것은 수백만 달러의 수익을 창출할 가능성이 있다.

113 그 고객 서비스 직원은 몇 차례의 배송이 창고에서 출하되지 않은 원인을 알아보려고 애쓰고 있다.

114 회사 보유 배송 트럭들의 업그레이드에 관한 제안이 이사진과 함께하는 분기별 Busy Bees Shipping Co. 회의에서 고려될 것이다.

115 Landers 씨는 새 Coryne 접시들을 찾아보러 나갔고, 쇼핑 센터에서 판매 중인 것들을 발견했다.

116 적절하게 관리하면, 여러분의 Bronoville 주방 도구들은 최소 7년간 지속될 것으로 예상됩니다.

117 종이 기반의 모든 의료 기록들은 환자들에 관한 기밀 정보를 포함하고 있기 때문에 잠금 장치가 된 파일 캐비닛에 보관된다.

118 Southfield Freight는 증가하는 유리 제품 배송 수량으로 인해 물품을 처리하는 자사의 직원들을 재교육했다.

119 Jackson Corporation의 자회사는 Cindy Mercer의 감독 아래 운영될 것이다.

120 면접은 가능한 한 많은 지원자들이 고려되는 것을 확실히 하려는 노력의 일환으로 하루 종일 실시될 것이다.

121 세부 사항들을 검토했음에도 불구하고 위원회에 의해 사고의 원인이 밝혀질 수 없었다.

122 남성복 코너에 있는 모든 제품들은 별도의 공지가 있지 않는 한 25퍼센트 할인 판매된다.

123 지역 내의 좋지 않은 날씨가 Symington 씨의 항공편이 제시간에 출발하지 못하게 했다.

124 Davidson 씨는 지원자들에게 직접 연락했지만, 그의 동료들 중 세 명이 면접을 도와주었다.

125 저희 회사의 그 자리를 수락하기를 원하시면, 반드시 첨부된 서류에 서명하신 후에 이메일 또는 팩스로 근무일 기준 3일 내에 돌려보내 주시기 바랍니다.

126 경영진은 항상 Whitner Inc. 직원들의 주요 업적을 치하하기 위해 노력한다.

127 〈Devon Times〉의 기자들은 Maxell Industries와 계속 진행 중인 분쟁에 관련된 개개인들과 인터뷰하는 것에 동의했다.

128 Jacobs 씨는 자신의 사무실에서 고객들과 화상 회의를 하는 것을 선호하여, 출장 가는 것을 피한다.

129 아동 도서 작가들은 지난달에 후보자 지명이 공표된 이후로 기대감을 갖고 Starling Writer's Award 수상자들의 발표를 기다려 왔다.

130 Street Bridge 마무리 공사를 위한 기간은 그 프로젝트 기술자에 의해 만들어진 단지 추정치였을 뿐이었다.

PART 6

신유형 ▶ 131-134는 다음 기사를 참조하시오.

Tokyo—Mayoto Mobile Inc.는 그 제품 라인을 내년에 인도와 필리핀으로 수출하기 시작할 것이라는 정보를 오늘 발표했다.

영업 부사장인 Haruki Kurosawa 씨는 새로운 시도가 회사의 수익을 거의 두 배로 만들 것으로 기대한다고 말했다. 예상되는 수요를 충족하기 위해, 공장들은 그 생산 능력을 확대할 것이다. 다섯 곳 모두 생산 비율을 40퍼센트까지 늘릴 예정이다.

인도와 필리핀의 휴대 전화 사용에 정통한 시장 분석가들은 Mayoto Mobile이 다른 회사들로부터 많은 고객들을 끌어들일 것이라고 생각한다. "그들의 매출은 빠르게 그 경쟁사들의 매출을 훨씬 앞지를 것입니다."라고 〈Tech Asia Weekly〉의 편집장인 Yani Jung이 말했다.

Mayoto Mobile은 또한 특별히 해외 시장들을 위한 더 낮은 가격의 신제품 라인을 개발할 것이다. 이렇게 하여, 그들은 더 폭넓은 고객 층에게 판매를 할 수 있을 것이다.

신유형 ▶ 135-138은 다음 공지를 참조하시오.

Saint Martha Hospital의 보수 공사가 6월 11일이 있는 주 동안 이루어질 것입니다. 작업은 서쪽 물품 보관실이 간호사실로 개조되는 것으로 시작할 것입니다. 또한 방문객과 가족들을 위한 셀프 서비스 커피 바도 설치될 것입니다. 이 프로젝트 동안, 병실 9208부터 9215까지의 병실은 이용할 수 없을 것입니다. 그 결과, 직원 규모도 병동의 환자 수에 맞도록 줄어들 것입니다. 서쪽 측면에 있는 화장실들은 이 기간 동안 이용하실 수 없다는 것을 유념해 주시기 바랍니다. 그로 인해 동쪽 홀 화장실들이 매우 붐빌 수 있습니다. 이 개선 과정을 위해 진행되고 있는 준비에 관해 어떠한 의문 사항이나 의견이 있으면, 9층 관리인인 Matt Whitaker에게 말해 주시기 바랍니다.

신유형 ▶ 139-142는 다음 이메일을 참조하시오.

수신: Tabitha Chun
발신: Allen Lundy
날짜: 9월 27일
제목: 가을 축제의 성공

Chun 씨에게,

저희가 지난번에 이야기했던 이후로, 연례 가을 축제 준비로 바빴습니다. 우선, 배치를 기존의 것에서 변경하라는 귀하의 조언을 받아들여, 무대가 공원의 중앙에 있을 것입니다. 말씀하신 대로, 다른 활동들을 무대에 다소 가까이서 하는 것이 행사를 더욱 통합되도록 만들 것입니다. 또한 페이스 페인팅과 풍선 아트 같은 추가적인 어린이 활동들도 마련했습니다. 이는 행사에 더 많은 가족들을 끌어들일 수 있게 할 것입니다. 조직 위원회와 저는 축제를 개선할 귀하의 아이디어들에 매우 만족스럽습니다. 추가 의견이 있으면 저에게 전화해 주세요.

안녕히 계십시오.
Allen Lundy
Starwood 가을 축제, 물류 관리자

신유형 ▶ 143-146은 다음 기사를 참조하시오.

〈Dried Out〉 작가를 초청한 지역 서점

Aukland (12월 3일)—Attic 서점의 소유주인 Natalie Yoon은 일요일에 12th Street에 위치한 자신의 서점으로 〈Dried Out〉 시리즈의 유명 작가인 Edmond George를 초청했다. George 씨와의 질의 응답 세션에 이어, 작가는 〈Eleventh Hour〉라는 부제의 시리즈의 최신작에서 발췌한 부분을 낭독했다. 그는 또한 참석한 이들에게 자신의 책에 사인을 해 주었다.

찬사를 받은 이 책 외에, George 씨는 또한 베스트셀러인 단행본 소설 〈Breach of Risk〉를 썼다. 그의 작품은 도서 평론가들 Marge Hass와 Benny White에 의해 "놀랄 만한 성과"라는 찬사를 받았다.

George 씨의 가장 최신 책을 찾을 수 있는 곳에 관한 상세 정보와 질의 응답 세션 녹화 영상을 위해 theatticbooks.net을 방문하라.

PART 7

147-148은 다음 기사를 참조하시오.

(Twin Falls—1월 12일) Twin Falls Ski Resort는 올겨울에 방문객 수가 예기치 못하게 감소했다고 알렸다. 올해 많은 적설량과 추운 기온을 감안할 때, 저조한 티켓 판매량은 많은 이들을 놀라게 했다. 공원 책임자인 Michael Lemme은 지역의 휘발유 가격 인상이 원인일 수 있다고 생각하고 있다. 방문객 수 감소에 대응해, 공원 측은 지금부터 시즌 종료 때까지 티켓을 할인 판매한다고 발표했다. www.skitwin.com을 방문하면 상세 가격 정보를 확인할 수 있다. 지역 주민들은 추가적인 특별 할인도 이용할 수 있다.

147 기사에 따르면, 무엇이 방문객들 수의 감소를 야기했는가?
(A) 공원 수의 감소
(B) 값비싼 스키 리조트 티켓들
(C) 과도한 적설량
(D) 휘발유 가격 인상

148 리조트는 최근의 매출 변화에 어떻게 대처하고 있는가?
(A) 겨울 동안 시즌 티켓을 판매함으로써
(B) 티켓에 할인을 제공함으로써
(C) 지역 주민들을 공원에 초대함으로써
(D) 휘발유 가격에 보조금을 지급함으로써

149-150은 다음 광고를 참조하시오.

소유자 게시: Perkins 잔디 깎이 4200X
제시 가격: 110달러

지역: Ontario, OR

게시물 상세

10개월 전 매장에서 구입함. 원래 가격 450달러. 1년 공장 품질 보증 서비스 중 2개월 남음.
상태는 좋지만 구매자가 망가진 바퀴 하나를 교체해야 하며, 품질 보증 서비스에 해당되지 않음.
현금만 가능. (사진은 없고 직접 봐야 함.)
구매자가 가져가야 함.
최고 가격 제시자에게 판매될 것임; 관심이 있다면, 전화로 예약.
길 안내를 받기 위해, (562) 272-1747로 전화 또는 문자 바람.

149 잔디 깎는 기계에 관해 설명된 것은 무엇인가?
(A) 가장 먼저 오는 이에게 판매될 것이다.
(B) 구매자는 품질 보증 서비스를 이용해 바퀴를 교체해야 한다.
(C) 한 명이 넘는 소유주에 의해 사용되었다.
(D) 1년 미만의 기간 동안 사용되었다.

150 소유자는 무엇을 하겠다고 제안하는가?
(A) 판매 전에 망가진 부분을 수리하기
(B) 요청 시에 할인을 고려하기
(C) 제품의 사진을 보여주기
(D) 잠재적인 구매자를 위해 제품을 보유해 두기

151-152는 다음 공지를 참조하시오.

이제 Evans Building의 6개월간의 개조 공사가 완료되었으므로, TTG Enterprises는 그 부서들을 재편할 것입니다. 4월 2일부터, 재무 팀의 사무실들은 건물의 남쪽 동에서 찾아볼 수 있습니다. 마케팅 사무실들은 동쪽 동에 있을 것인데, 그곳이 유일하게 이 직원들을 함께 모아둘 만큼 충분히 넓은 공간이기 때문입니다. 변동 사항은 몇 주 내로 새로운 건물 안내 정보에 반영될 것입니다. 그동안은 안내 데스크의 안내 직원들이 여러분이 갈 곳을 기꺼이 알려 드릴 것입니다.

151 공지는 왜 쓰여졌는가?
(A) 회사에 의해 제공되는 새로운 서비스를 홍보하기 위해
(B) 건물 관련 규정에 대한 최신 정보를 알리기 위해
(C) 일부 직원들의 이전을 알리기 위해
(D) 곧 있을 개조 공사 프로젝트를 설명하기 위해

152 TTG Enterprises에 관해 언급된 것은 무엇인가?
(A) 직원들이 4월 2일에 고객들을 만나지 못할 것이다.
(B) 마케팅 부서에 직원들이 가장 많이 있다.
(C) 남쪽과 동쪽 측면에 출입구가 있다.
(D) 6개월 동안 운영되어 왔다.

153-155는 다음 안내 정보를 참조하시오.

유지 보수 서비스 정보

Upton Station의 시설 관리부는 대략 15명의 직원들로 구성된 팀으로, 시설의 순조롭고 안전한 운영에 기여하고 있습니다. 엔지니어링 직원들이 열차와 선로의 수리를 하는 반면, 저희 부서는 조명과 화장실, 출입구 등을 포함하여, 역의 다른 모든 측면들을 책임지고 있습니다. 이것들은 직원 안내서에 개괄되어 있습니다.

업무는 시설의 요구 사항에 따라 매우 다양합니다. 각 교대 근무 시작 때,

긴급 업무들을 모두 먼저 수행하고 뒤이어 일상적인 유지 보수와 수리를
진행합니다. 저희는 무엇이 반납되고 대여되었는지를 보여주는 장비 일
지를 관리하고 있습니다. 이것은 물품 보관실의 문에 걸려 있습니다.

모든 출입구들은 매일 역을 열고 닫을 때 점검됩니다. 운영 시간 이후 시
설 이용에 대해서는 555-7878로 전화하세요.

153 이 안내 정보를 받도록 의도되는 대상은 누구인가?

(A) 버스 터미널의 승객들

(B) 전문 여행사 직원들

(C) 기차역의 직원들

(D) 현재 엔지니어링을 공부하는 학생들

154 안내 정보에 따르면, 읽는 이들은 장비 대여에 관한 추가 정보를
어떻게 얻을 수 있는가?

(A) 전화 상담 서비스에 전화함으로써

(B) 게시된 문서를 읽음으로써

(C) 상사에게 이야기함으로써

(D) 웹 페이지를 확인함으로써

155 출입구들은 얼마나 자주 확인되는가?

(A) 하루에 한 번

(B) 하루에 두 번

(C) 일주일에 한 번

(D) 일주일에 두 번

156-158은 다음 회람을 참조하시오.

Kathryn Morrison 마라톤 경기 후 연회

Kathryn Morrison 마라톤 경기 후 스파게티 먹기는 원래 예정된 대로
경기 후 저녁인, 9월 20일 오후 5시에 이어질 것입니다. 하지만 이중 예
약으로 인해, 그 행사는 Alphonsus Center 대신 Cole Road에 있는
Gold Gate Festivities Hall에서 열릴 것입니다.

Leif Stadium(경주 출발선)에서 Gold Gate Festivities Hall까지의
길 안내

Vermont Road의 서쪽에서 시작해, 그 길을 따라 두 개의 신호등을 지
나 Granite Street까지 가세요. Granite에서 1마일 계속 가세요. 그런
다음 Phillmore로 우회전하세요. Gold Street에서 곧장 좌회전하면 오
른쪽에 Gold Gate Hall의 주차장이 있을 것입니다. 안내 데스크의 직
원이 정확한 행사 장소로 안내해 드릴 것입니다.

현장 주차 공간이 많다는 점을 기억하세요. Festivities Hall의 주차장에
들어갈 때 주차권을 발급받게 될 것입니다. 그저 식사 자리를 떠나기 전
에 주차권을 확인받으시면 지불은 필요하지 않을 것입니다.

156 행사는 원래 어디에서 개최될 계획이었는가?

(A) Gold Gate Festivities Hall에서

(B) Alphonsus Center에서

(C) Cole Road에서

(D) 경기장의 입구에서

157 경주는 어디에서 시작될 것인가?

(A) Granite Street

(B) Phillmore Road

(C) Gold Street

(D) Vermont Road

158 회람에 따르면, 주차 요금은 어떻게 면제될 수 있는가?

(A) 유효한 주차 공간을 찾음으로써

(B) 저녁 식사가 끝나기 전에 떠남으로써

(C) 마라톤 경주에 참가함으로써

(D) 조건에 맞는 티켓을 보유함으로써

신유형 ▶ 159-160은 다음 문자 메시지 대화를 참조하시오.

Alita LaGrande	오전 10:14

제 회의가 오전 11시까지 지속될 거라 생각했는데, 끝났어요. 그래서 지
금 Birmingham으로 가요.

Walter Lind	오전 10:17

기차표 변경하는 데 아무 문제 없으셨죠, 그렇죠? 제가 유연한 요금으로
예약했으니 그 노선의 아무 열차나 타실 수 있으실 거예요.

Alita LaGrande	오전 10:18

문제없어요. 그런데 도착하는 대로 Ewell Hotel에 체크인할 수 있도
록 확실히 해 두고 싶어요. 2시에 체크인할 거라고 했는데, 거기 1시간
정도 일찍 도착할 거예요. 나 대신 전화해서 괜찮은지 확인해 주겠어요?

Walter Lind	오전 10:20

물론이죠. 확인을 끝낸 후에 문자를 보낼게요.

Alita LaGrande	오전 10:21

고마워요!

159 LaGrande 씨는 언제 호텔에 체크인하기를 원하는가?

(A) 오전 11시에

(B) 오후 1시에

(C) 오후 2시에

(D) 오후 5시에

160 오전 10시 20분에, Lind 씨가 "Of course"라고 썼을 때 의미하
신유형 는 것은 무엇인가?

(A) 그가 LaGrande 씨를 픽업할 것이다.

(B) 그가 기차 표를 예약할 것이다.

(C) 그가 호텔에 연락할 것이다.

(D) 그가 기차역에 전화할 것이다.

161-164는 다음 편지를 참조하시오.

Joyce Wallace
629 Park Boulevard
Roxbury, MA 02119

1월 8일

Sergio Bianchi
881 Valley Street
Collingswood, NJ 08108

Bianchi 씨께,

제 이름은 Joyce Wallace로, Vernon Pharmaceuticals의 연구 부
서의 책임자입니다. 귀사의 수석 실험실 연구원 자리가 공석이라는 것을
알고 있으며, 저는 James McCarty가 이 역할에 뛰어난 후보자일 것이
라고 생각합니다.

McCarty 씨는 자원 봉사 교육생으로 6년 전 저희 회사에 들어왔고, 3개
월 프로그램이 끝난 후에 정규직으로 채용되었습니다. 실험실 연구원으
로 단 6개월 근무한 후, 그는 프로젝트 책임자 역할을 맡게 되었는데, 그
것은 대개 훨씬 더 선임 직원들에게 주어지는 자리입니다. 저는 그 이후

로 McCarty 씨의 직속 상관으로 근무해 왔습니다. McCarty 씨와 함께 일하며, 저는 그가 프로젝트 지연과 예기치 않은 도전들에 대한 해결책을 생각해낼 수 있는 방식에 깊은 인상을 받았습니다. 그는 늘 에너지와 열정으로 업무를 완수해 냈고, 자신의 분야에 관련된 지식을 늘리기 위해 필요한 노력을 기꺼이 쏟아 부었습니다.

McCarty 씨를 영입하면 그의 직업의식과 경험에서 큰 혜택을 얻을 것이라고 확신합니다. 궁금한 점이 있으시면 기꺼이 답해 드릴 수 있으며 (617) 555-7041로 연락이 가능합니다.

안녕히 계십시오.

Joyce Wallace

161 Wallace 씨가 쓴 편지의 목적은 무엇인가?

(A) 공석에 대한 지원서를 제출하기
(B) Bianchi 씨에게 실험실 연구원 직을 제안하기
(C) 한 직책에 직원을 추천하기
(D) 신입 사원에게 직무를 설명하기

162 McCarty 씨에 관해 알 수 있는 것은 무엇인가?

(A) Wallace 씨와 6개월 동안 함께 일했다.
(B) 관리자 역할을 맡은 적이 없다.
(C) Wallace 씨의 직속 상관이었다.
(D) 늘 유급 사원이었던 것은 아니다.

163 두 번째 단락, 세 번째 줄의 단어 "assumed"와 의미가 가장 가까운 것은 무엇인가?

(A) ~을 할당했다
(B) ~을 제안했다
(C) ~을 수락했다
(D) ~을 만들었다

164 McCarty 씨가 지닌 자질들 중 하나로 나타나 있지 않은 것은 무엇인가?

(A) 시간 관리 능력
(B) 에너지 넘치는 태도
(C) 문제 해결 능력
(D) 배움에 대한 의지

신유형 165-167은 다음 기사를 참조하시오.

레스토랑 라이선스 관련 새 소식

Greater Detroit 지역의 수많은 레스토랑들은, 현재 주 공무원들에 의해 검토 중인 레스토랑 라이선스 법률에 있어 곧 있을 변경 사항에 영향을 받을 것이다. — [1] —. 법안의 지지자들은 증가된 정부 세입을 중요한 고려 사항으로 지적한다.

업계 관찰자들은 물가 상승률을 초과한 작년의 6퍼센트 증가율에 이어, 그 규정이 의결되어 1월 초에 시행될 경우 레스토랑 라이선스 비용이 약 8퍼센트까지 증가할 것이라고 예측한다. — [2] —. 그들은 서비스 업계의 고용 성장률에 부정적인 영향을 볼 것으로 예상하는데, 그것은 지난 2년 동안 각각, 10퍼센트와 11퍼센트의 증가를 누렸다.

"이 변경 사항은 식음료 업계에 전체적으로 해로운 결과를 초래할 수 있습니다,"라고 Restaurant Association 회장 Sol Adams가 말했다. — [3] —. 일부에게는 추가적인 행정 비용이 너무 큰 부담일 수 있습니다." 입법자들은 그 혜택이 비즈니스 업계에서 감수해야 할 위험보다 클지 여부를 결정해야 한다. — [4] —.

165 기사에 따르면, 내년에 라이선스 요금은 얼마나 오를 것 같은가?

(A) 6퍼센트
(B) 8퍼센트
(C) 10퍼센트
(D) 11퍼센트

166 전문가들이 법률 제정에 따른 가능한 결과라고 생각하는 것은 무엇인가?

(A) 더 적은 일자리들이 제공될 것이다.
(B) 인플레이션이 계속 증가할 것이다.
(C) 행정 비용이 간소화될 것이다.
(D) 폐업이 줄어들 수 있다.

167 [1], [2], [3], [4]로 표기된 위치들 중에서 다음 문장이 가장 잘 어울리는 곳은 어디인가?

신유형

"재료비의 증가로 인해, 많은 레스토랑들이 이미 긴장한 상태다."

(A) [1]
(B) [2]
(C) [3]
(D) [4]

신유형 168-171은 다음 온라인 채팅을 참조하시오.

Huan Wu 오후 5:24
오늘 우리가 만날 시간이 없었기 때문에, 고전 영화 기념 행사를 위한 모든 것이 어떻게 진행되고 있는지 알고 싶었어요.

Dale Gracey 오후 5:26
막 축제에 대한 광고를 시작했어요.

Ravi Gupta 오후 5:27
도시 전역의 모든 레스토랑과 상점에 우리 포스터를 갖다 놓았고, 그것들은 눈에 잘 띄는 곳에 게시될 거예요.

Huan Wu 오후 5:29
잘됐네요. 많은 사업주들이 그렇게 하겠다고 약속했다는 것을 알지만, 이행하지 않을 수도 있을 거라고 생각했어요.

Dale Gracey 오후 5:30
걱정하실 필요 없어요.

Ravi Gupta 오후 5:31
높은 참석률을 예상하고 있지만, 그것으로 또 다른 문제가 생기잖아요. 극장 뒤쪽의 주차장뿐만 아니라 길 건너편에 있는 주차장도 많은 차량들을 수용할 수 없어요.

Amber Vanuolo 오후 5:32
그래서 Tresson Mall 주차장을 이용하게 하고 두 지점 사이를 운행하는 셔틀 버스를 두도록 허가를 받는 작업을 진행 중이에요.

Huan Wu 오후 5:33
그러면 완벽하게 되겠네요. 고마워요! Amber, 어떤 특별 게스트들이 그쪽으로 올지 알고 있나요?

Amber Vanuolo 오후 5:34
감독님들 몇 분인데, 아직 최종 목록을 갖고 있지는 않아요. 또한 Carlton Fletcher가 그곳에 올 계획이고요. 그가 행사에 관한 자신의 기사가 〈Peoria Daily Times〉의 1면에 실리게 될 것 같다고 했어요.

168 온라인 채팅은 주로 무엇에 관한 것인가?

(A) 시상식 행사
(B) 지역 사회 퍼레이드
(C) 기념일 축하 행사

(D) 영화제

169 오후 5시 29분에, Wu 씨가 "but I thought they might not
follow through"라고 썼을 때 의미하는 것은 무엇인가?

(A) 그녀는 행사 참석률이 높을 것이라는 사실이 놀랍다.

(B) 그녀는 프로젝트가 제때 완료되지 않을 수 있다고 생각했다.

(C) 그녀는 광고를 내걸지 못할 수 있을까 봐 걱정했다.

(D) 그녀는 몇몇 사업주들은 기부하지 않을 것이라고 생각했다.

170 Gupta 씨는 무슨 일이 일어날 것이라고 생각하는가?

(A) 몰이 일찍 문을 닫을 것이다.

(B) 일부 주차 구역들이 가득 찰 것이다.

(C) 셔틀 버스가 제때 운행되지 않을 것이다.

(D) 일부 티켓들이 빠르게 판매될 것이다.

171 Fletcher 씨는 누구일 것 같은가?

(A) 감독

(B) 건물 소유주

(C) 연예인

(D) 기자

신유형 ▶ 172-175는 다음 이메일을 참조하시오.

수신: Katherine Jarvis 〈katherine.jarvis@phc.net〉
발신: Geraldine Grayson 〈g.grayson@reachcomp.com〉
날짜: 1월 17일
답장: PHC 제안서

Jarvis 씨에게,

지난주에 있었던 귀하의 유익한 발표에 대해 대단히 감사 드립니다. 귀하
께서는 PHC의 시장 점유 상태와 독자 참여도를 개괄하는 작업을 아주
잘해 주셨습니다. ― [1] ―. 유감스럽게도, PHC가 저희에게 잘 맞지는
않다는 결정을 내려, 이번에는 거절하려 합니다.

저희는 전반적으로 인쇄 매체 광고를 통한 수익이 줄어드는 것을 목격
해 왔습니다. ― [2] ―. 이는 지난 5년 동안 웹 기반 채널들의 영향 때
문으로 생각하며, 그것은 저희에게 주효하다고 판단했습니다. 저희는 또
한 고객들에게 직접 전단을 우편으로 발송하고 스포츠 행사를 후원하는
일과 같은, 현저한 실적이 있는 다른 프로젝트들에도 전념해 왔습니다.
― [3] ―.

게다가, 월간 잡지와 분기별 잡지에 있어서의 성과를 지켜보고 있고, 이
것들은 여전히 저희 전략의 핵심 부분을 형성합니다. 하지만, 일간지의
경우 과거에 귀사의 것에서 확인했듯이, 더 나빠져 때로 투자 대비 수익
을 제공하지 않고 있습니다. ― [4] ―.

귀하의 양해에 감사 드리며, 행운을 빌어 드립니다.

안녕히 계십시오.

Geraldine Grayson
마케팅 커뮤니케이션 책임자, Reach Computers

---

172 Grayson 씨는 왜 이메일을 썼는가?

(A) 비즈니스 협정을 제안하기 위해

(B) 컴퓨터 주문서를 전달하기 위해

(C) 한 업체에 제안을 하기 위해

(D) 광고 기회를 거절하기 위해

173 Reach Computers를 위한 효과적인 마케팅 기술로 언급되지 않
은 것은 무엇인가?

(A) 전시회 참가

(B) 기업 후원

(C) 온라인 채널들

(D) 광고용 우편물

174 PHC는 어떤 유형의 업체일 것 같은가?

(A) 월간 잡지사

(B) 뉴스 웹사이트

(C) 모바일 앱

(D) 일간 신문사

175 [1], [2], [3], [4]로 표기된 위치들 중에서 다음 문장이 가장 잘 어
신유형 울리는 곳은 어디인가?

"저희 이사진이 회의 중에 귀하의 자료를 검토했고 이 요점들을 장
시간 논의했습니다."

(A) [1]

(B) [2]

(C) [3]

(D) [4]

176-180은 다음 보고서와 기사를 참조하시오.

Kovar Aquarium and Marine Preservation (KAMP)
분기별 요약 사항 보고: Curtis Rafferty

업무/성과:

Marine Preservation Center의 새로운 부속 건물 기공을 위한 언론 행사를 마련했고, 그곳에서 내년에 펭귄 서식지 전시회를 개최할 것임. 16곳의 언론 매체 대표들이 참석했음. [4월]
Jamie Halstead의 도움을 받아, Dallas의 Avery Career Fair에 3년 연속으로 부스 설치를 계획하고 운영함. 우리 부스에 대한 관심이 작년보다 훨씬 더 높았음. [5월]
Lionella Monaldo 관장이 캐나다, Vancouver에서 열린 Progressive Environmental Conference에서 자신의 연구를 발표할 때 수행함. KAMP 프로젝트를 논의하기 위해 연구자들을 만났음. [5월]
직원들에게 동물 복지와 관련된 새로운 정부 규제에 관해 알리기 위한 교육 세션을 실시함. KAMP의 모든 부서들이 이 규정들을 준수하도록 했음. [6월].

신임 관장을 맞이하는 수족관
〈**Kovar Herald Community News**〉 기자
Dorothy Langston 작성

9월 14일—Kovar Aquarium and Marine Preservation(KAMP)은
신임 관장으로 Ruben Caro가 선임되었다고 발표했다. Caro는 해당
수족관에서 관장으로 15년 동안 재직했던 Lionella Monaldo의 후임으
로 근무할 것이다. Monaldo는 자리에서 물러나 은퇴할 예정이다. Caro
가 비록 KAMP에서 5년 동안 연구원으로 근무하기는 했지만, 그가 관장
으로 선임된 것은 일부 사람들에게는 놀라운 일이었는데, 기존의 모든 관
장들이 연구 직책이 아닌 운영 책임자로서의 경력을 지닌 사람들이었기
때문이다. 하지만 관련 분야에서의 뛰어난 이력 그리고 수족관에 대한 관
심을 이끌어 내는 혁신적인 아이디어들과 함께, 해당 시설에 대한 Caro
의 열정이 분명 KAMP에 긍정적인 영향을 미칠 것이다. Caro는 내년
호주의 Sydney에서 열리는 다음 번 Progressive Environmental
Conference에 참석해 구조된 해양 포유류에 관해 연설할 예정이다. 그
곳에서 그는 동종업계의 사람들을 교육하는 것뿐만 아니라 해양 환경을
위해 KAMP가 하는 대단히 중요한 일에 대해 사람들이 관심을 갖도록
만들려고 노력할 것이다.

326 정재현 新토익 실전 1000제 RC 문제집

176 4월에 KAMP에서 무슨 일이 있었는가?

　(A) 펭귄의 서식지 보호를 위한 기금이 마련되었다.

　(B) 새롭게 개장한 전시회에 온 방문객들이 환영을 받았다.

　(C) 몇몇 획기적인 연구가 발표되었다.

　(D) 새로운 건물 구역에 대한 공사가 시작되었다.

177 Rafferty 씨의 Dallas 방문 목적은 무엇이었을 것 같은가?

　(A) 잠재적인 기부자들과 네트워크를 형성하기

　(B) 새로운 규정들에 관해 배우기

　(C) KAMP의 공석을 홍보하기

　(D) 새로운 서비스를 광고하기

178 Langston 씨에 관해 알 수 있는 것은 무엇인가?

　(A) 최근에 수족관을 방문했다.

　(B) 한때 KAMP에서 일을 했었다.

　(C) 곧 자신의 직책을 그만둘 계획이다.

　(D) 지역 신문사에 고용되어 있다.

179 KAMP 관장 직책에 관해 암시된 것은 무엇인가?

　(A) 5년 동안의 경력이 요구된다.

　(B) 대개 연구원이 맡지 않는다.

　(C) 예기치 못하게 채워져야 했다.

　(D) 이사진에 의해 임명된다.

180 Progressive Environmental Conference에 관해 암시된 것은?

　(A) 주최 국가가 바뀐다.

　(B) 인기가 증가하고 있다.

　(C) 2년에 한 번 개최된다.

　(D) 과학자들만을 위해 의도된 것이다.

181-185는 다음 전단과 이메일을 참조하시오.

The Power of Art에 의해 변화하다!

회사가 시내 상업 지구에 위치해 있으신가요? 우리 지역 사회를 도우며 동시에 여러분의 회사에 관심을 불러일으키고 싶으신가요? 그렇다면 The Power of Art (TPOA) 프로그램에 가입하는 것을 고려해 보셔야 할 것입니다. TPOA는 Norfolk City에 더 많은 방문객들이 오도록 돕고자 도심부에 다채로운 벽화를 그리도록 의뢰하고 있습니다. 시의회는 지난 몇 년 동안 관광객 수가 지속적으로 감소해 왔다는 것을 알아냈습니다. 이는 방문객들이 더 줄어드는 일을 방지하는 데 필요한 조치를 취하는 데 있어 시 의회의 결정을 촉발했습니다.

TPOA에 가입함으로써, 여러분의 건물 외부에 벽화가 그려지도록 허용하게 됩니다. 저희 전문 미술가들 중 한 분이 만든 이미지를 선택하거나 여러분이 직접 디자인하실 수 있습니다. 직접 디자인하는 것으로 선택할 경우, 반드시 "역사적인 Norfolk City"의 주제를 따라야 합니다. 그 디자인에 업체의 이름이나 로고가 포함될 수 없습니다.

문의 사항과 등록 요청은 h.fletcher@norfolkcity.gov로 Hubert Fletcher에게 보내야 합니다. 등록은 무료이고, 제출 서류는 4월 15일까지 받을 것입니다. 선정된 장소의 소유주들은 늦어도 4월 25일까지 통지를 받을 것입니다. 소형 벽화(50~250 평방 피트) 그림 작업은 5월 10일에 시작되는 반면, 대형 벽화(251 평방 피트 이상) 그림 작업은 6월 1일에 시작될 것입니다.

페인트와 그림 붓, 양동이, 사다리 등을 기부하는 것에 관심이 있으시면 www.norfolkcity.gov/tpoa를 방문해 주세요. 이는 저희의 예산을 최대한 활용하고 가능한 한 많은 벽화를 제작하는 데 도움이 될 것입니다.

수신: Marilyn Raya 〈rayam@sunnydayflorist.com〉

발신: Hubert Fletcher 〈h.fletcher@norfolkcity.gov〉

날짜: 4월 20일

제목: The Power of Art (TPOA)

Raya 씨에게,

축하합니다! 귀하의 장소(154 Ames Street)가 TPOA 프로그램에 선정되었습니다. 귀하께서는 아래 설명과 함께, 자신의 이미지를 제출해 주셨습니다:

100년 전 Main Street의 모습을 그대로 보여주는 8′×15′ 벽화 (총 120평방 피트). 벽화에는 왼쪽 아래 모서리에 Sunny Day Florist 로고와 오른쪽 아래 모서리에는 미술가의 서명과 함께, 여러 건물들과 사람들이 포함되어 있다.

귀하의 제출물에 일부 수정을 했는데, 그 원래 상태가 저희의 기준에 맞지 않았기 때문입니다. 첨부된 수정 버전을 보시기 바랍니다. 벽화를 그릴 구역에 물품들을 치우는 것 외에 화가들을 위해 특별히 어떤 준비를 하실 필요는 없습니다. 나머지는 팀이 처리할 것이다.

감사합니다!

Hubert Fletcher

책임자, The Power of Art (TPOA)

---

181 TPOA의 목적은 무엇인가?

　(A) 시내 구역을 청소하기

　(B) 더 많은 지역 사업체를 시작하기

　(C) 미술가들을 위한 교육을 제공하기

　(D) 도시에 더 많은 사람들을 끌어들이기

182 전단에서, 첫 번째 단락, 여섯 번째 줄의 단어 "prompted"와 의미가 가장 가까운 것은 무엇인가?

　(A) ~을 시작하게 했다

　(B) 신속히 행동했다

　(C) ~을 허용했다

　(D) 도움을 제공했다

183 전단에 따르면, 웹사이트에서 할 수 있는 것은 무엇인가?

　(A) 프로젝트 아이디어들을 제출하는 것

　(B) 과거의 출품작들을 보는 것

　(C) 물품을 기부하는 것

　(D) 프로그램 규칙들을 검토하는 것

184 Raya 씨의 제출물의 문제는 무엇일 것 같은가?

　(A) 요구되는 주제를 따르지 않았다.

　(B) 특정 업체에 대한 언급이 포함되어 있었다.

　(C) 그 장소가 도심 지역 범위에 들어가지 않는다.

　(D) 전문 미술가에 의해 디자인되지 않았다.

185 팀이 언제 Raya 씨의 업체에서 작업을 시작할 것 같은가?

　(A) 4월 25일

　(B) 5월 10일

　(C) 5월 25일

　(D) 6월 1일

신유형 ▶ 186-190은 다음 공지와 후기, 그리고 기사를 참조하시오.

COOL BEANS COFFEE 고객들에게 공지

Cool Beans Coffee가 10월 1일에 Irving Street 176번지로 이전

할 것입니다. 새로운 장소까지의 운전 길 안내는 저희 웹사이트 www. coolbeansc.com에서 이용 가능합니다. 새로운 매장으로 저희를 방문해 계속해서 저희와 같은 지역 소유의 업체들을 성원해 주시기를 바랍니다. 저희는 지역 내에서 최고의 커피 음료를 제공하는 데 전념하고 있습니다. Wentzville Mall에서 저희의 마지막 영업일은 9월 20일이 될 것임을 유념해 주시기 바랍니다.

저희는 이전을 축하하기 위해 영업 첫 주 동안 특별 행사를 개최할 것입니다. 저희의 창의적인 바리스타들이 만들어 내는 특별 음료, 따뜻한 음료에 대한 할인, 그리고 라이브 포크 음악 공연이 있을 것입니다. 이 즐거움을 놓치지 않도록 10월 1일부터 7일까지 꼭 저희 매장으로 오세요. 앞으로 오래도록 여러분께 서비스하기를 고대합니다!

Cassandra Marquez
소유주, Cool Beans Coffee

---

www.wentzvillenow.com/chamber-of-commerce/reviews

업체: Aloha Coffee   게시일: 10월 28일

최근에 처음으로 Aloha Coffee에 가봤는데 이전에 Cool Beans Coffee가 사용했던 임대 공간에 들어섰기 때문이다. 커피 자체는 만족스러웠고, 그 커피숍은 사람들이 기대할 모든 일반적인 음료들을 제공한다. 하지만, 이곳과 같은 대형 체인점은 지역 소유의 업체들이 제공하는 것과 같은 수준의 개인적이고 친절한 수준의 서비스를 제공하지는 못한다. 이 지역 사회에서, Cool Beans Coffee가 고객 서비스에 있어 탁월함에 대한 기준을 세웠는데, Aloha Coffee가 그에 미치지 못하는 것이 유감이다.

비즈니스의 중심에 남아 있는 쇼핑 센터

200개가 넘는 소매점들이 있는, Wentzville Mall은 언제나 현지의 쇼핑객들과 관광객들을 모두에게 무료 링쇼기 되어 있다. 새로운 소유권하에, 주차장과 보안 시스템이 업그레이드되었고, 푸드 코트와 화장실을 개조하려는 계획이 진행 중이다. 하지만, 그 이면에서 일어나고 있는 변화들이 장기적으로 상당 부분 쇼핑몰의 모습을 만들게 될 것이다.

첫 변화들 중 하나는 몰 안의 매장들의 임대료가 증가한 것으로, 각 매장의 개별 임대가 만료됨에 따라 시행된 것이다. 이것이 Evelyn's Boutique와 Cool Beans Coffee 같은 지역 소유의 업체들을 포함한 여러 업체들이 밖으로 내몰리게 했다. 이런 유형의 업체들은 브랜드 인지도와 전국적인 광고 캠페인의 혜택을 볼 수 있는 대형 체인점들에 의해 대체되고 있다.

소규모 기업주들은 그런 경향을 우려하지만, 이는 몰의 이미지에 부정적으로 영향을 미치는 않는 듯하다. "저는 Wentzville Mall에서 쇼핑하는 것을 좋아해요."라고 쇼핑객 Alice Russell이 말했다. "한 지붕 아래 제가 필요한 모든 게 다 있거든요."

186 Marquez 씨는 왜 업체를 이전했을 것 같은가?
(A) 새로운 위치가 더 편리하다고 생각했다.
(B) 고객들을 위해 더 많은 좌석들이 필요했다.
(C) 더 이상 임대료를 감당할 수 없었다.
(D) 더 새로운 시설 안에 있고 싶었다.

187 Aloha Coffee에 관해 알 수 있는 것은 무엇인가?
(A) Cool Beans Coffee와 제휴를 맺고 있다.
(B) 때때로 라이브 음악 공연을 특별히 선보인다.
(C) Wentzville Mall 내에 위치해 있다.
(D) 단골 고객들이 많다.

188 후기에서, 첫 번째 단락, 다섯 번째 줄의 단어 "set"과 의미가 가장 가까운 것은 무엇인가?
(A) ~을 확립했다
(B) 쉬었다, 휴식을 취했다
(C) 계산했다
(D) ~을 놓아두었다

189 Wentzville Mall에 관해 언급된 것은 무엇인가?
(A) 최근에 매각되었다.
(B) 현재 직원을 모집하고 있다.
(C) 건물을 확장할 것이다.
(D) 전국적으로 광고를 한다.

190 Russell 씨가 Wentzville Mall에 관해 좋아하는 것은 무엇인가?
(A) 현대적인 외관
(B) 폭넓은 다양성
(C) 저렴한 가격
(D) 친절한 직원들

신유형 191-195는 다음 이메일과 편지, 그리고 일정표를 참조하시오.

수신: Saiki Kojima 〈kojimas@hoshinotech.com〉
발신: Namiyo Fujimoto 〈fujimoton@hoshinotech.com〉
날짜: 1월 9일
제목: 출장 상세 정보

Kojima 씨께,

3월에 싱가포르에 가는 출장에 관한 귀하의 문의에 대한 응답으로 글을 씁니다. 비용에 관한 규정들은 국내 출장과 동일하며, 아래와 같습니다.
- 회사가 직접 호텔비와 항공료를 지불할 것입니다.
- 다른 모든 비용에 대해 법인 신용카드를 써야 합니다. 식사와 교통, 그리고 고객 접대와 같은 최대 100달러까지의 소액 결제 영수증은 보관할 필요가 없는데, 이는 신용카드 거래 명세서에서 확인될 수 있기 때문입니다.
- 그 금액을 초과하는 비용에 대해서는, 돌아오는 대로 반드시 저에게 영수증을 제출하셔야 합니다.

교통편과 관련하여 다음 안내 사항들을 준수하시기 바랍니다.
- 공항과 Novena Convention Center, 그리고 Aspella Hall을 오가는 무료 셔틀 버스 서비스를 이용하실 수 있습니다.
- Sunrise Restaurant 방문을 위해 저희가 대여 차량을 마련해 드립니다.

갖고 계실 추가 문의 사항에 대해 기꺼이 답변해 드리겠습니다.

안녕히 계십시오.

Namiyo Fujimoto
인사 담당자, Hoshino Tech

Saiki Kojima
Hoshino Tech
33-4 Sakanoshita, Kamakura
Kanagawa Prefecture 248-0021, 일본

Kojima 씨께,

국제 기술 디자인 학회(ITDC)에 등록해 주셔서 감사합니다. 귀하의 예약과 300달러 등록비를 받았습니다. 동봉된 것에서 이 요금에 대한 영수증을 보실 수 있을 것입니다. 올해의 학회는 OBC의 Keith Noster를 포함하여, 업계의 저명한 리더들을 특징으로 할 것입니다. 아직 일부 일정의 세부 사항들을 작업 중인데, 연사 일정이 확정되는 대로 웹사이트에 게시해 드리겠습니다.

호텔 객실 예약을 미루지 마시라고 권해 드리는데, 근처 호텔들이 빠르게 채워질 것으로 예상되기 때문입니다. 예정된 학회 세션들에 더해, Global Technology Alliance 회원들을 위해 학회 첫날 환영 아침 식사가 있을 것임을 유념해 주시기 바랍니다. 또한 3월 24일에는 모든 학회 발표자들을 위한 폐회 만찬 행사도 있을 것입니다.

ITDC에서 즐거운 시간 보내시기 바랍니다!

Felicia Lim
행사 진행 책임자, 국제 기술 디자인 학회

주간 행사 일정 / Saiki Kojima

3월 21일	3월 22일	3월 23일	3월 24일	3월 25일
오후 2:10 DS384 항공편 Narita International Airport에서 출발	오전 8:00 Novena Convention Center에서 환영 아침 식사	오전 10:00 –오후 6:00 Novena Convention Center에서 학회 세션들	오전 10:00 –오후 2:00 Novena Convention Center에서 학회 세션들	오전 8:00 Jave Hotel 에서 Zi Mai 와 미팅
오후 8:55 Changi Airport 도착 Jave Hotel 체크인	오전 10:00 –오후 6:00 학회 세션들	오후 7:30 Sunrise Restaurant 에서 Norman Kelly와 저녁 식사	오후 3:00 Aspella Hall 투어	오전 11:50 DS1609 항공편 Changi Airport에서 출발 오후 8:11 Narita International Airport 도착

191 Fujimoto 씨의 말에 따르면, Kojima 씨는 100달러가 넘는 구매에 대해 무엇을 해야 하는가?

(A) 다른 신용카드를 사용하기
(B) 사전에 승인받기
(C) 구매 증명서 제출하기
(D) 은행 계좌 이체하기

192 편지에서, 첫 번째 단락, 다섯 번째 줄의 단어 "settled"와 의미가 가장 가까운 것은 무엇인가?

(A) 최종 확정된
(B) 지불된
(C) 종료된
(D) 완화된

193 Lim 씨가 하도록 제안하는 것은 무엇인가?

(A) 행사 일정표를 확인하는 것
(B) 숙소를 즉시 마련하는 것
(C) 학회 자료들을 다운로드하는 것
(D) 미리 저녁 식사 예약을 하는 것

194 Kojima 씨에 관해 암시된 것은 무엇인가?

(A) 그는 학회에서 발표를 할 것이다.
(B) 그는 한때 ITDC의 직원이었다.
(C) 그는 Lim 씨와의 회의에 참석할 것이다.
(D) 그는 Global Technology Alliance의 회원이다.

195 Kojima 씨는 언제 전용 차량을 이용할 것인가?

(A) 3월 22일에
(B) 3월 23일에
(C) 3월 24일에
(D) 3월 25일에

신유형 ▶ 196-200은 다음 공지와 두 이메일을 참조하시오.

제품 테스터 구함

RP Investigators가 현재 주요 식품업체들의 다양한 음료와 과자의 맛을 테스트할 소비자 패널의 구성원들을 모집하고 있습니다. 참여하려면 반드시 최소한 18세 이상이어야 합니다. 패널 구성원들은 여러 요소들에 대해 제품들을 평가하고 서면 양식과 소규모 토론을 통해 의견을 공유할 것입니다. 그 세션은 오후 1시부터 4시까지 진행될 것이고, 중단 없이 전체 세션에 참석할 수 있어야 합니다. 더 많은 정보를 원하시면 www.rpinvestigators.com을 방문하세요.

수신: Lila Valente
발신: Darshan Bassi
날짜: 8월 14일
제목: 소비자 패널 업데이트

Valente 씨께,

8월 28일 소비자 패널에 관하여, 저희의 목표 연령층(18-30세)에 해당하는 많은 분들이 낮 동안 일을 하시기 때문에, 그 세션을 오후 6시-9시로 옮겼습니다. 45명의 지원자들이 있었고, 그들 중 40명을 수락했습니다. 다른 분들은 밀이나 견과류에 알레르기가 있었기 때문에 거절되었는데, 그것들은 테스트될 일부 제품들에 들어 있는 재료입니다.

제가 회의실 두 곳을 사용하기로 결정했습니다. 참가자들은 회의실 A에서 시작할 것입니다. 그곳에 개별 테이블들을 놓을 공간이 있어, 참가자들이 이야기를 나눠 각자의 의견에 영향을 미치는 일은 없을 것입니다. 각자 각 제품을 맛보고 자신의 경험에 대한 자세한 설명을 작성하게 됩니다. 그런 다음 제가 모두를 회의실 B로 이동시킬 것이고, 그곳에는 소규모 토론을 위한 공간이 마련될 것입니다.

저희는 다음 회사들이 만든 제품들을 테스트할 것입니다:
Lee's Beverages: 3가지 맛 소다
Duncan Farms: 1가지 맛 과일 주스
Neosho: 4가지 맛 크래커
Jarmill Co.: 2가지 맛 감자 칩

세션이 완료된 후 제가 전체 보고서를 가지고 고객들에게 연락할 것입니다.

안녕히 계십시오.

Darshan

수신: Anthony Fowler
발신: Darshan Bassi
날짜: 8월 30일
제목: 소비자 패널 결과

Fowler 씨께,

RP Investigators가 귀사의 제품에 대한 소비자 테스트를 완료했습니다. 첨부된 것에서 저희 직원들의 추천 사항들뿐만 아니라 참가자들의 의견에 관한 완전한 보고서를 보실 것입니다. 간단히 말해, 고객들께서는 귀사 제품들의 맛을 좋아했고, 두 가지 제품 모두 90퍼센트보다 높게 평가했습니다. 추가 테스트를 실시하거나 포장 같은 다른 요소들에 관해 조사해 보고 싶으시다면, 주저하지 마시고 제게 연락 주시기 바랍니다.

안부를 전하며,

Darshan Bassi
수석 연구원, RP Investigators

196 소비자 패널 구성원에 관해 암시된 것이 아닌 것은 무엇인가?

(A) 반드시 3시간 동안 시간이 있어야 한다.

(B) 특정 음식에 알레르기가 없어야 한다.

(C) 최소 연령 요건을 충족해야 한다.

(D) 단골 쇼핑객들이어야 한다.

197 Bassi 씨에 따르면, 세션 시간은 왜 변경되었는가?

(A) 일부 회의실의 이중 예약을 피하기 위해

(B) 특정 연령 그룹을 수용하기 위해

(C) 정부 규제를 준수하기 위해

(D) 충분한 직원들이 참석할 수 있도록 보장하기 위해

198 첫 번째 이메일에서, 두 번째 단락, 세 번째 줄의 단어 "full"과 의미가 가장 가까운 것은 무엇인가?

(A) 상세한

(B) 사용 중인

(C) 만족한

(D) 붐비는

199 Bassi 씨는 왜 두 개의 회의실을 사용하기를 원하는가?

(A) 동시에 두 그룹을 맞이하기 위해

(B) 다양한 제품들이 섞이는 것을 피하기 위해

(C) 다양한 장비에 접근 권한을 갖기 위해

(D) 독립적인 의견을 얻기 위해

200 Fowler 씨는 어디에서 일하는가?

(A) Lee's Beverages에서

(B) Duncan Farms에서

(C) Neosho에서

(D) Jarmill Co.에서

PART 5

101 모든 직원들은 로비에 보수 공사가 진행되는 동안 뒷문을 이용해 건물에 출입해야 한다.

102 Marqui Flowers는 그들의 기존 고객들에게 매년 그들의 생일에 무료로 꽃다발을 제공한다.

103 이번 주 금요일에 쉴 계획인 직원들은 늦어도 이번 주 목요일까지 소속 부서장들에게 그들의 근로 시간을 제출해야 한다.

104 Two Oaks는 주택 및 사무 환경에 합리적인 가격의 품질이 좋은 가구 제품을 판매한다.

105 Parabolic Ventures 사는 앞으로 몇 년에 걸쳐 여러 가지 혁신적인 기기들을 출시할 계획이다.

106 Vecker Laboratories의 연구는 향후 몇 년 이내에 심장병을 치료하는 것이 가능할 수도 있다는 사실을 밝혀냈다.

107 지역 박람회는 그 행사를 위해 실시된 광고가 상대적으로 부족했음에도 불구하고 큰 성공을 거뒀다.

108 판매 중인 것으로 기재된 E. Grapewood Drive 2472번지의 주택은 넓은 정원에 필요한 충분한 공간 및 기존에 설치된 급수 시설을 가지고 있다.

109 부사장은 연구 개발 부서의 모든 직원들에게 내년 예산이 줄어들지 않을 것이라고 장담했다.

110 사내 야유회 준비 담당자는 오늘까지 준비를 완료할 것이라고 모든 사람들에게 말했다.

111 Pollard Clothes는 그들의 웹사이트 및 계산대의 안내판에서 회사의 제품 교환 정책을 간략히 보여 주고 있다.

112 Langford 씨가 Nugent 씨에게 할당된 일을 완료하자마자, 자신의 업무 진척 상황에 관해 부사장에게 보고하기 위해 부사장실로 보내졌다.

113 재활용의 중요성을 보여 주는 많은 연구 후에, 현재 총 135개의 지자체들이 일종의 의무적인 재활용 프로그램을 보유하고 있다.

114 테니스의 인기를 고려해 보면, 요즘 아주 많은 어린아이들이 테니스를 치기 시작하는 것을 보는 것은 놀라운 일이 아니다.

115 면접에서 성과를 열거할 때, 지원하는 일과 관련이 있는 것에만 초점을 맞추십시오.

116 주방 기기를 판매하는 사업을 해온 30년 동안, Dean & Gold Co.의 매출은 거의 매년 점진적으로 증가해 왔다.

117 독학으로 공부하기를 원하는 학생들과 다른 이들과 함께 배우기를 원하는 학생들 모두에게 러시아어와 독일어 수업이 제공된다.

118 해외 지사로 전근하는 직원들은 보통 자신 및 자신의 가족들에게 필요한 거처를 찾기 위해 인사부의 직원에게 의존한다.

119 Pollard Award는 공학 분야의 혁신을 인정하는 상이며, 매년 상을 받을 자격이 있는 사람에게 수여된다.

120 호텔의 고객과 손님들을 제외한 어느 누구도 Winchester Hotel의 수영장 시설을 이용할 수 없다는 점에 유의하시기 바랍니다.

121 대규모의 청중들에게 연설할 때, 연설하는 대부분의 시간 동안 메모를 보는 일을 피하는 것이 중요하다.

122 Johnson 씨는 Berlin에서 온 고객들에게 도움을 줄 수 있어서 기쁜데, 이는 그녀에게 독일어로 말할 기회를 줄 것이기 때문이다.

123 블로거들이 〈Greenwich News and Report〉 또는 소속 기고자들의 견해를 반드시 반영하는 것은 아니라는 점에 주의하시기 바랍니다.

124 Marshall 씨의 말에 따르면, 직원들에게 배부되는 정보는 오직

Bentley 프로젝트를 맡아 작업하는 사람들에게만 한정되어야 한다.

125 팀 내의 직원 수를 줄이려는 결정은 사무실에 있는 거의 모든 사람들에 의해 반대되었다.

126 Mandarin Hotel에서 걸어서 갈 수 있는 거리에 10곳이 넘는 이국적인 식당들이 있다.

127 재무 이사인 Meredith Wesley 씨는 내일 열릴 주주 회의에서 최근에 일부 직원들에게 지급된 보너스에 대해 다룰 것이다.

128 Hartford Manufacturing은 자사의 성공 원인이 Jefferson Media에 의해 진행된 마케팅 캠페인이 아니라 자사 제품의 품질 때문이라고 생각한다.

129 시장 전문가들은 이번 연휴 시즌에 매출의 감소를 오랜 기간 예상했었지만, 그럼에도 불구하고 기록적으로 많은 소비자들이 모습을 드러내면서 지속적으로 분석가들을 놀라게 했다.

130 Westmill Mall의 일부가 1월 한 달 동안 보수 공사로 인해 문을 닫을 것이고, 영향을 받는 매장들 목록은 저희 웹사이트에서 찾아볼 수 있습니다.

PART 6

신유형 ▶ 131-134는 다음 공지를 참조하시오.

새로운 레크리에이션 시설이 Hernsdale 지역에 찾아옵니다. 어제, 〈The Hernsdale Press〉는 3백만 달러의 비용이 드는 종합운동장이 시 의회 공원 위원회의 승인을 받았음을 알리는 기사를 실었습니다. 그 투표는 9월 2일 화요일에 실시되었습니다.

공사는 Willis Park 옆에 위치한 들판 부지에서 11월 10일에 시작됩니다. The Blue Ridge Sports Complex로 알려질 이 운동장은 6월 22일에 개장합니다. 이 시설물은 종종 지역 내 스포츠 팀들을 위해 예약될 수 있지만, 일반적으로 정규 개방 시간 동안 누구나 이용할 수 있을 것입니다.

신유형 ▶ 135-138은 다음 기사를 참조하시오.

Irving (7월 9일)—Jonathan Melle 씨가 Irving School District의 책임자로 승진했다. 그는 월요일 밤에 열린 이사회에서 만장일치로 선출되었다. Melle 씨는 6년 동안 JPC High School에서 교장으로 재직했다. 새로운 직책에서, 그는 그 구역 내 모든 학교의 예산과 직원, 그리고 시설물들을 관리하는 책임을 맡을 것이다. 더욱이, 그는 8월 11일에 열리는 다음 회의부터 교육 위원회 의장을 맡게 될 것이다. 이사회 의장 자리에서 물러나는 Adel Keene 씨는 지난 5년 동안 해당 직책을 맡아 왔다.

신유형 ▶ 139-142는 다음 편지를 참조하시오.

Karlee Wood
Habitat Advertising의 채용 책임자
342 Marsh Lane
Sun Valley, ID 83353

Wood 씨께,

Andrew Nelson 씨가 여기 Yountville Marketing Agency에서 3년이 넘는 시간 동안 저희와 함께 일하셔서 기뻤습니다. 저희 회사에 채용된 바로 그 순간부터, Nelson 씨는 신뢰할 수 있고 헌신적인 인재라는 것을 증명해 왔습니다. 지난 10개월 동안, 그는 신입 직원 교육을 담당했

습니다. 결과적으로, 저희는 직원들의 전반적인 생산성 향상을 목격해 왔습니다.

물론, Andrew 씨가 저희 Yountville Marketing을 떠나는 것을 보게 되어 진심으로 유감스럽게 생각하지만, 저는 그를 귀하의 회사에 아주 강력히 추천해 드리고자 합니다. 의심할 여지없이, 그는 저희 회사에서 그래왔던 것처럼 Habitat Advertising에 필요한 뛰어난 인재가 될 것입니다.

안녕히 계십시오.

Joshua Shroud
Yountville Marketing Agency, 팀장

신유형 ▶ 143-146은 다음 이메일을 참조하시오.

수신: Kyra Thompson 〈k.thompson@mail.org〉
발신: Trista Whitaker 〈trista@harvestgrain.com〉
날짜: 4월 4일
제목: 귀하의 지원

Kyra 씨께,

Capitol Street에 있는 저희 제과점에 게시된 제빵사 직에 대한 귀하의 지원서를 받았습니다. 그 자리는 아직 충원되지 않았습니다. 귀하께서 여전히 관심이 있으시다면, 다음 단계는 면접 날짜를 잡는 것입니다. 귀하께서 다른 제과점에서 빵과 케이크를 만든 경험이 있다는 점을 알고 있습니다. 그러니 이 일에 포함되는 몇 가지 업무를 이해하고 계실 겁니다. 제 동업자와 저는 귀하의 자격 사항이 매우 훌륭하다는 점에 대해 상당히 깊은 인상을 받았습니다. 저는 4월 9일 오후 3시에 면접을 할 시간이 있습니다.

만약 귀하께서 관심이 있으시면, 제게 전화 주셔서 약속을 확인해 주시기 바랍니다. 귀하의 관심에 감사 드립니다.

안녕히 계십시오.
Trista Whitaker
Harvest Grain Bakery, 공동 소유주

PART 7

147-148은 다음 이메일을 참조하시오.

수신: gamer1985@mail.com
발신: taladipro@shop.taladi.com
제목: 새로 나오는 Taladi Active Pro
날짜: 8월 31일

게임 애호가이신 귀하께서는 아마 Taladi Active Pro Gaming Console이 곧 출시된다는 얘기를 이미 들어 보셨을 것입니다.

Taladi Inc.의 기존의 고객으로서, 귀하는 11월 1일에 시장에 출시될 예정인 Taladi Active Pro 제품을 미리 주문하실 수 있는 특별 안내장을 받으실 것입니다. 공급량이 한정되어 있어 연휴 시즌이 다가오는 해당 시점에 빠르게 매진될 것으로 예상됩니다. www.taladi.com/activepro를 방문하시어, 귀하의 특별 안내장 코드인 W23YU1을 입력하셔서 주문하실 수 있습니다.

즐거운 게임 하시기 바랍니다.
Taladi Gaming Consoles 홍보팀

147 이메일의 목적은 무엇인가?

(A) 새롭게 문을 여는 게임 회사 알리기

(B) 자사 고객에게 시즌 할인 공지하기

(C) 곧 출시될 제품 소개하기

(D) 행사 초대장 발송하기

148 Taladi Active Pro에 관해 알 수 있는 것은 무엇인가?

(A) 신규 고객들만을 위한 것이다.

(B) 젊은 전문가들 사이에서 인기가 많다.

(C) 게임을 하기 위해서는 여섯 자리의 코드가 필요하다.

(D) 아직 구매할 수 없다.

149-150은 다음 청구서를 참조하시오.

Inside Out Pest Control
3510 Market Street
Milton, Nebraska 68858

날짜: 5월 9일	청구 대상:
계정 번호: X32433MV	Marito Resort and Spa
	PO Box 695
	Milton, Nebraska 68858

4월 23일에 실시한 계절별 종합 병충해 방지 처리 작업에 대한 내역서

물품 사용:	96.50달러
인건비:	135.20달러
소계:	231.70달러
세금:	13.90달러
총계:	245.60달러

다음 작업 날짜: 5월 23일

거래해 주셔서 심사합니다.

* 다음번 월간 작업 날짜 이전에 청구 금액을 납부해 주시기 바랍니다. 기한 내에 비용이 수납되지 않을 경우, 다음으로 예정된 예약은 지연되거나 취소될 수 있습니다. 또한 미납 금액의 10퍼센트에 해당되는 연체료가 청구서에 추가될 것입니다. 저희 기록에 따르면 귀사의 시설물에 대한 서비스는 8월까지만 예정된 것으로 나타나므로, 가을 서비스 일정을 잡으시려면 늦어도 8월 10일까지 저희 사무실 번호인 585-711-3620으로 전화 주시기 바랍니다.

149 Marito Resort and Spa는 무엇을 하도록 요청받는가?

(A) Inside Out Pest Control에 서면 답변하기

(B) 2주 내로 비용 지불하기

(C) 다음 작업 날짜 정하기

(D) 총 지불 비용 액수 확인하기

150 언제 작업이 실시되었는가?

(A) 3월 9일

(B) 4월 23일

(C) 5월 23일

(D) 8월 10일

151-152는 다음 공지를 참조하시오.

Manila에 거주 중이시며 영어가 가능하신 전문가들께 알립니다. The International Association of Business and Marketing(IABM)이 Manila에 첫 번째 지부를 개설합니다. 첫 번째 모임이 Rizal Avenue 2342번지에 위치한 3C 건물에서 6월 3일 오후 6~9시까지 열립니다.

임대한 시설의 크기 때문에, 참가자 수는 150명으로 제한됩니다. 첫 모임에 참가비는 필요치 않습니다. 하지만 관심이 있으신 분은 5442-5467로 전화하셔서 자리를 예약하셔야 합니다.

IABM의 Samyra Duete 부회장님께서 특별 연사로 참석하실 예정입니다. 그분께서 IABM의 여러 역할 및 전 세계의 회원들이 비즈니스와 마케팅 분야에 기여한 바를 개괄적으로 설명해 주실 것입니다. 참석하시는 분들께서는 IABM이 제공하는 전문성 향상을 위한 여러 기회에 관해 알게 되실 것입니다.

저희는 IABM이 필리핀으로 진출하게 되어 매우 흥분됩니다. 회원 자격 관련 상세 정보, 그리고 저희 지부에 예정된 연설자와 행사들은 www.iabm.org/manila에서 찾아보실 수 있습니다.

151 어디에서 볼 수 있는 공지인가?

(A) 방송 시설에서

(B) 비즈니스와 마케팅 관련 도서에서

(C) 국제 신문에서

(D) 지역 사회 소식지에서

152 IABM에 관해 알 수 있는 것은 무엇인가?

(A) 세계적으로 회원들을 모아 오고 있다.

(B) Manila는 처음 비즈니스를 시작한 곳이다.

(C) 신입 직원들에게는 참가비가 필요 않다.

(D) 지부 개설 요청은 온라인으로 할 수 있다.

153-155는 다음 안내 정보를 참조하시오.

Rosanna Cosmetics

전문 지식과 비즈니스 감각으로 동료 직원들에게 대단히 높이 평가받고 계신 William Terry 씨는 최근에 CEO 직책에서 물러나신 Judith Perkins 씨의 후임자입니다. Terry 씨는 이미 우리 Rosanna Cosmetics를 한 단계 더 끌어 올리고 우리 회사의 수상 브랜드를 유럽에 출시하기 위해 다섯 단계의 전략에 대한 윤곽을 그리신 상태입니다.

Terry 씨는 15년 전에 작은 화장품 유통 업체를 설립하셨으며, 5년 동안 이 회사를 성공적으로 운영하신 후에 Rosanna Cosmetics에 입사하셨고 최고 마케팅 이사 자리까지 오르셨습니다. 그분의 브랜드 관리 능력은 우리 회사가 분기마다 이윤을 내는 데 도움이 되었습니다. 최고 마케팅 이사로 재직한 6년 동안, Terry 씨는 본인의 인맥 관리 능력을 발휘해 국내외에서 놀라울 정도로 많은 동종 업계 종사자들과 연락을 주고받으셨습니다. 개인 사업을 하고 Rosanna Cosmetics에 입사하시기 전에, 그는 그의 고향에 있는 작은 병원의 수의사이셨습니다.

153 안내 정보는 왜 게시되었는가?

(A) 제품 출시를 홍보하기 위해

(B) 신임 임원을 소개하기 위해

(C) 수상자를 발표하기 위해

(D) 비즈니스 절차에 관한 개요를 설명하기 위해

154 Terry 씨에 관해 언급되지 않은 것은 무엇인가?

(A) 다른 사람들에게 존경받고 있다.

(B) 수익을 늘리는 데 도움이 되었다.

(C) 원래 유럽 출신이다.

(D) 폭넓은 비즈니스 인맥을 가지고 있다.

155 Terry 씨에 관해 알 수 있는 것은 무엇인가?

(A) Rosanna Cosmetics에서 15년 동안 근무했다.

(B) 경력상의 진로를 변경하기로 결정했다.

(C) 공개 연설 경험이 없다.

(D) 자신의 회사를 Rosanna Cosmetics에 매각했다.

신유형 ▶ 156-157은 다음 문자 메시지 대화를 참조하시오.

Lawrence Sosa [오전 11:38]
이곳 Nelson Avenue에 있는 건물은 준비가 거의 다 되었어요.

Dwight Bryant [오전 11:40]
알았어요, 저는 가는 중입니다.

Lawrence Sosa [오전 11:41]
좋습니다. 저희는 지금 막 짐 싸는 일을 완료했기 때문에, 정오쯤에 모든 물품들을 싣기 시작할 준비가 될 겁니다.

Dwight Bryant [오전 11:42]
평소와 마찬가지로, 부피가 큰 물품들부터 먼저 처리하고, 그다음에 상자들을 처리할 것입니다. 그렇게 해야 우리가 이용 가능한 공간을 최대로 활용하는 데 도움이 될 겁니다.

Lawrence Sosa [오전 11:44]
도착하시는 대로 소파와 침대를 잔디밭으로 내놓겠습니다.

Dwight Bryant [오전 11:45]
왜 기다리시죠? 지금 바로 하시면 시간을 절약할 수 있을 거예요.

Lawrence Sosa [오전 11:46]
알았어요, 작업 팀원들에게 알릴게요.

156 Sosa 씨는 누구일 것 같은가?

(A) 트럭 정비사
(B) 이사 전문 업체 직원
(C) 공사장 인부
(D) 건물 관리 책임자

157 오전 11시 45분에, Bryant 씨가 "Why wait"라고 썼을 때 의미하는 것은 무엇인가?

(A) 작업 팀원들이 지금 휴식을 취하게 하도록 제안한다.
(B) 마감 시한을 맞추지 못하는 것에 대해 혼란스러워한다.
(C) 일부 가구가 즉시 판매될 수 있다고 생각한다.
(D) 팀원들이 지금 당장 일을 시작하기를 원한다.

신유형 ▶ 158-160은 다음 기사를 참조하시오.

확장 예정인 서점

2월 9일—Intelecto Mundial Books는 올여름부터 사업을 확장할 계획이 완료됐음을 발표했다. 현재 세 곳의 서점들이 앞으로 몇 년 안에 각각 다른 국가에서 문을 열 계획이다. — [1] —. 전 세계의 희귀 도서 판매를 전문으로 하는 이 업체는 다양한 언어로 다양한 곳에서 출판되는 구하기 어려운 도서들의 주요 공급원이다. 현재 대부분의 수익은 온라인 매장에서 나오고 있지만, 이 업체는 2년 전에 이미 잉글랜드에 첫 번째 소매점을 운영하기 시작했다. — [2] —.

이 새로운 서점은 지역 주민들을 끌어들이면서 대단한 성공을 거둬 왔으며, 심지어 그 나라를 방문하는 관광객들이 찾는 주요 명소가 되고 있다.

Intelecto Mundial Books의 대표 이사인 Mariana de la Torre는 다음과 같이 말했다. "이것은 전 세계에서 독서를 되살리기 위한 첫 단계에 불과합니다. 저희가 처음 온라인 웹사이트를 시작했을 때, 저희의 목표는 모든 사람이 훌륭한 문학 작품을 읽을 수 있고 독서를 장려하는 것이었습니다. 저희 회사는 잉글랜드에서 저희와 같은 목표를 지닌 직원들을 채용할 수 있었습니다. 저희는 곧 이 비전을 스페인으로 옮겨갈 생각입니다. — [3] —. 이미 Barcelona에 있는 부지를 매입해 둔 상태이며, 아주 빠른 시일 내에 건축 공사를 시작할 것입니다. 저희 회사의 본사가 Madrid

에 있는데 드디어 여기서 매장을 열게 되어 좋습니다."

앞으로 몇 년 안에 멕시코와 캐나다에서도 더 많은 매장들이 문을 열 것으로 예상된다. — [4] —. 비록 첫 두 곳의 매장들만큼 클 것으로 예상되지는 않지만, 성공을 위해 신중한 계획이 여전히 필요할 것이다.

158 Intelecto Mundial Books에 관해 언급된 것은 무엇인가?

(A) 현재 대부분의 수익이 London 지점을 통해 나온다.
(B) 본사가 스페인에 지어질 계획이다.
(C) 신규 매장들은 첫 번째 지점보다 규모가 더 클 것이다.
(D) 사람들에게 더 많은 문학 작품을 읽을 기회를 제공한다.

159 다음 매장은 어디에서 문을 열 것으로 예상되는가?

(A) 잉글랜드에서
(B) 스페인에서
(C) 멕시코에서
(D) 캐나다에서

160 [1], [2], [3], [4]로 표기된 위치들 중에서 다음 문장이 가장 잘 어울리는 곳은 어디인가?

신유형

"유럽 내 세계 문학에 대한 대단한 관심으로 인해, London 지점은 결국에는 웹사이트를 통한 해외 매출을 능가할 추세에 있다."

(A) [1]
(B) [2]
(C) [3]
(D) [4]

161-163은 다음 이메일을 참조하시오.

수신: Pandara Nishad ⟨p_nishad@bellhurst.net⟩
발신: Ross Dillard ⟨r_dillard@bellhurst.net⟩
날짜: 4월 18일
제목: 배정 업무

Nishad 씨께,

저는 직원 투자 프로그램의 시행 가능성과 관련해 당신이 저에게 배정해 주신 일을 완료했습니다. 우리 회사에 필요한 선택권들을 조사해 본 결과, 이와 같은 프로그램을 시행하는 것은 제안하신 기간 이내에 실현이 가능할 것이라고 결론 내렸습니다. 세부 내용이 포함된 요약 파일을 첨부했습니다.

고려해야 할 많은 요소들이 있지만, Abner Investments가 우리의 요구에 가장 잘 맞을 것이라고 생각합니다. 이 업체는 정년과 아주 거리가 먼 직원들이 주로 근무하는 회사들과 함께 일해 본 경험이 있으며, 투자와 관련해 사람들이 제대로 알고 결정을 내리는 데 도움이 되는 폭넓은 정보들을 제공하기 때문에 Bellhurst에 이상적인 곳이라고 생각합니다. 최종 결정을 내리는 대로 계약을 추진할 수 있습니다.

오늘 이따가 사무실에 계시지 않을 거라는 것을 알고 있습니다. 저는 다음 주에 다른 지역에 가 있을 예정이기 때문에 그 전에 만나 뵙고자 합니다. 시간이 나시는지 알려 주시기 바랍니다.

감사합니다!

Ross Dillard

161 이메일의 목적은 무엇인가?

(A) 조사 내용 제출하기
(B) 제안 거절하기
(C) 승인 해 주기
(D) 업무 배정하기

162 Bellhurst에 관해 암시된 내용은 무엇인가?

(A) 금융 상품을 전문으로 한다.

(B) 직원들이 젊다.

(C) 직원 수가 빠르게 늘고 있다.

(D) 오랫동안 운영되어 온 회사가 아니다.

163 Dillard 씨는 언제 회의를 하고 싶어할 것 같은가?

(A) 오늘 늦게

(B) 이번 주 후반

(C) 다음 주

(D) 2주 후

164-167은 다음 웹 페이지를 참조하시오.

http://www.oakridgecleaning.com/company_information

홈	회사 정보	제품 목록	주문 페이지	연락처

회사의 제품

Oakridge Cleaning은 상업적 및 주거 환경에서 사용되는 청소 용품들을 공급하는 Oakridge 지역의 가장 큰 업체입니다. 저희가 보유한 제품들이 최상의 품질을 유지하고 있음을 보장하기 위해 최고의 제조사들과 협업하고 있습니다. 각 제품은 무독성이며, 특정 구역을 청소할 수 있도록 특별히 고안되었습니다. 저희 직원들은 힘든 청소 업무와 얼룩 제거 작업에 필요한 제품들을 추천해 드릴 수 있도록 모든 교육을 마쳤습니다.

회사 이야기

Oakridge Cleaning은 25년 전에 Joseph Jordan 씨에 의해 설립된 회사며, 그가 경영하던 호텔에서 사용할 청소 제품 선택의 폭이 부족하다는 것에 좌절감을 느꼈을 때 사업 아이디어를 얻었습니다. Jordan 씨께서는 사람들이 지역 경제를 뒷받침할 수 있도록 바로 이곳 Oakridge에 사시는 분들께 필요한 것은 쉽게 얻을 수 있게 만들고 싶어 하셨습니다. Jordan 씨께서 은퇴하시자마자 회사는 가족에 의해 유지되었으며, 당시에 회사를 따님에게 물려주셨습니다.

회사의 확장

오랜 고객들의 성원 덕분에, Oakridge Cleaning은 Evansville로 사업을 확장할 준비가 되었습니다. 그곳의 저희 매장은 그 지역에 더욱 신속한 배송 서비스를 제공해 드릴 것이며, 최초의 저희 지점과 마찬가지로 매장에서의 제품 구입을 위해 매일 문을 열 것입니다. 또한 그곳은 고객들께 모든 종류의 표면과 직물을 세척하는 최상의 방법을 가르쳐 드리는 것을 목적으로 하는 주간 제품 시연회의 전용 매장이 될 것입니다.

Oakridge Cleaning에서 진행되고 있는 모든 일과 관련된 최신 소식을 접하길 원하시는 분은 info@oakridgecleaning.com으로 이메일을 보내 주시면 저희 소식지 발송 명단에 추가해 드리겠습니다. Oakridge Cleaning에서 여러분을 위해 서비스를 제공해 드릴 수 있기를 고대합니다!

Paula Kirchner, 소유주

Craig Ramos, 지점장 (Oakridge 지점)

164 Oakridge Cleaning에 관해 알 수 있는 것은 무엇인가?

(A) 당사의 제품을 광고 방송을 통해 광고한다.

(B) 전국의 동종 업계 회사들 중에서 가장 크다.

(C) 당사의 제품에 유해한 화학 성분이 들어 있지 않다.

(D) 청소 용품 제조사다.

165 Kirchner 씨에 관해 알 수 있는 것은 무엇인가?

(A) Evansville로 이사할 계획이다.

(B) 그녀의 아버지는 호텔을 운영했다.

(C) 25년의 경력이 있다.

(D) 업체를 Ramos 씨에게 물려줄 것이다.

166 Evansville 지점은 Oakridge 지점과 어떻게 다를 것인가?

(A) 일주일 내내 문을 열 것이다.

(B) 더 많은 종류의 제품을 제공할 것이다.

(C) 청소 시연회를 제공할 것이다.

(D) 제품 배송 방법을 선택할 수 있을 것이다.

167 고객들은 왜 웹 페이지에 제공된 주소로 이메일을 보내야 하는가?

(A) 무료 샘플을 요청하기 위해

(B) 보상 프로그램을 신청하기 위해

(C) 제품에 관한 의견을 공유하기 위해

(D) 회사의 소식을 접하기 위해

신유형 168-171은 다음 편지를 참조하시오.

Adam Sanderson

428 Ridgewood Drive

Aberdeen, SD 57401

Sanderson 씨께,

귀하의 Dargo 4도어 세단, 일련번호 683495-97에 대한 연장된 품질 보증에 따라, 귀하께서는 6개월마다 무료 점검을 받으실 수 있는 자격이 있습니다. — [1] —. Tyson Garage에서 Dargo 브랜드의 차량을 보유하고 계신 모든 고객께 Basic Preventative Maintenance Package(BPMP)라고 불리는 이 점검을 제공합니다. 이 패키지는 차내 전기 회로 테스트, 에어컨 정상 가동 여부 확인, 브레이크 기능 점검 외의 여러 서비스를 포함합니다. — [2] —. 저희는 또한 귀하의 편의를 위해 진공 청소기로 청소해 드리고 차량 내부 표면을 닦아 드립니다. BPMP는 귀하의 차량 내 모든 부품이 문제 없이 작동되도록 보장하는 방법이며, 저희가 수리 작업이 필요할 수도 있는 부분들을 찾아낼 수 있는 기회를 주기도 합니다. — [3] —.

6월 8일에서 20일 사이에 귀하의 패키지 이용을 신청하실 수 있습니다. 이 기간 동안의 패키지 이용 신청은 예약에 의해서만 가능합니다. 예약을 하시려면 555-5950으로 연락 주시기 바랍니다. — [4] —. 말씀 드린 기간 내에 차량을 가져오지 못하실 경우, 나중에 이용하실 수 있는 상품권을 발급해 드릴 수도 있기는 하지만, 이는 저희 정비소 사장님의 재량에 따른 것입니다.

안녕히 계십시오.

The Tyson Garage Team

168 편지의 목적은 무엇인가?

(A) 긴급 안전 관련 경고하기

(B) 고객 충성도 프로그램 소개하기

(C) 고객에게 무료 서비스 알리기

(D) 품질 보증 관련 정보 업데이트하기

169 BPMP의 일환으로 언급된 사항이 아닌 것은 무엇인가?

(A) 차량 내부를 청소하는 일

(B) 전자 부품을 확인하는 일

(C) 닳은 브레이크를 교체하는 일

(D) 냉방 장치를 테스트하는 일

170 Sanderson 씨는 무엇을 하도록 요청받는가?

(A) 더 새로운 패키지로 업그레이드하기

(B) 전화로 예약하기

(C) 상품권의 만료일을 확인하기

(D) 일련 번호를 확인하기

171 [1], [2], [3], [4]로 표기된 위치들 중에서 다음 문장이 가장 잘 어 [신유형] 울리는 곳은 어디인가?

"어떤 것이라도 발견될 경우, 작업을 더 진행하기 전에 귀하께 알려 드리겠습니다."

(A) [1]
(B) [2]
(C) [3]
(D) [4]

[신유형] ▶ 172-175는 다음 온라인 채팅을 참조하시오.

Madison Lynch [오후 1:11]
저기, Evan. 방해해서 죄송해요. 데이터베이스와 관련된 기술적인 문제에 대해 저 좀 도와주시겠어요?

Evan Norris [오후 1:13]
제가 할 수 있는 일이면요. 하지만 그와 관련해서 당신보다 더 많이 알고 있을 것 같지 않은데요.

Madison Lynch [오후 1:14]
저는 그저 접속하려고 했을 뿐인데, 에러 메시지가 떴어요. HF Enterprises의 Kent Feldman 씨에게 필요한 정보에 접속하려고 하는 중이에요. 그들의 새로운 탄산음료 제품 라인에 필요한 마케팅 전략을 준비해야 해서, 정부의 몇몇 규정들을 살펴보고 싶었거든요.

Evan Norris [오후 1:16]
얘기 못 들으셨어요? 그 시스템이 업그레이드되었어요. 어제 있었던 직원회의에서 배정받은 새로운 비밀번호를 입력하셔야 해요.

Madison Lynch [오후 1:17]
저는 그 자리에 없었어요.

Evan Norris [오후 1:18]
IT 부서에 있는 Ben에게 얘기해 보세요. 그분이 비밀번호를 배정해 드릴 거예요. 저도 오늘 아침에 같은 문제를 겪었어요.

Madison Lynch [오후 1:19]
그렇게 할게요. 감사합니다!

172 오후 1시 13분에, Norris 씨가 "If I can"이라고 썼을 때 의미하는 [신유형] 것은 무엇인가?

(A) 나중에 Lynch 씨를 만나기를 바란다.
(B) 자신의 일정에 대해 확신이 없다.
(C) 도움을 주려 할 것이다.
(D) 기술적인 문제점을 보고할 것이다.

173 Feldman 씨는 어디에서 근무할 것 같은가?

(A) 음료 제조사에서
(B) 연구 기관에서
(C) 마케팅 회사에서
(D) 정부의 부처에서

174 Lynch 씨에 관해 알 수 있는 것은 무엇인가?

(A) 신입 직원이다.
(B) 회의에 참석하지 않았다.
(C) 데이터베이스에 파일을 추가했다.
(D) 자신의 컴퓨터를 업그레이드했다.

175 Norris 씨는 오전에 무엇을 했는가?

(A) 고객에게 연락했다.
(B) Lynch 씨에게 비밀번호를 배정해 주었다.
(C) IT 부서의 직원과 이야기했다.

(D) 자신의 컴퓨터를 맡겨서 수리했다.

176-180은 다음 광고와 이메일을 참조하시오.

Ride the Rails 추첨 콘테스트: 모험을 찾아 떠나는 티켓

특별한 경험을 위해, 차창으로 Pacific Northwest의 아름다운 풍경을 즐겨 보시기 바랍니다! Northwest Folk Festival이 Seattle Train Tours와 제휴해 동반 2인을 포함한 무료 기차 여행 티켓을 받으실 수 있는 기회를 제공해 드립니다.

8월 한 달 동안 개최되는 Northwest Folk Festival에서 어떤 물품이든 구매하시면 경품 추첨 행사를 위한 6자리 코드를 발급해 드립니다. 응모를 위해 저희 웹사이트 www.northwestff.org/contest에서 이 코드를 입력하세요. 반드시 최소 18세 이상이어야 참여가 가능합니다. 1인당 1회로 응모가 제한됩니다. 추첨은 코드 입력 기간이 끝난 다음 날 아침에 진행되며, 당첨자께는 추첨 당일에 연락을 드립니다. 아래에 기재된 아주 멋진 상품들을 확인해 보세요!

상품	코드 입력 기간
Mount Rainier 기차 투어	8월 1~7일
Cascade 기차 투어	8월 8~14일
해변 기차 투어	8월 15~21일
Heritage Park 기차 투어	8월 22~28일

Seattle의 주민이시든 방문객이시든 상관없이, Northwest Folk Festival을 방문해 이 콘테스트에 참여하셔서 여름을 최대한 즐기실 수 있기를 바랍니다. 행운을 빕니다!

수신: Lillian Brewer 〈brewer.l@star-inbox.net〉
발신: Curtis Flynn 〈curtis@northwestff.org〉
날짜: 8월 15일
제목: Ride the Rails에 당첨되셨습니다!

Brewer 씨께,

축하 드립니다! 귀하께서 이번 주 Ride the Rails 추첨 콘테스트의 당첨자라는 사실을 알려 드리게 되어 기쁘게 생각합니다. 첨부해 드린 파일을 보시면 앞으로 제공될 예정인 투어의 일정표를 확인하실 수 있습니다. 투어를 떠나기 원하시는 두 가지 날짜를 제게 이메일로 보내 주시기 바라며, 요청 사항을 수용해 드릴 수 있도록 최선을 다하겠습니다. 가능한 한 빨리 제게 이메일을 보내 주시기를 권해 드리는데, 이는 투어가 많은 인기를 얻고 있어서 짧은 기간에 표가 매진되는 경향이 있기 때문입니다. 귀하의 티켓은 참가 신청서에 기재된 주소로 8월 27일쯤 우편으로 도착할 것입니다. 투어는 진행 시간에 약간씩 차이가 있으며, 최대 6시간까지 진행됩니다. 저희 회사에서는 또한 회사의 서비스를 한층 더 개선할 수 있는 방법을 알아보기 위해 주기적으로 설문 조사를 실시하고 있으므로, 투어가 끝나는 시점에 조사 양식을 작성하도록 요청받으실 수 있습니다. 문의 사항이 있으실 경우, 제게 알려 주시기 바랍니다.

안녕히 계십시오.

Curtis Flynn

176 Ride the Rails 추첨 콘테스트에 관해 언급되지 않은 것은 무엇인가?

(A) 참여하기 위해서는 물품 구입이 필수이다.
(B) 각 상품은 세 명에게 유효하다.
(C) 참여자들은 단 한 번 응모할 수 있다.
(D) 지역 내에서 해마다 열린다.

177 Brewer 씨는 어느 상품에 당첨됐을 것 같은가?

(A) Mount Rainier 기차 투어
(B) Cascade 기차 투어

(C) 해변 기차 투어

(D) Heritage Park 기차 투어

178 Brewer 씨에 관해 알 수 있는 것은 무엇인가?

(A) Northwest Folk Festival에 참석했다.

(B) 일정표를 다운로드하는 데 어려움을 겪었다.

(C) 투어 시간을 변경하고 싶어 한다.

(D) 티켓을 이메일로 받도록 요청했다.

179 Brewer 씨는 무엇을 제공하도록 요청받는가?

(A) 우편 주소

(B) 신분증

(C) 선호하는 날짜

(D) 유효한 영수증

180 이메일에서, 첫 번째 단락, 일곱 번째 줄의 단어 "conducts"와 의미가 가장 가까운 것은 무엇인가?

(A) ~을 완수하다

(B) ~을 시행하다

(C) ~을 안내하다

(D) ~을 행동하다

181-185는 다음 이메일과 설문지를 참조하시오.

수신: Albert Chapman ⟨alchapman@grantviewmail.com⟩
발신: BB-Card ⟨info@bb-card.com⟩
날짜: 5월 23일
제목: BB-Card에서 전하는 메시지

Chapman 씨께,

BB-Card를 대신해, 저희 서비스를 이용하고 계신 고객님께 감사 드리고자 합니다. 저희 기록을 보면 귀하께서는 최근에 처음으로 보상 포인트를 상품으로 교환하신 것으로 나타납니다. 저희가 고객들의 구매 경험을 관찰하는 데 도움을 얻기 위해, 첨부해 드린 양식을 작성해 주시기를 요청 드립니다. 이것은 설문 조사용 양식으로서 귀하께서 자유롭게 의견을 공유해 주실 수 있습니다. 작성된 양식은 위의 이메일 주소를 통해 되돌려 보내 주시면 됩니다.

귀하께서 시간을 내 주신 것에 대해 감사 드리기 위해, 해당 양식이 6월 15일 또는 그 이전에 작성되어 제출될 경우에 가죽으로 제본한 무료 BB-Card 데이 플래너를 받으실 수 있습니다. 이 날짜 이후에 양식을 제출하시는 고객들께서는 BB-Card 펜 세트를 받으시게 됩니다. 저희가 드리는 무료 선물을 즐겁게 사용하시기를 바랍니다.

안녕히 계십시오.

Kevin Salas
고객 서비스부장, BB-Card

저희 BB-Card 설문 조사 양식을 작성해 주셔서 감사합니다!

성명: Albert Chapman   설문지 작성 날짜: 6월 29일

1. BB-Card를 신청하신 이유는 무엇입니까? 제 친구 한 명이 추천해 주셨습니다.

2. 보통 얼마나 자주 BB-Card를 사용하시며, 어디에서 사용하십니까? 거의 매일 사용하며, 주로 주유소나 슈퍼마켓과 같은 곳에서 주기적으로 구입하는 물품에 대해 사용합니다.

3. 귀하의 보상 포인트 사용 경험에 대해 어떻게 평가하십니까?

[✔] 아주 만족   [   ] 만족   [   ] 보통   [   ] 불만족

의견: 제 BB-Card 포인트로 구입할 수 있는 아주 다양한 물품들이 있어서 좋았습니다. 처음에는 남아 있는 포인트를 확인하기 위해 제 계정을 이용하는 방법을 알아내느라 고생했는데, 온라인 사용자 가이드를 읽고 난 후에는 모든 것이 명확해졌습니다. 주문을 한 후에, 불과 며칠 만에 제 주문품을 받게 되어서 놀랐습니다. 더 많은 포인트를 받을 수 있도록 이 카드를 이용해 계속 쇼핑할 생각입니다.

181 이메일의 목적은 무엇인가?

(A) 서비스를 업그레이드한 고객에게 감사하기

(B) 고객에게 의견 얻기

(C) 고객에게 비용을 지불하도록 상기시키기

(D) 주문 양식에 필요한 정보 요청하기

182 BB-Card에 관해 사실인 것은 무엇인가?

(A) 보상 프로그램을 제공한다.

(B) 저금리 혜택을 제공한다.

(C) 해외에서 사용할 수 있다.

(D) 처음 이용하는 고객에게 선물을 준다.

183 이메일에서, 첫 번째 단락, 두 번째 줄의 단어 "monitor"와 의미가 가장 가까운 것은 무엇인가?

(A) ~을 감독하다

(B) ~을 유지하다

(C) ~을 감지하다

(D) ~을 지켜보다

184 BB-Card로부터 Chapman 씨에게 보내질 것은 무엇인가?

(A) 주유 상품권

(B) 필기구 세트

(C) 슈퍼마켓 샘플 제품

(D) 가죽 데이 플래너

185 Chapman 씨가 BB-Card에 관해 말한 것은 무엇인가?

(A) 온라인 사용자 가이드의 내용이 헷갈린다.

(B) 물품이 신속히 배송되었다.

(C) 정책의 변화가 타당하다.

(D) 웹사이트 접속이 일시적으로 불가능했다.

신유형 ▶ 186-190은 다음 광고와 양식, 그리고 이메일을 참조하시오.

Glitz Cleaning
저희에게 청소 작업을 맡겨주세요!

저희 Glitz Cleaning은 청소를 하는 허드렛일이 여러분의 바쁜 생활 양식에 맞추기에 어려운 일이라는 것을 알고 있습니다. 이것이 바로 저희가 1회 청소 서비스 및 주간 청소 서비스를 제공해 드리는 이유입니다. 저희는 여러분의 주택에 상쾌하고 안락한 분위기의 환경을 만들어 드리는 데 전념하고 있으며, 전문가들로 구성된 저희 팀이 어떠한 규모의 일이든지 처리해 드릴 수 있습니다.

저희는 세 명의 청소 작업자들로 구성된 팀을 보내 드리며, 이용 요금은 다음과 같이 일괄적으로 계산됩니다. 1시간에 80달러, 2시간에 150달러, 3시간에 215달러, 4시간에 280달러입니다. 4시간을 초과하는 작업은 사전에 협의되어야 합니다.

저희 직원들이 모든 청소 용품과 기기들을 가져갈 것이므로 아무것도 준비하실 필요가 없습니다. 특별한 주의를 필요로 하는 일이 있으실 경우, 예약을 잡으실 때 저희에게 알려 주십시오. 오늘 www.glitzcl.com으로 저희에게 연락 주십시오.

http://www.glitzcl.com/booking
Glitz Cleaning / 작업 요청서

요청 날짜: 10월 14일   요청 번호: 9820
고객: Vivian Pharr   주소: 592 Brook Road, Fredericksburg, VA 22401
연락처: [ ] 전화 _____ / [✔] 이메일 vpharr@espinozainc.com
Glitz Cleaning을 이용해 보신 적이 있으신가요? [ ] 네 [✔] 아니오
청소되어야 할 건물의 규모: 침실 5개 짜리 주택, 모든 방

선호하는 서비스 제공 날짜: 10월 20일   하루 중 선호하는 작업 시간대: 오전
서비스 종류: [✔] 1회 [ ] 주간   작업 시간: 2시간

고객 메모: 청소 작업자들께서 천장에 있는 조명 기기의 먼지를 털어 내려면 높은 사다리가 필요할 거예요. 제게 사다리가 없기 때문에 가져 오셔야 할 겁니다.

특별 지시 사항: 거실에 보시면, 치워 버리고 싶은 오래된 안락의자가 하나 있는데, 이것을 처리해 주실 수 있는지 궁금합니다. 제게 알려 주세요.

수신: Vivian Pharr ⟨vpharr@espinozainc.com⟩
발신: Glitz Cleaning ⟨appointments@glitzcl.com⟩
날짜: 10월 14일
제목: 청소 작업 요청

Pharr 씨께,

귀하의 청소 작업이 10월 20일 오전 10시에 예약되었음을 확인해 드리고자 합니다. 귀하의 건물 크기로 인해, 요청하신 작업 시간보다 1시간 더 예약해 드렸습니다. 건물의 크기 때문에 이렇게 하는 것이 필요할 것으로 보이는데, 특히 저희가 처음 방문하기 때문입니다. 귀하의 주택으로 세 명의 직원들이 보내질 것이며, 녹색으로 된 Glitz Cleaning 명찰을 통해 신분을 확인하실 수 있습니다. 저희 직원들은 고객들로부터 현금으로 지불되는 금액을 수납하지 않는다는 점을 기억해 주시기 바랍니다. 따라서, 최소한 예약 시간보다 24시간 전에 은행 계좌 이체로 지불하도록 준비해 주셔야 합니다. 제가 거래 내역서 및 계좌 이체를 위한 안내 사항들을 첨부해 드렸습니다. 귀하께서는 이메일로 영수증을 받게 되실 것입니다. 기록을 위해 이를 보관해 두셔도 되지만 저희 직원들에게 보여 주실 필요는 없습니다.

저희 작업 요청서의 특별 지시 사항 항목에 기재해 주신 요청 사항과 관련해, 해당 내용을 수용해 드릴 수 있다는 점을 말씀 드리게 되어 기쁩니다. 그리고 귀하께서는 신규 고객이시므로 이 서비스는 무료로 진행해 드리겠습니다.

질문이 있으시면 주저하지 마시고 이 이메일 주소로 연락하시거나 555-2907로 전화하시기 바랍니다.

안녕히 계십시오.

Alan Jordan
Glitz Cleaning 고객 서비스 담당

186 광고에서, 첫 번째 단락, 두 번째 줄의 단어 "committed"와 의미가 가장 가까운 것은 무엇인가?

(A) 제한된
(B) 기부된
(C) 익숙한
(D) 전념하는

187 Pharr 씨가 자신의 주택에 관해 말한 것은 무엇인가?

(A) 망가진 조명들이 있다.
(B) 1개가 넘는 층으로 되어 있다.

(C) 천장이 높다.
(D) 최근에 개조되었다.

188 Pharr 씨의 청구 비용은 얼마일 것 같은가?

(A) 80달러
(B) 150달러
(C) 215달러
(D) 280달러

189 Jordan 씨는 Pharr 씨에게 무엇을 하도록 상기시키는가?

(A) 물건들 치워 놓기
(B) 미리 비용 지불하기
(C) 주소 확인하기
(D) 계좌번호 확인하기

190 Glitz Cleaning에 관해 알 수 있는 것은 무엇인가?

(A) 직원 규모를 늘릴 계획이다.
(B) 가구를 치우는 서비스를 제공한다.
(C) 지역 내에서 자사의 비즈니스를 광고한다.
(D) 옥외의 유지 관리 서비스를 실시한다.

신유형 191-195는 다음 공지와 이메일, 그리고 이용 후기를 참조하시오.

공지

경영 팀에서는 우리 호텔이 ⟨Urban Outdoors Magazine⟩에 특집으로 소개된다는 점을 알려 드리게 되어 기쁩니다. 우리 호텔이 소유한 정원에 관한 기사가 실릴 것입니다. 정원을 유지 관리하는 데 도움을 주는 관련 직원들의 단체 사진과 정원을 찍은 사진들이 기사와 함께 실릴 것입니다. 사진 기자가 5월 20일 화요일, 오후 2시에 사진 촬영을 위해 우리 호텔을 방문할 것입니다. 단체 사진의 일원에 해당되는 분이시라면, 사진 촬영을 위해 단추를 잠그는 방식으로 된 전문적인 스타일의 셔츠와 바지(청바지는 안 됩니다)를 착용해 주십시오. 촬영 후에 근무를 계속하실 수 있도록 갈아입을 것을 가져오시기 바랍니다. 질문이 있으신 분은 Antonia Suhr 씨께 말씀하십시오.

수신: Antonia Suhr ⟨antoniasuhr@merrillhotel.net⟩
발신: Jessie Weiss ⟨jessie@urbanoutdoorsmag.com⟩
날짜: 5월 16일
제목: 곧 있을 사진 촬영

안녕하세요, Suhr 씨,

다음 주에 있을 사진 촬영 당일에 날씨가 따뜻하고 화창할 예정이므로 저는 사진이 잘 나올 것이라고 생각합니다. 저는 사람들이 일자리로 돌아갈 수 있도록 단체 사진을 먼저 찍을 것입니다. 단체 사진 촬영에 걸리는 시간은 10분이 넘지 않을 것이며, 분수대 근처가 가장 좋은 장소일 것 같으니 이곳에서 사람들을 만날 수 있게 해 주시기 바랍니다. 그 후에 정원의 나머지 부분들의 촬영을 진행할 것이며, 오후 4시에는 모든 촬영을 마무리할 계획입니다. 화요일에 직접 뵐 수 있기를 바랍니다.

안녕히 계십시오.

Jessie Weiss

Merrill Hotel: 자연과 함께 하는 도심 속 휴양
Ralph Cross 작성

Hammond City에 머무르시는 분들에게, 건물을 둘러싼 4에이커 크기의 정원을 갖고 있는 Merrill Hotel은 도시의 바쁘고 부산한 생활에서 벗어나 반가운 휴식을 제공합니다. 호텔의 북쪽에 있는 중앙 출입구에서, 12가지 다양한 종류의 장미들을 특징으로 하는 아름다운 장미 정

원이 손님들을 맞이할 것입니다. 건물의 뒤편인 남쪽 방면에는 미술가인 Fausta Udinesi 씨가 디자인한 대리석 분수대가 가동되고 있습니다. 서쪽 방면에서는, 손님들이 호텔 구내에 있는 레스토랑으로 이어지는 야외 테라스 구역을 즐길 수 있습니다. 그리고 동쪽 방면에는 6개의 정교한 울타리 조각 작품이 있습니다.

매년, Merrill Hotel이 여행 시즌을 맞아 봄에 개장하면, 방문객들과 지역 주민들이 이곳의 아름다움을 즐기기 위해 호텔에 모여듭니다. "정원에 꽃들이 만발하면, 눈을 즐겁게 하는 축제가 됩니다"라고 이 호텔을 주기적으로 찾는 손님인 Andrew Deleon 씨는 말합니다. "저는 이 정원에서 느낄 수 있는 차분한 분위기가 정말 좋아요. 항상 제가 휴식을 취하는 데 도움이 됩니다."

Merrill Hotel은 웹사이트 www.merrillhotel.net을 통해 예약을 받습니다.

191 Weiss 씨는 누구의 사진을 촬영할 것 같은가?
(A) 객실 청소 직원들
(B) 접수 담당 직원들
(C) 정원 관리 직원들
(D) 호텔 손님들

192 일부 직원들은 5월 20일에 무엇을 하도록 요청받는가?
(A) 정원 구역 밖에 있기
(B) 여분의 옷을 갖고 출근하기
(C) 일찍 교대 근무를 하러 오기
(D) 사원증을 착용하기

193 어디에서 단체 사진 촬영을 할 것인가?
(A) 호텔의 북쪽 구역
(B) 호텔의 동쪽 구역
(C) 호텔의 남쪽 구역
(D) 호텔의 서쪽 구역

194 Merrill Hotel에 관해 알 수 있는 것은 무엇인가?
(A) 일 년 내내 여는 곳이 아니다.
(B) 한 곳이 넘는 지점이 있다.
(C) 해당 도시에서 가장 큰 호텔이다.
(D) 연례 꽃 축제를 주최한다.

195 Deleon 씨는 호텔 정원의 무엇을 마음에 들어 하는가?
(A) 야생 동물들
(B) 화초들의 종류
(C) 편안한 좌석
(D) 평화로운 주변 환경

신유형 ▶ 196-200은 다음 정보와 두 이메일을 참조하시오.

Laurel Community Center에서 열리는 가을 강연 시리즈

9월 15일, 목요일 / "의사 결정 능력 개선" / Granite Room / 오후 7:30-오후 9:30
Bergan University에서 심리학을 가르치시는 JieKuo 교수님이 사람들이 결정을 내리는 방법의 이면에 숨어 있는 원리를 설명해 드리며, 가장 흔히 하는 실수를 피하는 방법을 가르쳐 드립니다. 강연 후에는 Laurel Homeless Shelter를 위한 모금 행사가 있을 예정입니다. 모든 분들께서 후하게 기부해 주시기 바랍니다.

9월 29일, 목요일 / "건강 과학" / Slate Room / 오후 7:30-오후 9:00
Russell University의 Arthur Cardoso 박사님께서 건강과 행복 분야에서의 최신 연구 내용에 관해 말씀해 주실 것이며, 여기에는 예방 접종과 업무 관련 스트레스, 그리고 컴퓨터 앞에 너무 오래 앉아 있는 것의 영향 등과 같은 주제들이 포함됩니다. Cardoso 박사님께서는 8th Avenue Clinic을 대표해 기부금을 받으실 것입니다.

10월 13일, 목요일 / "국제 정치" / Granite Room / 오후 7:00-오후 9:00
정보를 얻을 수 있는 좋은 기회입니다! Cynthia Ebert 씨께서 다른 곳에서 절대 들으실 수 없는 통찰력과 함께 가장 뜨거운 정치적 현안들을 다루실 것입니다. 참가자들께서는 Worldwide Relief Fund에 재정적인 기부를 하실 수 있는 기회를 가지실 수 있습니다.

10월 27일, 목요일 / "고전 문학 탐구" / Granite Room / 오후 7:00-오후 9:30
Charlotte College의 Isabella Folliero 교수님께서 역사적으로 가장 잘 알려진 소설들을 살펴볼 것이며, 이 소설들을 걸작으로 분류하게 만드는 요소들을 강조해 설명해 주실 것입니다. 참가자들께서는 행사장에서 Laurel Library에 기부금을 내실 수 있습니다.

입장권(1인당 6.50달러)을 구입하실 분은 b.maxwell@laurelccenter.org로 Britney Maxwell 씨에게 이메일을 보내시기 바랍니다. 앞줄의 좌석은 오로지 지방 정부 근무자들을 위해서만 예약되어 있다는 점에 유의하시기 바랍니다.

수신: Britney Maxwell ⟨b.maxwell@laurelccenter.org⟩
발신: Hayden Lester ⟨lesterhayden@epic-mail.com⟩
날짜: 9월 10일
제목: Autumn Lecture Series

Maxwell 씨께,

저는 Autumn Lecture Series에 참석할 수 있는 입장권 한 장을 예매하는 데 관심이 있습니다. 저는 이미 "의사 결정 능력 개선" 강연에 대한 제 입장권을 주문해서 받았습니다. 저는 첫 번째 줄에 앉을 수 있게 되어 매우 기쁘게 생각합니다. 제가 추가 예매하려고 하는 입장권은 "국제 정치" 강연에 대한 것입니다. 제게 성인 입장권 1장을 보내 주시고 제가 처음 입장권을 구매하기 (거래 번호 7592) 위해 제공해 드렸던 신용카드로 비용을 청구해 주십시오. 감사합니다!

Hayden Lester

수신: Hayden Lester ⟨lesterhayden@epic-mail.com⟩
발신: Britney Maxwell ⟨b.maxwell@laurelccenter.org⟩
날짜: 9월 11일
제목: 회신: Autumn Lecture Series

Lester 씨께,

귀하께서 어제 요청하신 부분을 진행해 드릴 수 없다는 점을 알려 드리게 되어 죄송합니다. 안타깝게도, 해당 강연은 취소되어 Glenda Fesno 씨께서 진행하실 "소셜 미디어 시대"라는 이름의 강연으로 대체되었습니다. 그런데 취소된 강연에 대한 입장권이 이미 귀하께 발송되었으며, 귀하의 신용카드로 비용이 청구되었습니다. 새로운 강연에 참석하시기를 원하시면, 기존의 입장권을 새 입장권으로 교환해 드리겠습니다. 저희는 안내 데스크에 입장권을 보관할 것이며, 행사 당일에 오셔서 수령하실 수 있습니다. 제게 이메일로 답장하셔서 새로운 강연에 참석하기를 원하시는지, 아니면 환불받기를 원하시는지 알려 주시기 바랍니다.

안녕히 계십시오.

Britney Maxwell
발권 담당, Laurel Community Center

196 모든 강연에 대해 공통점은 무엇인가?

(A) 모두 같은 방에서 열린다.

(B) 모두 같은 시간 동안 지속된다.

(C) 모두 기부금을 받는다.

(D) 모두 대학 교수들에 의해 진행된다.

197 Lester 씨에 관해 알 수 있는 것은 무엇인가?

(A) 자신의 첫 번째 입장권을 잃어버렸다고 생각한다.

(B) 작년 행사에 참석했다.

(C) 지역 문화 센터의 회원이다.

(D) 정부 부처에서 근무한다.

198 "소셜 미디어 시대"라는 제목의 강연은 언제 열리는가?

(A) 9월 15일에

(B) 9월 29일에

(C) 10월 13일에

(D) 10월 27일에

199 두 번째 이메일에서, 첫 번째 단락, 다섯 번째 줄의 단어 "hold"와 의미가 가장 가까운 것은 무엇인가?

(A) ~을 주최하다

(B) ~을 옮기다

(C) ~을 움켜쥐다

(D) ~을 보관하다

200 Lester 씨는 무엇을 하도록 요청받는가?

(A) 우편 주소 제공하기

(B) 선호하는 사항 알리기

(C) 비용 지불 증명서 보여 주기

(D) 좌석 선택하기

PART 5

101 Lexon Construction의 부서장은 건축 자재를 재활용함으로써 공사 작업을 덜 낭비하는 변화를 제안했다.

102 회사는 본관 실험실에 대한 출입을 선임 기술자들로 제한하는데, 그곳에서 실시되는 연구가 매우 민감한 것이기 때문이다.

103 이번 여름의 쾌적한 날씨 덕분에 밀 수확이 매우 좋을 것으로 예상된다.

104 Mahawai Resort Hotel은 고객들의 요청 사항이 큰 것이든 작은 것이든 상관없이 그 일에 세심히 귀 기울이는 것으로 명성이 나 있다.

105 Waterstone Road의 양쪽 어느 곳이든 주차하는 것이 허용되지 않는데, 그곳이 Clarksville 마을 전체에서 가장 좁은 거리이기 때문이다.

106 Brotan-630 프린터에 사용된 최신 기술 덕분에, 그 프린터는 전문적으로 인쇄된 출력물을 대량 복사할 수 있다.

107 최근 설문 조사에 따르면, Harding's를 찾는 많은 고객들이 이 회사의 쇼핑객 전용 클럽의 존재에 대해 모르고 있다.

108 Camping Express에 대한 전국적인 마케팅 캠페인은 그 회사의 최신 텐트 제품 라인에 대해 많은 관심을 이끌어 냈다.

109 공무원들은 도시 남부 교외 지역의 인구가 놀라울 정도로 빠른 속도로 증가하고 있다고 보고했다.

110 오직 7.99달러의 추가 요금만 내시면 귀하께서 선택하신 배송 방식은 당일 항공 배송으로 업그레이드될 수 있습니다.

111 Gold's Gym에서, 1월부터 단체 수업의 참가 비용이 달라질 것이라는 공지가 있었다.

112 사장은 수출 시장의 침체를 방지하기 위한 방법들을 논의하기 위해 여러 유명 경제학자들과 만났다.

113 Moreland Department Store에서는 고객 만족도를 평가하기 위해 앞으로 2주에 걸쳐 설문 조사가 실시될 것이다.

114 연례 저널리즘 학회와 관련된 더 깊이 있는 상세 정보는 www. hughesjournalism.org/conference에서 찾아볼 수 있다.

115 Sustainability for Life 행사에 참가하는 것은 기업가들이 그들의 프로젝트에 재정적으로 지원해 줄 투자자들에게 폭넓게 알려질 수 있는 기회를 준다.

116 연례 연회에서 모금된 기금은 도움을 가장 필요로 하는 어느 자선 단체에게든지 나눠질 것이다.

117 기업들은 일반적으로 한 직원이 같은 직책에서 최소 6개월 동안 근무를 할 때까지 부서 간의 이동에 대한 요청을 승인하지 않는다.

118 Luther 씨의 감독하에 있는 Carthage 프로젝트는 내일부터 2주 후에 완료될 것으로 예상된다.

119 Municipal Transit Department는 승객들이 한 번의 요금 지불로 버스, 지하철 그리고 택시를 타고 이동할 수 있게 하는 카드를 개발하고 있다.

120 피아니스트 Melissa Keen의 콘서트에 참석했던 평론가들은 그녀의 특유의 정확한 연주에 깊은 인상을 받았다.

121 Wrenton University의 정치학 교수인 Marie Hollister의 연구는 〈Journal of Current Events〉에 주기적으로 게재된다.

122 공립 학교와 공원, 그리고 쇼핑 센터와의 근접성 때문에, Meadow Lake Village는 사람들 사이에서 매우 인기가 있다.

123 항공사가 Camacho 씨의 분실 수하물을 찾았을 무렵, 그녀는 이미 돌아오는 항공편에 탑승했다.

124 중앙아메리카에서 가장 인기 있는 휴양지 중 한 곳이라는 점 외에도, Belize는 놀랄 만한 야생 동물로 자연을 사랑하는 사람들 사이에서 알려져 있다.

125 건물 꼭대기 층에 있는 VIP 휴게실은 오직 임원들과 그들의 손님들에 의해서만 사용되어야 한다.

126 주차장의 안전을 개선하기 위해, 시설 관리 팀이 어두운 조명을 더 밝은 것으로 교체할 것이다.

127 3월 9일에, 전국에서 가장 판매가 잘 되는 브랜드 회사의 영업 사원들이 브랜드 마케팅 학회를 위해 모였다.

128 국제 학회의 주최 측은 30명이 넘는 통역사들을 고용했는데, 이들 중 대부분은 번역의 목표어를 모국어로 사용하는 사람들이다.

129 모든 팩스 기기는 1년 동안 무료로 서비스를 제공하거나 수리를 해 준다는 내용의 약정서를 포함하고 있다.

130 Zaga Inc. 제조 공장들은 이용 가능한 가장 시간 효율이 좋은 기계를 사용하고 있으며, 그에 따라 생산 능력을 늘리고 있다.

PART 6

신유형 ▶ 131-134는 다음 광고를 참조하시오.

천연 온천, 맛있는 음식과 아름다운 나무들이 우거진 산 사이에 자리 잡은 평화로운 강이 여기 Sawtooth Spa에서 여러분을 기다리고 있습니다. 84번 주간 고속도로의 21B 출구에서 불과 15분 거리에 위치해 있어 쉽게 찾아오실 수 있습니다. 다양한 스타일과 가격대로 이용하실 수 있는 숙박 시설들이 근처에 많이 있어, 저희 Sawtooth Spa는 모든 분들의 예산을 충족해 드립니다.

더 자세한 정부가 필요하시거나 입장권을 구매하기 위해서는 sawtoothspa.com을 방문해 주세요. 질문은 '이용 분의 상독홀 통해 히실 수 있습니다. 모든 질문과 요청 물품들에 대해 즉시 답변해 드릴 것이며, 이는 휴가를 계획하는 일이 절대로 스트레스가 되지 않아야 한다고 생각하기 때문입니다!

신유형 ▶ 135-138은 다음 정보를 참조하시오.

청색 4사이즈의 Belmore Evening Gown을 구입해 주셔서 감사 드립니다. 저희는 귀하의 거래를 가치 있게 생각하고 있으며, 저희 제품에 대해 매우 만족하시기를 바랍니다. 만약 불만족스러우실 경우, 귀하께서는 구매 시점으로부터 60일 이내에 사용하지 않은 제품에 대해 환불을 요구하실 수 있습니다. 조건에 해당되는 상품을 반품하시기 위해서는, 온라인 계정을 통해 신청서를 제출하시면 저희가 물품 배송용 라벨을 보내드릴 것입니다. 상품은 원래의 가격표와 함께 보내 주셔야 합니다. 귀하의 요청이 처리되기까지 30일이 소요된다는 점을 감안해 주시기 바랍니다. 반송 요금과 처리 비용이 전체 가격에서 공제될 수 있습니다. 귀하의 거래에 감사 드리며, 다시 저희 제품을 구매하시기를 바랍니다.

신유형 ▶ 139-142는 다음 편지를 참조하시오.

Manning's Groceries
945 East Front Street
Placerville, CA 95667
5월 19일

Jon Mauk 또는 현 거주자
2700 Foothills Dr.
Placerville, CA 95667

소중한 고객님께,

저희 Manning's Groceries는 주 전역에서 시행되는 비닐 사용을 줄이기 위한 노력에 6월 1일부터 동참하기 시작할 것입니다. 저희는 귀하께 이 계획이 저희 식료품점에 미칠 영향에 대해 알려 드리고자 합니다. 저희는 계산대에 비닐 봉투를 없애고, 그것들을 구매된 재사용 봉투나 제품 배송에서 남은 박스로 대체하는 것으로 시작할 것입니다. 두 가지 선택 사항 중 하나를 요청하시려면, 계산대 직원에게 말씀해 주시기만 하면 됩니다.

이 프로젝트의 결과로, 저희는 판매 비용을 더 낮출 수 있을 것이라 예상하며, 이로 인해 고객들께서는 매년 약 10달러를 절약할 수 있게 됩니다.

지구를 지키는 일에 저희와 함께 해 주셔서 감사 드립니다. 더 많은 정보는 manningsfood.com에 접속하시거나 매장 매니저에게 문의하시기 바랍니다. 귀하께서 이 프로젝트의 참여를 자랑스럽게 여기시기를 바랍니다.

안녕히 계십시오.

Silvia Bundy, 매장 매니저
Manning's Groceries

신유형 ▶ 143-146은 다음 편지를 참조하시오.

Hanson 씨께,

저희는 귀하께서 1월 6일에 저희 웹사이트를 통해 제출하신 대출 신청서를 접수해 처리했습니다. 저희는 고객님들께서 필요로 하시는 자금을 제공해 드리는 것뿐만 아니라, 계약이 실행 가능하도록 보장해 드릴 수 있기를 바라고 있습니다. 귀하의 파일은 신중히 검토되었고, 요청 사항은 승인되었습니다. 저희 대출 담당 직원인 Sienna Toledo 씨에게 253-5545로 연락 주시면, 귀하께 자세한 정보를 제공해 드릴 것입니다. 그녀가 귀하의 질문에 답변해 드릴 것입니다.

저희 Zenque Credit Union은 이 계약을 최종 완료해 앞으로 귀하의 금융 상황을 개선하기 위한 동반자가 될 수 있기를 고대합니다.

진심으로,

Gwen Hughes
대출 담당 책임
Zenque Credit Union

PART 7

147-148은 다음 이메일을 참조하시오.

수신: Cedarstone Planning Team 〈planningmembers@cedarstone1.com〉
발신: Mario Schreiber 〈m.schreiber@cedarstone1.com〉
날짜: 4월 18일
제목: 월간 회의

안녕하세요 여러분,

제가 어제 보내 드린 안건에 언급된 바와 같이, 다음 기획 회의 때 건물 위치에 관해 논의할 것입니다. 비록 현재 건물에서 지낸 지 3개월밖에 안 되었지만, 이미 우리의 필요보다 너무 협소합니다. 우리의 논의 시간을 최대한 활용할 수 있도록, 여러분 각자가 우리에게 적합할 것 같은 건물들을 몇 개씩 조사해 주셨으면 합니다. 월간 임대료, 크기, 그리고 편의 시설에 관해 파악해야 합니다.

감사합니다!

Mario Schreiber
Cedarstone 기획팀, 관리자

147 Schreiber 씨는 Cedarstone에 관해 무엇을 암시하는가?

    (A) 하나가 넘는 지사가 있다.

    (B) 현재 직원들을 모집하는 중이다.

    (C) 빠르게 성장해 왔다.

    (D) 그 기획 회의가 변경되었다.

148 이메일 수신자들은 무엇을 하라고 요청받는가?

    (A) 조사를 실시하는 것

    (B) 논의 그룹들로 나누는 것

    (C) 건물들의 사진을 찍는 것

    (D) 선호하는 건물을 이메일로 보내는 것

149-150은 다음 광고를 참조하시오.

Wildview Youth Ranch에는 현재 세 명의 학생 인턴 자리가 비어 있으며, 동물들과 함께 일하는 것의 인간의 심리적인 이점과 관련된 여러 프로젝트를 연구팀이 진행하는 일을 돕게 됩니다.

– 합격자는 심리학 또는 상담 분야에서 6월 10일까지 최소 1년의 대학원 교육을 이수하시는 분이어야 합니다.

– 동물 교육에 대한 기본적인 업무 지식은 해당 직무 수행에 필수이며, 어린이들과 어울리기 좋아하는 성향 또한 필수입니다.

– 응급 처치 자격증이 있는 지원자는 적극 우대합니다.

관심 있으신 분들께서는 과거의 현장 경험, 서면 보고서, 또는 통계 분석 자료를 상세히 기술한 포트폴리오를 제출하셔야 합니다.

11월 10일 이전까지 wvyouthranch.org/summerinternship을 방문해 온라인으로 지원하시기 바랍니다.

149 인턴의 자격 요건이 아닌 것은 무엇인가?

    (A) 동물 서식지 분야에 관한 지식

    (B) 동물 교육에 대한 익숙함

    (C) 응급 상황에 대비한 의료 기술

    (D) 상담 분야에 대한 대학원 교육

150 Wildview Youth Ranch에 관해 명시된 것은 무엇인가?

    (A) 제약회사다.

    (B) 심리학에 대한 연구를 실시한다.

    (C) 프로젝트 책임자 자리가 공석이다.

    (D) 여러 개의 작은 농장을 관리하고 있다.

151-152는 다음 정보를 참조하시오.

Providence Electronics

저희 Providence Electronics는 품질과 신뢰성을 위해 전념하고 있다는 사실을 고객 여러분께서 인식하고 신뢰하고 계신다는 점을 알고 있습니다. 저희는 여러분께 최고의 제품을 보장해 드리고 있으며, 여러분의 행복이 저희에게는 중요합니다. 이것이 바로 저희가 Spirit-22 충전기 팩을 자발적으로 회수하기로 결정한 이유입니다. 저희는 이 장치가 과열되어 화재 위험을 초래할 수 있다는 보고를 받았습니다.

이 제품을 구입하신 고객님들은 환불을 받으실 자격이 있습니다. 저희 소매점에 있는 작업실에서 이 장치를 수리해 드리지는 않을 것이라는 점에 유의하시기 바랍니다. 저희는 그저 이 장치를 수거하고 환불을 해 드릴

것입니다. 자세한 정보를 원하시면, 동부 표준시로 매일 오전 7시에서 오후 9시까지 저희 전화 상담 서비스 1-800-555-7676으로 전화 주시거나, www.providenceelectronics.com을 방문하시기 바랍니다. 거래해 주셔서 감사 드립니다.

151 정보는 왜 쓰였는가?

    (A) 단골 고객들에게 의견을 요청하기 위해

    (B) 새로운 제품 주문 방식을 소개하기 위해

    (C) 고객들에게 안전 관련 문제를 알리기 위해

    (D) 고객들의 충성도에 감사하기 위해

152 Providence Electronics에 대해 사실인 것은 무엇인가?

    (A) 당사의 기기는 평생 품질 보증 서비스가 딸려 있다.

    (B) 당사의 전화 상담 서비스는 24시간 이용 가능하다.

    (C) 영수증이 제시될 경우에만 제품에 대한 환불이 가능하다.

    (D) 당사의 소매점에서 수리 서비스를 제공한다.

신유형 153-154는 다음 문자 메시지 대화를 참조하시오.

Natasha Mann [오후 3:02]
George, 저에게 분량을 줄여 달라고 하셨던 TV 뉴스 영상에 관해 뭔가 확인을 좀 해도 될까요?

George Atkins [오후 3:04]
물론이죠.

Natasha Mann [오후 3:05]
제가 보니 자막이 전혀 없더라고요. 그것들을 제가 추가해야 하나요, 아니면 다른 누군가가 할 건가요?

George Atkins [오후 3:07]
그건 나중에 완료될 거예요. 아직 일부 정보를 기다리고 있어서요.

Natasha Mann [오후 3:08]
알겠어요. 그럼 그 영상을 뉴스 팀으로 보낼게요.

George Atkins [오후 3:09]
저라면 아직 그러지 않겠어요.

Natasha Mann [오후 3:10]
아, 그래요?

George Atkins [오후 3:10]
Marty가 승인할 수 있도록 먼저 검토하게 하는 게 나을 거예요. 그렇지 않으면, 나중에 수정해야 할 수도 있어요.

Natasha Mann [오후 3:11]
맞아요.

George Atkins [오후 3:12]
그저 그게 당신한테 다시 돌려보내지는 건 원치 않아서요.

153 Mann 씨는 누구일 것 같은가?

    (A) TV 수리 작업자

    (B) 광고 담당 임원

    (C) 신문 기자

    (D) 동영상 편집자

154 오후 3시 11분에, Mann 씨가 "That's true"라고 썼을 때 의미하**신유형** 는 것은 무엇인가?

    (A) 그녀는 혼동을 피하기 위해 팀에 직접 이야기해야 한다.

    (B) 그녀는 Marty가 최고의 자막 작업일 것이라고 생각한다.

    (C) 그녀는 업무가 검토되도록 해야 한다는 데 동의한다.

(D) 그녀는 나중에 수정할 수 있는 시간이 더 많이 있을 것이다.

155-157은 다음 편지를 참조하시오.

〈Easton Times〉 편집자께,

지난주에 대규모 폭풍이 Easton을 통과해 지나갔을 때, 시에서 그것을 어떻게 처리할지 우려했습니다. 자연 재해는 늘 한 지역 사회가 대처하기 어려운 일입니다.

도심에서, 쓰러진 나무들이 Roosevelt Street를 가로질러 놓여 있어, 차들이 지나갈 수 없었습니다. 또한 정전도 발생해 몇몇 지역의 건물들에 영향을 미쳤습니다. 게다가, Tyce River는 둑을 넘쳐 흘러 Jackson Park의 일부를 물에 잠기게 했습니다.

이 문제들이 매우 신속히 처리되었다는 것에 깊은 인상을 받았다고 말씀드려야겠고 지자체 직원들 모두를 칭찬하고자 합니다. Daniel Roberts가 운영하는 우리 시의 소셜 미디어 페이지가 특히 도움이 되었다는 것을 알았습니다. 그것이 시의 모든 사람들이 최신 소식을 쉽게 확인할 수 있게 해 주었습니다. 일이 잘 처리되도록 관여해 주신 모든 분들께 감사 드립니다.

Amelia Cho

155 Cho 씨는 왜 편지를 보냈는가?

(A) 폭풍에 대한 경고를 하기 위해
(B) 지자체 정책을 추천하기 위해
(C) 관리 절차를 설명하기 위해
(D) 비상 사태 대응 시스템을 칭찬하기 위해

156 Easton의 문제로 나타나지 않은 것은?

(A) 전기가 끊겼다.
(B) 도로가 차단되었다.
(C) 강이 오염되었다.
(D) 공원이 침수되었다.

157 Roberts 씨에 관해 알 수 있는 것은 무엇인가?

(A) 그는 자연 재해를 예측했다.
(B) 그는 주민들에게 계속 최신 소식을 전했다.
(C) 그는 시의 일부 직원들을 관리했다.
(D) 그는 시설물 수리를 담당했다.

158-160은 다음 기사를 참조하시오.

새로운 장르로 영역을 넓히는 Ian Danley
Shelly Haagenson 작성

Los Angeles (12월 9일)—Ian Danley는 광고와 영화에 자주 사용되는, 모든 장르의 수많은 히트곡을 제작하는 것으로 알려져 있다. 〈Zippy Cakes〉 디저트 광고에 사용된 인기 있는 시엠송에서 그의 작품을 알아차릴 수 있을 것이다. 〈Twilight Breeze〉와 〈Mint Leaves〉 같은 그의 작품들 중 일부는 미국 전역과 유럽의 일부 지역에서 그를 유명하게 만들었다. 현재, 과거에 다른 일로 함께 작업을 한 적 있는 작곡가 Kate Evans와의 공동 작업으로, Danley는 내년 여름에 스크린을 강타할 작품을 위한 음악을 제작 중이다. 두 사람은 Michael Straight가 제작하는 장편 애니메이션 영화 〈Zoo Run〉을 위해 곡을 쓰기로 계약을 맺었다. Straight 씨는 〈Mully's Day Out〉 작업으로 Trendy Award를 수상했다.

Danley가 애니메이션 영화를 위해 곡을 쓰는 것은 이번이 처음이지만, 그는 자신의 노력에 낙관하고 있다. "애니메이션이 참으로 색다르고 재미있어 정말 즐겁습니다. 제가 작업했던 다른 영화들보다 훨씬 더 마음이 가벼워요. 장면에 맞는 곡을 만드는 것과 같은 많은 면에서 동일하지만,

좀 더 실험적으로 작업하게 됩니다."

이 영화는 6월 1일에 Los Angeles에서 상영할 준비가 되었고, 6월 22일에 전국적으로 개봉된다. 6월 24일에는 London과 Sydney에서 상영될 것이고, 이후에 곧 세계의 각지에서도 상영될 것이다.

Straight 씨의 경우, 그는 이 영화가 인기 있을 것이라고 예상한다. 지난주 인터뷰에서 그는 "〈Zoo Run〉이 박스 오피스에서 1위에 오르지 못할 이유가 없다고 보는데, 특히 Kate와 Ian 같은 재능 있는 작곡가들이 함께하니 말이죠. 줄거리도 아주 흥미롭고 모든 연령층이 즐길 것입니다."라고 말했다.

158 Danley 씨는 누구인가?

(A) 광고 제작자
(B) 애니메이션 영화 감독
(C) 시나리오 작가
(D) 작곡가

159 Straight 씨에 관해 알 수 있는 것은 무엇인가?

(A) 그는 새로운 영화에 필요한 음악을 작곡할 것이다.
(B) 그는 전에 Kate Evans와 공동 작업을 한 적이 있다.
(C) 그는 Haagenson 씨와 최근에 이야기를 나눴다.
(D) 그는 지난주에 Kate와 Ian 씨를 인터뷰했다.

160 영화 〈Zoo Run〉에 관해 언급된 것은 무엇인가?

(A) Straight 씨가 대본을 쓴 첫 애니메이션 영화이다.
(B) 모든 연령층 사이에서 인기를 얻었다.
(C) 애니메이션 장면들로만 구성되어 있다.
(D) 제작자가 더 마음 편히 즐길 영화들을 제작했었다.

신유형 ▶ **161-163은 다음 웹 페이지를 참조하시오.**

홈	회사 소개	제품	고객 서비스	직원 채용

Flintglass Eyewear는 전 연령층을 대상으로 처방전이 필요하거나 그렇지 않은 교정용 안경과 선글라스 제품을 판매하는 온라인 소매점입니다. 1928년부터 영업해 오며, 저희는 고객들의 시력과 패션 관련 요구 사항을 충족시켜 드리는 것을 전문으로 합니다. — [1] —.

3천 가지가 넘는 다양한 스타일로, 저희는 어디서든 구매 가능한 가장 다양한 종류의 전문화된 안경을 제공해 드립니다. 그리고 각 스타일은 고객이 필요한 사이즈에 맞게 변경될 수 있습니다. — [2] —.

주문 과정은 매우 간단합니다. — [3] —. 그저 계정을 하나 만들고 카메라를 정면으로 보고 찍으신 사진을 업로드 하세요. 간단한 몇 가지 단계를 거치고 나면 저희 소프트웨어가 다양한 안경테를 착용한 모습을 미리 볼 수 있게 해 드립니다. — [4] —. 그 다음에 원하시는 렌즈 사양을 입력하고 주문 버튼을 클릭하세요. 저희 제품은 보통 영업일 기준으로 2~3일이면 배송되며, 전 세계 어디로든 보내드릴 수 있습니다.

질문이나 우려 사항이 있으신 분은, 저희 고객 서비스 전문가들이 24시간 내내 전화 또는 온라인 채팅으로 도와 드릴 수 있습니다. 거주하고 계신 나라의 특정 전화번호 목록은 저희 고객 서비스 페이지에서 확인해 보시기 바랍니다.

161 Flintglass Eyewear에 관해 사실이 아닌 것은 무엇인가?

(A) 고객들의 요구를 충족하기 위해 주문 제작된 안경을 제공한다.
(B) 배송까지 평균 일주일이 채 걸리지 않는다.
(C) 고객들은 언제든지 우려 사항을 문의할 수 있다.
(D) 고객들은 소매점에서 다양한 스타일의 안경을 착용해 볼 수 있다.

162 웹 페이지에 따르면, 주문 과정의 일부분은 무엇인가?

(A) 선택된 사진에 맞는 안경테를 디자인하기

(B) Flintglass Eyewear가 미리 보기를 위해 제공한 소프트웨어를 이용하기

(C) 안경테를 추천받기 위해 사진을 직접 업로드하기

(D) 이메일을 통해 고객 서비스로 사진을 보내기

163 신유형 [1], [2], [3], [4]로 표기된 위치들 중에서 다음 문장이 가장 잘 어울리는 곳은 어디인가?

"여러분은 원하는 안경테를 고르기만 하면 됩니다!"

(A) [1]

(B) [2]

(C) [3]

(D) [4]

신유형 164-167은 다음 문자 메시지 대화를 참조하시오.

Mina Yoon [오전 9:07]
여러분 모두 즐거운 주말 보내셨기를 바랍니다. 지난주 7월 5일 인사부 기획 회의를 갑자기 끝내야 해서 죄송합니다. 좋지 않았던 설문 조사 결과와 관련해 무엇을 해야 할지 아이디어 회의를 할 기회가 없었기 때문에, 여러분의 생각을 듣고 싶습니다.

Stan Berry [오전 9:08]
우리 모두 지난달 설문 조사의 응답 내용에 놀랐어요. 우리가 뭘 해야 할지 모르겠어요.

Andrew Geneva [오전 9:10]
네, 보통 직원들에게 설문지를 배부하면, 그들은 업무 환경에 대해 전반적으로 만족하는 것으로 답해요. 그러니, 그들에게 다시 한 번 동기를 부여할 방법을 찾아야 합니다.

Stan Berry [오전 9:11]
맞아요. 직원들의 성과를 인정해 주기 위한 특별 연회를 여는 것은 어떨까요?

Megan Dawson [오전 9:12]
못할 것 없죠? 우리의 감사를 표할 재밌는 방법이 될 거예요. 그런데 요즘은 대부분의 콘퍼런스 센터들이 바쁜 시기잖아요. 제가 오늘 전화해서 장소를 예약하는 건 어떨까요? 기회를 놓치고 싶지 않잖아요.

Mina Yoon [오전 9:14]
먼저 재무팀장님께 승인을 받는 것이 나을 거예요. 예산에 여유가 있는지 확실히 해 둬야 하니까요.

Megan Dawson [오전 9:15]
좋은 지적이에요. 제가 지금 그렇게 해 보고 나중에 어떻게 됐는지 알려드릴게요.

164 Yoon 씨는 왜 문자 메시지 대화를 시작했는가?

(A) 결과를 알려 주기 위해

(B) 해결책을 요청하기 위해

(C) 프로젝트를 발표하기 위해

(D) 회의를 연기하기 위해

165 설문 조사는 언제 실시되었는가?

(A) 5월에

(B) 6월에

(C) 7월에

(D) 8월에

166 신유형 오전 9시 12분에, Dawson 씨가 "Why not"이라고 썼을 때 의미하는 것은 무엇인가?

(A) 그녀는 일정이 겹칠 것이 의심스럽다.

(B) 그녀는 연회가 좋은 아이디어라고 생각한다.

(C) 그녀는 정책에 관해 혼란스러워하고 있다.

(D) 그녀는 Berry 씨가 상을 받을 만하다고 생각한다.

167 Dawson 씨는 다음에 무엇을 할 것 같은가?

(A) 부서장에게 이야기하기

(B) 예산 제안서 승인하기

(C) 콘퍼런스 장소에 연락하기

(D) 직원들에게 정보 보내기

신유형 168-171은 다음 이메일을 참조하시오.

수신: Carla Earhart ⟨earhartc@falcoind.com⟩
발신: Benjamin Reeves ⟨ben.reeves@ddcsecurity.com⟩
날짜: 7월 19일
제목: 읽어 보시기 바랍니다

Earhart 씨,

7월 3일에 저희 기술자들 중 한 명의 방문에 시간을 내주셔서 다시 한 번 감사 드립니다. 방문을 마친 후에 저희가 추천을 하는 보안 업그레이드 목록을 보내 드렸지만 이 업그레이드 작업을 진행하고 싶으신지에 대해 아직 답변을 듣지 못했습니다. — [1] —. 저희가 귀하의 정확한 사양에 맞도록 초기 계획을 고안해 두었습니다. — [2] —. 저희는 최근 이 지역에 문을 열었으며, 이미 많은 고객들이 만족하셨습니다. — [3] —. 이들은 쇼핑 센터와 미술관으로부터 건설 회사에 이르기까지 다양하므로, 저희는 현재 이용 중이신 제공업체의 서비스만큼 만족시켜 드리거나 그것을 뛰어 넘는 높은 수준의 서비스를 Falco Industries에 제공해 드릴 수 있다고 확신합니다. 원본을 찾기 위해 이전 이메일들을 다시 확인할 필요가 없도록, 편의를 위해 이 이메일에 귀하의 회계 법인 회사에 필요한 문서를 다시 첨부했습니다. — [4] —.

곧 소식 전해 주시기를 바랍니다,

Benjamin Reeves

168 이메일의 목적은 무엇인가?

(A) 업데이트된 가격 견적서를 제출하기

(B) 추천 사항들을 다시 보내기

(C) 한 장소를 방문하는 일정을 잡기

(D) 제안서에 오류를 지적하기

169 Reeves 씨에 의해 암시된 것은 무엇인가?

(A) DDC Security가 몇몇 신입 기술자들을 채용했다.

(B) Reeves 씨와 Earhart 씨가 직접 만난 적이 있다.

(C) Earhart 씨는 현재 DDC Security의 경쟁사를 이용하고 있다.

(D) Falco Industries는 최근에 해당 지역에 문을 열었다.

170 Falco Industries는 어떤 유형의 업체일 것 같은가?

(A) 회계 회사

(B) 쇼핑 센터

(C) 건설 회사

(D) 미술관

171 신유형 [1], [2], [3], [4]로 표기된 위치들 중에서 다음 문장이 가장 잘 어울리는 곳은 어디인가?

"추가적으로, 시간이 지나면서 귀하께 필요한 것이 달라짐에 따라

저희 서비스를 조정해 드릴 수 있습니다."

(A) [1]

(B) [2]

(C) [3]

(D) [4]

172-175는 다음 기사를 참조하시오.

밝은 전망을 보이는 Stansbury 지역의 노동 시장

STANSBURY—Ziemer Software가 우리 Stansbury에 지사를 열어 Stansbury를 중심으로 점점 더 늘어나고 있는 기술 회사들 중의 하나로 만들 예정이라고 발표하면서 Stansbury의 취업 전망이 밝은 상황이다. 비록 Belding City가 기술 업계에서는 여전히 지역 내에서 가장 많은 일자리를 제공하는 곳이기는 하지만, 기업들을 유치하기 위한 폭넓은 세금 감면 혜택에 부분적으로 힘입어 Stansbury는 스스로 명성을 얻기 시작하는 과정에 있다. Vanderhoof University의 Stansbury 캠퍼스에서 운영 중인 최고 수준의 프로그램들과 함께, 현지 출신의 뛰어난 자격 요건을 갖춘 수많은 대학생들이 최근에 배출되고 있다.

로봇 공학 회사인 Emeral Inc.는 지역 내에서 수년 동안 많은 직원들을 채용한 업체였으며, 최근에 Stansbury에서 사업을 지속하려는 계획을 재확인해 주었다. Emeral Inc.의 대변인은 Stansbury 내의 인력 상황에 대해 만족해 왔다고 말했다. "러시아의 St. Petersburg, 스페인의 Madrid와 마찬가지로 몇몇 저희 지사에서는 제대로 된 지원자들을 모집하는 데 오랜 시간이 걸리는데, 저희가 오직 최고의 재능을 지닌 분들만 채용하기 때문입니다. Stansbury에서는 직원 채용이 항상 더 쉽다고 느끼는데, 이는 선택할 수 있는 뛰어난 후보자들이 아주 많기 때문입니다. 저희는 다행히도 아주 커다란 성공을 거둬 왔습니다. 투자자들의 재정적 지원과 최상급의 상품들은 이 상황의 일부에 지나지 않습니다. 일이 진행되도록 하기 위해서는 창의적인 직원들이 필요합니다."

Stansbury에서는 민간 기업 부문에서만 채용 기회를 늘리는 것이 아니다. Business Connect는 정부가 운영하는 프로그램으로, 지역 내에서 일자리를 찾도록 구직자들에게 도움을 준다. 이 프로그램은 2년 전에 더 많은 사람들과 기업들을 Stansbury로 유치하기 위한 노력의 일환으로 시작되었다. 불과 두 명의 직원들과 함께 시간제로 운영되기 시작했던 것이 성장을 거듭해 여섯 명의 정규직 직원들이 있는 규모가 되었다. Business Connect의 운영 책임자인 Marjorie Barnes 씨는 이 프로그램이 지역 기업들을 지탱하는 힘을 제공하는 데 기여하고 있다고 말했다. "우리 지역의 기업들이 성공을 거두면, 우리 지역 사회는 풍요로워집니다,"라고 Barnes 씨는 말했다. "저희는 그것을 실현하기 위해 이곳에 있는 겁니다."

172 기사에 따르면, 업체들은 왜 Stansbury가 매력적이라고 생각하는가?

(A) 대규모 교통 네트워크를 갖추고 있다.

(B) 인구가 빠르게 증가하고 있다.

(C) 능력 있는 직원들을 찾기가 쉽다.

(D) 업체들에게 세금 서비스를 제공한다.

173 Emeral Inc.에 관해 사실인 것은 무엇인가?

(A) 해외 투자자들을 유치하기 위해 노력한다.

(B) 본사를 Stansbury로 옮겼다.

(C) 해외 지사들을 가지고 있다.

(D) 채용 업무를 외부에 위탁했다.

174 Emeral Inc.의 성공 요인으로 나타나지 않은 것은 무엇인가?

(A) 고품질의 제품들

(B) 혁신적인 직원들

(C) 투자 자금

(D) 효율적인 검토 과정

175 Barnes 씨에 관해 암시된 것은 무엇인가?

(A) 그녀는 Emeral Inc.의 이전 직원이다.

(B) 그녀는 Stansbury에서 개인 사업을 시작했다.

(C) 그녀는 기술 분야에 학위가 있다.

(D) 그녀는 정부에 의해 고용된 사람이다.

176-180은 다음 이메일과 일정표를 참조하시오.

수신: Gateway 회계법인 직원들 〈allstaff@gatewayaccounting.com〉

발신: Robert Garza 〈r.garza@gatewayaccounting.com〉

날짜: 3월 7일

제목: MTC 주식회사

안녕하세요 여러분,

어제 회의에서 발표했던 대로, MTC 주식회사와의 합병에 관한 협의가 완료되었고, 협정이 마무리되었습니다. 여러분들 중 다수가 이 합병이 회사와 여러분 각자의 역할에 어떤 영향을 미칠 것인지에 대해 우려하셨다는 것을 알고 있습니다. 이 결정에 여러 가지 명확한 이점들이 있다는 것으로 여러분을 안심시켜 드리고 싶습니다. 새롭게 형성된 회사 (MTC Gateway)는 약 35퍼센트의 시장 점유율을 확보할 것이며, 이는 우리에게 경쟁적 우위를 가져다 줄 것입니다. Gateway 회계 법인과 마찬가지로, MTC 주식회사는 복잡한 세금 신고를 처리하는 것으로 명성이 나 있습니다. 게다가, MTC 주식회사는 법적 자문을 제공하는 부서가 있어, 우리 회사를 새로운 차원에 이르도록 해 줄 수 있을 것입니다.

그 변화가 더 순조로워지도록 돕기 위해, 다음 주에 각 회사에서 선정한 한 명의 회의 진행자와 함께하는 부서별 회의가 열릴 것입니다. Gateway 회계 법인의 직원은 두 회사의 인력을 가장 잘 통합할 방법을 찾기 위해 모두의 책무를 평가할 것입니다. MTC 주식회사 직원은 앞으로 MTC Gateway아에 시행될 정책들에 관해 이야기할 것입니다.

안녕히 계십시오.

Robert Garza
Gateway 회계 법인, 사무장

부서별 회의: Gateway 회계 법인 본사

3월 16일 화요일, 오후 1시~4시

부서	회의 장소	회의 진행자
영업	회의실 A	Semhar Tewelde [Gateway 회계 법인] Carol Nicols [MTC 주식회사]
마케팅	304호실	Rohini Sharaf [Gateway 회계 법인] Mitsuo Daijou [MTC 주식회사]
인사	회의실 B	Terry Woodard [Gateway 회계 법인] Joseph Decker [MTC 주식회사]
재무	직원 라운지	Gabriel Cardoso [Gateway 회계 법인] Yan Siu [MTC 주식회사]

두 회사의 현 CEO들은 그 직원들이 이미 자신들과 개별 미팅을 가졌던 인사부를 제외한 모든 부서들을 방문할 것입니다.

176 Garza 씨가 이메일을 보낸 한 가지 이유는 무엇인가?

(A) 변화에 따른 이점들을 강조하기 위해

(B) 직원들의 노고에 감사하기 위해

(C) 기업 합병을 발표하기 위해

(D) 협의 과정을 설명하기 위해

177 MTC 주식회사에 관해 암시된 것은 무엇인가?

(A) 35퍼센트의 시장 점유율을 보유하고 있었다.

(B) 어려운 세무를 처리하는 것으로 알려져 있다.

(C) 개인과 업체들의 요구를 충족시켜 준다.

(D) 몇몇 해외 지사들이 있다.

178 이메일에서, 첫 번째 단락, 여덟 번째 줄의 단어 "dimension"과 의미가 가장 가까운 것은 무엇인가?

(A) 장애물

(B) 특징

(C) 헌신

(D) 비율

179 Cardoso 씨에 관해 사실일 법한 것은 무엇인가?

(A) 그는 일부 직원들의 직무를 평가할 것이다.

(B) 그는 사무장과 만날 것이다.

(C) 그는 Siu 씨의 자리를 이어받을 것이다.

(D) 그는 새로운 정책들을 논의할 것이다.

180 3월 16일 회의에 관해 알 수 있는 것은 무엇인가?

(A) 지도자들이 직원들에 의해 선정되었다.

(B) 인사부 회의는 갑자기 끝날 것이다.

(C) 부서들이 점심 시간 전에 모일 것이다.

(D) CEO들이 회의실 B는 방문하지 않을 것이다.

181-185는 다음 전단과 이메일을 참조하시오.

자택 또는 회사에 필요한 빗물받이 통을 무료로 드립니다!

우리 시가 필요로 하는 수준을 충족할 만큼 충분한 물을 확보하지 못해 자주 물 부족에 시달리는 Burwell City Water System에 대한 부담을 줄이기 위한 노력의 일환으로, 5월 3일에 Valencia Park에서 Burwell 시민들에게 빗물받이 통을 나눠 드립니다. 주민들은 한 개의 무료 빗물받이 통(각 주소지당)을 받으실 수 있는 자격이 있으며, 기업 소유주들은 소매가보다 훨씬 저렴한 불과 40달러의 비용으로 통 하나를 구입하실 수 있습니다. 이 행사는 Burwell 시와 Association for Environmental Responsibility의 후원을 받는 행사입니다. 빗물받이 통은 반드시 직접 가져가셔야 하며, 오직 비스듬한 형태의 지붕과 배수 시스템을 갖춘 주택과 상업용 건물에서만 적합하게 쓰일 수 있습니다. 크기에 따라 통을 옮기는 데 픽업 트럭이 필요할 수도 있다는 점에 유의하시기 바랍니다.

이 통을 이용해 모은 물은 정원 작업, 세차, 그리고 그 외의 여러 용도로 사용될 수 있습니다. 시에서는 자연 환경에 미치는 영향을 급격히 줄일 수 있는 이와 같은 창의적인 해결책을 찾기 위해 지속적으로 노력할 것입니다. 더 많은 정보를 보시려면, www.cityofburwell.gov/water를 방문하시기 바랍니다.

수신: Tammy Damian 〈damiant@telebiz.com〉

발신: Hinako Okamura 〈h_okamura@cityofburwell.gov〉

날짜: 5월 18일

제목: 빗물받이 통 프로그램

Damian 씨께,

5월 3일에 Valencia Park에서 열린 행사에서 구입하신 빗물받이 통과 관련해 이메일을 보내 드립니다. 사용자한테서 불만을 접수한 끝에, 저희는 통 아래 부분에 있는 배수 꼭지의 크기가 잘못된 것이라는 사실을 알게 되었습니다. 따라서 정확하게 조립하더라도, 통에서 물이 샐 것입니다. 저희가 새로운 배수 꼭지를 보내 드릴 수 있도록 첨부해 드린 양식을 작성해 주시기 바랍니다. 원래 갖고 계신 것을 돌려주실 필요는 없습니다. 실은, 내년 행사에 쓸 빗물받이 통에 그 사이즈로 된 것을 사용할 예

정이므로 해당 프로그램에 다시 참여하실 계획이시라면 가지고 계시는 편이 좋을 것입니다. 작성하신 양식은 우편 또는 이메일로 보내 주시면 됩니다.

귀하의 행사 참여에 감사 드립니다.

Hinako Okamura

프로그램 진행 책임자

---

181 전단에 제공되지 않은 것은 어떤 유형의 정보인가?

(A) 건물 요건들

(B) 이용 가능한 통의 크기

(C) 행사의 후원자들

(D) 행사의 목적

182 Burwell에 관해 언급된 것은 무엇인가?

(A) 물 공급량 부족을 겪고 있다.

(B) 비가 가장 많이 오는 달은 5월이다.

(C) 새로운 공원이 문을 열었다.

(D) 인구가 빠르게 증가하고 있다.

183 전단에서, 두 번째 단락, 세 번째 줄의 단어 "dramatically"와 의미가 가장 가까운 것은 무엇인가?

(A) 엄격하게

(B) 예술적으로

(C) 상당히

(D) 환경적으로

184 Damian 씨에 관해 알 수 있는 것은 무엇인가?

(A) 그녀는 자신의 업체에서 통을 사용하고 있다.

(B) 그녀는 물품을 나눠 주는 일에 자원했다.

(C) 그녀는 Burwell의 주민이 아니다.

(D) 그녀는 Okamura 씨에게 불만을 제기했다.

185 Okamura 씨가 하도록 제안하는 것은 무엇인가?

(A) 조립 설명서를 검토하는 것

(B) 내년 행사에 등록하는 것

(C) 장비에 문제가 있는지 확인하는 것

(D) 향후 사용을 위해 부품을 보관하는 것

신유형 186-190은 다음 이메일들과 회의록을 참조하시오.

수신: 행사 기획 위원회 〈ep@marietta-co.com〉

발신: Melissa Trevino 〈m_trevino@marietta-co.com〉

날짜: 10월 10일

제목: Kovar 씨의 은퇴

여러분 안녕하세요,

모두 아시다시피, Jack Kovar 씨께서 우리 Marietta Co.에서 거의 30년간 근무하신 끝에 다음 달에 은퇴하십니다. 행사 기획 위원회에서는 우리 회사에서 보낸 Kovar 씨의 시간을 기념하고 멋지게 송별회를 열어 드리기 위해 은퇴 기념 연회를 준비하는 일을 담당합니다. 저는 이번 주 중으로 회의 일정을 정하고자 합니다. 여러분께 가장 적절한 날짜와 시간을 제게 알려 주시면, 모든 분들의 일정을 맞춰 보겠습니다.

장소는 제가 이미 예약해 뒀는데요, 11월 21일에 Laredo Center의 연회실로 했습니다. 하지만 준비 과정의 나머지 일들이 여전히 완료되어야 합니다. 우리의 시간이 다소 제한되어 있기 때문에 출장 요리 업체를 찾을 수 있도록 Chelsea Ebert 씨께 사전 조사를 해 달라고 요청해 두었

습니다. 과거에 우리가 이용해 본 적이 있지만 현재는 새 주인이 운영하는 Fairfield Catering을 포함해, Ebert 씨가 몇몇 업체를 평가할 것입니다.

이 파티에 대해 생각해 보시고 회의에서 가장 좋은 아이디어를 제시해 주시기 바랍니다. Kovar 씨는 최고의 진실성과 결단력으로 업무를 수행해 주신 분이십니다. 그러므로 Kovar 씨께 제대로 경의를 표해 드리는 것이 중요합니다.

안녕히 계십시오.

Melissa Trevino

수신: 행사 기획 위원회 〈ep@marietta-co.com〉
발신: Chelsea Ebert 〈c_ebert@marietta-co.com〉
날짜: 10월 11일
제목: 출장 요리 업체 선택안

안녕하세요, 여러분,

Trevino 씨께서 저에게 Kovar 씨의 은퇴 연회를 위해 이용 가능한 출장 요리 업체들을 조사해 달라고 요청하셨습니다. 제가 Bryant Creations와 Fairfield Catering으로 범위를 좁혔는데, 이 중 어느 곳이든 행사에 적합할 것 같습니다. 회의에서 더 자세한 정보를 제공할 것이지만, 간략한 비교가 아래 제시되어 있습니다.

메뉴 옵션: Bryant Creations는 세련된 입맛을 가진 분들을 위한 고급 음식에 초점을 맞춥니다. 높은 수준의 음식은 전반적으로 행사에 긍정적인 영향을 미칠 것입니다. 반면, Fairfield Catering은 훨씬 더 많은 메뉴들이 있고, 채식주의자들과 극단적 채식주의자들, 글루텐 없는 음식을 먹는 분들 등에게 맞춰줄 수 있습니다.

가격: Bryant Creations가 Fairfield Catering보다 약 50퍼센트 정도 더 비쌉니다. 하지만, 다른 목록들의 예산에 유연성이 좀 있다면, 여전히 이용할 여유가 있습니다.

이용 가능성: 두 회사 모두 행사일에 이용 가능하지만, 서비스를 확보하기 위해 빨리 결정을 해야 합니다. 추가로, 두 회사 모두 손님 10명당 1명의 종업원을 고용하는 것을 추천했는데, 우리가 뷔페가 아닌 자리에 앉아 먹는 식사를 원하기 때문입니다.

회의: 행사 기획 위원회
날짜와 시간: 10월 13일 목요일 오전 10시 – 11시
장소: 회의실 2
사회자: Melissa Trevino
참석자: William O'Connor, Deborah Hughes, Chelsea Ebert
불참자: Lewis Eastman

회의 내용 메모:

1. Ebert 씨께서 Fairfield Catering과 Bryant Creations 간의 상세한 비교를 제시해 주셨습니다. 위원회는 만장일치 표결로 Fairfield Catering을 선정했습니다. Ebert 씨가 Fairfield Catering에 연락해 선금을 지불하고 Bryant Creations에도 그 서비스를 이용하지 않을 것이라고 알릴 것입니다. 예상 참석 손님 수는 150명이고, Fairfield Catering은 필요한 숫자의 종업원을 제공할 수 있습니다.

2. 각 행사 항목에 대한 예산이 확정되었으며, 행사 기획 위원회가 단체로 주요 결정을 내리겠지만, 조사 작업을 도울 수 있도록 각 항목에 위원회 위원들이 한 명씩 배정되었습니다. 그 항목들은 행사 장소(Melissa), 음식과 음료(Chelsea), 오락(William), 그리고 실내 장식(Deborah)입니다. Lewis는 필요한 곳에 도움을 주도록 요청받을 것입니다.

3. 다음 회의는 10월 21일 금요일 오후 1시에 열릴 것입니다. 행사 장소를 어떻게 장식할지 알 수 있도록 색상과 주제를 선정할 것입니다.

---

186 Trevino 씨가 쓴 이메일의 목적은 무엇인가?

(A) 회의 시간의 변경을 알리기
(B) 위원회에 자원봉사자들을 모집하기
(C) 은퇴 파티 준비를 위한 회의 시간을 정하기
(D) 한 동료 직원의 은퇴를 알리기

187 첫 번째 이메일에서, 세 번째 단락, 두 번째 줄의 단어 "performed"와 의미가 가장 가까운 것은 무엇인가?

(A) ~을 제시했다
(B) ~을 즐겁게 했다
(C) ~을 달성했다
(D) ~을 수행했다

188 Fairfield Catering에 관해 암시된 것이 아닌 것은?

(A) Bryant Creations보다 더 다양한 음식이 있다.
(B) 행사에 뷔페식 저녁 식사를 제공하는 것을 전문으로 한다.
(C) 과거에 Marietta Co.의 행사에 음식을 제공한 적이 있다.
(D) Bryant Creations에 비해 더 저렴한 옵션이다.

189 회사는 종업원을 몇 명 고용할 것 같은가?

(A) 10명
(B) 15명
(C) 20명
(D) 25명

190 다음 회의에서 무슨 일이 있을 예정인가?

(A) 음식 시식하기
(B) 초대장 준비하기
(C) 초대 연사 선정하기
(D) 장식물에 관해 논의하기

신유형 ▶ 191-195는 다음 이메일과 의제, 그리고 기사를 참조하시오.

수신: 모든 회원 〈membetslist@sunnydalecommunity.org〉
발신: Sally Fordwich 〈s.fordwich@sunnydalecommunity.org〉
날짜: 9월 23일
제목: 업데이트

회원 여러분께,

우선, 지난주 기금 마련 행사 동안의 여러분의 노고에 대해 모두에게 감사 드리고 싶습니다. 우리의 목표치를 12퍼센트나 초과했습니다! 내년에 우리의 재정 상태는 현재 매우 견실해 보이고, 곧 여러 가지 흥미로운 프로젝트들을 발표할 것입니다.

또한, 여러분들 중 일부가 아시다시피, Bob Harknett이 병원 예약으로 인해 다가오는 시의회 회의에 참석할 수 없을 것입니다. Karl Rogers가 발표를 대신 하는 것에 동의하셨습니다. 그가 우리를 대표하여 다음 세 가지 사안들을 제시할 것입니다:

- 연세가 많은 주민들의 입장료를 줄일 수 있도록 공공 기금 이용하기
- 안전을 개선하기 위해 주민 센터의 중앙 출입구 바깥에 과속방지턱을 추가하기
- 야간에 상시 감시가 가능하도록 두 명의 보안 요원들을 고용하기

안녕히 계십시오.

Sally Fordwich
센터장, Sunnydale 지역 주민 센터

Sunnydale 시의회 회의 제안 의제
9월 28일 오후 3시 [9월 18일 최종 업데이트]

오후 3:00   개회 선언과 출석 확인, 이전의 회의록 낭독과 승인
오후 3:15   초청 연사: Daniel Fashanu, 부 주지사
            연설 내용: "지역 사회 연계 확립"
오후 3:45   교육 보고: Elise LeBlanc, Sunnydale High School
            교장
오후 4:00   주민 발표: Alice Rickards
오후 4:15   주민 발표: Bob Harknett
오후 4:30   주민 발표: Shannon Jackson
오후 4:45   제시된 주제에 관한 의회 의원들 간의 토론
오후 5:15   Millie Lentz를 대체해 노동 개발 위원회장직을 맡을 시의
            회 의원 선출(불참이 예상되는 의원들은 미리 투표권을 행
            사할 수 있습니다.)
오후 5:30   회의 종료

Sunnydale 지역 주민 센터에 있을 변화

10월 25일—시의회와 함께 많은 노력 끝에, Sunnydale 지역 주민
센터(SCC)는 지난달 회의 이후에 많은 성공 사례들을 축하할 수 있었
다. 새로운 과속방지턱이 설치된, 센터 출입구 외부에서 한 연설에서,
SCC의 Sally Fordwich 센터장은 차량 저속 조치들이 "충돌할 뻔한"
사고들이 보고되는 횟수가 더 줄어든 형태로 이미 긍정적인 결과를 낳았
다고 말했다. 게다가, 그녀는 시의회가 노인들을 위한 주민 센터 요금에
보조금을 지급하기로 합의한 것에 기뻐했다. Fordwich 씨는 그들의 조
치에 대해 시의회 의원들을 칭찬했고, 또한 다음 달 추가 재정 지원을 요
청할 계획도 이미 가지고 있다고 언급했다.

---

191 Fordwich 씨는 왜 그룹 구성원들에게 감사하는가?

(A) 그들이 건물 개조 공사에 참여했다.
(B) 그들이 유용한 프로젝트 제안을 했다.
(C) 그들이 시의회 회의에 참석했다.
(D) 그들이 성공적인 기부 운동에 도움을 줬다.

192 Rogers 씨는 몇 시에 시의회 의원들에게 연설했을 것 같은가?

(A) 오후 3:45에
(B) 오후 4:00에
(C) 오후 4:15에
(D) 오후 4:30에

193 9월 28일 회의에 관해 사실인 것은 무엇인가?

(A) 그 주요 연설이 회의 마지막에 진행되었다.
(B) 시의회 의원들과 주민들 사이의 토론을 특징으로 했다.
(C) 한 관리를 선출하기 위한 투표가 포함되었다.
(D) 언론 기자들에게 공개되지 않았다.

194 Rogers 씨에 의해 요청된 변화 중 시의회에 의해 이뤄지지 않은
것은?

(A) 센터 외부에 과속방지턱을 설치하는 것
(B) 고령자들을 위해 입장료를 내리는 것
(C) 보안 직원들의 수를 늘리는 것
(D) 장애인들의 출입을 개선하는 것

195 Fordwich 씨는 11월에 무엇을 할 것 같은가?

(A) 시의회 의원 자리에 출마하기
(B) 더 많은 자금을 요청하기
(C) 몇몇 새 프로젝트를 시작하기
(D) 건물 확장을 요청하기

신유형 196-200은 다음 이메일과 정보, 그리고 기사를 참조하시오.

수신: Finn Holmberg
발신: Graycliff Outfitters
날짜: 4월 8일
제목: 회신: 문의

Holmberg 씨께,

귀하의 신규 자연 여행 가이드 사업을 위해 20개의 배낭을 구매하는 것
에 대한 관심에 감사 드립니다. 오로지 격렬한 신체 활동에 익숙하지 않
은 초보 등산객들의 구미를 맞추기 위해, 가벼운 모델을 찾고 계신다고
말씀하셨습니다. 게다가, 등산이 날씨에 상관없이 진행될 것이기 때문에,
방수 또는 내수 재질로 만들어진 배낭이 필요하시다고요. 저희 재고에는
아주 다양한 종류의 배낭들이 있으니, 요구에 맞는 것을 찾으실 수 있을
것으로 확신합니다. 귀하께서 명시해 주신 가격 범위 내의 품목에 관
한 제품 정보를 첨부했습니다. 질문이 있으시면 저에게 알려 주시기 바랍
니다.

안녕히 계십시오.

Trina Sherman
고객 서비스 담당, Graycliff Outfitters

Graycliff Outfitters

배낭: 150.00달러 – 199.99달러
품질 보증서를 별도로 구매해야 하는 Trailz를 제외하고, 모든 배낭은
3년 무료 품질 보증서가 딸려 있다.

Trailz – 154.99달러
무게를 고르게 배분해 주는 넓은 어깨 끈. 다양한 사이즈로 된 12개의 수
납 공간. 방수 천으로 제작.
색상: 파란색, 빨간색, 회색.
용량: 36리터.

Camplife – 169.99달러
하루 종일 편안함을 제공하는 패드가 있는 허리 밴드. 내수 기능이 있는
캔버스 천이 약한 비에도 내부를 젖지 않게 함. 손쉬운 정리를 가능하게
하는 외부 주머니 6개와 내부 주머니 3개. 시중에서 가장 가벼운 프레임
으로 된 것들 중 하나임.
색상: 검정색.
용량: 34리터

Sierra – 174.99달러
내부 공간 5개와 외부 주머니 4개가 있는 경량 디자인. Sierra는 경쟁
제품들보다 거의 2대 1의 비율로 많이 판매됨. 접어 넣을 수 있는 열쇠용
체인.
색상: 검정색, 진한 녹색.
용량: 60리터

Cougarex – 189.99달러
젖은 물품들을 말릴 망사 주머니 하나를 포함해 내부 공간 2개와 외부 주
머니 5개. 내열 및 내수 직물로 제작됨. 중간 무게의 프레임.
색상: 검정색, 파란색, 빨간색
용량: 80리터

업체들이 관광 산업의 변화에 반응하다
Rebecca Keiser 작성

6월 20일—여름은 늘 호텔과 항공사, 그리고 기타 관광 관련 업체들에
게 분주한 시기이다. 하지만, 이번 시즌은 또한 야생 동물 보호구역과 국
립 공원과 같은 자연 지역의 방문 수가 상당한 증가세를 보여줬다. 등산
과 캠핑 여행 경험이 많은 가이드들의 수요 증가로 인해, 그 간극을 메우
기 위해 업체들이 갑자기 생겨났다. 방문객들이 혼자서 공원을 여행하는

것이 허용되어 있기는 하지만, 많은 곳에서 등산로에 위험 구역들이 포함되어 있다. 안전이 중요하기 때문에, 사람들은 기꺼이 전문적인 도움을 받기 위해 추가 비용을 지불하고 있다. 수년간 관광 사업을 이끌어 왔던 두 업체는, Hickman Mountains에서 고급과 중급 투어를 운영하고 있는 Forrista와 Evergreen Park에서 초급 투어를 운영하고 있는 Ace Tours이다. 눈여겨봐야 할 두 곳의 신생 업체는 Mesa Park에서 오직 초보자들에게만 등산 프로그램을 제공하는 DC Excursions와 Marshall Nature Reserve에서 모든 수준의 등산 프로그램을 제공하는 Sunshine Tours이다.

196 Sierra에 관해 알 수 있는 것은 무엇인가?
(A) 가장 큰 배낭이다.
(B) 가장 인기 있는 제품이다.
(C) 패드가 들어간 벨트가 있다.
(D) 전문가들에 의해 추천된다.

197 네 브랜드 모두의 공통된 특징은 무엇인가?
(A) 그것들은 모두 한 가지가 넘는 색상으로 나온다.
(B) 그것들은 모두 빠르게 건조되도록 디자인되어 있다.
(C) 그것들은 모두 수납 공간들이 많이 있다.
(D) 그것들은 모두 무료 품질 보증을 받는다.

198 어떤 배낭이 Holmberg 씨의 회사에 가장 적합할 것인가?
(A) Trailz
(B) Camplife
(C) Sierra
(D) Cougarex

199 기사에서, 첫 번째 단락, 일곱 번째 줄의 단어 "counts"와 의미가 가장 가까운 것은 무엇인가?
(A) 고려하다
(B) 포함하다
(C) 계산하다
(D) 중요하다

200 Holmberg 씨의 회사는 어디에서 운영되고 있을 것 같은가?
(A) Hickman 산
(B) Evergreen 공원
(C) Mesa 공원
(D) Marshall 보호 구역

PART 5

101 농산물 직판 시장에서 사용되는 제품 진열용 탁자는 매주 토요일마다 판매자가 부분적으로 설치해야 했지만, 현재는 완전히 조립되어 있는 상태로 유지된다.

102 Lambert 씨의 비서는 Stewart 씨가 6월 5일에 그를 만나도록 조치하기 위해 전화했다.

103 안타깝게도 자금 부족으로 인해, 사상 최초의 National Reader's Education Conference가 내년으로 일정이 재조정될 것이다.

104 고객들이 자신의 호텔 객실과 관련해 어떤 문제라도 알릴 경우에는 가능한 한 빨리 그 문제를 해결하기 위해 노력해 주시기 바랍니다.

105 시골 지역에서 제공되는 시간당 급여는 도심 지역에 있는 회사들에 의해 지급되는 것보다 훨씬 더 낮다.

106 Taylor 씨는 자신이 실수로 연락을 받았다고 생각했기 때문에, 다시 전화를 걸지 않았다.

107 다과가 필요한 사람들은 건물 1층의 엘리베이터 맞은편에 있는 직원 휴게실을 찾을 것이다.

108 신입 직원들은 어떤 불만 사항이든지 직접 처리하려 하기보다는 부서장에게 전달하도록 권장된다.

109 그 출판사는 늦어도 10월 1일까지 완전한 형태로 편집된 책을 요청하고 있다.

110 금요일에 있을 직원회의에 참석하실 때, 당신은 제안된 사업 모델에 관한 분석 자료를 보고할 준비가 되어야 합니다.

111 승인될 수 있는 대출 액수는 업체의 신용 기록뿐만 아니라 연간 수익에 따라 달라진다.

112 Yoon Financial Consultants는 고객들의 개별 목표 및 소득 능력에 적합한 계획을 세우기 위해 고객들과 긴밀히 협력한다.

113 그들 일의 민감한 속성 때문에, 의료 전문가들은 환자들과 관련된 모든 사안에 있어 엄격한 비밀 유지 규정을 준수한다.

114 Harrisville 지점의 지붕이 수리되는 동안, 직원들은 반드시 부지 내의 모든 재고 물품을 부지 밖의 창고로 옮겨야 한다.

115 도서관의 이사회 임원들은 심사숙고한 끝에 새로운 컴퓨터실에 필요한 자금을 풀기로 결정했다.

116 Johno's Wool은 개인 및 호주 전역에 위치한 기업을 대상으로 최고급 양털 제품을 판매한다.

117 Roof Videos에서는, 모든 대여물이 7일 이내에 반납되어야 하며, 연체된 대여물은 추가 요금 부과 대상이다.

118 모든 그림들이 접수되어 전시된 상태이므로 미술 경연대회를 책임지고 있는 위원회가 참가작들을 검토할 것이다.

119 〈Journal of Rock and Soil〉에 따르면, 연구원들은 화장품에 사용되는 광물에 대한 수요가 앞으로 20년 동안 최고조에 달할 것으로 추정한다.

120 최근의 한 보고서는 더 많은 고객들이 다른 곳에서 상품을 구입하는 일을 방지하기 위해 가격을 낮출 필요성이 있음을 보여 주었다.

121 Maguire 씨는 곧 있을 회사의 신제품 운동화 출시 행사를 열기 위해 선호하는 장소 목록을 제공하도록 요청받았다.

122 Herbert 씨의 주택 담보 대출을 위한 서류 작업이 불완전했기 때문에, 은행은 그의 요청을 처리할 수 없었다.

123 Carter 박사는 풍부한 전문 지식을 갖고 있기 때문에, 지역 병원에 알려지지 않은 질병을 지닌 환자가 올 경우에 병원 측으로부터 자주 연락을 받는다.

124 포장 음식을 배달하는 사람은 고객이 현금보다 신용카드를 선호

할 경우에 신용카드로 지불하는 금액을 결제할 기기를 갖고 다닌다.

125 내일 오전 2시에서 4시 사이로 예정된 설치 작업에 대비해 반드시 모든 문서를 저장하고 백업해 두십시오.

126 그 어느 누구도 보안 검색대에서 자신의 신분증을 스캔하지 않고는 건물 밖으로 나갈 수 없도록 되어 있다.

127 업계 내에서의 높은 실패율로 인해, 투자자들은 식당을 지원하는 일에 대해 재정적으로 신중하다.

128 Ragland Theater에서의 긴급하고 예기치 못한 수리 작업으로 인해, 그 지역 연극은 대신 6월 5일에 첫 번째 공연을 개최할 것이다.

129 Symington 씨가 베이징으로의 전근을 받아들였다면, 자신의 회사로부터 많은 액수의 급여 인상을 받았을 것이다.

130 업무와 관련되지 않은 활동에 대해 회사의 컴퓨터를 사용하는 일은 지정된 휴식 시간 동안 외에는 직원들에게 적절한 것으로 간주되지 않는다.

PART 6

신유형 131-134는 다음 기사를 참조하시오.

3년 전 첫 제과점을 개장한 후에, Hogan's Donuts는 북미 전역에서 빠르게 성장해 왔으며, 현재 해외로 확장하려고 한다. 이 체인점은 이미 캐나다에 위치한 두 곳의 매장을 운영하고 있다. 최근에 있었던 〈Timely Business〉와의 인터뷰에서, 최고경영자인 Kirk Mason 씨는 올해 안에 같은 국가 내에서 두 곳의 추가 지점이 개장될 것으로 예상된다고 말했다. 하지만 회사는 이 국가에서 매장을 개장할 수 있는 가맹점 점주들을 아직 확보하지 못했다. 지원 희망자들은 hogansdonuts.com을 방문해 자격 요건과 절차를 담은 목록을 확인해 봐야 한다. 회사는 국제 상법과 관련해 문제점이 있는 가맹점들을 도울 준비가 되어 있다.

신유형 135-138는 다음 기사를 참조하시오.

Emmet(5월 28일)—시에서 가장 인기 있는 중고차 및 신차 판매 업체인 Lewiston Auto Dealer는 자사의 알림 시스템을 변경할 예정이다. 이 대리점은 매달 수백 명의 고객들에게 정기적인 자동차 서비스를 제공한다. 이제 곧, 이 회사는 주로 모바일 알림 기능을 이용하여 서비스 알림 날짜를 전송할 것이다. 현재의 시스템은 시간이 많이 소요되고 있는데, 편지를 출력해 우편으로 발송하는 방식에 의존하고 있기 때문이다. "우리는 이 변화가 훨씬 더 효율적일 것이라고 예상합니다."라고 매장 책임자인 Tanya Kay 씨가 말했다. 문자 알림 서비스는 7월 1일부터 시작될 것이다. 하지만 누구나 STOP이라고 답장을 보내 새 시스템에서 탈퇴할 수 있으며 계속해서 편지로 알림을 받을 수 있다.

신유형 139-142는 다음 보도자료를 참조하시오.

Billington Air Group의 최고경영자 Gretchen Hun 씨에 따르면, 추가 비행기들이 이착륙하는 것을 가능하도록 하기 위해 Westmore Airport 활주로가 확장될 것이다. 지난 5년간 도시의 인구가 꾸준히 증가해 왔기 때문에, 공항은 항공 교통량의 증가를 경험했다. Hun 씨는 이 확장 사업이 대략 6개월 정도 걸릴 것으로 기술자들이 현재 예상하고 있다고 말했다. 일일 보안 점검이 가능하도록 하기 위해 원래 4개월로 추산한 것이 변경되었다. Hun 씨는 비행장 보안이 반드시 최우선 사항으로 유지되어야 한다고 언급했다. 더불어, "여행자들은 이용 가능한 항공편이

줄어들어 비행기표 가격이 인상되는 결과가 생길 가능성이 있다고 예상할 수 있습니다. 유감스럽게도, 이것이 실행 가능한 유일한 선택입니다." 라고 최고경영자 Hun 씨가 말했다.

신유형 143-146은 다음 회람을 참조하시오.

발신: Alyssa Brundige
수신: 전 직원
날짜: 1월 2일
제목: 개발 이사직 충원 완료

저는 Alex Yoon 씨가 Alumbaugh University의 신임 개발 이사로 임명되었음을 알리게 되어 기쁩니다.

Yoon 씨는 기금 모금 및 홍보 활동으로 10년간 일해 오신 분이며, 고등 교육 기관을 위해 5백만 달러가 넘는 금액을 모금해 오셨습니다. 이와 같은 경험이 그가 우리 대학에 기여할 수 있을 만한 능력을 갖출 수 있게 해 주었지만, 이것이 유일한 이유는 아닙니다.

Yoon 씨는 우리 Alumbaugh University의 졸업생일 뿐만 아니라, 학생 수가 늘어남에 따라 우리 학교를 성공적으로 만드는 데 이용할 많은 독창적인 아이디어를 갖고 계신 카리스마 있는 분입니다. 저는 Yoon 씨가 Alumbaugh의 가족으로서 매우 소중한 분이 될 것이라고 확신합니다.

올해 첫 직원회의가 열리는 1월 7일에 Alex를 만나는 것을 기대하셔도 좋습니다.

안녕히 계십시오.

Alyssa Brundige

PART 7

147-148은 다음 편지를 참조하시오.

Skylark Air Rewards
2310 Kings Avenue
Auckland, NZ
0800-313-555

Jenny Smith
1600 First Street
아파트 12B
Auckland, NZ

3월 15일

Smith 씨께,

Skylark Air Rewards 프로그램을 찾아 주신 것을 환영합니다! 회원 여러분께서는 어느 컴퓨터나 모바일 기기를 통해서든 보상 포인트를 확인하고 사용할 수 있는 혜택을 받으십니다. 애플리케이션은 무료이며, 보상 프로그램 페이지를 둘러보시는 데 기술적인 사항에 능숙하지 않으셔도 됩니다. 더 많은 정보를 원하시거나 무료 가입 신청을 원하시면, 오늘 skylarkair.com/rewards를 방문해 보시기 바랍니다.

이 페이지의 뒷면에 가입 과정을 안내해 드리는 간단한 핵심 가이드가 있습니다.

즐거운 항공 여행 되십시오.

Isaac Yoon

Skylark Air Rewards
책임자

147 편지의 목적은 무엇인가?

(A) 이전의 고객에게 프로그램을 다시 이용하도록 권하기

(B) Skylark Air Rewards 프로그램의 서비스를 홍보하기

(C) Smith 씨에게 애플리케이션 사용 방법에 관해 안내하기

(D) 새로운 버전의 컴퓨터 소프트웨어를 홍보하기

148 편지에 무엇이 포함되어 있는가?

(A) 광고 전단

(B) 설명서

(C) Smith 씨의 포인트 적립 상태

(D) 프로그램 가입 양식

149-150은 다음 웹사이트를 참조하시오.

홈 》 서비스 》 온라인 계정 》 fujisawa_yuiri

환영합니다, Fujisawa 씨! 귀하의 전기 서비스 계정과 관련된 기능들을 더욱 편리하게 이용하실 수 있도록 저희 웹사이트를 업데이트했습니다. 새로운 사이트를 이용하시면서, 다음과 같은 일들을 하실 수 있습니다.

－ 온라인 계좌 이체를 통해 전기 요금을 납부하실 수 있습니다.

－ 정전 사태와 안전 경고에 관련된 문자 알림 서비스를 설정하실 수 있습니다.

－ 전선과 관련해 어떤 문제가 있으시든 저희 고객 서비스팀에 연락하실 수 있습니다.

－ 자택 또는 사무실에서 에너지를 절약하는 방법에 관한 팁을 읽어보실 수 있습니다.

여기를 클릭하시면 저희 약관을 읽어 보실 수 있습니다.

149 Fujisawa 씨는 누구일 것 같은가?

(A) 고객 서비스 직원

(B) 온라인 금융 서비스 이용객

(C) 공공 서비스 회사의 고객

(D) 구직 지원자

150 웹사이트에서 할 수 있는 일로 나타나 있지 않은 것은 무엇인가?

(A) 계정에 대한 요금을 납부하는 일

(B) 서비스에 대한 문제점을 알리는 일

(C) 안내 정보 메시지의 수신을 요청하는 일

(D) 안전 관련 상담 일정을 잡는 일

신유형▶ 151-152는 다음 문자 메시지 대화를 참조하시오.

Marilyn Cooper [오후 1:15]
저는 오늘 밤 연회에 사용할 케이크를 구입하려고 제과점에 와 있어요. 제가 사무실에 다시 들를 시간이 없을 것 같아요. 저 좀 도와주시겠어요? 시설 관리부의 Eric 씨와 연락이 되지 않네요.

Ettore Arcuri [오후 1:18]
뭘 도와 드리면 될까요?

Marilyn Cooper [오후 1:19]
제 사무실에 장식 물품들이 담긴 상자가 세 개 있어요. 그 상자들을 컨퍼런스 센터로 가져와 주시겠어요?

Ettore Arcuri [오후 1:20]
물론입니다. 몇 시에 필요하신가요?

Marilyn Cooper [오후 1:22]
2시 30분쯤이면 좋겠어요. 하지만 제 사무실이 잠겨 있으니 Eric 씨에게 도와 달라고 하셔야 할 거예요.

Ettore Arcuri [오후 1:23]
알겠습니다. 아마 지금쯤이면 점심 식사를 마치고 돌아오셨을 겁니다. 제가 확인해 보겠습니다.

Marilyn Cooper [오후 1:24]
감사합니다! 약 1시간 후에 뵙겠습니다.

151 오후 1시 20분에, Arcuri 씨가 "For sure"라고 썼을 때 의미하는
신유형 것은 무엇인가?

(A) 회사 연회에 참석할 계획이다.

(B) 상자들을 옮기는 데 동의한다.

(C) 정보가 정확하다는 것을 확신한다.

(D) 장식품을 구입할 수 있는 장소를 안다.

152 Arcuri 씨는 곧이어 어디로 갈 것 같은가?

(A) 시설 관리부 사무실로

(B) 컨벤션 센터로

(C) Cooper 씨의 사무실로

(D) 제과점으로

153-155는 다음 영수증을 참조하시오.

Hannigan's   5월 1일

200 Bannock St.
Eagle, Montana
(435) 555-9293

구매 영수증 #2742953

#1040	육각 렌치(1/4인치)	7.99달러
#2311	2갤런짜리 주문 제작 혼합 인테리어 페인트(갤런당 21.25달러)	42.50달러
#0232	섬유 유리용 장도리	8.35달러
#5499	소형 전동 공구 콤보 세트	127.00달러

소계	185.84달러
세금(7%)	13.00달러
총계	198.84달러

지불 방법:
상품권 013945   100달러(잔액 0달러)
현금   98.84달러
보상 포인트 68점을 획득하셨습니다!
총 보상 포인트: 325

이번 보상 포인트 누적 기간은 4월 1일부터 5월 31일까지입니다.

이달 말까지 다음번 방문 시에 이 영수증을 제시하시면 보상 포인트를 사용해 가격 할인을 받으실 수 있습니다.

60일 이내에 구입한 제품에 대해서는 아무런 이유도 묻지 않고 반품과 교환을 해 드리는 정책이 적용됩니다.

반품 시에 이 영수증을 갖고 계시지 않을 경우, 매장 포인트가 발급됩니다.

저희 Hannigan's를 이용해 주셔서 감사합니다.

153 할인을 받기 위해서는 무엇을 해야 하는가?

(A) 5월 1일부터 60일 이내에 매장을 방문해야 한다.

(B) 6월이 시작되기 전에 매장으로 영수증을 가져가야 한다.

(C) 한 달 이내에 상품권을 사용해 제품을 구입해야 한다.

(D) 더 많은 제품을 구입해 더 많은 보상 포인트를 받아야 한다.

154 영수증에 제시된 내용이 아닌 것은 무엇인가?

(A) Hannigan's의 환불 정책

(B) 구입한 제품에 대한 배송 날짜

(C) 보상 포인트의 누적이 끝나는 날짜

(D) 주문 제작 혼합 인테리어 페인트의 갤런당 가격

155 무슨 종류의 업체가 이 영수증을 발급했을 것 같은가?

(A) 미술용품 매장

(B) 철물점

(C) 선물 가게

(D) 자동차 수리소

156-157은 다음 기사를 참조하시오.

3월 17일—시 당국자들은 Tyler Valley 지역에 짓는 대규모 스포츠 경기장 건설 공사를 승인한다고 발표했다. 일반적인 매점 시설뿐만 아니라, 이 건물에는 고급 식당을 포함해 여러 식당들도 들어서게 될 것이다. 이 경기장은 이전의 VF Plastics 공장 부지 일부를 포함할 예정인데, 이 공장은 4년 전에 폐쇄하기 전까지 수십 년 동안 우리 지역에서 성장의 동력이 되었던 곳이다. 새로 지어질 경기장은 태양열 전지판, 그리고 경기장에 물을 대는 데 필요한 물을 재활용하는 시스템 등과 같이 지속 가능한 기술을 활용할 것이다. 또한, 화창한 날에 개방할 수 있는 지붕도 설치될 예정이다. 경기장 전역에는 증폭기가 설치되어 팬들이 항상 와이파이를 이용할 수 있도록 할 예정이며, 설계자들은 이 장치가 실시간으로 팬들이 자신의 경험을 공유함으로써 자연스레 소셜 미디어를 이용한 홍보가 가능해질 수 있기를 바라고 있다. 부지 내의 주차장은 25,000개의 주차 공간을 보유하게 될 것이며, 일부 공간에는 보호용 지붕이 설치될 것이다. 이 경기장은 지역의 관광객들을 끌어들일 것으로 예상되며, 불과 10마일 떨어진 Evergreen 지역에 위치한 초대형 건물인 Alexia Convention Center를 완벽히 보완해 주는 장소가 될 것이다.

156 Tyler Valley 지역에 관해 알 수 있는 것은 무엇인가?

(A) 그곳의 주요 사업은 컨벤션 센터다.

(B) 여러 식당들이 있는 곳이다.

(C) 한때 제조 사업의 본거지였다.

(D) 그곳의 스포츠 경기장이 확장될 것이다.

157 경기장의 특징으로 언급되지 않은 것은 무엇인가?

(A) 지하 주차장

(B) 재활용수 시스템

(C) 개폐 가능한 지붕

(D) 신뢰할 만한 인터넷 연결

신유형 ▶ 158-160은 다음 편지를 참조하시오.

11월 8일

Lanae Harding 박사

5498 Newport Beach Road

Newport Beach, OR 97352

미국

Harding 박사님께,

Evergreen Convention Center에서 사상 최초로 열리는 '신경 유전학 학회'에 참가하시기로 결정해 주셔서 감사드립니다. — [1] —. 남은

100달러의 비용은 11월 30일까지 전액 납입 완료되어야 합니다. 귀하의 학회 참가비에는 행사에 필요한 모든 자료들뿐만 아니라 금요일과 토요일, 그리고 일요일의 아침 식사와 점심 식사가 포함되어 있습니다. 컨벤션 센터에서 걸어서 갈 수 있는 거리에 저녁 시간에 영업하는 다양한 식당들이 있습니다. 이용 후기가 포함된 전체 목록을 학회 웹사이트에서 확인해 보실 수 있습니다. — [2] —.

컨벤션 센터 근처에는 선택 가능하신 여러 숙박 시설이 있지만, 숙박 비용은 귀하의 행사 참가비에 포함되어 있지 않다는 사실에 유의하시기 바랍니다. — [3] —.

이 안내 자료 묶음에는 호텔 편의시설과 그 가격에 대한 상세 목록이 컨벤션 일정표와 함께 동봉되어 있습니다. 행사 기간에 열리는 많은 세미나와 워크숍들 중에서 선택하실 수 있도록 미리 일정표를 확인해 보시기를 권해 드립니다. — [4] —.

다시 한 번, '신경 유전학 학회'에 등록해 주셔서 감사합니다.

안녕히 계십시오.

Jon Simmons

Jon Simmons

Association for Neuro Genetics 의장

158 Simmons 씨는 왜 편지를 썼는가?

(A) 11월에 있을 연례 학회를 알리기 위해

(B) 비용에 포함되는 범위를 명확히 하기 위해

(C) 정확한 위치에 관한 정보를 제공하기 위해

(D) 등록이 완료되었음을 확인해주기 위해

159 Harding 박사는 무슨 정보를 미리 확인하도록 권고받는가?

(A) 개최될 것으로 계획된 행사들

(B) 각 호텔에서 이용 가능한 시설과 서비스들

(C) 등록비에 포함되어 있는 자료들

(D) 저녁 식사를 할 수 있는 식당들의 위치

160 [1], [2], [3], [4]로 표기된 위치들 중에서 다음 문장이 가장 잘 어

신유형 울리는 곳은 어디인가?

"귀하께서 지불하신 100달러의 비용은 처리되었으며, 귀하의 자리도 예약되었습니다."

(A) [1]

(B) [2]

(C) [3]

(D) [4]

161-164는 다음 이메일을 참조하시오.

수신: Neil Bergeron ⟨neilb@thismail.com⟩

발신: Caroline Wells ⟨cwells@mercuryfinancial.com⟩

날짜: 4월 3일

제목: Mercury Financial

Bergeron 씨께,

신중히 고려해 본 결과, 귀하께서는 Mercury Financial의 선임 재정 분석가 직책에 지원한 모든 지원자들 중에서 가장 뛰어난 자격을 갖춘 분이라는 것을 확인하게 되어 해당 직책에서의 근무를 제안하고자 합니다. 선임 재정 분석가로서, 귀하께서는 직접 일부 최우수 고객들의 계좌를 담당하시게 될 것으로 예상됩니다. 또한, 직급이 낮은 몇몇 분석가들을 관리하고, 그들에게 조언을 제공해 멘토의 역할을 하시게 될 것입니다. 마지막으로, 모든 선임 재정 분석가들에게 경제의 여러 분야에 대한 주간 보

고서를 제공하도록 요청합니다. 귀하께서 맡으실 분야는 해외 및 국내 자동차 산업입니다.

귀하께서는 매년 12만 달러의 연봉을 지급받게 될 것이며, 회사의 주식뿐만 아니라 분기별 성과급도 받게 됩니다. 늦어도 5월 1일에는 근무를 시작해야 하므로, St. Louis를 떠날 준비를 하시는 동안 이 날짜가 되기 전에 Dallas에서 머물 곳을 찾으셔야 합니다. 회사에서는 귀하의 이사 비용을 지불할 것이며, 계속 머무를 주택을 찾으실 때까지 귀하의 숙박비도 지불해 드릴 것입니다.

이 제안을 수락하신다면, 인사부에 근무하는 Melissa Patterson 씨의 연락을 받게 될 것입니다. Melissa Patterson 씨는 여러 가지 채용 관련 양식을 귀하께 보내 드릴 것이며, 이 중에는 늦어도 4월 20일까지 모두 작성하셔서 서명을 한 후에 돌려 보내 주셔야 하는 계약서도 포함되어 있습니다.

조만간 함께 일할 수 있기를 고대합니다.

안녕히 계십시오.

Caroline Wells

161 이메일의 목적은 무엇인가?

(A) 합동 프로젝트를 맡도록 제안하기
(B) 세미나 초대장을 보내기
(C) 채용 문제에 관해 조언을 구하기
(D) 채용 결정에 관해 이야기하기

162 선임 재정 분석가의 책무 중 하나로 언급되지 않은 것은 무엇인가?

(A) 다른 직원들에게 도움을 주는 것
(B) 매주 보고서를 작성하는 것
(C) 다른 분석가들과의 회의를 진행하는 것
(D) 특정 고객들과 밀접하게 근무하는 것

163 Bergeron 씨에 관해 언급된 것은 무엇인가?

(A) Wells 씨를 한 번도 직접 만난 적이 없다.
(B) 업계에서 10년의 경력을 지니고 있다.
(C) 현재 St. Louis에 살고 있다.
(D) 인사부장 직속으로 근무하고 있다.

164 Wells 씨는 Bergeron 씨에게 무엇을 하도록 요청하는가?

(A) 문서를 작성할 것
(B) 주문에 대한 비용을 지불할 것
(C) St. Louis 사무실을 방문할 것
(D) Patterson 씨에게 연락할 것

신유형 165-168은 다음 온라인 채팅을 참조하시오.

Brian Roebuck [오후 5:31]
안녕하세요, 여러분. 제가 지금 막 Danielle Roy 씨한테서 한 가지 요청을 받았어요. Roy 씨는 우리 팀이 자기 사업체의 인테리어 디자인 작업을 한 달 빨리 완료해 주시기를 원하고 계세요. 저는 이 일이 가능한지 궁금합니다.

Rick Lloyd [오후 5:32]
제 생각에는 시간이 충분할 것 같아요. 물품 보관실과 운동 공간들은 계획을 해 두었지만, 로비 구역은 체육관 회원들에게 좋은 인상을 남길 수 있어야 해요.

Chang Tung [오후 5:34]
제가 로비 구역에 대한 예비 도안을 완료했는데, 자재의 예산 견적이 완

료되어야 무엇이든 제시할 수 있어요. 이 일이 어디까지 진행되어 있죠, Amanda?

Amanda Vicini [오후 5:35]
시간이 더 있을 거라고 생각해서 아직 시작하지 않았어요.

Brian Roebuck [오후 5:37]
얼마나 빨리 완료하실 수 있으시죠? 우리가 정확히 언제 공사를 시작할지 알고 난 후에 작업자들을 예약하고 싶어요.

Amanda Vicini [오후 5:39]
저는 추가로 시간을 들여 일해도 상관없어요. 내일 아침에 제일 먼저 책상에 올려놓겠습니다.

Brian Roebuck [오후 5:40]
좋아요! 감사합니다! 그렇게 하면 새로운 마감시한인 3월 15일을 맞출수 있을 것 같아요.

Chang Tung [오후 5:43]
Roy 씨께서는 우리가 최근에 비용을 올린 것을 알고 계신가요?

Rick Lloyd [오후 5:44]
네. 우리가 계약서를 준비할 때 제가 새롭게 바뀐 비용 수치가 포함된 안내 책자를 전달해 드렸어요.

165 오후 5시 31분에, Roebuck 씨가 "I'm wondering if that's possible"이라고 썼을 때 의미하는 것은 무엇인가?

(A) 예산이 충분한지 분명히 해 두고 있다.
(B) 한 정책에 대해 잘 알지 못한다.
(C) 일정을 바꾸고 싶어한다.
(D) 서비스가 제공되고 있다고 확신하지 못한다.

166 Roy 씨는 무슨 종류의 업체를 개장하는가?

(A) 피트니스 시설
(B) 호텔
(C) 아파트 단지
(D) 연구 기관

167 오늘 누가 늦게까지 일할 것 같은가?

(A) Roebuck 씨
(B) Lloyd 씨
(C) Tung 씨
(D) Vicini 씨

168 Roy 씨에 관해 알 수 있는 것은 무엇인가?

(A) 한 사업체를 추천했다.
(B) 여러 지점에서 서비스를 필요로 한다.
(C) 계약 협상을 하고 싶어 한다.
(D) 새로운 비용에 관해 통보받았다.

신유형 169-172는 다음 이메일을 참조하시오.

수신: 전 직원
발신: Oliver Sondreal
날짜: 10월 23일
제목: 즉각적인 확인이 필요한 메시지입니다.

직원 여러분,

시간 제약으로 인해, 오늘 아침 직원회의에서 안건의 모든 사항들을 논의할 수 없었습니다. 따라서 저는 다가오는 Toronto Design Contest (TDC)에 관해 잠시 여러분께 말씀드리고자 합니다. — [1] —. 이 경연대회는 해마다 열리는 행사이며, 캐나다 내에서 12개월 미만의 기간 동

안 운영되어 온 모든 회사들을 대상으로 합니다. 우리 Media Max의 경영 관리팀은 여러분 모두가 TDC 행사를 최우선 사항으로 여겨 주시기를 바랍니다. — [2] —.

이 경연대회는 재능 있는 우리 직원들을 더 넓은 시장에 소개할 수 있는 아주 좋은 기회입니다. 작년 행사의 우승자는 이 대회로 인해 대단히 큰 주목을 받았으며, 이것은 광고에 엄청난 투자를 하지 않고는 다른 방법으로 달성해 내기 매우 어려운 성장을 이뤄내는 데 동력이 되었습니다. — [3] —.

다른 분들과 함께 참가 작품을 준비할 의향이 있고 그것이 가능한 분이라면 총무부의 Marcus Ness 씨를 만나 보십시오. — [4] —. 가이드라인에 관한 최신 정보는 다음 주에 다시 전해 드리겠지만, 가능하다면 금요일까지 어느 분께서 관심이 있으신지 대략적으로 파악하고자 합니다. 여러분 모두가 이 행사 참여를 고려해 보시기 바랍니다.

안녕히 계십시오.

Oliver Sondreal

169 Sondreal 씨는 왜 이메일을 썼는가?

(A) 대회의 가이드라인을 설명하기 위해
(B) 수신자들에게 직원회의에 관해 상기시켜 주기 위해
(C) 행사 참가를 장려하기 위해
(D) 직원들에게 의견을 요청하기 위해

170 Media Max에 관해 언급된 것은 무엇인가?

(A) Sondreal 씨에 의해 설립되었다.
(B) 1년이 채 되지 않은 회사이다.
(C) Toronto에 본사가 있다.
(D) 작년에 경연대회에서 우승했다.

171 Sondreal 씨는 TDC의 어떤 혜택을 언급하는가?

(A) 업계 종사자들과 인적 관계를 형성하는 일
(B) 정부가 제공하는 기금을 신청하는 일
(C) 신제품을 시장에 소개하는 일
(D) 증대된 홍보 효과를 얻는 일

172 [1], [2], [3], [4]로 표기된 위치들 중에서 다음 문장이 가장 잘 어 `신유형` 울리는 곳은 어디인가?

"이는 우리가 최상의 가능한 팀을 조직하는 데 도움이 될 것입니다."

(A) [1]
(B) [2]
(C) [3]
(D) [4]

173-175는 다음 기사를 참조하시오.

시카고(5월 17일)—투기자들을 놀라게 한 조치를 통해, Tilliman Beverages의 창립자이자 오랜 기간 대표로 재직해 온 Norman Chapin 씨가 대표직에서 물러날 것이라고 발표했다. Chapin 씨는 레스토랑과 같은 상업적인 판매 업체에 자사의 음료 제품 라인을 마케팅하는 것에서 소비자들에게 직접 제품을 판매하는 방식으로 변화하는 과정에서 회사를 성공적으로 이끈 것으로 잘 알려져 있다. 기업 고객에서 개인 고객으로 초점을 바꾸는 방법으로, 이 회사는 고객 기반을 확장했으며 가장 인기 있는 음료 제조사들 중의 하나가 되었다.

이 회사의 성공 덕분에, Milton Snacks는 시장의 선두주자를 인수하겠다는 희망을 안고 작년 11월에 Tilliman Beverages의 소유주들에게

입찰 가격을 제시했다. 몇 달간의 협상과 회의를 거친 끝에, 거래가 성사되어 업계의 두 거대 기업은 합병하기에 이르렀다. 이 합병은 다음 달에 있을 예정이다.

Milton Snacks의 Heather Moore 대표 이사는 어제 오후에 열린 기자 회견에서 두 회사는 자신들을 각자 인기 있는 회사로 만들어 준 뛰어난 제품의 맛을 그대로 계속 유지할 것이지만, 또한 신제품 제조 연구를 위해서도 협력할 것이라고 말했다. 자세한 사항은 밝혀지지 않았지만, Moore 씨는 Chapin 씨가 이 과정에서 중요한 역할을 할 것이라고 말했다.

173 기사의 목적은 무엇인가?

(A) 두 스낵 업체들 간의 합병을 제안하기
(B) Milton Snacks 창업주의 사임을 발표하기
(C) 고객들에게 생산 라인의 변화에 관해 알리기
(D) Tilliman Beverages에서 일어나는 변화를 발표하기

174 Tilliman Beverages는 최근 몇 년간 어떤 방법으로 변화했는가?

(A) 새로운 라인의 음료 제품을 만들었다.
(B) 자사의 음료 제품 라인을 레스토랑에 판매하기 시작했다.
(C) 고객 범위를 확장했다.
(D) 다른 거대 업체를 인수하려고 했다.

175 합병에 관해 사실이 아닌 것은 무엇인가?

(A) 결과적으로 Tilliman Beverages 음료 유형을 바뀌게 될 것이다.
(B) 여러 달 동안 논의되었다.
(C) 가장 성공적인 회사들 중 두 곳 사이에서 일어나는 일이다.
(D) 6월에 있을 예정이다.

176-180은 다음 편지와 이메일을 참조하시오.

Arya Sehgal, 인사부장
NWT Sports 기업 사무실
4355 Drummond Street
Dallas, TX 75207

4월 10일

Sehgal 씨께,

저는 현재 Austin에 있는 NWT Sports 매장에서 지점장으로 근무하고 있습니다. Laredo 지점의 지점장이신 Patrick Soto 씨가 곧 은퇴를 한다고 들었고, 제가 그 매장의 지점장으로 고려될 수 있기를 바랍니다. 저는 Austin 매장에서 많은 성공을 이뤄 왔습니다. 근무 첫날 출근했을 때, 매장은 엉망이었습니다. 직원들은 의욕도 없고 제대로 교육을 받지도 못했으며, 매출은 지역에서 가장 저조했습니다. 또한, 고객 만족도 평가는 끔찍했습니다. 불과 몇 개월 만에, 저는 이 문제점들을 바로잡아 Austin 지점을 지역 내에서 두 번째로 가장 높은 수익을 올리는 매장으로 바꿔 놓을 수 있었습니다. 저는 현재 새로운 도전을 찾는 중이며, Laredo 지점이 제 능력을 발휘하는 데 최적의 장소라고 생각합니다.

이 사안에 관해 더 논의할 수 있도록 면접 일정을 잡을 수 있다면 (전화 면접 또는 방문 면접) 더없이 기쁠 것입니다. 가급적 빨리 제게 연락 주시기 바랍니다.

안녕히 계십시오.

Susan Quinn
Austin 지점장, NWT Sports

수신: Laredo 지점 전 직원
발신: Susan Quinn
날짜: 1월 8일
제목: 전 직원 여러분께

여러분 안녕하세요.

제가 막 마감한 분기에 대한 수치 자료들을 검토했으며, 우리가 매출 목표에 도달했다는 사실을 여러분께 알려 드리게 되어 기쁩니다. 여러분 모두 수고 많으셨습니다! 이 목표치는 연휴 기간을 감안하더라도 야심적인 목표였지만, 여러분 모두가 합심해 우리가 목표로 삼았던 것을 달성해 내었습니다. 매장을 잘 관리된 상태로 유지하고 뛰어난 고객 서비스를 제공함으로써, 우리는 작년과 비교해 매출액을 상당히 향상시킬 수 있었습니다.

저는 또한 여러분께서 보여 주신 협동 정신에 깊은 인상을 받았습니다. 아시다시피, 우리 제품에 대한 수요가 증가해 왔기 때문에, 우리는 약 20명의 추가 직원들을 고용했습니다. 여러분 모두가 이 신입 사원들이 우리 근무 환경에 적응할 수 있도록 도움을 준 방식은 대단했습니다. 이와 같은 행동은 우리 NWT Sports를 근무하기 좋은 곳으로 만드는 데 도움이 됩니다. 저는 이 매장을 책임지고 있다는 것을 기쁘게 생각하며, 앞으로의 한 해가 매우 기대됩니다. 여러분 모두 지금처럼 잘 해주시기 바랍니다!

Susan

176 Quinn 씨는 왜 편지를 썼는가?

(A) 요청받은 일자리 수를 제공하기 위해

(B) 회사의 사명에 관해 문의하기 위해

(C) 한 직책에 동료 직원을 추천하기 위해

(D) 공석에 관심을 표현하기 위해

177 편지에서, 첫 번째 단락, 네 번째 줄의 어구 "turned up"과 의미가 가장 가까운 것은 무엇인가?

(A) 이동했다

(B) 발견했다

(C) 도착했다

(D) 증가했다

178 이메일을 쓴 한 가지 목적은 무엇인가?

(A) 변화의 이유를 설명하기

(B) 성과에 대해 직원들을 축하하기

(C) 직원들의 제안에 대해 감사하기

(D) 내년의 목표를 간략히 말하기

179 Laredo 지점에 관해 알 수 있는 것은 무엇인가?

(A) 가장 인기 많은 지점이다.

(B) 주기적으로 교육 프로그램을 개최한다.

(C) 직원 규모가 늘어났다.

(D) 점검을 받아야 했다.

180 Quinn 씨에 관해 사실일 것 같은 것은 무엇인가?

(A) 전근 요청이 승인되었다.

(B) 보너스를 받을 자격이 있었다.

(C) 연휴 세일 행사에 대한 제안이 시행되었다.

(D) 한때 Sehgal 씨의 사무실에서 근무한 적이 있었다.

181-185는 다음 전단과 웹 페이지를 참조하시오.

Towry Center

Goldcliff Building, 1488 34th Street, Indianapolis, IN 46203

Towry Center는 민간 자본으로 운영되어 지역 사회에 이바지하는 기관입니다. 저희는 무료 강좌와 온라인 자료들을 제공해 개인과 가족이 금융 자산을 운용하는 가장 좋은 방법을 배우도록 함으로써 부채와 소비를 관리하는 데 도움을 드리고 있습니다. Reynalda Palermo 씨께서 진행하시는 그룹 강좌가 매달 열립니다. 강좌 등록비는 무료입니다. 저희는 또한 소액의 요금만을 받고 Scott Brenner 씨와 함께하는 1대1 상담 서비스를 제공하고 있습니다.

유익한 기사를 받아 보는 것 외에도, 월간 소식지를 구독하시는 분들께서는 Jeremy Caruso 씨께서 펴낸 예산 책정에 관한 무료 전자책을 받으시게 됩니다. 단계별로 설명하는 이 지침서는 수천 명의 사람들에게 도움이 되었습니다.

더 많은 정보를 원하시면 저희 웹사이트 www.towrycenter.org를 방문하시거나, 저희 업무 시간인 월요일부터 금요일, 오전 10시에서 오후 5시 사이에 들르셔도 됩니다.

---

www.towrycenter.org/upcomingevents

홈	다가오는 행사	연락처	자주 하는 질문들

8월 3일, 화요일

월간 그룹 강좌 (무료입장)

이달의 주제: 세금 대책 마련하기

오후 7:30 – 오후 9:00, Logan Hotel (회의실 106호)

8월 28일, 토요일

Hickory Convention Center에서 열리는 Annual Indianapolis Fair에 설치된 저희 부스를 방문하시면 무료 10분 상담 서비스를 통해 귀하의 금융 자산을 평가해 드립니다. 또한, 저희가 제공해 드리는 프로그램들에 관해 더 많은 것을 알아보시려면 저희 직원들에게 문의하실 수 있습니다.

9월 1일, 수요일

Affordable Housing Commission(AHC)은 9월 1일부터 생애 첫 주택 구매자들을 위한 보조금을 제공할 것이라고 발표했습니다. 우리 지역에서는 오직 25명에게만 보조금 혜택이 돌아가며, 선착순으로 제공됩니다. 지원서는 9월 1일부터 접수되며 접수 개시일 후 며칠 안에 보조금 혜택자가 모두 정해질 것으로 예상됩니다. Rex Building(475 Searcy Street)에 위치한 AHC 사무실로 직접 방문하거나, Margaret Garza 씨에게 555-4856으로 전화해 더 많은 정보를 얻으실 수 있습니다.

181 Towry Center의 목적은 무엇인가?

(A) 소기업들을 지원하기

(B) 사람들에게 돈을 관리하는 법을 조언해 주기

(C) 사람들에게 가계자금 대출금을 제공하기

(D) 지역 사회의 프로젝트에 필요한 기금을 마련하기

182 전단에 따르면, 사람들은 어떻게 무료 책자를 받을 수 있는가?

(A) 우편물 수신 대상자 목록에 추가됨으로써

(B) 상품을 구매함으로써

(C) 각자의 의견을 공유함으로써

(D) 강좌에 출석함으로써

183 누가 8월 첫째 주에 있을 행사를 진행할 것 같은가?

(A) Scott Brenner

(B) Jeremy Caruso

(C) Margaret Garza

(D) Reynalda Palermo

184 Towry Center의 직원들은 어디에서 무료 상담 서비스를 제공할 것인가?

(A) Goldcliff Building에서

(B) Hickory Convention Center에서

(C) Logan Hotel에서

(D) Rex Building에서

185 AHC에 관해 암시된 내용은 무엇인가?

(A) 주택 견학을 제공할 계획이다.

(B) 9월에 이전할 것이다.

(C) Towry Center에서 행사를 개최한다.

(D) 제공하는 서비스에 대한 수요가 높다.

신유형 186-190은 다음 일정표와 이메일들을 참조하시오.

제3회 연례 Woodridge 환경 축제
10월 15일 토요일, 오전 9시-오후 8시, Fleming Park에서

환경을 지키는 전사들, 야외무대에서 모입니다, 오전 9시-정오
이 청소 프로젝트에서 자원봉사함으로써 여러분의 관심을 환경으로 돌려보세요. 저희는 James River 기슭에서 쓰레기를 수거해 이 구역을 아주 깨끗한 상태로 만들 것입니다. 장갑은 직접 챙겨 오세요.

쓰레기에서 보물로, Loredo Gallery 주최, 오후 1시-오후 3시
재활용 제품들을 이용해 독특한 공예품을 만듦으로써 여러분의 창의성을 발휘해 보세요. 대회 참가작들은 하루 종일 축제 방문객들에 의해 심사될 것이며, 우승자는 폐회식에서 발표될 것입니다. 1인당 1개의 참가작만 가능.

엉뚱한 동물원, Woodridge Health Association 주최, 오후 4시
즐겁고 기억에 남을 만한 5킬로미터 달리기를 하는 동안 가장 좋아하시는 동물처럼 입어 보세요. 상품은 가장 빠른 경주자와 최고의 의상 착용자에게 모두 수여될 것입니다.

특 가판대, Environmental Alliance 주최, 하루 종일
지역 내 가장 큰 야외 시장으로, 건강식품과 천연 미용 제품, 재활용품을 업그레이드한 의류, 그리고 그 외의 여러 물품들을 판매하는 매우 다양한 가판대들을 만나실 수 있습니다. 우리 지역 내의 지속 가능한 제품 판매를 성원해 주세요.

폐회식은 오후 7시 30분 야외무대에서 열림

수신: Addison Evans ⟨addisonevans@communityconnex.org⟩
발신: Jackson Lewis ⟨j.lewis@woodbridgecity.gov⟩
날짜: 10월 12일
제목: Woodridge 환경 축제

Evans 씨께,

이번 주말의 일기 예보를 확인해 봤는데, 축제 당일 아침에 꽤 쌀쌀할 것 같습니다. 차가운 기온으로 인해 참가자들이 강변 청소 행사에 오지 못하게 될까 걱정됩니다. Community Connex가 이미 이 행사에 20명의 사람들을 데려오는 데 전념했다는 것을 알고 있지만, 당신이 도움을 줄 사람들 5명에서 10명을 추가로 찾아줄 수 있는지 궁금합니다. 급하게 말씀드려서 죄송하지만, 폐회식에서 사회자가 당신이 속한 그룹의 노고에 감사의 인사를 전해 드릴 것이니 믿으셔도 됩니다.

감사합니다!

Jackson Lewis

수신: Cai Tan ⟨tancai@gt1post.com⟩
발신: Paul Watson ⟨p.watson@stauntonco.com⟩
날짜: 10월 16일
제목: 감사합니다!

안녕하세요 Cai,

어제 제가 폐회식을 진행하는 동안 사진 촬영을 해 주셔서 감사합니다. 웹사이트에 추가할 멋진 사진들을 찍어 주셨습니다. 또한, 귀하께서 조직하신 경주 대회에 관해 많은 긍정적인 의견들을 이미 들었습니다. 사람들은 의상을 차려입고 즐거운 시간을 보냈으며, 저는 내년에도 이 행사를 꼭 포함해야 한다고 생각합니다.

또 연락드리겠습니다!

Paul

186 일정표에서, 첫 번째 단락, 첫 번째 줄의 단어 "Turn"과 의미가 가장 가까운 것은 무엇인가?

(A) 향하게 하다

(B) 조정하다

(C) 전환하다

(D) 회전시키다

187 공예품 대회에 관해 알 수 있는 것은 무엇인가?

(A) 오후 3시에 우승자가 발표될 것이다.

(B) 대회 참가자들은 전문 미술가가 아니어야 한다.

(C) 갤러리 소유주에 의해 심사될 것이다.

(D) 한 사람의 참가작의 수를 제한하고 있다.

188 Lewis 씨는 왜 첫 번째 이메일을 보냈는가?

(A) 장소 변경을 알리기 위해

(B) 더 많은 자원봉사자들을 모집하기 위해

(C) 일정을 조정하기 위해

(D) 일기 예보를 확인하기 위해

189 Watson 씨에 관해 유추할 수 있는 것은 무엇인가?

(A) Tan 씨와 직접 만나고 싶어 한다.

(B) Woodridge Health Association의 회원이다.

(C) 작년에 열린 Woodridge 환경 축제에 참여했다.

(D) 행사에서 Community Connex를 언급했다.

190 Tan 씨는 어느 행사를 이끌었는가?

(A) 환경을 지키는 전사들

(B) 쓰레기에서 보물로

(C) 엉뚱한 동물원

(D) 특 가판대

신유형 191-195는 다음 편지와 이메일, 그리고 광고를 참조하시오.

관계자께:

Sapphire Theater Association은 Sapphire Theater의 복원 프로젝트에 필요한 기금 마련을 위해 장기자랑 대회를 개최합니다. 예산 부족 문제가 필수 수리 작업과 복구공사에 있어 여러 번의 지연 사태를 야기했지만, 저희는 단순히 이를 더 이상 참을 수 없습니다. 지금이 바로 조치를 취해야 할 때이며, 여러분의 도움이 필요합니다.

여러분의 회사를 알림과 동시에 후원자가 되어 이 가치 있는 프로젝트를 지원해 주십시오.

기부 단계	기부 금액	무료 광고 게재	기타 혜택
브론즈 레벨	250달러	극장 웹사이트	–
실버 레벨	500달러	극장 웹사이트와 인쇄된 공연 안내 책자	–
골드 레벨	1,000달러	인쇄된 공연 안내 책자와 무대 현수막	중앙 구역의 VIP 좌석(6명)
플래티넘 레벨	2,500달러	무대 현수막과 신문 광고	전용 고급 관람 구역 내의 VIP 좌석(8명)

골드 레벨과 플래티넘 레벨의 기부자들은 Ryan Campbell 시장님, Nino Shaw 극장 총괄 매니저님과 함께 장기자랑 대회에서 사진 촬영을 할 수 있도록 직원 한 명을 선택해야 하며, 이 사진은 〈Stone Valley Times〉의 일요일 호에 실릴 것입니다.

저희는 여러분께서 이 아름답고 역사적인 건물과 시내의 중요 명소를 보존하는 데 함께해 주시기를 바랍니다.

안녕히 계십시오.

Elise Hart
협회장, Sapphire Theater Association

수신: Elise Hart 〈e.hart@sapphiretheater.com〉
발신: Neerav Chambal 〈chambaln@bramptonltd.com〉
날짜: 5월 14일
제목: 회신: Sapphire Theater 기금 마련 행사

Hart 씨께,

귀하께서 1천 달러에 해당하는 저희 Brampton Ltd.의 수표를 받으셨다니 기쁩니다. 저희는 이 중요한 대의행사에 재정적인 기부를 하게 되어 기쁩니다. 저희 회사를 대표할 사람으로 선정한 분은 Shannon Gardner 씨입니다. 요청하신 대로, 이분께서 행사 당일 오후 6시 45분에 무대에 오르실 예정입니다. 기금 마련을 위한 노력에 대해 귀하의 단체에 행운을 빌며, 목표치를 달성하시거나 심지어 초과하실 수 있기를 바랍니다.

안녕히 계십시오.

Neerav Chambal

Sapphire Theater Talent Show
Sapphire Theater Association 제공
6월 2일 토요일, 오후 7시 30분

사상 최초로 열리는 Sapphire Theater Talent Show에 참가하실 가수, 코미디언, 마술사, 그리고 그 외의 여러분들을 찾습니다. 여러분의 재능을 지역 사회와 공유해 주시고 Sapphire Theater의 개조 공사 프로젝트에 필요한 기금을 마련하는 데 도움을 주세요. 오디션은 필요치 않습니다! 시상은 대회가 끝나고 이 극장의 총괄 매니저님께서 하실 것입니다.

공연자가 아니시라고요? 관객의 일부가 되시는 방법으로도 행사를 후원하실 수 있습니다. 입장권은 1인당 불과 15달러밖에 하지 않으며, 중간 휴식 시간에 받으실 수 있는 무료 청량음료가 포함되어 있습니다.

191 편지는 누구에게 보내졌을 것 같은가?
(A) 연극 비평가들
(B) 전문 음악인들
(C) 동호회 회원들
(D) 지역 기업들

192 편지에서, 첫 번째 단락, 세 번째 줄의 단어 "stand"와 의미가 가장 가까운 것은 무엇인가?
(A) 위치를 찾다
(B) 올리다
(C) 참다
(D) 남아 있다

193 Brampton Ltd.는 어디에 무료 광고를 할당받을 것인가?
(A) 웹사이트에만
(B) 웹사이트와 공연 안내 책자에
(C) 공연 안내 책자와 현수막에
(D) 현수막과 신문에

194 Gardner 씨에 관해 알 수 있는 것은 무엇인가?
(A) 사진이 신문에 실릴 것이다.
(B) Brampton Ltd.의 소유주다.
(C) 좌석이 전용 고급 관람 구역에 있을 것이다.
(D) 장기자랑 대회에서 노래를 부를 계획이다.

195 6월 2일 행사에 관해 사실인 것은 무엇인가?
(A) Campbell 씨가 연설을 할 것이다.
(B) 공연자들은 한 시간 전에 미리 도착해야 한다.
(C) 시상은 Shaw 씨가 할 것이다.
(D) 입장권에는 경품 추첨 참가권이 포함되어 있다.

신유형 196-200은 다음 웹 페이지와 일정표, 그리고 이메일을 참조하시오.

---

www.musicshop99.com

홈	장르	오늘의 서비스	연락처

검색: Janice Brown

4개의 검색 결과를 찾음:
〈On the Edge〉
밝은 분위기의 이 앨범은 도심 생활에 초점을 맞춰 여러 음악 스타일을 독특하게 접목하기 위해 Brown이 힙합 스타인 Ferrari G와 합작함에 따라 Brown의 작사 능력을 잘 드러내고 있습니다. 싱글 곡인 'Wouldn't You'는 차트에서 18주 동안 1위에 올라 있었습니다.

〈For Always〉
Brown이 빠른 속도의 이 록 앨범을 위해 음악계의 여러 전설들과 협력했습니다. 앨범의 모든 수익금은 Hurricane Relief Fund로 전달되며, 이 성금은 전 세계에서 자연재해로 고통받는 지역 사회에 제공되고 있습니다.

〈Simple Things〉
Brown의 평소 스타일인 빠른 비트와 전자 사운드에서 벗어나, 〈Simple Things〉는 느린 사랑 노래 발라드를 특징으로 합니다. 각 노래는 다른 아티스트와의 듀엣곡으로, 오직 어쿠스틱 기타만 반주로 사용되었습니다.

〈Footsteps〉
Texas 주의 Dallas에서 열린 순회공연의 라이브 녹음. Brown은 자신의 투어 밴드 및 가수 Rhonda Cook과 함께 수천 명의 열광적인 팬들로 구성된 관객들 앞에서 공연을 펼쳤습니다. 이 앨범은 Brown의 새로운 음악뿐만 아니라 히트곡들도 포함하고 있습니다.

103.5 FM 라디오 오후 일정표: 6월 4일, 월요일

오후 1시 Politics and Promises / 이 6부작 시리즈의 두 번째 에피소드는 주 전역과 전국적인 차원의 부패를 파헤칩니다. / 내레이션, Joe

Rayburn

오후 2시 Jazz Hour / Tara Watkins가 진행하는 이 프로그램은 여러분께 즐거움을 드리는 다양한 재즈 히트곡들을 특징으로 합니다. 신청곡은 205-555-2940으로 방송국에 전화해 신청해 주세요.

오후 3시 On the Pulse / 음악가와 배우, 감독, 그리고 그 외의 연예업계 종사자들에 관한 최신 소식과 함께 연예계의 상세 뉴스를 전하는 프로그램. 이번 주에는, 진행자 Gregory King이 허리케인 피해자들을 돕기 위한 자선기금 마련 앨범을 낸 가수 Janice Brown과 이 앨범에 관한 인터뷰를 진행합니다.

오후 4시 News Corner / 시사에 관해 알려 드리기 위해 전하는 전 세계의 다양한 이야기와 청취자들이 가장 관심 있어 하는 사안들에 관한 최신 뉴스

일기 예보와 교통 관련 보도는 각 방송 시간이 시작될 때 전해 드립니다.

수신: ⟨feedback@103-5radio.com⟩
발신: Ashley Lemon ⟨lemona@scopemail.net⟩
날짜: 6월 6일
제목: 프로그램 의견

관계자께:

저는 귀사의 훌륭한 오후 프로그램들, 특히 On the Pulse에 대해 감사의 뜻을 전하고자 합니다. 저는 팝 문화의 대단한 팬이기 때문에 Lee Parker 씨가 진행자였던 몇 년 전에 이 프로그램에 빠져들었습니다. 제 생각에 Gregory King 씨는 맡은 바를 훌륭히 해내고 계시며, 이 프로그램을 맡으신 지 불과 몇 주밖에 되지 않았음에도 방송 중에 매우 자연스럽게 느껴집니다. 다른 사람들과 의사소통을 하고 그들 삶의 가장 매력적인 측면들을 끌어내는 데 대단한 능력을 지니고 계신 분이라는 점을 쉽게 알 수 있습니다. 또한, 초대 손님 선정도 마음에 들고, Janice Brown 씨와의 인터뷰를 들을 수 있어 기뻤습니다. 저는 Janice Brown 씨가 라이브 녹음을 했던 공연에 참석했었는데, 대단히 깊은 감명을 받았습니다. Janice Brown 씨의 창의적인 작업 과정과 음악 이면에 숨어 있는 영감에 관한 이야기를 듣는 것이 흥미로웠습니다. 저는 계속해서 이 프로그램의 단골 청취자가 될 것입니다. 계속 좋은 프로그램 만들어 주세요!

안녕히 계세요.

Ashley Lemon

196 Janice Brown의 모든 앨범이 지닌 공통점은 무엇인가?
(A) 다른 음악가들과의 공동 작업을 포함하고 있다.
(B) 오직 어쿠스틱 기타만이 반주로 사용되었다.
(C) 사랑을 주제로 담고 있다.
(D) 빠른 리듬의 곡들을 포함하고 있다.

197 어느 앨범이 King 씨 프로그램의 중심이었는가?
(A) ⟨On the Edge⟩
(B) ⟨For Always⟩
(C) ⟨Simple Things⟩
(D) ⟨Footsteps⟩

198 King 씨에 관해 알 수 있는 것은 무엇인가?
(A) 한때 전문 가수였다.
(B) 자신의 프로그램 시간대를 변경했다.
(C) 자신의 자리를 새롭게 맡았다.
(D) 잘 알려진 라디오 진행자이다.

199 이메일에서, 첫 번째 단락, 네 번째 줄의 단어 "see"와 의미가 가장 가까운 것은 무엇인가?
(A) 알아차리다
(B) 보장하다
(C) 상담하다
(D) 예상하다

200 Lemon 씨에 관해 유추할 수 있는 것은 무엇인가?
(A) 노래를 신청하기 위해 방송국에 전화했다.
(B) Dallas에서 열린 콘서트에 갔다.
(C) Janice Brown의 모든 앨범을 소장하고 있다.
(D) 매일 오후에 103.5 FM을 청취한다.

PART 5

101 매장 관리자의 책무는 직원들의 성과를 검토하는 것이 포함된다.

102 건물 1층에 있는 직원 식당은 모든 지역 보건 지침들을 준수하도록 요구된다.

103 누군가는 지난밤 폭풍우로 인해 실험실에 대규모의 침수 피해가 있다는 것을 보고해야 한다.

104 영화제의 웹사이트에 따르면, 입장료는 모든 영화 상영과 워크숍에 입장할 허가가 포함되어 있다.

105 아파트 임대료는 지역에 따라 상당히 다른데, 고급 건물들은 저가인 곳의 거의 세 배이다.

106 여행 비용에 대해 환급 받기 위해서는, 출장에 대한 모든 영수증들이 연말까지 제출되어야 한다.

107 Haritas Express는 널리 광고함으로써 그 공석에 자격이 있는 지원자들을 찾을 계획이다.

108 역사 지구 내에 있는 건물들에 대한 변경은 관련 허가 신청서가 제출되고 승인이 될 때까지 이루어질 수 없다.

109 해로운 화학 물질을 섭취하는 것에 대한 우려의 증가 때문에, 유기농으로 재배한 농산물에 대한 수요가 급격히 증가했다.

110 귀하의 요청에 따라, 저희는 귀하의 최근 24팩 바닐라 향 소이 캔들 구매를 취소했습니다.

111 Lee 씨가 아침 9시에 시작하는 주간 예산 회의에 늦게 도착할 것이기 때문에, 회의를 예정대로 시작할 수 없다.

112 대표단의 다음 주 일정이 다양하기 때문에, Collins Inc.의 대표단은 띄고띄고 지능치로 학회에 갈 것이다.

113 CDV Apparel의 Graphic Center는 고객들이 각자의 티셔츠 앞면에 보이는 디자인을 맞춤 제작하는 것을 가능하게 한다.

114 지난달부터 시작된 시스템 업데이트는 직원들이 사용하는 컴퓨터의 4분의 1에 대해 여전히 완료될 필요가 있다.

115 Indianapolis Homeless Shelter의 책임자는 다가오는 해의 그곳의 예산 필요에 대해 숙고하고 있다.

116 Thompson 씨는 대기업들에게 해외 시장으로 진입하는 방법에 관한 조언을 제공해 엄청나게 부유해졌다.

117 그 작품집에 포함되어 있는 이야기들은 시골 지역 사람들에 의해 전해지는 민간 설화들을 바탕으로 하고 있다.

118 학회 참가자들 모두에게 무료 점심 식사가 제공될 것이지만, 기부금은 환영합니다.

119 폭넓은 전문 지식으로 팀이 소프트웨어 작업을 끝내는 것을 가능하게 했던, 수석 컴퓨터 프로그래머가 다가오는 대회에서 강연을 할 것이다.

120 Stephenson 시장은 시립 경기장의 개조 공사 자금에 재정적으로 기여했던 이들에게 감사를 표하기 위한 행사에 참석할 것이다.

121 조직의 관행들은 그것들이 합리적이고 의미 있는 방식으로 회사의 비전을 반영하고 있는지 확실히 하기 위해 정기적으로 다시 논의된다.

122 그 주제에 대한 관심 부족이 학교에서 생물학 수업을 제공하려던 계획을 취소하는 결과를 초래했다.

123 정부 법률가들 집단이 두 회사의 합병 중에 어떠한 법률이 위반되었는지에 관해 밝혀내고 있다.

124 Oh 씨는 수요일 월간 업무 회의 안건을 늦어도 금요일 오후 5시까지는 보낼 것이다.

125 Grand View Hospital의 의사들은 진료실을 떠나 연속으로 4일이 넘게 보내는 것이 좀처럼 허용되지 않는다.

126 Morrow 씨는 마케팅을 공부한 적이 없지만, 나노 기술에 관한 한 회사에서 가장 박식한 직원이다.

127 호의적인 평가를 받은 후에, Karen Smith는 〈Show Mountain Daily Newspaper〉의 의견 칼럼에 또 다른 기사를 쓰는 것에 동의했다.

128 〈Warren Global News Magazine〉을 1년 구독 신청해서, 당신은 〈Modern Travel Weekly〉 한 부를 무료로 받을 것입니다.

129 Genome Software Inc.의 London으로의 이전은 그 도시 내에 컴퓨터 엔지니어들에 대한 상당한 수요를 만들어 낼 것으로 예상된다.

130 지난 10년 동안, Rosewood 씨는 자신의 개인 소장품의 많은 미술 서적들을 그 대학의 도서관에 기부해 왔다.

PART 6

신유형 ▶ 131-134는 다음 기사를 참조하시오.

연례 Sentinel Springs Marathon

제 23회 연례 Sentinel Springs Marathon의 사전 등록이 시작되었다. 장거리 도보 경주는 늘 그렇듯이 4월의 마지막 일요일에 개최될 것이다. 올해 경주 날짜는 4월 30일이고 오전 7시에 시작될 것이다. Hide Park에서 시작되는 이 26.2마일 코스는 참가자들과 경치 좋은 Coastal Boulevard를 따라가다 Meyer Stadium에서 끝이 난다.

작년 참가자 수를 바탕으로, 올해 참가자 수는 10,000명이 넘을 것으로 예상된다. 모든 주자들은 늦어도 4월 15일까지 등록을 완료해야 한다.

2월 1일 이전 입장료는 70달러이다. 사전 등록 마감 기한 후에 등록하는 이들은 90달러를 지불해야 할 것이다.

신유형 ▶ 135-138은 다음 공지를 참조하시오.

Hanauma Children's Community Center가 Diamond Head Park Amphitheater에서 11월 3일 오후 4시에 열릴 콘서트를 후원합니다. 센터는 그 모임의 목표는 상호작인 자연 과학 아동 박물관 건립을 위한 기금을 조성하는 것이라고 발표했습니다.

Oahu Youth Jazz Ensemble이 Kailua Children's Choir와 함께 공연할 것입니다. 솔로 연주자인 Ailani Kane이 가수로 특별 출연할 것입니다. 이 행사는 가족 친화적이고 12세 미만의 어린이들 모두에게는 무료일 것입니다. 좌석은 hanaumaccc.org에서 예약할 수 있으며, 잔디 공간은 공연 당일에 선착순으로 이용 가능할 것입니다. 티켓 가격은 위치와 이용 가능 여부에 따라 달라질 것입니다. 모든 수익금은 지역 아동 박물관 프로젝트에 보탬이 될 것입니다.

신유형 ▶ 139-142는 다음 이메일을 참조하시오.

발신: m.hassel@d&bequipment.com
수신: D&B Equipment 직원들
제목: 스키장 입장권 할인
날짜: 10월 31일

많은 분들이 아시다시피, Millet Basin Ski Park를 운영하는 회사인 Hatons Resorts는 우리의 가장 오래된 고객들 중 하나입니다. 우리는 그들을 위해 전국적으로 17개의 거의 전 지점에 스키 리프트 장비를 공

입장권을 제공할 것입니다. 이는 어느 직원이든 정가의 20퍼센트로 이용이 가능할 것입니다. 이 특별 할인을 이용할 계획이시라면, 확인을 하기 위해 저에게 답장을 보내주시기 바랍니다. 정규 시즌 입장권의 가격은 300달러이니, 각 직원은 60달러만 내면 됩니다. 이 입장권에 많은 관심이 있을 것으로 기대합니다.

여러분의 노고에 감사 드립니다.

Marge Hassel
D&B Equipment, 관리자

신유형 143-146은 다음 회람을 참조하시오.

발신: olivestone@advantagedental.org
수신: 전 직원
제목: 최우수 치과상
날짜: 4월 7일
첨부 파일: 식사 선택

Advantage Dental 전문의들께,

저는 이 지역 주민의 구강 건강과 행복에 크게 기여를 하고 있는 우리 치과 전문의들이 매우 자랑스럽습니다. 우리 환자들은 우리 서비스에 대해 높이 평가해 오고 있습니다. 실제로, 우리는 3년 연속으로 Dental Excellence Award를 받게 됩니다. 이것이 우리 환자들의 수가 계속 증가하는 이유 중 하나입니다. 그래서 Advantage Dental의 운영진은 4월 23일에 Running Y Resort에서 축하 만찬 행사를 열게 되어 기쁩니다. 식사 선택을 위해 첨부된 목록을 봐 주시기 바랍니다.

감사합니다.

Olive Stone
Advantage Dental 관리자

PART 7

147-148은 다음 서식을 참조하시오.

Angwin Gardens Vineyard: 결혼식장

축하 드리며 Angwin Gardens Family가 되신 것을 환영합니다! 귀하의 인생에서 이런 중요한 순간을 축하하기 위해 Angwin Gardens Vineyard를 선택해 주셔서 대단히 기쁩니다. 잠시 시간을 내어 이 특별한 날을 위한 귀하의 계획에 관해 말씀해 주시기 바랍니다

저희 행사 기획자들 중 한 명이 귀하의 결혼식의 요구를 충족시키는 데 필요한 계획과 가격 상세 정보를 가지고 연락을 드릴 것입니다.

- 결혼 당사자 성함: ________ 와(과) ________.
- 이메일: ____________ 연락처: ________ 날짜: ________
- 장소 선택: St. Helena: { } 1200 Blue Vintage
  Calistoga: { } 9530 Hot Springs Dr.
  Angiwn: { } 913 Clark Road { } 25 Angwin Way
- 필요 시설물: { } 예배당 { } 탈의실 { } 연회장 { } 기타: ______
- 예상 하객 수: { } 15-29 { } 30-69 { } 70-99 { } 100-149
  { } 150 이상
- 필요 장비: { } 탁자 { } 의자 { } 음향 시스템

147 행사 기획자는 다음에 무엇을 할 것 같은가?
(A) 특별한 날을 위한 시설물과 장비를 준비하기
(B) 결혼식 참석자들을 위한 온라인 공지 게시하기
(C) 호텔 숙박 비용에 관한 정보를 제공하기
(D) 이 양식에 제공된 상세 정보를 기반으로한 견적서 전달하기

148 Angwin Gardens Vineyard에 관해 알 수 있는 것은 무엇인가?
(A) 요청 시에 손님들을 위해 식사를 제공한다.
(B) 선택할 수 있는 네 개의 다른 지점이 있다.
(C) 다양한 도구들을 갖추고 있다.
(D) 이용 가능한 고객용 객실이 있다.

149-150은 다음 공지를 참조하시오.

8TH STREET HARDWARE 고객들께 공지

8th Street Hardware의 경영 팀이 여러분께 중요한 변동 사항을 알려 드리고자 합니다. Jackson가에 의해 13년 동안 운영되어 온 뒤에, 저희 업체는 지역의 기업가인 Carl Lugo에게 매각되었습니다. 그분의 노력에 행운을 빌며, 그가 여러분께서 8th Street Hardware에 기대해 오셨던 최고의 고객 서비스를 유지해 주실 것이라고 확신합니다. 새로운 경영진 하에 있는 첫 3개월 동안, 교환 정책에 변경은 없을 것입니다. 제품 가격 또한 현재의 수준으로 유지될 것입니다. 여러분의 건물과 자택 수리에 필요한 모든 것을 위해 앞으로도 8th Street Hardware가 여러분이 가장 먼저 방문할 곳이 되기를 바랍니다.

149 공지는 왜 쓰여졌는가?
(A) 수상자를 소개하기 위해
(B) 소유주의 변경을 알리기 위해
(C) 기념 행사를 홍보하기 위해
(D) 교환 정책을 설명하기 위해

150 매장의 상품에 관해 언급된 것은 무엇인가?
(A) 고품질일 것으로 여겨진다.
(B) 수리 작업을 무료로 해 줄 것이다.
(C) 3개월 이내에 반품할 수 있다.
(D) 가격이 동일하게 유지될 것이다.

151-152는 다음 편지를 참조하시오.

Smithson Educational Conference

12월 4일
Andrew McCoy
726 McKinley Street
Westborough, MA 17344

McCoy 씨께,

이 편지는 12월 20일부터 22일까지 New Jersey, Princeton에서 열리는 Smithson Educational Conference에 귀하가 참석하심을 확인하기 위한 것입니다. 귀하의 발표는 12월 22일에 진행될 것입니다.

학회 마지막 날에, 세미나의 모든 참석자들을 위한 저녁 만찬이 있을 것입니다. 그것은 Triple Crown Hotel에서 열릴 것이고, 세미나가 진행될 곳의 바로 아래층입니다. 그것은 오후 9시에 시작될 것입니다. 가능하시다면 만찬에 함께하셔도 됩니다.

제 비서인 Jordan Genovia가 Grand Tree Hotel에 귀하의 숙박을 예약해 놓았습니다. 그 호텔은 도시의 시내 지역에 편리하게 위치해 있고, 학회 장소는 호텔에서 불과 걸어서 5분 거리에 있습니다. 귀하의 숙박에 관한 질문이 있으실 경우, jgenovia@smithsonec.com으로 제 비서에게 연락하시기 바랍니다.

연설을 하시기 전에 저희가 양질과 타당성을 검토해 볼 수 있도록 발표

내용과 관련 자료의 사본을 제출해 주셔야 한다는 점을 상기시켜 드립니다. 가능한 한 빨리 이를 해 주시기를 요청 드립니다.

귀하의 동료들로부터 Johnson Education Center에서의 귀하의 경력에 관한 좋은 이야기를 많이 들었습니다. 세미나에서 귀하의 발표를 듣게 되어 더없이 기쁘게 생각합니다.

안녕히 계십시오.

Grace Page
Smithson Educational Conference, 행사 운영자

151 편지는 왜 보내졌는가?

(A) 세미나 대표를 모집하기 위해
(B) 학회에 관한 세부 사항을 전달하기 위해
(C) 교육 행사를 광고하기 위해
(D) 객실 예약에 관한 문의를 하기 위해

152 McCoy 씨는 어디서 발표를 할 것인가?

(A) Grand Tree Hotel에서
(B) 저녁 만찬회장에서
(C) Johnson Education Center에서
(D) Triple Crown Hotel에서

153-155는 다음 광고를 참조하시오.

고객 참여형 이탈리아 미술사 투어에 함께 하세요!

미술과 역사, 그리고 문화를 좋아하시나요? 내년 여름에 미술사 전문가가 진행하는 이 세 가지가 통합된 2주간의 이탈리아 투어를 떠나 보세요. 여행 일정에 포함된 것은:

• 이탈리아의 가장 유명한 박물관 방문
• 르네상스 시대에 관한 상세 강연
• 스케치와 채색, 그리고 조각 기법을 직접 적용해 보는 수업
• 정통 이탈리안 레스토랑에서의 맛있는 식사

고객들께서는 Florence, Venice, 그리고 Rome 같은 도시들의 고급 호텔에서 숙박하실 것입니다. 모든 박물관 입장권과, 식사 그리고 숙박이 포함될 것입니다. 하지만 참가자들은 매일 가볍거나 중간 정도의 몇 시간 걷기가 가능해야 합니다. 투어는 Rome에서 시작되며, 고객들은 각자 항공권을 확보해 두셔야 합니다.

현재 3번의 투어가 여전히 이용 가능합니다. 이것들은 5월 30일과 6월 18일, 그리고 7월 5일에 출발합니다. 최대 15퍼센트까지 아끼시려면 1월 1일 이전에 등록하세요.

가격 상세 정보와 자세한 여행 일정표를 위해 www.italianarthistory culture.org을 방문하시기 바랍니다.

153 무엇이 광고되고 있는가?

(A) 휴가 패키지 여행
(B) 미술관 티켓
(C) 이탈리아에서 열리는 특별 행사
(D) 미술과 역사에 관한 세 가지 강연

154 고객들은 무엇을 하도록 요청받는가?

(A) 온라인 후기를 작성하도록
(B) 미술사 강좌에 등록하도록
(C) 호텔에 빈 객실이 있는지 확인하도록
(D) Rome행 항공편을 예약하도록

155 광고에 따르면, 웹사이트에서 무엇이 이용 가능한가?

(A) 지역 명소들까지의 길 안내
(B) 활동 일정표
(C) 고급 호텔 목록
(D) 박물관 입장료

신유형 ▶ 156-157은 다음 문자 메시지 대화를 참조하시오.

MARY SCHMIDT	오후 12:40

오늘 아침에 금요일에 열릴 Comic Book Expo에 관하여 문자 메시지를 보냈어요. 받았나요?

MARSHALL GRIMES	오후 12:55

방금 전에 메시지들을 막 확인했어요. 티켓이 많이 남아있지 않다고 되어 있는데, 그렇죠? 우리가 참가할 수 있으면 좋겠는데. 제 〈Cloaked Rider〉 시리즈에 그 작가 사인을 꼭 받고 싶거든요.

MARY SCHMIDT	오후 1:00

아직 티켓을 안 샀다는 뜻인가요?

MARSHALL GRIMES	오후 1:03

네, 하지만 큰 문제가 되지는 않을 거예요. 집에 가는 길에 매표소가 있어요. 지금 바로 가서 2장 살게요.

MARY SCHMIDT	오후 1:04

너무 늦었어요. 1시간 전에 매진됐어요.

MARSHALL GRIMES	오후 1:07

다 잘될 거예요. 온라인에서 다른 누군가에게 사면 될 거예요. 값이 2배나 비싸지기는 하겠지만.

MARY SCHMIDT	오후 1:13

그럴 필요 없어요. 제 친구 중 한 명이 그 행사에서 일하는데, 티켓을 구해줄 수도 있을 거예요.

MARSHALL GRIMES	오후 1:15

알겠어요. 계속 희망을 가지고 있을게요.

156 글쓴이들은 어떤 유형의 행사에 참석할 계획인가?

(A) 스포츠 경기 대회
(B) 도서 컨벤션
(C) 거리 퍼레이드
(D) 패션쇼

157 오후 1시 07분에, Grimes 씨가 "It will work out"이라고 썼을 **신유형** 때 의미하는 것은 무엇인가?

(A) 계획이 변경되지 않을 것이라고 확신한다.
(B) Schmidt 씨가 자신에게 한 말을 믿지 않는다.
(C) 많은 사람들이 행사에 올 것이라 기쁘다.
(D) 자신의 일정을 변경할 의향이 없다.

신유형 ▶ 158-160은 다음 기사를 참조하시오.

지역 뉴스
Andrea Vaughn 작성

8월 19일—여름 방문객들이 집으로 돌아감에 따라 지역 업체들이 성수기로 인한 긴장을 풀고 있다고 소비자 행동 조사 회사인 Stats Watch의 CEO인 Chad Nelson이 발표한다. — [1] —. 지역 내 서비스를 제공하는 대부분의 호텔과 항공사들이 작년과 비슷한 수치를 경험하기는 했지만, 자연과 관련된 모험 활동을 제공하는 업체들은 수익의 증가가 있었다. Cliff Inc.와 Campex 같은 회사들은 방문객들을 이끌고 국립 공원을 둘러 보는 야간 여행을 통해 많은 수익을 거둬들이고 있다.

— [2] —. Campex는 불과 가이드 다섯 명으로 개업했지만, 수요를 맞추기 위해 다음 달에 두 명을 더 고용할 계획이고, 이 수요는 날씨가 더 추워지기 시작하는 늦가을까지 지속될 것으로 예상된다. — [3] —.

"이런 종류의 업체들이 지닌 매력은 그들이 참가자들에게 독특한 경험을 약속한다는 것입니다. — [4] —. 사람들이 지역의 자연이 최상인 상태일 때 그것을 보기 위해 줄 서는 것은 놀라운 일이 아니죠,"라고 Nelson은 말했다.

지역 공무원들은 그 추세가 내년 그리고 이후에도 지속될지 의문스러워 한다. 방문객들의 안전을 보장하기 위한 규제 확대 관련 사안들이 앞으로 몇 달에 걸쳐 논의될 것이다.

158 기사는 왜 쓰여졌는가?
(A) 기업 합병에 대한 계획을 발표하기 위해
(B) 관광 분야에 관한 새로운 소식을 제공하기 위해
(C) 한 회사의 신임 CEO를 소개하기 위해
(D) 업체들을 후원할 제안 사항을 설명하기 위해

159 Campex는 9월에 무엇을 할 것인가?
(A) 직원을 늘리는 것
(B) Cliff Inc.와 제휴 관계를 맺는 것
(C) 국립 공원에 기부금을 내는 것
(D) 실내 서비스를 제공하기 시작하는 것

160 신유형 [1], [2], [3], [4]로 표기된 위치들 중에서 다음 문장이 가장 잘 어울리는 곳은 어디인가?

"아름다운 Winona Falls로의 도보 여행은 현재 제공 중인 여행 서비스의 하나의 사례에 불과합니다."
(A) [1]
(B) [2]
(C) [3]
(D) [4]

신유형 161-164는 다음 편지를 참조하시오.

Sunshine Home and Garden 고객
1149 Lindale Avenue
Berkeley, CA 94707
5월 15일

고객님께,

Home and Garden에서, 저희는 매장과 쇼핑 선택 폭을 개선하기 위한 변화를 시행하기 위해 노력하고 있습니다. 다음 달에 개선된 것을 확인하러 오시기 바랍니다. — [1] —.

최근에 Sunshine Home and Garden을 방문하셨다면, 아마도 건물의 북쪽 끝에서 진행되는 공사를 알아차리셨을 것입니다. — [2] —. 6월 1일부터, 저희 정원용 기구 코너가 원래 크기의 두 배가 될 것입니다. 추가된 공간은 또한 처음으로 판매 목록에 실외용 의자들과 테이블을 추가하는 것을 가능하게 합니다.

저희는 6월 7일 일요일에 이 흥미로운 개선 사항을 기념할 계획입니다. — [3] —. 하루 종일 무료 다과뿐만 아니라 무료 정원 가꾸기 시연을 제공할 것입니다. 또한, 저희 매장은 매일 저녁 8시 대신 저녁 9시까지 문을 열 것입니다. — [4] —. 꾸준한 이용에 감사를 표하기 위해, 6월 30일까지 유효한 매장 쿠폰을 동봉했습니다. 더불어 Venetar 브랜드 꽃씨 샘플 한 팩도 보내드립니다.

고맙습니다.

Jessica Cerrone
Sunshine Home and Garden, 매장 관리자

161 편지의 목적은 무엇인가?
(A) 독자를 매장 이전 파티에 초대하기
(B) 전동 공구 브랜드를 홍보하기
(C) 매장의 확장을 알리기
(D) 계절 세일의 조건을 명확히 하기

162 Sunshine Home and Garden에서 언제 특별 행사가 열릴 것인가?
(A) 5월 15일
(B) 6월 1일
(C) 6월 7일
(D) 6월 30일

163 편지에서 나타나 있지 않은 것은?
(A) 매장 운영 시간이 연장될 것이다.
(B) 원예 정원용 기구 코너가 더 커질 것이다.
(C) 고객 카드가 도입될 것이다.
(D) 실외용 가구가 판매될 것이다

164 신유형 [1], [2], [3], [4]로 표기된 위치들 중에서 다음 문장이 가장 잘 어울리는 곳은 어디인가?

"이는 7,500평방 피트만큼 매장의 진열 구역을 확장하기 위한 프로젝트의 일부였습니다."
(A) [1]
(B) [2]
(C) [3]
(D) [4]

165-167은 다음 웹사이트를 참조하시오.

http://www.hotelencounter.com/info

Hotel Encounter 스마트폰 앱으로 최저가 호텔을 찾아 보세요!

Hotel Encounter는 한 번의 버튼을 터치하는 것만으로 가장 저렴한 호텔을 찾도록 도와 드립니다. 막판 예약을 하든 미리 계획을 하든, 필요에 맞는 호텔을 찾으실 수 있습니다. 위치, 가격, 또는 등급으로 검색할 수 있습니다. 프리미엄 회원들은 또한 공항 교통편, 고급 식사, 여행자 보험 등에 대한 특별 제공 할인 서비스도 받으실 수 있습니다.

일단 선택을 하시면, 예약을 마무리하기 위해 해당 호텔의 웹사이트로 이동될 것입니다. 저희가 그 호텔에 관한 정보를 제공해 드릴 수 있지만, 환불과 취소는 해당 호텔을 통해서만 처리된다는 점을 유념해 주시기 바랍니다. 하지만 저희 표시 가격이 호텔의 가격과 일치하지 않는 것을 발견하시면, 1-800-555-6879로 저희에게 전화하셔서 그 문제에 관해 알려 주실 수 있습니다. 저희가 온라인상의 오류를 바로잡아 여러분께서 반드시 광고된 가격으로 이용하실 수 있도록 할 것입니다.

165 Hotel Encounter에 관해 알 수 있는 것은 무엇인가?
(A) 고객들이 각자의 호텔 체험을 평가할 수 있다.
(B) 경쟁사의 가격과 동일하게 제공한다.
(C) 다양한 기준을 바탕으로 검색 결과를 얻을 수 있다.
(D) 막판 예약이 가장 저렴하다.

166 프리미엄 회원들에게 무엇이 제공될 것인가?
(A) 관련 서비스들에 대한 할인

(B) 무료 여행자 보험

(C) 상품 판매에 대한 사전 공지

(D) 빠른 공항 탑승 수속

167 웹사이트에 따르면, 고객들은 왜 Hotel Encounter에 연락해야 하는가?

(A) 호텔에 관해 불만을 제기하기 위해

(B) 취소에 따른 환불을 요청하기 위해

(C) 지불 상세 정보를 제공하기 위해

(D) 가격 불일치를 알리기 위해

신유형 ▶ 168-171은 다음 온라인 채팅을 참조하시오.

Fang Qin [오후 4:20]

오늘 회의에 참석해 주셔서 감사합니다, 여러분. Sharber Enterprises 를 잃은 것을 만회하기 위해 앞으로 우리가 할 일이 많다는 것을 알고 있습니다.

Raktim Maraj [오후 4:21]

그들이 우리 경쟁사로 옮기기로 결정했다니 너무나 실망스러웠어요.

Ashley Cohen [오후 4:22]

네, 그 손실을 보완하려면 몇몇의 신규 회사들이 필요할 겁니다.

Fang Qin [오후 4:24]

그래서 제가 우리 팀이 더욱 효율적이 되도록 영업 구역을 개편할 계획을 세운 거예요. 회의 시간에 맞춰 지도가 포함된 유인물을 준비하지 못해 죄송합니다. 프린터에 문제가 있었어요.

Victor Rocha [오후 4:25]

이메일로 보내줄 수 있나요?

Fang Qin [오후 4:29]

방금 보냈어요. 제가 어떻게 나눴는지 한번 봐 주세요.

Ashley Cohen [오후 4:32]

선임과 후임 영업 사원들이 함께가기보다 각자의 구역이 있는 것 같네요. 하지만 많은 연습을 먼저 하지 않고 신규 고객에게 아이디어를 홍보하는 일은 어려울 텐데요.

Victor Rocha [오후 4:33]

맞아요. Waleck 씨는 여기서 3월에 일을 시작했잖아요.

Fang Qin [오후 4:34]

원래 계획을 고수하고 싶지만, 역할극 활동이 포함된 워크숍이 신입 사원들에게는 더 유용할 수 있겠네요. 워크숍을 맡아줄 시간 있는 분 계세요?

Raktim Maraj [오후 4:35]

제가 준비할 수 있을 것 같아요.

168 Sharber Enterprises에 관해 암시된 것은 무엇인가?

(A) 직원들이 최근에 Qin 씨와 만났다.

(B) 회사를 해외로 옮길 계획이다.

(C) 글쓴이들의 회사의 주요 고객이었다.

(D) 이전 중에 계약서를 분실했다.

169 Qin 씨는 왜 사과를 하는가?

(A) 고객을 화나게 만들었다.

(B) 새로운 프린터를 주문하는 일을 잊었다.

(C) 부정확한 이메일 주소를 사용했다.

(D) 문서를 준비해 두지 못했다.

170 오후 4시 33분에, Rocha 씨가 "Ms. Waleck started here in March"라고 썼을 때 의미하는 것은 무엇인가?

신유형

(A) 동료 직원이 일을 처리하지 못할 것이라고 생각한다.

(B) 변동 사항에 대한 이유를 발견했다.

(C) 동료의 실수를 명확히 밝혀 내고 싶어 한다.

(D) 팀원에게 도움을 요청하고 있다.

171 Maraj 씨는 무엇을 하는 것에 자원하는가?

(A) 교육을 이끄는 것

(B) 신입 사원들을 모집하는 것

(C) 몇몇 가구들을 조립하는 것

(D) 일부 보고서들을 교정보는 것

172-175는 다음 기사를 참조하시오.

Nutriglow 이사로 임명된 Peter Tulip

〈Finance Monthly〉

Los Angeles(7월 6일)—영양제 제조업체인 Nutriglow가 이번 주 Peter Tulip을 합류시켜 이사회의 업계 전문가 명단을 보강할 것이라고 발표했다. Tulip 씨는 마케팅 분야의 선도적인 권위자들 중 한 명으로 경쟁 회사인 WellEat, Inc.의 성공적인 발전을 감독하며, 그의 업계에서 널리 인정받고 있다. Nutriglow는 이사회에서의 그의 존재로 수익에서 유사한 증가를 볼 것으로 기대한다. 회사는 올해 1월부터, 당시 시행되었던 가격 전략의 변동과 관련됐던 것으로 생각되는 수익 감소로 고군분투하고 있다.

Tulip 씨를 고용하기로 한 결정은 5월 회의 후에 내려졌고, 그 회의에서 중역들은 회사가 나아가고 있는 방향에 대해 우려를 표했다. Sean Masters 회장의 말에 따르면, Tulip 씨는 그 역할에 자격을 갖춘 몇 안되는 사람들 중 한 명이었다. "저희는 Nutriglow를 호전시켜야 하는 당면 문제의 규모에 대해 환상을 가지고 있지 않습니다." Masters 씨가 기자 회견에서 말했다. "저희는 Tulip 씨가 최근 몇 개월간 크게 결여되어 온 새로운 시각을 불러올 것이라고 확신합니다. 역시 기자 회견에 참석한 Tulip 씨도 자신의 새로운 역할에 만족한다고 덧붙였다. "Nutriglow의 잠재력에는 의심의 여지가 없습니다." 그가 모인 기자들에게 말했다. "반드시 여기 있는 모두의 잠재력을 키우게 하는 것이 저의 일이죠."

Peter Tulip은 계속해서 그 이야기를 다루는 기자들에게, 그의 첫 행보는 인기 있는 영양제 Strawberry Supreme을 다시 출시하는 것으로, 현재 가격은 미정 상태라고 말했다. 이는 젊은 고객들 사이에서는 인기 있는 맛이었지만, 새로운 맛의 개발을 위하여 이전에 생산이 중단됐었다.

기자 회견을 마무리하면서, Tulip은 또한 그의 예전 고용주들에게 감사하는 시간을 가졌고, 자신의 관리하에 성취된 일들에 대한 만족감을 표했다. "제가 있는 동안, WellEat, Inc.가 소규모 가족 업체에서 국내 최고의 영양제 회사로 발전한 것을 지켜봤습니다. 좋았던 기억만 가지고 떠납니다."라고 말했다.

172 무엇에 관한 기사인가?

(A) 두 회사의 합병

(B) 전문가의 고용

(C) 새로운 공장의 개업

(D) 업체의 폐업

173 기사에 따르면, 5월에 무슨 일이 일어났는가?

(A) 간부회의가 열렸다.

(B) 새 관리자가 고용되었다.

(C) 가격 전략에 변화가 이루어졌다.

(D) 판촉 행사가 시작되었다.

174 다시 출시되는 영양제에 관하여 여전히 결정되어야 하는 것은 무엇인가?

(A) 포장 색상

(B) 성분 목록

(C) 가격을 얼마로 할지

(D) 어디에서 판매할지

175 WellEat, Inc.에 관해 언급된 것은 무엇인가?

(A) 당사의 제품들은 우편 주문으로 구매가 가능하다.

(B) 100개가 넘는 제품을 제공한다.

(C) Los Angeles에서 설립되었다.

(D) 시장의 선두 주자이다.

176-180은 다음 공지와 일정표를 참조하시오.

Bloomfield Community Center 공지

우리 지역 주민들 중 한 분의 후한 기부금 덕택에, Bloomfield Community Center가 프로그램을 확대할 수 있게 되었습니다. 저희 일정에 추가될 첫 활동은 태극권입니다. 그 강좌는 일주일에 두 번 오전에 무술 전문가이신 Sheng Hou가 가르칠 것입니다. 참가자들은 헐렁한 옷과 튼튼한 운동화를 착용하실 것을 권장합니다. 첫 강좌는 15명이 신청하는 대로 시작할 것입니다. 하지만 강좌가 정기적으로 운영되기 시작한 후에는, 사전 등록이 필요하지 않을 것입니다. Bloomfield Community Center에 새로운 활동을 제안하고 싶으시면, 안내 데스크에서 의견 카드를 작성해 주시기 바랍니다. 저희 시설의 목적은 지역 사회를 위해 건강에 도움이 되는 아주 다양한 활동들을 제공하는 것이니, 여러분의 의견이 저희에게 중요합니다.

Bloomfield Community Center 활동 일정표: 2월
본관 활동들

일요일
오후 12:30 가족 에어로빅, 모든 연령을 위한 심장 강화 운동
오후 3:00 초보자들을 위한 발레(첫째 주와 둘째 주만), 발레화 대여 가능

월요일(휴무)

화요일
오전 11:00 실내 테니스, 단식 또는 복식
오후 2:00 태극권, 모든 레벨 환영

수요일
오전 10:00 초보자 요가(첫째, 둘째, 넷째 주)
오후 3:00 실내 테니스, 단식 또는 복식

목요일
오전 10:00 실내 테니스, 단식 또는 복식
오후 5:00 청장년 농구

금요일
오후 2:00 태극권, 모든 레벨 환영
오후 6:00 킥복싱, 사전 등록 필수

토요일
오후 1:00 청장년 농구(이달 마지막 토요일은 본관이 지역 토너먼트를 위해 사용될 수 있어 취소됨)

활동들을 인쇄한 일정표는 안내 데스크에서 받거나, www.bloomfield cc.org에서 다운로드할 수 있습니다.

---

176 공지는 왜 쓰여졌는가?

(A) 지역 문화 센터에 필요한 기부금을 요청하기 위해

(B) 피트니스 강사를 소개하기 위해

(C) 공원 직원으로 일할 사람들을 모집하기 위해

(D) 새로운 활동에 참여자들을 초대하기 위해

177 공지에서, 첫 번째 단락, 여덟 번째 줄의 단어 "aim"과 의미가 가장 가까운 것은 무엇인가?

(A) 방향

(B) 목적

(C) 인식

(D) 표시

178 태극권 강좌에 관해 사실일 법한 것은?

(A) 특별한 도복이 필요하다.

(B) 가장 인기 있는 활동들 중 하나다.

(C) 애초에 계획된 것보다 늦은 시간에 모인다.

(D) 2월 강좌를 맡은 강사가 변경되었다.

179 2월에 어떤 활동이 정확히 세 번 열릴 예정인가?

(A) 가족 에어로빅

(B) 실내 테니스

(C) 청장년 농구

(D) 초보자 요가

180 Bloomfield Community Center에 관해 알 수 있는 것은 무엇인가?

(A) 2월에 경기 대회를 주최할 것이다.

(B) 토너먼트 일정이 변경될 수 있다.

(C) Sheng Hou에 의해 설립되었다.

(D) 한 개가 넘는 농구 코트가 있다.

181-185는 다음 이메일들을 참조하시오.

수신: Elaine Andell 〈andell.e@ibsconsulting.net〉
발신: Chen Li 〈li.chen@ibsconsulting.net〉
날짜: 3월 28일
제목: 문의

Andell 씨께,

저에게 뭔가 도움을 주실 수 있을지 궁금합니다. 회사는 지난달에 몇 명의 제 팀원들과 함께 저를 해외로, Taipei에서 열린 International Leadership Conference에 보냈습니다. 저희는 그곳에서 아주 많은 정보를 얻었고 저는 집단 역학에 관한 세션을 이끌었던 Chennai University의 Arnav Gera 박사님의 강연에 특히 깊은 인상을 받았습니다. 저는 곧 있을 오리엔테이션 세션에 제 강연에서 데이터를 이용할 수 있도록, 이 주제에 관해 그분께서 쓰신 연구 논문을 읽어 보고 싶습니다.

유감스럽게도, 제가 저희 온라인 참고 도서관을 찾아봤을 때, 저희가 이 논문이 발행된 저널인 〈The Journal of Strategic Management〉를 구독하지 않는다는 것을 알게 되었습니다. IBS Consulting이 이 저널에 구독 서비스를 구입하는 것이 가능할지 궁금합니다. 우리가 이 옵션을 선택한다면, Gera 박사님의 연구 자료뿐만 아니라 우리 회사에 귀중한 자산이 될 것으로 생각되는 다른 기사들도 이용할 수 있게 됩니다.

오리엔테이션 날짜인 4월 8일 이전에 이 구독 신청을 해 주실 수 있을지 여부를 알려 주시기 바랍니다.

감사합니다.

Chen Li

수신: Chen Li 〈li.chen@ibsconsulting.net〉
발신: Elaine Andell 〈andell.e@ibsconsulting.net〉
날짜: 3월 29일
제목: 회신: 문의

Li 씨께,

회사의 올해 예산이 이미 정해져 있어 항목들이 추가될 수 없음을 알려 드리게 되어 유감입니다. 따라서 이번에는 요청하신 구독 서비스를 구매할 수 없을 것입니다. 하지만 다른 방법이 있을 수도 있습니다. 제가 Gera 박사의 이메일 주소를 얻기 위해 Chennai University의 웹사이트를 둘러봤습니다. 그가 목록에 기재되어 있지 않아, 최근에 대학을 그만두신 것으로 보이는데, Gera 박사와 공동 저자였던 Leya Sahota 교수에 대한 상세 정보가 있었습니다. 제가 그 명부의 사본을 첨부했으니 직접 연락해 보실 수 있을 것입니다. 필요한 것을 그분께서 제공해 주실 수도 있을 것입니다. 문의 사항은 저에게 자유롭게 이메일을 보내시거나, 내일 주간 직원 회의에서 말씀해 주시기 바랍니다.

안녕히 계십시오.

Elaine Andell

181 Li 씨는 무엇을 하는 데 어려움이 있었나?

(A) 자료실에 접속하는 것
(B) 오리엔테이션 일정을 정하는 것
(C) 연구 자료에 관한 정보를 찾는 것
(D) 학회를 위해 연사들을 고용하는 것

182 첫 번째 이메일에서, 두 번째 단락, 네 번째 줄의 어구 "go with"와 의미가 가장 가까운 것은 무엇인가?

(A) 선택하다
(B) 논의하다
(C) 동반하다
(D) 세다

183 Andell 씨는 도움을 제공하기 위해 무엇을 했나?

(A) 몇몇 연락처를 보냈음
(B) 다른 연사를 추천했음
(C) 보고서의 오류들을 확인했음
(D) 행사 날짜를 변경했음

184 Sahota 씨에 관해 알 수 있는 것은 무엇인가?

(A) Li 씨와 직접 연락할 계획이다.
(B) 최근에 Chennai University를 그만두었다.
(C) 자신의 연구가 저널에 실리도록 했다.
(D) Li 씨의 행사에 참가하는 데 동의했다.

185 IBS Consulting에 관해 나타난 것이 아닌 것은?

(A) 예산 변경을 허용하지 않는다.
(B) 해외 행사들에 직원들을 보낸다.
(C) 한 대학교와의 제휴 관계를 추구하고 있다.
(D) 일주일에 한 번 직원회의를 연다.

신유형 ▶ 186-190은 다음 웹 페이지들을 참조하시오.

http://roxburyinstitute.com/classes

홈	강좌	등록	후기	연락처

Roxbury Institute의 미술 강좌: 6월

Roxbury Institute는 Maryville의 미술계에 새로 추가된 곳으로, 불과 몇 주 만에 이미 인기를 얻고 있습니다. 저희 강사들은 주당 한 강좌만을 가르칩니다. 저희는 참가자들이 다양한 기술을 배울 수 있도록 매달 다른 강좌들을 제공합니다.

풍경 수채화: 매주 월요일 오후 7:00-9:00 / 강사: Donald Bernier

학생들은 사진을 가이드로 활용해 풍경들을 재현하게 됩니다. Donald Bernier는 학생들의 수준에 상관없이 적용될 수 있는 실제 그림 기법들을 보여줄 것입니다.

유화 초상화: 매주 화요일 오후 6:30-8:30 / 강사: Geneva Winters
초상화에 개인의 특성을 담는 일은 즐거운 도전이며, Geneva Winters가 자신의 전문 지식을 이용해 그렇게 하도록 도움을 드릴 것입니다. 등록하려면 유화 기초 또는 동등한 강좌를 반드시 수강해야 한다는 것을 유념해 주시기 바랍니다.

명암과 색채 혼합: 매주 수요일 오후 6:30-8:30 / 강사: Chantel Hernandez
이 강좌는 특히 초보자들에게 도움이 되지만, 모든 수준의 화가들이 이 필수 기법들을 연습함으로써 각자의 결과물을 향상시킬 수 있습니다.

사생화: 매주 목요일 오후 7:00-9:00 / 강사: James Roble
동물과 꽃에서부터 산과 시내에 이르기까지, 자연은 참가자들에게 영감을 줄 끝없는 가능성을 가지고 있습니다. 최종 프로젝트들은 Hadley Gallery에서 열리는 지역 사회 전시회에 포함될 것입니다.

National Arts Association의 회원들은 25퍼센트의 할인을 받을 것입니다.

등록하려면 여기를 클릭하세요!

http://roxburyinstitute.com/register

홈	강좌	**등록**	후기	연락처

등록일: 5월 19일　　　수강기간: 6월
학생: Cynthia Morton　　이메일: c.morton@crmpost.net
National Arts Association의 회원이신가요? 아니오

강좌 설명	수강 날짜	등록비
풍경 수채화	6월 5일, 12일, 19일, 26일	89달러
사생화	6월 8일, 15일, 22일, 29일	112달러

비용이 수납되는 대로, 이메일로 확인 코드를 받을 것입니다. 이 코드를 강좌 첫날 강사에게 제시해 주시기 바랍니다.

http://roxburyinstitute.com/reviews

홈	강좌	등록	**후기**	연락처

후기 작성자 Cynthia Morton / 게시일, 7월 5일

저는 Roxbury Institute에서 들었던 그림 강좌에 대해 대단히 만족했습니다. 이 취미를 시작한 지 얼마 되지 않았는데, 제 강사님들 둘 다 박식하시고 인내심이 많다는 것을 알았습니다. Donald Bernier는 특히 강좌에 열정적이셨습니다. 그는 확실히 미술에 깊은 애정이 있고, 더불어 그것을 다른 이들과 공유하는 재능도 있습니다.

Roble 씨의 강좌에 약 50명의 사람들이 있을 것이라는 사실을 알았을 때, 개별적인 관심을 많이 받지 못할 것으로 생각했습니다. 하지만 저에게는 개별적인 그림 작업과 강사의 피드백을 받는 것 사이의 균형이 완벽했습니다. 다음 달, 저는 다른 강좌에 등록할 계획이며, 함께 다닐 제 친구들을 모으려고도 합니다.

186 Roxbury Institute에 관해 알 수 있는 것이 아닌 것은?

(A) 매달 강좌를 변경한다.
(B) 최근에 문을 열었다.
(C) 대량 할인을 제공한다.
(D) 강사들이 시간제로 근무한다.

187 어떤 강좌가 이전의 경험이 필요한가?

(A) 풍경 수채화

(B) 유화 초상화

(C) 명암과 색채 혼합

(D) 사생화

188 Morton 씨에 관해 사실일 것 같은 것은 무엇인가?

(A) 초상화에 관해 더 배우는 것에 관심이 있다.

(B) 자신의 작품을 공개적으로 전시할 기회가 있었다.

(C) 25퍼센트의 할인을 받을 자격이 있었다.

(D) Hernandez 씨가 가르치는 강좌에 등록했다.

189 Morton 씨는 자신의 후기에서 무슨 말을 했는가?

(A) 풍경 수채화 강좌에 사람이 너무 많았다.

(B) 사생화 강좌는 예상했던 것보다 더 어려웠다.

(C) 풍경 수채화 강좌의 강사가 열정적이었다.

(D) 사생화 강좌는 전문가가 가르쳤다.

190 Morton 씨는 8월에 무엇을 할 것이라고 말하는가?

(A) 같은 강사들과 다시 한 번 작업할 것이다.

(B) 친구들에게 강좌 수강을 권장할 것이다.

(C) 두 개의 그림 강좌들을 등록할 것이다.

(D) 학원에 관한 또 다른 후기를 게시할 것이다.

신유형 191-195는 다음 두 이메일과 첨부 자료를 참조하시오.

수신: Jia Bansal, Timothy Reeves, Genji Taihei

발신: Lara Strehlow

날짜: 11월 4일

제목: 연회

첨부: venue_details.dox

안녕하세요 여러분,

11월 2일에 Spirit Café에서 한 회의 중에 우리 회사의 기념일 파티 계획에 관한 일을 진척시켜서 좋았습니다. 우리 회사가 출간했던 소설들을 쓰신 몇몇 작가들을 만날 수 있을 것이기 때문에 저는 이번 행사를 고대하고 있습니다. 파티 기획 서비스를 이용하지 않기로 결정한 것이 기쁜데, 우리가 적은 비용으로 직접 준비할 수 있기 때문입니다. 약속대로, 제가 도시 전역에 여러 장소 소유주들과 이야기했고 첨부된 문서에 최고 선택 사항들을 요약해 놓았습니다. 어느 곳이 우리 목적에 가장 적합한지 결정할 수 있도록 그것을 검토해 주시기 바랍니다. 우리가 모두 요즘 바쁘기 때문에, 11월 19일까지는 다시 직접 만나지 않을 것입니다. 하지만 그동안에 이메일로 아이디어들을 공유할 수 있습니다.

힘냅시다.

Lara Strehlow, Doyle Incorporated

Hatton Hall / 공항 근처에 있는 현대적인 건물인 Hatton Hall에는 손님들을 위한 많은 무료 지하 주차 공간이 있습니다. 본관이 최근에 최신 음향 시스템을 갖추게 되었고, 그 서비스에 대해 최고의 평가를 받았습니다. 본관 대여 비용: 1,950달러

The Lexington / The Lexington 옥상 테라스에서 도심의 환상적인 경관을 볼 수 있고, 그곳은 대여가 가능합니다. 공항에서 차로 아주 가까운 거리에 있습니다. 날씨가 추울 경우 외부에 이동 가능한 히터가 설치될 수 있습니다. 옥상 테라스 대여 비용: 1,600달러

Morgan Plaza / Morgan Plaza는 야간 투숙객들을 위한 넓은 객실들이 있고 공항에서 불과 몇 분 거리에 떨어져 있습니다. 그랜드 홀은 넓은 무대뿐만 아니라 아름다운 나무 공예품을 특징으로 하며, 무대는 그

장소에서 무료로 장식해 줄 수 있습니다. 그랜드 홀 대여 비용: 1,800달러

Wakefield Center / 시내에 위치한 Wakefield Center는 Riley Street Mall을 오가는 무료 셔틀버스 서비스를 제공합니다. 상층부에는 야간 투숙객들을 위한 객실들이 있고 건물 내에서 열리는 행사에 참석하는 고객들을 위해 할인된 요금을 제공합니다. 중앙 연회장 대여 비용: 1,750달러

수신: Jia Bansal, Timothy Reeves, Lara Strehlow

발신: Genji Taihei

날짜: 11월 5일

제목: 회신: 연회

위원회 동료 위원 여러분,

최근 Spirit Café에서의 회의에 참석하지 못해 죄송합니다. 그곳에 갈 계획이었지만, 매우 유망한 고객과의 계약을 논의하느라 San Francisco에 있었고, 집으로 돌아오는 항공편이 몇 시간 지연되었습니다. Lara, 이 유용한 목록을 준비해 줘서 고마워요. 마침내 그것을 살펴볼 시간이 좀 있었습니다. 다른 분들은 장소에 관하여 어떻게 생각하시는지 모르겠지만, 저는 공항 근처에 있는 장소를 선택하는 것이 좋을 것 같습니다. 많은 참석자들이 다른 지역에서 비행기를 타고 오실 것이며, 도착해서 멀리 이동하는 것을 원치 않으실 것입니다. 추가로, 그들 대부분은 야간 숙박을 하셔야 하니 숙박 시설도 제공하는 장소로 하는 것이 최선이라고 생각합니다. 여러분들의 생각을 듣고 싶습니다.

다양한 항목들(장소, 음식, 그리고 장식물)에 대한 가격 견적을 보내 주셔서 여러분 모두에게 감사드립니다. 또한, Timothy, 초대장 작업을 위해 당신이 추천해 줬던 그래픽 디자이너의 전화번호가 아직 필요합니다. 11월 19일 회의 때까지 샘플 작업이 완료되었으면 합니다.

감사합니다!

Genji

191 Strehlow 씨는 어디에서 일할 것 같은가?

(A) 금융 기관에서

(B) 출판사에서

(C) 커피숍에서

(D) 파티 기획 서비스 업체에서

192 장소들 중 한 곳에서 제공되는 편의시설로 언급된 것은 무엇인가?

(A) 붙박이 좌석 공간

(B) 건물 내 식당 시설

(C) 현대식 보안 시스템

(D) 무료 교통 서비스

193 Taihei 씨는 11월 2일에 무엇을 했는가?

(A) 위원회를 임명했음

(B) 출장에서 돌아왔음

(C) 장소를 견학했음

(D) 일부 계약서들을 제자리에 두지 않았음

194 Taihei 씨는 어느 장소를 선택할 것 같은가?

(A) Hatton Hall

(B) The Lexington

(C) Morgan Plaza

(D) Wakefield Center

195 Reeves 씨에 관해 알 수 있는 것은 무엇인가?

(A) 다음 회의에 참석하지 않을 것이다.

(B) Taihei 씨에게 몇 가지 수치를 보냈다.

(C) 그래픽 디자이너로 일하고 있다.

(D) Strehlow 씨와 함께 몇몇 장소를 방문했다.

신유형 196-200은 다음 웹 페이지와 이메일, 그리고 공지를 참조하시오.

Cerda National Park: 크로스컨트리 스키 코스

Arrowhead 코스 / 난도: 초급 / 길이: 9.3마일
평평한 지형으로 인해 이 코스는 초보자들에게 훌륭한 곳입니다. 이 코스는 과거 군사 진지였던 Fort Robinson을 지나갈 뿐만 아니라 아름다운 숲속의 경치를 가로지르는 곳입니다.

Prairie 코스 / 난도: 중급 / 길이: 18.1마일
이 코스는 가파른 경사가 포함되어 있지만, 코스에서 보는 White Lake의 경관은 시도해 볼 만한 가치가 충분히 있습니다.

Bell Valley 코스 / 난도: 중급 / 길이: 15.8마일
현재 야생 동물 보호 구역과의 근접성 덕택에, 우리의 가장 인기 있는 코스가 되었습니다. 피크닉용 쉼터가 코스 동쪽 방면에 위치해 있고, 방문객께서는 쓰레기를 모두 수거해 가야 함을 명심하시기 바랍니다.

Harmony 코스 / 난도: 고급 / 길이: 19.4마일
이 코스는 고급 장대 사용과 회전 능력을 요구하므로, 숙련된 스키어들에게만 추천됩니다. 문제가 발생할 경우, 공원 관리소는 코스를 따라가다 보면 나오는 Mile 7에 있습니다.

수신: 동호회 회원들 〈members@ccskiclub.org〉
발신: Lawrence Agan 〈lawrencea@ccskiclub.org〉
날짜: 12월 3일
제목: 스키 활동

크로스커트리 동호회 회원 여러분께,

우리의 다음 스키 활동을 위한 장소로 Cerda National Park를 선정했으며, 이번 활동은 12월 8일 토요일에 있을 예정입니다. 많은 분들께서 지난달의 코스가 너무 쉬웠다는 의견을 주셔서, 이번에는, 중급 코스를 이용할 것입니다. Cerda National Park에 이용 가능한 두 코스가 있는데, 활동 당일에 어느 곳이 더 나은지 결정할 수 있습니다. 우리는 오전 9시에 방문객 센터에서 만날 것입니다. 공원에서 오후 3시나 4시 정도까지 머물 예정이니, 반드시 각자 도시락과 간식을 가져오시기 바랍니다.

여러분 모두 뵙기를 고대합니다!

Lawrence

공지

낙석으로 초래된 안전 위험 문제로 인해, Prairie 코스는 남은 겨울 시즌 동안 폐쇄됩니다. 암석들이 치워지고 그 구역이 안전하다고 여겨지면 봄에 다시 개장될 것인데, 그 후에는 일 년 중 남은 기간 동안 개장된 상태를 유지할 것으로 예상됩니다. 적색 표지판이 코스의 시작점을 나타냅니다. 이 지점 너머는 출입이 허용되지 않습니다. 더 많은 정보를 위해, 공원의 서쪽 출입구 근처에 위치한 방문객 센터에 들르시기 바랍니다.

12월 6일부터 시행됨

196 스키어들이 가장 긴 코스를 따라가다 방문할 수 있는 곳은 무엇인가?

(A) 공원 관리소

(B) 호수

(C) 피크닉 쉼터

(D) 군사 지역

197 동호회는 어느 코스를 이용할 것 같은가?

(A) Arrowhead 코스

(B) Prairie 코스

(C) Bell Valley 코스

(D) Harmony 코스

198 Cerda National Park에 관해 알 수 있는 것은 무엇인가?

(A) 일 년 내내 문을 연다.

(B) 새로운 코스를 지을 것이다.

(C) 스키 강습을 제공한다.

(D) 입장료를 부과한다.

199 공지에서, 첫 번째 단락, 다섯 번째 줄의 단어 "point"와 의미가 가장 가까운 것은 무엇인가?

(A) 특징

(B) 목적

(C) 위치

(D) 아이디어

200 동호회는 12월 8일에 어디에서 만날 것인가?

(A) 코스 시작 지점 근처

(B) 중앙 출입구에서

(C) 서쪽 출입구 근처

(D) 주차장에서

TEST 06 해석

PART 5

101 Yang 씨는 자신과 같은 소비자들이 몇몇 장소에서 불공평하게 대우를 받고 있었기 때문에 지역 사업체들의 등급을 매기는 웹사이트를 개발했다.

102 프로 농구 선수인 Bryan Jones는 최근 Bevelia Athletic Shoes를 5년 동안 홍보하는 데 합의하는 계약서에 서명했다.

103 신중한 계획 덕분에, 상당한 경기 침체가 지속된 기간 동안 Hiltz-Steen Inc.의 재정은 놀랍게도 안정적인 상태로 유지되었다.

104 Bain Capital은 자사 고객들의 불만 사항들을 신속히 처리함으로써 좋은 평판을 얻어 왔다.

105 정문 근처에 있는 고객 서비스 데스크가 모든 반품 및 교환 업무를 처리한다.

106 3개월마다, Ralph Electronics Corporation은 각 부서장에게 직원 업무 능력 평가를 실시하고 보고서를 제출하도록 요구한다.

107 대부분의 소비자들은 HG Electronics의 새로운 평면 TV의 가격이 비교적 낮다는 말을 듣고 놀랐다.

108 온라인 마케팅 계획에 대한 새로운 제안서가 승인을 받는 대로, 부서장이 외부 디자인 업체를 고용할 것이다.

109 HT Corporation 직원 수의 감소는 주로 회사가 더 나은 혜택을 제공하지 못한 것의 결과였다.

110 어떤 사소한 제품 결함이라도 있는 상품은 할인된 가격에 제공되어야 하며 재고 정리 코너에 있어야 한다.

111 일단 매장에서 제품들의 완전한 재고 조사를 확고히 해 두면, 주기적으로 재고를 업데이트하는 것이 꽤 쉬울 것이다.

112 컨설턴트로 구성된 팀이 회사의 회계 기록을 철저히 검토한 끝에 결국 실수를 발견했다.

113 최근 개업한 이탈리안 레스토랑인 La Ciccia의 사장은 주 반대편에 위치한 Durham 지역에 두 번째 지점이 곧 영업을 시작할 것이라고 말했다.

114 팀장이 보낸 체크리스트는 최종 검토자가 문서에 모든 상세 정보가 포함되어 있는지를 확인하는 데 도움이 될 수 있다.

115 Sunset Beach 인근에 편리하게 위치한 Heaven Resort는 최고의 여행지 중 하나로 널리 알려져 있다.

116 Filomena Books는 제품이 재고로 남아 있는 동안 팸플릿에 기재되어 있는 가격에서 50퍼센트 할인을 제공하고 있다.

117 기술 콘퍼런스에 참가하는 마케팅 팀이 컴퓨터 보안 소프트웨어의 가장 최신 라인을 홍보하기 위해 종합적인 발표를 준비할 것이다.

118 몇 달의 공사 끝에, 리모델링 프로젝트가 마지막 단계에 있으며 다음 주에 완료될 예정이다.

119 밤 10시 이후에 지불된 비용은 저희가 다음 날 영업을 위해 문을 열 때까지 대금 청구서에 나타나지 않을 수 있습니다.

120 지난달에, 지역 회사인 Birdwell Inc.는 통신 기술 발전에 대한 뛰어난 기여로 인해 상을 받았다.

121 J&T Enterprises의 연간 영업 수치 목표는 서비스 품질에 대한 직원들의 헌신으로 인해 이미 초과되었다.

122 ACN Co. 소속의 직원들은 업계 전문가들이 매일 진행한 대부분의 활동들과 프로그램들이 매우 매력적이라고 생각했다.

123 보안상의 이유로, 인사부는 개인으로부터 서명을 받은 공개 동의서 없이는 제 3자에게 어떠한 개인의 신상 정보도 유출하지 않을 것이다.

124 규칙적인 운동은 매우 추천되는데, 특히 대부분의 시간을 책상에 앉아 일하는 데 보내는 사무직 종사자들에게 그렇다.

125 Franz Daily Deli는 여름 휴가 시즌 동안에 높아진 수요를 감당하기 위해 추가로 3명의 웨이터를 고용할 것이다.

126 Keller Institute는 Jackson Foundation으로부터 많은 보조금을 받았기 때문에, 앞으로 몇 달 안에 더 많은 연구원들을 채용할 계획이다.

127 세금 인상에 합의하도록 지역 주민들을 설득하기 위한 여러 번의 시도가 있었지만, 한 번도 성공하지 못했다.

128 Froth Beverages Inc.는 아시아와 유럽 지역으로 자사의 존재를 확장하기 위해 현재 국제 시장 전문가들과 협업하고 있다.

129 근무 일정이 알맞게 조정될 수 있도록 Kennedy 씨에게 이번 여름에 떠나는 휴가 계획을 알려 주시기 바랍니다.

130 Newmont Tech가 개발한 새로운 온라인 게임 시리즈는 다양한 연령대의 사람들에게 홍보되고 있다.

PART 6

신유형▶ 131-134는 다음 소책자를 참조하시오.

Galington-Ling Partners는 고급 주택 시장에서 세계적으로 유명한 회사입니다. 저희 회사의 전문 건축 설계사들은 규모와 스타일을 하나의 도면 안에 통합하는 데 전문가들입니다.

여러분들께서 필요로 하시는 것이 크든 작든, 정교한 것이든 단순한 것이든 상관없이, 저희 전문가들은 여러분의 만족을 보장해 드릴 수 있습니다. 919-736-4291로 전화하셔서 예약 일정을 잡으시기 바랍니다. 저희 컨설턴트가 필요한 모든 정보와 견적을 제공해 드릴 것이며, 절차의 모든 단계를 안내해 드릴 것입니다.

신유형▶ 135-138은 다음 이메일을 참조하시오.

수신: Cody Black, 현장 감독
발신: Darrel Reagan, 안전 관리부
날짜: 3월 12일
제목: 회신: 장비 점검

Black 씨께,

C2 창고 내에 있는 온도 측정기에 관한 귀하의 우려 사항에 대해 안전 관리부에 연락 주셔서 감사합니다. 저희 팀이 그 문제를 조사해 보았습니다.

이 측정기는 신선한 농산물을 적절하게 보관하는 데 필요한 설정보다 훨씬 더 높은 온도를 나타내고 있었습니다. 문제는 있어 보였지만, 측정기는 작동하고 있는 것으로 판명되었습니다. 측정기는 냉장 시스템에 문제가 될 수 있는 것을 제대로 감지하고 있습니다.

그럼에도 불구하고, 기술자들은 왜 냉각 시스템이 제대로 작동하지 않는지를 파악하기 위해 테스트하고 있습니다. 그러는 동안, 모든 부패성 품목들을 C2 창고 밖으로 옮겨 주시기 바랍니다.

협조해 주셔서 감사합니다.

안녕히 계십시오.
Darrel Reagan

신유형▶ 139-142는 다음 편지를 참조하시오.

6월 3일

Peralta 씨께,

5월 28일에 제품을 구매해 주셔서 감사합니다. Steel and Stone Hardware는 귀하의 거래와 관련된 비판들뿐만 아니라, 여러분의 모든 문의 사항을 소중히 여깁니다.

저희는 언제나 고객들의 관점을 최우선으로 생각합니다.

이러한 이유로, 간략한 설문 조사를 작성하시어 저희 제품이나 서비스, 가격, 그리고 그 외의 귀하께서 경험하신 질에 관련된 여러 가지 요소들에 대해 귀하의 의견을 말씀해 주시기를 요청 드립니다.

이 설문 조사는 저희 회사의 장점은 향상시키고 단점을 파악하는 것을 돕기 위해 고안되었습니다. 가장 중요한 점은, 이 조사에 대한 귀하의 답변이 고객들께서 원하시는 수준의 서비스를 받을 수 있게 해줄 것입니다. 귀하의 의견에 미리 감사의 말씀을 드립니다.

안녕히 계십시오.
Steel and Stone Hardware

신유형 143-146은 다음 편지를 참조하시오.

내부 지원자

St. Luke's National Real Estate와 같은 대기업에서 일하는 것의 한 가지 장점은 1년 후 해외 전근이나 승진을 요청할 수 있는 자격이 주어진다는 것입니다. 관심 있는 사람들은 회사의 내부 전산망에서 공석을 찾을 수 있습니다. 내부 지원자들은 외부 지원자보다 꼭 우선 선발되는 것은 아닙니다. 그러나 만약 그 직책에 자격을 갖추셨다면, 내부 지원자들은 항상 특혜를 받을 것입니다.

PART 7

147-148은 다음 수료증을 참조하시오.

이 수료증은 4월 26일에 "재정 분야의 윤리: 거래의 공정한 관행에 대한 원칙"이라는 제목으로 Stansfield Professional Institute에서 진행된 일련의 워크숍에 Rachel Torsten 씨가 참가했음을 증명합니다. 강좌 후 실시된 테스트에서 86점을 기록해, 기관의 등급 시스템에 따라 '매우 우수함' 등급을 획득하였습니다.

Daniel Payet
Daniel Payet, 워크숍 지도자
Stansfield Professional Institute

147 Torsten 씨는 4월 26일에 무엇을 했는가?
(A) 그녀는 워크숍을 진행했다.
(B) 그녀는 강좌에 참석했다.
(C) 그녀는 교사 직책에 지원했다.
(D) 그녀는 호텔에서 체크아웃했다.

148 Torsten 씨는 누구일 것 같은가?
(A) 운동선수
(B) 컴퓨터 교수
(C) 증권 중개인
(D) 부동산 개발업자

149-150은 다음 공지를 참조하시오.

한 달에 한 번, 〈The Bartlett Journal〉은 세 페이지 분량의 "Bartlett

Looks Back" 칼럼에 사용하기 위해 제출된 오래된 사진들을 특집으로 싣습니다. 이 월간 특집 코너는 우리 지역 주민들에 의해 기록된 우리 시의 역사 속 순간들을 기념합니다.

시의 역사 속에서 주목할 만한 장소나 행사를 담은 40년보다 더 오래 전에 찍힌 사진들이 특히 관심의 대상입니다.

사진은 이메일 주소 jencook@bartlettjournal.com을 통해 Jennifer Cook 씨에게 제출하시면 됩니다. 사람들의 이름과 장소, 그리고 대략적인 날짜 등을 포함해 가능한 한 사진에 관한 많은 정보를 제공해 주시기 바랍니다. 사진은 늦어도 출간되는 달의 두 번째 금요일까지는 반드시 제출되어야 합니다. 우리 신문에 실리는 모든 사진들은 흑백으로 인쇄된다는 점에 유의하시기 바랍니다.

149 이 공지는 누구를 대상으로 하는 것인가?
(A) 잡지 편집자들
(B) 역사학 저자들
(C) 지역 유명 인사들
(D) Bartlett 지역 주민들

150 〈The Bartlett Journal〉이 제출된 것을 언제 거절할 것인가?
(A) 발신인이 컬러 사진을 제출할 때
(B) 제출되는 것이 세 페이지보다 적을 때
(C) 제출 마감일이 지났을 때
(D) 발신인이 개인 정보를 공유할 때

신유형 151-152는 다음 문자 메시지 대화를 참조하시오.

Tariq Jha 오후 2:07
이세 공항에 노착했나요? 예성보나 늦게 사무실에서 나가는 바람에 택시를 타셔야 했던 것으로 알고 있어요.

Valarie Cortez 오후 2:09
약 10분 정도면 도착할 수 있을 것 같아서 어렵지 않게 비행기를 탈 수 있을 거예요.

Tariq Jha 오후 2:10
그 말씀을 들으니 다행이네요.

Valarie Cortez 오후 2:11
Parsons Co.에서 보내 온 계약서는 택배 회사가 배송해 주었나요?

Tariq Jha 오후 2:13
네, 막 도착했습니다. 그런데, 이 서류를 어떻게 해야 할지 모르겠어요.

Valarie Cortez 오후 2:15
Cynthia 씨에게 주세요. 그분이 그 일을 처리하고 있었거든요.

151 Cortez 씨는 현재 어디에 있을 것 같은가?
(A) 사무실에
(B) 택시에
(C) 공항에
(D) 버스에

152 오후 2시 15분에, Cortez 씨가 "She was handling it"이라고 **신유형** 썼을 때 의미하는 것은 무엇인가?
(A) Cynthia 씨가 Cortez 씨를 위해 출장 계획을 짰다.
(B) Cynthia 씨가 서류에 실수를 했을 수도 있다.
(C) Cynthia 씨가 Parsons Co.와 관련된 일처리에 익숙하다.
(D) Cynthia 씨가 배송 비용 지불에 대해 후속 조치를 할 것이다.

153-154는 다음 이메일을 참조하시오.

수신: b.cooper@bcauto.net
발신: terrypritchard@quickmail.com
날짜: 10월 2일
제목: 수리 작업

Bradley 씨께,

저희는 회사의 차량들 중 한 대를 지난주에 귀하로부터 가져왔으며, 그 이후로는 작동이 잘 되어왔습니다. 하지만 오늘 오후에 워크숍에 그 차를 몰고 가려고 했을 때, 시동이 걸리지 않더니 계기판에 몇몇 오류 표시등이 깜빡였습니다. 사용 설명서에 따르면, 이는 오일이 교환되어야 하며, 엔진의 일부가 교환을 필요로 한다는 것을 가리킵니다. 저는 가능한 한 신속히 이 문제가 해결되기를 진심으로 바라고 있는데, 회사 보유 차량들 중의 한 대가 오랫동안 사용되지 못한다면 상당한 비용 손실이 발생할 것이기 때문입니다. 오늘 수리 작업을 해 주실 수 있으신가요? 신속한 서비스를 보장해 주신다면 추가 비용을 지불할 용의가 있습니다.

안녕히 계십시오.

Terry Pritchard
Terry Pritchard

153 이메일의 목적은 무엇인가?

(A) 차량 가격을 협의하기
(B) 서비스를 요청하기
(C) 사용 설명서를 주문하기
(D) 워크숍 일정을 정하기

154 Cooper 씨에 관해 알 수 있는 것은 무엇인가?

(A) 그는 회사에 지각을 했다.
(B) 그는 조명 부품들을 제공한다.
(C) 그는 지난 청구서에 실수를 했다.
(D) 그는 정비공이다.

신유형 ▶ 155-157은 다음 공지를 참조하시오.

승객 여러분께 알립니다.

Atlantic Airlines의 항공권을 구매해 주셔서 감사합니다. 체크인하시기 전에, 다음 사항들에 유의해 주십시오.

– 승객들은 20킬로그램을 넘지 않는 가방 하나만 체크인하는 것이 허용됩니다. 추가로 가방을 체크인하시거나 허용 무게를 초과하는 분들은 체크인 시 정해진 요금의 부과 대상이 됩니다. — [1] —.

– 승객들은 기내에 하나의 휴대용 가방을 들고 탑승하실 수 있습니다. — [2] —. 인화성 물질이나 무기류는 어떤 휴대용 가방 안에도 넣고 탑승하실 수 없습니다. — [3] —. 휴대용 가방은 Atlantic Airlines의 직원에 의해 탑승 전에 확인될 것이며, 불법이거나 허용되지 않은 물품은 압수될 것입니다. — [4] —.

문의 사항이 있으신 분은 1-888-555-4094로 전화하시어 새로운 자동 응답 시스템을 이용하시기 바랍니다. 삐 소리 후에 5번을 누르시면, 연결됩니다.

Atlantic Airlines를 이용해 주셔서 감사합니다.

155 공지의 목적은 무엇인가?

(A) 예약 취소 방법을 설명하기
(B) 몇몇 새로운 무게 규제를 공표하기
(C) 회사의 정책을 개괄적으로 설명하기
(D) 항공사의 최신 노선을 홍보하기

156 승객들은 왜 돈을 더 지불할 수도 있는가?

(A) 탑승 두 시간 전에 체크인하지 못했기 때문에
(B) 휴대용 가방에 불법 물품들을 가지고 있기 때문에
(C) 두 가지 수하물을 체크인하기 때문에
(D) 휴대용 가방에 대한 무게 제한을 초과했기 때문에

157 [1], [2], [3], [4]로 표기된 위치들 중에서 다음 문장이 가장 잘 어
신유형 울리는 곳은 어디인가?

"이것은 노트북 가방과 배낭을 포함하지만 각 승객들은 지갑이나 핸드백도 가지고 탑승하실 수 있습니다."

(A) [1]
(B) [2]
(C) [3]
(D) [4]

신유형 ▶ 158-161은 다음 온라인 채팅을 참조하시오.

Renee Alocer 오후 2:24
커피 드실 분 있으세요? Café Reno에 한 잔 값에 두 잔을 주는 라떼가 있어요. 제가 곧 주문할 거예요.

Fiona Brown 오후 2:25
네, 저요!

Kenneth Graham 오후 2:26
저도 한 잔 할게요.

Oliver Whitworth 오후 2:26
저는 괜찮습니다.

Fiona Brown 오후 2:28
Kenneth, 오후 회의에 마실 것을 가져가도 문제가 되지 않죠, 맞죠?

Kenneth Graham 오후 2:31
미리 마셔 두는 게 좋을 거예요. 제가 새 보안 장비를 시연할 예정이라서 거기서 음료를 쏟는 일이 생기면 안 돼요.

Fiona Brown 오후 2:32
알겠습니다. 여러분 모두 회의에 가시죠?

Renee Alocer 오후 2:33
물론이죠. 선택의 여지가 없잖아요.

Oliver Whitworth 오후 2:35
Kenneth, 당신이 발표하는 거예요? 저는 Larry 씨가 하는 줄 알았는데요.

Kenneth Graham 오후 2:37
Larry 씨가 올 수 없다고 해서 마지막 순간에 Larry 씨를 대신해 달라고 요청받았어요.

Fiona Brown 오후 2:38
아, 그렇군요. 제가 듣기로는 어제 아프셔서 일찍 퇴근하셨다고 하더라고요. 도움이 필요한 일이 있으신가요?

Kenneth Graham 오후 2:39
Larry 씨가 이미 슬라이드 쇼 발표를 준비해 두셨어요. 하지만 제 사원증을 쓸 수 없기 때문에 시스템을 시연해 보이기 위해서는 누군가의 사원증을 빌려야 해요. 제가 보안팀 소속이라서 사원증이 다르게 반응하더라고요.

Renee Alocer 오후 2:41
제 것을 사용하셔도 돼요. 미리 빌려 드릴까요?

Kenneth Graham 오후 2:42
아뇨, 그냥 회의 장소로 가져 오시기만 하면 됩니다. 감사합니다!

158 오후 2시 25분에, Brown 씨가 "Yes, please"라고 썼을 때 의미
신유형 하는 것은 무엇인가?

(A) 쿠폰을 사용할 것이다.
(B) 음료를 한 잔 마시고 싶어 한다.
(C) Alocer 씨와 함께 갈 것이다.
(D) 몇몇 사무용품이 필요하다.

159 오후 회의에 관해 암시된 것은 무엇인가?

(A) 신입 사원을 소개할 것이다.
(B) 마지막 순간에 일정이 잡혔다.
(C) 직원들에게 의무적인 일이다.
(D) Whitworth 씨에 의해 진행될 것이다.

160 Larry 씨에 관해 알 수 있는 것은 무엇인가?

(A) 오늘 결근했다.
(B) 시스템을 설치하고 있다.
(C) 사무실에 일찍 도착했다.
(D) 발표 파일을 분실했다.

161 누구의 사원증이 발표에서 사용될 것인가?

(A) Alocer 씨의 것
(B) Brown 씨의 것
(C) Graham 씨의 것
(D) Whitworth 씨의 것

162-164는 다음 광고를 참조하시오.

Connect Media: 세상과의 연결

여러분의 회사를 위해 전문적인 웹사이트를 제공하는 데 숙련된 전문가를 찾고 계십니까? 그렇다면, 외식 업계를 대상으로 메뉴와 재료, 영업 시간 및 예약 상세 사항 등과 같은 정보들을 포함한 고급 웹사이트를 제작하는 것을 전문으로 하는 디자인 회사, Connect Media의 서비스를 받아 보시는 것은 어떠십니까?

저희 Connect Media는 지역 내에 있는 40곳 이상의 업체에 고급 인터페이스를 제작했으며, 이전의 고객들로부터 많은 호의적인 사용 후기를 받아 왔습니다. 이달 말까지 저희 서비스를 요청하거나 1년 넘게 저희 서비스를 이용하시는 고객들은 20퍼센트의 할인을 받으실 수 있습니다.

www.connectmedia.net을 방문하셔서 시작해 보세요. 이곳에서, 귀하께서는 색상 배치를 선택하고 고객 후기를 읽어보실 수 있으며, 서비스 신청 비용을 지불하실 수 있습니다.

다음 사항에 유의하세요. 사이트에 넣으실 서면으로 된 내용을 저희에게 제공해 주셔야 합니다. 이를 직접 제공해 주실 수 없다고 생각되시는 분들은 저희 회사의 내부 필자의 도움을 요청하실 수 있고, 555-3920-4225로 연락이 가능하며, 시간당 30달러의 비용이 청구됩니다.

162 이 광고는 누구를 대상으로 할 가능성이 큰가?

(A) 전문 작가들
(B) 인터넷 블로거들
(C) 재정 고문들
(D) 레스토랑 매니저들

163 Connect Media에 관해 알 수 있는 것은 무엇인가?

(A) 잘 알려진 요리 학교이다.
(B) 1년 약정을 필요로 한다.
(C) 판촉 행사를 진행하고 있다.
(D) 40명의 직원을 고용하고 있다.

164 Connect Media의 웹사이트에서 할 수 있는 일로 언급되지 않은 것은 무엇인가?

(A) 예약하는 것
(B) 고객 이용 후기를 읽어보는 것
(C) 비용을 지불하는 것
(D) 선호하는 색상을 선택하는 것

165-167은 다음 초청장을 참조하시오.

운영팀에서 다음 직원을 기리는 행사에 여러분의 참석을 바랍니다.

Dean Lewis 씨

Capital Automotive의 부장으로서
그의 기록적인 영업 수치를 축하합니다.

9월 19일, 금요일
Pinetree Hotel Ballroom
Pine Valley
Massachusetts 84932

오후 7시 연회
오후 8시 연설 및 축배
오후 8시 30분 DJ Turquoise와 함께 하는 디스코

선물 대신에, Lewis 씨는 불우한 아이들을 위한 Bexley 기금에 대한 기부금이 더 의미 있을 것이라고 말씀하셨습니다.

555-3455-2214나 ysetts@capital.com으로 가능한 한 빨리 영업 보조 직원인 Yvonne Setts 씨에게 회신 바랍니다.

165 행사의 목적은 무엇인가?

(A) 일부 직원들을 교육하기
(B) 호텔의 개장을 축하하기
(C) 한 직원의 업적을 치하하기
(D) 승진을 기념하기

166 손님들은 무엇을 하도록 권고받는가?

(A) 선물을 가져올 것
(B) 자선 단체에 기부할 것
(C) 깔끔하게 차려 입을 것
(D) 선금을 지불할 것

167 Setts 씨에 관해 알 수 있는 것은 무엇인가?

(A) Capital Automotive에 고용된 직원이다.
(B) 파트 타임 DJ이다.
(C) Lewis 씨의 보조이다.
(D) 새로운 이메일 주소를 가지고 있다.

신유형 ▶ 168-171은 다음 이메일을 참조하시오.

수신: John Heyward
발신: Wilma Caraway
제목: 귀하의 주문
날짜: 3월 27일

Heyward 씨께,

귀하께서 방금 보내주신 이메일에 대해 감사 드립니다. 저희 Simpson's Sporting Goods는 고객의 소리를 듣는 것을 기뻐하고 있으며, 가능한 모든 방법을 통해 고객 여러분을 돕기 위해 최선을 다하고 있습니다. — [1] —.

귀하의 이메일에 따르면, 귀하께서 최근에 주문하신 물품에 문제가 있었습니다. 귀하께서는 제품 번호 495-RRE3(오른손잡이용 야구 글러브)과 제품 번호 302-WAW2(32온스 야구 배트)를 구입하셨다고 써 주셨습니다. 하지만 32온스 야구 배트 대신에, 귀하께서는 무게가 30온스인 제품을 받으셨습니다. — [2] —. 안타깝게도, 주문하신 두 가지 물품에 대해 비용이 청구됨과 동시에, 귀하께서 원하시지 않는 배트 제품에 대해서도 추가로 비용 청구가 되었습니다.

귀하께서 주문하셨던 배트를 특별 배송 서비스를 이용해 오늘 아침 일찍 보내 드렸으므로 오늘 저녁쯤이면 해당 물품을 받아 보실 수 있습니다. — [3] —. 귀하께서는 비용을 부담하지 않으시고 돌려보내 주시거나 50 퍼센트 할인된 가격으로 구입하실 수 있습니다. 이 두 가지 방법들 중에서 어느 것이 더 좋으신지 알려 주십시오. 배트를 돌려보내시길 원한다는 의사를 나타내시면, 반송하실 때 사용하실 수 있도록 우편 요금이 선납된 상자를 보내 드릴 것입니다. — [4] —. 배트를 사용하시는 것이 더 좋으시면, 귀하의 계좌에 필요한 조치를 취할 것입니다.

불편을 끼쳐 드려 진심으로 사과 드리며, 이 불미스러운 일로 인해 귀하께서 저희 Simpson's Sporting Goods에서 쇼핑하시는 일이 중단되지 않기를 바랍니다.

안녕히 계십시오.

Wilma Caraway
고객 서비스 직원

168 이메일의 목적은 무엇인가?

(A) 제품을 반송한 것에 대해 고객에게 감사하기
(B) 한 물품을 왜 더 이상 구매할 수 없는지를 설명하기
(C) Heyward 씨에 의해 알려진 문제를 해결하기
(D) Heyward 씨가 이용 가능한 특가 상품 설명하기

169 Heyward 씨는 요청 시에 무엇을 받을 것인가?

(A) 배송 상자
(B) 야구 글러브
(C) 회사 카탈로그
(D) 새로운 거래 내역서

170 제품 번호 302-WAW2에 관해 언급된 것은 무엇인가?

(A) 3월 27일에 도착할 것이다.
(B) 정가의 반값에 제공되고 있다.
(C) Heyward 씨에게 제품 번호 495-RRE3과 함께 보내졌다.
(D) 더 이상 Simpson's Sporting Goods에서 판매되지 않는다.

171 [1], [2], [3], [4]로 표기된 위치들 중에서 다음 문장이 가장 잘 어울리는 곳은 어디인가?
신유형

"귀하께서 이미 받으신 배트와 관련해, 두 가지 선택 가능한 방법이 있습니다."

(A) [1]
(B) [2]
(C) [3]
(D) [4]

172-175는 다음 기사를 참조하시오.

Eccleston Theme Park를 방문해 보세요.

Eccleston, CA (6월 9일)—여름 휴가 기간 동안 가족 모두를 위한 즐거운 일일 여행을 찾고 계신가요? 그렇다면 Eccleston Theme Park를 방문해 보시는 것은 어떠십니까? 비록 이 놀이공원이 일 년 내내 방문할 수 있게 문을 열기는 하지만, 다음 달은 돌고래 쇼를 즐기기에 가장 좋은 때인데, 동물들은 일반적으로 여름의 따뜻한 물속에서 더 즐거워하기 때문입니다. 이와 더불어, 물을 이용한 새로운 놀이기구인 'The Drencher'도 곧 공개될 것입니다.

Eccleston은 친환경적인 놀이공원으로서, 고객들이 개인 교통 수단을 이용해 찾아갈 수 없기 때문에 도심에서 셔틀 버스를 이용하는 방법으로만 방문할 수 있습니다. 이는 지역 사회에 교통 및 공해로 인한 영향을 최소화하기 위한 것입니다. 버스의 좌석은 버스 회사의 웹사이트를 통해 미리 예약할 수 있습니다. 가족들을 위한 할인 요금은 12세 이하의 아이들과 동행하는 가족들에게 제공됩니다.

공원에 입장하는 티켓은 공원 매표소에서 직접 구입하시거나 지역에 있는 많은 독립 소매업체 중의 하나를 통해서도 구입할 수 있습니다. 고객들은 공인된 판매업체를 이용하는 것이 권고되는데, 정직하지 못한 업자들이 판매하는 위조 입장권에 대한 보도가 있었기 때문이며, 이 입장권으로는 공원에 입장할 수 없습니다. 입장권은 현재 Adventurex에서 할인된 요금으로 판매되고 있으며, 고객들은 이 업체의 컴퓨터나 TV 제품을 구입할 때 이 판촉 행사를 이용할 자격을 갖게 됩니다.

입장권 가격과 개장 시간 및 예정된 쇼에 관한 더 많은 정보가 필요하신 분은 www.ecclestonpark.net를 방문하시기 바랍니다.

172 기사에 따르면, 어느 달에 Eccleston Theme Park를 방문하는 것이 추천되는가?

(A) 4월
(B) 5월
(C) 6월
(D) 7월

173 Eccleston Theme Park에 관해 유추할 수 있는 것은 무엇인가?

(A) 겨울 기간에는 문을 닫는다.
(B) TV 다큐멘터리에 특집 방송되었다.
(C) 자동차 주차 공간이 없다.
(D) 새로운 직원들을 고용하고 있다.

174 방문객들에게 권고되는 일은 무엇인가?

(A) 회사의 소식지를 받을 수 있도록 신청하는 것
(B) 인증된 업체로부터 입장권을 구입할 것
(C) 물을 이용한 기구를 탈 때 특수 의류를 착용할 것
(D) 동물 공연을 관람하기 위해 자리를 예약할 것

175 Adventurex는 무슨 종류의 업체일 가능성이 큰가?

(A) 아동 보육 시설
(B) 광고 대행사
(C) 전자제품 판매업체
(D) 규제 기관

176-180은 다음 소책자와 이메일을 참조하시오.

최신 세미나 일정
Pumisville College 제공

Pumisville College는 변호사 및 관련 전문가들을 위한 최신 세미나 일

정을 최종 확정했습니다. 이 세미나들은 우리 대학의 Darkford Road 캠퍼스에서 열릴 예정이며, 다년간의 경험을 통해 터득한 지식을 전달해 주길 열렬히 원하는, 업계에서 존경받는 분들께서 진행하시게 됩니다. 각 세미나의 참가 비용은 20달러입니다. 참가자들은 예정된 시작 시간보다 10분 미리 도착하시기 바랍니다.

3월 24일, 월요일, 오후 8시, 강연장 B
연설자: Robin Terrance, Thompson Solicitors
문서 준비: 업계 기준에 준하는 파일을 준비하는 방법에 대해 배우세요.

3월 26일, 수요일, 오후 6시, 강연장 A
연설자: Brian Pinkman, 퇴직 판사
법정 진술: 의뢰인을 가장 잘 대변할 수 있는 가장 설득력 있는 화법을 알아보세요.

3월 28일, 금요일, 오후 4시, 72호실
연설자: Sue Perm, Acorn Advertising
사업 홍보: 귀사에 신규 고객들을 유치하는 방법을 배워 보세요.

3월 30일, 일요일, 오후 12시, 8c호실
연설자: Freddie Campbell, Campbell & Frazer Ltd 사업 파트너
기업 내 승진: 상사에게 깊은 인상을 남기는 방법과 회사에서 더 높은 자리로 승진하는 방법에 대해 알아보세요.

모든 문의 사항은 Lucy Wilcox 씨에게 l.wilcox@pumisville.net 또는 555-2929-5036으로 연락하시기 바랍니다.

수신: Lucy Wilcox 〈l.wilcox@pumisville.net〉
발신: Joseph Whitel 〈josephwhitel@hmail.com〉
제목: 세미나 시리즈
날짜: 3월 29일

Wilcox 씨께,

저는 최신 세미나 시리즈에 참석했습니다. 저는 퇴직한 판사님께서 진행하시는 시간에 참가하는 것에 상당히 기뻤는데, 그분의 경험을 통해 많은 것을 배울 수 있다고 생각했기 때문입니다. 하지만, 제가 세미나실에 들어갔을 때, 저는 갑작스런 통보와 함께 그분이 다른 연설자로 대체되었음을 알게 되었습니다. 그로 인해, 저는 그 자리에 참석하는 것에 더 이상 흥미를 느끼지 못했고, 즉시 자리를 떠났습니다. 제가 미리 지불한 세미나 참가 비용을 환불해 주시면 대단히 감사하겠습니다.

안녕히 계십시오.
Joseph Whitel

176 소책자에서, 첫 번째 단락, 세 번째 줄의 단어 "figures"와 의미가 가장 가까운 것은 무엇인가?
(A) 통계
(B) 도표
(C) 교과서
(D) 사람들

177 세미나에 관해 언급된 것은 무엇인가?
(A) 무료로 참석할 수 있다.
(B) 일정보다 10분 늦게 진행될 수 있다.
(C) 법률과 관련된 분야에서 일하는 사람들을 위해 고안된 것이다.
(D) 모두 같은 장소에서 열린다.

178 3월 28일에 열리는 세미나의 주제는 무엇인가?
(A) 법정에서 설득력 있게 말하는 방법
(B) 잠재 고객을 유치하는 방법
(C) 문서를 준비하는 방법
(D) 승진하는 방법

179 Whitel 씨는 누구의 세미나에 참석하는 것에 관심이 있었는가?
(A) Terrance 씨의 세미나
(B) Pinkman 씨의 세미나
(C) Perm 씨의 세미나
(D) Campbell 씨의 세미나

180 Whitel 씨는 왜 이메일을 썼는가?
(A) 교직에 지원하기 위해
(B) 소책자를 받기 위해
(C) 찾아가는 길을 묻기 위해
(D) 환불을 요청하기 위해

181-185는 다음 공지와 양식을 참조하시오.

패키지 변경

고객님께,

고객 여러분께 가능한 한 최고의 서비스를 제공하기 위한 노력의 일환으로, Teleview Cable은 Viewpoint Media와 협력 관계의 조건에 관해 재협상을 해 왔으며, 모든 프리미엄 고객들께서는 다음 달부터 3가지의 새로운 영화 채널 서비스를 받게 된다는 점을 알려 드리게 되어 기쁩니다. 이 계약을 기념하기 위해, 기존의 기본 요금 고객들께서는 현재 프리미엄 서비스로 등급을 올리실 경우에 월간 청구서 비용에서 5달러를 절감하실 수 있습니다. 더욱이, 기존의 계약을 변경하는 것에 대해 통상적으로 발생되던 50달러의 수수료를 부담하지 않으시게 됩니다. 고객들께서는 이 조건에 적용을 받기 위해서는 이달 말 전에 등급을 올리셔야 합니다.

프리미엄 서비스로 등급을 올리기를 원하시는 고객들께서는 직통 서비스 전화 555-923-5894로 연락하시기 바랍니다. 고객께서는 또한 www.teleview.net/upgrade를 방문하여 온라인으로도 등급을 변경하실 수 있습니다. 등급 상향 조정 절차를 완료하기 위해서는 계정 번호와 비밀번호를 말씀해 주셔야 합니다. 추가로, 위에 언급해 드린 혜택을 받으실 수 있도록 판촉 행사 코드인 SWITCHME를 반드시 말씀해 주시기 바랍니다. 이 혜택을 받으시려면, 반드시 18세 이상의 미국 거주자이어야 합니다.

Teleview Cable 고객 의견 양식

고객 상세 정보
성명: Helen Webbings
계정 번호: 939238
날짜: 8월 18일
이메일 주소: hwebbings@quickmail.net
상세 불만 사항: 구독

저는 지난주에 케이블 방송 패키지를 업그레이드했으며, 어제부터 변경 사항이 적용되었습니다. 지금까지는 대부분의 서비스에 대해 만족하고 있으며, 특히 Viewpoint Media에 의해 제공되는 세 가지 영화 채널을 보는 것이 즐거웠습니다. 하지만 저는 어젯밤에 이 채널들을 틀어 보려 했지만 '채널 이용 불가'라는 에러 메시지를 보게 되었습니다. 저는 귀사의 서비스 이용 조건 내용을 신중하게 읽어 보았고 이 채널들은 제가 신청한 패키지의 특징이기 때문에 뭔가 실수가 있었던 것이 분명합니다. 가능한 한 빨리 이 상황이 바로잡힐 수 있다면 감사하겠습니다. 이는 귀사와 같은 유명 회사로부터 제가 기대하는 서비스의 수준이 아닙니다.

181 공지의 주된 목적은 무엇인가?
(A) Viewpoint Media와의 협력 관계가 중단되었음을 알리기
(B) 고객들에게 업그레이드가 의무임을 알리기
(C) 고객들에게 회사 소유권 변경에 대해 알리기
(D) 몇몇 케이블 채널의 추가를 알리기

182 50달러의 청구 금액에 관해 알 수 있는 것은 무엇인가?

(A) 즉시 납입되지 않으면 이자가 붙을 것이다.
(B) 기존의 고객들이 등급을 올릴 때 적용되지 않을 것이다.
(C) 신규 고객들에게 적용되지 않을 것이다.
(D) 지역 자선 단체에 기부될 것이다.

183 특별 혜택을 이용하기 위해 요구되는 사항이 아닌 것은 무엇인가?

(A) 비밀번호
(B) 할인 코드
(C) 인터넷 연결
(D) 계정 번호

184 Webbings 씨에 관해 사실일 가능성이 큰 것은 무엇인가?

(A) 프리미엄 패키지를 신청했다.
(B) Viewpoint Media에 입사 지원을 했다.
(C) 신규 서비스를 위해 5달러를 지불해야 한다.
(D) 3가지가 넘는 채널을 요청했다.

185 Webbings 씨는 Teleview Cable이 무엇을 하기를 기대하는가?

(A) 우편물 전달 목록에서 자신의 이름을 삭제하는 것
(B) 리모컨을 자신에게 보내주는 것
(C) 자신에게 새 비밀번호를 발급해 주는 것
(D) 서비스 오류를 바로잡는 것

신유형 186-190은 다음 기사와 이메일, 그리고 배치도를 참조하시오.

Community Beat
438권, 4월 28일

제5회 연례 여름 음악 축제가 7월 6일부터 8일까지 Redding Park에서 다시 한 번 열릴 예정입니다. 이번 축제는 3일 동안의 기간에 걸쳐 매우 다양한 음악가들이 특별 출연하며, 올해는 프로그램 중에 Annie Jarvis, the Gray Foxes와 the Dallas Quartet이 포함될 것입니다. 음악 공연 외에도, 지역 기업들은 자사의 제품을 판매할 수 있도록 야외 부스를 대여할 수 있습니다. 이 부스들은 음악과 관련될 필요는 없습니다. 과거의 행사 수치 자료를 보면 음악과 의류, 그리고 공예품 부스가 가장 큰 성공을 거둔 것으로 나타납니다.

부스 대여에 대한 등록은 이미 시작되었고, 자리들이 채워지기 시작하고 있으며, 특히 중앙의 무대와 야구 경기장 근처에 있는 부스들이 그렇습니다. 관심이 있는 업체들은 실망하지 않으시려면 가능한 한 빨리 부스를 확보하시길 권해 드립니다. 이를 위해서는, www.mysummer-fest.com을 방문하셔서 소매 업체 페이지에 기재된 안내사항을 따르시기 바랍니다. 모든 부스는 같은 크기이며, 3일에 해당하는 전체 기간 동안 350달러의 이용 요금에 제공됩니다. 작년에 열린 행사에 참가하셨던 업체 소유주들께서는 올해 다시 등록하실 경우 이용 요금에서 15퍼센트를 할인받게 됩니다.

축제 중의 음악 관련 활동에 관한 더 많은 정보는 확정되는 대로 업로드될 것입니다. 문의 사항은 m.adkinson@mysummerfest.com으로 행사 진행 책임자인 Melody Adkinson 씨께 보내시면 됩니다.

수신: Melody Adkinson ⟨m.adkinson@mysummerfest.com⟩
발신: Raymond Colby ⟨raymondcolby@colbyprints.com⟩
날짜: 6월 2일
제목: 여름 음악 축제

Adkinson 씨께,

저는 Redding Park에서 열리는 제5회 연례 여름 음악 축제에서 부스를 대여하는 데 관심이 있습니다. 제 친구들 중의 한 명인 Sabrina Ta가

작년에 이 행사에서 부스를 대여해 큰 성공을 거뒀다고 말해 주었습니다. 이 친구는 올해 다시 한 번 부스를 대여할 것이며, 저도 똑같이 하도록 적극 추천해 주었습니다. 제가 웹사이트에서 등록하려고 해 봤지만, 시스템이 무슨 이유에서인지 제 신청서를 처리하지 못하고 있습니다. 따라서, 그 대신에 이메일로 부스를 하나 예약할 수 있기를 바랍니다.

웹사이트에서 이용 가능한 부스를 볼 수 있는 배치도를 확인해 봤습니다. 저는 공원의 서쪽 구역에 자리잡고 싶습니다. 가능한 한 중앙 출입구와 가까운 곳에 있는 것을 선호하지만, 가장 중요한 점은, 제가 티셔츠 판매 업체를 운영하기 때문에 의류를 판매하는 부스 바로 옆에 있지 않은 자리를 제게 배정해 주셨으면 합니다. 가능한 한 빨리 제게 이메일로 답신 주시기 바랍니다.

감사합니다.

Raymond Colby
사장, Colby Prints

주차장	중앙 출입구	(이용 가능) W1	Jill's Dresses W2	Games Plus W3	Wonder Crafts W4	(이용 가능) W5
		(이용 가능) W6	Ace Florists W7	Candy Creations W8	Scoops Ice Cream W9	(이용 가능) W10

186 기사는 왜 쓰여졌는가?

(A) 지역의 한 기관을 평가하기 위해
(B) 공연할 음악가들을 모집하기 위해
(C) 축제에 업체들을 유치하기 위해
(D) 공원 개조 공사 프로젝트를 발표하기 위해

187 Redding Park에 관해 알 수 있는 것은 무엇인가?

(A) 물가에 있다.
(B) 공원 내에 스포츠 시설을 갖추고 있다.
(C) 한 곳이 넘는 주차장을 갖추고 있다.
(D) 도심 구역에 자리잡고 있다.

188 기사에서, 두 번째 단락, 네 번째 줄의 단어 "follow"와 의미가 가장 가까운 것은 무엇인가?

(A) 추구하다
(B) 관찰하다
(C) 붙잡다
(D) 따르다

189 Ta 씨에 관해 알 수 있는 것은 무엇인가?

(A) 판매 상품이 Colby 씨의 것과 비슷하다.
(B) 할인을 받을 자격이 있다.
(C) 서쪽 구역에 부스를 얻을 것이다.
(D) 올해는 두 개의 부스를 대여할 것이다.

190 어느 공간이 Colby 씨에게 가장 적합할 것인가?

(A) W1
(B) W5
(C) W6
(D) W10

Seattle Science Museum에서 열리는 다가오는 전시회:
로봇 혁명: 7월 10일-8월 1일

"로봇 혁명"은 직접 참여 가능한 전시회로서 인공 지능 분야의 최신 상황을 집중 조명합니다. Todd Vega 씨가 창안한 이 전시회는 사람들의 명령과 행동에 반응하는 독특한 로봇들을 특징으로 합니다. 말하기 능력을 활용하는 것에서부터 물리적인 일들을 수행하는 것까지, 로봇들은 사람들과 교감함으로써 "배웁니다." 전시회가 진행될수록 이 로봇들은 점점 더 많은 능력들을 보여줄 것이므로, 최소한 두 번은 전시회장을 방문하도록 적극 권해 드립니다.

상호 교류하는 로봇과 함께 하는 활동 외에도, 방문객들은 로봇 공학의 역사에 관한 글을 읽어볼 수도 있고 이 분야의 미래 가능성에 대해서도 알아볼 수 있습니다. 실제 사실과 즐거움의 완벽한 조합으로, "로봇 혁명"은 아이들과 어른들 모두에게 즐거움을 줄 것입니다.

이 분야에 관해 더 많은 것을 배우시려면, Hillside Hall(7월 12일)과 Bartlett Hotel(7월 20일)에서 Todd Vega 씨가 진행하는 학술적인 강연을 놓치지 마십시오. 또한 Jacqueline Stanfill와 공동으로 저술한 〈로봇 세상〉에서 그의 작업에 관해 더 많은 것을 읽어 보실 수도 있습니다.

전시회 입장권은 1인당 18달러이며, 현장에서 구매 가능합니다. Seattle Science Museum은 화요일부터 일요일까지, 오전 9시에서 오후 8시까지 문을 엽니다.

수신: Todd Vega 〈t.vega@lexingtonmail.com〉
발신: Georgina Mizrahi 〈mizrahi_g@techtracking.com〉
날짜: 7월 21일
제목: 인터뷰 제안

Vega 씨께,

Seattle Science Museum에서 열린 귀하의 놀라운 전시회를 본 후에, 저는 귀하의 강연 중 하나를 신청했습니다. 어제 열린 강연에 참석했는데, 귀하의 아이디어에 강한 호기심을 느꼈습니다. 저는 Tech Tracking이라고 불리는 기술 관련 블로그를 운영하고 있으며, 제 구독자들이 로봇과 인공 지능과 관련해 귀하의 지식에 관한 내용을 즐겁게 읽어볼 수 있을 것 같습니다. 이는 또한 귀하의 연구에 대한 아주 좋은 노출이 될 수 있는데, 제 블로그에는 매달 20만 명이 넘는 특별한 방문객들이 찾아오고 있으며, Doyle Center로부터 최고의 웹 상을 받은 블로그입니다.

저는 현재 Seattle에 살고 있습니다. 귀하와 전화로 인터뷰를 실시할 수 있으며, 또는 제가 8월 1일과 4일 사이에 언제든지 Los Angeles에 있는 귀하의 사무실로 기꺼이 방문할 수 있는데, Hendrix Innovation Expo 행사로 인해 제가 그곳으로 갈 예정이기 때문입니다. 귀하의 고려에 대해 감사 드립니다. 귀하로부터 답변을 들을 수 있기를 바랍니다.

안녕히 계십시오.

Georgina Mizrahi
www.techtracking.com

수신: Georgina Mizrahi 〈mizrahi_g@techtracking.com〉
발신: Todd Vega 〈t.vega@lexingtonmail.com〉
날짜: 7월 22일
제목: 회신: 인터뷰 제안

Mizrahi 씨께,

귀하의 인터뷰 초청에 감사 드립니다. 저는 제 사무실에서 직접 만나 뵙는 것이 가장 좋을 것 같습니다. 이렇게 해야 귀하께서 저희 제품 모델들과 시제품들 일부를 사진 촬영하실 수 있을 것입니다. 제 비서인 Jamie

Lucas에게 555-5934로 전화하셔서 귀하의 엑스포 활동에 방해되지 않는 시간을 정하시기 바랍니다. 또한 저와 함께 저술 작업을 하는 파트너도 함께 자리하도록 할 텐데, 함께 공유할 만한 특별한 통찰력을 보여 드릴 것이라 확신합니다.

안녕히 계십시오.

Todd Vega

---

191 사람들은 왜 한 번보다 많이 박물관을 방문하도록 권고받는가?

(A) 방문객들이 입장권 할인을 받을 수 있다.
(B) 다른 전문가들이 강연을 할 것이다.
(C) 전시회가 시간이 지날수록 달라질 것이다.
(D) 박물관의 마지막 전시회가 될 것이다.

192 전시회에 관해 언급된 내용은 무엇인가?

(A) 한 달 동안 진행될 것이다.
(B) 아이들은 무료로 입장할 수 있게 해준다.
(C) 주말 내내 문을 닫는다.
(D) 모든 연령층의 방문객들을 대상으로 한다.

193 Mizrahi 씨는 어디에서 강연에 참석했는가?

(A) Hillside Hall
(B) Bartlett Hotel
(C) Seattle Science Museum
(D) Doyle Center

194 Vega 씨에 관해 무엇이 사실일 것 같은가?

(A) Los Angeles에서 만나고 싶어 한다.
(B) 자신의 투어에 더 많은 강연을 추가할 것이다.
(C) 수상 후보자로 지명되었다.
(D) Mizrahi 씨에게 시제품을 보낼 것이다.

195 Vega 씨는 무엇을 할 것이라고 말하는가?

(A) Stanfill 씨를 만남에 초대할 것이다.
(B) 자신의 비서에게 양식을 출력하도록 시킬 것이다.
(C) Hendrix Innovation Expo에서 강연을 할 것이다.
(D) 자신의 웹사이트에 인터뷰를 홍보할 것이다.

수신: Steve Irving 〈steve.i@hmtllc.com〉
발신: Colin Mountebank 〈colin.m@hmtllc.com〉
날짜: 2월 2일
제목: 계약 - 긴급 사항!

안녕하세요, Steve 씨,

제가 오늘 할당해 드린 다른 일들 외에, TransState Couriers에 전화하셔서 물건을 좀 가져가도록 조치해 주시겠어요? 저는 오늘 사무실로 다시 돌아가지 않을 것이며 (제 회의가 애초에 예상한 것보다 훨씬 더 오래 진행되고 있어요), 제가 Adam Harrison 씨와 그분의 파트너를 위해 준비한 계약서들이 오늘 오후에 발송되어야 합니다. 특별한 배송 서비스는 필요치 않지만 이 서류들이 내일까지는 도착했으면 합니다. 이 서류들은 제 책상의 왼쪽 맨 위 서랍 안에 있는 두 개의 봉투에 들어 있습니다. 배송 비용이 우리 회사의 계좌로 곧바로 청구될 수 있도록 이 배송회사의 온라인 예약 화면에서 우리 회사의 계정 번호인 #563886A를 사용하십시오.

감사합니다!

Colin Mountebank
대표, Hope, Mountebank & Tweed

---

http://www.transstatecouriers.com/services

TransState Couriers

홈	회사 관련	서비스	배송 추적	연락처

서비스 〉〉 0.7kg 이하 〉〉 서류

저희 TransState Couriers에서는 여러분의 서류가 제때 전송되는 것의 중요성을 잘 알고 있습니다. 저희의 경쟁력 있는 요금과 신뢰도에 대한 명성으로 인해, 여러분께서는 저렴한 가격에 원하시는 마음의 평안을 얻으실 수 있습니다.

	기본 계정	기업 계정
일반 (영업일로 3일 이내에 전달)	16.95달러	12.95달러
특급 (익일 오후 5시까지 전달)	23.95달러	19.95달러

내용물 보험, 배송 증명서(서명 포함), 그리고 냉장 운송 등과 같은 추가 서비스에 대한 비용을 보시려면 여기를 클릭하세요.

저희는 두 번에 걸쳐 배송이 완료되도록 시도할 것입니다. 저희가 배송 물품을 전해 드릴 수 없을 경우에는, 가장 가까운 곳에 있는 창고로 돌려보내질 것이며 (주소와 지도를 보시려면 여기를 클릭하세요), 오후 11시까지 이곳에 직접 오셔서 찾아가실 수 있습니다. 문자 메시지를 통해 수취인께 알려 드립니다.

수신: (312) 555-8922
발신: (312) 555-1001

수취인 Adam Harrison 씨께: 저희 TransState Couriers에서 배송 물품(참조 번호822744532)을 전달해 드리려고 했으나, 귀하께서 계시지 않았습니다. 이 배송 물품은 Doyle Lane 283번지에 있는 저희 창고로 보내졌으며, 오후 11시 이전에는 언제든지 찾아가실 수 있습니다. 그렇지 않을 경우, 배송 일정을 재조정하실 수 있도록 저희 웹사이트를 방문해 주세요.

---

196 Mountebank 씨는 누구일 것 같은가?

(A) Irving 씨의 상사
(B) Irving 씨의 비서
(C) Harrison 씨의 부서장
(D) Harrison 씨의 파트너

197 이메일에서, 첫 번째 단락, 세 번째 줄의 단어 "originally"와 의미가 가장 가까운 것은 무엇인가?

(A) 처음에
(B) 정식으로
(C) 창의적으로
(D) 일반적으로

198 TransState Couriers에 의해 제공되는 서비스로 언급되지 않은 것은 무엇인가?

(A) 배송 물품 안에 들어 있는 것에 대해 보험에 가입하는 일
(B) 배송 물품이 전달되었다는 증명서를 제공하는 일
(C) 온도를 조절한 운송 서비스를 이용하는 일
(D) 위험한 물품들을 운송하는 일

199 Irving 씨는 물품 배송에 얼마의 비용을 소비했을 것 같은가?

(A) 12.95달러
(B) 16.95달러
(C) 19.95달러
(D) 23.95달러

200 Harrison 씨의 배송 물품에 관해 알 수 있는 것은 무엇인가?

(A) 배송 주소가 잘못 되었다.
(B) 배송 회사가 두 번 배송을 시도했다.
(C) 발신인에게 되돌려 보내질 것이다.
(D) 운송 중에 손상되었다.

PART 5

101 직원의 사기를 높이려는 Dickinson 씨의 열정은 생산성과 매출 증대 모두에 상당한 영향을 끼쳐 왔다.

102 분기별 매출 보고서는 투자자들을 위해 회사 저널에 실리지만, 월례 보고서는 오직 직원들만 이용 가능하다.

103 아침에, Patricia Cooper는 곧 팩스로 전송될 서류들이 자신의 것이라고 사람들에게 알렸다.

104 지난밤에 있었던 기자 회견에서, GLM Biomedical의 최고경영자인 Godfrey Miranda는 정반대로 진술된 보도에도 불구하고 은퇴하지 않겠다는 결정을 알렸다.

105 Cranton-Taft Mechanics는 새 제조 공장을 열고 특별히 자사 브랜드의 다양한 자전거 제품들을 조립하기 위해 150명의 기술자들을 고용할 것이다.

106 Happy Beauty 성형외과는 30일 이내에 납부할 경우 무이자 결제 방식을 제공한다.

107 훌륭한 팀 리더는 팀원들이 생산적으로 일할 수 있도록 각각의 업무를 명확히 규정하는 방법을 알아야 한다.

108 많은 전문가들은 기기 공업이 국가 경제의 다른 어떤 분야보다 훨씬 더 빠르게 성장하고 있다는 점에 주목했다.

109 First Tech의 최고경영자인 Jansen 씨는 비상 회의를 소집했지만, 그 회의 자체는 회사의 재정적 문제를 즉각적으로 처리하지 못했다.

110 나이와 상관없이, 유효한 입장권이 있는 사람은 누구든지 박물관의 최신 전시회에 입장하는 것이 허용될 것이다.

111 다음 주 내내 개최될 예정인 교육 워크숍은 업무 효율성을 향상시킬 것으로 기대된다.

112 최고의 그리스 식당 중 하나가 시내에 있는 역사 박물관 맞은편에 있고, 유명한 거미 동상도 근처에 있다.

113 Morning Star Clothing은 자사 제품에 최고의 직물을 사용하고 있다고 강조했지만 설문 조사 결과는 이와 다른 내용을 보여준다.

114 Brown 씨는 직원용 소책자에 넣을 새 전자 데이터베이스에 관한 상세한 설명을 작성하겠다고 자원했다.

115 AME Industries는 사용자 친화적인 기능들과 새로운 배치를 특징으로 하는 완전히 새로 디자인된 웹사이트를 공개했다.

116 고객들은 만족스럽지 못하다고 여겨지는 제품들을 모두 반품했고 매장으로부터 환불을 받았다.

117 여름 시즌 동안, Little Critters Apparel은 추가 고객들을 유치하려는 노력의 일환으로 운영 시간을 연장하고 매주 판촉 행사를 제공할 것이다.

118 업계에서 가장 숙련된 협상가 중 한 명인 Thomson 씨는 우리 회사가 Falaman Hotel 보수 공사에 대한 적절한 계약을 따내도록 돕는 데 중요한 역할을 했다.

119 영업 분야에 경험이 풍부한 Poe 씨는 우리 부서에 환영할 만한 추가 인원이다.

120 어제 이사회에 보내진 보고서는 조직 개편 가이드라인에 관한 Quantum Enterprises의 새로운 비즈니스 전략을 강조한다.

121 Hill 씨의 이력서에 기록된 많은 성과들 중에 언론인으로서 상을 받았던 경력이 있다.

122 Rewster Pharma의 교육 담당자는 월간 〈Pharmacist's Reading List〉를 위해 학술 자료에서 기사를 선택한다.

123 Terragin Beverage Company의 혁신적인 마케팅 팀 덕분에,

회사의 수익이 지난해의 이윤을 계속 뛰어넘고 있다.

124 대학의 관행에 따라, 매 학기 말까지 찾아가지 않는 주인 없는 물건들은 지역 자선 단체로 보내질 것이다.

125 Henderson 씨는 새 사무실 건물의 디자인에 대한 아이디어를 구상하기 위해 4개월간 광범위한 조사를 해야 했다.

126 만약 온라인 판매가 계속해서 경쟁업체의 판매를 앞선다면, New York에 대리점을 여는 계획이 가속화될 것이다.

127 어느 마케팅 전략을 시행할지 결정하기 위한 프로젝트 팀원들과의 일련의 회의가 있을 것이다.

128 우리 데이터는 3년 이상 우리 인터넷 서비스를 이용해 온 고객들이 신규 고객들보다 서비스 업체를 바꿀 가능성이 더 적다는 것을 보여준다.

129 조사관들은 모든 장비가 안전 기준을 준수하고 있는지 확인하기 위하여 Merriweather 공장에 도착할 예정이다.

130 Peterson 씨는 시장 트렌드에 관한 그의 연구 결과 분석 보고서에서 구성과 명확성에 주의를 기울이지 않았다.

PART 6

신유형 131-134는 다음 공지를 참조하시오.

Pocatello Medical Equipment를 선택해 주셔서 감사합니다. 저희들은 항상 결제 확인 후 24시간 내에 주문하신 제품을 배송하고 있습니다. 만약 언제라도 주문한 제품의 소재에 대한 문의 사항이 있으시면, 이 중요한 세부 사항을 주목해 주십시오. 모든 고객들은 계산 시 배송 방법을 선택하도록 요청받습니다. 배송 시간은 운송 방법에 따라 2일에서 15일이 소요됩니다. 항상 정시에 제품을 배송하는 것이 우리의 목표지만, 몇몇 지연은 피할 수 없는 경우도 있습니다. 이는 물건이 도착하는 데 더 오랜 시간이 걸리게 됩니다. 문의 사항이나 우려되는 부분이 있으시다면, 800-245-1000으로 전화하셔서 배송 상황에 대한 세부 사항을 문의해 주세요.

신유형 135-138은 다음 이메일을 참조하시오.

수신: Melissa Ryan 〈mryan@mail.com〉
발신: Benjamin Raja 〈braja@ejconsultants.org〉
제목: 최종 단계
날짜: 2월 29일

Ryan 씨께,

축하합니다! 귀하께서 지원하신 직책의 최종 선발 단계에 도달하셨습니다. 귀하의 경력과 자격 증명 사항들이 이 자리에 적합하고도 남는 것으로 보입니다.

마지막 검토 단계에 필요한 지원자 필수 요건에 따라 3명의 추천인 목록을 저에게 보내 주시기 바랍니다. 이 추천인들은 이전 직장의 상사 1명, 동료 직원 1명, 그리고 1명의 교수나 강사를 포함시키는 것이 가장 좋습니다.

이 요청된 정보들을 가능한 한 빨리 제게 이메일로 보내 주십시오. 모든 일이 순조롭게 진행된다는 가정 하에, 선발된 지원자는 5월 10일에 곧바로 근무를 시작할 수 있을 것입니다. 저희의 답변을 들으실 때까지, 이 이메일 계정을 계속해서 주의 깊게 살펴 보시기 바랍니다.

안부를 전하며,

Benjamin Raja
인사부장
EJ Consulting Firm

신유형 ▶ 139-142는 다음 편지를 참조하시오.

Mr. Kenneth Grey
5100 Front Street
Cincinnati, OH 45205
4월 15일

Grey 씨께,

저희 Reba Sheer Clothing Co.의 그래픽 디자인 인턴직에 시간 내어 지원해 주셔서 감사합니다. 하지만 신중히 고려한 끝에, 귀하께서는 올해의 인턴 프로그램에 참여하도록 선발되지 않았다는 점을 알려 드리게 되어 유감스럽게 생각합니다.

저희는 이전에는 5명의 인턴을 선발할 수 있었습니다. 하지만, 최근의 예산 감축으로 인해, 저희 부서는 올해 단 2명의 상근 디자인 인턴과 계약하도록 제한되었습니다.

선발되지 않았음에도 불구하고, 귀하의 포트폴리오에 들어 있는 광고들, Tippy Electronics and Young's Jewelry을 위한 광고들은 전망이 좋습니다.

귀하의 재능은 저희 회사에서 높이 평가받을 수 있습니다. 학교를 졸업하시는 대로, 저희 신규 졸업자 교육 인턴직에 지원하는 것을 고려해 보시기 바랍니다.

안부를 전하며,

Naomi Lang
부장, 그래픽 디자인 앤 마케팅부
Reba Sheer Clothing Co.

신유형 ▶ 143-146은 다음 공지를 참조하시오.

직원 여러분께 알립니다.

저희 사무실에서 최근에 회사 컴퓨터에 접근하려는 컴퓨터 바이러스에 관한 여러 보고서를 받았습니다. 안타깝게도, 저희는 아직 그 문제의 원인을 알아내지 못했습니다. 귀하의 업무용 컴퓨터가 소프트웨어 바이러스에 감염된 것을 발견하시는 경우에는, 즉시 컴퓨터를 끄고 IT 전문가에게 연락하십시오.

인터넷에서 프로그램을 다운로드하실 때 예방 조치를 취하시기 바랍니다. 더욱이, 원하지 않는 어떤 이메일이라도 받으시는 경우에, 특히 알 수 없는 주소로부터 오면 이메일을 열지 않으시길 바랍니다.

실수로 의심스러운 메시지를 열게 되시면, 어떠한 링크도 클릭하지 않거나 발신자에게 답변하지 않는 등의 예방 조치를 꼭 취하십시오. 이러한 사항들이 지켜지면, 컴퓨터 바이러스에 감염되는 위험을 크게 줄일 수 있을 것입니다.

IT 서비스 부
내선. 3203

PART 7

신유형 ▶ 147-148은 다음 온라인 채팅을 참조하시오.

Veronica Stroud [오후 3:22]
안녕하세요, Gustavo. 당신이 휴게실에 커피 기계를 설치했죠, 맞아요?

Gustavo Baretto [오후 3:24]
네, 오늘 아침에요. 왜요? 커피가 벌써 다 떨어졌나요?

Veronica Stroud [오후 3:24]
그런 건 아닌데, "에러" 메시지가 계속 깜빡이고 있어요.

Gustavo Baretto [오후 3:25]
뚜껑이 꽉 닫혀 있는지 확인해 보셨어요?

Veronica Stroud [오후 3:26]
네. 그리고 신선한 분말로 가득 채워져 있어요.

Gustavo Baretto [오후 3:27]
아마 기계를 재설정해야 할 겁니다.

Veronica Stroud [오후 3:27]
저는 한 번도 그렇게 해 본 적이 없어요. 설명서를 가져 와야 하나요?

Gustavo Baretto [오후 3:28]
아뇨. 오른편에 있는 버튼을 5초 동안 누르고 있기만 하면 됩니다.

Veronica Stroud [오후 3:29]
그게 전부예요? 그런 줄 알았더라면, 당신을 귀찮게 하지 않았을 거예요. 감사합니다!

147 Stroud 씨가 겪는 문제점은 무엇인가?
(A) 중요한 메시지를 받지 못했다.
(B) 휴식 일정표에 오류가 있었다.
(C) 일부 물품이 다 떨어졌다.
(D) 기기 하나가 제대로 작동되지 않고 있다.

148 오후 3시 29분에, Stroud 씨가 "Is that it"이라고 썼을 때 의미하는 것은 무엇인가?
신유형
(A) 그녀는 Baretto 씨가 아주 빨리 도착할 수 없다고 생각한다.
(B) 일부 지시 사항이 그녀가 예상한 것보다 더 쉽다.
(C) 그녀는 사무실에 설명서가 하나밖에 없어서 놀라워하고 있다.
(D) 버튼이 쉽게 다시 부착될 수 있다.

149-150은 다음 광고를 참조하시오.

Premier Getaways

어느 회사도 유럽 최고의 여행지로 가는 가격 면에서 저희를 앞서갈 수 없습니다.

Rome 349달러
London 265달러
Paris 299달러
Barcelona 388달러
Athens 321달러

여러분이 꿈꾸는 여행을 예약하기 위해 저희 웹사이트 www.premiergetaways.com을 방문해 보세요. 또한 저희가 제공하는 투어 및 특별 호텔 이용 서비스를 웹사이트에서 확인하는 것도 잊지 마세요.

거래 조건:
가격은 Boston에서 출발하는 개별 왕복 항공권에 대한 것입니다.
웹사이트를 통해 예약하시는 분들께서는 공항에서 호텔로 가는 무료 셔틀 버스 서비스를 이용하실 수 있습니다.
저희를 통해 호텔을 예약하시는 분들께서는 일일 무료 뷔페 저녁 식사 쿠폰을 받으실 것입니다.

149 Premier Getaways는 무엇일 것 같은가?
(A) 대중 교통 사무소
(B) 차량 판매 대리점
(C) 여행 리조트
(D) 여행사

150 항공권을 구매하는 사람들은 무엇을 받을 것인가?

(A) 호텔에 대한 특별 가격 할인

(B) 무료 저녁 식사

(C) 셔틀 버스 이용 서비스

(D) 가이드를 동반한 도심 투어

151-152는 다음 정보를 참조하시오.

구입 가능한 공간

Cloverdale Shopping Mall의 2층에 있는 푸드코트 내 레스토랑 시설. 패스트푸드 업체에 가장 적합합니다. 주방, 카운터 공간, 그리고 함께 식사를 하는 공간이 있으며, 소유주가 신속히 매각하기를 원하기 때문에 시세보다 낮은 가격에 구입할 수 있습니다. 냉장고와 현금 등록기는 추가 비용 없이 이용하실 수 있습니다. 더 많은 정보를 원하시거나 시설을 둘러보실 수 있도록 예약을 하기 위해서는 1-800-409-4334로 전화 주세요.

151 시설물에 관해 알 수 있는 것은 무엇인가?

(A) 쇼핑 센터의 1층에 위치해 있다.

(B) 소유주가 임대하고자 한다.

(C) 주변의 다른 레스토랑들보다 구매 비용이 저렴하다.

(D) 개별 좌석 공간이 딸려 있다.

152 판매 가격에 무엇이 포함되어 있는가?

(A) 몇몇 장비

(B) 저장 공간

(C) 전기세 및 가스비

(D) 주차 공간

153-154는 다음 정보를 참조하시오.

The City Arts Committee가 전시회를 개최합니다.

전시품: Mountainville의 학생 미술 콘테스트
수상자들의 그림과 조각품들

6월 23일 화요일, 오후 6시부터 오후 9시까지

Ed Klein Community Center
94 Southeast Front Street
Mountainville, TX 77028

입장료는 1인당 5달러이며, 다양한 음료와 간단한 간식이 포함됩니다.
입장권은 Mountainville Municipal Center에서
정규 업무 시간 동안 구입 가능합니다.

153 무슨 종류의 행사가 열리는가?

(A) 연극

(B) 미술 전시회

(C) 콘서트

(D) 콘테스트

154 행사에 관해 알 수 있는 것은 무엇인가?

(A) 학생들은 무료이다.

(B) Ed Klein에 의해 개최될 것이다.

(C) 주말 행사이다.

(D) 지역 예술가들을 특징으로 한다.

155-157은 다음 비즈니스 프로필을 참조하시오.

Wimberley, Inc.

Wimberley Inc.는 파나마의 Panama City에 본사를 두고 있는 소규모의 의약품 제조업체입니다. 이 회사는 파나마의 열대 우림에서 찾아낸 천연 물질에서 추출한 의약품을 생산합니다. 대부분의 제품들은 파나마를 비롯해 인근에 있는 중미 국가들에서 판매되지만, 유럽과 미국에도 적은 양을 수출하기 시작했습니다. 지난 2년에 걸쳐 35%가 넘게 매출이 상승했으며, 수익도 거의 비슷하게 증가해 왔습니다. 결과적으로, 올해 65명이 넘는 신입사원들을 채용했으며, 머지 않아 연구 개발에 수백 만 달러를 사용할 것입니다. 이 회사는 두 곳의 제조 시설을 갖추고 있는데, 두 시설 모두 파나마에 위치해 있습니다. Ernesto Carrera 부사장이 지난 12월에 회사에 입사했으며, 환경 문제에 민감한 사람들의 관심을 끌 수 있는 제품들을 개발하기 위해 회사의 연구를 확대할 것으로 기대를 모으고 있습니다.

Wimberley Inc.는 앞으로 유망한 미래를 바라보고 있으며, 10년 안에 파나마에서 가장 뛰어난 기업들 중 하나가 될 것입니다.

155 Wimberley Inc.의 제품을 구매할 가능성이 큰 사람은 누구인가?

(A) 정비공

(B) 환자

(C) 행사 주최자

(D) 출장 요리 제공업자

156 Wimberley Inc.는 작년에 무엇을 했는가?

(A) 여러 개의 새 지점을 열었다.

(B) 신임 임원을 채용했다.

(C) 세계적으로 제품을 광고했다.

(D) 주기적으로 직원들을 교육했다.

157 Wimberley Inc.에 관해 알 수 있는 것은 무엇인가?

(A) 파나마에 있는 가장 큰 회사들 중 하나이다.

(B) 자사의 연구 능력을 향상시킬 것이다.

(C) 지난 2년 동안 회사의 주가가 올랐다.

(D) 지난 분기에 35%만큼 수익이 증가했다.

158-160은 다음 기사를 참조하시오.

Micon 행사

Micon은 이전에 Wexley Fabrics 공장이었던 건물을 아파트로 개조하는 다가올 건설 프로젝트를 위해 자사의 인원 부족을 충당하기 위한 채용 행사를 개최할 예정이라고 발표했다. 전기 기사와 배관 담당자, 그리고 건설 현장 인부들이 급히 필요하다. Wexley Fabrics 건물의 개조는 저소득층 가정을 위해 도시 내 주택 숫자를 늘리는 것을 목표로 최근에 제정된 정책에 따른 대응이다. 이번 행사는 2월 17일 Fairway Center에서 오전 8시부터 오후 3시까지 예정되어 있다.

면접은 행사 당일에 실시될 예정이므로 지원자들은 작성을 완료한 지원서를 가져올 것이 요구된다. 양식은 www.micon-inc.net/forms에서 다운로드 받을 수 있다. 그곳에서 행사 참가 신청도 할 수 있다. 2월 17일 전에 신청을 하는 사람들에게는 Micon의 사명과 근무 조건, 그리고 채용 절차에 관한 상세 정보를 담은 회사 소책자와 함께 지원 관련 자료집이 보내질 것이다.

158 사람들은 왜 이 행사에 참여하기를 원하겠는가?

(A) 아파트 단지를 건학하기 위해

(B) 재정 지원을 신청하기 위해

(C) 구직 기회를 찾기 위해

(D) 지역 사회 단체에 가입하기 위해

159 기사에 언급된 정책의 목적은 무엇인가?

(A) 일부 시민들에게 주택을 공급하기
(B) 도시로 관광객들을 끌어들이기
(C) 도시 지역의 공해를 줄이기
(D) 역사적인 건물들을 보호하기

160 사전에 등록하는 사람들에게 무슨 일이 있을 것인가?

(A) 그들은 시설 안으로 일찍 들어가도록 허용될 것이다.
(B) 그들은 경품권을 받을 것이다.
(C) 그들은 회사 관련 정보를 받을 것이다.
(D) 그들은 요금을 할인받을 것이다.

`신유형` 161-164는 다음 문자 메시지 대화를 참조하시오.

Prabha Shah [오후 2:33]
저는 Nero Hotel에서 뷔페 행사를 준비하고 있어요. 그런데 보온용 트레이가 하나 더 필요할 것 같습니다.

Funato Ozaki [오후 2:37]
제가 Olivia Gardens의 오찬 행사를 마무리하는 중인데, 끝나면 하나 가져다 드릴 수 있어요.

Prabha Shah [오후 2:38]
그렇게 해 주시면 완벽할 겁니다.

Funato Ozaki [오후 2:39]
Carly가 아프기 때문에 오늘 밤에 있을 행사에 서버가 한 명 모자라요. 8명만으로 괜찮을까요?

Prabha Shah [오후 2:40]
안될 것 같아요. 우리는 Bridge Enterprises에 정기적으로 출장 요리를 제공하고 있는데, 서비스가 느려지는 것을 원하지 않아요.

Funato Ozaki [오후 2:40]
이 대화에 Jason을 초대하죠.

Prabha Shah [오후 2:41]
Jason, Carly가 일하던 6~10시 교대 근무를 대신 맡아 줄 사람이 필요해요. 혹시 시간 되나요?

Jason Irving [오후 2:45]
저를 넣어 주세요.

Prabha Shah [오후 2:46]
감사합니다! 상세 정보는 문자로 보내 드릴게요. Glendale Hall 행사에 입고 오셨던 것과 같은 유니폼으로 입고 오세요.

Jason Irving [오후 2:47]
알겠습니다. 다행히도, 지금 막 세탁해 두었어요.

Funato Ozaki [오후 2:48]
곧 뵙겠습니다, Prabha. 그리고 고맙습니다, Jason.

161 Shah 씨는 어떤 종류의 업체에서 근무하고 있을 것 같은가?

(A) 레스토랑 물품 공급 업체
(B) 출장 요리 제공 업체
(C) 운송 서비스 업체
(D) 호텔 체인점

162 오후 2시 45분에, Irving 씨가 "Sign me up"이라고 썼을 때 의
`신유형` 미하는 것은 무엇인가?

(A) 그는 Bridge Enterprises 직원들에게 연설을 할 수 있다.
(B) 그는 교육 행사에 등록하고 싶어 한다.

(C) 그는 동료 직원의 자리를 대신할 수 있다.
(D) 그는 사업 협정이 좋은 아이디어라고 생각한다.

163 Irving 씨는 무엇을 하도록 요청받는가?

(A) 청소 업무 수행하기
(B) Carly 씨로부터 지시받기
(C) Shah 씨에게 장비 가져다 주기
(D) 특정 의류 착용하기

164 Ozaki 씨는 다음에 어디로 갈 계획인가?

(A) Bridge Enterprises 사무실
(B) Glendale Hall
(C) Nero Hotel
(D) Olivia Gardens

`신유형` 165-167은 다음 공지를 참조하시오.

Silvertown Transportation Department
서비스 이용 주의

이번 주 토요일 오전 6시부터 일요일 오후 10시까지 Liberty Stadium과 Broadwell Boulevard 사이에 도로 보수 공사가 있을 예정입니다. — [1] —. 이 버스는 두 구간에서 운행될 예정입니다. Liberty Stadium에서 Madison Street까지, 그리고 Riverside Park에서 Broadwell Boulevard까지 운행됩니다. Apple Avenue는 도로 보수 공사로 인해 이용이 불가할 것입니다. — [2] —. Madison Street 정류장에서 Broadwell Boulevard 정류장까지 이동하길 원하시는 분들은, 이 두 거리를 잇는 셔틀 버스가 있을 것입니다. — [3] —. 이 셔틀 버스는 20분마다 운행될 것이며, 버스 승객들은 무료로 이용 가능합니다. 이 셔틀 버스는 도로 보수 공사가 완료되는 대로 운행이 중단됩니다. — [4] —. 다른 버스 노선들은 이 공사의 영향을 받지 않습니다.

승객 여러분께 불편함을 드려 사과 드립니다.

165 작업은 어디에서 있을 예정인가?

(A) Liberty Stadium에서
(B) Riverside Park에서
(C) Apple Avenue에서
(D) Broadwell Boulevard에서

166 공지에 따르면, 셔틀 버스의 목적은 무엇인가?

(A) 공사의 영향을 받는 승객들을 지하철역으로 옮기기 위해
(B) 두 버스 정류장을 연결하기 위해
(C) 사람들을 Liberty Stadium으로 데려다 주기 위해
(D) 버스에서 발생하는 승객 과잉을 보완하기 위해

167 [1], [2], [3], [4]로 표기된 위치들 중에서 다음 문장이 가장 잘 어
`신유형` 울리는 곳은 어디인가?

"이 기간 동안, 10번 버스 서비스에 일부 변동이 있을 것입니다."

(A) [1]
(B) [2]
(C) [3]
(D) [4]

168-171은 다음 이메일을 참조하시오.

발신: Ted Sanders, 대표이사
수신: 전 직원
날짜: 9월 10일

제목: 지부장으로 임명된 Greg Henderson

Ernest Mathieu가 9월 말에 퇴직하겠다는 의사를 밝힌 이후로, 우리 JPR Corporation 사는 그의 후임자를 찾아 왔습니다. 저는 여러분 모두에게 현재 Chicago에 있는 본사에서 근무하고 있는 Greg Henderson이 10월 초부터 남미 지역 지부장 자리를 이어받게 되었다는 것을 알려 드리고자 합니다. Henderson 씨는 남미 지역의 모든 운영 업무를 감독하게 될 것이며, 이 지역에서 우리 회사는 지난 수 개월 동안 엄청난 성장을 보여왔습니다.

Henderson 씨는 지난 7년 동안 우리 JPR에서 근무해 왔기 때문에 여러분 중 많은 분들이 잘 알고 있습니다. 이곳에서 근무하기 전에, 그는 Krieg International에서 근무했으며, Rio de Janeiro와 Brasilia에 있는 그 회사의 브라질 지사에서 5년간 일했습니다. Henderson 씨는 남미의 근무 환경에 익숙한 분이고, 그곳의 기업에 근무하는 많은 중요한 연락책이 있어서 새로운 직책에서 근무하는 데 분명 도움이 될 것입니다. 그는 아르헨티나의 Buenos Aires를 기반으로 근무하게 되지만 일년 중 여러 차례에 걸쳐 남미 전역에 있는 우리 시설들을 방문할 것으로 기대하고 있습니다.

우리 JPR에서 32년 넘게 근무한 Mathieu 씨의 업적을 기리기 위해, 우리는 9월 29일 금요일에 그를 위한 작별 행사를 열 예정입니다. 이 행사는 본사 근처에 위치한 이탈리안 레스토랑인 Marino's에서 오후 6시부터 9시까지 열립니다. 이 행사에 대해 더 알고 싶으신 분께서는, 제 비서인 Corrine Wise에게 내선 번호 5830으로 연락주세요. 인사 변동에 관해 질문이 있으신 분은, 인사부장이신 Stephanie Bush에게 내선 번호 9043을 통해 이야기하시기 바랍니다.

168 Mathieu 씨는 무슨 직책에서 퇴직하는가?
   (A) 대표이사
   (B) 인사부상
   (C) 남미 지부장
   (D) 비서

169 Henderson 씨에 관해 언급된 것은 무엇인가?
   (A) 그는 남미 출신이다.
   (B) 그는 작년에 Krieg International에서 근무했다.
   (C) 그는 업계에 있는 많은 사람들을 안다.
   (D) 그는 JPR의 본사를 기반으로 근무할 것이다.

170 행사는 왜 9월 29일에 열리는가?
   (A) Henderson 씨의 승진을 축하하기 위해
   (B) Sanders 씨의 퇴직을 알리기 위해
   (C) Mathieu 씨의 업적을 인정하기 위해
   (D) 남미 시장을 대상으로 한 JPR의 계획을 논의하기 위해

171 행사는 어디에서 열릴 것인가?
   (A) Buenos Aires에서
   (B) Chicago에서
   (C) Rio de Janeiro에서
   (D) Brasilia에서

신유형 172-175는 다음 메모를 참조하시오.

발신: Julie Hamilton 〈jhamilton@skydreamsairlines.com〉
수신: 알 수 없는 수신자
제목: 연례 회의
날짜: 11월 5일

이 메모는 Sky Dreams Airlines의 연례 회의가 11월 6일, 금요일에

열린다는 것을 다시 한 번 알려 드리기 위한 것입니다. — [1] —. 예상보다 많은 분들이 회의 참석 의사를 밝혀 주셨다는 점에 유의하시기 바랍니다. 이로 인해, 회의 장소를 변경했습니다. — [2] —. 대신, East Rutherford Convention Center로 변경되었습니다. 일정을 포함한 행사의 나머지는 10월 25일로 날짜가 표기된 제 이메일에 언급된 그대로입니다.

모든 Sky Dreams Airlines 직원들께서는 행사에 참석하실 수 있습니다. 대표이사님과 이사회, 그리고 대부분의 고위 운영진들이 참석할 예정입니다. 더불어, 모든 주요 주주들과 일부 잠재 투자자들도 참석할 것입니다. — [3] —. 회의에서는 질의 응답 시간이 있을 예정이며, 직위를 막론하고 누구나 이 질의 응답 시간에 참여할 수 있습니다. 회의가 끝난 후에는, Travis Carter 대표이사님께서 다과가 제공되는 연회를 주최하실 예정입니다. — [4] —. 직원들은 참석을 위해 반드시 등록을 해야 하며, 회의에 입장하는 것이 허용되기 전에 이름을 확인할 것입니다. 문의 사항이 있으신 분은 언제든지 제게 연락하시기 바랍니다.

172 메모는 왜 쓰여졌는가?
   (A) 새로운 회의 장소를 알리기 위해
   (B) Carter 씨가 대표이사 자리에서 사임한다는 것을 언급하기 위해
   (C) 몇몇 새로운 투자자들을 찾았다는 것을 말하기 위해
   (D) 행사에 등록하도록 직원들을 장려하기 위해

173 Hamilton 씨에 관해 언급된 것은 무엇인가?
   (A) 그녀는 지난달에 행사에 관한 이메일을 보냈다.
   (B) 그녀는 대표이사 사무실에서 근무한다.
   (C) 그녀는 내일 회의에 참석할 예정이다.
   (D) 그녀는 회의를 위해 컨벤션 센터를 예약했다.

174 Hamilton 씨가 참가자들에게 무엇을 하라고 요청하는가?
   (A) 연회를 위해 미리 예약하기
   (B) 미리 질문을 준비하기
   (C) 회의 참가 신청하기
   (D) 안내를 받기 위해 Hamilton 씨에게 연락하기

175 [1], [2], [3], [4]로 표기된 위치 중에서 다음 문장이 가장 잘 어울
신유형 리는 곳은 어디인가?

   "이는 더 이상 Sky Dreams Airlines의 본사에 있는 강당에서 열리지 않을 것입니다."
   (A) [1]
   (B) [2]
   (C) [3]
   (D) [4]

176-180은 다음 공지와 이메일을 참조하시오.

Historical Preservation Society(HPS)

HPS가 여러분에게 "역사적인 문서들을 보존하는 방법"이라는 제목으로 곧 열릴 인터넷 세미나 참석을 권합니다. 이 세미나는 역사적인 성격을 지닌 오래된 문서들이 보존되도록 하고 어떠한 종류의 손상도 입지 않도록 하는 최고의 방법들에 초점을 맞출 것입니다.

이번 행사는 역사학 박사 학위를 소지하고 있으며 현재 Parker University에서 교수로 재직 중인 Steven Rohm이 진행할 예정입니다. 이 세미나는 7월 30일 오후 1시부터 오후 4시까지 진행됩니다. 참석을 원하시는 분들께서는 늦어도 7월 1일까지 등록하셔야 합니다. 세미나 비용 및 기타 세부 사항들에 관한 정보는 www.hps.org/seminar를 방

문하시면 확인하실 수 있습니다.

등록하실 때, Rohm 씨에게 질문할 내용 한 가지를 제출하실 수 있습니다. Rohm 씨는 세미나가 진행되는 동안 가능한 한 많은 질문에 답변해 드리도록 최선을 다할 것입니다. 현장에서 답변하지 못한 질문들은 늦어도 8월 10일까지 웹사이트에 서면으로 답변이 게시될 것입니다.

발신: srohm@inthistfound.org
수신: sarahhallstead@hps.org
참조: guybouchrad@parker.edu
제목: 유감스러운 일
날짜: 6월 12일

Hallstead 씨께,

귀하의 단체로부터 후원을 받아 곧 열리는 세미나에서 제 역할을 수행할 수 없다는 점을 알려 드리게 되어 유감입니다. 세미나 당일에, 저는 14세기에 쓰여진 필사본의 복원 작업에 참석하기 위해 Paris로 비행기를 타고 가야 합니다. 저는 예전에 저와 함께 공부를 했고 현재 Parker University의 역사학 교수로 재직 중인 Guy Bouchard에게 세미나에서 저의 역할을 대신해 줄 것을 얘기했고, 그분이 승낙했습니다. 필요한 사항들을 준비하기 위해 곧 귀하께 연락을 드릴 것입니다.

Bouchard 씨는 15년이 넘는 기간 동안 역사적인 문서의 복원 및 보존을 전문으로 해 오신 분입니다. 이분은 American Smithsonian Insitue 및 Vatican 두 곳과 함께 일하고 계시니, 매우 뛰어난 능력을 지닌 분입니다. 귀하께서 그를 저의 적합한 대체자로 생각하시길 바랍니다.

다시 한 번, 세미나 당일에 참석할 수 없다는 점에 대해 진심으로 사과드립니다.

안녕히 계십시오.
Steven Rohm

176 행사에 관해 알 수 있는 것은 무엇인가?
(A) 대학 교수들을 대상으로 한다.
(B) 이틀의 기간에 걸쳐 열릴 예정이다.
(C) HPS의 본사에서 열릴 것이다.
(D) 문서를 관리하는 법에 대한 정보가 제공될 것이다.

177 행사에 참여하고자 하는 사람들에 관해 언급된 것은 무엇인가?
(A) Hallstead 씨에게 질문을 할 수 있다.
(B) 미리 등록해야 한다.
(C) 모두 대학에 재학 중인 학생들이다.
(D) HPS 회원 자격이 있어야 한다.

178 Rohm 씨는 언제 비행기로 Paris에 갈 것인가?
(A) 6월 12일에
(B) 7월 1일에
(C) 7월 30일에
(D) 8월 10일에

179 Rohm 씨는 무엇을 했다고 알리는가?
(A) 행사에서 자신을 대신하도록 동료에게 요청했다.
(B) Vatican을 위해 복원 작업을 했다.
(C) 세미나에 필요한 15세기 문서를 확보했다.
(D) 참석할 수 없는 사람들에게 보여주기 위해 세미나를 녹화했다.

180 Bouchard 씨에 관해 알 수 있는 것은 무엇인가?
(A) 그는 최근에 현재 맡고 있는 자리에 임명되었다.
(B) 그는 자신의 분야에서 폭넓은 경험을 지니고 있다.

(C) 그는 Smithsonian Institute에서 정규직으로 근무하기를 희망하고 있다.
(D) 그는 유럽에서 일하는 데 대부분의 시간을 쓴다.

181-185는 다음 전단과 웹 페이지를 참조하시오.

판매: Ninkovich NK100 공업용 스테이플러

2주 전에, 저는 제 회사에서 작성되는 대규모의 보고서들을 철하기 위해 NK100 제품을 구입했습니다. 하지만 저는 NK100 제품이 오직 적은 수의 페이지밖에 철할 수 없다는 점을 알지 못했습니다. (저는 130페이지를 철할 수 있는 기기를 구입할 생각입니다.)

NK100 제품은 50페이지 또는 그보다 적은 분량의 보고서를 철하기를 원하시는 분들에게 적합합니다. 제가 구입한 스테이플러는 한 번도 사용하지 않았으며, 여전히 원래의 포장 상자에 들어 있습니다. 이 회사의 웹사이트에 따르면, Ninkovich Inc.는 스테이플러가 제대로 작동하지 않는 경우에는 언제든 제품에 대한 서비스를 제공한다고 되어 있습니다. 또한 월요일부터 Ninkovich에서 이 특정 제품이 더 이상 만들어지지는 않을 것임에도 불구하고, 이 제품의 어느 부품이든 교체되어야 하는 경우에는 여분의 부품을 제공할 것입니다. 제가 지금 막 읽은 이러한 공지 때문에, 25달러가 아닌 15달러만 받고자 합니다.

이 물품을 구매하길 원하시는 분은 아래에 기재된 전화번호로 제게 연락해 주시기 바랍니다. 제품의 외관을 보기를 원하시면 휴대전화로 사진 몇 장을 보내 드릴 수 있습니다.

Jeremy Summers (617) 905-1743

모델 번호	철할 수 있는 최대 페이지 수	가격
NK50	50	25달러
NK100	100	35달러
NK150	120	45달러
NK200	150	60달러

Ninkovich Inc.

Ninkovich Inc.는 모든 사무실의 요구를 충족할 수 있는 공업용 스테이플러를 제공합니다. 이 제품들은 아주 두꺼운 보고서를 관통해 철심을 고정할 수 있으며, 헐거워지는 것과 같은 문제를 일으키지 않습니다. Ninkovich Inc.의 모든 공업용 스테이플러에 사용되는 철심은 동일한 사이즈이기 때문에 저희 회사를 통해 구입하는 철심은 서로 바꿔 사용하실 수 있습니다. 위 도표를 보시면 어느 공업용 스테이플러가 귀하의 사무실에 적합한 것인지 확인하실 수 있습니다. 제품 시연을 원하시는 분은 (405) 444-3854로 전화하셔서 개별 예약을 하시기 바랍니다.

181 Summers 씨는 왜 자신의 기기를 판매하려 하는가?
(A) 그는 더 이상 스테이플러가 필요하지 않다.
(B) 그는 비슷한 모델이 있다.
(C) 그것은 종종 고장이 난다.
(D) 그것은 많은 양의 보고서를 처리할 수 없다.

182 전단에 따르면, 기기는 왜 낮은 가격에 판매되는가?
(A) 그것은 더 이상 생산되지 않는다.
(B) 그것은 오랫동안 사용되어 왔다.
(C) 그것은 새로운 상태가 아니다.
(D) 그것은 여분의 부품을 필요로 한다.

183 Summers 씨의 기기에 관심이 있는 사람들은 어떻게 제품을 볼 수 있는가?
(A) 그의 홈페이지를 방문함으로써

(B) 그에게 사진을 보내줄 것을 요청함으로써
(C) 그의 사무실을 방문함으로써
(D) 지역 상점에 찾아감으로써

184 웹사이트에 따르면, 모든 Ninkovich Inc.의 공업용 스테이플러의 공통된 특징은 무엇인가?

(A) 동일한 페이지 수의 문서를 철한다.
(B) 동일한 철심을 사용한다.
(C) 같은 색상으로 나온다.
(D) 무게가 아주 많이 나가지 않는다.

185 Summers 씨는 이전에 구입했던 것을 대체하기 위해 어느 모델을 구입할 가능성이 큰가?

(A)NK50
(B)NK100
(C)NK150
(D)NK200

신유형 186-190은 다음 광고와 보고서, 그리고 문자 메시지를 참조하시오.

Delarosa Co.의 인턴 모집 행사
전국 최고의 소매업체 중 한 곳의 본사에서 여러분의 여름을 보내세요!

Delarosa Co.는 New York City에서 근무할 여름 인턴을 찾고 있습니다. 인턴으로 근무함으로써, 소중한 경험을 얻을 수 있고, 소속 부서 운영 방법에 관해서도 배울 수 있으며, 유용한 업계 내 인맥을 쌓을 수도 있습니다. 저희는 Mendoza Building(127th Street 348번지)에 있는 본사에서 4월 28일 단 하루 동안만 인턴 모집 행사를 개최합니다. 모든 지원자들은 그룹 면접에 참석할 것이며, 가장 유력한 후보자들이 개별 면접 단계로 넘어갈 것입니다. 지원자들은 또한 작문 능력을 평가하기 위한 테스트를 치를 것입니다. 지원자들은 오직 하나의 부서에만 지원해야 하며, 이력서와 자기 소개서를 powellg@delarosaco.com을 통해 Glenn Powell 씨에게 보내 지원하실 수 있습니다. 다과가 제공될 예정이기는 하지만, 면접 대상자들은 각자 점심 식사 계획을 세워야 한다는 점에 유의하시기 바랍니다.

부서	그룹 면접	개별 면접	위치
회계	오전 8:00 – 오전 10:00	오전 10:00 – 정오	회의실 A
재무	오전 8:00 – 오전 10:00	오전 10:00 – 정오	회의실 B
홍보	오후 1:00 – 오후 3:00	오후 3:00 – 오후 5:00	205호실
마케팅	오후 1:00 – 오후 3:00	오후 3:00 – 오후 5:00	206호실

채용 위원회 요약 보고
Glenn Powell 작성, 4월 30일 제출

4월 28일에 열린 인턴 모집 행사 이후, Delarosa Co.의 채용 위원회는 구직 지원자들에 관해 논의하기 위해 만났습니다. 경력과 학력, 시험 점수, 그리고 인성을 포함해 여러 가지 요소들이 고려되었습니다. 위원회에서는 인턴직에 대해 다음과 같이 추천하고자 합니다.

회계: Colleen Mack
재무: Kyle Atherton
홍보: Patricia Silas
마케팅: Benjamin Avila

위와 같이 선정된 최종 후보자들이 여의치 않을 경우, 대체 후보자로

Harvey Elliot (회계), William Duffy (재무), Joelle Hudson (홍보), 그리고 Yolanda Greer (마케팅)를 추천합니다.

발신: Glenn Powell
수신 시간: 5월 4일, 오후 2:48
수신: Samuel Walbaun

안녕하세요, Sam. 당신의 부서를 위해 첫 번째로 선택한 후보자인 Kyle Atherton 씨가 인턴직을 거절했습니다. 안타깝게도, 이분은 Benson Inc.의 일자리를 대신 수락하기로 결정했습니다. 제가 대체 후보자에게 연락해 보고 더 찾아야 하는지 알려 드리겠습니다. 만일 그렇게 해야 한다면, 검토하실 수 있도록 이력서들을 보내 드리겠습니다. 그동안에, 교육에 필요한 물품들을 신청하시는 데 필요하신 양식을 이메일로 보내 드렸습니다. 이 물품들은 다음 주 수요일에 주문될 것입니다.

186 4월 28일의 행사에 관해 사실이 아닌 것은 무엇인가?

(A) 회사의 본사에서 열렸다.
(B) 참가자들에게 식사가 제공되었다.
(C) 필기 시험이 포함되었다.
(D) 지원자들은 한 개가 넘는 면접에 참석할 수도 있다.

187 Silas 씨는 어디에서 면접을 봤을 것 같은가?

(A) 회의실 A에서
(B) 회의실 B에서
(C) 205호실에서
(D) 206호실에서

188 Powell 씨는 무슨 문제점을 언급하는가?

(A) 그는 후보자들 사이에서 선택하는 데 어려움이 있다.
(B) 한 지원자가 적합한 자격을 지니고 있지 않았다.
(C) 일부 면접이 예상보다 더 오래 진행되었다.
(D) 한 후보자가 다른 곳의 일자리를 수락했다.

189 Powell 씨는 누구에게 연락할 계획인가?

(A) Harvey Elliot
(B) William Duffy
(C) Joelle Hudson
(D) Yolanda Greer

190 Walburn 씨에게 무엇이 보내졌는가?

(A) 주문 양식
(B) 교육 일정표
(C) 면접용 질문들
(D) 몇몇 이력서들

신유형 191-195는 다음 안내와 이메일, 그리고 온라인 후기를 참조하시오.

제품 정보/커튼

브랜드: Orem

Orem 커튼은 100퍼센트 폴리에스테르로 만들어졌으며, 햇빛을 차단하기 위해 안감이 두껍습니다. 이 커튼 제품은 이중의 천으로 된 세트로 판매되며, 윗부분에 고리 장식이 가려져 있습니다.

천 너비(인치): 54
천 길이(인치): 63, 84, 95, 108, 그리고 120
선택 가능한 직물: Gray-Black Diamonds, Solid Forest Green,

Black-White Stripes, Navy Floral, and Solid Navy
가격: 세트당 25–50달러, 길이에 따라 다름

모든 Orem 커튼 제품에 대해, 고객들께서는 두 개 이상의 세트를 구매하시면 커튼 고정용 장식 끈 한 쌍을 무료로 받으실 수 있습니다.

수신: 영업사원들
발신: Jessie Austin
날짜: 8월 29일
제목: Orem 커튼

영업사원 여러분께,

저는 공급업자이신 Rick Brody 씨로부터 Sophia Mills 씨가 준비했던 Orem 브랜드 커튼에 대한 안내서가 오래된 것이라는 통보를 받았습니다. 문양 중의 하나인 Navy Floral은 이 제품 라인에서는 더 이상 구매할 수 없습니다. 추가로, 120인치 길이의 제품도 단종되었습니다. 다음 주중으로 새로운 안내서가 휴게실에 구비될 것입니다. 그 사이에, 제품 정보 설명서에 있는 기존의 것을 뜯어 내셔서 폐기하시기 바랍니다. 이렇게 하면 새로 제작된 안내서가 추가될 때 혼동을 방지할 수 있습니다.

저는 9월 1일부터 9일까지 휴가로 자리를 비울 예정이지만, 긴급한 질문들은 부 지점장인 Michelle Rowe에게 전달하실 수 있습니다. 그렇지 않을 경우, 제가 돌아왔을 때 저에게 얘기를 꺼내셔도 됩니다.

안녕히 계십시오.

Jessie Austin
지점장, Perrine Home Supplies

---

https://www.perrinehome.com/reviews

홈	목록	매장 찾기	**후기**	연락처

제품 카테고리: 실내 장식용품, 커튼 　　브랜드: Orem
후기 작성자: Walter Kuhl 　　게시일: 9월 8일

제가 최근에 Perrine Home Supplies를 방문했을 때, 제 안방과 손님 방에 쓸 커튼을 구입했습니다. 차광막 커튼에 대한 종류가 다소 제한되어 있기는 했지만, 현재 제 집의 실내 장식과 어울리는 스타일 두 개를 발견했습니다. 저는 제공된 치수가 혼란스러웠으며, 아는 것이라곤 이 커튼들이 바닥에 닿는 것인지 확실히 하고 싶다는 것뿐이었습니다. 저를 도와준 영업사원은 신입이어서 그리 경험이 많지 않았습니다. 하지만 저는 부 지점장으로부터 아주 좋은 조언을 얻었습니다. 전반적으로, 제 구매에 매우 만족합니다. 거리에서 들어오는 빛이 완벽히 차단되기 때문에 훨씬 숙면합니다. 저는 분명 이 브랜드의 제품을 다시 구매할 것입니다.

191 고객들은 몇 개의 문양에서 선택할 수 있는가?

(A) 두 가지
(B) 세 가지
(C) 네 가지
(D) 다섯 가지

192 이메일 수신자들은 무엇을 하도록 요청받는가?

(A) 공급물품이 있는지 보관 구역 확인하기
(B) 설명서에서 한 페이지 없애기
(C) 고객들에게 변동 사항 알리기
(D) 매출액을 이메일로 보내기

193 Kuhl 씨에 관해 알 수 있는 것은 무엇인가?

(A) 그는 Perrine Home Supplies에서 주기적으로 쇼핑한다.
(B) 그는 특정 문양의 제품을 특별 주문했다.
(C) 그는 무료 선물을 받을 자격이 있었다.

(D) 그는 자신의 커튼 제품을 할인가에 구매했다.

194 후기에서, 첫 번째 단락, 네 번째 줄의 단어 "reach"와 의미가 가장 가까운 것은 무엇인가?

(A) 닿다
(B) (특정 수준에) 달하다
(C) 덮다
(D) 개발하다

195 Kuhl 씨는 방문 중에 누구와 이야기했는가?

(A) Jessie Austin
(B) Rick Brody
(C) Sophia Mills
(D) Michelle Rowe

신유형 ▶ 196-200은 다음 이메일들과 업무 보고서를 참조하시오.

수신: Alliance Property Management ⟨info@alliancepm.net⟩
발신: Dawn Koffler ⟨d_koffler@citytimemail.com⟩
날짜: 1월 14일
제목: 답변 부탁 드립니다

관계자분께:

저는 Raymond Tower 4층에 거주하고 있으며, 3일 전에 제 거실에 있는 에어컨에 대한 수리 작업을 요청했습니다 (신청 번호 4950). 제가 아직 아무런 답변도 듣지 못해서, 유지보수를 위한 방문 일정을 얼마나 빨리 잡아주실 수 있는지 궁금합니다. 제가 이 에어컨을 작동할 때마다, 오른쪽 측면에서 물이 뚝뚝 떨어지기 시작합니다. 제 생각에는 배수 장치에 문제가 있는 것 같아서, 이 기기를 점검하러 오실 때 여분을 하나 가져오시는 게 좋을 것 같습니다. 직접 들어 오실 수 있도록 405호에 사시는 제 이웃인 Charles Wade에게 열쇠를 맡겨 놓겠습니다. Wade 씨는 자택 근무를 하셔서 하루 종일 집에 계실 겁니다. 이 문제와 관련해 신속한 조치에 감사 드립니다.

안녕히 계십시오.

Dawn Koffler

Alliance Property Management
관리 작업 보고서, 1월 15일 / 기술자: Edward Hinton

건물	동	작업 시간	상태
Jewel Apartments	406	오전 9:00 – 9:25	부품 주문 필요
Jewel Apartments	315	오전 9:30 – 11:45	작업 완료
Raymond Tower	404	오후 1:30 – 1:50	작업 완료
Raymond Tower	218	오후 1:55 – 2:35	부품 주문 필요

수신: Dawn Koffler ⟨d_koffler@citytimemail.com⟩
발신: Jonah Rodriguez ⟨rodriguezj@alliancepm.net⟩
날짜: 1월 15일
제목: 회신: 답변 부탁 드립니다

Koffler 씨께,

귀하께서 요청하신 수리 작업이 완료되는 데 며칠 동안 기다리게 해 드려 죄송합니다. 기술자 두 명이 최근에 저희 팀에서 그만 두는 바람에 요청 사항들을 맞춰 드리는 데 어려움이 있습니다. 이 문제는 곧 해결될 것입니다. 어쨌든, Edward Hinton이 오늘 귀하의 자택에서 작업을 완료했습니다. 그가 배수 장치를 직접 가져갔기 때문에 지체 없이 수리를 할 수 있었습니다. 앞으로 며칠 동안, 에어컨을 가동하실 때 물이 떨어지는지 주의 깊게 확인해 보시기 바랍니다. 만일 물이 떨어진다면, 저희에게 즉

시 알려 주십시오.

안녕히 계세요.

Jonah Rodriguez
관리 책임자, Alliance Property Management

196 첫 번째 이메일의 목적은 무엇인가?
(A) 정책에 관해 문의하기
(B) 수리 일정을 재조정하기
(C) 요청 사항에 대해 후속 조치를 하기
(D) 물에 의한 손상을 알리기

197 Koffler 씨에 관해 유추할 수 있는 것은 무엇인가?
(A) 그녀의 아파트 열쇠가 되지 않는다.
(B) 그녀는 보통 집에서 일을 한다.
(C) 그녀의 권고 사항이 시간을 절약해 주었다.
(D) 그녀는 해당 아파트 건물에 새로 온 입주자다.

198 Koffler 씨의 아파트는 언제 방문되었을 것 같은가?
(A) 오전 9시에
(B) 오전 9시 30분에
(C) 오후 1시 30분에
(D) 오후 1시 55분에

199 Rodriguez 씨는 Alliance Property Management에 관해 뭐라고 말하는가?
(A) 그곳은 출장 수리에 대해 요금을 부과한다.
(B) 그곳은 작업 주문서 일부를 분실했다.
(C) 그곳의 관리 팀에 인원이 부족하다.
(D) 그곳의 소속 기술자가 Keffler 씨를 다시 방문할 것이다.

200 두 번째 이메일에서, 첫 번째 단락, 여섯 번째 줄의 단어 "run"과 의미가 가장 가까운 것은 무엇인가?
(A) 보여주다
(B) 관리하다
(C) 흐르다
(D) 작동하다

PART 5

101 Ledge Sporting Goods Store는 어린이들을 위한 여름 레크리에이션 프로그램의 일환으로 많은 야외 활동들을 제공합니다.

102 언론 보도에 따르면, 지역 기업가들이 지역 내 자선 단체에 기부한 금액이 올 한 해에만 3백만 달러를 넘어섰다.

103 잠정적으로 12월 19일로 예정된 회사 파티는 경영진의 승인 없이 진행될 수 없다.

104 H&J Corporation은 매력적인 광고를 만들어 내지 못했기 때문에 회사에서 바랐던 연간 수익의 5% 증가를 달성할 수 있을 것으로 보이지 않는다.

105 연례 취업 박람회의 모든 참가자들은 행사 장소에 도착하는 즉시 접수 부스에 보고해야 합니다.

106 ABX International은 긴 논의 끝에 채용을 줄일 것을 확정했다.

107 사업을 해 온 30년 동안, Aerocom Inc.는 고급 항공기를 위한 고품질의 인테리어를 디자인하는 것으로 명성을 쌓아 왔다.

108 Mason 씨는 그의 후임자가 고용될 때까지 마케팅 부사장으로 남아 있으려고 한다.

109 최근에 있었던 제조상의 문제로 인해, 이달의 첫 주에 주문되었던 모든 주문품이 7~10일 지연될 것 같다.

110 일일 업무 과정에 몇몇 간단한 단계를 도입함으로써, Devon Energy는 제품 하자를 상당히 줄였다.

111 CRP Bank와 North Broad Bank는 Piedment 지역에서의 서비스 이용 가능성을 높이기 위한 노력으로 합병할 것이라고 발표했다.

112 Herman Olerud가 쓴 〈Financial Strategems〉의 두 번째 판이 내년 여름에 온라인으로 공개될 것이다.

113 더 나은 고객 서비스를 제공하기 위해서, Eureka Family Insurance의 홈페이지는 실시간 상담과 같은 새로운 특징들을 포함하도록 최근에 업그레이드되었다.

114 Salamanca Cuisine은 '올해의 최고 레스토랑'으로 지명된 이후 그 도시에서 사람들이 가장 많이 방문하는 식당들 중 하나가 되었다.

115 모든 출장 비용 환급 신청서는 사무실로 돌아온 후 늦어도 5 영업일 전에 제출되어야 한다.

116 Outback Trails는 호주 전역에서 가장 높은 등급을 받은 어드벤처 여행사들 중 하나이다.

117 작업 관련 사고를 가장 잘 예방하기 위해서, 일상적인 안전 점검이 주 단위로 실시된다.

118 연말 파티에서 채식주의자용 식사를 하기를 원하는 사람들은 내선 번호 504로 Teresa Masters에게 연락해야 한다.

119 Ducky's 식당을 제외하고, Springfield 지역에 위치한 모든 식당들은 올해 3분기 동안에 증가된 수익을 신고했다.

120 소비자들의 엄청난 수요에 대한 대응으로, Cooper's Sporting Goods는 아동 스포츠 의류의 더 많은 선택 사항들을 개발하기로 결정했다.

121 전산화된 의료 기록 시스템으로 전환하기 위해 Kolpacoff 박사의 사무실 직원들은 먼저 모든 환자들의 기록을 수집했다.

122 Aqua, Inc.의 Tammy Butler는 그녀 회사의 주요 경쟁사의 제조 부서를 인수하는 데 관심을 표했다.

123 Aropagus Water Purification Center는 관심이 있는 사람이라면 누구에게든 상을 받은 시설물에 대한 견학을 제공한다.

124 당신의 운동을 더욱 효과적으로 만들기 위해서 개인 트레이너가 이끄는 집중 강좌 수강이 강력히 권고된다.

125 등록 양식을 작성하기 전에 안내 책자의 각 페이지를 꼼꼼히 검토할 것이 권장된다.

126 International Healthcare Awards를 수상하는 건강 전문가가 다음 달에 교육 강좌 시리즈를 이끌 예정이다.

127 내년부터 TR Motors가 생산 라인을 확대하고 아시아에 조립 공장들을 열기 시작할 것 같다.

128 Jackson 씨는 몇 달 전에 회사에서 은퇴했지만 그 공석은 아직 채워지지 않았다.

129 누구든지 마감 연장이 필요하면, Hampton 씨에게 즉시 알리시기 바랍니다.

130 Cartwright Group과 함께 일한 그녀의 경험을 고려해 볼 때, Mary Landers는 San Antonio에 기반을 둔 새로운 프로젝트를 위한 이상적인 선택이었다.

PART 6

신유형 131-134는 다음 공지를 참조하시오.

Starbuilt Construction Co.는 산업 재해가 없는 근무지를 조성하는 데 전념하고 있습니다. 실제로, 저희들은 지난 3년 동안 안전한 업무 환경을 유지해 왔습니다.

공사 현장에서 직원들의 안전을 유지하는 기록을 이어 가기 위해서, 사내 세미나가 마련되었습니다.

모든 정규직 및 계약직 직원들은 5월 17일에 있을 8시간짜리 공사 현장 교통 안전 안내 교육에 참석해야 합니다. 추가로, 모든 직원들은 교육 시간 동안 설명될 근무지 안전에 대한 최신 권고 사항들을 강조하는 업데이트된 설명서를 제공받을 것입니다.

신유형 135-138은 다음 편지를 참조하시오.

6월 13일

Pacheco 씨께,

귀하께서 Greenwall Bakery를 위해 구매하신 방송 시간이 6월 12일에 방영을 시작하기로 예정되어 있었습니다. 안타깝게도, 저희 방송국의 방송이 잠시 동안 중단되었었습니다. 이 문제가 귀하의 광고 방송 송신에 지장을 주었습니다.

저희 기술자들이 그런 일이 재발되지 않도록 하기 위해 문제를 조사하고 있습니다. 이는 극심한 기상 상황과 관련되어 있었던 것으로 보입니다.

이와 같은 불편함에 대해 사과 드리기 위해, 저희는 귀하의 광고를 3일 연장해 드릴 것입니다.

만일 어떠한 추가적인 문제가 발생한다면, 귀하께 즉시 연락 드리겠습니다. 문의 사항이 있으시면 언제든지 332-878-5645로 제게 전화 주시기 바랍니다. 귀하의 양해에 감사 드립니다.

안녕히 계십시오.

Jason Fromme
KGRM 방송국 매니저

신유형 139-142는 다음 공지를 참조하시오.

모든 Sureway Grocery Store 쇼핑객 여러분께 알립니다.

다음 달 동안 여러분께서는 Sureway의 계산 절차에 있어 몇 가지 변화

를 보실 수 있을 것 같습니다. Fremont 매장이 전산화된 새로운 계산대를 테스트하는 장소가 될 것입니다.

현재, 계산 과정은 수작업으로 이뤄지고 있습니다.

5월 10일을 시작으로, 자동 금전 등록기 사용으로 인해 계산 과정이 전산화될 것입니다. 그것들은 구매를 위해 상품을 스캔하고 상품을 가방에 담아줄 것이며, 비용 지불을 처리할 것입니다.

저희는 이 새로운 기술이 고객의 계산을 용이하게 해 드릴 것으로 기대하고 있으며, 결과적으로 대기 시간이 줄어들 것입니다. 이 기기들이 비효율적인 것으로 판명될 것이라는 우려가 있지만, 생산성에서 전반적인 증대가 있을 것으로 생각합니다.

다음 달에 방문하셔서 이 새로운 방식을 시도해 보시길 바랍니다.

안녕히 계십시오.

Flora Alvarez
총무부장, Sureway Grocery Store

신유형 143-146은 다음 이메일을 참조하시오.

수신: Arianne Fredericks 〈afredericks@MaritonHerald.com〉
발신: Susan Lee 〈slee@MaritonPostOffice.gov〉
날짜: 12월 18일
제목: 이전 공고
첨부: 사진들

Fredericks 씨께,

Mariton City 우체국이 Twelfth Avenue의 4010으로 이전할 것이며, 1월 30일에 정상 업무를 재개할 것입니다. 그에 따라, 〈Mariton Herald〉 신문에 광고를 내고자 합니다.

주민들께서 새로운 주소를 쉽게 찾는 데 도움이 될 수 있도록 작은 지도뿐만 아니라 날짜 및 새로운 위치의 주소를 포함한 간단한 광고를 만들어 주시기 바랍니다.

광고에 포함될 새 건물의 사진들을 첨부했습니다. 이 이미지들을 자유로이 넣어 주시고, 우리의 이전을 가장 명확하게 알리는 데 있어 가장 효과적이라고 판단하시는 모든 방법을 활용해 주시기 바랍니다.

광고란 비용에 관한 정보를 기다리고 있겠습니다.

Susan Lee, 부장
Mariton Post Service

PART 7

147-148은 다음 엽서를 참조하시오.

식사를 하시기 위해 Archie's Restaurants의 지점을 방문하시면 저희 매니저들 중 한 사람에게 이 엽서를 보여 주세요. 총액이 50달러가 넘으면 30% 할인을 받으실 것입니다!

고객 한 분당 한 번만 제공됩니다. 이것은 여름 시즌 특별 할인이나 겨울 대 할인과 함께 사용될 수 없습니다. 이 할인은 공항 지점들에서는 사용이 불가능합니다. 전체 사용 조건이 궁금하시면, 저희 웹사이트에 방문해 주십시오.

비고: 지난번에 Archie's를 방문하셨을 때 100달러 이상 주문하셨기에 이 특가 제공을 받으셨습니다. 계신 곳에서 가까운 지점에 대해 더 알

Archie's
Restaurants
Ltd.
PO Box 93250
Seattle,
Washington
93027

Thomas King
57b King James
Street

147 엽서에서 King 씨에 관해 암시하는 것은 무엇인가?

　　(A) Archie's Restaurant의 매니저이다.

　　(B) 전에 식당을 방문했었다.

　　(C) 관리직에 지원하고 있다.

　　(D) 웹사이트 디자이너이다.

148 수신자는 왜 문자를 보낼 것인가?

　　(A) 새 전화를 개통하기 위해

　　(B) 주문 사항이 맞는지 확인하기 위해

　　(C) 식당 위치에 관한 정보를 받기 위해

　　(D) 몇 가지 조건을 보기 위해

149-150은 다음 문자 메시지를 참조하시오.

발신: Jack Chalmers, 014-4325-2392

수신: 12월 12일 월요일 오전 12시 15분

Anthony 씨 안녕하세요.

활주로에 눈이 많이 쌓여서 제 비행기가 취소되었어요. 저는 호텔을 예약 해서 오늘 밤 여기 머물러야 할 거예요. 학교에서 제 딸을 데리고 와 줄 수 있나요? 아이의 할머니께서 집에서 기다리고 계실 테지만 지금은 차 가 없어요. 가능한 한 빨리 저에게 연락을 주길 바랍니다.

Jack

149 Jack은 왜 메시지를 보냈는가?

　　(A) 그의 딸을 데려오도록 하기 위해

　　(B) 일기예보에 대해 묻기 위해

　　(C) 자동차 대여를 준비하기 위해

　　(D) 호텔 객실료에 대해 문의하기 위해

150 Anthony는 무엇을 빨리 하도록 요청받는가?

　　(A) 교통편 마련하기

　　(B) 연락하기

　　(C) 그의 할머니를 방문하기

　　(D) 예약 확인하기

151-152는 다음 광고를 참조하시오.

Kavariso Sandwich Shop

2320 East Fulton St

Jefferson, WY 82310

(307) 555-1212

www.kavarisosandwich.com

저희 가게에 방문하지 않고 Kavariso 샌드위치의 좋은 맛을 친구들, 가 족들 그리고 동료들과 함께 하기를 원하신 적이 있으신가요? 지금부터 가능 하다고 말씀 드리게 되어 기쁩니다! 8월 1일부터, Kavariso는 단체 행 사에 맛있는 샌드위치를 제공할 것입니다.

우리는 기본 세트부터 다양한 옵션이 있는 세트까지 세 가지 샌드위치 세 트를 제공합니다.

Monster Sandwich (10-15인분) 미리 자르거나 통째로 제공되는 2 미터짜리 샌드위치, 병에 든 탄산음료. 64달러

Monster Sandwich Meal (15-20인분) Monster Sandwich, 신

선한 야채 샐러드, 병에 든 탄산음료. 88달러

Monster Sandwich Full Meal (20-30인분) Monster Sandwich, 신선한 야채 샐러드, 병에 든 탄산음료, 1인분씩 담은 여러 가지 감자칩, 디저트 (브라우니와 쿠키). 116달러

3개 이상의 세트를 주문하시면 20퍼센트 할인을 받습니다. 최소 4시간 전에 미리 전화나 웹사이트를 통해 주문하셔야 합니다.

151 이 광고의 목적은 무엇인가?

　　(A) 가게 개업 홍보하기

　　(B) 새로운 출장연회 서비스 알리기

　　(C) 최근의 메뉴 변경 설명하기

　　(D) 샌드위치 크기 비교하기

152 고객들은 어떻게 Kavariso에서 할인을 받을 수 있는가?

　　(A) 웹사이트를 통해 주문함으로써

　　(B) 미리 식사를 주문함으로써

　　(C) 최소한 3세트를 주문함으로써

　　(D) 단체 행사에서 주문함으로써

신유형▶ 153-154는 다음 문자 메시지 대화를 참조하시오.

Lucy Crouse　　　　　　　　　　오전 8:38

좋지 않은 소식이 있어요. 제 차가 오늘 아침에 시동이 걸리지 않아서, 시 내로 가는 버스를 타야 해요. 약 20분 정도 늦을 것 같습니다.

Jane Levy　　　　　　　　　　　오전 8:40

아, 이런! 그럼, 이곳에 제때 도착하셔서 오전 9시에 있을 제 발표에 필요 한 프로젝터를 설치해 주시지 못하시겠네요.

Lucy Crouse　　　　　　　　　　오전 8:41

프로젝터가 내장되어 있는 다른 방으로 옮기실 수 있을까요? 아니면 대 신 9시 30분에 시작하시는 건요?

Jane Levy　　　　　　　　　　　오전 8:42

안타깝게도, 발표 시간은 변경할 수 없고 모든 방들이 예약이 되어 있어 요. 하지만 이 작업을 대신 해 주실 다른 분을 찾아 볼게요. 누가 이 일 을 처리할 수 있는 전문적인 기술을 갖고 있을까요? IT 부서에 계신 Jim Burke 씨인가요?

Lucy Crouse　　　　　　　　　　오전 8:44

바로 그분이죠. 다시 한 번 사과 드려요. 그리고 그분께 저 대신 감사의 말씀 좀 전해 주세요.

153 Levy 씨는 무엇을 할 계획인가?

　　(A) 다른 방으로 옮기기

　　(B) 몇몇 장비를 설치하기

　　(C) 동료 직원에게 도움을 요청하기

　　(D) 대중 교통을 이용하기

154 오전 8시 44분에, Crouse 씨가 "He's the one"이라고 썼을 때 의미하는 것은 무엇인가?

　　(A) Burke 씨에게 문제점을 알렸다.

　　(B) Burke 씨의 능력에 대해 확신한다.

　　(C) 몇몇 장비를 Burke 씨에게 맡겨 놓았다.

　　(D) Burke 씨가 방을 예약했다고 생각한다.

155-157은 다음 이메일을 참조하시오.

수신: 위원회 회원들
발신: Susan Coyle
제목: 기금
날짜: 1월 27일

Cubix 미술관에서 현대 예술 전시회를 유치할 수 있도록 도와주신 것에 여러분 모두에게 다시 한 번 감사를 전하고 싶습니다. 여러분의 노고가 없었다면 절대 해낼 수 없었을 것입니다.

저는 항상 미술관에서 전시할 흥미로운 새 예술품을 찾고 있습니다. 이는 우리 시의 사람들이 현대 문화를 직접 경험할 수 있는 기회를 얻게 하기 위해서입니다. 지금 이 순간, 저는 예술가 Patrick Cabaye 씨와 현재 협상 중에 있습니다. 저희 미술관은 여름에 그의 작품을 전시하기를 바라고 있습니다.

여러분들도 아시다시피, 운영비를 감당하기 위하여 저희는 회원들의 기금에 의존하고 있습니다. Cabaye 전시회의 자금 조달을 돕기 위해, www.cubix.com/members에 방문하셔서 가능한 한 많은 도움을 주시기 바랍니다. 저희 미술관은 여러분의 지속적인 후원에 진심으로 감사드립니다.

귀하께서 미술관의 이와 같은 최근의 노력을 지원해 주시길 바랍니다. Cubix 미술관은 Redbridge 시에 빈번히 여행객들을 끌어들이고 있고, 이는 모든 지역 사업체에 도움이 되고 있습니다. 여기 모든 이들을 대표하여, 다시 한 번 여러분의 지속적인 지원에 감사를 전하고 싶습니다.

Susan Coyle
수석 큐레이터, Modern Art Exhibits

155 이메일의 목적은 무엇인가?

(A) 회의에 참석한 것에 대해 직원들에게 감사를 전하기
(B) 예술가의 약력을 제공하기
(C) 회원들에게 기부를 요청하기
(D) 한 지역 업체로 가는 길을 안내하기

156 Coyle 씨에 대하여 언급된 것은 무엇인가?

(A) Cubix에서 전시의 주제를 담당한다.
(B) 최근 Redbridge로 이사했다.
(C) 올여름에 작품을 출품할 것이다.
(D) 흥미롭게 뜨고 있는 예술가이다.

157 Cubix에 관하여 언급된 것은 무엇인가?

(A) 티켓을 온라인으로 판매한다.
(B) 10년 넘게 운영되고 있다.
(C) 보수공사 때문에 문을 닫고 있다.
(D) 관광 명소가 되었다.

158-160은 다음 정보를 참조하시오.

비즈니스 운용을 위해 Geronimo Inc.를 선택하세요!

귀사의 직원들이 판매 교섭을 통해 거래를 확보하는 것에 종종 실패합니까? 그들이 다른 사업체의 경영진에게 발표할 때 자신감이 부족합니까? 그러면 Geronimo Inc.가 귀사의 모든 문제를 해결할 수 있을 것입니다!

저희의 차별화된 교육 DVD는 귀사의 직원들에게 다양한 발표 기술을 가르쳐서 중요한 거래를 더 잘 획득할 수 있도록 할 것입니다. 자료는 할리우드 배우 Ryan Minute 씨의 음성으로 전달되어 집중할 수 있고 재미있게 들을 수 있습니다. 평균적으로, 사업체들은 저희의 제품을 사용한 후 매출이 12퍼센트 증가했다고 보고합니다.

주문을 하기 위해서는, www.geronimo.org를 방문해 주세요. 만약 200달러 이상 구매하시면, 저희 회사 운영 담당자 Dan(dan@geronimo.inc)에게 이메일을 보내셔서 15퍼센트 할인을 적용받으시기 바랍니다. 우리 배송 기사들은 가능한 한 빨리 귀하의 주문을 배송하기 위해서 대기하고 있을 것입니다.

Geronimo Inc.

158 정보의 목적은 무엇인가?

(A) 몇몇 교육용 DVD를 홍보하기
(B) 배송비를 알리기
(C) 영업 회의를 알리기
(D) 곧 나올 영화를 광고하기

159 Geronimo Inc.의 제품들을 사용하면 누가 직접적으로 이익을 얻겠는가?

(A) 사업 관리자들
(B) 세미나 리더들
(C) 컴퓨터 판매자들
(D) 판매직원들

160 Geronimo Inc.에 관하여 언급된 것은 무엇인가?

(A) 새 운영 담당자를 찾고 있다.
(B) 자사의 증가된 매출액을 보고했다.
(C) 자격이 있는 고객들에게 할인을 제공한다.
(D) 전화 주문 시스템이 있다.

신유형 161-164는 다음 온라인 채팅을 참조하시오.

Nicole Gannon [오전 10:23]
제 이메일에 이렇게 신속히 답변해 주신 것에 대해 두 분께 감사 드립니다. 두 분께서 우려하시는 부분이 있었던 것 같아서 이 대화를 통해 제가 해결해 드려야겠다고 생각했습니다.

Denise Shulte [오전 10:24]
로고를 만드는 일에 대한 우리 팀의 업무 일부를 다시 배정하시겠다고 말씀하셨을 때 저는 혼란스러웠습니다.

Youngsik Park [오전 10:26]
맞습니다. 저희의 현재 프로젝트들은 중단되는 건가요?

Nicole Gannon [오전 10:27]
그건 프로젝트에 따라 다릅니다.

Denise Shulte [오전 10:28]
저는 현재 Bond Tech를 위해 몇몇 이미지 작업을 하고 있습니다. 이전의 프로젝트들 때문에, 그들의 취향을 알고 있어서 이 프로젝트를 포기하지 않는 편이 좋을 것 같습니다.

Nicole Gannon [오전 10:31]
이해합니다. 하지만 가장 경험이 많은 디자이너께 크게 주목 받고 있는 고객들을 배정하기로 결정했습니다. 그것이 바로 Youngsik 씨께서 Bond Tech를 맡으시게 되는 이유입니다.

Youngsik Park [오전 10:33]
제가 경험이 더 많을 수는 있겠지만, 좀 더 큰 틀에서 생각해 보시죠.

Nicole Gannon [오전 10:34]
무슨 말씀이시죠?

Youngsik Park [오전 10:35]
Bond Tech의 직원들은 아마 자신들이 익숙한 사람과 일하는 것을 선호할 겁니다.

Nicole Gannon [오전 10:36]

일리 있는 말씀이세요.

Denise Shulte [오전 10:38]

그럼, 제가 일을 계속 진행하고 Youngsik 씨께서 검토하시는 건 어떨까요?

Nicole Gannon [오전 10:41]

그렇게 하셔도 좋습니다. 제가 배정 업무 목록을 좀 수정해서 곧 두 분께 새로운 목록을 보내 드리겠습니다.

161 Gannon 씨는 어느 부서를 책임지고 있을 것 같은가?

(A) 영업부
(B) 정보통신 기술부
(C) 그래픽 디자인부
(D) 회계부

162 Shulte 씨에 관해 암시된 것은 무엇인가?

(A) Park 씨보다 경험이 더 많다.
(B) 예전에 Bond Tech와 일해 본 적이 있다.
(C) Gannon 씨의 이메일에 답하지 않았다.
(D) 한 프로젝트의 마감 시한을 지킬 수 없다.

163 **신유형** 오전 10시 33분에, Park 씨가 "let's look at the bigger picture"라고 썼을 때 의미하는 것은 무엇인가?

(A) 전략에 대해 동의하지 않는다.
(B) 고객과 함께 일하는 것을 요청했다.
(C) 회사가 성장할 것이라고 생각한다.
(D) 회의를 열고 싶어 한다.

164 Gannon 씨는 곧이어 무엇을 할 것 같은가?

(A) 새로운 계약서를 발송하기
(B) Bond Tech의 직원에게 연락하기
(C) 직원들의 배정 업무를 변경하기
(D) Shulte 씨가 작업한 것을 검토하기

신유형 ▶ 165-167은 다음 기사를 참조하시오.

Spartsville을 방문하는 〈Attack of the Drones〉

12월 2일 — [1] —. 새 영화 〈Attack of the Drones〉가 12월 19일부터 20일까지 주말 동안 팬들에게 시사회에 참석할 기회를 주기 위하여 Spartsville Movie Theater를 방문할 예정입니다. 이것은 예술적 관심을 높이기 위한 시의 노력의 일환으로 Russell Padrino 시장에 의해 마련되었습니다. 영화는 그 다음 주에 일반인들에게 공개될 것입니다.

— [2] —. 각각의 관객들은 또한 따뜻한 음료를 무료로 제공받을 것입니다. 모든 참석자들은 영화의 장면이 실린 무료 잡지도 받을 것입니다.

영화는 토요일 오후 4시와 일요일 오후 5시에 시작할 예정입니다. — [3] —. 추가로, 일요일에는 Dan Scremington 감독이 영화와 관련하여 관객들에게 질문을 받기 위해 참석할 것입니다. 이 추가 행사는 상영 후에 극장의 Room E에서 있을 것입니다. — [4] —. 전체 시간표가 보고 싶고 행사에 참가하고 싶으시면, www.attackofthedrones.net을 방문해 주세요.

165 이 기사의 목적은 무엇인가?

(A) 영화 시사회를 광고하기
(B) 잡지 구독을 제안하기
(C) 시장 선거를 알리기

(D) 컨벤션 센터의 개관식을 알리기

166 Scremington 씨에 대해 언급된 것은 무엇인가?

(A) 억만장자이다.
(B) 대회 우승자이다.
(C) 최소한 일 년에 한 번은 Spartsville에 방문한다.
(D) 12월 20일에 질문에 답변을 할 것이다.

167 **신유형** [1], [2], [3], [4]로 표기된 위치들 중에서 다음 문장이 가장 잘 어울리는 곳은 어디인가?

"영화 시사회는 모든 사람들에게 무료이며, 티켓은 선착순으로 교부됩니다."

(A) [1]
(B) [2]
(C) [3]
(D) [4]

168-171은 다음 공지를 참조하시오.

공고: Stockholm 무역 박람회

게시 날짜: 2월 22일

우리 경영진은 Readyflex Electronics의 직원들이 다음 달에 Quantum Future 무역 박람회 참석을 위해 다시 한 번 스웨덴으로 가게 되었음을 알리게 되어 기쁩니다. 모든 팀장들은 Chilview Hotel에 객실을 마련하고 비용을 지불하셔야 하고, 그 비용은 회사가 무역 박람회 마지막 날에 상환할 것입니다. 또한 영업팀의 6명이 행사에 참석해야 합니다. 이 기회에 자원하길 원하시는 직원들은 2월 26일까지 Mark Kennedy 씨에게 연락을 주셔야 합니다.

무역 박람회는 The Alexander White Building에서, 3월 20일부터 24일까지 매일 오전 9시부터 오후 5시까지 열릴 것입니다.

우리 제품들이 다음과 같이 전시될 예정입니다.
> Readyflex T500d 모델: 화요일과 목요일, Quantum Main Hall; 스탠드 B
> 고급 배터리 및 메모리 카드 세트: 수요일, Quantum Main Hall; 스탠드 B
> Readyflex Bluejaw 모델: 금요일, 외부 구역 C
> 차체 수리 작업의 혁신: 목요일, Quantum Main Hall; 스탠드 B

신규 고객들을 유치하기 위하여 무역 박람회에서 우리의 모든 제품 가격은 20% 할인됩니다. 제품에 판매 가격을 반드시 표시해 두세요.

계약 조건에 따라, 직원들은 이 행사에 참여할 의무가 없습니다. 그러나 여기에 지원하시는 직원들은 다음 달 본봉에 500달러의 보너스를 추가로 받을 수 있을 것입니다. 다시 한 번 말씀드립니다, 참석을 희망하시면 Kennedy 씨에게 연락해 주세요.

Leonard Schulz, 이사
Readyflex Electronics 인사과

168 이 공지의 목적은 무엇인가?

(A) 특정한 고급 호텔 체인을 홍보하기
(B) 신상품의 출시에 대해 세부 사항들을 제공하기
(C) 관리직 공석을 알리기
(D) 해외 출장에 관한 정보를 제공하기

169 Readyflex Electronics에 관해 알 수 없는 것은 무엇인가?

(A) 그곳의 제품이 주중에 매일 전시될 것이다.
(B) 전에 Quantum Future 무역 박람회에 참석한 적이 있었다.
(C) 할인 가격으로 제품 이용이 가능할 것이다.

(D) 제품이 한 곳보다 더 많은 곳에서 전시될 것이다.

170 언제 숙박료가 상환될 것인가?

(A) 2월 22일에

(B) 3월 20일 전에

(C) 3월 24일에

(D) 2월 26일 전에

171 공지에 따르면, 직원들은 왜 행사에 참석하는 것에 관심이 있을 것 같은가?

(A) 금전적인 보상을 받을 것이다.

(B) 승진 자격을 얻을 것이다.

(C) 새로운 절차에 대해 테스트를 받을 것이다.

(D) 신제품을 고객들에게 설명해야 한다.

신유형 172-175는 다음 편지를 참조하시오.

Antonio's Stationery

Claire Darras
Supervisor, Shawcross Services 193 Bridge Street
Chicago, IL

11월 4일

Darras 씨께,

저희 Antonio's가 운영 방식에 있어 몇 가지 변화를 계획하고 있음을 알려드리기 위해 편지를 드립니다. — [1] —. 그러기 때문에, 이제 저희 보관 창고의 확장 공사가 몹시 필요합니다. 일단 완료되면, 현재보다 더 많은 고객님들께 문구류 서비스를 제공할 수 있을 것입니다. 저희는 12월 10일에 다시 문을 열 수 있을 것으로 예상합니다.

— [2] —. 저희 업체는 11월 14일과 12월 9일 사이에 문을 닫을 것이며, 이는 고객님의 평상시 서비스가 일시적으로 중단되는 것을 의미합니다. 다시 문을 여는 날에, 고객님들을 저희 매장에 초대해서 축하 바비큐 파티를 열 것입니다. 참석하시는 모든 고객님들은 다음 구매 시 15 퍼센트 할인 적용이 가능한 쿠폰을 받을 것입니다. 저희는 가능한 한 많은 분들께서 참석하시기를 바랍니다.

— [3] —. 저희 매장에 매우 필요한 변화를 단행하는 동안 기다려 주시길 바랍니다. 저희는 매주 정기적으로 물품을 구매해 주시는 귀사와 같은 회사들에게 진심으로 감사를 전하고 싶습니다. 게다가, 불편함을 드린 데 대한 사과의 의미로 내년에 무료 배송 서비스를 제공해 드릴 것을 약속합니다. — [4] —.

만약 위의 정보와 관련하여 문의 사항이 있으시면, 주저하지 마시고 연락주세요. 555-3954-322로 전화 연락이 가능합니다. 저희 업체는 정상적으로 서비스를 재개하여 귀사가 필요하신 문구 제품을 제공할 수 있기를 바랍니다.

안녕히 계십시오.

Antonio Cinelli
CEO, Antonio's Stationery

---

172 Antonio's Stationery에 관해 알 수 있는 것은 무엇인가?

(A) 배송 서비스를 업그레이드할 것이다.

(B) 3월에 다른 곳으로 이전할 것이다.

(C) 곧 더 많은 고객들을 응대할 것이다.

(D) 웹사이트를 가지고 있다.

173 두 번째 단락, 두 번째 줄의 어구 "cut off"와 의미가 가장 가까운 것은 무엇인가?

(A) 향상되는

(B) 나누어지는

(C) 줄여지는

(D) 중단되는

174 Shawcross Services에 관하여 언급되지 않은 것은 무엇인가?

(A) Chicago에 위치해 있다.

(B) Antonio's Stationery에서 정기적으로 제품을 받는다.

(C) 회계 회사이다.

(D) 내년에 배송비를 면제받을 것이다.

175 [1], [2], [3], [4]로 표기된 위치들 중에서 다음 문장이 가장 잘 어울리는 곳은 어디인가?

신유형

"올해 3월에 개업한 이래로, 정기 구매자들의 꾸준한 증가를 보이고 있습니다."

(A) [1]

(B) [2]

(C) [3]

(D) [4]

176-180은 다음 이메일들을 참조하시오.

발신: Tony Burrows ⟨tburrows@supersaver.com⟩
수신: Lucy Vixen ⟨lucyvixen3@guardian.net⟩
날짜: 3월 7일 월요일 오전 11:40
제목: 사업 제휴

Vixen 씨께,

저와 제 동료는 지난 목요일(3월 3일) 귀하를 뵙게 되어 반가웠습니다. 저희들끼리 추가로 더 논의한 후에, Guardian Inc.의 제품을 우리 초대형 아울렛에 들여놓을 가능성에 기쁘다는 것을 알려드리고자 합니다. 저희 사무실로 다시 오셔서 계약 조건을 정하면 좋겠습니다. 그때 말씀 드렸듯이, 이 회의는 상무이사 Robert Ruins 씨가 주관할 것입니다. 그는 또한 개인적으로 귀사의 메이크업 상품에 깊은 인상을 받았고 SuperSaver가 보유하고 있는 친환경적인 제품을 갖추는 정신을 완벽히 대변한다고 생각합니다.

이번 주 목요일(3월 10일)에 우리 사무실에 들르실 수 있으신가요? 만약 불가능하시다면, Ruins 씨는 금요일 오후에 스케줄이 빌 것이고 그때 회의를 하셔도 됩니다. 예상하신 대로, 그의 스케줄은 시간이 지날수록 매우 빠르게 다른 일정이 잡히기 때문에 가능한 한 빨리 선호하시는 시간대를 알려주세요. 아니면, 그의 개인 비서인 Tina Coggins 씨에게 555-292-5200번으로 직접 연락하셔서 약속을 정하셔도 됩니다. 추가적인 논의를 고대합니다.

안녕히 계십시오.

Tony Burrows
제품 결정 책임자

발신: Lucy Vixen ⟨lucyvixen3@guardian.net⟩
수신: Tony Burrows ⟨tburrows@supersaver.com⟩
날짜: 3월 7일 월요일 오후 4:00
회신: 사업 제휴

Burrows 씨께,

귀사의 매장에 저희 회사의 상품을 들여놓고자 하신다는 이메일을 읽고 저는 매우 기뻤습니다. 상상하실 수 있는 것처럼, 이것은 저희 같은 작은 제조업체들에게는 대단히 성공적인 일입니다. 안타깝게도, 제 일정을 확인했는데 제안하신 목요일에 예정되어 있는 출장이 있습니다. 그러나 금요일에는 귀하를 뵐 수 있을 것이고 정오 이후에 언제든 가능합니다.

추가로, 저는 지난주에 저희가 논의했듯이 몇 가지 홍보 제품을 만드는 것의 가능성에 대하여 제 동료 Phil Satters와 얘기했습니다. 그는 이것이 귀사의 고객들에게 저희 제품을 홍보하는 데 매우 도움이 될 것임에 동의했습니다.

금요일을 고대합니다.

안녕히 계십시오.
Lucy Vixen

176 첫 번째 이메일의 목적은 무엇인가?

(A) 배송 일정 정하기
(B) 회의 주선하기
(C) 주문하기
(D) 몇 가지 지시 사항 제공하기

177 Guardian Inc.는 어떤 종류의 제품을 제조할 것 같은가?

(A) 전자제품
(B) 화장품
(C) 주방용품
(D) 사무용품

178 첫 번째 이메일에 따르면, Burrows 씨는 왜 Vixen 씨와 회의를 하기를 원하는가?

(A) 제품 세부 사항을 의논하기 위해
(B) 불만을 제기하기 위해
(C) 계약을 협상하기 위해
(D) 광고물을 제작하기 위해

179 Vixen 씨는 언제 출장을 갈 것으로 예상하고 있는가?

(A) 3월 3일에
(B) 3월 7일에
(C) 3월 10일에
(D) 3월 11일에

180 SuperSaver Inc.의 직원이 아닌 사람은?

(A) Ruins 씨
(B) Burrows 씨
(C) Coggins 씨
(D) Satters 씨

181-185는 다음 기사와 소책자의 서문을 참조하시오

Kingsville Business Weekly

예정된 확장 공사로 도시 공항이 일주일 동안 폐쇄되기 2주 전인 6월 14일에, Kingsville Association of Businesses(KAB)는 〈Keep Your Business Flying〉이라는 제목의 소책자를 발행했다. 이 책자는 예정된 폐쇄 기간 동안 정상적인 사업 운영에 미칠 영향을 완화시키기 위한 전략을 지역 사업체들에게 제공하기 위해 만들어졌다. 책자는 KAB에 등록된 모든 사업체로 직접 배송되었고, 다른 업체들의 요구가 지대하여 추가 인쇄가 필요했다.

KAB는 현재 새로운 버전을 만들기 위해 처음 출판물을 수정하고 있다. 이는 필수적인 보수 공사를 위해 예정된 High Road의 한 달간 폐쇄로 인해 향후의 지역 내 사회 기반 시설 작업에 영향을 주는 시의회의 최근 발표를 고려한 것이다.

협회가 9월 초에 발표하길 원하는 새 버전은 공항 폐쇄에 대응하기 위해 조치를 취해야 했던 업체 대표가 작성한 서문을 실을 것이다. 비싼 인쇄 비용을 줄이기 위하여, 책자의 온라인 전용 버전이 발간될 것이다.

KAB는 이전의 지장으로 영향을 받은 다른 회사들에게 의견을 요청하고 있다. 인터뷰 준비가 된 점주들은 Marcus Holmes 씨에게 연락하도록 요구된다. 전화번호 555-3934-3178이나 이메일 marcusholmes@kab.gov.com로 연락할 수 있다.

Keep Your Business Flying (제2판)
서문

웹사이트에서 받은 많은 주문 때문에, 우리 Ryan Clothing은 많은 제품들을 전국에 배송하기 위해 장거리 수송에 의존하고 있고, 우리 사업의 60%가 Kingsville Airport을 통해 이루어지고 있습니다. 그리하여, 우리는 공항이 일주일간 폐쇄된다고 발표되었을 때 거대한 수익 손실이 일어날 것이라고 예상했습니다. KAB에서 책자가 집에 오기 전까지 그랬습니다. 책자는 이 기간 동안 국내의 광범위한 철도망을 이용하는 방법과 같이 많은 유용하고 실용적인 정보를 담고 있었습니다. 공항은 결국 3주간 폐쇄되었지만, 우리는 회계사가 예상한 60%의 매출 감소와 비교하여 오직 20%만 매출이 감소했습니다. 그들의 조언이 우리 회사의 피해를 최소화하게 하였으므로 이 공적에 대해 KAB는 인정을 받을 만합니다.

귀사의 피해를 최소화하는 데 있어 비슷한 조언뿐만 아니라, 이 새로운 책자는 예상보다 시간이 더 소요된 공항 공사에 대처한 방법을 설명한 CEO들의 경험담도 실었습니다. 귀사가 이렇게 힘든 시기를 헤쳐나가는 데 도움이 될 그들의 경험에서 혜택을 얻기를 바랍니다.

Ryan Waynefield

181 기사에서 KAB의 출판물에 대해 언급된 것은 무엇인가?

(A) 2주 전에 디자인되었다.
(B) 유료로 배포되었다.
(C) 매우 인기가 많았다.
(D) 오직 한 작가에 의해서 쓰였다.

182 회사의 대표는 왜 KAB 직원과 연락할 것인가?

(A) 공항 폐쇄에 항의하기 위해
(B) 일자리에 지원하기 위해
(C) 책을 구매하기 위해
(D) 그들의 의견을 말하기 위해

183 서문에서, 첫 번째 단락, 여덟 번째 줄의 단어 "credit"과 의미가 가장 가까운 것은 무엇인가?

(A) 기부
(B) 인터뷰
(C) 힘
(D) 인정

184 Ryan Clothing에 관하여 언급되지 않은 것은?

(A) 얼마간의 수익 감소를 경험했다.
(B) Waynefield가 소유하고 있다.
(C) 제품을 배송할 때 철도는 제외했다.
(D) 온라인 주문을 받는다.

185 공항 폐쇄에 관해 알 수 있는 것은 무엇인가?

(A) Ryan Clothing에 이익을 주었다.
(B) 많은 사업체들의 파산 원인이 되었다.
(C) 계획보다 오랫동안 폐쇄되었다.
(D) 도시 관광 산업에 피해를 주었다.

Berkshire Film Festival
전 연령층을 위한 시대를 뛰어 넘는 영화들

Berkshire Artists Association은 5월 12일 화요일부터 5월 15일 금요일까지 Cessna Theater에서 지역 역사상 최초로 개최되는 영화제를 후원합니다. 축제 기간 동안 매일 저녁 관객들은 다른 고전 영화들을 즐길 수 있습니다. 모든 영화는 오후 7시에 시작되며, 입장권은 Cessna Theater 매표소 및 시내 여러 곳에서 구입이 가능합니다. 예정된 어느 영화든지 5장 이상의 입장권을 구입하시면 10퍼센트의 할인을 받으실 수 있습니다.

상영 시간표:
   5월 12일: 〈The Journey to New Orleans〉
   5월 13일: 〈Mystery of Silver Cave〉
   5월 14일: 〈Susanne's Dream〉
   5월 15일: 〈Train in the Night〉

수신: Conrad Varga 〈c.varga@npinbox.com〉
발신: William Riggs 〈riggsw@trujilloinc.com〉
참조: Annie Lockwood 〈lockwooda@trujilloinc.com〉
날짜: 5월 2일
제목: 다가오는 방문

Varga 씨께,

귀하께서 Berkshire에 위치한 Trujillo Inc.의 지사에 오실 수 있다니 기쁩니다. 채용 위원회의 위원들이 전화상의 질문에 대한 귀하의 답변에 깊은 인상을 받았으며, 저희는 귀하와 직접 면접을 볼 수 있기를 고대하고 있습니다. 저희는 잠재 직원들을 그룹 A와 그룹 B로 나눴으며, 이 그룹들은 각각 5월 13일과 14일에 저희 지사를 방문할 것입니다. 귀하께서는 그룹 A에 배정되셨습니다. 당일 일정을 마치고 나면, 그룹 구성원들은 지역 영화제에 참석할 것입니다. 이는 저희가 감사의 뜻을 전하는 방법입니다. 질문이 있으시면 제게 알려 주시기 바랍니다.

안부를 전하며,

William Riggs

수신: Annie Lockwood 397-555-1695
발신: William Riggs 397-555-7940

기차 일정상의 오류로, Conrad Varga 씨는 그룹 B로 옮겨져야 합니다. Amelia Raff씨가 그룹 A로 옮겨질 것이기 때문에 우리는 티켓에 대해서는 아무것도 변경하지 않아도 됩니다. 따라서, 여전히 두 그룹 모두에 대해 티켓 대량 구매 할인을 받을 수 있습니다. 모든 분들께서 오시면 반드시 방문객 출입증을 전부 준비해 주시기 바랍니다. 출입증에 넣을 각 방문객의 사진을 이메일로 보내 드렸습니다. 감사합니다!

186 Berkshire Film Festival에 관해 언급된 내용은 무엇인가?
   (A) 시의 후원을 받았다.
   (B) 처음으로 열릴 것이다.
   (C) 오직 성인들만을 대상으로 한다.
   (D) 하루에 2회 상영을 할 것이다.

187 Varga 씨가 Trujillo Inc.를 방문하는 목적은 무엇인가?
   (A) 점검을 실시하기
   (B) 교육 프로그램을 진행하기
   (C) 면접에 참석하기
   (D) 매매 협의하기

188 Varga 씨는 원래 어느 영화를 관람하기로 되어 있었는가?
   (A) 〈The Journey to New Orleans〉
   (B) 〈Mystery of Silver Cave〉
   (C) 〈Susanne's Dream〉
   (D) 〈Train in the Night〉

189 Riggs 씨는 Lockwood 씨에게 무엇을 하도록 요청하는가?
   (A) 출입증 준비하기
   (B) 축제 티켓 한 장 더 구입하기
   (C) 식사 예약하기
   (D) 초대 손님 목록 확인하기

190 Riggs 씨에 관해 알 수 있는 것은 무엇인가?
   (A) 기차역에서 몇몇 방문객들을 만날 것이다.
   (B) Berkshire Artists Association의 회원이다.
   (C) 예전에 Raff 씨를 직접 만난 적이 있다.
   (D) 최소 10장의 티켓을 구입할 것이다.

www.weddingbliss.net

Wedding Bliss
여러분의 결혼식에 큰 힘이 되어 드립니다!

홈	서비스	포토 갤러리	이용 후기	연락처

결혼식을 계획하는 일은 기쁨과 즐거움의 시간이지만, 또한 스트레스가 될 수도 있습니다. 저희 Wedding Bliss를 고용하셔서 아래의 서비스 일부 또는 전부를 경험해 보세요.
   – 직접 선택하신 색상을 완벽하게 만들어 주는 품격 있는 꽃과 장식
   – 행사 내내 음악을 제공해 주는 피아니스트 또는 오르간 연주자
   – 저녁 만찬 및 축하 연회를 위한 DJ
   – 손님들을 위한 발레 파킹
   – 추억을 담아 드리는 전문 사진 기사
   – 매우 다양한 종류의 출장 요리 선택권

저희는 Columbia Building(288 Chapman Lane)과 Ritter Complex(1434 Jefferson Street)에 지점이 있으며, 다른 장소에서의 결혼식도 도와 드립니다. 고객이 원하는 방식으로 모든 일이 진행될 수 있도록 하기 위해 모든 과정을 고객과 함께 합니다. 여기를 클릭하셔서 경험 많은 저희 행사 기획 전문가들 중의 한 명에게 오늘 연락하세요.

수신: Alysa Frederick 〈fredericka@whitleyinc.com〉
발신: Jennifer Morton 〈j_morton@garlandsales.com〉
날짜: 9월 14일
제목: Wedding Bliss

Frederick 씨께,

저는 현재 제 결혼식을 계획하는 과정에 있으며, Wedding Bliss의 고용을 고려하고 있습니다. 회사에서 참고 정보들을 제공해 주었지만, 저는 누군가를 통해 따로 확인해 보고 싶었습니다. 저는 Jackson Center에서 근무하고 있으며, 제 사무실에 근무하는 회계사인 Daniel Crawford 씨께서 제게 당신의 연락처를 알려 주셨습니다. 그는 당신이 4월에 Wedding Bliss의 서비스를 이용하셨다고 말씀하셨습니다. 제게 당신의 경험에 관해 말씀해 주실 수 있으신지 궁금하며, Wedding Bliss의 장소를 이용하셨는지 아니면 다른 장소를 이용하셨는지도 궁금합니다. 출장 요리 업체로부터 제공받는 선택 사항들이 충분하셨나요? 또한, 식중에 연주했던 피아니스트는 어땠나요? 제게 어떤 정보라도 제공해 주시면 매우 감사하겠습니다.

감사합니다!

Jennifer

수신: Jennifer Morton 〈j_morton@garlandsales.com〉
발신: Alysa Frederick 〈fredericka@whitleyinc.com〉
날짜: 9월 14일
제목: 회신: Wedding Bliss

Morton 씨께,

제게 연락 주셔서 기쁩니다. 결혼식 계획이 얼마나 중압감이 큰지 알고 있기 때문에 제가 도와 드릴 수 있어 기쁩니다. 전반적으로, 저는 Wedding Bliss의 서비스에 매우 만족했습니다. 처음에는, 저희는 다른 결혼식장인 Villa Hall에서 서비스를 이용하고 싶었지만, 저희가 원했던 날짜에 예약이 있었습니다. 저희는 Jefferson Street에 있는 Wedding Bliss의 시설을 사용하기로 결정했는데, 당시에는 Chapman Lane에 있는 것은 아직 열지 않았기 때문입니다. 저희 결혼식에는 약 300명의 손님들이 있었으며, 많은 분들이 채식주의자들이었습니다. 출장 요리 업체에서 제공한 음식은 저희의 모든 손님들의 입맛을 맞출 수 있을 만큼 충분히 다양했습니다. 저는 또한 Wedding Bliss의 직원들이 준비해 준 장식이 정말로 마음에 들었습니다. 축제 느낌이 나면서도 품격이 있었으며, 제가 원하는 스타일을 완벽하게 충족해 주었습니다.

이와 같은 행사는 아주 개인적인 것이기 때문에, 그곳의 컨설턴트들 중 한 분과 약속을 잡으실 것을 권해 드립니다. 이는 무료로 가능하며, 업체 측에서 제공하는 것을 정확히 파악하는 데 도움을 줄 것입니다.

행운을 빕니다!

Alysa

---

191 Wedding Bliss에 관해 언급된 것은 무엇인가?

(A) 장식은 행사 전날에 설치된다.
(B) 저녁 만찬을 위해 피아노 연주자를 제공한다.
(C) 사진 촬영 서비스를 제공한다.
(D) 제공되는 서비스가 모두 함께 이용되어야 한다.

192 Morton 씨는 어디에서 Frederick 씨의 이메일 주소를 얻었는가?

(A) Wedding Bliss의 웹사이트에서
(B) 친척에게서
(C) Wedding Bliss의 직원에게서
(D) 그녀의 동료에게서

193 Morton 씨가 물어본 것 중에서 Frederick 씨에 의해 답변되지 않은 부분은 무엇인가?

(A) 장식
(B) 가격 정보
(C) 메뉴 선택권
(D) 음악 연주자

194 Frederick 씨가 조언한 것은 무엇인가?

(A) 제안 사항을 협의하기
(B) 상담 일정을 잡기
(C) 무료 카탈로그를 요청하기
(D) 다른 곳의 시설을 이용하기

195 Wedding Bliss의 최신 시설은 무엇인가?

(A) Columbia Building
(B) Jackson Center
(C) Ritter Complex
(D) Villa Hall

신유형 ▶ 196-200은 다음 안내 정보와 온라인 포럼, 그리고 메시지를 참조하시오.

Lloyd Designs의 스탠딩 책상 및 부대용품

연구 결과는 장시간 앉아 있는 것은 신체에 해로울 수 있음을 보여줍니다. Lloyd Designs의 스탠딩 책상은 완벽한 해결책입니다. 책상은 대부분의 사람들에게 적합하도록 조절될 수 있으며, 완벽한 업무 공간을 만드는 데 필요한 부대용품도 있습니다.

– 스탠딩 책상 　　32인치x52인치의 표면적으로 되어 있으며, 24인치에서 50인치 사이의 높이 조절 가능 범위. 검은색, 흰색, 회색 구매 가능. 가격: 499달러 / 모델명: G284

– 조절 가능한 의자 　쿠션이 들어가 있고 검은 가죽으로 덮인 등받이 없는 의자로, 22인치에서 36인치 사이의 높이 조절 가능 범위. 가격: 149달러 / 모델명: T175

– 모니터 암 　　화면을 완벽히 위치시키는 가장 쉬운 방법. 최대 20파운드까지 지지 가능. 검은색 테두리로 된 회색 디자인. 가격: 99달러 / 모델명: W422

– 스탠딩 매트 　　서 있는 동안 피로를 방지하도록 돕는 부드러운 표면. 미끄럼 방지 재질의 표면이 특징. 검은색 구매 가능. 가격: 29달러 / 모델명: K398

lloyddesigns.com에서 온라인 주문하세요.

---

http://www.realfeedbackforum.com

회사명: Lloyd Designs　　　　　　　　　스레드 개설: 1월 8일

Fabian Roscoe　　51분 전에 게시됨

저는 제 자택 사무실에서 사용할 Lloyd Designs의 스탠딩 책상을 구입했는데, 전반적으로 사용 결과에 만족합니다. 제 업무 공간에 이 책상을 추가한 것이 제가 겪고 있는 요통을 상당히 줄여 주었습니다. 하루 중에 앉거나 일어서서 다양한 자세로 일할 수 있는 기능이 마음에 듭니다. 서 있는 것은 또한 제 다리 근육을 튼튼하게 하고 신체 균형을 향상시키는 데 도움이 되었습니다.

이 책상을 적극 추천하기는 하지만, 부대용품들에 대해서는 같은 의견을 말할 수 없습니다. 저는 T175 모델에 관해 분명히 우려되는 점이 있습니다. 이 제품은 소형 사이즈이기는 하지만 성인 한 명을 지탱하기에 충분히 튼튼하지 않은 것 같습니다. 저는 또한 K398 모델도 구입했지만 바닥에 검은색 자국을 남겼습니다.

---

http://www.realfeedbackforum.com

개인 메시지　　　　수신: Fabian Roscoe　　　　발신: Lloyd Designs

Roscoe 씨께,

저는 Lloyd Designs의 고객 서비스 담당 직원입니다. 귀하께서 저희 스탠딩 책상에 만족하고 계신다는 점에 기쁘게 생각하며, 친절한 의견에 감사 드립니다. 저희 부대용품이 자국을 남기는 것과 관련해, 귀하께서는 이와 같은 문제점을 겪고 계신 유일한 고객이 아니십니다. 귀하께서 설명해 주신 바로 그 이유에 때문에 저희는 그 제품을 회수했습니다. 저희는 현재 새로운 재료를 사용하고 있으며, 귀하께 기꺼이 무료 대체품을 배송해 드리겠습니다. 귀하의 이메일 주소를 제게 개인 메시지로 보내 주시면, 무료 대체품을 받기 위해 필요한 양식을 이메일로 보내 드리겠습니다. T175 모델에 대한 귀하의 우려와 관련해서는, 이 제품이 저희 연구소에서 철저히 테스트되었으며 350파운드가 넘는 무게를 견딜 수 있는 제품이라는 점을 장담합니다.

안녕히 계십시오.

Kevin Siegel, Lloyd Designs

196 Roscoe 씨는 자신의 책상에 관해 무엇이라고 언급하는가?

(A) 세련된 디자인으로 되어 있다.

(B) 해당 제품 사용이 통증 완화로 이어졌다.

(C) 소형 사이즈로 나온다.

(D) 조립하기가 쉬웠다.

197 온라인 포럼에서, 첫 번째 단락, 다섯 번째 줄의 단어 "balance"와 의미가 가장 가까운 것은 무엇인가?

(A) 나머지

(B) 안정적임

(C) 생산성

(D) 조화

198 Siegel 씨는 Roscoe 씨에게 무엇을 보내겠다고 제안하는가?

(A) 할인 쿠폰

(B) 모니터 암

(C) 스탠딩 매트

(D) 제품 카탈로그

199 Roscoe 씨는 무엇을 하도록 요청받는가?

(A) 우편으로 제품을 반품하기

(B) 손상 부위 사진을 이메일로 보내기

(C) 개인 메시지로 답변하기

(D) 전화번호를 제공하기

200 Lloyd Designs의 등받이 없는 의자에 관해 무엇이 사실일 것 같은가?

(A) 재료가 바뀌었다.

(B) 회수되었다.

(C) 다양한 색상으로 나온다.

(D) 내구성이 매우 좋다.

PART 5

101 재무 부서가 월급 지급을 준비할 수 있도록 신입 사원들은 각자의 은행 통장 사본을 팩스로 보내야 한다.

102 저희 금융 기관에서 주택 담보 대출을 신청하실 때 공인된 부동산 가치 평가액을 포함해 주시기 바랍니다.

103 무역 박람회의 등록 서류들은 Grayson 씨 사무실의 안전한 곳에 수치에 따라 정리 보관되어 있다.

104 Helena Building의 우편물실의 직원들은 보통 소포와 편지들을 수령하고 약 30분 후에 전달해 준다.

105 주방에 있는 조리대와 기기들이 교체되어야 하지만, 조명 설비는 여전히 좋은 상태를 유지하고 있다.

106 공동 창립자인 Samuel Lars 씨가 은퇴할 때 그와의 협의를 통해 Gail Hendricks 씨는 그 회사의 상당한 지분을 얻을 수 있었다.

107 제때 계약 조건을 이행하려는 노력에도 불구하고, 2월 말까지 충분한 제품이 시설로부터 운송되지 못했다.

108 고객 서비스 담당 직원들은 각각의 Mariana Resort 손님들이 최상의 편안함과 편리함을 경험하는 것을 보장하기 위해 항상 열심히 일하고 있다.

109 비록 많은 사람들이 그 박물관은 지나치게 야심적이라고 생각했지만, 박물관은 단 5년 만에 세계적 수준의 작품들을 획득해냈다.

110 회사의 최고 경영자인 Hu Chang은 여러 부서들 사이에서 폭 넓은 협력을 필요로 하는 계획을 시행했다.

111 Seaside Express를 이용하는 모든 승객들은 유효한 신용카드로 표를 구매해야 하며 환불이나 교환이 필요할 경우에 대비해 영수증을 보관해야 한다.

112 주말과 야간, 그리고 종종 초과 근무를 할 수 있는 유연성은 Fremont City Hospital의 비서 직책에 있어 필수 요건이다.

113 Jules Electronics Inc.는 새로운 태블릿 견본이 개선되어 연휴 시즌 전에 시장에 나오길 바라고 있다.

114 기술팀은 Hamilcar Moreno 씨가 유용한 해결책을 생각해 낼 때까지 다리와 관련된 무게 문제를 해결하는 데 어려움을 겪고 있었다.

115 수상 경력이 있는 작가 Jeremy Keith는 12권의 소설을 출간했는데, 이들 중 여러 권이 몇 년간 베스트 셀러였다.

116 Ralling 인터넷 및 전화 서비스 비용이 한 달에 10달러만큼 증가되었다.

117 내년부터, Chula Vista 지역의 주민들은 그들의 공과금 고지서를 우편이 아닌 전자 메일로 받을 것이다.

118 태양열 발전 시스템은 지역 호텔의 수요를 충족하기 위해 특별히 고안되었다.

119 비록 시즌에 따라 운영 시간이 변경되기는 하지만, 그 주의 공원과 레크리에이션 센터는 일년 내내 개장한다.

120 대안들을 조사한 후에, 새 에어컨을 설치하는 것이 가까운 미래에 이용 가능한 모든 해결책들 중에서 가장 저렴한 것이라는 결론이 내려졌다.

121 오랜 지연 끝에 새 건물 공사 프로젝트에 대한 예산 제안서가 이사회에 의해 마침내 승인되었다.

122 마케팅 부서는 다가오는 몇 달 동안 회사의 인지도를 높이기 위한 전략적 계획의 개요를 설명할 예정이다.

123 맛있는 저희 아이스크림의 샘플은 저희 매장 방문자 누구든 요청하면 맛보실 수 있습니다.

124 헌신적인 직원들의 노력 덕분에, 재정 지원 요청서 제출의 마감 기한이 지켜질 수 있었다.

125 Total Catering Services가 자사의 패밀리 레스토랑 사업을 남미로 확장시킬지는 그 회사의 자금과 노동력을 활용하는 능력에 달려 있다.

126 공립학교 식당에서 제공되는 모든 식사는 정부의 영양 요구량을 준수해야 한다.

127 신입 회원은 미리 등록비를 지불하면 연례 세미나에 참석하는 것이 허용된다.

128 분기 보고서에 인용된 Henderson 지역의 부동산 가격은 지역 중개인들이 모은 정보를 통해 수집된 것이다.

129 회사의 부사장인 Mark Poe가 Kit Foods의 새 회장으로 임명된 것을 발표할 것이다.

130 Hullet Laboratory는 저렴한 가격의 제약품을 개발한 업적으로 많은 권위 있는 연구 관련 상들을 받은 것으로 잘 알려져 있다.

PART 6

신유형 131-134는 다음 공지를 참조하시오.

Dilantin Windows and Doors에 오신 것을 환영합니다! 35년 전 회사가 설립된 이후로, 저희 엔지니어들은 업계에서 최상의 품질로 제작된 창문과 문을 디자인해 왔습니다. 저희의 가장 큰 목표는 저희 로고를 지니고 있는 각각의 제품이 브랜드 기준에 부합되게 기능하도록 하는 것입니다.

저희는 기꺼이 고객들의 이야기를 듣고자 합니다. 저희 직원들은 모든 고객 제안 사항을 마치 회사의 제품 관리 담당자들 중 한 명에게서 들은 것처럼 여깁니다.

저희는 고객 여러분께 양질의 제품과 서비스를 제공하기를 원합니다. 그 목적을 달성하기 위해서, 저희는 여러분께서 저희 직원들 중 한 명과 함께 하는 실시간 채팅에 참여하시기를 요청합니다. 직원들이 저희 제품과 관련해 여러분께서 가지고 계실 모든 문의 사항에 대해 기꺼이 답변해 드릴 것입니다.

신유형 135-138은 다음 공지를 참조하시오.

Santorini Bank 직원 여러분께,

여러분의 컴퓨터에 어떤 문제가 생길 경우, IT 서비스 부서로 연락 주시기 바랍니다. 그 부서의 전문가들이 각 시스템이 사용 목적에 맞게 작동하도록 해줄 것입니다.

특히, 마음에 걸리시는 어떠한 문제라도 발생하면, santorinibank.itservices.com에서 보고서를 작성하실 수 있습니다. 귀하의 연락처와 어느 컴퓨터를 사용하시는지, 그리고 문제점에 대한 설명을 반드시 명시해 주시기 바랍니다.

또한, 수리 과정을 용이하게 하기 위해서 모든 가능한 상세 정보를 제공해 주시기 바랍니다.

IT 서비스 부서에서 문제점들을 완전히 분석하고 그에 따라 대응하는 데 때때로 24시간이 넘게 필요할 수도 있다는 점을 유념해 주시기 바랍니다.

귀하의 협조 및 양해에 감사 드립니다.

신유형 139-142는 다음 이메일을 참조하시오.

발신: jhill@westernwaterplant.gov
수신: heather.kim@uod.edu
날짜: 4월 22일
제목: 회신: 흙 사용

Kim 씨께,

저희가 도시의 상수도를 정화할 때 제거된 흙을 지역의 농장 및 화원에 비료로 마케팅하여 활용할 것을 제안해 주신 이메일에 감사 드립니다.

신중히 고려한 후에, 저희 경영진은 이것이 저희가 이전에 사용한 폐기물을 처리하는 방식에 대한 매우 현실적인 대안이라고 생각하고 있습니다. 가장 비용 효율적인 마케팅 및 분배 방식을 확립하기 위해 이미 위원회가 결정되었습니다.

이 문제는 저희에게 매우 중요한 것이며, 저희에게 글을 써서 보내는 데 귀하의 시간을 내어주셔서 감사 드립니다.

University of Dranton에서의 귀하의 학업이 잘 되시기를 바랍니다. 여름에 대학생 인턴십에 지원하는 것을 고려해 보십시오. 귀하의 진취성과 혁신적인 생각이 Western Water에서 매우 높은 평가를 받을 것입니다.

안녕히 계십시오.

Joe Hill
Western Water Plant 담당자

신유형 143-146은 다음 공지를 참조하시오.

모든 승객 여러분께 알립니다.

3월 한 달 동안, 지하철 시스템이 다양한 변화를 겪을 것이며, 이것은 수정된 열차 운행 일정을 필요로 합니다. 이러한 변화에는 승객 탑승 칸의 현대화와 열차 정류장의 보수 작업이 포함될 것입니다.

저희는 이 과정을 3월 25일 이전에 완료할 계획입니다.

3월 2일부터 시행될 임시 시간표는 대중 교통 스마트폰 애플리케이션을 통해 이용하실 수 있습니다. 대체 시간표는 불편함을 줄이기 위한 것입니다.

이 프로젝트와 관련된 모든 최신 상황은 Public Transit Authority 웹사이트(PTA.gov/CloverCity)에 게시될 예정입니다. 문의 사항은 subway@ccpta.gov로 보내실 수 있습니다. 제목에 "3월 보수 공사"라고 기재해주세요.

감사합니다.

Samuel Lee
Clover City Public Transit Authority

PART 7

147-148은 다음 공지를 참조하시오.

귀하의 편의를 위해

저희는 고객들께서 빌려 가실 수 있는 열선 담요가 있습니다. 여러분께서 예약을 하실 때 이 담요를 객실에 놓아 두도록 요청하실 수 있습니다. 또한 안내 데스크에서 근무하는 직원에게 얘기하시면 커피메이커나 믹서기 같은 기기를 빌려 가실 수 있으며, 이 기기들은 선착순으로 이용이 가능합니다.

외국에서 전기 면도기나 기타 소형 기기들을 가져오시는 분들은 가져오시는 물품들이 거의 확실히 변환기를 필요로 하기 때문에 전압 변환기를 요청하셔야 합니다. 안내 데스크에 전화하시면, 객실로 즉시 보내 드릴 것입니다.

147 이 공지는 어디에서 찾아볼 수 있을 것 같은가?
(A) 호텔에서
(B) 미용실에서
(C) 슈퍼마켓에서
(D) 전자 기기 매장에서

148 공지를 읽는 사람들이 요청할 수 없는 물품은 무엇인가?
(A) 커피메이커
(B) 믹서기
(C) 전기 면도기
(D) 전압 변환기

신유형 ▶ 149-150은 다음 문자 메시지 대화를 참조하시오.

Timothy, 오후 1:21
안녕하세요, Caroline. 저는 Jasper 씨와의 회의를 위해 버스를 타고 지금 막 Sampson Building에 왔는데, 그분의 성함이 건물 층별 안내에 기재되어 있지 않아요. 제 책상에 있는 노트를 좀 확인해 주시겠어요? 제가 거기에 그분의 사무실 번호를 적어 놨거든요.

Caroline, 오후 1:24
508호실이에요. 회의 후에 Jasper 씨를 모시고 Vivian's Restaurant에 가시는 게 맞으시죠? 그곳은 보통 금요일에 바빠요.

Timothy, 오후 1:25
좋은 지적입니다. 지금 자리를 하나 예약할게요.

Caroline, 오후 1:27
좋습니다. 즐거운 시간 보내세요!

149 Caroline은 Timothy에게 문자를 쓸 때 어디에 있는가?
(A) 레스토랑에
(B) 버스에
(C) Sampson Building에
(D) 그의 사무실에

150 오후 1시 24분에, Caroline 씨가 "It's usually busy on Friday"라고 썼을 때 의미하는 것은 무엇인가?
신유형
(A) Jasper 씨가 아마도 늦을 것이다.
(B) 저녁 식사 예약을 해야 한다.
(C) Timothy가 교통 체증에 갇힐 수도 있다.
(D) 그녀는 예약을 할 수 없었다.

151-152는 다음 영수증을 참조하시오.

고객 명세서

고객 성명: Jacob Irwin　　　예약 코드: 459-549MV
회사명: T.Y. Saks　　　　　　예약 날짜: 4월 11일
주소: 45 Robinson Road, Des Moines, IA

도착 날짜: 4월 20일　　　　고객 수: 성인 1명
출발 날짜: 4월 22일　　　　객실 종류: 디럭스

날짜	내역	금액	참고 사항
4월 20일	디럭스 룸	150.00달러	
4월 20일	룸 서비스 (저녁)	42.99달러	
4월 21일	디럭스 룸	150.00달러	
4월 21일	룸 서비스 (점심)	18.00달러	
4월 21일	국제 전화 통화	12.75달러	통화 시간 10분
4월 22일	룸 서비스 (아침)	22.00달러	

소계: 395.74달러
세금: 27.29달러
총계: 423.03달러
지불 액: 423.03달러
미지불 총액: 0.00달러

Rudolph Hotel
45 Baker Street, Seattle, Washington

비용 지급인: T.Y. Saks
신용카드 번호: ****9804

Rudolph Hotel을 이용해 주셔서 감사합니다. 다시 찾아 주시기를 바랍니다.

151 Irwin 씨는 언제 Rudolph Hotel에서 체크아웃했는가?
(A) 4월 11일에
(B) 4월 20일에
(C) 4월 21일에
(D) 4월 22일에

152 영수증에서 알 수 있는 것은 무엇인가?
(A) Irwin 씨는 매일 그의 객실에서 저녁을 주문했다.
(B) 전체 호텔 청구 비용이 지불되지 않았다.
(C) Irwin 씨가 묵었던 호텔은 Des Moines에 위치해 있다.
(D) Irwin 씨의 고용주가 숙박비를 지불했다.

153-154는 다음 광고를 참조하시오.

Cousteau Pro Pool Care

Crestville에서 가장 신뢰할 수 있는 30년이 넘은 수영장 관리 서비스 업체!

날씨가 점점 따뜻해지고 있고, 지금이 바로 여름에 대비해 여러분의 수영장을 준비할 시기입니다! 5월 한 달에 한해, Cousteau Pro Pool Care가 "Season Starter" 장비 점검 서비스와 수영장 오픈 패키지에 대해 특별 할인가를 제공합니다. "Season Starter" 서비스의 일정을 온라인으로 신청하시든 전화로 하시든 상관없이, 할인 코드 MAY16를 제시하시고 정가에서 50달러를 할인 받으세요. 저희 기술자들은 전문적으로 교육을 받았으며, 그들은 이틀 안에 여러분의 수영장을 깨끗하고 사용할 준비가 되도록 할 것을 보장해 드립니다.

수영장이 문을 연 후에는, 주간 관리 패키지를 통해 여름 내내 여러분의 수영장을 빛이 나도록 깨끗하게 유지하세요. 또한 사설 및 상업용 수영장 모두를 대상으로 공인된 안전 점검과 적당한 가격의 수리 서비스도 제공해 드리고 있습니다. (314) 555-1212로 Cousteau Pro Pool Care에 전화하시거나 저희 웹사이트 cousteauppc.com을 방문하시기 바랍니다.

153 회사에 관해 알 수 있는 것은 무엇인가?

(A) 신입 직원들을 위해 교육을 제공한다.

(B) 확고히 자리를 잡은 회사이다.

(C) 공공 수영장을 위한 서비스 업체이다.

(D) 개업 기념일로 인해 세일을 하고 있다.

154 이 회사는 "Season Starter" 패키지에 무엇을 약속하는가?

(A) 신속한 결과

(B) 무료 수리

(C) 안전 관련 강좌

(D) 수영 강습

155-157은 다음 편지를 참조하시오.

Great Harvest Bank
2300 Windsor Street
Atlanta, Georgia

10월 5일

Peter Oh
2511 Amberidge Trail
Unit 3
Sandy Springs, GA 30319

저희 Great Harvest Bank는 귀하께서 금융 선물을 보호하기 위해 저희를 선택해 주신 것을 대단한 영광으로 생각합니다. 저희 은행에 회원으로 가입하신 귀하께서는 대단히 소중하므로 귀하의 개인 정보 보안은 저희 은행에서 가장 우선시 하는 일들 중 하나입니다. 11월 1일부로, 저희 온라인 서비스에 로그인하실 때마다 귀하의 신분을 확인하는 비밀번호가 필요할 것입니다.

이 비밀번호를 설정하기 위해, 귀하께서는 저희 파일에 있는 전화번호 xxx-xxx-0693으로 자동 녹음된 전화를 한 통 받게 되실 것입니다. 이 시스템이 귀하께 귀하의 계좌에 로그인하실 때 사용하실 6자리 숫자를 입력하도록 할 것입니다. 문의 사항이 있으시거나 실제 직원을 통해 비밀번호를 설정하기를 선호하시는 경우, 800-232-5242로 전화 주셔서 저희 Great Harvest Bank의 직원과 통화하시기 바랍니다.

안녕히 계십시오.

Jenny Kim
Great Harvest Bank

---

155 편지를 쓴 이유는 무엇인가?

(A) Oh 씨가 Great Harvest Bank에 회원 가입을 했다.

(B) 최근에 보안상의 위반이 발생되었다.

(C) 현재의 로그인 시스템에 변동 사항이 생겼다.

(D) 신규 온라인 계정이 가동될 준비가 되어 있다.

156 비밀번호 설정에 관해 언급된 내용은 무엇인가?

(A) 기존의 비밀번호를 대체할 것이다.

(B) 비밀번호를 설정하기 위해서 모든 회원들이 각자의 계정에 로그인해야 한다.

(C) Oh 씨는 비밀번호 사용 여부를 선택할 수 있다.

(D) 은행 직원과 이야기하는 방법으로 완료될 수 있다.

157 두 번째 단락, 두 번째 줄의 단어 "prompt"와 의미가 가장 가까운 것은 무엇인가?

(A) 설득하다

(B) 이끌다

(C) 중단시키다

(D) 활성화하다

신유형 ▶ 158-160은 다음 편지를 참조하시오.

Trenton Courier
67 Fairmont Drive
Vancouver, 캐나다

Bill Hamilton
Hamilton Consulting 309 W. Pacific Avenue
Vancouver, 캐나다

Hamilton 씨께,

저희 Trenton Courier는 귀하와 5년이 넘는 기간 동안 사업 파트너 관계를 유지해 오고 있다는 사실에 대해 감사 드립니다. — [1] —. 귀하와 귀하의 회사에 캐나다와 미국의 전 지역을 대상으로 한 신속한 익일 서비스를 제공하는 것에 대해 대단히 기쁘게 생각합니다. — [2] —. Trenton Courier는 중요한 소포를 빠르고 가장 저렴한 가격에 배송하는 것과 관련해 한치의 실수도 하지 않습니다. — [3] —. 귀하께 저희 회사에서 제공하는 서비스를 확대했다는 것을 알려 드리고자 합니다. — [4] —.

* 현재 유럽 전 국가를 대상으로 익일 항공 우편 서비스를 제공합니다.
* 현재 아시아와 남미의 전 국가를 대상으로 3일 항공 우편 서비스를 제공합니다.
* 현재 캐나다와 미국의 어느 지역으로든 피아노와 같은 대형 물품(최대 2톤) 맞춤 운송 서비스를 제공합니다.

새로운 서비스에 관해 더 많은 정보를 원하시거나 비용 제도에 관해 알고 싶으시면, 언제든지 전화 주시기 바랍니다.

안녕히 계십시오.

Russell Peterson
대표, Trenton Courier

---

158 편지는 왜 쓰여졌는가?

(A) 사업 파트너에게 할인을 제공하기 위해

(B) 새로운 사무실이 개업하는 장소를 언급하기 위해

(C) 새로운 서비스에 관한 정보를 제공하기 위해

(D) 다른 국가에 있는 직책을 광고하기 위해

159 Trenton Courier에 관해 알 수 있는 것은 무엇인가?

(A) 선택된 고객들에게 요금을 할인했다.

(B) 규격이 큰 소포에 대한 운송 서비스를 제공한다.

(C) 본사를 미국으로 이전한다.

(D) 다양한 아시아 언어를 말할 수 있는 직원들이 있다.

160 [1], [2], [3], [4]로 표기된 위치들 중에서 다음 문장이 가장 잘 어울리는 곳은 어디인가?

신유형

"다음은 저희가 이룬 것들입니다."

(A) [1]

(B) [2]

(C) [3]

(D) [4]

161-163은 다음 광고를 참조하시오.

Springwater의 모든 주민들께서는 이번 토요일에 있을 독특한 행사에 참석하시기 바랍니다. Springwater Community Center가 마침내 문을 열 준비가 되었습니다. 2년이 넘는 공사 끝에, 이 주민 센터가 이제 완공되었습니다. 이 센터에는 테니스 코트와 조깅 트랙, 공원, 그리고 수영

장을 포함한 다양한 야외 시설이 갖추어져 있습니다. 또한 농구 코트와 에어로빅 공간, 그리고 언어 및 미술 강좌를 위한 여러 강의실과 같은 많은 실내 시설도 있습니다.

주민 센터를 찾아오시는 방문객들은 20에이커가 넘는 모든 구역을 견학하실 수 있습니다. 그들은 센터의 회원이 되는 것의 혜택에 대해서 알게 될 것입니다. 그리고 회원들에게만 독점적으로 제공될 모든 강좌와 스포츠 행사에 대해서도 알게 될 것입니다. 센터 내 직원들이 현장에 있어서 어떤 질문에 대해서도 답변해 드릴 것입니다.

이 센터는 Springwater의 Golden Fields 인근에 있는 Valley Road 90번지에 위치해 있습니다. 방문객들께서는 토요일 오전 9시에서 오후 6시 사이에 언제든지 찾아오실 수 있습니다. 개장 행사에 참석하실 수 없는 분들은 웹사이트 www.springwatercommunitycenter.org에서 언제든지 확인해 보실 수 있습니다. 회원 가입 비용과 관련된 정보는 온라인으로 찾아보시거나 센터에 있는 직원과 함께 논의하실 수 있습니다.

161 Valley Road 90번지에서 무슨 행사가 열리는가?
(A) 주민들에게 제공되는 강좌에 대한 세미나
(B) 새 시설물 건축에 관한 회의
(C) 새 공공 편의 시설 소개
(D) 지역 사회에 참여하는 것에 관한 발표

162 Springwater Community Center에 관해 알 수 있는 것은 무엇인가?
(A) 공사 과정에서 예산을 초과했다.
(B) 사람들은 그곳에서 다양한 활동에 참여할 수 있다.
(C) 오직 회원들만 센터의 야외 시설물을 이용할 수 있다.
(D) 이번 주말에 회원 가입에 대한 특별 할인을 제공한다.

163 웹사이트에서 무엇이 제공되는가?
(A) 서비스 비용 지불에 관한 정보
(B) 주민 센터의 사진
(C) 직원들의 이름 목록
(D) 다음 달에 제공되는 모든 강좌

신유형▶ 164-167은 다음 기사를 참조하시오

시설물을 업그레이드한 Chapman Manufacturing

AUGUSTA (6월 12일)—미국 내에서 가장 큰 전자 제품 제조업체들 중의 하나인 Chapman Manufacturing이 Augusta 지역에 있는 자사의 공장 시설물을 업그레이드할 예정이라고 발표했다. "우리 회사는 스페인과 일본에 있는 기업들과 몇몇 새로운 계약을 막 체결했습니다. — [1] —."라고 Gerald Powell 사장이 밝혔다. "우리는 노동력 규모를 그대로 유지하면서 동시에 생산을 증가해야 합니다."

Powell 씨는 회사의 공장 내에 있는 조립 라인이 최신 기기를 추가함으로써 향상될 것이라고 말했다. — [2] —. 결과적으로, 직원들의 효율성이 최대 40퍼센트까지 개선될 것으로 기대되고 있다. 설치될 예정인 이 기기들은 Deco, Inc.에서 제조되는 제품들이다.

Powell 씨는 Chapman Manufacturing이 회사 내의 인력을 축소할 계획이 없다고 언급했다. — [3] —. "우리는 올해 여러 추가 계약을 맺을 것으로 기대하고 있습니다."라고 기자 회견에서 말했다. "그리고 우리는 어느 직원도 해고할 계획이 없는데, 이는 우리 직원들과 같이 고도로 훈련된 사람들을 어느 경쟁사에서든 데려가도록 하는 것은 어리석은 일이 될 것이기 때문입니다."

그는 대부분의 직원들이 새로운 기계를 사용하도록 교육을 받아야만 할 것이라고 덧붙였다. Chapman Manufacturing은 Deco 사 소속 엔지니어들이 진행하는 기계에 관한 세미나와 교육 과정을 열 예정이다. Mastroeni 씨는 교육 받는 것을 기대하는 직원들 중의 한 사람이다. — [4] —. "저는 제 일을 더 잘할 수 있고 빠르게 할 수 있는 방법을 배우길 기대하고 있습니다"라고 그는 말했다. "그리고 새로운 기술을 습득하는 것은 또한 대단한 일이 될 겁니다."

164 Chapman Manufacturing이 자사의 기기를 업그레이드하려는 이유로 언급되지 않은 것은 무엇인가?
(A) Chapman Manufacturing은 더 많은 직원을 고용하는 것을 원하지 않는다.
(B) Chapman Manufacturing은 해외에서 추가적인 사업을 계약했다.
(C) 기계가 직원들이 일을 더 잘할 수 있게 해 줄 것이다.
(D) Chapman Manufacturing의 경쟁사들이 새로운 기계를 구입하고 있다.

165 Powell 씨에 따르면, Chapman Manufacturing의 일부 직원들은 무엇을 할 것인가?
(A) 다른 나라에 있는 시설로 전근 가기
(B) 기술을 향상시키는 것에 대한 지도 받기
(C) 같은 분야에 있는 새로운 일 찾기
(D) 승진되고 급여 인상 받기

166 Mastroeni 씨가 현재 하는 일의 종류는 무엇인가?
(A) 그는 더 나은 기계를 위해 새로운 디자인을 만들어 낸다.
(B) 그는 조립 라인에서 기기를 조작한다.
(C) 그는 공장의 직원들을 관리한다.
(D) 그는 새로운 기계에 대한 교육을 받는다.

167 [1], [2], [3], [4]로 표기된 위치들 중에서 다음 문장이 가장 잘 어울리는 곳은 어디인가?

신유형

"이는 이전보다 직원들이 각자의 업무를 훨씬 더 신속하고 정확하게 완수할 수 있게 해 줄 것이다."

(A) [1]
(B) [2]
(C) [3]
(D) [4]

신유형▶ 168-171은 다음 온라인 채팅을 참조하시오.

Acrex 고객 서비스 온라인 상담 센터

직원 James Turner 오전 9:42
안녕하세요. 저는 Acrex 고객 서비스팀의 James입니다. 오늘 무엇을 도와 드릴까요?

Charlotte Farrell 오전 9:43
저는 귀사의 Book Tracker 230 소프트웨어 프로그램을 구입했고 귀사의 웹사이트에서 다운로드 받았어요. 그런데 등록을 할 수 없어요.

직원 James Turner 오전 9:44
제가 도와 드릴 수 있습니다. 먼저, 등록 페이지로 가시기 바랍니다. 구입하실 때 사용하신 성함에 따라 자동으로 사용자 이름이 보이실 겁니다.

Charlotte Farrell 오전 9:46
지금 등록 페이지를 보고 있어요. 여기에 사용자 이름이 cfarrell로 나와 있고요.

직원 James Turner 오전 9:47

좋습니다. 이제, 소프트웨어를 설치하실 때 선택하신 비밀번호를 입력하세요.

Charlotte Farrell 오전 9:48
지금 처음 사용하는 거예요.

직원 James Turner 오전 9:50
알겠습니다. 그러시면 직접 고르신 비밀번호를 사용하시는 대신, 저희 회사에서 생성한 초기 비밀번호를 사용하셔야 합니다. 문자와 숫자가 포함한 12개의 글자로 된 일련번호입니다.

Charlotte Farrell 오전 9:51
그걸 어디에서 찾을 수 있죠?

직원 James Turner 오전 9:52
구매 영수증이 포함된 이메일을 받으신 후에 12개의 글자로 된 이 일련번호가 있는 환영 이메일을 하나 더 받으셨어야 합니다.

Charlotte Farrell 오전 9:53
저는 영수증만 받았어요. 제 스팸 편지함을 확인해 볼게요.

Charlotte Farrell 오전 9:56
거기에도 없어요.

직원 James Turner 오전 9:57
괜찮습니다. 제가 이메일로 새로운 비밀번호를 발급해 드릴 수 있습니다. 시간이 잠깐 걸릴 겁니다.

Charlotte Farrell 오전 9:59
감사합니다.

직원 James Turner 오전 10:00
채팅 창에 잠시 대기하고 계시다가 이메일을 받으시면 알려 주십시오.

Charlotte Farrell 오전 10:01
알았어요, 그럴게요.

---

168 Farrell 씨는 왜 도움이 필요한가?

(A) 그녀가 구입한 소프트웨어를 받지 못했다.
(B) 그녀는 엉뚱한 프로그램을 다운로드했다.
(C) 그녀는 일부 필수 데이터를 삭제했다.
(D) 그녀는 소프트웨어 프로그램에 접속할 수 없다.

169 오전 9시 48분에, Farrell 씨가 "It's my first time using it"이라 신유형 고 썼을 때 의미하는 것은 무엇인가?

(A) 그녀는 그녀의 컴퓨터를 다시 시작해야 한다.
(B) 그녀는 비밀번호를 만들지 않았다.
(C) 그녀는 그녀의 사용자 이름을 알지 못한다.
(D) 그녀는 등록 페이지를 찾을 수 없다.

170 Turner 씨는 환영 이메일에 관해 무슨 말을 하는가?

(A) 사용자 이름을 변경하는 것에 대한 설명이 들어 있다.
(B) 도착하는 데 며칠 걸릴 것이다.
(C) 영수증과 별도로 발송되었다.
(D) 구매 가격을 확인해 준다.

171 Farrell 씨는 왜 채팅 창에 남아 있도록 요청받는가?

(A) 이메일을 받았는지 확인해 주기 위해
(B) 품질 보증 관련 정보를 받기 위해
(C) 다른 제품을 다운로드하기 위해
(D) 더 자세한 설명을 듣기 위해

172-175는 다음 편지를 참조하시오

Standish Metals, Inc.
2020 Watson Road
Dublin

10월 17일

Daniel Hampton
매니저, Hampton's Place
209 Burlington Avenue
Dublin

Hampton 씨께,

10월 12일 금요일에 제 동료 직원들 중의 한 분을 위한 시상식 연회를 개최해 주신 것에 대해 감사 드리기 위해 이 편지를 씁니다. 저는 귀하의 식당을 자주 찾는 즐거움을 누린 적은 없었지만, 그날 밤에 상을 받은 Roy Capers 씨가 가장 좋아하는 장소들 중의 한 곳입니다. 저는 귀하의 식당에서 제공하는 음식을 정말 맛있게 먹었기 때문에 제 아내나 친구들과 함께 조만간 방문할 생각입니다.

특별히 말씀 드리고 싶은 것 중의 하나가 모든 직원들이 보여준 전문성의 수준이었습니다. 서빙을 담당하는 분들은 기분 좋게 만들어 주었고, 요리사는 심지어 몇 분 동안이나 저희와 이야기를 나눌 정도로 친절했습니다.

다시 한 번, 매우 즐거운 저녁이 되었던 것에 대해 대단히 감사 드립니다. 이번 12월에 연말 파티를 열 장소를 찾기 위해 노력하고 있기 때문에 곧 다시 귀하께 연락 드릴 것으로 기대합니다.

안녕히 계십시오.

Ed Standish
CEO, Standish Metals, Inc.

---

172 Hampton's Place는 무엇인가?

(A) 광업회사
(B) 레스토랑
(C) 출장 요리 업체
(D) 요리 학원

173 Capers 씨에 대해 알 수 있는 것은 무엇인가?

(A) 그는 최근에 승진되었다.
(B) 그는 재직 5년째를 기념했다.
(C) 그는 Standish Metals, Inc.를 위해 새로운 계약을 따냈다.
(D) 그는 Standish Metals, Inc.에 의해 인정을 받았다.

174 두 번째 단락, 첫 번째 줄의 단어 "degree"와 의미가 가장 가까운 것은 무엇인가?

(A) 수준
(B) 종류
(C) 외관
(D) 기대

175 Standish 씨가 편지에서 암시하는 것은 무엇인가?

(A) 그는 Hampton's Place의 가격이 너무 비싸다고 생각했다.
(B) 그는 자신의 친구들 중의 한 명을 통해 Hampton's Place에 대해 알게 되었다.
(C) 그는 Hampton's Place와 앞으로 거래를 할 것으로 기대하고 있다.
(D) 그는 Hampton 씨가 자신의 편지에 빨리 답변하기를 바란다.

176-180은 다음 일정표와 웹 페이지를 참조하시오.

제9회 연례 마케팅 콘퍼런스
The Rocky Point Hotel
발표회 일정

오전 10:00 제품을 마케팅하기 위해 어떻게 소셜 미디어를 이용할 수 있는가?
Tillis Media의 Persephone Jones 씨가 잠재 광고주들뿐만 아니라 고객들에게도 제품에 대해 알리기 위해 소셜 미디어를 활용하는 가장 좋은 방법에 대해 이야기할 것입니다. 그녀는 소셜 미디어를 활용하는 데 있어 성공적이었던 최근의 몇몇 시도들을 분석할 것입니다.

오전 11:30 광고 예산을 최대로 활용하기
Watson Advertising의 부장인 Shamus O'Conner 씨가 제한된 자금을 가지고 있는 마케팅 책임자들이 그 자금을 최대한으로 이용할 수 있는 방법에 대해 이야기할 것입니다. 광고 예산이 잘 활용된 예시에 대한 두 개의 사례 연구를 제시할 것입니다.

오후 1:30 설문 조사: 유용한 것인가?
이 패널 토론회는, Kilburn Advertising의 Jessica Wilder, Sanderson, Inc.의 Mark Lemay, 그리고 Green Media의 Mary Harper 씨가 참여할 것이며, 설문 조사에 대한 식견과 가장 잘 활용될 수 있는 방법에 대해 알려 드릴 것입니다.

오후 4:00 인쇄 매체를 통한 마케팅
Central University의 Karl Jesse 마케팅 교수가 인쇄 매체를 통한 제품 및 서비스 마케팅의 장점과 단점에 관해 이야기할 것입니다. Jesse 교수는 인쇄 매체 활용을 옹호하는 분이기 때문에, 오직 인터넷에만 집중하기 위해 인쇄 매체를 기피하지 말아야 하는 이유와 관련해 다양한 아이디어를 제시해 주실 것입니다.

제9회 연례 마케팅 콘퍼런스
참가자 피드백

저는 마케팅에 관해 그렇게 많이는 생각하지 않는 작은 회사에 다니고 있습니다. 실제로, 제가 다니는 회사는 제가 사용할 수 있는 자금의 양이 제한되어 있기 때문에, 자금이 가능한 한 잘 사용될 수 있도록 열심히 노력하고 바쁘게 일해야 합니다. 제가 참석했던 시간에, 저는 모든 자금을 소중하게 만드는 뛰어난 방법들을 배웠으며, 저는 앞으로 이 방법들을 반드시 활용할 겁니다.
Tammy Howell, 작성일 7월 19일, 오전 9:14

저는 제가 참석했던 모든 행사에 확실히 제시간에 참석했음에도 불구하고, 항상 자리를 찾을 수가 없었습니다. 특히 패널 토론 시간이 그랬습니다. 참석한 사람들 중에서 반이 넘는 사람들이 벽에 기대거나 통로에 서 있었습니다. The Rocky Point Hotel은 이러한 행사들을 더 넓은 장소에서 열 필요가 있었습니다. 아니면 주최 측에서 내년에는 다른 곳으로 옮겨야 합니다.
Joe Buckley, 작성일 7월 20일, 오후 4:55

안타깝게도, 저는 행사 당일에 제 일정이 고객들과의 회의로 대부분 차 있었기 때문에 마지막 행사에만 참석했습니다. 저는 Jesse 교수님이 제안한 아이디어가 정말 마음에 들었습니다. 그 아이디어들은 제가 지난 몇 년 동안 대부분 무시하고 지냈던 인쇄 매체에 대해 생각해 보게 만들었습니다.
Naomi Watkins, 작성일 7월 20일, 오후 6:33

여러분의 의견을 환영합니다. 의견을 제출해 주세요.
성명:
의견:

176 O'Conner 씨의 발표 주제는 무엇이었는가?
(A) 효율적인 자금 사용

(B) 소셜 미디어의 장점
(C) 광고에 필요한 자금 마련 방법
(D) 설문 조사를 활용하는 최고의 방법

177 Jesse 교수에 관해 언급된 것은 무엇인가?
(A) 과거에 한때 신문 기자로 일했다.
(B) 인터넷에서 제품을 마케팅하는 방법에 익숙하지 않다.
(C) 매년 콘퍼런스에서 발표를 한다.
(D) 신문과 잡지를 통한 마케팅들을 지지한다.

178 Howell 씨는 언제 발표회에 참석했는가?
(A) 오전 10:00
(B) 오전 11:30
(C) 오후 1:30
(D) 오후 4:00

179 어느 발표가 가장 많은 사람들을 끌어모았을 것 같은가?
(A) 제품을 마케팅하기 위해 어떻게 소셜 미디어를 이용할 수 있는가?
(B) 광고 예산을 최대로 활용하기
(C) 설문 조사: 유용한 것인가?
(D) 인쇄 매체를 통한 마케팅

180 Howell 씨와 Watkins 씨는 어떻게 비슷한가?
(A) 광고 회사에서 일한다.
(B) 같은 도시에서 생활하며 일한다.
(C) 두 사람 모두 일로 바쁘다.
(D) 소속 회사가 작은 회사이다.

181-185는 다음 기사와 편지를 참조하시오.

〈The Saratoga Daily〉
8월 30일
식사 장소: Jimmy's Lakehouse
작성자, Daniel Simon

Jimmy's Lakehouse는 이달에 개업한 이후로 장안의 화제가 되고 있다. 이 레스토랑은 Patterson Lane 65번지에 위치해 있으며, Lake Hamilton을 내려다보고 있다. 호수와 가까운 곳에 있음에도 불구하고, 이 레스토랑은 여행지 및 상업 구역과 모두 가깝기 때문에 최상의 장소에 위치하고 있다. 식사 손님들은 특히 넓은 주차 공간을 마음에 들어 하는데, 이는 이곳에서 주차할 자리를 찾는 데 시간을 허비할 필요가 없다는 것을 의미한다.

자리에 앉은 후에, 나뿐만 아니라 함께 동석한 사람들은 메뉴를 살펴 보는 것이 즐거웠다. 메뉴의 선택폭이 중간 크기의 레스토랑치고는 유난히 넓었기 때문에 우리는 모든 것을 조금씩 시식해 보기 위해 뷔페로 결정을 내렸다. 아니나 다를까, 생선 메뉴, 특히 연어는 완벽하게 조리가 되었다. 프라이드 치킨과 소고기 안심은 맛이 있었다. 수많은 야채 메뉴들은 신선하고 다채로운 음식들로 가득했다. 비교적 저렴한 가격에도 불구하고, 음식의 질은 높았으며, 이는 기분 좋은 놀라움이었다. 와인 리스트 또한 훌륭했으며, 저렴한 가격에 뛰어난 와인들이 많은 것이 특징이었다.

한 가지 단점은 대기 시간이었다. 우리는 예약을 하지 못했기 때문에 자리에 앉을 때까지 1시간이 넘게 기다려야 했다. 우리의 테이블이 준비되기까지 그저 프런트 쪽에 있는 로비에서 기다려야 했는데, 이는 나와 함께 동행한 몇몇 사람들이 불평한 것이었다. 하지만 레스토랑의 사장은 이는 앞으로 오랫동안 계속될 문제는 아니라고 내게 알려주었다.

Jimmy's Lakehouse는 일주일 내내 오후 5시에서 밤 11시까지 영업을 한다. 이곳은 확실히 꼭 찾아가 봐야 하는 레스토랑이다. 단, 가기 전에 904-2900으로 전화를 걸어 반드시 예약을 해야 한다.

〈The Saratoga Daily〉
편집장에게 보내는 편지
9월 3일

편집장께,

저희 Jimmy's Lakehouse는 8월 30일에 작성된 저희 레스토랑의 방문기를 읽고 기뻤습니다. 저희는 음식 가격이 너무 높지 않다는 사실뿐만 아니라 손님들에게 제공하는 음식에 대해서도 자랑스럽게 생각합니다.

하지만, 한 가지 짚고 넘어가고 싶은 것이 있습니다. 이 기사에서 작성자가 자리에 앉기까지 오랫동안 기다려야 했다고 언급하셨습니다. 저는 저희 레스토랑이 확장 공사를 진행하는 과정에 있기 때문에 현재보다 30퍼센트 더 많은 좌석을 확보하게 될 것이라는 점을 알려 드리고 싶습니다. 따라서 9월 20일부로, 저희 레스토랑은 손님들이 예약을 하지 않더라도 일단 도착하면 훨씬 더 짧게 대기하실 것으로 기대하고 있습니다.

안녕히 계십시오.

Tim Morrow
사장, Jimmy's Lakehouse

---

181 Jimmy's Lakehouse에 관해 언급된 것은 무엇인가?

(A) 특별히 새롭지는 않다.

(B) 비싼 음식들이 많이 있다.

(C) 상업용 건물들이 있는 곳과 가깝다.

(D) 음식을 조리하는 데 시간이 오래 걸린다.

182 기사에서, 첫 번째 단락, 세 번째 줄의 단어 "prime"과 의미가 가장 가까운 것은 무엇인가?

(A) 이상적인

(B) 받아들일 수 있는

(C) 관련된

(D) 가까운

183 기사 작성자는 레스토랑의 어떤 측면이 흔치 않다고 생각하는가?

(A) 음식의 양

(B) 장소의 크기

(C) 음식의 선택 사항들

(D) 고객들의 숫자

184 편지는 왜 보내졌는가?

(A) 최신 정보를 제공하기 위해

(B) 실수를 수정하기 위해

(C) 실수에 대해 사과하기 위해

(D) 새로운 메뉴를 언급하기 위해

185 Morrow 씨는 언제 Simon 씨와 이야기했는가?

(A) 7월에

(B) 8월에

(C) 9월에

(D) 10월에

신유형 186-190은 다음 광고와 양식, 그리고 온라인 후기를 참조하시오.

Pyramid Security Systems

여러분께서는 회사를 설립하시느라 고생하셨으니, 저희 Pyramid Security Systems는 여러분의 회사를 보호하기 위해 열심히 일하겠습니다. 여러분의 회사에 필요한 것이 무엇이든, 저희는 그에 적합한 해결책을 찾아 드릴 수 있습니다. 저희는 30일 무료 체험을 제공해 드리므로 저희 서비스가 적합한 것인지 확실히 확인해 보실 수 있습니다. 추가로, 저희 장비는 다른 여러 시스템 회사들이 하는 것처럼 벽에 구멍을 남기지 않습니다. 이는 회사 사무실을 임대해 사용하는 분들에게 아주 적합합니다. 오늘 저희에게 1-800-555-9778로 전화하셔서 저희 직원들 중의 한 명과 말씀을 나누시면, 더욱 발전하실 수 있는 방법을 제안해 드릴 수 있을 것입니다. 또는, www.pyramidsecsys.com에서 '문의하기' 항목의 양식을 작성해 주셔도 됩니다. 아래에 있는 저희 일반 패키지들을 확인해 보세요.

패키지 타입	카메라 수	동작 감지 조명	디지털 녹화	긴급 상황 대처
Starter	2	2		
Pyramid-Pro	3-5	4	✔	
Pyramid-Premium	6-9	6	✔	✔
전체 포함	10+	8	✔	✔

---

https://www.pyramidsecsys.com/contactus

Pyramid Security Systems: 문의하기

성명: Sharon Wenzel   날짜: 7월 24일

귀하의 문의 사항 요약: 저는 Bonner City에 있는 그의 제과점에서 귀하의 서비스를 이용하고 있는 제 친구 Carl O'Connor를 통해 귀사에 관해 들었습니다. 귀사의 본사가 Stevensville에 있는 것으로 알고 있습니다. 저도 거기서 업체를 운영하고 있어서 첫 만남 일정을 잡기 편리할 것으로 생각합니다. 저는 제 안과 병원 때문에 보안 서비스에 관심이 있습니다. 제 문제는 진찰을 하는 동안 십부 남녀 직원이 때때로 뒤쪽에 있는 방에서 안경 수리를 하거나, 제품 진열 구역에서 고객들이 안경테를 고르는 것을 돕는다는 것입니다. 우리 두 사람이 모두 바쁠 때는, 병원 내 일부 구역이 방치된 상태가 된다는 것을 의미합니다. 귀사에서 제공하는 서비스에 관해 더 많은 것을 알아보고 싶습니다. 감사합니다.

---

https://www.pyramidsecsys.com/testimonials

저는 약 2개월 전에 Pyramid Security Systems에 의뢰해 제 업체에 카메라를 설치했습니다. 원래는 대기실과 중앙 복도, 진열 공간, 그리고 접수 데스크에 각각 카메라가 하나씩 있었습니다. 몇 주 후에, 제 개인 사무실 내부와 바깥에 카메라를 추가하기로 결정했습니다. 저는 높은 수준의 고객 서비스에 만족하고 있으며, 디지털 녹화 기능이 마음에 드는데, 제 컴퓨터에 동영상을 쉽게 백업할 수 있어서 나중을 위해 저장할 수 있게 해 주기 때문입니다. 게다가, 지역 내에 위치한 업체인 관계로 10퍼센트의 할인도 받았습니다. 저는 어느 소규모 업체 소유주에게든지 Pyramid Security Systems를 적극 추천해 드리고 싶습니다.

– Sharon Wenzel

---

186 Pyramid Security Systems에 관해 알 수 있는 내용이 아닌 것은 무엇인가?

(A) 제품이 벽에 손상을 초래하지 않는다.

(B) 가격이 경쟁사들보다 더 저렴하다.

(C) 제한된 기간 동안 서비스가 무료로 이용될 수 있다.

(D) 직원들이 고객들에게 추천해 줄 수 있다.

187 O'Connor 씨에 관해 유추할 수 있는 것은 무엇인가?

(A) 할인을 받을 자격이 없다.

(B) Wenzel 씨에게 안경을 납품한다.

(C) Pyramid Security Systems에서 근무했었다.

(D) 자신의 업체를 Stevensville로 옮길 것이다.

188 Wenzel 씨는 그녀의 업체에 관해 무엇을 암시하는가?

(A) 새로운 접수 담당 직원을 필요로 한다.

(B) 무료 시력 검사를 제공한다.

(C) 최근에 보안 관련 문제가 있었다.

(D) 매우 적은 규모의 직원을 보유하고 있다.

189 양식에서, 첫 번째 단락, 일곱 번째 줄의 단어 "unattended"와 의미가 가장 가까운 것은 무엇인가?

(A) 외로운

(B) 회피된

(C) 가구가 갖춰지지 않은

(D) 비어 있는

190 Wenzel 씨는 현재 어느 보안 패키지를 이용하고 있는가?

(A) Starter

(B) Pyramid-Pro

(C) Pyramid-Premium

(D) 전체 포함

신유형 ▶ 191-195는 다음 웹 페이지와 두 이메일을 참조하시오.

www.cleanwatersymposium.co.uk/about

| 홈 | 관련 정보 | 연설자 | 부스 | 등록 |

Clear Water Symposium은 증가하는 세계의 인구 때문에 직면한 수자원 관련 문제들을 논의하기 위해 영국에서 열리는 연례 행사입니다. 이 심포지엄의 인기로 인해, 올해의 행사는 Valle Complex에서 열릴 것이며, 이곳은 작년의 행사장보다 훨씬 더 많은 사람들을 수용할 수 있습니다.

이용 가능한 몇몇 활동들을 아래에서 확인해 보실 수 있습니다. 완전한 목록을 보시려면 연설자 및 부스 페이지를 방문하시기 바랍니다.

– Water United Foundation의 설립자이신 Sheng Kang 박사의 기조 연설

– Kieran Harper 국회의원과 함께 하는 질의응답 시간

– Stokes University의 Lauren Wilkinson 교수가 진행하는 공예 활동: 자신만의 정수 필터 만들기

– National Environmental Association의 협회장인 Jodie Mellor가 이끄는 현장 견학: St. Ives Bay로 가는 가이드 동반 견학

수신: Elizabeth Palmer 〈e.palmer@eil1.co.uk〉
발신: Curtis Volk 〈c.volk@eil1.co.uk〉
날짜: 3월 18일
제목: Clear Water Symposium

Palmer 씨께,

저는 Clear Water Symposium에서 알찬 시간을 보내고 있으며, 저를 이곳에 보낸 것은 좋은 생각이었다고 생각합니다. 저는 우리 구독자들의 관심을 끌 것이라고 생각하는 많은 소중한 정보들을 배우고 있습니다. Kieran Harper 씨께서 오신 후에 만나 뵐 기회가 있었습니다. 게다가, 해안만을 견학하는 중에 멋진 사진들도 찍었습니다. 지금까지 가장 즐거웠던 활동은, 이 활동은 교육적이기도 했는데요, 자연에서 흔히 찾아볼 수 있는 재료들로 정수기 필터를 만드는 일이었습니다. 이는 또한 사람들이 집에서도 시도해 볼 수 있는 것이기 때문에 제 기사에 단계별 안내 사항들을 포함할 수도 있을 것입니다.

내일 저는 태양열 양수기 시연회를 볼 예정이며, 이를 발명하신 분과의 인터뷰를 이미 잡아 두었습니다. 나머지 시간은 다양한 부스에 있는 직원들과 이야기를 나누는 것으로 보낼 것입니다.

곧 또 소식 전하겠습니다.

Curtis

수신: Amil Kota 〈kotaamil@atwmail.com〉
발신: Curtis Volk 〈c.volk@eil1.co.uk〉
날짜: 3월 20일
제목: 감사합니다!

Kota 씨께,

어제 있었던 시연회가 끝난 후에 저를 만날 수 있도록 시간을 내 주신 것에 대해 다시 한 번 감사의 인사를 드리고 싶었습니다. 세계의 수자원 위기에 대한 해결책들과 관련해 귀하의 통찰에 관한 이야기를 들을 수 있어 정말 흥미로웠습니다. 저에게 귀하의 우편 주소를 알려 주시면, 귀하의 모습이 실릴 출판물 한 부를 보내 드리겠습니다.

안녕히 계십시오.

Curtis Volk

191 웹 페이지에 따르면, 올해 열리는 Clear Water Symposium에 관해 사실인 것은 무엇인가?

(A) 다른 장소에서 열릴 것이다.

(B) 몇몇 연설자들이 여러 연설을 할 것이다.

(C) 입장료가 인상되었다.

(D) 모두 합쳐 3일 동안 지속될 것이다.

192 Volk 씨는 누구일 것 같은가?

(A) 잡지 발행인

(B) 사진가

(C) 기자

(D) 업체 소유주

193 Volk 씨는 누구의 활동이 가장 마음에 들었다고 말하는가?

(A) Kang 박사의 활동

(B) Harper 씨의 활동

(C) Wilkinson 씨의 활동

(D) Mellor 씨의 활동

194 첫 번째 이메일에서, 두 번째 단락, 두 번째 줄의 단어 "rest"와 의미가 가장 가까운 것은 무엇인가?

(A) 지지, 후원

(B) 나머지

(C) 휴식

(D) 과제, 임무

195 Kota 씨에 관해 알 수 있는 것은 무엇인가?

(A) 장치를 발명했다.

(B) 최근에 이사했다.

(C) 심포지엄 장소를 일찍 떠났다.

(D) Volk 씨의 동료 직원이다.

신유형 ▶ 196-200은 다음 보고서와 이메일, 그리고 기사를 참조하시오.

근무지 부상 관련 보고

Everest Manufacturing에서 요청한 바와 같이, Ashford Automotive Consulting(AAC)은 그 회사의 근무 안전 기록의 검토를 실시했습니다. 여러 사소한 부상 사례들이 공식적으로 보고되지 않기 때문에, AAC에서는 해당 제조사의 공장에서 발생되는 일에 관한 정확한

상세 자료를 수집하기 위해 설문지를 만들었습니다. 그것들은 교대 근무 책임자들에게 배부되었는데, 이들은 이와 같은 사안들에 관한 정보를 얻을 수 있는 가장 좋은 출처로 여겨집니다.

설문 조사는 Everest Manufacturing의 Elmhurst, St. Charles, 그리고 Pine Valley 지점에서 8월 15일부터 28일까지 실시되었습니다. 초기의 결과를 바탕으로, 세 가지 주요 개선 영역이 확인되었습니다. 이는 제조 장비의 잘못된 사용이나 필수 안전 장비의 미착용에 의해 초래된 부상과, 낡아서 오작동되는 기계 또는 부정확하게 설치된 부품들에 의한 부상, 그리고 미끄러운 바닥에서 넘어지거나 사다리와 기타 높은 장소에서 떨어지는 것에 의한 부상들입니다. AAC는 이와 같은 문제점들을 해결하기 위한 권고 사항들을 제출해 드릴 것입니다.

수신: Jin Ni ⟨jin.ni@everestmfg.com⟩
발신: Alex Vinson ⟨alex.vinson@everestmfg.com⟩
날짜: 9월 20일
제목: AAC 보고서

Ni 씨께,

저는 장비 교육을 해마다 실시하는 것에서 6개월마다 실시하는 것으로 변경하라는 AAC의 조언에 전적으로 동의합니다. 제조 일정의 지연 없이 이를 실시하기 위해서는, 직원들이 정규 근무 일정 외의 시간에 참석할 수 있도록 초과 근무 수당이 지급되어야 할 것입니다. 이를 위한 자금을 확보하는 것은 큰 문제가 되지 않을 텐데, 우리 직원들의 안전뿐만 아니라 정부의 점검을 통과해야 하는 회사의 능력에도 필수적이기 때문입니다. 다음 점검이 10월 27일로 예정되어 있으므로 이 시점이 되기 전에 우리가 조치를 취할 수 있기를 바랍니다.

감사합니다.

Alex Vinson

Everest Manufacturing 사보
Pine Valley 지사, 127호

전 직원을 대상으로 하는 의무 워크숍

우리 Everest Manufacturing의 직원들은 Ashford Automotive Consulting(AAC)의 권고에 따라 이번 달에 안전 교육을 받을 것입니다. AAC에서 8월에 실시한 초기의 설문 조사들 외에도, 두 곳의 Everest Manufacturing의 지점들(Beachville과 Wright City)이 해당 컨설팅 회사의 점검을 받았습니다. 추가 안전 교육이 필요한 것으로 밝혀졌습니다. 이 문제를 해결하기 위한 첫 워크숍이 10월 20일에 열릴 것이며, Alex Vinson 씨께서 진행하실 예정입니다. 이번 워크숍에 참석하실 수 없는 분들은 추가 지시 사항을 들을 수 있도록 각자의 직속 상사에게 알려야 합니다.

196 교대 근무 책임자들에게 왜 설문지가 주어졌는가?

(A) 새로운 절차에 관한 의견을 요청하기 위해
(B) 사고에 관한 정확한 정보를 얻기 위해
(C) 승진되어야 하는 직원들을 확인하기 위해
(D) 운영비를 줄이기 위한 방법을 찾기 위해

197 AAC에 의해 총 얼마나 많은 장소가 점검되었는가?

(A) 두 곳
(B) 세 곳
(C) 네 곳
(D) 다섯 곳

198 AAC는 Everest Manufacturing에 무슨 권고를 했는가?

(A) 더 현대적인 장비를 설치할 것
(B) 직원 안전 관리 책자를 배부할 것
(C) 교육 시간의 빈도를 높일 것
(D) 직원들을 위해 보호 장비를 구입할 것

199 이메일에서, 첫 번째 단락, 네 번째 줄의 단어 "secure"와 의미가 가장 가까운 것은 무엇인가?

(A) 얻다
(B) 확인하다
(C) 단단히 조이다
(D) 보호하다

200 Vinson 씨에 관해 알 수 있는 것은 무엇인가?

(A) 점검이 있기 일주일 전에 워크숍을 진행할 것이다.
(B) Ni 씨와의 회의 일정을 잡고 싶어 한다.
(C) AAC의 일부 권고 사항에 동의하지 않는다.
(D) 최근에 Pine Valley 지사로 전근했다.

TEST 10 해석

PART 5

101 업계의 전문가들은 Karl Amundson 씨가 창작 소설 〈Westward Adventures〉 시리즈로 인해 올해의 작가로 지명될 것이라고 예상하고 있다.

102 잠재 투자자들과의 회의를 진행하는 동안, Demitri 씨는 회사의 새로운 무선 헤드폰 제품에 대한 과감한 마케팅 전략을 제안했다.

103 보험 가입 목적으로, 생산 작업장 내의 모든 직원들은 매년 대단히 까다로운 안전 교육을 이수해야 한다.

104 저명한 호주 건축가 Jackson Black의 작품들이 유명한 Drake Center 컨벤션 빌딩에 전시되고 있다.

105 NewPage Hotel Group은 다양한 경쟁사들과의 계약에 서명이 되는 대로 자사의 호텔 체인을 확장할 것이다.

106 널리 알려진 세계적인 공급업체인 Interpublic Incorporated는 현재 다양한 새 소프트웨어 프로그램들을 출시할 계획을 갖고 있다.

107 MGU Holdings Corp.는 지역의 중소기업에 좀처럼 투자를 하지 않는 회사들 중의 하나이다.

108 콘서트 조직 위원회를 대표해, 행사 조직 책임자인 Wilson 씨가 공연의 지연으로 인해 야기된 모든 불편함에 대해 사과할 것이다.

109 시설 내에 있는 모든 사람들은 오후 6시 이후에 시설 부지 내에서 모습이 보일 경우에 경비 직원에게 그들의 신분 확인 명찰을 보여주도록 요청을 받을 것이다.

110 Ghepo Tech의 마케팅 부서는 자사의 연례 기술 박람회의 입장을 위한 무료 출입증을 배부하고 있다.

111 계속되는 가뭄으로 인해, 많은 지역 농부들이 농작물의 가격을 어쩔 수 없이 올린다.

112 저희 고객 서비스 직원들은 여러분께서 전화를 거실 때마다 문제를 해결해 드리기 위해 연중 매일 24시간 대기하고 있습니다.

113 비즈니스 학회 발표자인 Jillian Hull의 핵심 전문 분야는 국제 마케팅 법률과 전략이다.

114 Carlos Falconi는 부서 내에 있는 회계사들이 새로운 소프트웨어 사용법에 익숙해지게 하기 위해 그 소프트웨어에 관한 세미나를 주도할 것이다.

115 주차 허가증을 원하는 어떤 직원이든지 반드시 매달 15달러의 요금을 지불해야 한다.

116 고객들은 웹사이트의 내용에 관한 상세 정보를 위해 회사의 직원에게 연락해 보는 것이 권장된다.

117 회사 대변인에 따르면, 대부분의 공장 보수 작업은 두 달간 진행될 것이다.

118 직원들은 근무 일정에 대한 모든 변경 사항들에 대해 채용 담당 부서장의 승인을 받아야 한다.

119 Bissell Business Magazine은 소비자 경향의 최근 변화를 보여주기 위해 설문 조사 결과를 간략히 정리한 기사를 종종 게재한다.

120 새롭게 채용된 인턴들은 3월에 열린 워크숍에 참석한 이후로 생산적이었다.

121 Space Technology에서 제조된 새로운 제품 라인은 전자제품 및 가전제품에 대한 취향이 고급스러운 소비자들의 관심을 끌 수 있다.

122 Nixon 씨는 그가 운영하는 소매점이 계속해서 다른 경쟁 대리점들보다 더 나은 실적을 올리면 상당한 승진을 할 것으로 기대된다.

123 ABT Industries는 새롭게 도입된 생산 시스템에 대한 장기 안정화 계획을 확실히 하기 위한 현실적인 방안을 강구해야 한다.

124 Paper Planes International은 Hero Graphics, Ltd를 인수하면서 비디오 게임 업계에 위험을 무릅쓰고 뛰어들었다.

125 Peterman International은 유럽에서 컨설팅 서비스를 제공하고 있지만, 아직 아시아 시장에는 진입하지 않았다.

126 Lere Kitchen Appliances는 우리 제품의 질과 기능성을 향상시키기 위한 계속되는 노력을 하고 있다.

127 Kim 씨는 자신의 직원들이 그들의 생각을 잠재적인 투자자들에게 알리는 데 도움이 될 수 있도록 한 고문을 고용했다.

128 Jason Cochran이 제출한 포트폴리오를 신중히 검토한 끝에, 인사부장은 그와 면접을 갖기로 결정했다.

129 모든 참가자는 전시를 위한 진열 물품들을 싣기 전에 입구에 게시되어 있는 설명을 꼼꼼히 읽어야 한다.

130 소포가 배송될 것으로 예정된 시간 1시간 전에 수신자가 택배 회사와 연락할 수 있다면 주소 변경이 가능하다.

PART 6

신유형 131-134는 다음 편지를 참조하시오.

3월 24일
Stephen Garland 씨
162 Strathtay Road
Dundee, 스코틀랜드, 영국
Garland 씨께,

〈The British Journal of Electrical Engineering〉과 〈Contemporary Econ Journal〉에 대한 귀하의 주문을 처리해 드렸음을 확인하기 위해 편지드립니다. 〈Contemporary Econ Journal〉은 어제 배송되었습니다. 그것은 일주일 안에 도착할 것입니다.

안타깝게도, 배송 물품에는 인쇄 문제로 인해 〈The British Journal of Electrical Engineering〉이 포함되지 않을 것이며, 현재 저희 웹사이트의 보수로 인해 4월 15일까지 몇몇 온라인상의 기능들을 보실 수 없을 것입니다. 저희의 온라인 잡지 보관소는 4월 말까지 열람하는 것이 불가능할 것입니다.

웹사이트와 잡지 보관소가 완전히 제 기능을 하게 되면, 귀하께서 제공해 주신 이메일 주소로 알림 메시지를 보내 드리겠습니다.

안녕히 계십시오.

Mary Chilton
구독 서비스 팀장

신유형 135-138은 다음 이메일을 참조하시오.

수신: Winny Lancet
발신: Edwind Real Estate Online
날짜: 2월 15일
제목: 회원 자격 관련 문제

Lancet 씨께,

저희는 최근 귀하의 Edwind Real Estate Online 연간 계정을 자동으로 갱신하려 했습니다. 하지만 귀하의 지불 관련 정보에 오류가 있었습니다. 귀하의 온라인 계정에 로그인하셔서 귀하의 성함과 주소가 저희가 파일로 보관 중인 신용 카드에 있는 정보와 일치하는지 확인 바랍니다. 둘 중 하나라도 변경된 경우, 10일 안에 정보를 업데이트해 주시길 바라며,

그렇지 않으면 귀하의 계정은 삭제될 수 있습니다.

추가로, 귀하의 계정상에 판매 또는 임대를 목적으로 귀하께서 보유 중이신 부동산에 대한 소유권 증명서를 반드시 제출해 주시기 바라며, 이는 이미 그렇게 처리하시지 않은 경우에만 해당합니다.

귀하께서 처음으로 목록에 오를 당시에는 시행되지 않았던 새로운 회사 정책은 이제 Edwind Real Estate Online을 통해 광고되고 있는 각 부동산이 오로지 현 소유주의 계정하에 있는 것을 요구합니다.

안녕히 계십시오.

Edwind Real Estate Online

신유형 ▶ 139-142는 다음 기사를 참조하시오.

Hudson Lanny Gallery는 Tara Hidalgo 씨의 전원생활 사진들을 8월 한 달 내내 특별 전시할 예정이다. 갤러리 입장은 기부에 의해서만 가능할 것이다. 기부금은 Hidalgo Children's Art Education Fund로 전달될 것이다.

작은 농촌 마을의 가난에 초점을 맞춘 그녀의 독특한 작품으로 세계적으로 알려져 있기 때문에, Hidalgo 씨만큼 작품 속에 그런 풍부한 연관성을 갖고 있는 예술가들은 많지 않다. 그녀의 사진들은 자신의 어린 시절의 많은 부분을 반영하는 것으로 알려져 있다.

미국 중서부 지역에 걸쳐 다양한 시골 환경에서 산 경험에서 영감을 받아, Hidalgo 씨는 자신의 작품에 그 배경을 예술적인 방법뿐만 아니라 자선가의 입장에서도 지속적으로 반영하고 있다.

신유형 ▶ 143-146은 다음 이메일을 참조하시오

수신: Danielle Lim
발신: Huckle Books 고객 서비스부
제목: 교재 주문
날짜: 11월 3일

Lim 씨께,

다음 도서들에 대한 10월 30일 자 귀하의 주문을 처리했습니다.
〈Epidemiology: A Microscopic World〉 8판 저자 Jennifer Schwarzen 67.85달러
〈Hospital Administration〉 4판 저자 Adrian Flemming 84.00달러
〈Nursing Research: A Look into Change〉 5판 저자 Michelle Stevenson 45.50달러

〈Epidemiology〉와 〈Nursing Research〉는 모두 오늘 배송되었습니다. 하지만 데이터베이스를 찾아본 끝에, 귀하께서 주문하신 세 번째 도서는 현재 재고가 없다는 것을 알게 되었습니다. 저희는 한 권을 요청했으며, 이용 가능하게 되는 대로 귀하께 무료로 긴급 배송해 드릴 것입니다.

지연된 것에 대해 사과드리며, 이로 인해 귀하께 어떠한 불편함도 초래되지 않았기를 바랍니다. 다음 구매 시에 사용할 수 있는 첨부된 10퍼센트 할인 쿠폰을 받아 주시기 바랍니다.

안녕히 계십시오.

Dana Henry
Huckle Books 고객 서비스부

PART 7

147-148은 다음 정보를 참조하시오.

Zenith Supplies
상세 주문 내역

제품 설명 / 수량	가격
16인치 둥근 섬유 유리 서빙 쟁반 / 12개, 개당 18.99달러	227.88달러
20인치x20인치 헝겊 냅킨 (12개 들이 팩) / 10개, 개당 23.99달러	239.90달러
8쿼트 스테인리스 스틸 예열 접시 / 3개, 개당 169.99달러	509.97달러
13인치 스테인리스 스틸 서빙 스푼 / 6개, 개당 3.99달러	23.94달러
소계	1,001.69달러
배송비 및 세금	134.95달러
총계	1,136.64달러
지불 방식: 8946로 끝나는 신용 카드 / 1,136.64달러의 청구 비용이 2월 3일에 적용됨.	

주문 날짜: 2월 3일 　　　　　 예상 배송일: 2월 9일
고객 성함: Anuj Misra 　　　 조회 번호: F53R98

특이 사항: 냅킨에는 Misra Co.의 로고가 새겨질 것입니다.

147 Misra 씨는 무슨 종류의 사업을 운영할 것 같은가?
(A) 의류 매장
(B) 철물점
(C) 출장 요리 제공 업체
(D) 세탁소

148 주문에 관해 언급된 것은 무엇인가?
(A) Misra 씨의 집으로 배송될 것이다.
(B) 비용이 전액 지불되었다.
(C) 정리 할인 판매 제품을 포함했다.
(D) 배송 비용이 면제되었다.

149-150은 다음 웹 페이지를 참조하시오.

http://www.lunjaninc.com

Lunjan, Inc.

기존의 저희 보유 승용차 및 트럭과 함께 현재 이삿짐 전용 트럭도 제공하고 있습니다!

일일 이용 요금이 부과되는 서비스와 더불어, 다음과 같이 여러분의 요구 사항에 적합한 여러 가지 기능들을 추가하실 수 있습니다.

- GPS 내비게이션 장치
- 튼튼한 접이식 카트
- 자전거 거치대
- 스키 거치대

요금은 선택하시는 패키지에 따라 다를 수 있으며, 이용 보증금은 필수입니다. 여기를 클릭해 더 많은 정보를 확인해 보시기 바랍니다. 저희는 회사 내에 현금을 두지 않으므로 모든 비용 지불은 반드시 신용 카드나 은행 계좌 이체를 통해서만 이뤄져야 한다는 점에 유의하시기 바랍니다.

149 Lunjan, Inc.는 무슨 종류의 업체일 것 같은가?

(A) 스포츠 용품 매장
(B) 부동산 중개업체
(C) 이삿짐 전문 회사
(D) 차량 대여 업체

150 보증금에 관해 알 수 있는 것은 무엇인가?

(A) 할부로 납부할 수 있다.
(B) 단골 고객들에게는 할인된다.
(C) 현금으로 수납되지 않는다.
(D) 신속히 돌려받을 수 있다.

신유형 151-152는 다음 온라인 채팅을 참조하시오.

Ken Johnson [오전 10:43]
안녕하세요, Blake. Nicky Sutton 씨의 작업 팀원들에게 필요한 호텔은 정해 놓으셨나요?

Blake Hurst [오전 10:45]
오늘 아침에 막 정했습니다. 그분들께서는 Columbus Inn에 머무실 겁니다. 걸어서 갈 수 있는 거리에 있는 곳이기 때문에 그분들께서 이쪽으로 오셔서 무대 설치 작업을 하시기 수월하실 겁니다.

Ken Johnson [오전 10:46]
좋아요. Sutton 씨의 대리인에게 예약 정보를 전송해 주세요.

Blake Hurst [오전 10:47]
그렇게 하겠습니다. 그리고 Sutton 씨께서 6월 1일 오후 2시 5분에 Buena Airlines 항공편으로 도착하실 예정입니다. 우리가 리무진을 보내서 모셔 오도록 해야 할까요?

Ken Johnson [오전 10:49]
물론이죠. 그분은 대단한 유명 인사입니다.

Blake Hurst [오전 10:51]
그렇다면 그분을 멋지게 맞이할 수 있도록 필요한 조치를 취하겠습니다.

151 메시지 작성자들은 어디에서 근무할 것 같은가?

(A) 여행사에서
(B) 호텔에서
(C) 극장에서
(D) 공항에서

152 오전 10시 49분에, Johnson 씨가 "Certainly"라고 썼을 때 의미
신유형 하는 것은 무엇인가?

(A) 제안된 교통편이 좋은 아이디어라고 생각한다.
(B) Buena Airlines를 이용하는 것이 가장 좋은 선택이라는 데 동의한다.
(C) 자신이 직접 공항에서 Sutton 씨를 모셔 올 계획이다.
(D) 과거에 Columbus Inn에서 숙박한 적이 있다.

153-154는 다음 초대장을 참조하시오.

Harrison Towers
372 Stratford Drive
개장 행사, 8월 28일, 토요일

Woodland, Inc.를 대표하여, Harrison Towers가 제공하는 고급 주택을 둘러보실 수 있도록 귀하를 정중히 초청합니다.

다양한 규모의 임대 선택이 이용 가능합니다!

오후 1시부터 7시 사이에 한가하실 때 방문하시어 둘러보시기 바랍니다.

개별 배치도나 샘플 임대 계약서를 원하시는 분은 (212) 555-2054로 Erin Varner 씨에게 전화하십시오.

153 행사의 목적은 무엇인가?

(A) 공사 계획을 알리기
(B) 더 많은 직원을 모집하기
(C) 새로운 복합 거주 건물을 홍보하기
(D) 경영진의 교체를 발표하기

154 Erin Varner는 누구인 것 같은가?

(A) 박물관 견학 가이드
(B) 부동산 중개 직원
(C) 건축 인부 책임자
(D) 재정 전문가

신유형 155-158은 다음 문자 메시지 대화를 참조하시오.

오전 8:11
PAUL: 저는 3층에 있는 비즈니스 센터로 가는 길이에요. 행사 일정표를 추가로 더 복사하고 의자도 하나 더 가지고 내려갈게요.

오전 8:12
VANESSA: 저는 우리 부스에 있어요. 우리가 가져온 현수막이 너무 작지 않을까 생각했었는데, 우리가 부스의 절반만 사용하기 때문에 크기가 딱 알맞아요. 그리고 Ralston Co.의 색상 조합 때문에 우리가 운이 좋게 되었어요.

오전 8:13
WILLIAM: 무슨 얘기이신지 모르겠어요.

오전 8:15
VANESSA: 제 말은 그 회사의 장식품들이 우리 것들과는 완전히 달라서, 서로 다른 회사라는 게 명확하다는 뜻이에요.

오전 8:17
PAUL: 잘됐네요. 한 시간 후면 방문객들이 도착하기 시작할 거예요. 돌아다니면서 엑스포 행사장의 나머지 부분을 볼 수 있도록 순서를 정해 돌아가면서 부스를 지킵시다.

오전 8:18
WILLIAM: 좋은 생각이에요. 저는 오늘 오후에 중앙 무대에서 있을 Jarvis Enterprises의 시연회를 정말로 보고 싶어요.

오전 8:19
VANESSA: 저도요. Nixon-44는 올해 가장 크게 기대되는 스마트폰들 중의 하나예요.

오전 8:21
PAUL: 네, 좋은 제품일 거예요. 그건 그렇고, 제가 있는 이곳에 전시 업체들을 위한 선물 가방들이 있는데, 한 번에 전부 가지고 내려갈 수 없어요.

오전 8:22
WILLIAM: 제가 비즈니스 센터로 가서 도와 드릴게요.

155 이 그룹의 부스에 관해 알 수 있는 것은 무엇인가?

(A) 많은 방문객들이 찾아올 것이다.
(B) 무료 현수막이 딸려 있다.
(C) 다른 그룹과 공유하고 있다.
(D) 비즈니스 센터에서 가깝다.

156 오전 8시 13분에, William 씨가 "I'm not following you"라고 썼
신유형 을 때 의미하는 것은 무엇인가?

(A) 일부 장식품이 바뀌어야 한다고 생각한다.

(B) 무슨 말인지 이해하지 못하고 있다.

(C) 자신이 내놓은 아이디어를 활용하고 싶어 한다.

(D) Vanessa와 함께 갈 시간이 없다.

157 Nixon-44에 관해 암시된 내용은 무엇인가?

(A) 그 제품의 시연회가 한 시간 후에 시작될 것이다.

(B) 메시지 작성자들의 회사의 베스트셀러 제품이다.

(C) Jarvis Enterprises에 의해 제조된다.

(D) 전시 업체에 증정될 것이다.

158 William은 곧이어 무엇을 할 것 같은가?

(A) 3층으로 간다.

(B) 주차할 공간을 찾는다.

(C) 일정표를 복사한다.

(D) 중앙 무대에서 Paul을 만난다.

신유형▶ 159-161은 다음 광고를 참조하시오.

Sardis
직원 채용

마사지 치료 전문가: 파트타임 마사지 치료 전문가 자리(총 3명). 지원자들은 반드시 주에서 받은 자격증이 있어야 하며, 최소 2년의 관련 경력이 있어야 합니다. — [1] —. 저희는 매일 오전 7시에서 밤 10시까지 영업하므로 지원자들은 반드시 주간, 야간, 그리고 주말 근무가 가능해야 합니다. 일주일에 5일을 근무하실 것입니다. — [2] —.

접수 담당자: 정규직 접수 담당자(총 1명). 접수 담당자는 전화 응대, 마사지 및 기타 미용 치료에 대한 예약 조정, 그리고 수신 및 발신 청구서 처리를 담당합니다. — [3] —. 근무 시간은 일요일부터 목요일까지, 오전 7시에서 오후 4시까지입니다. 경력이 있는 지원자가 선호되지만, 적합한 지원자가 있으면 교육을 제공하고자 합니다.

6월 14일 또는 그 이전까지 www.sardis.net/careers에서 온라인 지원서를 작성하시기 바랍니다. — [4] —.

159 Sardis는 무슨 종류의 업체일 것 같은가?

(A) 교육 기관

(B) 스파 시설

(C) 정신 건강 클리닉

(D) 보험 회사

160 광고에 따르면, 두 직책의 직원들에게 모두 요구되는 것은 무엇인가?

(A) 과거의 경력이 있는 것

(B) 밤 10시까지 근무가 가능한 것

(C) 일주일에 5일을 근무하는 것

(D) 주에서 발급한 유효 자격증이 있는 것

161 [1], [2], [3], [4]로 표기된 위치들 중에서 다음 문장이 가장 잘 어울리는 곳은 어디인가?

신유형

"또한, 저희 소셜 미디어 페이지를 업데이트하는 일을 요청받으실 수도 있습니다."

(A) [1]

(B) [2]

(C) [3]

(D) [4]

162-164는 다음 계약서를 참조하시오.

Maritime Event Supply
1024 Maritime Street
Miami, Fl 33114

임대 계약서

오늘 날짜: 6월 10일   예약 날짜: 8월 1일

임차인: Marshal Wendt

선호하는 연락 방법: ___ 이메일 ___ 자택 전화 X 휴대 전화: 305-208-6666

임대 시간:

___ 오전(오전 6시부터 오후 1시까지)

___ 종일(오전 6시부터 오후 8시까지)

X 야간 포함(오전 6시부터 익일 오전 10시까지)

품목	수량	가격
의자(천연 원목; 접이식)	100	300달러
탁자(원형, 6피트)	12	168달러
테이블보(살구색; 원형)	12	60달러
탁자(긴 것, 8피트)	6	90달러

총계		618.00달러
지불 완료 금액		309.00달러
환급용 임차 보증금 지불액		100.00달러
7월 25일까지 지불 예정인 남은 금액		309.00달러

유의사항: 물품 수령 시 사진이 부착된 신분증을 제시하신 후 서명하셔야 합니다. 남은 대여료는 반드시 제때 지불되어야 하며, 그렇지 않을 경우 예약이 취소될 수 있습니다. 보증금은 물품의 상태와 반환 시점에 따라 전액 지급될 수 있습니다. 지정된 시간이 지난 후에 반환되는 물품에 대해서는, 시간당 10퍼센트의 연체 요금이 적용될 수 있습니다. 정상적으로 사용하지 않아서 발생한 물품 손상에 대한 비용 또한 보증금에서 공제될 것입니다. 기본적인 세척 작업에 대한 요금이 대여료에 포함되어 있기는 하지만, 탁자와 의자에 음식이 묻지 않도록 사용해 전반적으로 잘 관리된 상태를 유지하시기를 요청드립니다. 물품에 얼룩이 남아 있거나 특별 세척 작업이 필요한 경우에 추가 요금이 적용된다는 점에 유의하시기 바랍니다. 해당 요금은 100달러가 초과되지 않는 경우에는 보증금에서 공제되지만, 초과하는 경우에는 추가 비용 청구서를 받으실 수 있습니다.

162 Maritime Event Supply에 관해 알 수 있는 것은 무엇인가?

(A) 고객 신용 카드상의 정보를 요구한다.

(B) 주방에서 사용되는 물품들을 대여해 준다.

(C) 물품들이 반환되는 대로 보증금을 되돌려 준다.

(D) 최대 10시간 동안 물품 대여를 허용한다.

163 임대 물품들은 언제 반환될 예정인가?

(A) 오전 6시까지

(B) 오전 10시까지

(C) 오후 1시까지

(D) 오후 8시까지

164 어느 비용이 보증금에서 공제되지 않는가?

(A) 세척 비용

(B) 시간당 연체료

(C) 손상에 대한 비용

(D) 남아 있는 대여료

165-167은 다음 이메일을 참조하시오.

수신: Diane Hines ⟨d.hines@ingrammail.com⟩
발신: Roy Monroe ⟨monroeroy@stepbystepgoods.com⟩
날짜: 4월 20일
제목: 제품 R-490 (Gigi Cube)

Hines 씨께,

저희 회사가 장난감 용품 라인에 포함하기 위해 현재 개발하고 있는 유아들을 위한 안전한 놀이 구조물인 Gigi Cube를 테스트하는 데 참여해 주셔서 감사드립니다. 귀하께서는 저희에게 제공해 주신 주소지로 다음 주중에 배송 업체를 통해 제품을 받으실 것입니다. 다음 코드를 이용하셔서 저희 웹사이트에서 택배의 배송 상황을 언제든지 확인해 보시기 바랍니다: TWLHO90.

귀하께서 Gigi Cube를 댁에서 사용하시거나 친구, 가족, 공공장소를 방문하실 때 가져가셔서 귀하의 일상생활에서 활용해 보시길 요청드립니다. 앞서 제공해 드린 로그인 정보를 이용하여 저희 웹사이트인 stepbystepgoods.com/testing에서 제품에 관해 매주 의견을 작성해 주셔야 합니다. 사용의 편리성 및 외관, 그리고 품질뿐만 아니라 저희가 알아 두면 도움이 될 만하다고 생각하시는 모든 것들에 대해 가능한 한 상세하게 써 주시기 바랍니다. 저희는 현재의 개발 과정 단계에서 전문가들이 아닌 실제 고객들을 활용하고 있기 때문에, 고객들이 정말로 원하고 필요로 하는 것을 파악할 수 있습니다.

6주간의 테스트 기간이 종료되면, Gigi Cube는 귀하께서 소유하실 수 있습니다. 이것이 이 과정에 참여해 주신 것에 대해 감사를 전하는 저희의 방식입니다.

안녕히 계십시오.

Roy Monroe
연구 개발 부장, Step by Step

165 이메일의 목적은 무엇인가?

(A) 배송이 지연된 이유를 설명하기
(B) 일에 관한 지시 사항을 전하기
(C) 제품을 구매한 것에 대해 고객에게 감사하기
(D) 새로운 아동복 제품 라인을 소개하기

166 Step by Step에 관해 언급된 것은 무엇인가?

(A) 제품을 개발할 때 일반 소비자들을 참여시킨다.
(B) 연구 개발 부서가 현재 직원이 부족하다.
(C) 웹사이트에 대대적인 변화를 줄 것이다.
(D) 자원자들에게 할인 쇼핑 코드를 제공한다.

167 Gigi Cube에 관해 알 수 있는 것은 무엇인가?

(A) 재활용할 수 있는 재질로 만들어진다.
(B) 세탁기로 세척할 수 있다.
(C) 여러 종류의 직물로 구성되어 있다.
(D) 들고 다닐 수 있도록 고안되었다.

신유형 ▶ 168-171은 다음 편지를 참조하시오.

Diego Milanesi
4368 Oliverio Drive
Satanta, KS 67870

Milanesi 씨께,

귀하께서 Globe Photography Contest에 출품하신 것과 관련해 편지를 보냅니다. ⟨Walk in the Woods⟩라고 제목이 붙여진 귀하의 풍경

사진은 빛의 독특한 사용 때문에 저희 심사위원단에 깊은 인상을 남겼습니다. 따라서 저는 귀하의 사진이 이번 대회 최종 라운드에 진출했음을 알려 드리게 되어 기쁘게 생각합니다. 축하드립니다! ─ [1] ─. 최종 단계까지 진출하신 것만으로도, Russell Printing에서 제공하는 50달러 상당의 상품권을 받게 될 것이며, 그곳에서 모든 크기로 사진을 인화하실 수 있습니다.

귀하의 사진은 다른 준결승 진출자들의 작품들과 함께 18th Street에 있는 Middleton Gallery에 확대되어 전시될 것입니다. ─ [2] ─. 이 사진들은 9월 6일, 화요일부터 9월 10일, 토요일까지 일반인들이 관람하실 수 있게 됩니다. 토요일에는, 오후 7시에 와인 및 치즈가 제공되는 축하 연회에서 수상자들이 상패와 상품을 받을 것입니다. 우승자의 사진은 ⟨Nature Monthly⟩ 잡지에 실리게 될 것입니다. ─ [3] ─. 그리고 우승자에게 있어 대중들에게 노출되는 것은 대단히 이로울 것이라고 확신합니다.

저희가 적절한 양의 다과를 준비하는 데 도움이 되도록, 동봉해 드린 양식을 작성해 다시 보내 주셔서 귀하께서 축하 연회에 참석하실 계획인지를 알려 주시기 바랍니다. ─ [4] ─. 늦어도 8월 23일까지는 보내 주시기를 요청드립니다. 문의 사항이 있으시면, 555-4950, 내선 번호 45로 언제든지 연락 주시기 바랍니다.

Joyce Parker

168 Parker 씨는 왜 Milanesi 씨에게 편지를 보냈는가?

(A) 출품작이 원저작물이라는 것을 확인하기 위해
(B) 자신이 가장 좋아하는 사진에 투표하도록 요청하기 위해
(C) 심사위원단에 합류하는 것을 요청하기 위해
(D) 대회에서 그의 현재 상황에 대해 알리기 위해

169 결승 진출자들은 언제 행사에 참석할 것 같은가?

(A) 8월 23일에
(B) 9월 1일에
(C) 9월 6일에
(D) 9월 10일에

170 Milanesi 씨는 무슨 정보를 제공해 달라는 요청을 받는가?

(A) 그의 작품의 추가 샘플
(B) 작품을 보내길 원하는 곳
(C) 행사 참석 여부
(D) 선호하는 사진 크기

171 [1], [2], [3], [4]로 표기된 위치들 중에서 다음 문장이 가장 잘 어
신유형 울리는 곳은 어디인가?

"이는 저희가 지금까지 제공했던 것 중에서 가장 흥미로운 상입니다."

(A) [1]
(B) [2]
(C) [3]
(D) [4]

172-175는 다음 기사를 참조하시오.

Meadowbrook(10월 15일)─Reynolds Street 지하철역 근처의 야구 경기장이 지역 내 수천 명의 사람들에게 일자리를 제공한 지역 사업체인 Hennepin Manufacturing의 공로를 인정하여 이제 공식적으로 이름이 Hennepin Stadium으로 변경된다.

"Hennepin Manufacturing의 업적을 기리기 위해 경기장의 이름을 바꾼 것은 지역 사회 내 회사의 명망뿐만 아니라 작년에 경기장 부지 개선을

위한 계획에 아낌없이 3백만 달러를 투자한 것에 준한 결정이었습니다." 라고 어제 기자회견에서 시의회 위원장 John Ross 씨가 언급했다.

"야구 경기장은 지역 사회의 주요한 시설이므로 Hennepin이란 이름을 갖게 될 것이라는 소식을 듣고 저희는 기뻤습니다."라고 Hennepin Manufacturing의 홍보담당자 Kelly Woodruff 씨가 말했다. "이는 또한 저희 회사의 창립 20주년 기념일과 함께 일어난 즐거운 이벤트입니다. 저희는 저희 직원들이 경기장 개선 사업을 후원하는 것을 자랑스러워한다는 것을 알고 있고, Meadowbrook 주민들이 향후 몇 년 동안 그 시설에서 즐거운 시간을 갖기를 바랍니다."

방문객들을 대상으로 한 설문조사에서 가장 큰 불만 사항이 경기장 출입에 대한 어려움이라는 것이 드러난 후 경기장 개선 사업이 승인되었다. 이에 따라, 더 많은 차량을 수용하기 위하여 경기장의 다층형 주차 건물이 확장되었다. 더불어 두 개의 버스 정류장이 시내버스 노선에 추가되었는데, 하나는 동쪽 끝에 다른 하나는 서쪽 끝에 있다.

설계자들은 남은 자금을 경기장 지붕 일부에 태양 전지판을 설치하는 데 사용했다. 이는 건물이 도시 전력망에서 전기를 덜 이용할 수 있도록 해 줄 것이다.

172 기사에 따르면, 최근 무엇이 발표되었는가?
(A) 야구 경기의 승리
(B) 생산 시설의 개업
(C) 스포츠 복합단지의 이름 변경
(D) 시의회 의원의 사임

173 Hennepin Manufacturing은 작년에 무엇을 했는가?
(A) 방문객들로부터 받은 피드백을 검토했다.
(B) 본사를 Meadowbrook으로 옮겼다.
(C) 프로젝트에 돈을 기부했다.
(D) 직원들이 봉사활동을 하도록 장려했다.

174 세 번째 단락, 두 번째 줄의 단어 "bear"와 의미가 가장 가까운 것은 무엇인가?
(A) 상기시키다
(B) 알아내다
(C) 노력하다
(D) 지니다

175 개선의 이점으로 언급된 것이 아닌 것은?
(A) 에너지 사용의 감소
(B) 대중교통 노선의 확장
(C) 더 많은 주차 공간의 추가
(D) 건설 사업 조성

176-180은 다음 광고와 편지를 참조하시오.

Simpson Industries는 Detroit 지점에서 일할 근면하고 팀 중심으로 일하는 공장 관리자를 찾고 있습니다. Simpson Industries는 우리나라에서 선도적인 자동차 부품 생산업체 중 하나이고 지난 30년 동안 운영해 왔습니다. 이 부품들은 고품질로 명성을 갖고 있고, 전 세계에서 사용되고 있습니다.

공장 관리자는 생산 작업장의 모든 활동을 감독할 것입니다. 이 직책의 업무는 주와 연방 정부 규정에 따라 안전한 작업 환경을 보장하고, 유지보수와 장비 구입을 계획하고, 회사 정책들을 직원들에게 전달하는 일이 포함됩니다. 최소 3년의 관리 경력이 요구됩니다.

저희 공장은 대부분의 국가 공휴일을 포함하여 1년에 363일 운영하고

있고, 지원자들의 시간이 이 일정을 수용할 수 있어야 합니다. 직급 관리와 변화하는 인력 수요를 조정하는 것은 저희 인력 예산을 유지하는 데 매우 중요합니다. 저희는 현장에서 COBRA 일정 관리 소프트웨어를 사용하므로 지원자들은 이 프로그램을 사용하는 것에 능숙해야 합니다.

저희 팀에 합류하시는 것에 관심이 있으신 분들은 www.simpsonind.com/careers에서 지원서를 다운받으셔야 합니다. 빠짐없이 작성하신 후에 두 장의 추천서와 함께 Manuel Watts, Simpson Industries, 405 Woodbridge Street, Detroit, MI 48205로 보내셔야 합니다.

10월 16일

Manuel Watts 귀하
Simpson Industries
405 Woodbridge Street
Detroit, MI 48205

Watts 씨께,

저는 Simpson Industries의 공장 관리자 직에 지원한 Pai 씨를 위해 이 글을 씁니다. Pai 씨가 저희와 함께한 8년 중에서 지난 6년 동안, 저는 그의 직속 상관이었고 그와 매일 함께 일했습니다. Newton Co.에서 생산 작업장 관리자로서 일하는 동안, Pai 씨는 팀원들 사이에서 협력을 증진하는 데 뛰어났고, 그 결과 업계 평균과 비교하여 낮은 이직률을 야기했습니다. 또한, 저는 주간 간부회의에서의 그의 공헌에 매우 만족했습니다. 그는 여러 도움이 되는 아이디어를 공유했고, 그중 많은 것들이 저희 회사에서 시행되기도 했습니다.

저는 귀사의 채용 공고에 명시된 자격 요건을 검토했고 Pai 씨가 모든 요건에 적합하다고 확신합니다. 더욱이, 내부 조사뿐만 아니라 직원들의 설문조사에서도 Pai 씨는 사고를 막고 우수한 근무 환경을 만드는 데 완전히 헌신한다는 것을 보여주었습니다. 저희는 심지어 다른 시설의 관리자들에게 조언을 해 주도록 그를 보내기도 했습니다.

만약 Pai 씨를 고용하기로 결정하신다면, 그의 재능과 태도에 더없이 만족하시리라 확신합니다. 만약 필요하시다면, 저희 회사에서 그의 고용에 대해 기꺼이 더 자세히 말씀드리겠습니다. 사무실 번호 555-8923에 내선 번호 24로 저에게 연락하실 수 있습니다.

안녕히 계십시오.

Jessie Hoyle
시설 책임자, Newton Co.

176 Simpson Industries에 대해 언급된 것은 무엇인가?
(A) 몇몇 부서에 채용 공고가 있다.
(B) 사업을 Detroit로 확장할 계획이다.
(C) 차량의 부품 제조를 전문으로 한다.
(D) 3년간 운영해 왔다.

177 광고에 따르면, 공장 관리자는 무엇이 요구되는가?
(A) 무거운 물건을 운반하는 것
(B) 건강검진을 통과하는 것
(C) 출장을 가는 것
(D) 휴일에 근무하는 것

178 편지의 목적은 무엇인가?
(A) 한 지원자에게 일자리를 제안하기
(B) 공석에 대해 더 알아보기
(C) 한 직원에 대해 호의적인 평가를 해 주기
(D) 고용 과정을 설명하기

179 Pai 씨에 관해 알 수 있는 것은 무엇인가?

(A) COBRA 일정 관리 소프트웨어 사용법을 알고 있다.

(B) 웹사이트에 그의 이력서를 올렸다.

(C) 팀 구축 강좌를 수강했다.

(D) 정책을 개발한 경험이 있다.

180 Pai 씨는 얼마나 오랫동안 Newton Co.에서 근무했는가?

(A) 3년

(B) 6년

(C) 8년

(D) 10년

181-185는 다음 일정표와 이메일을 참조하시오.

Gazelle Wine Merchant 배송 일정

	화요일	수요일	목요일	금요일
오전	Lynwood	Seattle (북쪽)	SeaTac	Renton
오후	Edmonds	Seattle (남쪽)	Tukwila	Bellevue (북쪽)
저녁	Shoreline	Burien	Kent	Bellevue (남쪽)

휴일을 제외한 Seattle 지역 내 상점들의 배송 일정은 위와 같습니다.

지역 양조장에서 물건을 가지고 오기 위해 일정을 비워 두기 때문에 월요일에는 정기 배송 일정이 없습니다. 만약 통상 예정된 시간에 배송을 받을 수 없다면, 배송 책임자 Sabine Korovina에게 s.korovina@gazellewinemerchant.com으로 연락 주십시오.

수신: George Hoffman 〈george@regalgoods.net〉
발신: Sabine Korovina 〈s.korovina@gazellewinemerchant.com〉
날짜: 10월 28일
제목: 답장: 배송 요청

Hoffman 씨께,

귀하가 어제 이메일에서 언급하신 혼동된 부분을 제가 명확히 설명할 수 있기를 바랍니다. 먼저, 11월 11일 금요일이 국경일이기 때문에 11월 7일로 시작되는 그 주는 통상적인 배송 일정이 변경되는 것이 맞습니다. 우리는 그 주에만 모든 배송을 하루씩 앞당길 예정입니다. 이는 배달원이 귀하의 가게를 11월 10일 목요일 대신 11월 9일 수요일에 방문할 것을 의미합니다. 귀하의 경우에는 평상시 배달 시간인 점심시간 직후에 제품을 받게 될 것입니다. 저희 팀은 11월 7일 월요일에 배송 업무를 할 것이므로 판촉용 전시의 설치를 도와 달라는 귀하의 요청을 수락할 수 없음을 양해해 주시기 바랍니다.

통상 배송 일정은 11월 14일부터 재개될 것이며, 우리 판촉 전문가들 중 한 명을 그날 오전 10시에 가게로 보내서 휴일 맞이 Cordova Wines 전시를 준비하는 것을 돕도록 하겠습니다. 잊지 마시고 진열장이 세워지기를 원하시는 곳의 선반과 표지판, 그 밖에 다른 물품을 치워 주세요. 그렇게 하시면 일을 더 신속하게 처리할 수 있을 겁니다. 만약 추가로 문의 사항이 있으시면, 언제든 제게 이메일을 보내 주세요.

안녕히 계십시오.

Sabine Korovina 드림

181 월요일마다 무슨 일이 있는가?

(A) 배송에 추가 비용이 있다.

(B) 창고가 문을 닫는다.

(C) 새 물품이 들어온다.

(D) 배송 차량이 점검을 받는다.

182 Korovina 씨는 왜 이메일을 보냈는가?

(A) 신상품을 소개하기 위해

(B) Hoffman 씨에게 구매에 대해 감사하기 위해

(C) 품절된 물품에 대해 사과하기 위해

(D) 일정 변경을 설명하기 위해

183 Hoffman 씨의 가게는 어디에 있을 것 같은가?

(A) Bellevue

(B) Burien

(C) Seattle

(D) Tukwila

184 Hoffman 씨는 언제로 제품 판촉 관련 도움을 요청했을 것 같은가?

(A) 11월 7일

(B) 11월 9일

(C) 11월 10일

(D) 11월 11일

185 Korovina 씨는 Hoffman 씨에게 무엇을 하도록 상기시키는가?

(A) 전시를 위한 재료를 주문하는 것

(B) 이메일로 공식 요청서를 제출하는 것

(C) 전시를 위한 공간을 치워 두는 것

(D) 직원들이 할 수 있는지 확인하는 것

신유형 ▶ 186-190은 다음 이메일과 메모, 그리고 웹 페이지를 참조하시오.

수신: Newcast Radio 〈feedback@newscastradio.net〉
발신: Wesley Vincent 〈w.vincent@wv-enterprises.com〉
날짜: 4월 21일
제목: 청취자 의견

관계자께:

저는 수년 동안 Newscast Radio의 열혈 팬이었으며, 제가 소규모 철강 제조회사의 소유주이기 때문에 특히 국제 비즈니스 방송을 좋아했습니다. 제가 Newscast Radio의 회원권을 구입하는 것을 고려했었지만, 회원들이 이용할 수 있는 서비스가 일반 대중들에게 무료로 제공되는 것과 크게 다르지 않은 것처럼 보입니다. 하지만 회원들을 위한 섹션에 라디오 방송의 대본을 추가해 주신다면 저는 분명 가입할 것입니다. 제 생각엔 많은 사람들이 각자의 일정으로 인해 귀사의 라디오 채널을 제대로 듣지 못할 수도 있기 때문에 방송 대본을 볼 수 있기를 원할 것 같습니다. 제 의견을 고려해 주셔서 감사합니다.

안녕히 계십시오.

Wesley Vincent

수신: Newscast Radio 기자 여러분
발신: Kong Wei
날짜: 5월 3일
제목: 주간 회의

오늘 아침 회의에 참석하지 않으신 분들을 위해, 우리가 다뤘던 것에 관해 간략한 개요를 설명해 드리고자 합니다.

우리의 새 본사 건물이 될 Florence Tower의 공사는 아주 잘 진행되고 있습니다. 우리는 모든 공사가 완료되면 9월 중에 이전할 예정입니다. 건물 이전 준비에 관한 세부 사항은 이사 날짜가 가까워지는 대로 제공될 것입니다.

일상적인 소식 외에, 심층 분석이 필요한 여러 주제들을 확인했으며, 각각은 네 파트의 시리즈로 구성되어 다음 달에 방송됩니다. 선정된 주제들은 전자 화폐의 인기 증가, 캐나다 총리 경선, 그리고 Reyna Enterprises의 파산 절차입니다. 이 주제들은 각각 Sara와 Yuiko, 그리고 Manjit 씨에 의해 취재될 것입니다.

IT 부서의 Patrick 씨가 새로운 화상 회의 장비에 대해 시연할 예정이었지만, 아직 물품 배송을 기다리고 있어서 연기되었습니다. 이는 다음 주에 수행될 가능성이 가장 큽니다.

---

https://www.newscastradio.net/updates

Newscast Radio의 변화   게시일 11월 4일

Newscast Radio는 자사의 회원 서비스 향상을 알려 드리게 되어 매우 기쁩니다. 모든 방송의 대본을 이제 저희 웹사이트의 회원 섹션에서 다운로드받을 수 있게 될 것입니다. 여기를 클릭하셔서 매달 단 3.95달러에 이용 가능한 회원 프로그램에 가입하시기 바랍니다.

저희는 이번 달에 새로운 본사 건물로 이전할 예정입니다. 직원들에게 더 넓은 공간을 제공하는 것 외에, 1층에 방문객 공간이 생길 것이며 이곳에서 일반인 회원분께서 저희 회사에 대해 더 많은 것을 아실 수 있고 생방송을 듣거나 건물 내 카페에서 음료를 즐기실 수도 있습니다.

또한, 저희 팀에 다시 돌아오신 Reynaldo Carter 씨를 환영하게 되어 대단히 기쁩니다. 많은 분들께서 '사실 집중' 인터뷰로 이분을 기억하고 계실 것입니다.

186 Vincent 씨에 관해 알 수 있는 것은 무엇인가?

(A) 사업상 해외로 출장을 다닌다.
(B) Newscast Radio의 새로운 청취자이다.
(C) 회원으로 가입할 가능성이 클 것이다.
(D) Newscast Radio 신호가 믿을 만하지 못하다고 생각한다.

187 누가 전국 선거를 취재할 것인가?

(A) Kong
(B) Sara
(C) Yuiko
(D) Manjit

188 화상 회의 장비에 관해 언급된 것은 무엇인가?

(A) 사용자들이 작동하기 쉽다.
(B) Patrick으로부터 대여될 수 있다.
(C) 여분의 예산으로 비용이 충당되었다.
(D) 5월 3일까지 배송되지 않았다.

189 Florence Tower에 관해 유추할 수 있는 것은 무엇인가?

(A) 공사가 지연되었다.
(B) 대중교통과 가까운 곳에 있다.
(C) 보안 수준이 엄격하다.
(D) 뉴스 소식에서 다뤄질 것이다.

190 Carter 씨에 관해 알 수 있는 것은 무엇인가?

(A) 과거에 Newscast Radio에서 일했다.
(B) 회원 프로그램을 책임지고 있다.
(C) 지역의 유명 인사를 인터뷰할 것이다.
(D) Florence Tower 견학을 제공한다.

신유형 191-195는 다음 이메일들과 보고서를 참조하시오.

수신: Derek Mohr ⟨d.mohr@jarvissolutions.com⟩
발신: Clara Campbell ⟨c.campbell@jarvissolutions.com⟩
날짜: 3월 14일
제목: ERS United

Mohr 씨께,

저는 Seattle로 돌아가는 항공편을 타기 위해 공항에서 기다리고 있습니다. 저는 ERS United에서 근무하는 직원들을 대상으로 영업 발표를 했습니다. 우리 회사의 정수기 시제품이 비행기에 싣기에는 너무 커서 Dobbs Couriers를 이용해 ERS United의 사무실로 곧바로 배송했습니다. 하지만 배송 중에 발생한 문제로 인해, 발표 마지막 부분으로 계획해 두었던 30분 길이의 시연회를 건너뛰어야 했습니다. 다행스럽게도, 제 슬라이드 자료의 일부에 이 기기를 사용하는 모습을 담은 동영상이 포함되어 있기는 했지만, 그것으로 충분하다고 생각하지 않습니다. 저는 완전한 시연회를 하기 위해 이곳으로 오는 또 다른 출장을 준비해야 할 것입니다.

저는 오늘 일찍 Dobbs Couriers에 연락해서 이 문제점에 관해 공식적으로 불만을 제기했습니다. 내일 사무실에서 ERS United에 관해 더 상세한 내용을 말씀드리겠습니다.

안녕히 계십시오.

Clara Campbell
영업 사원, Jarvis Solutions

Dobbs Couriers 주간 사고 보고서: 3월 10일 – 16일

제출자 Jacqueline Roberts

고객 배송 물품과 관련된 사고 건수는 지난주보다 높았지만 여전히 용인되는 범위 내에 있었습니다. 요약 내용은 아래에 포함되어 있습니다.

사고 보고일	거래 ID	사고 설명	보험 비용	처리 상황
3월 11일	48502	물품 분실	100달러	물품 위치 추적됨
3월 12일	59641	잘못된 주소	없음	배송 경로 재지정
3월 14일	29482	내용물 손상	500달러	미해결
3월 16일	37709	늦은 배송	200달러	미해결

수신: Clara Campbell ⟨c.campbell@jarvissolutions.com⟩
발신: Dobbs Couriers ⟨cservice@dobbscouriers.com⟩
날짜: 3월 16일
제목: 귀하의 배송 물품
첨부: voucher_#01125

Campbell 씨께,

Dobbs Couriers를 대표해, 귀하의 최근 배송 물품(거래 번호 29482)과 관련해 귀하께서 겪으신 실망스러운 경험에 대해 진심으로 사과의 말씀을 드리고자 합니다. 저희는 이번 일이 귀하께 대단히 불편한 일이었다는 점을 알고 있습니다. 귀하께서는 이번 사안과 관련해 1,200달러에 해당하는 출장 비용 배상을 요청하셨습니다. 안타깝게도, 저희는 물품과 직접적으로 관련된 것 외에는 어떠한 손실에 대해서도 귀하께 배상해 드릴 수 없습니다. 귀하께서는 내용물에 대해 보험 가입을 하셨으므로 보험 처리 비용 전액을 받게 되실 것이며, 이 금액은 귀하의 회사 은행 계좌로 곧바로 송금될 것입니다. 또한, 사과의 의미로 다음번에 저희 회사를 통한 배송에 대해 50달러를 할인해 드리는 쿠폰을 첨부해 드렸습니다.

귀하의 양해에 감사드립니다.

191 Campbell 씨의 발표에 관해 알 수 있는 것은 무엇인가?

(A) Mohr 씨에 의해 진행될 예정이었다.

(B) 새로운 고객과의 계약으로 이어졌다.

(C) 질의응답 시간이 포함되어 있었다.

(D) 애초에 계획된 것보다 더 짧았다.

192 ERS United에 관해 알 수 있는 것은 무엇인가?

(A) 제휴 관계를 맺을 계획이다.

(B) Seattle에 위치해 있다.

(C) 다시 방문될 것이다.

(D) 회의가 취소되었다.

193 보고서에서, 첫 번째 단락, 두 번째 줄의 단어 "range"와 의미가 가장 가까운 것은 무엇인가?

(A) 갖가지

(B) 허용치

(C) 거리

(D) 능력

194 Campbell 씨는 자신의 배송 물품에 대해 무슨 문제점을 겪었는가?

(A) Dobbs Couriers에 의해 찾을 수 없었다.

(B) 잘못된 주소로 보내졌다.

(C) 손상된 상태로 배송지에 도착했다.

(D) 예정보다 늦게 배송되었다.

195 Jarvis Solutions의 은행 계좌로 얼마가 송금될 것인가?

(A) 100달러

(B) 200달러

(C) 500달러

(D) 1,200달러

신유형 ▶ 196-200은 다음 안내와 편지, 그리고 문자 메시지를 참조하시오.

음악 제출에 관한 안내

Coburn Studios에서 곧 제작될 영화에 귀하의 음악이 실리도록 선정된 것을 축하합니다. 승인 절차를 신속히 진행할 수 있도록 아래에 기재된 안내사항들을 따라 주시기 바랍니다.

– 서명하시기 전에 특허권 협약의 조항과 조건들을 신중히 검토해 보십시오.

– 일부 단어들이 이해하기 어려울 수 있으니 저희가 사용할 노래 가사를 제공해 주십시오.

– 다른 음악가들이 귀하의 녹음에 함께할 경우에(예를 들어, 코러스 가수, 드럼 연주자, 기타리스트 등), 반드시 곡이 사용되는 것에 대해 그분들의 동의를 받으십시오. 이는 귀하께서 작곡자 본인이시라 하더라도 반드시 행해져야 하는 일입니다. 이와 같은 목적에 필요한 동의서 양식은 www.coburn-studios.com/consent에서 이용 가능합니다. 서명된 양식은 우편으로 제출하시거나 스캔 후 이메일로 보내시면 됩니다.

– 귀하의 음악이 감독의 재량에 따라 오직 일부만 사용되거나 전체가 사용될 수 있다는 점에 유의하시기 바랍니다.

Coburn Studios

469 Athens Avenue

New York, NY 10021

www.coburn-studios.com

9월 27일

Daphne Gallagher

3198 Ferguson Street

Westborough, MA 01581

Gallagher 씨께,

필요한 모든 동의서 양식들을 받았으니 곧 제작될 저희 다큐멘터리 〈Beyond Politics〉에 귀하의 음악 〈Daylight Dreams〉가 사용될 것임을 확인해 드릴 수 있습니다. 저는 또한 12월 10일에 저희 스튜디오에서 열리는 개봉 기념 시사회에 귀하께서 참석하실 수 있다는 얘기를 듣게 되어 기쁩니다. 귀하와 귀하께서 모시고 오시길 원하시는 손님들을 위해 4장의 티켓을 동봉해 두었습니다. 제 팀원 중 누군가가 귀하와 일행 분들께서 스튜디오로 이동하실 수 있도록 귀하의 호텔에 차로 모시러 갈 것입니다.

저희는 귀하께서 이번 행사에 참여하시게 된 것에 대해 기쁘게 생각하며, 귀하의 공헌에 다시 한 번 감사드립니다. 궁금하신 점이 있으시면 언제든지 제게 (212) 555-9785로 전화 주셔도 좋지만, 업무 시간에는 이 번호로 오는 전화만 받는다는 점에 유의하시기 바랍니다.

안녕히 계십시오.

Jerald Hornsby

부 제작 책임자, Coburn Studios

발신: Michael Spence

전송: 12월 10일, 오후 5:35

수신: Daphne Gallagher

안녕하세요, 저는 Michael Spence입니다. 귀하를 모셔서 스튜디오로 데려다 드리기 위해 가는 중입니다. 약 20분 후에 머물고 계신 호텔에 도착할 것이며, 중앙 출입구 근처에서 기다리고 있겠습니다. 저는 차량 측면에 CS 로고가 표기된 흰색 SUV를 운전하고 있습니다. 곧 뵙겠습니다.

196 안내는 음악가들에게 무엇을 하라고 말하는가?

(A) 노래 길이를 줄일 것

(B) 노래의 다른 버전을 제공할 것

(C) 노래 가사를 제공할 것

(D) 노래 사본을 이메일로 보낼 것

197 〈Daylight Dreams〉에 관해 알 수 있는 것은 무엇인가?

(A) 재생 시간이 평균보다 훨씬 더 길다.

(B) 여러 다큐멘터리 영화에 수록됐었다.

(C) 원래 Hornsby 씨가 쓴 것이다.

(D) 여러 음악가의 연주를 포함한다.

198 Hornsby 씨에 따르면, Coburn Studios는 12월에 무엇을 할 것인가?

(A) 영화에 공헌한 사람들에게 비용을 지급할 것이다.

(B) 〈Beyond Politics〉를 위한 광고 캠페인을 시작할 것이다.

(C) 영화 한 편을 처음으로 선보일 것이다.

(D) 다큐멘터리 대회에 참가할 것이다.

199 편지에서, 두 번째 단락, 세 번째 줄의 단어 "take"와 의미가 가장
가까운 것은 무엇인가?

(A) 선택하다
(B) 받아들이다
(C) 나르다
(D) 제거하다

200 Spence 씨는 누구일 것 같은가?

(A) 〈Beyond Politics〉의 감독
(B) Hornsby 씨의 동료직원
(C) 호텔 직원
(D) Gallagher 씨의 매니저

자르는 선

ANSWER SHEET
TEST _____

수험번호						
성명	한글					
	영자					

응시일자	20 . .
맞은 개수	/ 100
환산 점수	/ 495

Listening Comprehension (PART I ~ PART IV)

1	ⓐⓑⓒⓓ	26	ⓐⓑⓒⓓ	51	ⓐⓑⓒⓓ	76	ⓐⓑⓒⓓ
2	ⓐⓑⓒⓓ	27	ⓐⓑⓒⓓ	52	ⓐⓑⓒⓓ	77	ⓐⓑⓒⓓ
3	ⓐⓑⓒⓓ	28	ⓐⓑⓒⓓ	53	ⓐⓑⓒⓓ	78	ⓐⓑⓒⓓ
4	ⓐⓑⓒⓓ	29	ⓐⓑⓒⓓ	54	ⓐⓑⓒⓓ	79	ⓐⓑⓒⓓ
5	ⓐⓑⓒⓓ	30	ⓐⓑⓒⓓ	55	ⓐⓑⓒⓓ	80	ⓐⓑⓒⓓ
6	ⓐⓑⓒⓓ	31	ⓐⓑⓒⓓ	56	ⓐⓑⓒⓓ	81	ⓐⓑⓒⓓ
7	ⓐⓑⓒ	32	ⓐⓑⓒⓓ	57	ⓐⓑⓒⓓ	82	ⓐⓑⓒⓓ
8	ⓐⓑⓒ	33	ⓐⓑⓒⓓ	58	ⓐⓑⓒⓓ	83	ⓐⓑⓒⓓ
9	ⓐⓑⓒ	34	ⓐⓑⓒⓓ	59	ⓐⓑⓒⓓ	84	ⓐⓑⓒⓓ
10	ⓐⓑⓒ	35	ⓐⓑⓒⓓ	60	ⓐⓑⓒⓓ	85	ⓐⓑⓒⓓ
11	ⓐⓑⓒ	36	ⓐⓑⓒⓓ	61	ⓐⓑⓒⓓ	86	ⓐⓑⓒⓓ
12	ⓐⓑⓒ	37	ⓐⓑⓒⓓ	62	ⓐⓑⓒⓓ	87	ⓐⓑⓒⓓ
13	ⓐⓑⓒ	38	ⓐⓑⓒⓓ	63	ⓐⓑⓒⓓ	88	ⓐⓑⓒⓓ
14	ⓐⓑⓒ	39	ⓐⓑⓒⓓ	64	ⓐⓑⓒⓓ	89	ⓐⓑⓒⓓ
15	ⓐⓑⓒ	40	ⓐⓑⓒⓓ	65	ⓐⓑⓒⓓ	90	ⓐⓑⓒⓓ
16	ⓐⓑⓒ	41	ⓐⓑⓒⓓ	66	ⓐⓑⓒⓓ	91	ⓐⓑⓒⓓ
17	ⓐⓑⓒ	42	ⓐⓑⓒⓓ	67	ⓐⓑⓒⓓ	92	ⓐⓑⓒⓓ
18	ⓐⓑⓒ	43	ⓐⓑⓒⓓ	68	ⓐⓑⓒⓓ	93	ⓐⓑⓒⓓ
19	ⓐⓑⓒ	44	ⓐⓑⓒⓓ	69	ⓐⓑⓒⓓ	94	ⓐⓑⓒⓓ
20	ⓐⓑⓒ	45	ⓐⓑⓒⓓ	70	ⓐⓑⓒⓓ	95	ⓐⓑⓒⓓ
21	ⓐⓑⓒ	46	ⓐⓑⓒⓓ	71	ⓐⓑⓒⓓ	96	ⓐⓑⓒⓓ
22	ⓐⓑⓒ	47	ⓐⓑⓒⓓ	72	ⓐⓑⓒⓓ	97	ⓐⓑⓒⓓ
23	ⓐⓑⓒ	48	ⓐⓑⓒⓓ	73	ⓐⓑⓒⓓ	98	ⓐⓑⓒⓓ
24	ⓐⓑⓒ	49	ⓐⓑⓒⓓ	74	ⓐⓑⓒⓓ	99	ⓐⓑⓒⓓ
25	ⓐⓑⓒ	50	ⓐⓑⓒⓓ	75	ⓐⓑⓒⓓ	100	ⓐⓑⓒⓓ

Reading Comprehension (PART V ~ PART VII)

101	ⓐⓑⓒⓓ	126	ⓐⓑⓒⓓ	151	ⓐⓑⓒⓓ	176	ⓐⓑⓒⓓ
102	ⓐⓑⓒⓓ	127	ⓐⓑⓒⓓ	152	ⓐⓑⓒⓓ	177	ⓐⓑⓒⓓ
103	ⓐⓑⓒⓓ	128	ⓐⓑⓒⓓ	153	ⓐⓑⓒⓓ	178	ⓐⓑⓒⓓ
104	ⓐⓑⓒⓓ	129	ⓐⓑⓒⓓ	154	ⓐⓑⓒⓓ	179	ⓐⓑⓒⓓ
105	ⓐⓑⓒⓓ	130	ⓐⓑⓒⓓ	155	ⓐⓑⓒⓓ	180	ⓐⓑⓒⓓ
106	ⓐⓑⓒⓓ	131	ⓐⓑⓒⓓ	156	ⓐⓑⓒⓓ	181	ⓐⓑⓒⓓ
107	ⓐⓑⓒⓓ	132	ⓐⓑⓒⓓ	157	ⓐⓑⓒⓓ	182	ⓐⓑⓒⓓ
108	ⓐⓑⓒⓓ	133	ⓐⓑⓒⓓ	158	ⓐⓑⓒⓓ	183	ⓐⓑⓒⓓ
109	ⓐⓑⓒⓓ	134	ⓐⓑⓒⓓ	159	ⓐⓑⓒⓓ	184	ⓐⓑⓒⓓ
110	ⓐⓑⓒⓓ	135	ⓐⓑⓒⓓ	160	ⓐⓑⓒⓓ	185	ⓐⓑⓒⓓ
111	ⓐⓑⓒⓓ	136	ⓐⓑⓒⓓ	161	ⓐⓑⓒⓓ	186	ⓐⓑⓒⓓ
112	ⓐⓑⓒⓓ	137	ⓐⓑⓒⓓ	162	ⓐⓑⓒⓓ	187	ⓐⓑⓒⓓ
113	ⓐⓑⓒⓓ	138	ⓐⓑⓒⓓ	163	ⓐⓑⓒⓓ	188	ⓐⓑⓒⓓ
114	ⓐⓑⓒⓓ	139	ⓐⓑⓒⓓ	164	ⓐⓑⓒⓓ	189	ⓐⓑⓒⓓ
115	ⓐⓑⓒⓓ	140	ⓐⓑⓒⓓ	165	ⓐⓑⓒⓓ	190	ⓐⓑⓒⓓ
116	ⓐⓑⓒⓓ	141	ⓐⓑⓒⓓ	166	ⓐⓑⓒⓓ	191	ⓐⓑⓒⓓ
117	ⓐⓑⓒⓓ	142	ⓐⓑⓒⓓ	167	ⓐⓑⓒⓓ	192	ⓐⓑⓒⓓ
118	ⓐⓑⓒⓓ	143	ⓐⓑⓒⓓ	168	ⓐⓑⓒⓓ	193	ⓐⓑⓒⓓ
119	ⓐⓑⓒⓓ	144	ⓐⓑⓒⓓ	169	ⓐⓑⓒⓓ	194	ⓐⓑⓒⓓ
120	ⓐⓑⓒⓓ	145	ⓐⓑⓒⓓ	170	ⓐⓑⓒⓓ	195	ⓐⓑⓒⓓ
121	ⓐⓑⓒⓓ	146	ⓐⓑⓒⓓ	171	ⓐⓑⓒⓓ	196	ⓐⓑⓒⓓ
122	ⓐⓑⓒⓓ	147	ⓐⓑⓒⓓ	172	ⓐⓑⓒⓓ	197	ⓐⓑⓒⓓ
123	ⓐⓑⓒⓓ	148	ⓐⓑⓒⓓ	173	ⓐⓑⓒⓓ	198	ⓐⓑⓒⓓ
124	ⓐⓑⓒⓓ	149	ⓐⓑⓒⓓ	174	ⓐⓑⓒⓓ	199	ⓐⓑⓒⓓ
125	ⓐⓑⓒⓓ	150	ⓐⓑⓒⓓ	175	ⓐⓑⓒⓓ	200	ⓐⓑⓒⓓ

www.engdangi.com

ANSWER SHEET
TEST _____

수험번호

성명	한글							
	영자							

응시일자	20 . .
맞은 개수	/ 100
환산 점수	/ 495

Listening Comprehension (PART I ~ PART IV)

	a b c d		a b c d		a b c d
1	ⓐ ⓑ ⓒ ⓓ	26	ⓐ ⓑ ⓒ ⓓ	51	ⓐ ⓑ ⓒ ⓓ
2	ⓐ ⓑ ⓒ ⓓ	27	ⓐ ⓑ ⓒ ⓓ	52	ⓐ ⓑ ⓒ ⓓ
3	ⓐ ⓑ ⓒ ⓓ	28	ⓐ ⓑ ⓒ ⓓ	53	ⓐ ⓑ ⓒ ⓓ
4	ⓐ ⓑ ⓒ ⓓ	29	ⓐ ⓑ ⓒ ⓓ	54	ⓐ ⓑ ⓒ ⓓ
5	ⓐ ⓑ ⓒ ⓓ	30	ⓐ ⓑ ⓒ ⓓ	55	ⓐ ⓑ ⓒ ⓓ
6	ⓐ ⓑ ⓒ ⓓ	31	ⓐ ⓑ ⓒ ⓓ	56	ⓐ ⓑ ⓒ ⓓ
7	ⓐ ⓑ ⓒ ⓓ	32	ⓐ ⓑ ⓒ ⓓ	57	ⓐ ⓑ ⓒ ⓓ
8	ⓐ ⓑ ⓒ ⓓ	33	ⓐ ⓑ ⓒ ⓓ	58	ⓐ ⓑ ⓒ ⓓ
9	ⓐ ⓑ ⓒ ⓓ	34	ⓐ ⓑ ⓒ ⓓ	59	ⓐ ⓑ ⓒ ⓓ
10	ⓐ ⓑ ⓒ ⓓ	35	ⓐ ⓑ ⓒ ⓓ	60	ⓐ ⓑ ⓒ ⓓ
11	ⓐ ⓑ ⓒ ⓓ	36	ⓐ ⓑ ⓒ ⓓ	61	ⓐ ⓑ ⓒ ⓓ
12	ⓐ ⓑ ⓒ ⓓ	37	ⓐ ⓑ ⓒ ⓓ	62	ⓐ ⓑ ⓒ ⓓ
13	ⓐ ⓑ ⓒ ⓓ	38	ⓐ ⓑ ⓒ ⓓ	63	ⓐ ⓑ ⓒ ⓓ
14	ⓐ ⓑ ⓒ ⓓ	39	ⓐ ⓑ ⓒ ⓓ	64	ⓐ ⓑ ⓒ ⓓ
15	ⓐ ⓑ ⓒ ⓓ	40	ⓐ ⓑ ⓒ ⓓ	65	ⓐ ⓑ ⓒ ⓓ
16	ⓐ ⓑ ⓒ ⓓ	41	ⓐ ⓑ ⓒ ⓓ	66	ⓐ ⓑ ⓒ ⓓ
17	ⓐ ⓑ ⓒ ⓓ	42	ⓐ ⓑ ⓒ ⓓ	67	ⓐ ⓑ ⓒ ⓓ
18	ⓐ ⓑ ⓒ ⓓ	43	ⓐ ⓑ ⓒ ⓓ	68	ⓐ ⓑ ⓒ ⓓ
19	ⓐ ⓑ ⓒ ⓓ	44	ⓐ ⓑ ⓒ ⓓ	69	ⓐ ⓑ ⓒ ⓓ
20	ⓐ ⓑ ⓒ ⓓ	45	ⓐ ⓑ ⓒ ⓓ	70	ⓐ ⓑ ⓒ ⓓ
21	ⓐ ⓑ ⓒ ⓓ	46	ⓐ ⓑ ⓒ ⓓ	71	ⓐ ⓑ ⓒ ⓓ
22	ⓐ ⓑ ⓒ ⓓ	47	ⓐ ⓑ ⓒ ⓓ	72	ⓐ ⓑ ⓒ ⓓ
23	ⓐ ⓑ ⓒ ⓓ	48	ⓐ ⓑ ⓒ ⓓ	73	ⓐ ⓑ ⓒ ⓓ
24	ⓐ ⓑ ⓒ ⓓ	49	ⓐ ⓑ ⓒ ⓓ	74	ⓐ ⓑ ⓒ ⓓ
25	ⓐ ⓑ ⓒ ⓓ	50	ⓐ ⓑ ⓒ ⓓ	75	ⓐ ⓑ ⓒ ⓓ

	a b c d
76	ⓐ ⓑ ⓒ ⓓ
77	ⓐ ⓑ ⓒ ⓓ
78	ⓐ ⓑ ⓒ ⓓ
79	ⓐ ⓑ ⓒ ⓓ
80	ⓐ ⓑ ⓒ ⓓ
81	ⓐ ⓑ ⓒ ⓓ
82	ⓐ ⓑ ⓒ ⓓ
83	ⓐ ⓑ ⓒ ⓓ
84	ⓐ ⓑ ⓒ ⓓ
85	ⓐ ⓑ ⓒ ⓓ
86	ⓐ ⓑ ⓒ ⓓ
87	ⓐ ⓑ ⓒ ⓓ
88	ⓐ ⓑ ⓒ ⓓ
89	ⓐ ⓑ ⓒ ⓓ
90	ⓐ ⓑ ⓒ ⓓ
91	ⓐ ⓑ ⓒ ⓓ
92	ⓐ ⓑ ⓒ ⓓ
93	ⓐ ⓑ ⓒ ⓓ
94	ⓐ ⓑ ⓒ ⓓ
95	ⓐ ⓑ ⓒ ⓓ
96	ⓐ ⓑ ⓒ ⓓ
97	ⓐ ⓑ ⓒ ⓓ
98	ⓐ ⓑ ⓒ ⓓ
99	ⓐ ⓑ ⓒ ⓓ
100	ⓐ ⓑ ⓒ ⓓ

Reading Comprehension (PART V ~ PART VII)

	a b c d		a b c d		a b c d
101	ⓐ ⓑ ⓒ ⓓ	126	ⓐ ⓑ ⓒ ⓓ	151	ⓐ ⓑ ⓒ ⓓ
102	ⓐ ⓑ ⓒ ⓓ	127	ⓐ ⓑ ⓒ ⓓ	152	ⓐ ⓑ ⓒ ⓓ
103	ⓐ ⓑ ⓒ ⓓ	128	ⓐ ⓑ ⓒ ⓓ	153	ⓐ ⓑ ⓒ ⓓ
104	ⓐ ⓑ ⓒ ⓓ	129	ⓐ ⓑ ⓒ ⓓ	154	ⓐ ⓑ ⓒ ⓓ
105	ⓐ ⓑ ⓒ ⓓ	130	ⓐ ⓑ ⓒ ⓓ	155	ⓐ ⓑ ⓒ ⓓ
106	ⓐ ⓑ ⓒ ⓓ	131	ⓐ ⓑ ⓒ ⓓ	156	ⓐ ⓑ ⓒ ⓓ
107	ⓐ ⓑ ⓒ ⓓ	132	ⓐ ⓑ ⓒ ⓓ	157	ⓐ ⓑ ⓒ ⓓ
108	ⓐ ⓑ ⓒ ⓓ	133	ⓐ ⓑ ⓒ ⓓ	158	ⓐ ⓑ ⓒ ⓓ
109	ⓐ ⓑ ⓒ ⓓ	134	ⓐ ⓑ ⓒ ⓓ	159	ⓐ ⓑ ⓒ ⓓ
110	ⓐ ⓑ ⓒ ⓓ	135	ⓐ ⓑ ⓒ ⓓ	160	ⓐ ⓑ ⓒ ⓓ
111	ⓐ ⓑ ⓒ ⓓ	136	ⓐ ⓑ ⓒ ⓓ	161	ⓐ ⓑ ⓒ ⓓ
112	ⓐ ⓑ ⓒ ⓓ	137	ⓐ ⓑ ⓒ ⓓ	162	ⓐ ⓑ ⓒ ⓓ
113	ⓐ ⓑ ⓒ ⓓ	138	ⓐ ⓑ ⓒ ⓓ	163	ⓐ ⓑ ⓒ ⓓ
114	ⓐ ⓑ ⓒ ⓓ	139	ⓐ ⓑ ⓒ ⓓ	164	ⓐ ⓑ ⓒ ⓓ
115	ⓐ ⓑ ⓒ ⓓ	140	ⓐ ⓑ ⓒ ⓓ	165	ⓐ ⓑ ⓒ ⓓ
116	ⓐ ⓑ ⓒ ⓓ	141	ⓐ ⓑ ⓒ ⓓ	166	ⓐ ⓑ ⓒ ⓓ
117	ⓐ ⓑ ⓒ ⓓ	142	ⓐ ⓑ ⓒ ⓓ	167	ⓐ ⓑ ⓒ ⓓ
118	ⓐ ⓑ ⓒ ⓓ	143	ⓐ ⓑ ⓒ ⓓ	168	ⓐ ⓑ ⓒ ⓓ
119	ⓐ ⓑ ⓒ ⓓ	144	ⓐ ⓑ ⓒ ⓓ	169	ⓐ ⓑ ⓒ ⓓ
120	ⓐ ⓑ ⓒ ⓓ	145	ⓐ ⓑ ⓒ ⓓ	170	ⓐ ⓑ ⓒ ⓓ
121	ⓐ ⓑ ⓒ ⓓ	146	ⓐ ⓑ ⓒ ⓓ	171	ⓐ ⓑ ⓒ ⓓ
122	ⓐ ⓑ ⓒ ⓓ	147	ⓐ ⓑ ⓒ ⓓ	172	ⓐ ⓑ ⓒ ⓓ
123	ⓐ ⓑ ⓒ ⓓ	148	ⓐ ⓑ ⓒ ⓓ	173	ⓐ ⓑ ⓒ ⓓ
124	ⓐ ⓑ ⓒ ⓓ	149	ⓐ ⓑ ⓒ ⓓ	174	ⓐ ⓑ ⓒ ⓓ
125	ⓐ ⓑ ⓒ ⓓ	150	ⓐ ⓑ ⓒ ⓓ	175	ⓐ ⓑ ⓒ ⓓ

	a b c d
176	ⓐ ⓑ ⓒ ⓓ
177	ⓐ ⓑ ⓒ ⓓ
178	ⓐ ⓑ ⓒ ⓓ
179	ⓐ ⓑ ⓒ ⓓ
180	ⓐ ⓑ ⓒ ⓓ
181	ⓐ ⓑ ⓒ ⓓ
182	ⓐ ⓑ ⓒ ⓓ
183	ⓐ ⓑ ⓒ ⓓ
184	ⓐ ⓑ ⓒ ⓓ
185	ⓐ ⓑ ⓒ ⓓ
186	ⓐ ⓑ ⓒ ⓓ
187	ⓐ ⓑ ⓒ ⓓ
188	ⓐ ⓑ ⓒ ⓓ
189	ⓐ ⓑ ⓒ ⓓ
190	ⓐ ⓑ ⓒ ⓓ
191	ⓐ ⓑ ⓒ ⓓ
192	ⓐ ⓑ ⓒ ⓓ
193	ⓐ ⓑ ⓒ ⓓ
194	ⓐ ⓑ ⓒ ⓓ
195	ⓐ ⓑ ⓒ ⓓ
196	ⓐ ⓑ ⓒ ⓓ
197	ⓐ ⓑ ⓒ ⓓ
198	ⓐ ⓑ ⓒ ⓓ
199	ⓐ ⓑ ⓒ ⓓ
200	ⓐ ⓑ ⓒ ⓓ

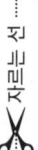

✂ 자르는 선

ANSWER SHEET
TEST

수험번호								응시일자	20 . .
성명	한글							맞은 개수	/ 100
	영자							환산 점수	/ 495

Listening Comprehension (PART I ~ PART IV)

No.	a b c d	No.	a b c d	No.	a b c d	No.	a b c d
1	ⓐ ⓑ ⓒ ⓓ	26	ⓐ ⓑ ⓒ ⓓ	51	ⓐ ⓑ ⓒ ⓓ	76	ⓐ ⓑ ⓒ ⓓ
2	ⓐ ⓑ ⓒ ⓓ	27	ⓐ ⓑ ⓒ ⓓ	52	ⓐ ⓑ ⓒ ⓓ	77	ⓐ ⓑ ⓒ ⓓ
3	ⓐ ⓑ ⓒ ⓓ	28	ⓐ ⓑ ⓒ ⓓ	53	ⓐ ⓑ ⓒ ⓓ	78	ⓐ ⓑ ⓒ ⓓ
4	ⓐ ⓑ ⓒ ⓓ	29	ⓐ ⓑ ⓒ ⓓ	54	ⓐ ⓑ ⓒ ⓓ	79	ⓐ ⓑ ⓒ ⓓ
5	ⓐ ⓑ ⓒ ⓓ	30	ⓐ ⓑ ⓒ ⓓ	55	ⓐ ⓑ ⓒ ⓓ	80	ⓐ ⓑ ⓒ ⓓ
6	ⓐ ⓑ ⓒ ⓓ	31	ⓐ ⓑ ⓒ ⓓ	56	ⓐ ⓑ ⓒ ⓓ	81	ⓐ ⓑ ⓒ ⓓ
7	ⓐ ⓑ ⓒ	32	ⓐ ⓑ ⓒ ⓓ	57	ⓐ ⓑ ⓒ ⓓ	82	ⓐ ⓑ ⓒ ⓓ
8	ⓐ ⓑ ⓒ	33	ⓐ ⓑ ⓒ ⓓ	58	ⓐ ⓑ ⓒ ⓓ	83	ⓐ ⓑ ⓒ ⓓ
9	ⓐ ⓑ ⓒ	34	ⓐ ⓑ ⓒ ⓓ	59	ⓐ ⓑ ⓒ ⓓ	84	ⓐ ⓑ ⓒ ⓓ
10	ⓐ ⓑ ⓒ	35	ⓐ ⓑ ⓒ ⓓ	60	ⓐ ⓑ ⓒ ⓓ	85	ⓐ ⓑ ⓒ ⓓ
11	ⓐ ⓑ ⓒ	36	ⓐ ⓑ ⓒ ⓓ	61	ⓐ ⓑ ⓒ ⓓ	86	ⓐ ⓑ ⓒ ⓓ
12	ⓐ ⓑ ⓒ	37	ⓐ ⓑ ⓒ ⓓ	62	ⓐ ⓑ ⓒ ⓓ	87	ⓐ ⓑ ⓒ ⓓ
13	ⓐ ⓑ ⓒ	38	ⓐ ⓑ ⓒ ⓓ	63	ⓐ ⓑ ⓒ ⓓ	88	ⓐ ⓑ ⓒ ⓓ
14	ⓐ ⓑ ⓒ	39	ⓐ ⓑ ⓒ ⓓ	64	ⓐ ⓑ ⓒ ⓓ	89	ⓐ ⓑ ⓒ ⓓ
15	ⓐ ⓑ ⓒ	40	ⓐ ⓑ ⓒ ⓓ	65	ⓐ ⓑ ⓒ ⓓ	90	ⓐ ⓑ ⓒ ⓓ
16	ⓐ ⓑ ⓒ	41	ⓐ ⓑ ⓒ ⓓ	66	ⓐ ⓑ ⓒ ⓓ	91	ⓐ ⓑ ⓒ ⓓ
17	ⓐ ⓑ ⓒ	42	ⓐ ⓑ ⓒ ⓓ	67	ⓐ ⓑ ⓒ ⓓ	92	ⓐ ⓑ ⓒ ⓓ
18	ⓐ ⓑ ⓒ	43	ⓐ ⓑ ⓒ ⓓ	68	ⓐ ⓑ ⓒ ⓓ	93	ⓐ ⓑ ⓒ ⓓ
19	ⓐ ⓑ ⓒ	44	ⓐ ⓑ ⓒ ⓓ	69	ⓐ ⓑ ⓒ ⓓ	94	ⓐ ⓑ ⓒ ⓓ
20	ⓐ ⓑ ⓒ	45	ⓐ ⓑ ⓒ ⓓ	70	ⓐ ⓑ ⓒ ⓓ	95	ⓐ ⓑ ⓒ ⓓ
21	ⓐ ⓑ ⓒ	46	ⓐ ⓑ ⓒ ⓓ	71	ⓐ ⓑ ⓒ ⓓ	96	ⓐ ⓑ ⓒ ⓓ
22	ⓐ ⓑ ⓒ	47	ⓐ ⓑ ⓒ ⓓ	72	ⓐ ⓑ ⓒ ⓓ	97	ⓐ ⓑ ⓒ ⓓ
23	ⓐ ⓑ ⓒ	48	ⓐ ⓑ ⓒ ⓓ	73	ⓐ ⓑ ⓒ ⓓ	98	ⓐ ⓑ ⓒ ⓓ
24	ⓐ ⓑ ⓒ	49	ⓐ ⓑ ⓒ ⓓ	74	ⓐ ⓑ ⓒ ⓓ	99	ⓐ ⓑ ⓒ ⓓ
25	ⓐ ⓑ ⓒ	50	ⓐ ⓑ ⓒ ⓓ	75	ⓐ ⓑ ⓒ ⓓ	100	ⓐ ⓑ ⓒ ⓓ

Reading Comprehension (PART V ~ PART VII)

No.	a b c d	No.	a b c d	No.	a b c d	No.	a b c d
101	ⓐ ⓑ ⓒ ⓓ	126	ⓐ ⓑ ⓒ ⓓ	151	ⓐ ⓑ ⓒ ⓓ	176	ⓐ ⓑ ⓒ ⓓ
102	ⓐ ⓑ ⓒ ⓓ	127	ⓐ ⓑ ⓒ ⓓ	152	ⓐ ⓑ ⓒ ⓓ	177	ⓐ ⓑ ⓒ ⓓ
103	ⓐ ⓑ ⓒ ⓓ	128	ⓐ ⓑ ⓒ ⓓ	153	ⓐ ⓑ ⓒ ⓓ	178	ⓐ ⓑ ⓒ ⓓ
104	ⓐ ⓑ ⓒ ⓓ	129	ⓐ ⓑ ⓒ ⓓ	154	ⓐ ⓑ ⓒ ⓓ	179	ⓐ ⓑ ⓒ ⓓ
105	ⓐ ⓑ ⓒ ⓓ	130	ⓐ ⓑ ⓒ ⓓ	155	ⓐ ⓑ ⓒ ⓓ	180	ⓐ ⓑ ⓒ ⓓ
106	ⓐ ⓑ ⓒ ⓓ	131	ⓐ ⓑ ⓒ ⓓ	156	ⓐ ⓑ ⓒ ⓓ	181	ⓐ ⓑ ⓒ ⓓ
107	ⓐ ⓑ ⓒ ⓓ	132	ⓐ ⓑ ⓒ ⓓ	157	ⓐ ⓑ ⓒ ⓓ	182	ⓐ ⓑ ⓒ ⓓ
108	ⓐ ⓑ ⓒ ⓓ	133	ⓐ ⓑ ⓒ ⓓ	158	ⓐ ⓑ ⓒ ⓓ	183	ⓐ ⓑ ⓒ ⓓ
109	ⓐ ⓑ ⓒ ⓓ	134	ⓐ ⓑ ⓒ ⓓ	159	ⓐ ⓑ ⓒ ⓓ	184	ⓐ ⓑ ⓒ ⓓ
110	ⓐ ⓑ ⓒ ⓓ	135	ⓐ ⓑ ⓒ ⓓ	160	ⓐ ⓑ ⓒ ⓓ	185	ⓐ ⓑ ⓒ ⓓ
111	ⓐ ⓑ ⓒ ⓓ	136	ⓐ ⓑ ⓒ ⓓ	161	ⓐ ⓑ ⓒ ⓓ	186	ⓐ ⓑ ⓒ ⓓ
112	ⓐ ⓑ ⓒ ⓓ	137	ⓐ ⓑ ⓒ ⓓ	162	ⓐ ⓑ ⓒ ⓓ	187	ⓐ ⓑ ⓒ ⓓ
113	ⓐ ⓑ ⓒ ⓓ	138	ⓐ ⓑ ⓒ ⓓ	163	ⓐ ⓑ ⓒ ⓓ	188	ⓐ ⓑ ⓒ ⓓ
114	ⓐ ⓑ ⓒ ⓓ	139	ⓐ ⓑ ⓒ ⓓ	164	ⓐ ⓑ ⓒ ⓓ	189	ⓐ ⓑ ⓒ ⓓ
115	ⓐ ⓑ ⓒ ⓓ	140	ⓐ ⓑ ⓒ ⓓ	165	ⓐ ⓑ ⓒ ⓓ	190	ⓐ ⓑ ⓒ ⓓ
116	ⓐ ⓑ ⓒ ⓓ	141	ⓐ ⓑ ⓒ ⓓ	166	ⓐ ⓑ ⓒ ⓓ	191	ⓐ ⓑ ⓒ ⓓ
117	ⓐ ⓑ ⓒ ⓓ	142	ⓐ ⓑ ⓒ ⓓ	167	ⓐ ⓑ ⓒ ⓓ	192	ⓐ ⓑ ⓒ ⓓ
118	ⓐ ⓑ ⓒ ⓓ	143	ⓐ ⓑ ⓒ ⓓ	168	ⓐ ⓑ ⓒ ⓓ	193	ⓐ ⓑ ⓒ ⓓ
119	ⓐ ⓑ ⓒ ⓓ	144	ⓐ ⓑ ⓒ ⓓ	169	ⓐ ⓑ ⓒ ⓓ	194	ⓐ ⓑ ⓒ ⓓ
120	ⓐ ⓑ ⓒ ⓓ	145	ⓐ ⓑ ⓒ ⓓ	170	ⓐ ⓑ ⓒ ⓓ	195	ⓐ ⓑ ⓒ ⓓ
121	ⓐ ⓑ ⓒ ⓓ	146	ⓐ ⓑ ⓒ ⓓ	171	ⓐ ⓑ ⓒ ⓓ	196	ⓐ ⓑ ⓒ ⓓ
122	ⓐ ⓑ ⓒ ⓓ	147	ⓐ ⓑ ⓒ ⓓ	172	ⓐ ⓑ ⓒ ⓓ	197	ⓐ ⓑ ⓒ ⓓ
123	ⓐ ⓑ ⓒ ⓓ	148	ⓐ ⓑ ⓒ ⓓ	173	ⓐ ⓑ ⓒ ⓓ	198	ⓐ ⓑ ⓒ ⓓ
124	ⓐ ⓑ ⓒ ⓓ	149	ⓐ ⓑ ⓒ ⓓ	174	ⓐ ⓑ ⓒ ⓓ	199	ⓐ ⓑ ⓒ ⓓ
125	ⓐ ⓑ ⓒ ⓓ	150	ⓐ ⓑ ⓒ ⓓ	175	ⓐ ⓑ ⓒ ⓓ	200	ⓐ ⓑ ⓒ ⓓ

ANSWER SHEET
TEST _____

수험번호						
성명	한글					
	영자					

응시일자	20 . .
맞은 개수	/ 100
환산 점수	/ 495

Listening Comprehension (PART I ~ PART IV)

1 2 3 4 5 6 7 8 9 10 11 12 13 14 15 16 17 18 19 20 21 22 23 24 25
26 27 28 29 30 31 32 33 34 35 36 37 38 39 40 41 42 43 44 45 46 47 48 49 50
51 52 53 54 55 56 57 58 59 60 61 62 63 64 65 66 67 68 69 70 71 72 73 74 75
76 77 78 79 80 81 82 83 84 85 86 87 88 89 90 91 92 93 94 95 96 97 98 99 100

Reading Comprehension (PART V ~ PART VII)

101 102 103 104 105 106 107 108 109 110 111 112 113 114 115 116 117 118 119 120 121 122 123 124 125
126 127 128 129 130 131 132 133 134 135 136 137 138 139 140 141 142 143 144 145 146 147 148 149 150
151 152 153 154 155 156 157 158 159 160 161 162 163 164 165 166 167 168 169 170 171 172 173 174 175
176 177 178 179 180 181 182 183 184 185 186 187 188 189 190 191 192 193 194 195 196 197 198 199 200

자르는 선

자르는 선

ANSWER SHEET

TEST ______________

수험번호							
성명	한글						
	영자						

응시일자	20 . . .
맞은 개수	/ 100
환산 점수	/ 495

Listening Comprehension (PART I ~ PART IV)

1	ⓐ ⓑ ⓒ ⓓ	26	ⓐ ⓑ ⓒ	51	ⓐ ⓑ ⓒ ⓓ	76	ⓐ ⓑ ⓒ ⓓ
2	ⓐ ⓑ ⓒ ⓓ	27	ⓐ ⓑ ⓒ	52	ⓐ ⓑ ⓒ ⓓ	77	ⓐ ⓑ ⓒ ⓓ
3	ⓐ ⓑ ⓒ ⓓ	28	ⓐ ⓑ ⓒ	53	ⓐ ⓑ ⓒ ⓓ	78	ⓐ ⓑ ⓒ ⓓ
4	ⓐ ⓑ ⓒ ⓓ	29	ⓐ ⓑ ⓒ	54	ⓐ ⓑ ⓒ ⓓ	79	ⓐ ⓑ ⓒ ⓓ
5	ⓐ ⓑ ⓒ ⓓ	30	ⓐ ⓑ ⓒ	55	ⓐ ⓑ ⓒ ⓓ	80	ⓐ ⓑ ⓒ ⓓ
6	ⓐ ⓑ ⓒ ⓓ	31	ⓐ ⓑ ⓒ	56	ⓐ ⓑ ⓒ ⓓ	81	ⓐ ⓑ ⓒ ⓓ
7	ⓐ ⓑ ⓒ	32	ⓐ ⓑ ⓒ ⓓ	57	ⓐ ⓑ ⓒ ⓓ	82	ⓐ ⓑ ⓒ ⓓ
8	ⓐ ⓑ ⓒ	33	ⓐ ⓑ ⓒ ⓓ	58	ⓐ ⓑ ⓒ ⓓ	83	ⓐ ⓑ ⓒ ⓓ
9	ⓐ ⓑ ⓒ	34	ⓐ ⓑ ⓒ ⓓ	59	ⓐ ⓑ ⓒ ⓓ	84	ⓐ ⓑ ⓒ ⓓ
10	ⓐ ⓑ ⓒ	35	ⓐ ⓑ ⓒ ⓓ	60	ⓐ ⓑ ⓒ ⓓ	85	ⓐ ⓑ ⓒ ⓓ
11	ⓐ ⓑ ⓒ	36	ⓐ ⓑ ⓒ ⓓ	61	ⓐ ⓑ ⓒ ⓓ	86	ⓐ ⓑ ⓒ ⓓ
12	ⓐ ⓑ ⓒ	37	ⓐ ⓑ ⓒ ⓓ	62	ⓐ ⓑ ⓒ ⓓ	87	ⓐ ⓑ ⓒ ⓓ
13	ⓐ ⓑ ⓒ	38	ⓐ ⓑ ⓒ ⓓ	63	ⓐ ⓑ ⓒ ⓓ	88	ⓐ ⓑ ⓒ ⓓ
14	ⓐ ⓑ ⓒ	39	ⓐ ⓑ ⓒ ⓓ	64	ⓐ ⓑ ⓒ ⓓ	89	ⓐ ⓑ ⓒ ⓓ
15	ⓐ ⓑ ⓒ	40	ⓐ ⓑ ⓒ ⓓ	65	ⓐ ⓑ ⓒ ⓓ	90	ⓐ ⓑ ⓒ ⓓ
16	ⓐ ⓑ ⓒ	41	ⓐ ⓑ ⓒ ⓓ	66	ⓐ ⓑ ⓒ ⓓ	91	ⓐ ⓑ ⓒ ⓓ
17	ⓐ ⓑ ⓒ	42	ⓐ ⓑ ⓒ ⓓ	67	ⓐ ⓑ ⓒ ⓓ	92	ⓐ ⓑ ⓒ ⓓ
18	ⓐ ⓑ ⓒ	43	ⓐ ⓑ ⓒ ⓓ	68	ⓐ ⓑ ⓒ ⓓ	93	ⓐ ⓑ ⓒ ⓓ
19	ⓐ ⓑ ⓒ	44	ⓐ ⓑ ⓒ ⓓ	69	ⓐ ⓑ ⓒ ⓓ	94	ⓐ ⓑ ⓒ ⓓ
20	ⓐ ⓑ ⓒ	45	ⓐ ⓑ ⓒ ⓓ	70	ⓐ ⓑ ⓒ ⓓ	95	ⓐ ⓑ ⓒ ⓓ
21	ⓐ ⓑ ⓒ	46	ⓐ ⓑ ⓒ ⓓ	71	ⓐ ⓑ ⓒ ⓓ	96	ⓐ ⓑ ⓒ ⓓ
22	ⓐ ⓑ ⓒ	47	ⓐ ⓑ ⓒ ⓓ	72	ⓐ ⓑ ⓒ ⓓ	97	ⓐ ⓑ ⓒ ⓓ
23	ⓐ ⓑ ⓒ	48	ⓐ ⓑ ⓒ ⓓ	73	ⓐ ⓑ ⓒ ⓓ	98	ⓐ ⓑ ⓒ ⓓ
24	ⓐ ⓑ ⓒ	49	ⓐ ⓑ ⓒ ⓓ	74	ⓐ ⓑ ⓒ ⓓ	99	ⓐ ⓑ ⓒ ⓓ
25	ⓐ ⓑ ⓒ	50	ⓐ ⓑ ⓒ ⓓ	75	ⓐ ⓑ ⓒ ⓓ	100	ⓐ ⓑ ⓒ ⓓ

Reading Comprehension (PART V ~ PART VII)

101	ⓐ ⓑ ⓒ ⓓ	126	ⓐ ⓑ ⓒ ⓓ	151	ⓐ ⓑ ⓒ ⓓ	176	ⓐ ⓑ ⓒ ⓓ
102	ⓐ ⓑ ⓒ ⓓ	127	ⓐ ⓑ ⓒ ⓓ	152	ⓐ ⓑ ⓒ ⓓ	177	ⓐ ⓑ ⓒ ⓓ
103	ⓐ ⓑ ⓒ ⓓ	128	ⓐ ⓑ ⓒ ⓓ	153	ⓐ ⓑ ⓒ ⓓ	178	ⓐ ⓑ ⓒ ⓓ
104	ⓐ ⓑ ⓒ ⓓ	129	ⓐ ⓑ ⓒ ⓓ	154	ⓐ ⓑ ⓒ ⓓ	179	ⓐ ⓑ ⓒ ⓓ
105	ⓐ ⓑ ⓒ ⓓ	130	ⓐ ⓑ ⓒ ⓓ	155	ⓐ ⓑ ⓒ ⓓ	180	ⓐ ⓑ ⓒ ⓓ
106	ⓐ ⓑ ⓒ ⓓ	131	ⓐ ⓑ ⓒ ⓓ	156	ⓐ ⓑ ⓒ ⓓ	181	ⓐ ⓑ ⓒ ⓓ
107	ⓐ ⓑ ⓒ ⓓ	132	ⓐ ⓑ ⓒ ⓓ	157	ⓐ ⓑ ⓒ ⓓ	182	ⓐ ⓑ ⓒ ⓓ
108	ⓐ ⓑ ⓒ ⓓ	133	ⓐ ⓑ ⓒ ⓓ	158	ⓐ ⓑ ⓒ ⓓ	183	ⓐ ⓑ ⓒ ⓓ
109	ⓐ ⓑ ⓒ ⓓ	134	ⓐ ⓑ ⓒ ⓓ	159	ⓐ ⓑ ⓒ ⓓ	184	ⓐ ⓑ ⓒ ⓓ
110	ⓐ ⓑ ⓒ ⓓ	135	ⓐ ⓑ ⓒ ⓓ	160	ⓐ ⓑ ⓒ ⓓ	185	ⓐ ⓑ ⓒ ⓓ
111	ⓐ ⓑ ⓒ ⓓ	136	ⓐ ⓑ ⓒ ⓓ	161	ⓐ ⓑ ⓒ ⓓ	186	ⓐ ⓑ ⓒ ⓓ
112	ⓐ ⓑ ⓒ ⓓ	137	ⓐ ⓑ ⓒ ⓓ	162	ⓐ ⓑ ⓒ ⓓ	187	ⓐ ⓑ ⓒ ⓓ
113	ⓐ ⓑ ⓒ ⓓ	138	ⓐ ⓑ ⓒ ⓓ	163	ⓐ ⓑ ⓒ ⓓ	188	ⓐ ⓑ ⓒ ⓓ
114	ⓐ ⓑ ⓒ ⓓ	139	ⓐ ⓑ ⓒ ⓓ	164	ⓐ ⓑ ⓒ ⓓ	189	ⓐ ⓑ ⓒ ⓓ
115	ⓐ ⓑ ⓒ ⓓ	140	ⓐ ⓑ ⓒ ⓓ	165	ⓐ ⓑ ⓒ ⓓ	190	ⓐ ⓑ ⓒ ⓓ
116	ⓐ ⓑ ⓒ ⓓ	141	ⓐ ⓑ ⓒ ⓓ	166	ⓐ ⓑ ⓒ ⓓ	191	ⓐ ⓑ ⓒ ⓓ
117	ⓐ ⓑ ⓒ ⓓ	142	ⓐ ⓑ ⓒ ⓓ	167	ⓐ ⓑ ⓒ ⓓ	192	ⓐ ⓑ ⓒ ⓓ
118	ⓐ ⓑ ⓒ ⓓ	143	ⓐ ⓑ ⓒ ⓓ	168	ⓐ ⓑ ⓒ ⓓ	193	ⓐ ⓑ ⓒ ⓓ
119	ⓐ ⓑ ⓒ ⓓ	144	ⓐ ⓑ ⓒ ⓓ	169	ⓐ ⓑ ⓒ ⓓ	194	ⓐ ⓑ ⓒ ⓓ
120	ⓐ ⓑ ⓒ ⓓ	145	ⓐ ⓑ ⓒ ⓓ	170	ⓐ ⓑ ⓒ ⓓ	195	ⓐ ⓑ ⓒ ⓓ
121	ⓐ ⓑ ⓒ ⓓ	146	ⓐ ⓑ ⓒ ⓓ	171	ⓐ ⓑ ⓒ ⓓ	196	ⓐ ⓑ ⓒ ⓓ
122	ⓐ ⓑ ⓒ ⓓ	147	ⓐ ⓑ ⓒ ⓓ	172	ⓐ ⓑ ⓒ ⓓ	197	ⓐ ⓑ ⓒ ⓓ
123	ⓐ ⓑ ⓒ ⓓ	148	ⓐ ⓑ ⓒ ⓓ	173	ⓐ ⓑ ⓒ ⓓ	198	ⓐ ⓑ ⓒ ⓓ
124	ⓐ ⓑ ⓒ ⓓ	149	ⓐ ⓑ ⓒ ⓓ	174	ⓐ ⓑ ⓒ ⓓ	199	ⓐ ⓑ ⓒ ⓓ
125	ⓐ ⓑ ⓒ ⓓ	150	ⓐ ⓑ ⓒ ⓓ	175	ⓐ ⓑ ⓒ ⓓ	200	ⓐ ⓑ ⓒ ⓓ

ANSWER SHEET
TEST _____

수험번호					
성명	한글				
	영자				

응시일자	20 . .
맞은 개수	/ 100
환산 점수	/ 495

Listening Comprehension (PART I ~ PART IV)

1	ⓐⓑⓒ	26	ⓐⓑⓒⓓ	51	ⓐⓑⓒⓓ	76 ⓐⓑⓒⓓ
2	ⓐⓑⓒ	27	ⓐⓑⓒⓓ	52	ⓐⓑⓒⓓ	77 ⓐⓑⓒⓓ
3	ⓐⓑⓒ	28	ⓐⓑⓒⓓ	53	ⓐⓑⓒⓓ	78 ⓐⓑⓒⓓ
4	ⓐⓑⓒ	29	ⓐⓑⓒⓓ	54	ⓐⓑⓒⓓ	79 ⓐⓑⓒⓓ
5	ⓐⓑⓒ	30	ⓐⓑⓒⓓ	55	ⓐⓑⓒⓓ	80 ⓐⓑⓒⓓ
6	ⓐⓑⓒ	31	ⓐⓑⓒⓓ	56	ⓐⓑⓒⓓ	81 ⓐⓑⓒⓓ
7	ⓐⓑⓒ	32	ⓐⓑⓒⓓ	57	ⓐⓑⓒⓓ	82 ⓐⓑⓒⓓ
8	ⓐⓑⓒ	33	ⓐⓑⓒⓓ	58	ⓐⓑⓒⓓ	83 ⓐⓑⓒⓓ
9	ⓐⓑⓒ	34	ⓐⓑⓒⓓ	59	ⓐⓑⓒⓓ	84 ⓐⓑⓒⓓ
10	ⓐⓑⓒ	35	ⓐⓑⓒⓓ	60	ⓐⓑⓒⓓ	85 ⓐⓑⓒⓓ
11	ⓐⓑⓒ	36	ⓐⓑⓒⓓ	61	ⓐⓑⓒⓓ	86 ⓐⓑⓒⓓ
12	ⓐⓑⓒ	37	ⓐⓑⓒⓓ	62	ⓐⓑⓒⓓ	87 ⓐⓑⓒⓓ
13	ⓐⓑⓒ	38	ⓐⓑⓒⓓ	63	ⓐⓑⓒⓓ	88 ⓐⓑⓒⓓ
14	ⓐⓑⓒ	39	ⓐⓑⓒⓓ	64	ⓐⓑⓒⓓ	89 ⓐⓑⓒⓓ
15	ⓐⓑⓒ	40	ⓐⓑⓒⓓ	65	ⓐⓑⓒⓓ	90 ⓐⓑⓒⓓ
16	ⓐⓑⓒ	41	ⓐⓑⓒⓓ	66	ⓐⓑⓒⓓ	91 ⓐⓑⓒⓓ
17	ⓐⓑⓒ	42	ⓐⓑⓒⓓ	67	ⓐⓑⓒⓓ	92 ⓐⓑⓒⓓ
18	ⓐⓑⓒ	43	ⓐⓑⓒⓓ	68	ⓐⓑⓒⓓ	93 ⓐⓑⓒⓓ
19	ⓐⓑⓒ	44	ⓐⓑⓒⓓ	69	ⓐⓑⓒⓓ	94 ⓐⓑⓒⓓ
20	ⓐⓑⓒ	45	ⓐⓑⓒⓓ	70	ⓐⓑⓒⓓ	95 ⓐⓑⓒⓓ
21	ⓐⓑⓒ	46	ⓐⓑⓒⓓ	71	ⓐⓑⓒⓓ	96 ⓐⓑⓒⓓ
22	ⓐⓑⓒ	47	ⓐⓑⓒⓓ	72	ⓐⓑⓒⓓ	97 ⓐⓑⓒⓓ
23	ⓐⓑⓒ	48	ⓐⓑⓒⓓ	73	ⓐⓑⓒⓓ	98 ⓐⓑⓒⓓ
24	ⓐⓑⓒ	49	ⓐⓑⓒⓓ	74	ⓐⓑⓒⓓ	99 ⓐⓑⓒⓓ
25	ⓐⓑⓒ	50	ⓐⓑⓒⓓ	75	ⓐⓑⓒⓓ	100 ⓐⓑⓒⓓ

Reading Comprehension (PART V ~ PART VII)

101	ⓐⓑⓒⓓ	126	ⓐⓑⓒⓓ	151	ⓐⓑⓒⓓ	176 ⓐⓑⓒⓓ
102	ⓐⓑⓒⓓ	127	ⓐⓑⓒⓓ	152	ⓐⓑⓒⓓ	177 ⓐⓑⓒⓓ
103	ⓐⓑⓒⓓ	128	ⓐⓑⓒⓓ	153	ⓐⓑⓒⓓ	178 ⓐⓑⓒⓓ
104	ⓐⓑⓒⓓ	129	ⓐⓑⓒⓓ	154	ⓐⓑⓒⓓ	179 ⓐⓑⓒⓓ
105	ⓐⓑⓒⓓ	130	ⓐⓑⓒⓓ	155	ⓐⓑⓒⓓ	180 ⓐⓑⓒⓓ
106	ⓐⓑⓒⓓ	131	ⓐⓑⓒⓓ	156	ⓐⓑⓒⓓ	181 ⓐⓑⓒⓓ
107	ⓐⓑⓒⓓ	132	ⓐⓑⓒⓓ	157	ⓐⓑⓒⓓ	182 ⓐⓑⓒⓓ
108	ⓐⓑⓒⓓ	133	ⓐⓑⓒⓓ	158	ⓐⓑⓒⓓ	183 ⓐⓑⓒⓓ
109	ⓐⓑⓒⓓ	134	ⓐⓑⓒⓓ	159	ⓐⓑⓒⓓ	184 ⓐⓑⓒⓓ
110	ⓐⓑⓒⓓ	135	ⓐⓑⓒⓓ	160	ⓐⓑⓒⓓ	185 ⓐⓑⓒⓓ
111	ⓐⓑⓒⓓ	136	ⓐⓑⓒⓓ	161	ⓐⓑⓒⓓ	186 ⓐⓑⓒⓓ
112	ⓐⓑⓒⓓ	137	ⓐⓑⓒⓓ	162	ⓐⓑⓒⓓ	187 ⓐⓑⓒⓓ
113	ⓐⓑⓒⓓ	138	ⓐⓑⓒⓓ	163	ⓐⓑⓒⓓ	188 ⓐⓑⓒⓓ
114	ⓐⓑⓒⓓ	139	ⓐⓑⓒⓓ	164	ⓐⓑⓒⓓ	189 ⓐⓑⓒⓓ
115	ⓐⓑⓒⓓ	140	ⓐⓑⓒⓓ	165	ⓐⓑⓒⓓ	190 ⓐⓑⓒⓓ
116	ⓐⓑⓒⓓ	141	ⓐⓑⓒⓓ	166	ⓐⓑⓒⓓ	191 ⓐⓑⓒⓓ
117	ⓐⓑⓒⓓ	142	ⓐⓑⓒⓓ	167	ⓐⓑⓒⓓ	192 ⓐⓑⓒⓓ
118	ⓐⓑⓒⓓ	143	ⓐⓑⓒⓓ	168	ⓐⓑⓒⓓ	193 ⓐⓑⓒⓓ
119	ⓐⓑⓒⓓ	144	ⓐⓑⓒⓓ	169	ⓐⓑⓒⓓ	194 ⓐⓑⓒⓓ
120	ⓐⓑⓒⓓ	145	ⓐⓑⓒⓓ	170	ⓐⓑⓒⓓ	195 ⓐⓑⓒⓓ
121	ⓐⓑⓒⓓ	146	ⓐⓑⓒⓓ	171	ⓐⓑⓒⓓ	196 ⓐⓑⓒⓓ
122	ⓐⓑⓒⓓ	147	ⓐⓑⓒⓓ	172	ⓐⓑⓒⓓ	197 ⓐⓑⓒⓓ
123	ⓐⓑⓒⓓ	148	ⓐⓑⓒⓓ	173	ⓐⓑⓒⓓ	198 ⓐⓑⓒⓓ
124	ⓐⓑⓒⓓ	149	ⓐⓑⓒⓓ	174	ⓐⓑⓒⓓ	199 ⓐⓑⓒⓓ
125	ⓐⓑⓒⓓ	150	ⓐⓑⓒⓓ	175	ⓐⓑⓒⓓ	200 ⓐⓑⓒⓓ

ANSWER SHEET
TEST _____

수험번호						
성명	한글					
	영자					

	20 . .
응시일자	
맞은 개수	/ 100
환산 점수	/ 495

Listening Comprehension (PART I ~ PART IV)

Reading Comprehension (PART V ~ PART VII)

www.engdangi.com

ANSWER SHEET
TEST ____

수험번호				
성명	한글			
	영자			

응시일자	20 · ·
맞은 개수	/ 100
환산 점수	/ 495

Listening Comprehension (PART I ~ PART IV)

1–100 answer bubbles (a)(b)(c)(d)

Reading Comprehension (PART V ~ PART VII)

101–200 answer bubbles (a)(b)(c)(d)

www.engdangi.com

✂ 자르는 선

ANSWER SHEET
TEST _____

수험번호						
성명	한글					
	영자					

응시일자	20 . .
맞은 개수	/ 100
환산 점수	/ 495

Listening Comprehension (PART I ~ PART IV)

1 ~ 25, 26 ~ 50, 51 ~ 75, 76 ~ 100

Reading Comprehension (PART V ~ PART VII)

101 ~ 125, 126 ~ 150, 151 ~ 175, 176 ~ 200

www.engdangi.com

✂ 자르는 선

ANSWER SHEET
TEST ________

수험번호								
성명	한글							
	영자							

응시일자	20 . . .
맞은 개수	/ 100
환산 점수	/ 495

Listening Comprehension (PART I ~ PART IV)

1	ⓐ ⓑ ⓒ ⓓ	26	ⓐ ⓑ ⓒ	51	ⓐ ⓑ ⓒ ⓓ	76	ⓐ ⓑ ⓒ ⓓ
2	ⓐ ⓑ ⓒ ⓓ	27	ⓐ ⓑ ⓒ	52	ⓐ ⓑ ⓒ ⓓ	77	ⓐ ⓑ ⓒ ⓓ
3	ⓐ ⓑ ⓒ ⓓ	28	ⓐ ⓑ ⓒ	53	ⓐ ⓑ ⓒ ⓓ	78	ⓐ ⓑ ⓒ ⓓ
4	ⓐ ⓑ ⓒ ⓓ	29	ⓐ ⓑ ⓒ	54	ⓐ ⓑ ⓒ ⓓ	79	ⓐ ⓑ ⓒ ⓓ
5	ⓐ ⓑ ⓒ ⓓ	30	ⓐ ⓑ ⓒ	55	ⓐ ⓑ ⓒ ⓓ	80	ⓐ ⓑ ⓒ ⓓ
6	ⓐ ⓑ ⓒ ⓓ	31	ⓐ ⓑ ⓒ	56	ⓐ ⓑ ⓒ ⓓ	81	ⓐ ⓑ ⓒ ⓓ
7	ⓐ ⓑ ⓒ	32	ⓐ ⓑ ⓒ ⓓ	57	ⓐ ⓑ ⓒ ⓓ	82	ⓐ ⓑ ⓒ ⓓ
8	ⓐ ⓑ ⓒ	33	ⓐ ⓑ ⓒ ⓓ	58	ⓐ ⓑ ⓒ ⓓ	83	ⓐ ⓑ ⓒ ⓓ
9	ⓐ ⓑ ⓒ	34	ⓐ ⓑ ⓒ ⓓ	59	ⓐ ⓑ ⓒ ⓓ	84	ⓐ ⓑ ⓒ ⓓ
10	ⓐ ⓑ ⓒ	35	ⓐ ⓑ ⓒ ⓓ	60	ⓐ ⓑ ⓒ ⓓ	85	ⓐ ⓑ ⓒ ⓓ
11	ⓐ ⓑ ⓒ	36	ⓐ ⓑ ⓒ ⓓ	61	ⓐ ⓑ ⓒ ⓓ	86	ⓐ ⓑ ⓒ ⓓ
12	ⓐ ⓑ ⓒ	37	ⓐ ⓑ ⓒ ⓓ	62	ⓐ ⓑ ⓒ ⓓ	87	ⓐ ⓑ ⓒ ⓓ
13	ⓐ ⓑ ⓒ	38	ⓐ ⓑ ⓒ ⓓ	63	ⓐ ⓑ ⓒ ⓓ	88	ⓐ ⓑ ⓒ ⓓ
14	ⓐ ⓑ ⓒ	39	ⓐ ⓑ ⓒ ⓓ	64	ⓐ ⓑ ⓒ ⓓ	89	ⓐ ⓑ ⓒ ⓓ
15	ⓐ ⓑ ⓒ	40	ⓐ ⓑ ⓒ ⓓ	65	ⓐ ⓑ ⓒ ⓓ	90	ⓐ ⓑ ⓒ ⓓ
16	ⓐ ⓑ ⓒ	41	ⓐ ⓑ ⓒ ⓓ	66	ⓐ ⓑ ⓒ ⓓ	91	ⓐ ⓑ ⓒ ⓓ
17	ⓐ ⓑ ⓒ	42	ⓐ ⓑ ⓒ ⓓ	67	ⓐ ⓑ ⓒ ⓓ	92	ⓐ ⓑ ⓒ ⓓ
18	ⓐ ⓑ ⓒ	43	ⓐ ⓑ ⓒ ⓓ	68	ⓐ ⓑ ⓒ ⓓ	93	ⓐ ⓑ ⓒ ⓓ
19	ⓐ ⓑ ⓒ	44	ⓐ ⓑ ⓒ ⓓ	69	ⓐ ⓑ ⓒ ⓓ	94	ⓐ ⓑ ⓒ ⓓ
20	ⓐ ⓑ ⓒ	45	ⓐ ⓑ ⓒ ⓓ	70	ⓐ ⓑ ⓒ ⓓ	95	ⓐ ⓑ ⓒ ⓓ
21	ⓐ ⓑ ⓒ	46	ⓐ ⓑ ⓒ ⓓ	71	ⓐ ⓑ ⓒ ⓓ	96	ⓐ ⓑ ⓒ ⓓ
22	ⓐ ⓑ ⓒ	47	ⓐ ⓑ ⓒ ⓓ	72	ⓐ ⓑ ⓒ ⓓ	97	ⓐ ⓑ ⓒ ⓓ
23	ⓐ ⓑ ⓒ	48	ⓐ ⓑ ⓒ ⓓ	73	ⓐ ⓑ ⓒ ⓓ	98	ⓐ ⓑ ⓒ ⓓ
24	ⓐ ⓑ ⓒ	49	ⓐ ⓑ ⓒ ⓓ	74	ⓐ ⓑ ⓒ ⓓ	99	ⓐ ⓑ ⓒ ⓓ
25	ⓐ ⓑ ⓒ	50	ⓐ ⓑ ⓒ ⓓ	75	ⓐ ⓑ ⓒ ⓓ	100	ⓐ ⓑ ⓒ ⓓ

Reading Comprehension (PART V ~ PART VII)

101	ⓐ ⓑ ⓒ ⓓ	126	ⓐ ⓑ ⓒ ⓓ	151	ⓐ ⓑ ⓒ ⓓ	176	ⓐ ⓑ ⓒ ⓓ
102	ⓐ ⓑ ⓒ ⓓ	127	ⓐ ⓑ ⓒ ⓓ	152	ⓐ ⓑ ⓒ ⓓ	177	ⓐ ⓑ ⓒ ⓓ
103	ⓐ ⓑ ⓒ ⓓ	128	ⓐ ⓑ ⓒ ⓓ	153	ⓐ ⓑ ⓒ ⓓ	178	ⓐ ⓑ ⓒ ⓓ
104	ⓐ ⓑ ⓒ ⓓ	129	ⓐ ⓑ ⓒ ⓓ	154	ⓐ ⓑ ⓒ ⓓ	179	ⓐ ⓑ ⓒ ⓓ
105	ⓐ ⓑ ⓒ ⓓ	130	ⓐ ⓑ ⓒ ⓓ	155	ⓐ ⓑ ⓒ ⓓ	180	ⓐ ⓑ ⓒ ⓓ
106	ⓐ ⓑ ⓒ ⓓ	131	ⓐ ⓑ ⓒ ⓓ	156	ⓐ ⓑ ⓒ ⓓ	181	ⓐ ⓑ ⓒ ⓓ
107	ⓐ ⓑ ⓒ ⓓ	132	ⓐ ⓑ ⓒ ⓓ	157	ⓐ ⓑ ⓒ ⓓ	182	ⓐ ⓑ ⓒ ⓓ
108	ⓐ ⓑ ⓒ ⓓ	133	ⓐ ⓑ ⓒ ⓓ	158	ⓐ ⓑ ⓒ ⓓ	183	ⓐ ⓑ ⓒ ⓓ
109	ⓐ ⓑ ⓒ ⓓ	134	ⓐ ⓑ ⓒ ⓓ	159	ⓐ ⓑ ⓒ ⓓ	184	ⓐ ⓑ ⓒ ⓓ
110	ⓐ ⓑ ⓒ ⓓ	135	ⓐ ⓑ ⓒ ⓓ	160	ⓐ ⓑ ⓒ ⓓ	185	ⓐ ⓑ ⓒ ⓓ
111	ⓐ ⓑ ⓒ ⓓ	136	ⓐ ⓑ ⓒ ⓓ	161	ⓐ ⓑ ⓒ ⓓ	186	ⓐ ⓑ ⓒ ⓓ
112	ⓐ ⓑ ⓒ ⓓ	137	ⓐ ⓑ ⓒ ⓓ	162	ⓐ ⓑ ⓒ ⓓ	187	ⓐ ⓑ ⓒ ⓓ
113	ⓐ ⓑ ⓒ ⓓ	138	ⓐ ⓑ ⓒ ⓓ	163	ⓐ ⓑ ⓒ ⓓ	188	ⓐ ⓑ ⓒ ⓓ
114	ⓐ ⓑ ⓒ ⓓ	139	ⓐ ⓑ ⓒ ⓓ	164	ⓐ ⓑ ⓒ ⓓ	189	ⓐ ⓑ ⓒ ⓓ
115	ⓐ ⓑ ⓒ ⓓ	140	ⓐ ⓑ ⓒ ⓓ	165	ⓐ ⓑ ⓒ ⓓ	190	ⓐ ⓑ ⓒ ⓓ
116	ⓐ ⓑ ⓒ ⓓ	141	ⓐ ⓑ ⓒ ⓓ	166	ⓐ ⓑ ⓒ ⓓ	191	ⓐ ⓑ ⓒ ⓓ
117	ⓐ ⓑ ⓒ ⓓ	142	ⓐ ⓑ ⓒ ⓓ	167	ⓐ ⓑ ⓒ ⓓ	192	ⓐ ⓑ ⓒ ⓓ
118	ⓐ ⓑ ⓒ ⓓ	143	ⓐ ⓑ ⓒ ⓓ	168	ⓐ ⓑ ⓒ ⓓ	193	ⓐ ⓑ ⓒ ⓓ
119	ⓐ ⓑ ⓒ ⓓ	144	ⓐ ⓑ ⓒ ⓓ	169	ⓐ ⓑ ⓒ ⓓ	194	ⓐ ⓑ ⓒ ⓓ
120	ⓐ ⓑ ⓒ ⓓ	145	ⓐ ⓑ ⓒ ⓓ	170	ⓐ ⓑ ⓒ ⓓ	195	ⓐ ⓑ ⓒ ⓓ
121	ⓐ ⓑ ⓒ ⓓ	146	ⓐ ⓑ ⓒ ⓓ	171	ⓐ ⓑ ⓒ ⓓ	196	ⓐ ⓑ ⓒ ⓓ
122	ⓐ ⓑ ⓒ ⓓ	147	ⓐ ⓑ ⓒ ⓓ	172	ⓐ ⓑ ⓒ ⓓ	197	ⓐ ⓑ ⓒ ⓓ
123	ⓐ ⓑ ⓒ ⓓ	148	ⓐ ⓑ ⓒ ⓓ	173	ⓐ ⓑ ⓒ ⓓ	198	ⓐ ⓑ ⓒ ⓓ
124	ⓐ ⓑ ⓒ ⓓ	149	ⓐ ⓑ ⓒ ⓓ	174	ⓐ ⓑ ⓒ ⓓ	199	ⓐ ⓑ ⓒ ⓓ
125	ⓐ ⓑ ⓒ ⓓ	150	ⓐ ⓑ ⓒ ⓓ	175	ⓐ ⓑ ⓒ ⓓ	200	ⓐ ⓑ ⓒ ⓓ

영단기 토익 RC 대표
정재현

가장 선호하는 신토익 교재 브랜드

영단기가 만든 <영단기 신토익 RC> 저자
영단기 신토익 입문서 <영단기 신토익 스타트 RC> 저자
<정재현의 신토익 RC 종결노트 3종 : 강의노트, 복습노트, 실전노트>저자
<영단기 신토익 개정판RC> 저자
<여기서 다 나온다 20일 속성 >교재 저자
<영단기 토익 보카 PLUS+> 교재 저자

*<정재현의 신토익 RC 종결노트 3종 : 강의노트, 복습노트, 실전노트>는 영단기에서만 구매 가능

결과로 증명된 BEST 강사!
영단기 적중특강 188만 View 이상
네이버 취업카페 스펙업 회원 선정
BEST 토익 강사 1위

토익 시험장 가기 전, 실전 감각을 더욱 높여줄
정재현 선생님만의 특별한 콘텐츠!

시험 직전 마지막 실전 마무리!
정재현의 적중특강!

토익 직전,
점수를 올려줄
적중 문제를 확인하라!

**핵심 출제 포인트까지
한 번에 잡을 무료 특강!**

시험장에 가져가야 할, 단 한 권의 노트
新토익 적중노트

시험 D-7, 하루 30분으로
시험 준비 끝!

시험 바로 직전까지
반드시 알아야 하는
전략만 제공합니다.

지금 영단기 홈페이지에 접속하시면 정재현 선생님의 모든 강좌를 확인하실 수 있습니다.

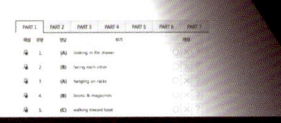

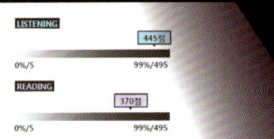

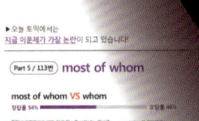

인공지능 출제 예측서비스

STELLA

STELLA가 예측한 토익 **PART 5 30문제 중 20문제*** 보기 및 유형 적중!

*17.12.30~18.07.29 시험대비 STELLA 예측문제 중 15회차 PART5 30문제 중 유형 및 보기 적중 평균 값 기준

토익 시험을 위한 모든 것을 준비해 두었습니다.
STELLA가 제안하는 '시기별 맞춤 콘텐츠'를 이용해보세요.

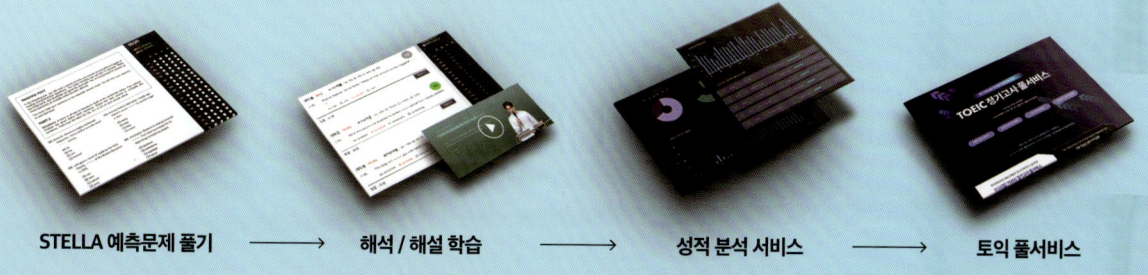

STELLA 예측문제 풀기 ⟶ 해석 / 해설 학습 ⟶ 성적 분석 서비스 ⟶ 토익 풀서비스

영단기 실전 예측 모의고사
REFINED AGING

매 월 2번 바뀌는 토익 트렌드에 맞춰 매 월 4회 제공되는
영단기만의 고퀄리티 모의고사입니다.

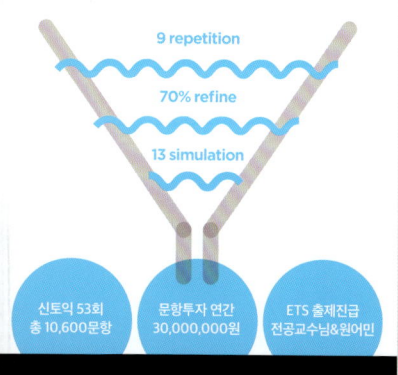

9 repetition

70% refine

13 simulation

신토익 53회
총 10,600문항

문항투자 연간
30,000,000원

ETS 출제진급
전공교수님&원어민

**Refined Aging Science로
최신 기출 분석**

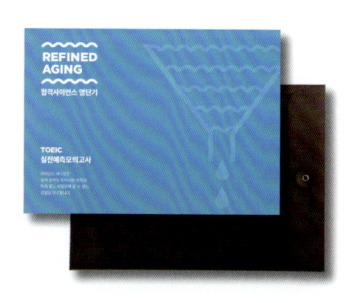

REFINED
AGING
합격사이언스 영단기

TOEIC
실전예측모의고사

**매 월 4회 고퀄리티 문제
모의고사 출제**

신토익 모의고사
해설강의

**영단기 1타강사진의
해설 강의 수강**

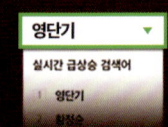
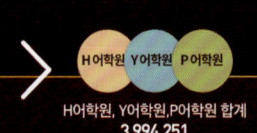